D1525013

The Inevitable Domination by Man
An Evolutionary Detective Story

Magdalenian (c.12,000 B.P.) spearthrower made of reindeer antler decorated with a carved image of a defecating fawn. Colored in hematite and manganese. Right eye of the fawn is an inserted piece of amber, the left, of lignite (see page 278). Musée des Antiquités Nationales, Saint-Germain-en-Laye, Paris

The Inevitable Domination by Man
An Evolutionary Detective Story

Seymour W. Itzkoff

PAIDEIA PUBLISHERS
Ashfield, Massachusetts

Library of Congress Cataloging-in-Publication Data

Itzkoff, Seymour W.
    The inevitable domination by man : an evolutionary detective story / Seymour W. Itzkoff.
        p. cm.
    Includes bibliographical references (p.).
    ISBN 0-913993-16-6 (alk. paper)
        1. Evolution (Biology)--Philosophy. I. Title

    QH360.5 .I89 2000
    576.8'01--dc21   00-021970

Paideia Publishers
P.O. Box 343
Ashfield, Massachusetts 01330

Printed in the United States of America

To Pat

BOOKS BY SEYMOUR W. ITZKOFF

Wherefore we decided to collect the diverse statements of the Holy Fathers, as they might occur to our memory, thus raising an issue from their apparent repugnance, which might incite the *teneros lectores* to search out the truth of the matter, and render them the sharper for the investigation. For the first key to wisdom is called interrogation, diligent and unceasing....By doubting we are led to inquiry, and from inquiry we perceive the truth.

Peter Abélard, *Sic et Non,* 1120 A.D.

Preface

The philosopher's challenge: to understand human nature, the meaning of the forms of knowledge, the damnably puzzling diversity in behavior and culture in our interbreeding species and, most crucial, the seemingly unstoppable aggression of humans against the natural world and against themselves.

In 1971 *Ernst Cassirer: Scientific Knowledge and the Concept of Man*, was published. It was the first of my two books on Cassirer. It was a study in the neo-Kantian tradition of the theory of knowledge, specifically dealing with the conundrum that this great 20th-century Kantian addressed in his attempt to locate the broader cultural and biological sources for the symbolic forms of knowledge. Cassirer's concern was to understand the historical/evolutionary position of the symbolic forms in the panorama of human progress. Human knowledge and communication seemed to be unique expressions in the biological world of signs. We humans are biological creatures. The selective function of animal communication has been consistent along a vast spectrum of time. Yet the motivations that undergirded the symbolic forms of knowledge seemed to be inconsistent with this biological heritage.

My hesitant solution focused on the great orthoselective transformation that had seemingly produced the sapient brain. Human knowledge indeed seemed to derive from no overt survivalistic yearnings. At the same time, we could not place its sources in a higher "metaphysical" reality. We seemed to be *sui generis* compared to the shared needs of rats, chimpanzees, and algae. Yet we were products of the same ultimate biophysical forces that created these other companions along the road.

My next exploration of this concern with the significance of human evolution was expressed in a four-volume series of books on the evolution of human intelligence, published between 1983-1990. This series confronted what to me had become a clear challenge to the universalistic civilizational vision of the neo-Kantians—the variability of human intelligence and its cultural products. How could we explain from the standpoint of human evolution this variability in individual capabilities and such great social differences? My conclusion: the variability was real, a product of a human species that was by no means homogeneous in its hegira forward in time and upward in corticalization from its root primate origins.

In the years since, many new evolutionary perspectives and controversies have overtaken our intellectual scene. *The Inevitable Domination by Man, An Evolutionary Detective Story* is the product of a more detailed investigation into a number of important challenges to our scientific understanding of *Homo*'s place in the evolutionary process and its present bio-cultural significance. These contemporary intellectual trends constitute a threat to our ongoing ability to take our future rationally in hand in the contemporary dynamic of both social and biological change.

The first is the view that we humans, with all of our unprecedented power over life and nature, are the *accidental* products of 4-plus billion years of evolution on the planet. Such a view would again lay us open to the kinds of 20th-century cultural and political manipulation by those who assert that we have no causally created "human nature." What else would we humans become then if not pawns to be indefinitely manipulated by those in power? I argue below, in demurral, that there is causal meaning in both our journey and arrival.

The second is the so-called adaptationist and sociobiological school. As devoted evolutionists, those espousing this ideology are too impressed by the orthodox evolutionary processes that seem to describe the creation of our mammal and primate heritage. The resulting interpretation of human behavior becomes a caricature of evolutionary understanding. There is no room here for that creature celebrated by the *Enlightenment* and held up as an ideal for human aspirations. In many ways, this was the same argument proffered several generations ago by the behaviorist psychologists, and fought by Cassirer. It is a metaphor for genetic tooth and claw.

Thus, the controversies are many and fascinating. Several of the scholars that I cite below as consultants and conversational partners do disagree with my "take" on the scientific evidence. It is for the reader to evaluate these controversies and await the empirical evidence, evidence that will ultimately confirm or confute the position that I present here. If ever we are able to plan for the future of the species and the biophysical environment that have provided for our coming into temporary dominance, the issues and facts that are here engaged will prove to be decisive.

My sincere thanks go out to: Christian de Duve, Rockefeller University; Ofer Bar-Yosef, Ernst Mayr, David Pilbeam, Harvard University; Jean-Jacques Hublin, Musée d'Histoire Nationale, Paris; Jeffrey Schwartz, University of Pittsburgh; Terry Deacon, Boston University; Bill Calvin, Peter Ward, University of Washington; Phillip Tobias, University of Wittwatersrand, South Africa; Walter Kistler, Bob Citron, and Sesh Velamor, Foundation for the Future; Russell Gardner, University of Texas Medical Branch; Clive Gamble, Southhampton University, U.K.; David Coming, City of Hope National Medical Center; Roger Pearson, Institute For the Study of Man; Dean Hamer, National Cancer Institute; Leon Sloman, University of Toronto.

Over a number of years, many Smith College students helped to obtain research materials as I worked on this book. Especially noteworthy was my most recent research assistant, Anne Booker. My wife, Pat, to whom I dedicate this book, has been heroic in the editing of the manuscript, disciplining the potential chaos. My appreciation is without end.

Contents

Illustrations

1

Accidental Human Nature?

"It is not in our genes." (R. Lewontin); "Mammals, victors by default." (C. Janis); "Extinction, bad genes or bad luck?" (D. M. Raup); "Humans have become, by the power of a glorious evolutionary accident called intelligence, the steward of life's continuity on Earth." (S. J. Gould)

- 1 -

Our Need to Understand

Can we have a rationally determined future without a meaningful past? If it is all a glorious accident, are our grandchildren and their descendants consigned to a chaotic and meaningless future? Without a scientific structure of reason and cause to explain how we humans arrived at our paradoxical historical situation, how can we defend a concept of natural human rights, fend off the opportunistic persuasions to power of the tyrants, Hitler, Stalin, Mao, Milosovic? They preach that we have no human nature. "Just trust us."

Is this what the scholars of the great human accident of becoming have preordained us for? Intelligence, and thus critical and skeptical thinking, equally replaceable by faith, belief, acquiescence, instinct. Are they so naïve as to think the membrane of knowledge between the biological and the political is impermeable?

It cannot be. Science and human rationality are rooted in the view that all things in nature can in principle be causally explained. What seems to be accidental is in reality our ignorance taking over our sense of determination to lift the curtains of unknowability and search ever deeper for the predictable causes of things. Understanding comes from relating in symbolic concept what heretofore seemed random and variable.

Even the mysteries of human evolution, human intelligence, our cultures and civilization, indeed the fearful depredations that this unfathomed human nature has wreaked upon our planet, must be subject to clear-eyed scientific study, and mastered. This is the philosopher's mandate as well as the scientist's particulate task.

The Inevitable Domination by Man, An Evolutionary Detective Story is an attempt to resolve some of the mystery surrounding the origin of modern humans, as well as the controversies that have attended the study of human nature and its evolutionary roots. The book is written by a philosopher who has long puzzled over these issues, written about them, and now, forced by new controversies and claims, returned to the search.[1] It is written to clarify, in the light of the most recent scientific research, the question inherent in the title of this book.

This recent retreat from scientific causality when it comes to the evolution of humans is the other side of the coin of an irrationalism, perhaps a naïve theism that today clouds the public mind. The position of this writer is that there is meaning in the coming to dominance of our species over the vast eukaryote domain of complex life forms.

There will be good scholarly minds that will take issue with the concept of "inevitability." Their view would focus on the moment-by-moment contingency of life forms, both coming into being, and disappearing over the edge of existence, the extinction of countless structures which at one time metabolized external energies for internal homeostasis and reproduction, at the least for a brief moment of sidereal time. However, the author believes that we are not the end result of a series of environmental accidents, extruded into happenstance existence. Neither are we a product of an act of "supernatural" creation.

Our extrusion from the evolutionary "fires" is not surprising given the parameters of the Earth's position in the solar system, *vis à vis* the energies and heat of the Sun. Other factors that conspired in our inevitable appearance include the Earth's internal chemistry, a fitness in the originating environment for the metabolizing of energy by various biochemical compounds, their ability to replicate a likewise functioning metabolic copy of themselves. Built into our evolutionary biochemistry was a tradition of variance in our environmental and ecological conditions, yet stability within the basic parameters necessary for the perdurance of living forms on the planet. In sum, the events that coordinated the evolutionary shaping of those pathways leading toward *Homo sapiens* created a zone of time-deep adaptive possibilities through which our ancestral lines inexorably moved toward the eventual dominance that now characterizes our species.

No rational thinker would ever think of this dominance as permanent. The planet Earth is only c.4.6 billion years old. And as we will point out, the possibility is that living molecules were metabolizing energy and replicating as early as 4 billion years ago. In all probability we still have quite a long scenario of life on the Earth into the future. Geophysical conditions will someday likely arise that will make life as we know it today, certainly for sexually reproducing, nuclear eukaryote plant and animal life, impossible to persist.

Philosophical Perspective
The philosophical stimulus for this book is Kantian (Immanuel Kant, 1724-1804). Kantians are persuaded that the structure of knowledge is a human creation.[2] It takes on its value and power for truth to the extent that it correlates with other knowledge structures, all of which build on a base of empirical, sensory, experiential information, ulti-

mately grounded in our universal human common sense. In evolutionary parlance, our vertebrate brain was and is an information-processing "machine." Implied is that the selective vindication of human knowledge, as with instinctual mammalian behavior, is to predict the future, hopefully to lead humans along the high road of evolutionary success.

But there is more to the Kantian vision than an adherence to the scientific method and away from metaphysical and ideological absolutes and non-empirically-based claims for knowledge. Kantians implicitly view the practicality of human knowledge as important, but not central. Central is a view of humans as creatures of knowledge, in the sciences, but also in the realm of moral and religious ideals, the arts, and political discourse. In sum, the knowledge-creating instincts in humans are *sui generis*, intrinsic to human existence, if not defining it.

Kantianism was a core element in the Enlightenment conception of the power and uniqueness of human reason. In a sense it was a glorification of the special gift of humans to think scientifically and logically, a special, yet natural endowment of all members of the species. This implicit view of the world of nature was not human *hybris* a denigration of the lower biological world of extinct and survival. But it was utopian, to the extent of its view that the universe was the locus of study by the rational human mind.

Coming to the 20th century and our vastly extended knowledge of the biological world and the scientific explication of evolutionary theory, it was clear that a challenge existed to the supposed suzerainty of human reason. Now the behavioristic and sociobiological challenge to see human mental functioning as part of an evolutionary continuity with the animal host was increasingly persuasive. We act so as to maximize our adaptive-reproductive-selective thrust for raw bio/political power. So-called rational motivations constitute a spurious cover that masks our eternally primeval drives.

Modern neo-Kantians, such as Ernst Cassirer (1874-1945) could not accept this blatant reductionism which interpreted our symbolic culture, science, philosophy, music and poetry, even religious communion and ethnic loyalty, as convenient phenotypes for the deeper reproductive power plays demanded by our biological inheritance.[34]

The full import of this analysis of the structure of human knowledge coalesced in Cassirer's enunciation of a perspective on humans in the world of life, the biological, symbolic domain of knowledge. Here Cassirer argued against the then (1930s 1940s) psychobiological infatuation with behavioristic reductions of human thought and action to the categories established through studies of rats or fish. Humans, he argued, were not instinct-driven creatures in their "information processing." For him, human thought and action could be epitomized in his use of the term, *animal symbolicum*.[5]

The symbolic animal, he averred, inhabited the natural world along with plants and other animals. The laws that humans would create to understand behavior in this world of chimpanzees, wolves, robins, and maple trees, needed to harmonize (cohere) with the principle of the continuity of nature. But in those more delimited intellectual domains where we study the sign behaviors of all animals, distinctions would have to be made between signal or instinctive responses and those behaviors that seemed to lack the clear-cut adaptive, survivalistic biological vector seen in most animals, the behaviors of *Homo*.

The Question of Human Nature

The 20th-century Kantians left us with an empirical as well as an intellectual challenge. We need to reconcile these many-sided dimensions of human behavior thus far unexplained by science or philosophy. We are animals, products of the evolutionary fires. Yet, we are so different, and now awesomely powerful. It is almost as if we war against the rest of eukaryote nature, including ourselves.

This "war" against life and self is sharply different from the usual selective struggle for physical and reproductive survival that is characteristic of the biological world before humans appeared in strength.[67] For the evolutionary line that led to humans, that struggle was secured several million years ago. The contemporary contrast is sharp. Six billion human souls now pour over the face of the planet. The ferocity that we unleash against nature and ourselves does not primarily issue from our physical selves. Our ammunition in this war against life is constructed from symbols, values, meanings. Oddly, we have the biological power, in the human brain, to interdict this behavior. How and why did we break with "nature"?

We humans recognize this violent, dominating potential in ourselves, and impotently fear its uncontrolled smothering of our lives and destiny. We also cherish and glorify the intellectual, richly symbolic productivity inherent in civilizational life. How to rationalize such paradoxical biological behavior with the evolutionary processes that produced it?

What has motivated the writing of this book is a dissatisfaction with existing philosophical and scientific solutions to the above conundrum. Also, it is the realization, after many years of study, that the only way supportable answers to the above critical human questions can be developed is by delving into the empirical research, posing those questions that only an independent inquirer can hope to have answered, through one's own "digging and asking."

Indeed, the philosopher is constrained to remain outside the cave or laboratory. Here we must depend on the clarity of the scientific researchers in the field. Only they can present us with a consensus delineation of the facts in question, and this in the many and diverse fields that contribute to our perspectives on human evolution. The issues leading to an understanding of the forces of nature that have produced *Homo sapiens sapiens* are contentious and numerous.

To have any hope for the clarification of the critical dilemmas of current and future history, other philosophers will also be required to roll up their intellectual sleeves and throw the evidential net out, widely and deeply.

- 2 -

The Arguments

1. General Scientific: This work should be seen as a naturalistic and secular perspective on the issue of the origins of living matter and the evolution of humans. The author eschews all attempts to read into our current lack of complete knowledge of all

dimensions of the evolutionary process as supporting those who would substitute for science, linguistically-inflated metaphysical "realities."

Many argue contentiously about all dimensions of the evolutionary processes. The reader should be forewarned that with so much of what we presume to "know" established interpretively on the basis of thin empirical evidence, it is inevitable that deviations from any current orthodoxy will be labeled "scientific error" (thus, the careful documentation of this author's argument). Any conclusions arrived at in this study are, along with all other hypotheses, "up for grabs," given the discovery of new empirical evidence.

2. Time Depth: This author views the ongoing scientific trend of opinion as tending to lengthen the time of creation and appearance of the various participants in the evolutionary process. The earlier error lay in jumping to the conclusion that the first fossil appearance of a form of life, denoted its simultaneous time of origin.

Scientists have discovered only a minuscule percentage of the possible fossil and other empirical evidence for the appearance of particular life forms. With each year new research, both theoretical as well as empirical, is driving the time parameters back in evolutionary history.

As the reader will note, this conclusion now seems to fit the scenario for the origin of the complex eukaryote cell and the origins of animal life. As developed here in some detail, the origin of the chordates and the vertebrate sub-phylum must also be pushed further back in evolutionary history. The amphibians are already deemed older than they were a few years ago, and now too the early reptiles and the synapsids, seeming ancestors to the mammals. Remember, some sharks were and are viviparous placentals. It would not surprise this writer if extremely early placental mammal progenitors will be discovered at the water's edge. Already the origins of the primates and before them true placental mammals are being traced into the deep Cretaceous, well before the demise of the dinosaurs. We will note below the truly contentious battles being waged over this "time of origins" issue with regard to human ancestors.

3. Dinosaur Fate: Not central to the argument of the book, but interesting in itself, other evidence, arguing contra the "giant Asteroid" scenario for the extinction of this line of reptiles, will be presented. It will be noted that these reptiles were already in serious decline at the time of K/T boundary c.65mya, when the asteroid presumably hit the Earth. By then, the placentals were already on an expansive pathway, many formerly competitive marsupials disappearing along with the dinosaurs. Clue: the lure of the egg.

4. Humans—Third Chimpanzee?: Based on molecular similarities and their presumed fixed rates of change, the two contemporary chimpanzee species and the hominids are now commonly thought to have separated between 5-6mya. Two chapters are here devoted to the evidence against this widely accepted mythology.

The necessary morphological changes required for such a recent dividing point verge on evolutionary creationism, unheralded among mainline mammals. There now exist hominid fossil fragments that date from 6-8mya, a time frame earlier than the hypothetical molecular point of separation of the two lines.

The problem here and in the "African-Eve" scenario, discussed below, is the willingness of sober scientific minds to be seduced by deductive molecular or mathematical models. Such theories are tantalizing to those in an empirical, field-oriented discipline, itself fraught with potential inaccuracies. But even "relativity theory" needed the discipline of empirical verification before it was widely accepted.

5. Modern Humans—African Eve?: A great mystery and a great debate now surround the origins of *Homo sapiens sapiens*. For a time, and still in the mass media, the mitochondrial DNA time clock seemed to point to a migration out of Africa of modern humans who now share a molecular history. Thus there are some Africans, and then other Africans with the rest of humanity in terms of the grouping of molecular affiliations. Also required by the theory was that these modern humans streaming out of Africa, some time in the last several hundred thousand years, would replace, without interbreeding, all the other human residents on the planet. Note, only the invading modernists and not any interbred or aboriginal resident could have survived. Quite a theoretical genocide!

It has long been clear to the scientific community that the true human modernists could only have been the Cro-Magnons of Eur-Asia, and they seem to have had no fossil antecedents from Africa. Their modern morphology and civilization were unique in comparison to all existing human cultures from around 45,000 B.P.

The mtDNA theoretical model has now been critically challenged along many conceptual avenues, resulting in an alteration that allows for an African emigration time frame of from c.150,000 B.P. to 400,000 B.P. This span of time is wide enough for dozens of "real-time" migrations to have taken place both into and out of Africa. Thus, which modern group came out, when, and from where?

It will be argued here over a number of chapters that the human modernists were indigenous to Eur-Asia, arriving there as part of the well-accepted originating Diaspora out of Africa c.2-1mya. The argument in TIDBM is in effect a compromise between a "Garden-of-Eden" scenario, now Eur-Asia, and the multi-regional view of parallel evolutionary lines of modernizing humans.

6. Inevitable Dominance: Once the physico/chemical fitness of the Earthly environment made it possible for counter-entropic metabolic molecular energy production and reproduction, then only time and natural selection would produce the basic nuclear, sexually reproducing eukaryote cell that now undergirds the so-called higher forms of life. The production of free oxygen by the eukaryote plant cells was also an inevitability given the Sun's position relative to the Earth and our indigenous chemistry.

From that point on, a time-deep zone of adaptation became available for mobile, predatory and intelligent forms of life, first in the water and then on land. The argument here is not that we are the end-all, the perfecting of the evolutionary process. Simply, some kind of highly intelligent, information-processing creature would eventually dominate the eukaryote plant and animal adaptive zone.

In the long run the prokaryote bacteria may inherit the mantle of dominance, if they do not already do so.

7. Intelligence and Our New Adaptive Zone: The long-term dominating selective impact of vertebrate animal evolution has been centered on the growth of the brain and its adaptive behavioral implications. Over time, in being focused on the primates and then on *Homo*, the selective power of abstract "g" general intelligence has drawn with it in deep genetic linkages a powerful mammalian heritage of structure and function.

The combination of an expansive iso-cortex and more general mammalian/primate brain reconstructions has created the great intelligence/culture biological tensions within the larger human species. In the process of learning to live with (adapt to) this unprecedented way of life, we can thus identify the source of *Homo*'s quick and disastrous impact on the ecology and destiny of the rest of eukaryotic life.

The evolutionary result of a brain whose growth was not constrained by close adaptive honing is an animal that behaves and lives in a new taxonomic biological realm-"culture." Traditional biological selective forces shaped by the ecological destiny of our planet will in the long term determine the future of this dominating species. However, it is clear that the information-processing capacity of the brain, and its intelligent behavior, has become an important factor in *Homo sapiens sapiens'* fate in this newest evolutionary zone of adaptation.

Endnotes, Chapter 1

[1] Itzkoff, S. W. 1983-1990. "The Evolution of Human Intelligence," 4 vols.: *The Form of Man*, 1983, N.Y.: Peter Lang; *Triumph of the Intelligent*, 1985, N.Y.: Peter Lang; *Why Humans Vary in Intelligence*, 1987, N.Y.: Peter Lang; *The Making of the Civilized Mind*, 1990, N.Y.: Peter Lang.

[2] Kant, I. 1755. *Universal Natural History and Theory of the Heavens*; 1758, *New Theory of Motion and Rest*.

[3] Cassirer, E. 1923-1929. *Philosophy of Symbolic Forms*, 3 vols., tr. by R. Manheim, New Haven: Yale Univ. Press.

[4] Langer, Susanne. 1967-1982. *Mind: An Essay on Human Feeling*, 3 vols., Baltimore: Johns Hopkins Univ. Press.

[5] Cassirer, E. 1944. *An Essay on Man*, New Haven: Yale Univ. Press.

[6] Cassirer, E. 1945. *The Myth of the State*, New Haven: Yale Univ. Press.

[7] Dewey, J. 1927. *The Public and Its Problems*, N.Y.: Henry Holt.

2

Why Ultimate Predator?

- 1 -
Arrival—Extinctions

New Actor, Old Extinctions/Creations

Humans had lived in the North for ages on end. This human, however, was a new type. The morphology was distinctive, different from the heavy-boned erectine-*heidelbergensis* prototype. So, too, was this form of man different from the large-skulled Neanderthals who had apparently "owned" the northern Eur-Asian land mass for over 100,000 years. These were tall, gracile people, indeed well muscled and sturdily adapted to the cool climates of the glaciated north. Their bones were thin, skulls and face freed of the massive bony structures of both erectines, early *sapiens*, and, of course, the Neanderthals.

The Cro-Magnons had arrived at the end of the Pleistocene Ice Ages, which had endured for almost two million years. Presently we may be living in an interstadial, one of those often relatively brief interregna between the coolings and ice descent that characterize this period. Indeed, these climatic changes are more important in determining consequences for animal and plant life, not to mention for predicting civilizational consequences, than is our own serious, potentially fatal, ill-conceived behavior. Two examples: 1) the alteration in the earth's axial tilt, between 22 and 25 degrees which the Yugoslavian physicist Milankovich has calculated as occurring approximately every 46,000 years, 2) the wobble in the earth's orbital motion around the sun. These are two cosmic variables that produce virtually unpredictable climatic changes that affect the entire earth.[1]

In essence, we could easily slip back into another cooling episode despite our self-imposed "greenhouse" heating of earth's atmosphere. What would result from the double impact of human-made heating and planetary gravitational perturbations boggles the imagination. Such climatic changes along with shifts in the continents and their associated oceans and seas have long been decisive in altering existing animal and plant balances on Earth.

In the context of a time line for recent hominid evolution, scientists such as paleontologist Elizabeth Vrba cite an earlier mass extinction of animal species beginning at the end of the Pliocene, some 2.5mya.[2] In contrast to the events of the terminal Pleistocene some 12,000-10,000 years ago, these extinctions also saw the coming into fossil reality of many new replacement forms of animal life, including modern forms of the horse, elephant, camel, and a variety of predators.

A. D. Barnosky suggests an extinction rate of 45% of major mammal genera at that time, but then an origination rate of well over 60% of new genera appearing in the fossil record.[3] This compares with an extinction rate of close to 40% at the end of the Pleistocene Ice Ages with an origination rate of near 0% in those same mammal genera leading into the Holocene, post-Ice-Age period.

	Extinct	Living	Total	Percent Extinct
Africa	7	42	49	19.3
North America	33	12	45	73.7
South America	45	12	57	78.9
Australia	19	3	22	86.4

2.1 Late-Pleistocene extinct and living genera of terrestrial megafauna (>44 kg adult body weight).

Savage argues that the late Pliocene, c.2.5mya, saw an extinction rate of mammals of all sizes, but mostly small.[4] In North America, the rate of extinction was almost double that of Europe, 31% to 17%. An even greater disparity occurred in the late Pleistocene, the end of the Ice Ages, in which the ratio of North American to European extinctions was 64% to 22%. The more recent episode saw large mammals making up 66% of the extinctions on both continents.

Peter deMenocal, at the Lamont-Doherty Earth Observatory, in analyzing the ocean sediments off the eastern and western African coasts, believes that Africa and thus presumptively the more northern latitudes, suffered sharp cycles of cold, dry climate at 2.8, 1.7, and 1.mya. These changes in climate probably coincided with the first expansion of the polar ice sheets over Eur-Asia and North America.[5]

In fact, the long-term perspective of evolution throughout the so-called Tertiary period, or the Cenozoic, from around 65mya, a period that saw the flourishing and dominance of mammalian vertebrate life, is one of an Earth gradually drying, if not cooling. How different this trend is when compared to the world of vast shallow seas that characterized earlier eras of domination by the amphibians and dinosaurian reptiles.

Genocide of Animals: Nature or Nurture

Humans are relative newcomers to this planet. They are still subject to its most fundamental physical laws, the push and pull of ecological and climatic changes over which animal life has so little control. These seemingly abstract material factors can be seen as the traditional driving force of evolutionary change and succession. True, such larger events are gradual both in their coming and their impact. Still, the difference in dynamic impact that *Homo sapiens sapiens* contributed to this traditional lethargic rhythm of life alterations is of crucial self-interest for our as-yet dim awareness of futurity and the limits of human control over earth's destiny.

At first, this impact was slow to be felt. The so-called Aurignacian culture that characterizes the first clearly-defined unity of cultural homogeneity, the product of *Homo sapiens sapiens'* unusual human morphology, extended from Spain to southern Russia, down to the Middle East, modern Israel, and Lebanon. Indeed, in time we should find evidence of its existence before this 45,000 B.P. Rubicon of arrival in the seemingly simultaneous and wide-spanning geographies of earliest impact.

Thirty-five-thousand years later, as the ice flows receded, the landscape had become denuded of a vast proportion of the magnificent mammalian and other fauna that flourished both during the eras of the expanding ice sheets and in the milder interstadials that interrupted this two-million-year yin and yang of climatic alterations. An additional perspective on the enormous extinction rates of large mammals, those over 44kg adult body weight, is given in table 2.1.[6]

According to Russian scientists, of the 182 species of terrestrial mammals that had existed in the late Pleistocene and early Holocene in the former USSR, contiguous with all European fauna, 30 have become extinct, approximately 17%. These include the hairy mammoth, great cave bear, cave hyena, cave lion, wooly rhinoceros, giant deer (Irish elk), and primitive bison.[7]

Many related genera, both in North America and Eur-Asia, also outside the above geographic confines, disappeared during this period. In the Eastern Hemisphere, others were able to move south into adaptable ecologies. Animals such as the horse, camel, rhinoceros, lion, panther, hyena survived, but in somewhat different form.

Modern humans were key players in this great evolutionary watershed, to what extent is still not clear, and may never be. For perhaps 25,000-35,000 years of their approximately 45,000-year presence in Eur-Asia, *Homo sapiens sapiens* seems to have coexisted with the resident large mammalian populations. True, the Aurignacian culture, in which is displayed both the physical and mental presence of these peoples, implies the concurrent existence in these populations of powerful social skills, skills that made possible their technology and art.

Their ability to live in large band and tribal associations—evidenced by the massive and calculated garbage trenches outside their caves in which were deposited the bones of animals from the hunt—reflects both organization as well as the discipline of political sociality over time. The cultural continuity, over thousands of years of esthetic and technological change, along with the extensive spread of this unified culture throughout Europe and West Asia, testifies to their life success.

The faunal extinction process has a relatively clear chronological movement, though its causes are highly controversial. The Great Wooly Mammoth can be used to illustrate the process and mystery of large mammal extinctions. The mammoth's climax seems to have been realized in Europe between 15,000 and 13,000 B.P. During that time, the mammoths became extinct in western Europe. The direction of their movement seems to have been both east and north into Siberia, then into North America.

From a period of 24,000-14,000 B.P., for example, hunters in European and Asiatic Russia never ventured north of 45-degrees latitude in their hunts. Evidence has been found of camps, seemingly temporary, located as far north as 60 degrees.[8] From 14,000 B.P., the massive hunting of mammoths is assumed to have taken place in the north, upwards of 57-degrees latitude, and east into Siberia, toward the land bridge of Beringia. To Paul Martin, it is almost as if humans were following the mammoth herds east into extinction.[9]

The final and most recent date of mammoth destruction is at Berelekh in northern Yakutia, in Siberia, at 70-degrees latitude. The date is 12,240 B.P. Approximately 140 mammoths were found here, in a disarticulated scattering of bone. The ivory tusks were removed from the skulls of the mammoths. It is assumed that the animals were either killed or died because of extreme environmental stress. The bodies were apparently dismembered and used for human sustenance.

At this point in the late Würm or Wisconsin glaciation, temperatures which at their extremes registered −30-degrees F. at latitudes equal to southern England and then due east, had suddenly begun to ameliorate. Snow and wetness in winter not only changed the food landscape for these beasts, but they also interposed new ecological factors, the formation of lakes, rivers, landslides into newly-formed ravines.[10]

Naturally, the chronology of climatic and ecological change at the transition to the Holocene is neither clear nor decisive. Thus, the destruction of such megafauna as the Wooly Mammoths could be a product of either human or climatic intervention into the existing ecological balance.

The migration of humans into North and then South America is fact. It is the timing of the migration that is still subject to controversy. The consensus is that sometime between 15,000 and 13,000 B.P. the melting of the ice packs broke up the Beringian land bridge and effectively closed off further migration, except for possibly the resident northwestern, North American Eskimo populations.

According to C. V. Haynes, the major killing of Alaskan megafauna by resident Amero-Indian populations began about 15,380 B.P. Many large mammals were extinct in Alaska by 13,000 B.P. The changing climatic conditions opened up a land route through the shrinking Rocky Mountain glaciers to about today's Edmonton, in Alberta, Canada. Mammoth deaths began here about 12,000 B.P. The use of the so-called Clovis point by the Amero-Indians dates to about 11,500 B.P. All megafauna except the traditional bison were extinct by 11,000 B.P.[11]

Paul Martin, citing Michanova, believes that all mammoths were destroyed in Siberia by 11,000 B.P. Simultaneously, a *Blitzkrieg* in North America was under way, in which up to 90,000 Amero-Indian migrants destroyed all the non-bison megafauna over a period of 300 to 600 years: "Virtually synchronous in the region extending from eastern Siberia to the southern U.S.A." By 11,000 B.P., migrating human populations were resident along both coasts in Mexico, possibly all the way south to Tierra del Fuego.[12] By 10,500 B.P., the North American mammoths, mastodons, camels, horses, ground sloths, scimitar cats, Harrington's goats, long-horned bison, (*Bison latifrons*), and other large mammals, plus many bird and small mammal species had disappeared forever.[13]

The transition to the Holocene period, starting c.11,000 B.P., was marked by a series of climatic eruptions. Sharply colder and dryer periods of hundreds of years periodically alternated with warm centuries. The Russian scholars, Vereshchagin and Baryshnikov have presented the argument for a climatic and ecological explanation of the vast northern extinction of large mammals.[14] For the North American perspective, R. Dale Guthrie has presented the most systematic analysis of the non-human physical forces that altered the climate and then the ecology within which these great animals had lived and prospered for hundreds of thousands of years.[15]

The Pleistocene of the north, Eur-Asia and North America, from c.2mya, except for the final, extremely harsh Würm-Wisconsin glaciation, c.20,000-11,000 B.P., Guthrie argues, was a time of much cooler, yet relatively equable climatic conditions. The northern plains of that time could be depicted as a mosaic of ecologies, plains, brush and forest, scattered woodlands, all with a much more mixed floral composition than today, about which numerous scientist have expressed both amazement and consternation. Throughout the range, up to the northernmost Arctic latitudes, plant types could be found that today are restricted either to the sub-tropical or to the most northerly temperate borderlands, all intermixed in ecologies that did not reveal a stringent climatic selectivity.

The result is that plants flowered and grew in their most protein-rich periods at various rhythms and moments up and down the geography of the Pleistocene. This allowed a wide variety of large mammals to find nutritious foods at all latitudes in periods when summers were cool yet productive and winters that were cold but not arctic. Thus are explained the numbers and varieties of animal life in this vast, extended, and very mixed ecological setting, which altered from cold to warm millennia and back again, but not to the degree of seasonal variations that we have experienced for the past 10,000 years.

Morphologically modern humans were drawn into this setting some 45,000 years ago, advancing west into Europe. Other human groups had been resident in Eur-Asia for at least 1.5 million years. The impact of these earlier human groups on the resident animal and plant life seems to have been negligible. Where the newcomers came from is unknown. Their potential power is reflected both in their tool culture as well as the seeming intensity of their tribal movements. That they lived in a relatively symbiotic and steady state of existence with the Pleistocene fauna is hinted at by the fact that for about 30,000 years of their early historical residency in Eur-Asia, from c.45,000 B.P. no great destruction of animal life seems to have taken place.

Their cave art, both painting and sculpting, reflects an appreciation of the power, mystery, and importance of that which sustained them in life. The conscious destruction of these animals, with the possible exception of the dislocation of resident cave animals, bears, sloths, cats, is thus questionable. It is hard to believe the claims that such limited populations could have destroyed the habitats of such a large proportion of the above cave inhabitants, or killed so many of the large and wide-ranging mammals during a fairly moderated climatic and mixed ecological setting. In addition, they would have to have accomplished these kills over vast distances and geographies.

Where Does the Blame Lie?

An extremely well-adapted predatory variant, *Homo sapiens sapiens*, was drawn late into the final Pleistocene Eur-Asian continent. The hunting-gathering experience of traditional million-year-old human patterns was extended and deepened by humans' new brain powers to create and engage in a complex symbolic world of abstract communication and expression. The full manifestation of the powers of the human mind was still limited by the necessities of earning a living in this stark, constraining, yet rich and stimulating faunal and floral environment. It is clear that the genetics of this once-small ethnicity quickly expanded far beyond its recognized cultural boundaries. It gave many other human populations the skills to amplify their own hunting-gathering powers.

The swift, decisive change of climate from the extreme cold of the final Würm, 20,000-12,000 B.P., to the Holocene pattern of sharp geographical boundaries of climate, and the extremes of continental patterns of temperature and rainfall throughout the latitudes, rendered the existing fauna extremely vulnerable.[16] Where their migratory or adaptive patterns were blocked by ice or behavioral specialization, mammals became vulnerable to an increasing population of humans themselves displaced from their existing ecological stabilities.

The 3.5+ billion years of the evolution of living forms have seen many mass extinctions. Several saw the wiping out of taxonomic families, even in the earliest phases, exotic phyla that appeared briefly, never again to be encountered. In every case, however, a few million years at the most, our planet has experienced renewed bursts of life. New forms and categories have been created that were able to adapt so as to meet new selective conditions.

So, too, the extinction of the late-Pleistocene fauna saw the bursting forth of a highly adaptable and new form of life. It, however, represented only one extended superspecies, *Homo sapiens*. That the subsequent behavior of this large mammal species led to further decimations both of floral and faunal life forms is uncontested. The future historically recordable behavior of *Homo sapiens sapiens* suggests this species' complicity in the decimation and extinction of the rich variety of mammal life that existed toward the end of the Pleistocene. But this suggestibility is not decisive.

By contrast, in the relatively brief successor term of perhaps 12,000 years, no other form of life by itself, and insinuated from within evolutionary history, has had such an irrevocable impact on competitive, even distantly-related faunal and floral families. From an objective standpoint, given the historical results of the presence of *Homo sapiens sapiens* on this planet, we are warranted in calling attention to the uniqueness of this *ultimate predator*.

- 2 -
Dominance, Obliteration, Genocide

First Demographic Expansion

The transition to the modern climatic patterns of sharp seasonal alternations began to affect the planet's ecological profile between 14,000 and 11,000 B.P. In the north, conifer and deciduous forests supplanted the ice sheets and tundras. The remnant hunting fauna disappeared within the tangled woodlands. Extremely harsh, frigid Eur-Asian climatic sequences completed the extinction of many large mammals that had once feasted in the lush spring-like verdancy and moderate coolness of these vast plains.

In the south, a considerable amount of the grazing plain of the Near East and North Africa was replaced by desert. Yet for centuries, many of the traditional African and European large mammals hung on, adapting marginally to the changes, even migrating with the alternating seasons wherever humans did not interfere to make this impossible.

Humans also dispersed. They sought out the river valleys, the Tigris/Euphrates, Nile, Indus, Volga, Don, Danube, Yellow/Yangtse. Also, the oases such as Jericho, where as early as 9,000-8,000 B.P., protective walls were in evidence, doubtfully to keep out predatory carnivores. Shortly, the dog, by-now domesticated, was joined by the horse, sheep, ox, camel, goat, and a variety of fowl.[17] The concentrated populations resident along the river banks soon precipitated the Neolithic era, characterized by an agricultural and technological revolution in economy that undergirded the subsequent urbanization of social life.

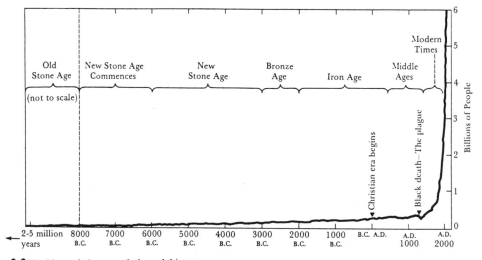

2.2 World population growth through history.

The human population at the close of the Pleistocene some 12,000 years ago (10,000 B.C.) can be estimated at two to four million worldwide.[18] A broader estimate has the expansion to be more rapid, to five to ten million between 8,000-6,000 B.C.[19] Anne and Paul Ehrlich estimate this population at the beginnings of urbanism, such as at Jericho, (about 8,000 B.C.) at five million.[20] The increased pace of economic and social organization, improvements in irrigation, and surge in city development throughout the post-glacial Holocene could account for this growth in human numbers.

The estimate for world population at about the time of Christ, at the height of the Roman Empire, and thus 8,000 years later, is estimated at between 100-200 million persons.[21] The population of the Roman Empire at its height, c.100 A.D., is estimated to have been 60-100 million.

By 1650 the world population had reached almost 500 million people. In two hundred years, 1850, it had doubled, to one billion. New industrial technologies, linked to scientific understandings of the causes of disease and the relation of health to sanitation, catapulted populations around the world by reducing traditional death rates. By 1996, the world population was 5.7 billion. Given the continuation of such growth rates in human populations, scientific experts were predicting a world population of close to 10 billion people by the end of the 21st century.

This enormous demographic explosion by the great replacement mammal of the Quaternary had its impact on surviving flora and fauna. It also afforded new ecological niches for bacteria, insects, birds, (sparrows, starlings, sea gulls), as well as mammals such as the rat, the domesticated cat and dog that could arrange a symbiotic peace with the new dominator at the top of the food chain.[22]

Rome's Sacrifice of Mammals

The *munus* was developed in late Republican times in Rome as a festival of filial celebration that involved the commemoration of the supreme sacrifice, human life, for the good of the city. Obviously this was a modern version of an ancient tradition of a people celebrating a communal victory over fallen foes. In the modern Roman transcription, in the grand arena of the *colossea*, the festival evolved into displays of gladiatorial valor and sacrifice, but increasingly punctuated by struggles against wild animals.

In prehistoric periods, decoration was a by-product of hunting or scavenging, in which bone, ivory, antler, teeth were utilized. The use of animals in the "game" became possible when humans established conditions for the live capture of the wild forms and their subsequent transport and slaughter in formal entertainment.

Caesar Augustus, at the turn of the Christian era, first institutionalized the *munus* as a regular festival. It was held once a year outside the city, semi-annually in Rome itself. It is recorded that as many as 120 gladiators and many animals were involved in each *munus* in the early period. Caesar Augustus himself is reported to have put on three spectacles in his own name, then five more for his children and grandchildren.[23]

The building of the Flavian Amphitheater (Colosseum), holding some 50,000 spectators, was completed in 80 A.D. It brought the *munus* to a new peak of mass entertainment. At its dedicatory performance, which continued from morning until dark, under the Emperor Titus (the second of the Flavians, and the conqueror of Jerusalem), it is reported that 5,000 beasts were sacrificed as well as a large number of gladiators.[24]

These mass killings of both human beings and animals, and in numerous Roman amphitheaters scattered throughout the Empire, continued for several hundred years, well into the Roman Christian fourth century A.D. As one Roman writer was proud to say, Rome had cleared the hippopotamus from Nubia, the lion from Mesopotamia, the tiger from Hyrcaneum. No longer could any of Hannibal's elephants be found in North Africa.

New Zealand and Madagascar Exemplars

More recent invasions, after 1000 A.D., of New Zealand by Polynesian Maoris, and of Madagascar by Indonesian peoples, brought with them new exemplifications of the delicate ecological balance that is necessary for the viability of animals. The moas, renowned giant, flightless, herbivorous New Zealand birds, some of them as much as ten feet tall, quickly became extinct with the coming of the Maoris,. An orgy of killing destroyed possibly 20 species of moas, plus at least half a dozen other bird species—geese, rails, swans, and a giant eagle. Europeans, entering New Zealand early in the 19th century, and bringing with them new mammal predators, are blamed for the extinction of at least half a dozen additional species of birds.[25]

Dewar, Trotter, and McCulloch have described the toll on wildlife after the coming of humans to Madagascar Island in the Indian Ocean in the ninth and tenth centuries A.D.[26] Fourteen genera of large ground-dwelling lemurs disappeared, totaling 17 species. Several species were as large as 200 pounds. Also, the entire rattie population (ground-dwelling elephant birds), similar to ostriches, and some 3 meters high, equal in height to Moas, totaling 12 species, disappeared, leaving behind only an enormous litter of broken egg shells on the beaches, clearly the direct result of human predation. In addition, a giant turtle, pigmy hippopotamus, and several other mammal species became extinct during the first several hundred years of the human occupancy of Madagascar.

Closures

From an evolutionary perspective, the impact of humans on a wide variety of living forms, not merely closely-related primates and mammals, but birds, reptiles, and amphibians, set the stage early in human history for an ever-widening band of forced competitive extinctions unrelated to wider climatic, geographical shifts of land and sea. Nature was now revealing the existence of one of the most powerful of its evolutionary children in its 4+ billion years in the history of life.

Geologist Peter Ward comments on the impact of humans on the highly specialized, isolated, and unique fauna on the islands of our planet: "The list of island extinctions is as numerous as the list of islands on our earth. On the Chatham Islands near New Zealand, between nineteen and twenty-seven species of birds have gone extinct. On Easter Island, the Polynesians eliminated virtually the entire flora, then eventually starved to death after eating most living things off the face of that bleak isle. In the Indian Ocean, Europeans killed off the dodo, while in the Atlantic, the great auk was exterminated in the arctic and rails disappeared from Ascension Island."[27]

David Day states that since 1680 and the destruction of the dodo, there have been 300 extinctions of vertebrate animals. Over half of these represent full species.[28] At the present moment, Day estimates that four hundred more vertebrates are at the brink of extinction, rendered thus by the decrease in their breeding numbers. In addition, an unknown number of thousands of plant species, many of which lived in a symbiotic relationship with the extinct animals, have also become extinct since 1680. The wildlife population of Africa alone has decreased more than 70% since 1900.[29]

In Plymouth Massachusetts, 1627, Isaack Rasieres is quoted as follows: "Sometimes we take them by surprise and fire amongst them with hail shot, immediately that we have made them rise, so that sixty, seventy, and eighty fall all at once, which is very pleasant to see."[30] And thus began the extermination of much of the indigenous population of fowl.

It was not only the Romans who showed a complete indifference for animal life, indulging themselves in the sport of killing the existing plenitude of animal life. Peter Ward quotes Roger Di Silvestro, in *The Endangered Kingdom.* The event: "A single eighteenth century hunt in Pennsylvania, where the hunters gathered from many parts of the state. They formed a circle 100 miles in diameter, with a hunter located each half mile. The hunters marched inward, killing all they found; the final tally included 41 cougars, 109 wolves, 18 bears, 111 bison, 112 foxes, 114 bob cats, 98 deer, and more than 500 smaller animals."[31]

One of the more interesting examples of the extinction of a mammal is that of the wild ox, the auroch, *Bos primigenius*, legendary from Greek mythology and before. The auroch probably constitutes the wild breeding stock from which domesticated cattle derive. Day believes that the auroch's closer genetic descendant may be the modern black Spanish fighting bull, which has the auroch's light-colored line running along its spine. The auroch is probably as different from modern cattle as the wolf is from the dog.[32]

Julius Caesar described these beasts, six foot high at the shoulder with long, forward-curving horns, in "*De Bello Gallico.*" "They are but little less than Elephants in size, and are of the species, colour, and form of a bull. Their strength is very great, and also their speed. They spare neither man nor beast that they see. They cannot be brought to endure the sight of men, nor be tamed, even when taken young. The people who take them in pitfalls, assiduously destroy them; and young men harden themselves in this labor, and exercise themselves in this kind of chase; and those who have killed a great number—the horns being publicly exhibited in evidence of this fact—obtain great honor."[33]

The last redoubt of the auroch was western Poland at the end of the 15th century. A number of Polish nobles had attempted to preserve these animals in protected forests under their control, this from the end of the 13th century when it became clear that the auroch was endangered. Typically, as their numbers were gradually reduced and their range increasingly delimited, they became ripe for extinction. This occurred near Warsaw in 1627.[34]

Some estimates are that, including the transition to the Holocene, when so many of the large mammals and their associated bird, insect, flora species were lost, some 10-20% of all species from pre-history to the present have become extinct. Bird species alone are down by approximately 25%, from 12,000 to 9,000 species.[35] E. O. Wilson estimates that at the present rate of species attrition, 20% more of the existing species will disappear in the next 30 years.[36]

Of the great tropical rain forests, especially in The Democratic Republic of the Congo (Zaire) and the Amazon River, Wilson estimated in 1992 a present loss of 1.8% of this tropical habitat cover each year, which would lead to a species loss of 0.5% each year.[37] Given his estimate of 10 million species living in these rain forests, this could equal the extinction of 50,000 species each year.[38] There is great controversy over the extent to which the great rain forests are disappearing. One estimate is that the greatest of the tropical rain forests, the Amazon, which produces 50% of its own rainfall, has lost 25% of its area, and that 10% of all Earth's species are in Amazonia.[39]

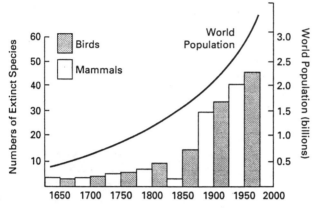

2.3 Rapid increase in human population is paralleled by rapid increase in extinction of birds and mammals.

New estimates of rates of extinction of plants and animals appear almost daily. Thus, even the most recent research is subject to immediate qualification. A meeting at the National Academy of Sciences in Washington, D.C., in October of 1997, elicited the following data: Sir Robert May of Oxford University put *described* species of existing flora and fauna at approximately 1.5 million; he places the total number of estimated living species at from 5 to 15 million. Sub-species extinction rates are put at 0.8% per year of the 1 to 6 billion hypothesized sub-species populations. Species extinctions in the tropics have been estimated at a rate of 0.1 to 0.3% per year. E. O. Wilson, as noted, put the tropical extinction rate at 0.5% per year. The above 1997 calculation by Stuart Pimm of the University of Tennessee sees the shrinkage of habitat for birds that would lead to an extinction rate of 50% of bird species in the next half-century and 75% in the next century.[40]

- 3 -

Ultimate Mystery

Fracture Within

Our experience with hunter-gatherer peoples, those who stood outside the great symbolic revolutions of literacy and urbanism, argues for the seemingly perennial existence of warfare, torture, cannibalism. Whether this was the pattern with those northern *Homo sapiens sapiens*, Cro-Magnon peoples who first gave us the symbolic products of civilized cultural life, we cannot know. Their contact with the neighboring Neanderthal peoples reveals few indications of mortal war and conflict.[41] Recent studies argue for only an indirect relationship, one that excludes genetic contact.[42]

The historical period for all humanity reveals widespread human conflict, personalized killing, deadly intra-political and ethnic conflict as well as inter-political, national, and ethnic warfare. Intra-species aggression is a commonly noted biological fact. Within species, usually between males, reproductive dominance appears to be the critical issue. In humans, evidence of overt individual competition for reproductive dominance is not as apparent as in other mammals. Conflict is more indirect, more between social and economic classes than between individuals for reproductive advantage.

In a parallel historical development, we can note, especially for the 20th century, the universal theme of social welfare, the redistribution of symbolic wealth from the advantaged socioeconomic classes to the weaker or less fortunate groups, the consequent wherewithal for reproductive self-maintenance, if not dominance. These possibly momentary historical turnabouts from traditional evolutionary selective patterns precipitate important questions about the nature of the human animal.

The pre-history of *Homo* is replete with the disappearance of less-evolved human forms, less evolved in their brain structure morphology and the culture produced by the more primitive morphologies. However, the actual patterns by which dominance has led to the disappearance of these earlier human types, whether through internal evolutionary transformation or through demographic replacement, war, economic, and/or ecological displacement, cannot be known as yet. (In a later chapter, we shall consider some of the presumed scenarios, using the Neanderthals and other recent vulnerable sub-species, as exemplars.)[43]

More recent events provide insights into the mysterious nature of this creature, *Homo sapiens*, who has had such a devastating impact on our planet, both on non-human fauna, as well as on our contemporary fellows. These facts seem to take us beyond traditional vertebrate evolutionary dynamics of dominance and displacement.

A comparative example within recent memory derives from the 19th century, the European discovery and takeover of Australia and its southern island of Tasmania, the latter the size of Ireland. The aboriginal peoples of Australia have survived, though now much diminished in numbers. The Tasmanians, an aboriginal population of about 5,000, physically of a Melanesian ethnic cast, as compared to the aboriginals of Australia, unable to make fire, and unaware of the relationship between sexual intercourse and child bearing, disappeared toward the end of the 19th century. A sub-population of hybrid Tasmanian peoples presumably still exists, intermixed with the dominant Europeans.

Many factors entered into the struggle of the Europeans against the Tasmanian aboriginals. Most important, the struggle was unequal. Also, the Tasmanians did not have vast spaces of the Australian outback into which to vanish, as did the Australian aborigines, and the Tasmanians, in contrast to the continental aboriginals, fought the invaders. By mid-century, they had been pressured into submission. An infamous *"cul de sac"* roundup concluded with the extirpation of these "annoying primitives." The remnant 200 individuals were exiled on Flinders Island in the Bass Straits between the mainland and Tasmania. The shock of expulsion and the complete destruction of their culture by a powerful foreign entity froze them into ultimate cultural suicide. No children, the last pure-blooded Tasmanian, a woman, Truganini died in 1876.[44]

Other, earlier genocidal destruction of weaker peoples had taken place against the Caribbean Indians in the period after the arrival of European Spaniards between 1492 and 1600. The Araucanian Indians of Argentina suffered destruction in the mid-19th century in defense of their lands against the oncoming ethnic Europeans of that nation.[45]

Surely, in many species of animal life, changes in the ecology and environment—such as those that occurred at the conclusion of the last glacial advance, 12,000 B.P.—unleash natural conditions that favor one form of the species, one race, over others. This is the grist of evolutionary change. And out of such dynamics, major shifts often occur in the faunal and floral balances of life, often ushering in the dominance of wholly new forms, and higher and precipitating taxonomic extrapolations.

It was much earlier, in Eur-Asia, as we shall develop later in greater factual and theoretical detail, that the great hominid revolution, still occurring today, began in earnest. Thus it is not unreasonable to consider the above historical events as part of a long-enduring and wider process of expansion.

However, what has happened since, and especially after at least 12,000 years of post-Ice Age cognitive human learning and experience, and into the 20th century, should bedevil our perception of the evolutionary process. Here, the events of the 20th century constitute an almost suicidal break with evolutionary principle and precedent. These occurrences inevitably raise once again the evolutionary question of explaining human behavior.

The Century of Genocide

For persons living in the 20th century, the meaning of this seemingly unlimited power and expansiveness of one species over the Earth is especially vexing. For, even after almost 12,000 years of settled agricultural and urban life, a time during which humans have seemingly gained mastery over a variety of symbolic vehicles of knowledge, literacy, philosophy, scientific method, medicine, historical self-consciousness, events have taken place, biologically unexplainable, incomprehensible.

The 20th century saw a series of wars between nations and peoples, some international and vast, but also a worldwide set of murders within nations, genocides, or, in the words one of the most serious chroniclers of these events, R. J. Rummel, "democides."[46] Another writer on these extraordinary bio/social events, Arno Mayer, placed the total figure derived from two world wars, internal national conflicts, and killings, at slightly over 200 million people dead up to 1988.[47] Rummel's own analysis, carefully broken down, produced a similar total, now comprising about 38 million in actual combat deaths, and almost 170 million innocent civilians killed as a by-product of government engagement in these wars, often conscious genocidal campaigns against the civilian enemy.

This proverbial nation of "Golgotha," the killed and dead,[48] constitutes one of the largest "nations" in the late-20th-century pantheon of peoples, a product of a world in which the power to protect life and security—vested by individuals in their social group—has been transformed into the unprecedented power of this self-same social group to kill its own. It is curious that Rummel's careful statistical and descriptive analysis does not include the Biafran genocide in Nigeria in the late 1960s.

2.4 Twentieth-century democide.

Twentieth-Century Democide

Regimes	Years	Democide (000) [a]			Annual Rate (%) [b]
		Total	Domestic	Genocide	
Megamurderers	1900-87	151,491	116,380	33,476	.92 [d]
Dekamegamurderers	1900-87	128,168	100,842	26,690	.18 [d]
USSR	1917-87	61,911	54,769	10,000	.42
China (PRC)	1949-87	35,236	35,236	375	.12
Germany	1933-45	20,946	762	16,315	.09
China (KMT)	1928-49	10,075	10,075	nil	.07 [e]
Lesser Megamurderers	1900-87	19,178	12,237	6,184	1.63 [d]
Japan	1936-45	5,964	nil	nil	nil
China (Mao Soviets) [c]	1923-49	3,466	3,466	nil	.05 [e]
Cambodia	1975-79	2,035	2,000	541	8.16
Turkey	1909-18	1,883	1,752	1,883	.96
Vietnam	1945-87	1,678	944	nil	.10
Poland	1945-48	1,585	1,585	1,585	1.99
Pakistan	1958-87	1,503	1,503	1,500	.06
Yugoslavia (Tito)	1944-87	1,072	987	675	.12
Suspected Megamurderers	1900-87	4,145	3,301	602	.24 [d]
North Korea	1948-87	1,663	1,293	nil	.25
Mexico	1900-20	1,417	1,417	100	.45
Russia	1900-17	1,066	591	502	.02
Centi-Kilomurderers	1900-87	14,918	10,812	4,071	.26 [d]
Top 5	1900-87	4,074	2,192	1,078	.89 [d]
China (warlords)	1917-49	910	910	nil	.02
Turkey (Atatürk)	1919-23	878	703	878	2.64
United Kingdom	1900-87	816	nil	nil	nil
Portugal (dictatorship)	1926-82	741	nil	nil	nil
Indonesia	1965-87	729	579	200	.02
Lesser Murderers	1900-87	2,792	2,355	1,019	.13 [d]
WORLD TOTAL	1900-87	169,202	129,547	38,566	.09 [f]

a Includes genocide, politicide, and mass murder; excludes war dead. These are most probable mid-estimates in low to high ranges. Figures may not sum due to rounding.

b The percent of a population killed in democide per year of the regime.

c Guerrilla period.

d Average.

e The rate is the average of that for three successive periods.

f The world annual rate is calculated for the 1944 global population.

Of course it could not include the most recent 1990s' killings of Bosnian and Albanian Muslims and other ethnic communities in the former Yugoslavia, heritage of genocidal slaughters of Jews and Serbs in World War II by Croats and Germans. The 1990s' genocides in Rwanda of almost 500,000 ethnic Tutsis are also not noted. Romania under Ceausescu is not listed. East Europe in general under post-World War II Communism constitutes a hidden horror that still requires enumeration. Nor are Iraq under Saddam Hussein or Iran under the Mullahs part of Rummel's inventory of human self-destruction. The totals, of 20th century death by human violence against fellow humans, given this additional information, would now be well over 210 million. Rummel understands this lack of complete accounting: "...it could conceivably be nearly 360 million."[49]

Brzezinski sees the total figure of 20th-century deaths as 87 million war deaths, including civilians. He cites 80 million more of civilian deaths, deliberate murders that he labels "the century of megadeath." The total is placed at 167 million killings of humans by humans thus far in the 20th century.[50]

A sliding list that pairs the most vicious genocides with their perpetrators is instructive. Stalin heads Rummel's demonology with almost 43 million of his own citizens' souls on his bloody hands. Mao is next, 38 million killings throughout his long career. Hitler killed 21 million, not including war casualties either on Germany's or Germany's opponents' side in Hitler's entire 12 years in power. During Chiang Kai-Shek's reign, over 10 million were killed over a 23-year period. These are only the worst examples.

Rummel's explanatory analysis is focused on the enormous increase in the power available within the political confines of a state, in technology, transportation, weaponry, communication. Tyrants, flaunting their ideological legitimacy, were now able to manipulate political institutions, and, without democratic controls, were able to gain temporary power by unleashing their various "holocausts," all in the name of the ideological ideal.[51] Democracies are absolved from this list of the damned, as their hands were relatively clean of massive brutality. Rummel argues for the democratic process as the best defense against such arbitrary power.

There is in Rummel's survey of this contemporary war of humans against humans evidence for a set of distinctions that could lend greater analytical power to renewed study of this bio/social phenomenon, and in its current 20th-century configuration.[52] For example, the traditional wars, those using 20th-century technology, such as World War I, exhibit the traditional characteristics of the struggle for power by national entities. Nations or blocs fought to limit or impede rivals, to gain what was thought rightfully to belong to their nation or group—land, trading advantages, for example. As such, World War I was not much different from Caesar's or Napoleon's wars.

But alongside traditional political adventurism, which could include massive ethnic genocide, as was true of many an internecine classical Greek city-state war, or of the Mongol advance into West Asia, is the ideological tonality of much of the human destruction of the present century. As with most religious fervor, the ideology of totalitarianism, with its absolute assumptions and visions of truth and futurity, claimed to necessitate the obliteration of all real or apparent opponents, for example, the intellectual opposition. Stalin came near to destroying the entire Soviet intelligentsia, many of whom were allies of Lenin (who had his own extermination list). Rummel estimates that Stalin killed one million Communists in the years 1936-38.

This is but one example, a relatively minor episode in the ideological killings. Recall, too, the wiping out of the Cambodian middle class by fellow ethnics Khmer Rouge, 2 million people. Gurr and Harff label these deaths "politicide," not genocide, as they involved the killing of one's own ethnic group.[53] But they do involve the killing of the "haves," not the "have nots." A closer analysis of the great majority of these internal non-ethnic genocides suggests that most examples of inter-ethnic genocide of the 20th century are accompanied by the targeting and destruction of higher socio-economic groups, the "haves," by the supposed representatives of the "have nots," thus constituting "genocide of the intelligent."

Finally, perhaps the most deadly focus of human killing, ethnicity. Rummel does not discuss the wars of religion in India and Pakistan at the time of partition, after the end of World War II, in which Muslims and Hindus of similar ethnic background slaughtered each other on the way to their respective new nations. An equally horrific but different ethnic dimension is exemplified by the government of Islamic Pakistan, in the west. This was the slaughter of its East Bengali citizens, who now comprise the nation of Bangladesh. In this case the religious allegiance is the same, Muslim. The racial and linguistic heritage among the citizens of this formerly united nation was different. Rummel estimates this death toll at 1.5 million people, mostly intellectuals.[54] The often-conscious, morally indifferent slaughter of people of another ethnicity—Jews, Tutsis, Ukrainians, Armenians, Ibos, Chechens—remains a core dimension of the violence of humans against humans.

Evolutionary Considerations

There is no simple or clear parallel to the human experience of both expansion and multiplication, destructive of fauna and flora on such a worldwide scale, and over such an apparently narrow sidereal time scale. It is believed that vast extinctions of species, even entire classes of animals have occurred a number of times in the history of life. The causes, invariably, have been laid at the door of climate and/or geology.

Because of changes in their plate tectonics, continents have been shifted to new positions relative to the equator or the two poles. In addition, shifts in the inclination of the planet, the so-called Milankovich cycles, have induced major climatic changes. Life itself, within the basic geo-physical parameters of the planets rotational movements and its orbital rotation around the Sun, has become a basic conditioning factor in the evolution of life. As we shall trace in subsequent chapters, new metabolic pathways, the powerfully photosynthesizing eukaryotic, nuclear cell, has unleashed vast amounts of oxygen, which in turn became the basis for the expansion of metazoan animal forms of life.

Some basic life forms may have disappeared as part of this vast revolution in the history of life. In the past, other forms were quickly extruded. Since the time of *Homo sapiens sapiens*, this seems no longer possible for the metazoa. Still, there is much room for the perdurance, indeed the flourishing of basic and new forms of prokaryotic, simple bacterial life. Humans today represent one dominating, but vulnerable, interbreeding super-species.

The environmental impact by one biological species, as chronicled above, is unprecedented, accompanied as it has been by the additional characteristic of massive self-destructive war and genocide. Twentieth-century events cannot be thought of as part of a traditional evolutionary process of biological selection, since apparently well adapted and exemplar evolutionary groups of humans were consciously subjected to obliteration. Any analysis of the 20th century must allow that what took place was largely the genocide of the most creative and archetypal representatives of the human species, those groups whose intelligence has been the key selective elements in the precipitation of *Homo sapiens sapiens*' dominance. A bizarre accompaniment to this destruction of over 200 million humans by their fellows has been the concomitant background increase in the world population of *Homo sapiens*, almost threefold in the 20th century, to 6 billion persons.

It is clear that some kind of evolutionary explanation is required. These events were not idiosyncratic, rather without parallel in the animal world. To understand these historical events, we need to go back to study the evolutionary conditions that brought this unique animal to power.

Such a study of the evolutionary, the natural biological conditions that rocketed humans into contemporary reality may help us better understand the inner physiological, the psychological and cultural behavior of this animal.

The self-investigation by humankind must always begin with the homeland itself.

Endnotes, Chapter 2

[1] Eldredge, Niles. 1991. *The Miner's Canary op. cit.*, pp. 91-192; Aitken, M. J., Stringer, C. B., and Mellars, P. A., eds. 1993. *The Origin of Modern Humans and the Impact of Chronometric Dating*, Princeton, N. J.: Princeton Univ. Press. p. 9.

[2] Eldredge, 1991, *op. cit.*, pp. 183, 187.

[3] Barnosky, A. D. 1989. "The Late Pleistocene Event as a Paradigm for a Widespread Mammal Extinction," in *Mass Extinctions: Process and Evidence*, S. K. Donovan, ed., N.Y.: Columbia Univ. Press, pp. 238-239.

[4] Savage, R. J. G. 1988. "Extinction and the fossil mammal record," in *Extinction and Survival in the Fossil Record*, G. P. Larwood, ed., N.Y.: Oxford Univ. Press, p. 331.

[5] deMenocal, Peter, in *Columbia*. Winter, 1996, 44.

[6] Elliott, David, K. ed. 1986. *Dynamics of Extinction*, N. Y.: John Wiley, Table 1, p. 108. Table excludes continents of Europe and Asia. (Note the relatively small rate of extinctions amongst the contemporary African mammal fauna.)

[7] Vereshchagin, N. K., and Baryshnikov, G. F. 1984. "Quaternary Mammalian Extinctions in Northern Eurasia," in *Quaternary Extinctions: a prehistoric revolution*, P. S. Martin and R. G. Klein, eds., Tucson: Univ. of Arizona Press, p. 484.

[8] Martin, P. S. 1984. "Prehistoric overkill: the global model," in *Quaternary Extinctions*, P. S. Martin and R. G. Klein, eds., *op. cit.*

[9] *Ibid.*

[10] Vereshchagin and Baryshnikov, 1984, *op. cit.*, p. 484.

[11] Haynes, C. V. 1984. "Stratigraphy and late Pleistocene extinctions in the United States," in *Quaternary Extinctions*, P. S. Martin and R. G. Klein, eds., *op. cit.*, pp. 345-353.

[12] *New York Times* articles on cultures in Brazil and Tierra del Fuego, southern Argentina: Wilford, J. N. 1996. "In an Amazon Cave, Light Is Shed on Early Americans," *The New York Times* April 19, p. A10. Reports on research in *Science*, April 19, 1996, by Dr. Anna Roosevelt of the Univ. of Illinois of a cave in Amazonia (Monte Alegre) with paintings on cave walls made by an Amero-Indian foraging community, c. 11,000 B.P., contemporaneous with the Clovis, New Mexico Amero-Indian spear point culture of the same time period; Wilford, J. N. 1997. "Human Presence in Americas Is Pushed Back a Millennium," *The New York Times*, Feb. 11, p. A1. Reports on discoveries in Southern Chile made by Dr. Tom Dillehay, Univ. of Kentucky, and Chilean archaeologists. Report to be published in March, 1997, issue of Smithsonian Institution. Artifacts in Monte Verde area dated to 12,500 B.P., 1,000 years earlier than the Clovis culture of New Mexico.

[13] Martin, P. S. 1984. "Prehistoric overkill: the global model," in P. S. Martin and R. G. Klein, eds., *op. cit.*, p. 405.

[14] Vereshchagin and Baryshnikov, 1984, *op. cit.*, p. 484.

[15] Guthrie, R. Dale. 1984. "Mosaics, Allelochemics and Nutrients," in P. S. Martin and R. G. Klein, eds., *op. cit.*, pp. 259-298.

[16] McDonald, J. N. 1984. "North American Selection Regime," in, P. S. Martin and R. G. Klein, eds., *op. cit.*, pp. 404-439.

[17] Wade, N. 1997. "Man Has Older Friend Than Thought," *The New York Times*, June 13, p. A-12. This article discusses researchers' possible DNA evidence that dogs were domesticated several hundred thousand years ago.

[18] McEvedy, C., and Jones, R. 1978. *Atlas of World Population*, N.Y.: Penguin, p.14.

[19] Ross, John T., ed. 1982. *International Encyclopedia of Population*, Vol. 2, N.Y.: Free Press, Macmillan Pub., p. 679.

[20] Ehrlich, Anne and Paul. 1981. *Extinction*, N.Y.: Random House.

[21] Soule, Michael. 1987. Cited in C. Tudge, *Evolution and Extinction*, Chaloner, W. G. and Hallam, A., eds., 1994, N.Y.: Cambridge Univ. Press, p.485; *World Almanac*, 1995, p. 510, says 200 million.

[22] Colinvaux, Paul. 1978. *Why Big Fierce Animals Are Rare*, Princeton, N.J.: Princeton Univ. Press.

[23] Carcopino, J. 1940. *Daily Life in Ancient Rome*, New Haven: Yale Univ. Press, p. 230.

[24] Carcopino, 1940, *op. cit.*, p. 239.

[25] Ward, Peter. 1994. *The End of Evolution*, N.Y.: Bantam Books, pp. 242-243; Trotter, M. M., and McCulloch, B., "Moas, Men and Middens," p. 708; Anderson, A., "The Extinction of Moa in Southern New Zealand," p. 728; Cassels, R., "Faunal Extinction and Prehistoric Man in New Zealand and the Pacific Islands," p. 741; Dewar, R. E., "Extinctions in Madagascar: The Loss of the Subfossil Fauna," pp. 574-593, all in, 1984, P. S. Martin and R. G. Klein, eds., *op. cit.*

[26] Cited in Martin, P. S., and Klein, R. G., eds. 1984. *Quaternary Extinctions, op. cit.*

[27] Ward, P. 1994. *op. cit.*., p. 243.

[28] Day, D. 1981. *The Doomsday Book of Animals*, N.Y.: Viking Press, p. 13.

[29] Day, D., 1981, *op. cit.*, p. 272.

[30] Jameson, J. Franklin, ed. 1959. "Letter of Isaack de Rasieres to Samuel Blommart, (1628?)" 'Narratives of New Netherlands' New York, in Patrick Malone. 1991. *The Skulking Way of War*, Lanham, Md.: Madison Books, p.62.

[31] Di Silvestro, Roger. 1994, in Peter Ward, *op. cit.*, p. 211.

[32] Day, D., 1981, *op. cit.*, p. 188.

[33] Day, D., 1981, *op. cit.*, pp. 188-189.

[34] Day, D., 1981, *op. cit.*, p. 189.

[35] Kellert, S., and Wilson, E. O., eds. 1993. *The Biophylia Hypothesis*, Washington, D.C.: Island Press p. 37.

[36] Wilson, E. O., and Kellert, S., eds., 1993, *op. cit.*

[37] Wilson, E. O. 1992. *The Diversity of Life*, Cambridge, MA: Harvard Univ. Press.

[38] Wilson, E. O., 1992, *op. cit.*, p. 36.

[39] Prance, G. T. 1983. N.Y. Botanical Garden, cited in Lovejoy, Thomas, and Salati, Eneas. 1983. *The Dilemma of Amazonian Development,* pp. 214-215; Prance, G. T. 1982. "Forest refuges: Evidence from woody angiosperms," in *Biological Diversification in the Tropics*, Prance, G. T., ed., N.Y.: Columbia Univ. Press, pp. 137-159.

[40] McDonald, K. A. 1997. "Scientists Refine Estimates of Number of Species and Their Rate of Extinction," *The Chronicle of Higher Education*, 11/14/97, A17; also see Ehrlich, P., *et al.* 1997. *Science*, 10/24/97; also see above estimates of Jared Diamond and E. O. Wilson.

[41] Trinkaus, E., and Shipman, P. 1993. *The Neanderthals*, N.Y.: Knopf.

[42] Wade, N. 1997. "Neanderthal DNA Sheds New Light On Human Origins," *N.Y. Times*, July 11. Wade discusses article by Svante Paabo in *Cell* (July 11, 1997). Further, Neanderthal mitochondrial DNA reveals no evidence of interbreeding with modern humans, mtDNA taken from five continents. *Hss* and Neanderthals presumably parted genetically at least 600,000 years ago.

[43] Simeons, A. T. S. 1962. *Man's Presumptuous Brain*, p. 276; Tattersall, I. 1995. *The Last Neanderthal*, N.Y.: Macmillan/U.S.A., p. 9.

[44] Moorehead, A. 1966. *The Fatal Impact*, N.Y.: Harper and Row.

[45] Diamond, Jared, 1992, *op. cit.*, pp. 278-285; also Moorehead, 1992, *op. cit.*

[46] Rummel, R. J. 1994. *Death By Government*, New Brunswick, N.J.: Transaction Publishers.

[47] Mayer, A. 1988. *Why Did The Heavens Not Darken?*, N.Y.: Pantheon.

[48] After Shakespeare, *King Richard II*; 4,1,144; Rummel, 1994, *op. cit.*, pp. 9-11.

[49] Rummel, 1994, *op. cit.*, p. 9; also fig. 1.9, p. 21.

[50] Brzezinski, Zbiegniew. 1994. *Out of Control*, N.Y.: Macmillan, pp. 10, 17; Conquest, R. 1986. *The Harvest of Sorrow: Soviet Collectivization and the Terror Famine*, N.Y.: Oxford Univ. Press.

[51] Rummel, 1994, *op. cit.*, see XV-XVI, pp. 15-16, 31-43.

[52] Rummel, 1994, *op. cit.*, see I. L. Horowitz "Foreword," p. XIV.

[53] Gurr, T. R., and Harff, B. 1994. *Ethnic Conflicts in World Politics*, Boulder, CO.: Westview Press, p. 8.

[54] Rummel, 1994, *op. cit.*, pp. 315-337.

3

Life Begins

"Time in fact is the hero of the plot....Given so much time, the impossible becomes possible, the possible
probable, and the probable virtually certain. One has only to wait: time itself performs the miracles."
George Wald

Earth Origins

The reports during the summer of 1996 of the possible existence of simple forms
of bacterial life on the planet Mars, based according to NASA scientists on a Martian
meteorite found in Antarctica, once again raises the question of the ubiquity of life in
our universe.[1] As scientists have argued for many years, the natural combining of certain
universally available elements into compounds which resemble amino acids and other
organic compounds is quite common and found in a variety of materials encountered
from outer space. J. William Schopf of U.C.L.A has noted that polycyclic aromatic hy-
drocarbons have been found on earth and again in meteorites but have origins that are
not biological.[2]

Thus, under the special conditions experienced by our Earth in its origination in the
solar system 4.6bya, and as compared with those physico-chemical conditions experienced by the other planets, and perhaps other bodies throughout our own galaxy and out
into our universe, the basic attractions exhibited by chemical elements in our originating
water based environment is not to be considered extraordinary or improbable. Of course,
duplicating these originating Earth conditions in the universe at large is *not* considered
probable.

The "lithosphere," the hard, solid, upper mantle of our Earth, began forming about
4.6 billion years ago. A consensus view is that a cloud of interstellar matter began to
condense and fall in upon itself through the action of gravitational forces. It is a view
proposed over two centuries ago by both Immanuel Kant and Pierre Laplace. Yet we are
still speculating as to the cause.[3]

It is possible that in the early period (4.6-4.3bya) of the contraction of the dust and
gaseous mass that became planet Earth, much interstellar material was drawn gravitationally into its orbit around the sun. At this time, a "Mars"-sized mass possibly collided

with the Earth that caused a tearing off of a large body of material, throwing it into a secondary orbit. This mass became a satellite of the Earth, *i.e.*, the Moon. It is also possible that as a result of this collision, the orbital configuration of the Earth was shaped and defined, as well as our day/night periodicity. The Earth's axis was consequently tilted to give us winter and summer seaonality.[4]

In this earliest period in the history of our planet, 4.6-4.3bya, the heat generated in the process of creation was, as with the Sun, extreme. The intense heat came from three sources: 1) heat generated from the collapse of the material in the gas and dust cloud, and produced by gravitational shrinkage; 2) bombardment of the sphere by extraterrestrial meteorites; 3) radioactive elements within the earth. For over 600 million years, the Earth was extremely hot. Most of the heat-causing asteroid bombardment by solar system debris (planetesimals) was concluded by 4bya. The Earth before this time was perhaps too hot for the existence of life.[5]

Controversy still occurs as to the makeup of the Earth's atmosphere some 4bya, the present speculation being that it consisted mostly of CO_2, hydrogen sulfide, molecular nitrogen, perhaps some methane, water vapor, perhaps trace amounts of oxygen because of the gravitational loss of light hydrogen atoms.[6] The Sun at about 4bya had only 75% of its present-day brightness, and a day on Earth was only ten hours long due to the tidal gravitational drag exerted by the Moon.[7]

A greenhouse effect existed on Earth that prevented its super-cooling. It is possible that it was a combination of water vapor, carbon dioxide, nitrogen, and possibly some methane, all of which existed in Earth's earliest atmosphere, that prevented the radiation into space of indigenous and atmospheric introjected heat.[8] It is estimated that without water, carbon dioxide, and some methane in the atmosphere, given the present existence of oxygen in the atmosphere, the temperature of the Earth's surface would be a steady, 0 degrees Fahrenheit. In fact, these atmospheric gases mediate the incoming sunlight (short wave length radiation) and the outgoing heat radiation which the atmosphere both encloses and absorbs, to create an average worldwide temperature of 59 degrees Fahrenheit.

Water is crucial to the origin and evolution of life. The surface of Earth at this time was covered by deep oceans, with volcanoes spewing interior heat onto the surface of the earth. The so-called hydrological cycle takes place when water evaporates, condenses, is transducted into deeper realms of the earth's mantle, a process called subduction. There it erupts again as gaseous extrusions, eroding the continental shelves, is then absorbed into the crust of the continents, cooling and constituting a vast self-regulating homeothermic system. In this way, the hydrological cycle stabilizes the climate and the ecological balances on the earth.[9] "The hydrothermal circulation is the radiator of the Earth's engine. It rapidly cools oceanic crust; it causes oceanic crust to be hydrated; it helps subduction to operate and thus helps the continents to exist; and it is an important control of the chemical composition of seawater."[10]

The oldest existing sedimentary rocks are at Isua in Greenland. They were laid down about 3.8bya and give evidence of an atmosphere with significant amounts of CO_2[11], also oxidized iron sediments.[12] One scientific school theorizes that such ancient rocks show early signs of oxidation, indicating the presence of oxygen in free form. The possibility of an early greenhouse effect that saved the early oceans from freezing over would imply the existence of some oxygen in the early atmosphere, as some of the light hydrogen fixed in water vapor, was transported through ultraviolet heating and molecular disassociation processes out of the atmosphere, freeing up some of the oxygen.[13]

Harold Blum argued, in a classic book, *Time's Arrow and Evolution* (1951), that the Second Law, often called "time's arrow," clarified how, in one specific thermodynamic system within our universe, structures of matter and energy have arisen that we define as "living things."[14] These temporarily surge against the prevailing and inevitable universal degradation of free energy (entropy). Finally, all counterentropic processes, information itself, life as well as the dampened sidereal fires of galaxies and their incandescent stars will be extinguished in the quiet of universal energic dispersal.

Life can be defined in its creation of free energy as it metabolizes available sources of food energy in the process of renewal and reproduction. Sources of energy may be metals available in moist clays—sulfur, iron—usually combining with CO_2 and water, the oxidation process giving off chemical energy. The use of the energy of the sun even under anaerobic, nonoxidizing conditions, given the availability of complex organic molecules to be absorbed within a confined cellular membrane, sufficed for respiratory/fermentation metabolism, whose products were energy and waste organic molecules such as alcohol.[15]

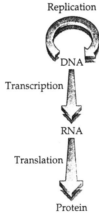

Replication

DNA

Transcription

RNA

Translation

Protein

3.1 The relationships between DNA and RNA that function during gene replication and protein synthesis.

The three basic molecular elements that form the structure of life that exists today are made up of DNA, Deoxyribonucleic acid, now represented as a double helix, and RNA, Ribonucleic acid, a single strand compound made up of carbon, oxygen, nitrogen, hydrogen, and phosphorous. Most advanced forms of life have coded in their DNA the informational structure that in the process of development produces the living form. RNA constitutes the transcription of the DNA into a working copy of the instructions to be communicated to the amino acids in the protein molecules. These amino acid chains—20 basic to all living things—are composed of carboxylic acids, COOH, and an amine, NH_2. These so-called peptide bonds, form polypeptides, which are the working model for the construction of the various cell structures of the animal, plant, fungus morphologies and physiological functions. According to Monod,[16] a simple bacterium, "Escherichia coli" could have as many as 2500 different protein molecules in its struc-

ture, derived from various combinations of these 20 basic amino acids; humans would
have over one million.

G. L.Stebbins believes that in this dynamic, pre-biotic soup of 4.3bya to 3.8bya,
possibly millions of pathways of metabolic activity existed as these molecules maintained themselves for a moment, then dissolved.[17] Gradually, the evolving Earth began
to produce less and less of the naturally occurring organic molecules that were excreted
from the interactions of hot lava, geothermal eruptions, and the flux of many molecular
minerals. As G. Pirie put it, in the evolution of living forms, the transition over time is
from chemical and metabolic diversity to increasing bio-chemical simplicity, specialization, and regularity. Then, morphological diversity.[18]

The Tree of Life

No longer do we consider the tree of life as consisting of two great kingdoms -
plants and animals. Our knowledge of the molecular structure of living entities, the
makeup of their DNA, RNA, and protein sequences allows us to create a map of relationships that presumably carries us back in time almost to that surviving Ur-bacterium
out of which have come and diverged the modern descendants of the primeval surviving
forms of life. These kingdoms are now six: two seemingly most ancient prokaryotic unicellular forms, the archaebacteria and the eubacteria, the latter comprising the most
common bacterial forms now encountered; four eukaryotic (complex cells) - protists
(unicellular forms), fungi, true plants, animals.

Therefore, at least three original "super-kingdoms": 1. Archaebacteria. 2. Eubacteria. 3. Eukaryote forms. 1 and 2 are prokaryote, if differently structured. The pending
question revolves around their evolutionary relationship and sequence of origination.[19]

The nucleotide sequences of the rRNA (ribosomal RNA) in both archaebacteria
and eubacteria, as well as higher forms of eukaryotes, have been analyzed by C. R.
Woese.[20] His conclusions, now the accepted orthodoxy, are that all three forms of life
contribute to a triangle of biological structures equidistant from each other in their evolutionary origin. They all have three similar primeval characteristics that point to a
common origin: 1) all use fermentation as an energy-generating metabolism; 2) all are
"thermophilic," needing very hot environments in which to mobilize their metabolisms;
3) all live by anaerobiosis, in a non-oxygenating environment, probably characteristic of
the early atmospheric environment on the Earth.

C. Woese has recently moved toward a view that favors the independent origins of
each of the super-kingdoms from a common pool of interacting cells that selectively
acquired over time a similar genetic code.[21]

> Cellular life appeared on our planet, after it had cooled down enough to allow chemi-
> cal self-organization, within less than one thousand million years. It is probable that the
> greatest part of this period was needed for the necessary molecules for the processes of life
> to accumulate in sufficient concentrations to encounter one another frequently and to or-
> ganize the first "social animal", the cell....The path led from molecules to integrated systems
> of molecules, from the single cell to the system of interacting cells, from the agglomeration
> of cells [stromatolites] to the integrated cellular society, from the organ to the higher organ-
> ism.[22]

There too came into functioning, eubacteria that utilized the still faint energies of the sun to anaerobically combine carbon dioxide and hydrogen sulfide and a metallic light sensitive compound, thence broken down by ATP, to produce energy plus other carbon compounds. Hartman argues that the earliest anaerobic photosynthetic bacteria were ancestors of contemporary purple bacteria.[23]

Eukaryote cells are the basic building blocks of modern one-celled protists (algae, paramecia), fungi, plants and animals, the other four of the six kingdoms of life. They are large and complex. Multicellular life would be impossible without them The model proposed by C. Woese thus has the two primeval forms of prokaryotic life representing the earliest victorious biochemical lines of heterotrophic (organic feeders) and autotrophic (non-organic molecules or photosensitive) metabolizers going their individual pathways as early as 3.5bya.[24] The eukaryotes, then, are viewed as extremely early competitors of the prokaryotes, possibly independent in origins, exhibiting a mix of characteristics of both archaebacteria and eubacteria, else a later, 2.5-1.5bya fabrication.

All four basic forms of eukaryote life, protists, plants, fungi, animals, would be tied together by certain common evolutionary features: the amino acids and their polymers, as a class; the proteins; the nucleotides and their polymers, the nucleic acids. Basic differences in proteins and their enzymes with their divergent metabolic pathways would eventually lead in the metazoa, multicellular forms of life, to the varied forms of development beyond the cell walls and membranes of individual life forms, to the larger systemic integration of differently structured and functioning cells into a complex organism. At the common core were the building blocks of life, the genetic code and its ribosomal machinery.[25]

By two billion years ago, half the present age of the earth, the oxygen-producing bacteria were pushing various archae- and eubacteria into the backwaters of the environment where they can be found today, in the root nodes of nitrogen-fixing plants, in the intestinal tracks of animals, in the vast thermal bottoms of the ocean floors. Bacteria that were without the enzymes to metabolize oxygen were driven, as part of this epochal transitional shift in evolutionary life and natural selection, into deep, airless, perhaps infinitely secure Earthly environments.[26]

Through the use of this free oxygen, newer biochemical processes were made possible in the availability of organic forms rich in nutrient energy for the metabolic food chain. They could now break down as "food" a vast array of organic molecules into CO_2 and H_2O, releasing unprecedented amounts of energy. Yet, even today: "Deep in the cells of oxygen-breathers the old machinery works to break down food into by products that it passes on to the newer oxygen-burning equipment for further conversion."[27] A new form of eukaryotic heterotrophic life, all building on the existence of the work of the autotrophic (non-organic) photosynthesizers, was now made possible.[28]

Thus began the transformation of pink skies into blue, the brownish seas to azure, an indication of a vast change coming over the biotic face of the planet.

The Eukaryote Cell

The eukaryote cell testifies to a now perhaps 2-billion-year process of experimentation on a material entity, the planet Earth, which had calmed, physically and geologically, in its own re-creation and evolution (from c.4.6bya). Within the parameters of our physico-chemical environment—the watery surfaces, the exterior and interior dynamics of the continental plates, an atmosphere increasingly invaded by oxygen exuded by eubacterial stromatolites —the race of life forms was now for stability of metabolism within this environment of seeming semi-permanence. This contextual (symbiotic-"Gaia") physico-chemical/biological environment would now exhibit increasing efficiency and versatility of energy production, far beyond the now specializing archaebacteria, the proliferating eubacterial autotrophic and heterotrophic forms.

The so-called protists of our contemporary world, single- eukaryote-celled animals, contained within their permeable membrane a well-defined nucleus containing chromosomes, genes, and DNA, plus assisting amino acids-proteins, the biochemical information and regulatory packet that programmed the moment-by-moment functioning of the cell. This basic structure also contributed to its biological reproductive perdurance over time.

An important evolutionary message can be derived from the probable originating events in the unique cosmic environment that existed on Earth after 4.6bya. It is communicated from those forms of life that seem to have survived the unknown, but certainly decisive, selective sieve of the succeeding 2.5-3.0-billion years of Earthly geophysical changes. This message is transmitted from the events contributing to the overwhelming percentage of bio-molecular extinctions that took place, as life forms, most likely slowly, but irresistibly, pushed against the eternal energic tide toward entropy. This message—and its lesson—was the need for life forms to gain the energic girth and stability that could resist momentary environmental anomalies, a homeostasis often at the edge of extinction.[29]

Combine chance events with a basic Earth environment of counterentropic possibility, an abundance of water, an atmosphere that protected and insulated, and we can understand the necessity for this at least 2 billion years of experimentation. In the end was created that mysterious and gigantic industrial entity, so many functions, internal semi-independence, fabricating the material and energetic basis for our self-maintaining and reproducing eukaryote entity. This living machine as we meet it, often at 10,000X the size of the typical prokaryote bacterial cell, early constitutes the great and enigmatic miracle in the evolution of life on our planet.

During the ongoing history of the prokaryotes, surviving in their various, sometimes extreme environments, biochemically constrained even given their random mutations, prokaryotes evolved a diversity of internal bio-chemical metabolic pathways. At the same time these physico-chemical arrangements were bereft of new structural forms. They remained tiny one-celled entities, even when forming dense-colonied stromatolite mats. Eukaryotes, by contrast, were able to mobilize the energy and transport systems that could organize a variety of interacting cells, (cooperating), having many nuclei and their surrounding morphologies, all within a single bodily cavity, the metazoa.[30]

The simplest green alga has, including the sex cells, four or five different kinds of cells functioning for the individual plant. In humans, the developmental DNA sequence from the moment of fertilization invokes the fabrication of about 250 differing kinds of cells in their diverse distribution and physiological functioning throughout the entire morphological entity, the individual.[31]

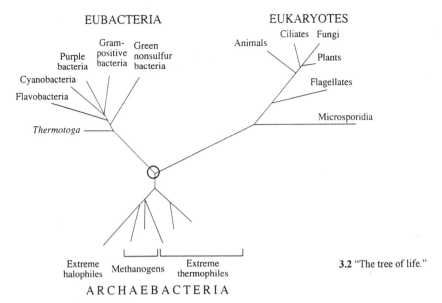

3.2 "The tree of life."

Selective Factors in Sexual Reproduction

1. Christian de Duve cites the cytoskeletal innovations in the eukaryote protist "*Giardia*," along with sexual reproduction, as most important pre-conditions for the evolution of advanced metazoa. The flagellum, which acts as a directional and movement organ, and the more temporary "mitotic spindle" that arises, then dissolves as part of the reproductive cycle, characterize a highly complex product of many interacting proteins created at some unknown point in the transition between prokaryote and eukaryote forms of life.[32]

2. The secured genome within the nucleus might have gained selective value as a means for the early eukaryotes to resist invasion and plundering of the genome by viruses.[33]

3. Sexual reproduction may seem to be disadvantageous because of its slower reproductive rate than pure bacterial mitosis. By the time two eukaryote cells have been created from one, one trillion bacteria will have been produced by mitotic division, along with several billion mutations, the latter due to replication errors.[34]

4. Richard Dawkins argues for the advantage of sexual reproduction over more ancient eubacterial forms of reproduction which share and/or exchange genetic material with each other on occasion, while still maintaining asexual reproduction. The selective advantage might lie in the use of shared (gametic) genetic DNA that might then be used to repair mutated or adaptively defective DNA in one or both of the parent cells, hence for its own "selfish" survival needs. In so doing it could create daughter forms that had no "errors" and thus that were more adaptive, thence to be favored by natural selection.[35]

5. The versatility of plants in terms of asexual and/or sexual reproduction hints at the early and powerful adaptive success of this kingdom of eukaryote life. Their evolutionary progression and direction seem to have had much more "leg room," by dint of

photosynthesis, than the constrained sexual and heterotrophic pathway taken by major lines of animal life.[36]

6. Sexual reproduction will facilitate the opportunity for the exploration of new habitats: coral polyps and sponges, also rhizopod flagellates, (*Naegeleria*), engage in asexual reproduction for stability, perdurance—mitotic division. Periodically they undergo meiosis, forming gametes of genetic variability under the stimulus of new environmental conditions, brought about by the opportunity for the colonization of new ecologies. Many will fail.[37]

"[Eukaryote] plant cells multiply by simple division, perpetuating the same genome. But let the survival of the cells be endangered by some environmental upheaval and they suddenly go into a frenzy of sexual debauchery...a frantic search for a genetic combination better adapted to the new conditions."[38]

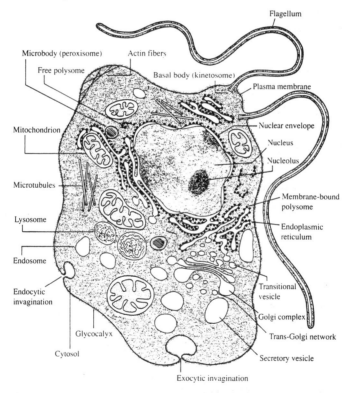

3.3 Eukaryotic organization. Hypothetical biflagellated protist illustrating the main components of animal cells

7. Sexual reproduction allows for death. The disappearance of mother cells opens up evolutionary opportunities for genetically variable daughter eukaryote cells. Here, the progeny might be somewhat better able to cope with a constantly changing environment without the competition of parent forms.

8. Prokaryotic bacteria can exchange genetic information with types of bacteria that are genetically far removed. Recombination can occur between distant relatives. Such diversity in bacteria, along with their propensity to err in mitotic division, can create new biochemical characteristics, thus foiling human antibiotic medicine and the inoculation of humans against bacterial infections. Eukaryote sexual reproduction, on the other hand, limits the range of reproductive partners because of the molecular need for the compatibility of the genes. The result is a much slower rate of biological change in eukaryote cells, as compared with the prokaryotes.

9. Natural selection has secured the internal homeostasis of the eukaryote type by dint of the millennial stability over billions of years of the Earth's environmental system. This relationship is further reinforced by the slow reproductive rhythms of sexual exchange. Eukaryotic life adaptively has opted for a relatively slow rate of genetic variability to meet the challenges of a slowly changing but physically and bio-chemically complex environment. Sexual reproduction adaptively coordinates the selective valences in a large, metabolically efficient, slower-maturing and longer-lived phenotype.[39]

The key to the future of complex sexually-reproducing cellular life, whether protozoa or metazoa, was the build-up of free oxygen in the planetary atmosphere, up to the present 20-21%, a process rooted in the photosynthetic transformation of sunlight into energy.

Endnotes, Chapter 3

[1] *Science*, August 1996.

[2] *The New York Times*, 8/13/96, p. c8.

[3] Sepkoski, J. J., Jr. 1993. "Foundations: Life in the Oceans," *Life*, S. J. Gould, ed., N.Y.: W. W. Norton, p. 38.

[4] Nisbet, E. G. 1991. *Living Earth*, N.Y.: Harper Collins, pp. 4-5.

[5] Sepkoski, 1993, *op. cit.,* p. 38.

[6] Sepkoski, 1993, *op. cit.,* p. 38.

[7] Nisbet, 1991, *op. cit.,* p. 15.

[8] Nisbet, 1991, *op. cit.,* pp. 9-13.

[9] Nisbet, 1991, *op. cit.,* pp. 25-26.

[10] Nisbet, 1991, *op. cit.,* p. 29.

[11] Hartman, H., *et al.* 1987. *Search for the Universal Ancestors: The Origin of Life*, Palo Alto, CA: Blackwell, pp. 68-69.

[12] Sepkoski, 1993, *op. cit.,* pp. 42-43.

[13] Nisbet, 1991, *op. cit.,* p. 15; see also, Fowler, C. M. R. 1990. *The Solid Earth*, N.Y.: Cambridge Univ. Press.

[14] Blum, H. F. 1951. *Time's Arrow and Evolution*, Princeton, N.J.: Princeton Univ. Press.

[15] Sepkoski, 1993, *op. cit.,* pp. 40-41.

[16] Monod, Jacques. 1971. *Chance and Necessity, op. cit.,* p. 48.

[17] Stebbins, G. Ledyard. 1982. *Darwin to DNA, Molecules to Humanity*, San Francisco: W. H. Freeman, p. 186ff.

[18] Pirie, N. W. 1957. "Some Assumptions Underlying Discussion of the Origin of Life," in *Modern Ideas on Spontaneous Generation*, Ross F. Nigrelli, ed., N. Y. Annals of the New York Academy of Science, pp. 369-376.

[19] Carl Woese, a number of years ago, suggested the term "Domain" for each of the three "super-kingdoms." Woese, C. S., Kandler, O., Wheelis, M. S. 1990. "Towards a Natural System of Organisms: Proposal for the Domains Archea, Bacteria and Eucarya," in *Proceed. Natl. Acad. Sci. U.S.A.*, 87:4576-4579.

[20] Woese, C. R. 1981. "Archaebacteria," *Scientific American*, 244:6; Stebbins, 1982, *op. cit.*, pp. 188-189; Dyer, B. D., and Obar, R. A. 1994. *Tracing the History of Eukaryotic Cells, op. cit.*, p. 32.

[21] Wade, Nicholas. 1998. "Tree of Life Turns Out to Have Surprisingly Complex Roots," *The New York Times*, April 14, C1.

[22] Eigen, Manfred. 1992. *Steps Toward Life*, N. Y.: Oxford Univ. Press, p.48.

[23] Hartman, H., *et al.*, 1987, *op. cit.*, pp. 38-39.

[24] Woese, C. R., Kandler, O., and Wheelis, M. L. 1990. "Towards a Natural System of Organisms: Proposal for the Domains Archea, Bacteria and Eucarya," in *Proc. Natl. Acad. Sci. USA87*, 87:4576-79.

[25] Hartman, H., *et al.*, 1987, pp. 39-40; see also Margulis, L. 1992. *Symbiosis and Cell Evolution*, 2nd ed., San Francisco: W. H. Freeman; Schopf, J. W., ed. 1983. *The Earth's Earliest Biosphere*, Princeton, N. J.: Princeton Univ. Press; Woese, C. R. 1981. "Archaebacteria," *Scientific American*, 244:6.

[26] Sepkoski, 1993, *op. cit.*, p. 44.

[27] *Ibid.*

[28] *Ibid.*

[29] Monod, Jacques. 1971. *Chance and Necessity, op. cit.*, pp. 123-124.

[30] Stebbins, 1982, *op. cit.*, p. 193.

[31] Stebbins, 1982, *op. cit.*, p. 210.

[32] de Duve, Christian. 1995. *Vital Dust, op. cit.*, pp. 154-156.

[33] Woese, C. R. 1987. "Bacterial Evolution," in *Microbiol. Rev.*, 51:221-271; Dyer, B. D., and Obar, R. A. 1994. *Tracing the History of Eukaryotic Cells, op. cit.*, pp. 228-230.

[34] de Duve, Christian. 1995. *Vital Dust, op. cit.*, p. 126.

[35] Dawkins, R. 1995. *River Out of Eden* , N. Y.: Basic Books.

[36] Stebbins, 1982, *op. cit.*, pp. 221-225.

[37] Williams, G. C. 1975. *Sex and Evolution*, Princeton, N.J.: Princeton Univ. Press.

[38] de Duve, 1995, *op. cit.*, p. 159.

[39] Nisbet, 1991, *op. cit.*, pp. 111-114.

4

Evolution of the Vertebrates

Prelude to Animals

> "....Comparative work on hemoglobin and calibrated rates of nucleotide sequence divergence suggested that there was an extended period of metazoan diversification that began earlier in the mid-Proterozoic, perhaps about 1 billion years ago."
>
> Chia-Wei Li, Jun-Yuan Chen, Tzu-En Hua[1]

A special crisis in the history of our planet is thought to have occurred after c.1bya. It was paralleled by the simultaneous breakup of an existing super-continent that apparently had long stabilized climatic conditions on Earth. The shifting continental tectonics seem to have coincided with the ending of a series of intense glaciations, considered by some to be the harshest in the history of the planet. The residue from these shifts left glacial deposits in Australia, identified as existing around 600mya, when that continent was within ten degrees of Earth's equator.[2]

By 1bya it is believed that the molecular and structural basis of animal life had been established. During the approximately 3.5by that had preceded this period of Earth's history, a number of crucial biochemical pathways for counter-entropic energic self-maintenance had been established.

The basic eukaryote cell was by then a reality. Controversy exists over the length of formation time, its relationship to both or either the archaebacteria or eubacteria, whether as a break-off form of life sometime down the time line from the early 4by-old formation of these living molecules. Else, as an originating form, thence taking on, in heterotrophic absorption (phagocytosis), various molecular-structural components—cytoplasm, mitochondria, nuclear structure.

Sexual reproduction was certainly, by 1bya an established reproductive pathway for both plant and animal lines, long differentiated as separate kingdoms. In fact there is consensus that by this time frame, the levels of oxygen in the air were close to 21%. So, too, well dissolved in water, oxygen no longer bound to iron, and the latter precipitated to the sea bottoms.

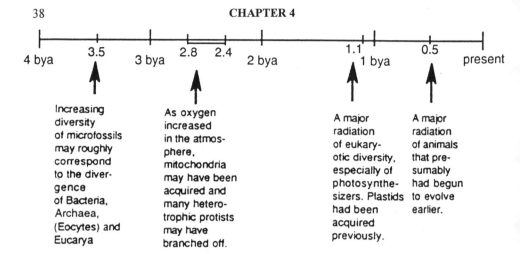

4.1 Major events in molecular evolution.

Shortly after 1bya, the so-called Varengian glaciation seems to have covered major portions of the planet, including land masses very close to the equator. Also in this time frame we seem to see the breaking up of the great super-continent Rodinia, presumably creating a number of shallow inland seas that may have established the possibility for a speedier dynamic in the evolution of the metazoa, those multi-cellular plants and animals now reproducing sexually, in great competition with a host of life forms. Those lines that were able to shift from vegetative to sexual reproductive patterns and back again seem invariably to have taken to the sexual patterns in times of stress or competition, thus arguing for the value of sexual reproduction as a concession to the need for chance taking into the evolutionary unknown by the particular line in question.

The Varengian glaciation, and the cold that it reflects, could have been a product of the breakthrough in photosynthetic efficiency of plant forms, mostly plankton, algae and mosses. The stimulus of the surplus oxygen now available in water through the extrusion of oxygen into the atmosphere, not only created the cold by depleting the protective warming atmospheric effect of CO_2, but also provided enormous food metabolic opportunities for the proliferating heterotrophic multi-cellular animal forms.

First products of this reasonable, if hypothetical, scenario are the Ediacaran fauna of the Riphean and Vendian periods, from c.800-650mya. These so-called soft path animals, mostly rooted filter feeders, flourished in the shallow post-Rodinian continental and inter-continental seas. Most evidence argues that these animal forms constitute an enormous number of different structural and metabolic pathways, and that they were productive of many now extinct phyla, many more than have come down to modern times since the Cambrian. In general, they seem to have been passive, soft-bodied creatures resembling the form of plants even more than modern animal forms.

The only other signs of possible animal life are the burrows and tracings found in various geological strata dating to that period, sometimes in conjunction with Ediacaran fossil indications. This indirect evidence points to worm-like bilateral forms of animal life.

The great evolutionary question relates to the transition to the seeming explosive burst of Cambrian animal life, exemplified in the variegated phyla found in the Burgess Shales (c.520mya) in British Columbia. How could such a transition from virtually no signs of modern hard-bodied forms of animal life in the Vendian period, 700-600mya, to the flourishing of so many modern forms of animal life 100-50my later, have so quickly occurred alongside the concomitant total disappearance of the Ediacaran forms?

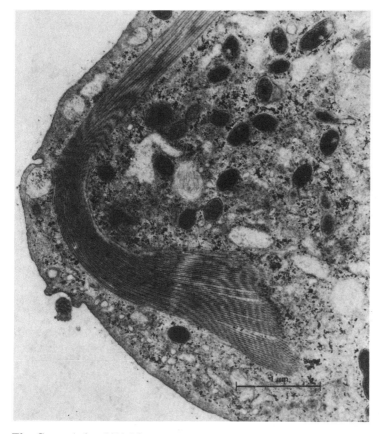

4.2 This electron micrograph shows bacterial endosymbionts living in the cytoplasm of the protozoon *Pyrsonympha*, which itself lives as a symbiont in the hindgut of the termite *Reticulitermes*.

The Great Animal Divide

Ancient animal body plans consisted of two types: a) Radial symmetry, cnidarians (jellyfish, corals), echinoderms—radial around a central axis. Four-fold radiation as in jellyfish; five-fold as in starfish. Also there is a tubular, pseudo bilaterality, as in echinoderm sea cucumbers, a pentameral symmetry along an elongated soft-body; in predatory priapulid worms—a five-fold axis of symmetry running length of body; b) most tubular animals are bilateral—two eyes, arms, legs, lungs; bilateral annelid worms can be traced in burrowings into the Vendian. It is the first coelomate animal, having a fluid-filled central cavity that often serves as a hydrostatic skeleton. Here we note the beginnings of frontal/lateral axis of behavior that will eventually lead to a nervous system and brain.

This will serve the adaptive need to differentiate between moving forward and excreting behind.[3]

The echinoderms (starfish, sea urchins, sea cucumbers) are considered, on the basis of early developmental similarities, to be the closest relatives of the ancient chordates, prelude to true vertebrates, our own main branch in the tree of life. Comparison of the larvae of Pterobranchia, sessile creatures, phylum—Hemichordata—they sweep in food through their tentacles, resemble the related modern acorn worm. The larvae of these creatures and those of the modern lancelet, amphioxus, a primitive chordate, as well as the larvae of the modern echinoderms all reveal a free-swimming stage with a hint of a notochord, stabilizing the swimming abilities of the larvae. Presumably the condition represents the ancestral type.

These developmental similarities in the larval stage suggest an ancient relationship for all three phyla. Subsequent mutational changes in the developmental and structural patterns of these creatures, and probably during the post-oxygen explosion of energy production, from at the most recent, c.800mya, allowed for the developmental and then the adaptive branching which on the one hand, in the two chordate phyla, re-created a fixed colonial sessile (Ediacarans, corals, sponges) feeding way of life for some, the Pterobranchia, a permanent mud-silt feeding (worms) life style for the lancelets, and for the line that led to the fish, a more mid-water food filtration way of surviving.[4]

G. Ledyard Stebbins notes that the split between the defensive, perhaps even defeatist adaptive tack taken by fixed sessile feeders such as the acorn worm colonies, the lancelet mud feeders, and contrasted with the free swimming opportunists who would become the true vertebrates, is reflected in the reproductive patterns taken by the two lines.[5]

With regard to the proto-vertebrates, the egg cell of the fertilized neonates while growing in the mother's ovary would have acquired a large amount of fatty yolk which the embryo could digest before becoming a free-swimming larva. This shift of nutrition from filter feeding to dependence on nutrition from mother and egg, apparently one of many random genetic changes, but an alternative subsequently often proffered in nature, (sharks are an example), which tended to shift animals from more stable environmental nutritive options to mother/daughter binding patterns, eventually made possible for some lines, more adventurous and opportune adaptive shifts. Here we may find one more adaptive key to the development of higher, behaviorally malleable life styles: the closer nurturing of the young by parents, and thus a lengthened state of infantile dependency offset by the correlative maturational delay leading to increased behavioral adaptiveness.

The fertilization of the female egg cell allowed for the internal development of the young metazoan animal in the first place. The moment in time that the fertilized egg or immature larva is expelled or born apparently is disciplined by selective conditions of survival. Clearly, just as plants and some simple animals can go back and forth from asexual stability of reproduction to sexual exploratory reproduction in times of environmental stress, a parallel exists in the animals, a parallel in the longer retention of the immature within the body of the mother's egg.[6]

The relationship of the ancient progenitors of the echinoderms to the chordates argues for a radical structural-behavioral departure toward a free-swimming adaptive life cycle. Amphioxus could be a modern chordate that represents a pattern of conservative deviation from an ancient pre-Cambrian free-floating form that has not yet been found in the fossil record. This evolutionary pivot, leading toward the true vertebrates, based on larval structural/developmental patterns could represent an early manifestation of heterochronic or neotenous development, in which the characteristics of the larval state are retained into the mature descendant forms, in this case, the vertebrates.

The Burgess Shale deposits represent one of the riches fossil deposits yet discovered of this distant era. In these deposits is *Pikaia*, a 2-inch, worm-like swimmer, a cephalochordate, also related to living lancelets such as amphioxus, a true chordate, but not a vertebrate. It gives us a hint about the pathway of chordate/vertebrate evolution, but also reveals even more clearly the adaptive alternatives that the early animal lines had before them in their breakthrough radiation of opportunity. Some must have been floaters, swimmers, as well as dominating Ediacaran fixed sessile filterers.

It is difficult to accept the close phyletic relationship between echinoderms such as sea lilies, hemichordates such as the acorn worms, and such different vertebrate fish that would appear in the fossil records just a few million years up the time line. Evolutionary sobriety argues that proto-fish-like vertebrates existed that were most probably long separated from the other lines of animals, chordates, hemichordates, and echinoderms, all long before the Cambrian.[7]

In fact, in the space of 30 million years we discern this seeming evolutionary leap forward from *Pikaia* to *Astraspis*, a 4-inch Ordovician jawless protochordate (agnathan) fish. This was a heavily-armored fish, thick bone exterior, clearly adapted for defense against enemies, which sucked in food through its mouth, had an eye and gill slits. Its armored tail section could be moved from side to side through the water for propulsion. It did not have an internal vertebrate structure. Michael Benton believes that a common chordate ancestor pre-dates *Pikaia*, to about 570mya.[8]

Perspective Forward: Stabilization of Animal Forms

In the Ordovician, 505-430mya, it is estimated that 70% of the ocean species were eliminated, the super-continent Gondwana drifted over the South Pole, and the cooling climate may have lowered ocean and lake water levels. Yet no new phyla appeared. The enormous changes of the more recent Permian, 300 million years after the Cambrian, during which the greatest destruction of species ever occurred, only served, after time, up to 10 million years, to give more dynamic impetus to the more change-oriented genotypes. In general, considering the stability of existing Cambrian phyla, the genetic fail-safe principle of "breeding true" over time inevitably cut down on the possibilities of animal and plant evolutionary innovation.

In addition, considering the wide-ranging adaptive niches occupied by the many metazoan animal phyla that established themselves on earth, it is quite possible that we may have here, at least for animal life, an exemplification of "orthoselection," in which the evolution of certain forms of life was permanently shaped to evolve in a given direction, over time, in part by means of the predatory nature of animal life. Here also may be an evolutionary exemplification of the "founder effect," in which the perfection of eukaryote biochemistry could precipitate into selective permanence forms of metazoan animal life that would henceforth block its recreation. Only the survivors would leave their time-bound imprint on the map of evolutionary life.

Solely in the bacterial world, where the molecular structure is simple enough for small random changes to have larger and rapid adaptive phenotypic impact, could the course of the evolution of life be said to continue to be a relatively open and unread book.

Ancient Mystery Recalled

The Ediacaran fauna seemed to have been two-layered, radially symmetrical animals. The most primitive living animals, the sponges, (Porifera), corals, jellyfish, (cnidaria-coelenterates), comb jellies (ctenophora), are two-layered diploblast-radially symmetrical creatures.[9]

The echinoderms and the two chordate phyla are triploblast, three-cell-layered creatures, as with approximately 30 other extant phyla. But these three phyla are deuterstomes, the blastospore opening becomes the anus, and not as all the other above 30 phyla, who are protostomes, blastospore (mouth) first, anus second, in embryological development.

> A cephalized, bilaterally symmetrical body composed of three germ layers predates the protostome-deuterostome split,..and thus probably evolved much earlier than is generally recognized...Seven independent data sets suggest that invertebrates diverged from chordates about a billion years ago, about twice as long as the Cambrian. Protostomes apparently diverged from chordates well before echinoderms, [1.2 bya] which suggests a prolonged radiation of animal phyla..[10]

Embryological development further relates the above three deuterstome phyla in terms of their free-swimming larval behavior. They are different from the earliest animal phyla, the two-layered forms, as well as the 30 triploblast protostome phyla. Most larvae are free floating at the upper ranges of the waters, reminiscent of the free-floating ciliated unicellular flagellates.[11]

The echinoderms, deuterstome, triploblast, however, by the Cambrian have long evolved into sessile, (except for the starfish), fixed and anchored in the bottom lands of the sea waters of the Earth, becoming radially symmetrical creatures. As such they resemble the hypothesized structure of the ancient Ediacaran fauna. No claims have as yet been made that the Ediacaran fauna were derived from free-floating forms, perhaps choanaflagellates, derived from the most ancient traditions of protist animal life.

Indeed, all the non-vertebrate chordates, in their mature forms turn into sea bottom dwelling sessile filter feeders. Among the protostomes: brachiopods, cephalopod mollusks, tiny calcareous ostracods represent adaptations in which food is passively filtered into their systems, else through tentacles, else body muscle flexing could move water and food through their nutritive systems.[12]

Therefore, the fixed passive life must have clearly been a recurrent genetic and adaptive option for animals of varying structural and evolutionary heritages. The shift from the presumed bilaterality of the free-swimming larval form in the echinoderms to their equally ancient reminiscence in the radial nerve net "symmetry" specialized in by the sponges, jellyfish and corals may flag an equally hoary past for all three deuterstome phyla.

One must puzzle at the genetic heritage that provided for the free-swimming destiny of the chordates and the vertebrates, the origin of the notochord, and its evolution into a flexible internal column of support for large free swimmers. To the skeptical observer, the solution to these evolutionary mysteries, their morphological and adaptive behavioral tangibility and divergences, the answer to the puzzle cannot lie in the current presumed time line that places the Cambrian as the time of vertebrate origins.

The above phyletic relationships can only be accommodated by the expansion of our evolutionary time frame. The chordate and vertebrate adaptive solutions probably go back much further than we currently dare to hypothesize, into the deepest levels of animal history and phylogeny. Only time and empirical evidence will clarify this mystery.

Phyla, Environmental Shapings

The fact that practically all the known contemporary animal phyla or pathways of adaptive life were in existence in the Cambrian, some one half billion years ago, with little in the fossil record to reveal a process of formation even a few tens of millions of years earlier, has raised puzzlement and controversy.

One proposal hypothesizes a sudden increase in the oxygen level that could have supported the expansion in size and structure of early animal forms, thence allowing for the proliferation of animal numbers and forms from the existing genetic repertoire. This event supposedly precipitated the variable adaptive routes and body plans evident in the Cambrian. It was a great evolutionary opportunity for animal life, built presumably upon the heterotrophic capabilities of these animals to live off an effulgence of plant and protist resources.

An alternative explanation is based upon the lack of continuing taxonomic evolution of new phyla after the Cambrian. This argues for a genetic "Rubicon," in which the possibilities for genetic variation were fully exploited in the pre-Cambrian once the opportunities for growth and radiation in the existing animal forms became opportune. This radiation, and the subsequent occupation of the available ecological niches, and given the genetic richness of the existing animal lines, subsequently blocked off appearance of new animal forms.

A third explanation, favored by McMenamin and McMenamin, is the predator-prey cycle that was put into place by the explosive radiation of animal opportunity. This occurred in the short period of transition between the flourishing of so-called soft path animal life and the hard path Darwinian selective balances, revealed in Cambrian animal forms.

McMenamin and McMenamin believe that the burrowing forms of life hinted at in pre-Cambrian geologies argue for the existence of bilateral predators already in search of plant and animal food, even of microscopic size. Here existed a level of animal life beyond passive radial/symmetrical food straining of the Ediacaran forms. The variability of the existing Cambrian phyla both in structure and behavior argues for an evolutionary context of strong selective pressures to diversify and specialize.

The term "browsing" is used to indicate the process by which both plant and fixed animal forms were utilized as food sources, now by animal forms that could move through their environments. So-called *Chaetognath* worms, revealed in their "fossil" worm tube imprints, are presumed evidence for this cause-and-effect disappearance of the Ediacaran fauna.[13]

The earliest and seemingly unique animal phylum to establish itself probably both within and beyond the Ediacaran Vendian, 700-600mya, were the sponges, phylum, Porifera. These primitive, two-layered colonial forms used flagella-like appurtenances to create currents whereby free-floating protists—algae, seaweed, and other food forms, including bacteria—would be caught in their cytoplasmic webs. Such animal forms flourished both through their efficient food access methods, as well as their massive reproductive growth—both sexual and asexual—and presumable versatility of metabolic accessing.

4.3 Rodinia, the Precambrian supercontinent, surrounded by the superocean Mirovia

The Cambrian reveals a large proportion of hard-shelled phyla, the early coelenterates, the corals and jellyfish, the related "comb jellies," with their two-layered nerve nets are next furthest in remove from the vertebrates, arthropods and mollusks. These latter groups are today the most diverse and seemingly successful lines. So, too, triploblast, three-layered flat worms, without a clear differentiation of mouth and anus, then existed in plenitude.

The vast variety of worm-like creatures, many phyla, multitudinous survivors into the present of these presumed borers and browsers who left their tracks in the Ediacaran, themselves then and now largely soft-bodied creatures, were able through muscular contractions, to both move, forage, and digest. Their evolutionary creation was a relatively simple one, through the innovation of duplicating genes. This genetic development produced the simple segmentation that allowed for both efficient movement and digestion.

What started out as cilia, flagella-like protein extrusions utilized for motility and sexual reproduction in both the prokaryote and early eukaryote unicellular forms, became the rudimentary, mineral-reinforced and resilient, bony, precursor skeletal structures.

McMenamin and McMenamin hypothesize that the break-up of Rodinia, the possible extension and erosion into the seas of large-scale continental shelving throughout the Riphean and Vendian periods could have extruded and dissolved enormous amounts of phosphate and carbonate mineral compounds into the seas. The pre-existing metabolic and thus genetic memory for dealing with and incorporating these minerals into other rudimentary external and internal hard cellular structures could have been given an enormous opportunistic boost at precisely the opportune and momentary selective juncture.

That dynamic interaction probably moved the existing proto-animal metazoan lines beyond the soft path adaptations of the various Ediacaran phylogenies, then at least 20 lines, into the 30-40 modern phyla, many of them with hard external skeletons or shells. These now were opportunistically incorporated as direct adaptive means for both defense and offense, as animals now struggled to establish a way of life in our planet's rapidly crowding aqueous environment.

Animal Contexts

Modern animal phylogeny is traced in its origins largely through ribosomal RNA molecular analysis.[14] Embryological development has revealed other interesting affinities that have been read back into the past to determine these phylogenetic relationships, the mystery of origins.

Two pieces of embryological evidence have been used to clarify the phylogeny of the vertebrates. In the phylum incorporating the "protostomes" pattern of embryological development, the mouth appears first, the anus developing second. These animal forms exclude the Porifera, *Coelenterates, Platyhelminthes*, sponges, corals, comb jellies, and flat worms. All other phyla are triploblasts, have three-layer tissues, organ systems, body cavities and blood circulatory systems, including the Chordates, two phyla: Hemichordata, Chordata, as well as the Echinodermata. These latter three phyla, known as deuterstomes, are exceptions to the "protostome" sequence noted above, because in their embryological development a reversal has taken place in which the anus forms first (out of the developing blastopore), the mouth second.

It is not known when and in which order this seeming embryological reversal of developmental sequence occurred. Possibly the ancestors of the chordates and the echinoderms evolved first and all the others came after. But this is questionable, because the protostomes generally are passive sessile filter feeders and seem more congruent with the adaptive patterns of the ancient Ediacaran phenotype, except that their hard shells apparently protect them against the more predatory animal forms.

"Starfish evolved from some armless echinoderm ancestor, probably to prey on sedentary shellfish" (mollusks).[15] The echinoderms, mostly stalked filter feeders, rooted to the sea floor, reveal both in their embryological development, as well as in their larvae, structure, and behavior, remarkable similarities with the chordates and their momentarily victorious vertebrate variants. The larval forms of modern echinoderms are free swimming, with a hint of a notochord-like internal stiffening, but in subsequent ontogenetic development, assume the typical rootedness and radial symmetry of sea cucumbers, sea urchins, starfish. As noted in the previous section, the radial symmetry of the echinoderms appears to be a significant archaic reversion.

What is additionally important about the phylum echinoderm is that contrary to most of the other invertebrate phyla it has *not* been able to find the mutations in any of its lines to make the transition to fresh water. Given its deuterstome relation to the vertebrates, this is an interesting molecular deviation in its genetic code as compared to the chordates.[16]

G. Ledyard Stebbins presents us with a persuasive explanatory model as to the differentiation of modern phyla from the root animal lines. He argues that the first truly multicellular animals derive from the jellyfish, corals, the *Coelenterates*. The sponges, Porifera, are an aberrant, early, largely successful individualistic, if colonial form; they do not represent the pathway to modern animal adaptation.[17] In fact it is possible that the sponges may be related to the now extinct Ediacaran group of animals.

These floating colonies of ciliated protozoan cells were bilateral in structure. The larvae, in a near universal pattern of reproductive development, floated on the water surfaces subsisting on microscopic plankton that they digested through their rudimentary mouth openings. Then they drifted to the water bottoms to catch passing food substances with their waving tentacles, conveying the food to their bag-like stomachs— passive sessile feeders.

Stebbins illustrates this universality of early animal adaptiveness in the patterns of the segmented worm or mollusk, trochophore larva, the echinoderm, sea urchin or starfish larva, and primitive chordates, the acorn worm, "Balanoglossus." "The tube-within-a-tube body plan [triploblast with coelom] may have evolved from the blind sac [two-layered diploblast] in at least three and possibly more separate groups. This means that the separation between the two major groups of land animals—joint legged [arthropods—insects and trilobites] and vertebrates goes back to the original jellyfish-like ancestor."[18]

The period between 680-530mya, a period of 150my, is seen by Stebbins as long enough for all the modern phyla to have been differentiated, given the assumed existing genetic variability and diversity of the extant animal lines, as well as an increasing level of selective competition for the available biotic ecologies within the ocean environments. Wheel animalcules—rotifers; brachiopods—lamp shells; mollusks—clams and mussels; marine worms; all are sessile suspension feeders sucking food through their bodies by means of the creation of currents by their mouth structures. At the same time they are relatively inert on the ocean bottoms. They have presumably developed their shelled exteriors for protection against predators: echinoderms—starfish; gastropods (mollusk phylum)—snails and winkles; cephalopods (mollusk phylum)—squid and octopus; arthropods—crabs, lobsters, barnacles, spiders, mosquitoes.

The triploblast solution is argued by Stebbins to be the answer to sedentary vulnerability at the ocean bottoms.[19] It is typical of sessile animals, as well as those worm-like burrowers whose trace fossils can be found associated with Ediacaran fossils. The hydrostatic internal skeleton allowed the worm to blow itself up to create a semi-vacuum into which water and food substances would be sucked in from an externally protruding mouth, to be excreted at the opposite anal end before it retreated into its defensive burrow.

But this argues, congruent with McMenamin and McMenamin, that early on in animal evolution, the predator-prey dialogue had already been put into place and was rapidly speeding up animal evolution. The existence of diploblasts such as jellyfish, which are more or less free floaters, but also predators with their often deadly sting, could support the hypotheses of Stebbins as well as McMenamin and McMenamin, *e.g.*, the offensive/defensive nature of triploblast body structure, and the early and genetically dynamic onset of the selective shaping of the animals that led toward the Cambrian effulgence.

Vertebrate Origins: The Path Forward

The phylum Hemichordata, today the acorn worms (*Balanoglossus*), and the Pterobranchia, today worm-like colonial animals that start out their larval existence as free swimmers with simple mouths and gill slits for food, oxygen, waste filtration and extraction. They show hints of a notochord supporting their inner tube like branches as they are developmentally transformed into fixed sessile feeders with tentacles.

The lancelet, amphioxus, a cephalochordate, is a transparent and primitive creature. Up to 2.5 inches in size, it has a mouth surrounded by tentacles, gill slits, a dorsal tubular nerve cord above, rod-stiffened discs of muscle surrounded by fluids that allow the rod to be pressurized and released for movement and flexibility. Amphioxus has long been thought to be the model of the primal chordate.

The sac-like tunicates (sea squirts), urochordates, have a well-developed pharynx with gill slits. Adult forms of any of these chordates could have undergone regulatory genetic mutations to allow the model of the youthful free-swimming tunicate larvae, having tails, to have become the paedomorphic prototype, as with vertebrates, in its retention of juvenile features into sexual maturity. As it is, all of the above chordate forms mature and opt for the safe and sure evolutionary adaptive route, a livelihood of fixed aqueous ground and under-the-sand, rooted filterers.

The earliest true chordate is *Pikaia gracilens*, from the Middle Cambrian Burgess Shale in British Columbia, from about 530mya. This fossil creature shows many structural similarities to modern lancelets. John Long believes that the tadpole-like characteristics of the tunicate larvae described above most closely resemble what would become a fish. He hypothesizes that here may lie the most direct line leading toward true vertebrates, with the lancelets a side branch.[20]

Recently so-called conodont fossils, tiny bits and pieces of innumerable Paleozoic remnants made up of phosphatic mineral composition have come under scientific attention. These very common and heretofore unidentified bits of fossil material are seen by some to be similar to vertebrate bone, with rod- and cone-like elements, blades with tooth like protuberances. If supported by other morphological evidence of vertebrate affinities, these fossil remnants might be assigned as true ancestors of the fish.[21]

All chordates have a dorsal neural tube as part of their bilateral symmetrical structure. These nerve fibres extend front to back and act as a conduit of information from the primitive receptors around its mouth to the tail. Underneath is the notochord, a stiff fibrous rod of tissue, discs of muscle surrounded by fluid that support and strengthen the elongated shape of the animal. Early on, many of the chordates evolved the ability to secrete phosphatic hard tissue, leading to the development of an inner skeletal structure, the spinal chord and vertebrae, first of softer cartilaginous tissue, then of bone.[22]

Differentiation of the Vertebrates

Considering the perdurance of filter feeding as a viable adaptive option for numerous lines of animal evolution into the Cambrian, 550mya, the pre-adaptive patterns of filter feeding in terms of the body plans of the early metazoa, +/- 1bya, was well established before the presumed worldwide environmental crises, the Varengian ice age, and the breakup of the super-continent Rodinia. Both events paralleled, over a period of several hundred million years, the final explosion of photosynthesis and the oxygenating metabolic environment described above.

McMenamin and McMenamin argue that the buildup of oxygen in the oceans as increasing amounts were released through photosynthesis was inhibited in its release as a gas and subsequent metabolic utilization by animals because of its first and immediate union with ocean-dissolved iron, gradually precipitating as iron oxide onto the sea beds of the world.[23] This view therefore implies an earlier origination of the plant photosynthesizers than 1bya.

Even at such a distance it may be helpful to utilize subsequent evolutionary patterns to help explain the shrouded events and processes that led to the extrusion of the vertebrates. Certain assumptions must be made in constructing a time line.

First, by +/-1bya, the choanoflagellate animals had been clearly differentiated from the fungi. They had spread and diversified due to the heterotrophic time of plenty now being exploded into the environment by photosynthetic plants, masses of algae, protists, slime mold. These provided a nutritious diet for the growing, reproducing, and diversifying animals.

Clearly sponges multiplied first, simple enigmatic colonial and filter feeding forms. The diploblast solution of the corals, jellyfish, sea pens was a second pathway that probably found its way in the early post-1bya seas. During this period we must factor in—as we should for the earlier Proterozoic eras—Milankovich cycles, during which the Earth's axis tilt, its inclination toward the Sun, and its orbit around the Sun act as interacting variables in creating periodic climate changes on the Earth.

It is possible that Martin Glaessner will be proved correct in that most of the Ediacaran fauna dating from after 700mya will be seen as precursor forms of coelenterates, cnidarians, arthropods, and various sorts of worms, perhaps even echinoderms, if not directly related. Dolf Seilacher and McMenamin and McMenamin agree with him, seeing these rooted bottom-living forms as filter feeders, two dimensional, with inflatable capabilities. This would place them as fading remnants of what was once a dominant body plan, the flat, two-layered pancake, diffuse, passive absorbers of a super-abundant free-floating food supply.

There is no doubt that an ecology opened up in this post-1bya period that propelled always opportunistic forms of life toward plenitude. But it is not likely that the seemingly major adaptive morphological and behavioral solutions represented in the Ediacaran fauna and the probable triploblast worm-like trace fossils in these same geologic strata, will be seen as only one adaptive pathway, especially after the previous 3+by of life experimentation and diversification.

The scenario for the origin of the vertebrates must therefore include an ancient surface to mid-water feeding adaptation amongst incipient metazoan animal life that dates back to or before the 1bya oxygenation explosion in the seas and the consequent plenitude of metabolic pathways for these heterotrophs. And it is likely that the relatively shallow continental shelves provided enormous amounts of plant and protist fodder to precipitate the growth and diversification of existing genetic experiments, both at the bottom of these seas and above.

Thus both the debris of dead organic matter, as well as swarming micro-organisms should have stimulated populations of soft-bodied rooted filter feeders, as well as burrowers in the organic mud, even browsers of plant and animal matter rooted to the ocean floors. As we know from subsequent evolutionary history, where there are forms of life that adaptively opt for that which is most readily at hand, there are other forms that must struggle at the edge of selective survival.

Natural Selection, the Precipitator
The assumed environmental events, c.700-600mya, including the fissuring of Rodinia, facilitated the production of both defensive and offensive protective coverings in an increasingly competitive environment within the proliferating metazoan animal lines. It also reflects the probability that the proto-chordates/vertebrates were having some adaptive success in growth and morphological specialization, therefore requiring an internal stabilizing skeleton to facilitate propulsion and feeding. As with the worms, the bilateral body plan necessitated in an elongated structure, now with a front and a rear, a neurological information-relaying set of cells to guide a more active searching creature. In the case of the proto-vertebrate, being a mid-water adapting animal rather than a slow-moving, mud-traversing worm, efficient quick reacting neurological nets were highly adaptive.

So, too, the vertebrates, surviving at the edge, and thus not available in plenitude for fossil identification today, defensively developed their own bilateral adaptations. The fact that the tunicate and lancelet, (perhaps even the still controversial "conodont") adaptive fulfillment of their chordate heritage evolved into ground dwelling, filter feeding should only emphasize the probable extended time span during which these pathways zigged and zagged through different environmental openings before settling into a permanent morpho-genetic adaptive commitment, some 650-500my later. By contrast, the echinoderms, later readapting to a genetically available recapitulation of an ancient radial symmetrical body plan opted for the post-Ediacaran plenty at the bottom of the seas.

The various chordate lineages were also adaptively repatterned toward easier survival pathways. Clearly, as genetic and positive adaptive opportunities presented themselves, they were taken. But if we view the Cambrian, from 550mya, as an intensely competitive environment with a myriad of predators: mollusks, arthropods, and then echinoderms (starfish), then the probability is that these protochordates reversed their evolutionary trend early enough in this cycle to have secured for themselves the early and fruitful adaptive niche that they now (and thus much later) precariously inhabit, securing themselves well, even before the Cambrian selective sieve.

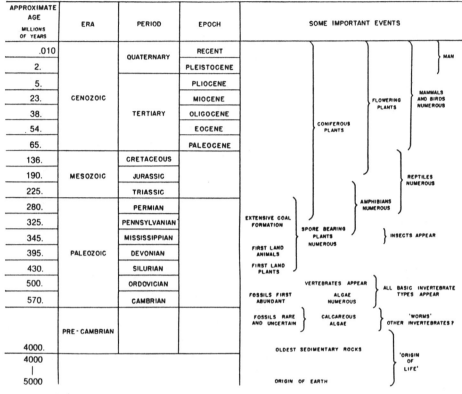

4.4 The geological
time scale.

At this point in evolution, the early Cambrian, 550mya, the earliest vertebrates lacked hard parts. The pharynx at the head acted as a food strainer, the mouth sucked mud and organic debris. Then, for they, too, eventually found the morphological means to exploit the relative plenty at the bottoms, there existed a long row of vertical slits through which water was expelled, food passed into a thin tube for digestion. Next was the gut, for absorption of nutrients. Muscles in the body wall between the slits created suction to operate the pharynx, expanded and contracted the volume of the pharynx to suck in water, then expel it through gill slits. Later thin sheets of folded blood vessels attached to walls of pharynx between the gill slits created a larger area of gas exchange so as to provide greater oxygenating power for a larger animal.

The gill arches in the wall of the pharynx between the slits provided the muscular support for the process. Later a heart pump would develop to move the nutrients through the blood fluid that carried greater amounts of molecular oxygen to the gut, passing it back to the gills where it was re-oxygenated as circulation. The heart developed strong muscular tissue to maintain the contractile process throughout the life of the growing vertebrate.[24]

Pathway for Dominance

The vertebrate adaptive plan, like the vertebrate body plan, needed much time for its eventual perfection and proliferation in the Ordovician, some 500mya. As in so many subsequent evolutionary transitions, the late success of one line should not necessarily suggest or imply its sudden revolutionary coming into being. Rather, the success of the vertebrates, given the embryological evidence of evolutionary affinities and origins, argues for an ancient and steady, if precarious adaptive tack. The survival of the line, and its gradual perfection of body plan, amidst the quick and distinct successes of other animal lines and their own particular adaptive pathways, tells us about the very variable and relatively open ecological possibilities existing on our planet during the metazoan animal expansion, after 1bya.

We now know the vertebrates to be survivors. Long hidden on the peripheries, they eventually burst into a form of dominance that has lasted for some 500 million years. It is a dominance characterized by the occupation of an adaptive ecology heretofore uncontested. The innovative character of the vertebrate design is its long-run ability to broaden and expand the environmental limits of its life ecology.

There does not here exist an augur of selective dominance into a limitless future. The early history of animal and chordate life tells us much about the ephemeral nature of biological success, success that can even last several hundred million years. Ultimately the conditions and possibilities for adaptive and selective perdurance are determined by the Earth's ecological and environmental conditions, conditions that can be determined only in part by the living actors on this planetary stage.

Endnotes, Chapter 4

[1] Li, Chia-Wei, Hua, Tzu-En, and Chen, Jun-Yuan. 1998. "Precambrian Sponges with Cellular Structures," *Science*, 2/6/98, 279:879-882.

[2] Sepkoski, J. J., Jr. 1993. "Foundations: Life in the Oceans," in *Life*, S. J. Gould, ed., *op. cit.*, p. 46.

[3] McMenamin, Mark A. S., and McMenamin, L. S. 1990. *The Emergence of Animals, the Cambrian Breakthrough*, N.Y.: Columbia Univ. Press, pp. 137-139.

[4] Stebbins, G. Ledyard. 1982. *Darwin to DNA, Molecules to Humanity*, San Francisco: W. H. Freeman, pp. 271-274.

[5] Stebbins, 1982, *op. cit.*, Illustration, Figs. 8-10, p. 267.

[6] Stebbins, 1982, *op. cit.*, pp. 271-273.

[7] Sepkoski, 1993, *op. cit.*, p. 56.

[8] Benton, M. 1993. "The Rise of the Fishes," in *Life*, S. J. Gould, ed., *op. cit.*, pp. 65-66.

[9] Sepkoski, 1993, *op. cit.*, p. 61.

[10] Wray, G. A., *et al.* 1996. "Molecular Evidence for Deep Precambrian Divergences Among Metazoan Phyla," *Science*, Vol. 274, 25 Oct., 568-573; also see, Vermeig, G. J. 1996. "Animal Origins," *Science*, Vol. 274, 25 Oct., 525-526.

[11] Stebbins, 1982, *op. cit.*, pp. 265-266.

[12] Sepkoski, 1993, *op. cit.*, pp. 58-59.

[13] Brasier, M. 1989. "On Mass Extinction and Faunal Turnover Near the End of the Pre-Cambrian," in *Mass Extinctions: Process and Evidence*, S. K. Donovan, ed., N.Y.: Columbia Univ. Press, pp. 81, 84-85.

[14] Sepkoski, 1993, *op. cit.*, p. 61, refers to the research of Rudolf Raff.

[15] Sepkoski, 1993, *op. cit.*, p. 59.

[16] McKinney, M. L. 1993. *Evolution of Life*, Englewood Cliffs, N.J.: Prentice Hall, p. 139.

[17] Stebbins, 1982, *op. cit.*, pp. 265-269.

[18] Stebbins, 1982, *op. cit.*, pp. 267-268; see de Duve, Christian. 1995. *Vital Dust, op. cit.*, p. 191, and footnote 4, p. 314, on the origin of diploblasts and triploblasts, independent from early protist, early choanoflagellate ancestor of animals and fungi, in Wainright, P. O., *et al.* 1993. *Science*, (1993):340-342; or different protists, Christen, R., *et al.* 1991. EMBO J. 10 (1991):499-503.

[19] Stebbins, 1982, *op. cit.*, p. 269.

[20] Long, John A. 1995. *The Rise of Fishes*, Baltimore: Johns Hopkins Univ. Press, p. 34.

[21] Long, 1995, *op. cit.*, pp. 35-37.

[22] Long, 1995, *op. cit.*, pp. 30-31.

[23] McMenamin and. McMenamin, 1990, *op. cit.*, p. 162.

[24] Radinsky, Leonard. 1987. *The Evolution of Vertebrate Design*, Chicago: The Univ. of Chicago Press, Chap. 3, "The Basic Vertebrate Body Plan," pp. 21-28.

5

From Sea to Land

Precipitating Environments

> The rock record from one billion years ago to the Pre-Cambrian-Cambrian boundary is replete with rocks of known or suspected glacial origin, and it is certain that during this interval there were times when many parts of the world experienced exceptionally low temperatures. Harland cites evidence for at least four major episodes of late Precambrian glaciation. This 400 million year "reign of glaciers" is unique in earth history...[1]

It is during this period, according to McMenamin and McMenamin that the animal kingdom emerged from the evolutionary mists. Emergence should not be thought of as formation. It is probable that the molecular, genetic, and phenotypic morphological structures were laid down well before. Most probably the differentiation of the various animal phyla did take place during this time, especially as it is likely that the glaciations themselves were in part caused by a burst of oxygen into the atmosphere, the suspended iron oxidation precipitated onto the ocean floor by eubacterial stromatolites, and then true plants. When this process was completed, newly released gaseous oxygen could well have been the underlying cause of this cold.

G. Ledyard Stebbins notes that fossilized worm burrow remains have been traced back to c.1bya. Citing the work of M. F. Glaessner, Stebbins accepts the existence of various kinds of worms and jellyfish phyla in the Ediacaran Formation of Australia, whose beginning dates back to about 700mya.[2]

Heterotrophic animal life feeding on plants and giving off CO_2 as a by-product of their metabolic oxidation could have depleted the oxygen levels and caused, by the Precambrian-Cambrian boundary, about 600mya, the warming and then stabilization of the Earth's climate. It should not be thought however that such violent climatic transitions, if indeed over a vast amount of time, a period which no doubt had an extraordinary selective impact on the evolutionary direction and pace of change in all forms of life, was unique to the history of our planet.

John Sepkoski has hypothesized that the 50-60my of the Cambrian were punctuated by at least five major extinctions of phyla and classes of animal and plant life.[3] It is possible that the Precambrian Ediacaran phyla disappeared because of animal predatory grazing and burrowing, behaviors that undercut their basic viability. Animals that cause the extinction of their prey are themselves endangered. It is possible that the worm like burrowers whose trace fossils we find alongside the Ediacaran impressions also died out. More likely, the climatic-environmental-ecological changes during this period could have degraded their adaptability, helped along by the pressures of predatory and more motile forms. It is clear from subsequent extinctions that Mother Earth herself, in her various climatic and geological alterations, has wreaked the greatest havoc on the status quo.

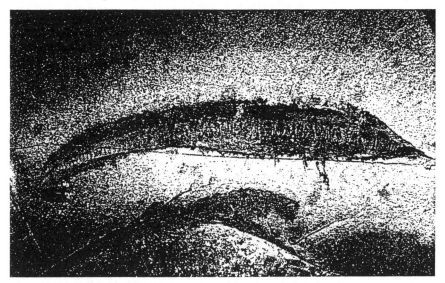

5.1 *Pikaia*: early chordate.

It is this constant ebb and flow of environmental change that gave the proto-vertebrates their hidden hold on adaptive viability, during the 400my of formative animal evolution. And it is this quality of instability in our environment that has precipitated ever more unspecialized, environmentally probing forms of life. These have avoided the ultimately vulnerable finality that is concluded by the extinction of the comfortably embedded formerly successful lines of life.

But who is to say that the arthropods, mollusks, the most widely dispersed and seemingly successful of the ecologically specialized animal phyla, with their literally millions of forms, will not outlast more environmentally adaptable types such as *Homo*? A great environmental catastrophe could render some insects and gastropods as specialized if yet non-demanding survivors in a much harsher Earthly home.

Fish as Vertebrates

Pikaia, a fossil cephalochordate from the mid-Cambrian, c.530mya, appears to have had a dorsal mass running behind its frontal areas. This may reflect a stiffening notochord and nerve cord, as in modern lancelets.

Almost 60my later in the Ordovician, c.470mya, both fossil impressions and fossil examples of the first jawless fish appear, the agnathans. They are found in what is now Australia and South America, once the region of a great super-continent, Gondwana. They were large creatures, 20-30 centimeters (8-12 inches).[4] Clearly they were already well-evolved representatives of a more ancient line that was developing in the Cambrian, 560-510mya.

The agnathan, jawless fishes are barely beyond the evolutionary stages of the larval tunicates or adult lancelets. They have a hard external phosphatic bone-like covering, but not an internal bony skeleton. Thus they are protochordates. But because they are swimmers during their entire ontogenetic development, unlike the lancelets or sea squirts, which become rooted creatures in the adult form, they constitute an important leap forward in the creation of a free-swimming predator.[5]

Respiration is achieved through the gills, organs composed of numerous thin walled soft tissues, filaments, supported by gill arch bones. These are gaseous exchange organs that place a large surface area of highly vascularized tissue in contact with water. The gills take oxygen out of the water and release carbon dioxide. Lampreys, modern jawless descendants of the agnathans, use their gills as supplementary excretory organs in addition to their kidneys. Modern teleost fish can sometimes excrete ammonia through glandular elements located near the gills.[6]

Modern lampreys and hagfish, vicious parasitic and carrion-eating forms, evolved from the period of great diversification of the jawless fish, from about 430-330mya. Their proximate ancestors had subsequently lost their bony external armor. The modern descendants are simplified and streamlined in their perfection of an ancient adaptive valence. In terms of sensory structure, they have visual capabilities with two median dorsal sensory openings and two orbit openings at the front of the head for eyes. The inner ear has two semi-circular canals (higher vertebrates have three), and the brain is segmented into discrete divisions, as in higher vertebrates. A large vein drains the blood from the head and a system of sensory fields extends over the body of the fish.[7]

Clearly, such fish evolving into adult forms with internal notochord, and sharing many similarities with Ur- and cephalochordates, point to a very ancient and gradual, but successful adaptation to life and survival in the waters of the ancient seas. Among the many varieties of agnathans that evolved, diversified, and competed during this period were forms that seem to have developed cartilaginous protective coverings around the eyes, and in turn may have had through associated connector genes, developed hard part lower jaw structures leading to tooth-like shearing instruments. In turn, building on the gill arches around the throat, the jaw could have gradually become hinged and lined with teeth. A mouth connected to a hinged jaw built around the gill arches could function adaptively to sweep in more food as well as pump more oxygen through the gills through rapid flexing.[8]

About 420mya the so-called placoderms appeared. They were fish with hard, bony armor-like plates covering both head and trunk, but with spino-occipital nerves extending back into the cranio-spinal process. Here, the beginnings of vertebrae and a backbone surrounding the notochord can be noted.[9] With simple jaws and arm-like pectoral fins, they represented a line of advanced shark-shaped fish. They moved into a wide variety of adaptive niches, even without a swim bladder. It is believed that, as with the agnathans, the placoderm was a bottom swimmer. A later representative of this line, *Bothriolepis*, lived in the seas as well as in fresh water lakes. It seems to have had paired lung-like organs that may have helped it gulp and pectorally push its way from muddy pool to clearer lakes. As a more developed version of the armored type of fish, it roared to an amazing proliferation of species and adaptations until the end of the Devonian, about 355mya, after a dominance of only 60my. Similar in shape to the more streamlined and obviously more mobile sharks, it became extinct, unlike the lampreys and hagfish, unable to find its long-term ecological niche.[10]

The acanthodians represent a controversial early group, Silurian, c.438mya, in terms of taxonomic placement. They were small spiny-finned fish, mostly filter feeders, some predators, having primitive tooth and jaw structures. Mid-water swimmers, they had lateral line canals (sensory detectors) that could identify small disturbances in the water. They flourished from about the Silurian, 430mya, to the Permian, 270mya.[11] They may have been related to the true bony fish.[12]

By 400mya the first jawed cartilaginous sharks were beginning to appear, apparently having transformed the hard external scales of earlier forms into an internal soft-boned structure. Fiercely predatory then, as today, they seem to have developed improved neurological means to assist them in seeking food. As yet without swim bladders, thus similar to the placoderms and acanthodians, but with a neural arch that connected brain and tail, they evolved a more streamlined and less heavy body structure to sweep the sea of the earlier forms.[13]

Bony Fish

The class, Osteichthyes, the bony fish, today represent the majority of the over 23,000 living species of fish. These fish first appear in the Silurian, about 410-400mya, as fully evolving competitors of the regnant agnathans and placoderms, then predating at the sea bottoms, the proliferating acanthodians, in the mid-waters, along with the soft-bodied sharks, the latter, as with the bony fish, still in their earliest evolutionary stages.

In the perspective of evolutionary time, the distance between the first sightings of the jawless fish, 470mya, still with many characteristics retained from the classes of early chordates—sea squirts, (tunicates), and the lancelets—and the appearance of modern fish, is about 70my. Bottom-swimming placoderms had appeared about 420mya.[14] The Cambrian period, to recall, which we tend to use as a yardstick for the appearance of all the modern animal phyla, as well as many which have now become extinct, is generally calculated at about 40-50 my, c.560-510mya.

In terms of structure, these osteichthyan fish show over time a gradual hardening of the internal bones, the spinal chord and the surrounding vertebrae. The bone structure of the skull, the pectoral girdle around the shoulder and neck areas (the latter highly developed in the placoderms and acanthodians) are streamlined. The loss of heavy armor around the external body and its replacement by masses of overlapping scales, light, rigid, and strong, along with truly enameled teeth, bone early on fused into the jaw, mark a series of structural adaptations which when fully evolved from their earliest sightings, 410mya, reveal a body plan with a selective future.[15]

Leonard Radinsky has detailed this forward looking sensory design leading toward land life and hearing.[16] The lateral line system detects vibrations in the water surrounding the fishes. The hair cells in the body alert the fish to such acoustic information.

> The size of the amplitude of the pressure change divided by the size or amplitude of the velocity change is called the acoustic impedance of the medium. When sound travels from one medium to another, the degree to which the sound is transmitted depends upon how close the acoustic impedances of the two media are. "Hearing" in fish is accomplished by the deformation of special processes of hair cells located inside the otic capsule (inner ear) of the fish. There is no connecting channel from the inner ear to the outside of the body, but sound travels from water through the body of the fish to the inner ear as though the body was transparent. This is because water and the fish body have similar acoustic impedances, in part because of their similar densities. On the other hand, 99% of the sound energy traveling from the air to the body of an organism is reflected rather than transmitted because of the difference in acoustic impedance between air and the body. (Remember the difference in density between air and muscles and bones).[17]

The transition from water to land required changes in the hearing structure of terrestrial animals: a) perilymphatic fluid in inner ear to improve how effectively small displacements in the tissues of the head could be transmitted to the hair cells of the inner ear; b) modification of the hyomandibula (the enlarged upper segment of the hyoid arch that had become a jaw brace in the early fishes) to transmit vibrations from the outer surface of the head to the perilymphatic system of the inner ear.[18]

Until recently most scientists studying the evolution of the fish postulated the early appearance of lungs as an accessory organ to the gill structures for obtaining and storing oxygen. Radinsky notes that both the placoderms and the osteichthyans, in contrast to the cartilaginous chondrychthyans (ancestors of modern sharks), were equipped with lungs, and also appear in the fossil record at about the same time period, 430-410mya.[19]

G. Ledyard Stebbins also argues in some detail that the ancestors of modern lungfish (*Dipnoi*) as well as the lobe fins (crossopterygians) were early on endowed with lungs, which allowed them to navigate the shallow, often oxygen-deprived inner lakes and estuaries.[20] He views the swim bladder as a secondary development of important adaptive advantage in waters of varying depth and turbulence, as an aid to rapid behavioral flexibility, especially in predation.[21]

In a more recent analysis, John Long argues that the distinction between the swim bladder and lung in fish is too sharp. Their function and structure are too similar to distinguish priority. Rather he opts for the use of the swim bladder, the earlier and generic organ, in oxygenating the blood as it came directly from the dorsal aorta. Inter-

estingly, he argues that the development of a swim bladder in the bony fish, the osteichthyans, replaced the highly-developed pectoral fins in early fish, which were used
mostly to maneuver along the lake and sea bottoms, but also to gain lift in the water
column. Henceforth, the bony fish used their fins to make sharp movements and brak-
ings.

The swim bladder, originally an out-pocketing from the gut, evolved to a gas
regulatory organ, having developed rich networks of capillaries to obtain oxygen to assist, as in a submarine, to move up and down as these gases were extruded or absorbed.
Gradually, in some fish, musculature was developed that more forcefully transferred
oxygen by means of an internal palatal nostril, which allowed for the gulping of air and
moving it directly into the swim bladder, now become a lung. It is probable that in the
early crossopterygian fish, the adaptive challenge presented by their shallow water
lunging predation, indicated by the shape and location of their fins, also strongly undergirded the selective development of such additional organs for supplementary oxygen intake.

Evolutionary Dynamics

What we are seeing in this dynamic of natural selection in the waters of the
oceans, lakes, estuaries, and rivers is the consecutive articulation of the genetic potential available from the basic pre-chordate body plan. This had evolved as a response to
climatic and ecological conditions among the multicellular heterotrophic forms of
animal life existing subsequent to 1bya, when the surge of photosynthesizing plants
produced a massive oxygen outflow into the oceans. Subsequent climatic turbulence
probably was a result of this injection of oxygen and an effulgence of autotrophic food
potential. Include in this dynamic evolutionary equation the periodic geological formation and disintegration of the continental land masses.

As in a play, the actors appear on stage to make their appearance and do their
"thing." Events turn their genetic potential into a rush for adaptive security, victory,
defeat, or tolerable survival at the edge, awaiting the second act for another appearance
onstage, and, hopefully, better luck. We see the results of this long process of presumptive hidden evolutionary dynamics in the proto-chordate line, which surely must
have been present along with the Ediacarans and the worms, probably in the form of
struggling survivors at the edges. They were there long before the above "famous" per-
sonages made their evolutionary hail and farewell. Closer in time we are able to trace
the rise and fall of these lines. It would be a mistaken evolutionary assumption to imply the succession of winners and losers to be strictly linear.

Even the relatively closely-related class of osteichthyans, the bony fish, with their
three sub-classes, are considered to have evolved in relatively removed geographies,
the actinopterygian ray fins and the *Dipnoi* lungfish from the Eur-American continent,
the crossopterygians from distant South China and East Gondwana.[22] Nature needs
time to work out its basic adaptive repertoires. And it is clear from the late Silurian,
early Devonian, 410-390mya, geographical remove of the above fossil lines that these
fish phylogenies with air-breathing preadaptations must have had a most ancient origi-

nating relationship, (Ordovician, 500mya?) to have thence evolved in these widely dispersed geographies.[23]

The placoderms, with their odd and extensive pectoral appendages, along with their heavy armored bodies that argue for a bottom water adaptation, still reflect the vertebrate design for mid-water stability. Their specializations along with their rapid proliferation argue for the adaptive advantage still provided by the abundant shellfish and other animal and plant life at the bottom of inter-reef basins.[24] Therefore, there probably came a presumptive re-adaptation from the classic, if peripheral mid-water vertebrate design to juicier pickings at the bottoms, now made selectively powerful by this long modernizing morphology.

For 300my, from the Proterozoic "Riphean," 700mya, to the Devonian, 390mya, the relatively shallow waters in which metazoan animal life evolved maintained inviting luxuriance of food supplies and secured ecological niches. It did so both for the comfortably adapted shelled filterers and scavengers, as well as for the more adventurous bilateral animal forms evolving in other, peripheral environments. These, like so many other animal phyla, were tempted to return at a more evolved structural/behavioral level (lancelets, agnathans, placoderms) to the abundant bottoms and their seeming security.

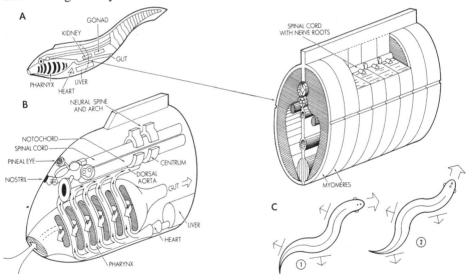

5.2 Basic vertebrate body plan. A. the ancestral vertebrate. B. major systems in head and trunk regions. C. top view of body showing how lateral undulations produce backward and sideway thrusts against the water.

Pre-Adapted Fish

A key evolutionary event may have been the development, in some fish, of an air filled pouch communicating with the pharynx. The air in the pouch came from the gills by way of the blood, which circulated through an increasingly rich network of capillaries surrounding the pouch. An advantage the fish derived from such a pouch was adjustable buoyancy, the main function of what is now the swim bladder. Another advantage was that the fish, in the manner of a scuba diver, carried a reserve of oxygen it could use in case of emergency, when its blood oxygen fell to a dangerously low level. In such an event, oxygen would diffuse in the reverse direction from the pouch into the blood. The adaptation opened the way to breathing, the pouch acting as a primitive lung. We can watch this in our fish bowl when a goldfish surfaces to take a breath of fresh air and. more dramatically, during the dry season in many a tropic lake of Africa, South America, and Australia, where lung-fish survive for months in the drying mud, awaiting the next rainy season.[25]

The lure for successful animal life on land was the possibility of extracting the rich trove of oxygen from the atmosphere, a supply which was only modestly dissolved in water, 0.0451 grams per liter, as compared to 6.70 grams of oxygen in a liter of air, approximately 150X greater, both at room temperatures.[26] In time this greater avail-ability of oxygen metabolizing potential would offer important selective advantages for those creatures sporting an adaptive valence of larger than average brain size and thus facility in information-processing.

A rich oxygenated environment combined with an available supply of food at the water's edge, else on land, would become the great adaptive beckoning that would be held out to a line of creatures structurally pre-adapted to make a move out of the mainlines of water specializations.

Recall that, to serve the metabolic needs of the metazoans, especially those still-exploring bilateral predators above the sea floors, the extraction of oxygen from water must have been perfected early in animal evolution. The larval sea squirts, urochor-dates, have gill slits, mouth, a primitive eye, a long thin tail with a notochord that trav-erses their body front to back. They propel themselves through the water much like the ciliated eukaryotes, 500my earlier, that absorbed their oxygenating sustenance through their cell walls as they moved toward and ingested their food near the water surfaces. In the adult stage, the sea squirt, now fixed on the sea bottom, still absorbs its food and oxygenating water through a large pharynx with gill slits.[27]

The generative and generalized swim bladder that provided a pathway out of the water as well as back into deeper waters for the different lines of fish reflects a shallow watery world of intense richness and violent and sharp selective pressures. This ecol-ogy increasingly shaped its denizens into specialized niches. But the genetic variability must have been there to allow for the flourishing of complex and evolving mobile and predatory forms, as well as to allow for new lines of adaptation for the successors of falterers, once both specialized and successful.

Thus it is that the early chordates and the even earlier proto-echinoderms, them-selves probably early on bilateral swimmers, ceded the open waters. So, too, the jaw-less fish, their domination thence to be shunted aside by the placoderms, both forms now fairly specialized gill breathers, with no hint of an air-breathing sub-specialization. The spiny-finned acanthodians are also gill breathers who succumbed to the competitive pressures of the sharks and the bony ray-finned fish. Only the early failed lancelets, sea squirts, then the hagfish and lampreys, the latter descendants of the jawless agnathans, produced descendants into the present.

It is probable that the ancestors of both the dipnoan lungfish, and the crossop-terygian lobe-finned fish, both equipped with swim bladders that could access atmospheric oxygen were developing their morphological and physiological specializations in parallel with these variously evolving lines, the failures as well as the winners. Both the above lines seemed to have been extremely successful predatory machines during their relatively brief period of florescence. The thick limb-like stabilizing adaptations of the crossopterygians, as compared to the ray-finned lines that would go on to evolve into the teleost explosion of the Cretaceous, some 300my down the line, give evidence for this shallow water specialization, one that would lead either to death for all but a very few forms of air breathers, or migration into a totally new adaptive plane.

We bear in mind the comment of C. de Duve with regard to the air breathing needs of goldfish (carp). This characteristic of air breathing both under conditions of oxygen distress in polluted or over heated water, as well as a widespread need to take a periodic breath of air can be found in a wide variety of fish, from catfish to cichlids, to gouramis, as any aquarium devotee will note. It is clear that the actinopterygians, who inherited the mid waters, as the crossopterygians and dipnoan lungfish waned, must have retained that ancient capacity for air breathing, either through direct adaptive re-tention, else within the genetic memory of the line, to be extruded into adaptive reality under conditions of changed oxygenization levels in the waters within which they lived.

Perhaps it is true that the air breathing adaptation in the evolving swim bladder came into use for this line some 70my before the development of feet.[28] Yet it is also persuasive that the lobe-finned organs that were used for stabilization and for facili-tating rapid predatory movements near the water bottoms contain the same basic bone structures that would be subsequently adapted for support of a now extremely "heavy" body in the much thinner atmospheric density of the air. The density of air is .001 g/cm^3, as compared with water, which is 1 g/cm^3. Muscle has a density of 1.05 g/cm^3; bone's density is 3 g/cm^3.

The always changing landscape and climate on the planet made the emergence of the proto-amphibians both possible and necessary. Additionally, this move was made as part of a general thrust of life above the water line. Both plant and animal forms (in-sects, scorpions) preceded the proto-amphibian crossopterygian panderychthyids, creatures who had probably been adaptively and selectively pressed to survive in ever more dangerously desiccating marine environments. For reasons unknown, chance op-portunism, else pressured specialization, they had been shunted *out* of the deeper, safer pools, and ever closer to that point of no return, Rubicon.

Amphibians and Mosaic Evolution
It is tempting to believe that the evidence scientists happen to find dating back hundreds of millions of years reflects a true and major picture of the events at that distant time remove. The picture of amphibian evolution to land has been suggested to be an example of extremely rapid macro-evolutionary changes, reflecting the theory of "punctuated equilibrium" developed by Gould and Eldredge. This hypothesis has been offered to accommodate the evidence of a "fits-and-starts" quality to evolution, the seemingly long periods of stasis in certain lines, then, in the same lines, explosive change and breakthroughs.[29]

An example of the above inevitably linear logic that occurs when the vast and probable domain of "unknowns" are not factored into our evolutionary models is reflected in a perspective that postulates a transition from an air- and water-breathing lobe-finned fish, Eusthenopteron, from the upper Devonian, some 380mya, through Panderychthys, from the late middle Devonian, 375mya, to *Acanthostega*, an early transitional amphibian (tetrapod) from the late Devonian 365mya. The evolutionary transition from fish to amphibian is thus presumed by R. L. Carrol, a follower of the "punctuated equilibrium" model, to have taken place in a blazing period of evolutionary "advance" of less than 15my.[30]

The changes in the limb structure and the skull roof and brain that mark a clear if gradual set of changes leading from fish to amphibian is rationalized by being compared to the similar time span during which supposedly the size of the ape brain as well as its patterns of locomotion were transformed into the human form, an hypothesized period of about 9-14my; many would argue 5-6my.

To further buttress this view of small mutations now occurring rapidly in time, processed by traditional adaptive and selective mechanisms, Carroll sets the divergence of the Osteichthyes line of crossopterygian lobe-finned fish from the ray-finned fishes, at about 405mya. But as noted above by Long, by 410mya, ray-finned fish with odd lobed fins, *Cheirolepis,* had already appeared, clearly a dimension of the existing mosaicism of this then proliferating line of bony fish. The existence of true fossil crossopterygians plus *Dipnoi* at this similar time boundary would argue, especially considering their wide geographical dispersal that the ray fins and lobe fins probably share an ancient common set of ancestors, at the least back to the Ordovician, some 100my earlier, c.500mya.[31] Note that the agnathan jawless fish were already flourishing, 470mya.[32]

5.3 *Acanthostega: early amphibian.*

Starting with a hypothetical vertebrate already differentiated from the ancestral specializing fossil chordates, the sea squirts and lancelets, some 550mya, it is a reasonable supposition that there were many lines of true free-swimming vertebrates evolving, radiating, specializing, and thus spiraling off a variety of forms as each line reached a point of morphological sophistication such that it could move into a previously unoccupied ecological niche and make its play. Thus we have the succession of the various classes and sub-classes of fish.

So, too, with the transition to the land by the radiating crossopterygians, and the appearance of *Acanthostega* in the late Devonian in Greenland, at about 365mya. Because we find examples of evolving crossopterygian panderichthyid fish that show a steady and seemingly rapid transition to amphibian structure and taxonomy, does not mean that these are the only true examples of a process of succession that seemingly took only 14my. They could well be fossil examples that reflect a wide variety of transitionals, diverse adaptive levels among the crossopterygians, responding either to selective pressures or opportunities to move toward the land. Further, it does not mean that all these creatures made it.

The massive regression of the crossopterygian sub-class of fish after 350mya, only a short time after some of their kind made the transition to life on the land, could argue for the existence of environmental selective pressures on creatures that were clearly adapted to shallow water predation Such creatures were diversifying in estuarial, coastal lagoons, inland seas and lakes, and other ecologies where limb-like stability for lurching predation was adaptive. Under drying conditions, else the creation of deep water geologies, these fish could have disappeared without trace except for lucky *Latimeria*.

A series of successive genetic moldings and restructurings had to be made, and probably was made over many million of years as the proto-amphibians made their transition to life on the land. The eight-toed *Acanthostega* was more a walking fish with much sturdier limbs than the typical lobe-finned fish, along with a spinal chord that was only loosely supported by a hip girdle, and without a sacrum, pre-existing structures that would make land traversal virtually impossible, yet supportable in water.[33]

A judicious time line for the evolution of fish to the land surfaces, making appropriate consideration for the many preadapted characteristics that this one line of panderichthyid fish was already developing as it evolved away from the order of crossopterygians, the osteolepiforms, argues for an evolutionary separation from the root air-breathing ancestor of the *Dipnoi* as well as the crossopterygians, certainly well before they appear in abundance, about 410mya. Here, too, we have to argue that the separation from the ray-finned fish should go back even further. We do not see their fossils yet, because they are rare and smaller the further back in time we go. But clearly, great structural and adaptive patterns take time to set themselves as functional evolutionary realities. Only if they survive their time of phylogenetic gestation and specialization will they subsequently appear. Only now, because their numbers make their fossil remains more discernible for retrieval, do we find them in the period after 400my.

One is persuaded to argue for a separation and evolution of these bony fish, as well as the cartilaginous ancestors of the sharks, occurring at the latest in the early Ordovician, 500mya. Further it is not overly speculative to hypothesize the primeval separation of free-swimming, true vertebrates, eventually to note the proliferation and temporary dominance both of the jawless fish (Agnatha) and the placoderms. These latter then must have originated at least 50my earlier, in the Cambrian, c.550mya. The problem: we still do not have evidence one way or the other that they were there.

This brings us back to the shaping of the amphibians. Consider the already pre-adapted large, flat and broad skull of the panderichthyids, with their top and frontally-positioned eyes, the lack of dorsal and anal fins, teeth and nostrils already in the amphibian mode. As described by Long, this was a line of creatures that lived and survived in a transitional adaptive zone, not fully aqueous, and yet not forced to move into strange terra firma.[34] Recall that the earliest tetrapods are found in this late Devonian time frame (c.365mya) throughout the world, in Greenland, Scotland, Russia, Australia. Thus even though Gondwana seems to have been the locus of osteolepiforme evolution, along with the ray fins, ancient Eur-America seems to encompass the current fossil record of the earliest amphibians.[35]

Can a time frame for the evolution of this line of evolved panderichthyid/crossopterygians to *Acanthostega/Icthyostega*-like amphibians be calculated at any less than from c.410mya to 365mya? Probably more, considering the fact that the earlier time period (410mya) already reveals the many other contemporaneous radiating lines of lobe-finned fish. Subsequently, a period of 40-50 million years of evolution adapting into the shallow water effulgence is not a break with traditional evolutionary rhythms. Finally, a substantial period of time was necessary to perfect the ancient lung/swim bladder preadaptation toward specialization for efficient lung/air breathing in bacterially deteriorated or stagnant waters, as well as alternate gill use, the development of limbs and toes (here, eight toes, but probably also, there, five toes) to traverse these shallow bottoms efficiently.

A hint as to the possible dynamics underlying this great ecological transition lies in the fact that juveniles of the osteolepiform fish that seem to have made the transition to tetrapod status show more similarities to subsequent amphibian structure, especially in the formation of the skull bones. This argues for an element of paedomorphosis, where the adult of the succeeding generation could retain many juvenile characteristics through a speeding up of sexual maturity. Such heterochronic rate gene activations usually are associated with increasing selective pressures on the earlier adult forms, allowing for the selection of variants that have come up with a genetically rooted paedomorphic solution. Thus the pressure exerted by an environment of greater aridity and falling water levels, perhaps increased mid-water selective pressures from expanding actinopterygians/ray-finned fish could have been elements in this equation.[36]

For a few lines of panderychthyid crossopterygians, the probably forced exploration of land was, with any luck, a halfway path back to the waters. Most perished. A few did find a solution in their genes and made it back. The coelacanth is an example: "It behaves more like a gymnast than a fish, with unusual twists and turns...its ears are similar to ours...it now bears live young."[37] One wonders whether these morphological characteristics were typical of other Devonian exemplars with the equipment to perdure and proliferate.[38]

Endnotes, Chapter 5

1 McMenamin, Mark A. S., and McMenamin, Dianna L. S. 1990. *The Emergence of Animals, the Cambrian Breakthrough*, N.Y.: Columbia Univ. Press, p. 93; Harland, W. B. 1983. "The Proterozoic glacial record," in *Geological Society of America Memoir*, 161:270-288.
2 Stebbins, G. Ledyard. 1982. *Darwin to DNA, Molecules to Humanity*, San Francisco: W. H. Freeman, p. 247.
3 Sepkoski, J. J., Jr. 1993. "Foundations: Life in the Oceans," in *Life*, S. J. Gould, ed., N.Y.: W. W. Norton, p. 59.
4 Long, John A. 1995. *The Rise of Fishes*, Baltimore: Johns Hopkins Univ. Press, p. 46.
5 Long, 1995, *op. cit.*, p. 38.
6 Long, 1995, *op. cit.*, p. 39.
7 Janvier, P. (Paris), in Long, 1995, *op. cit.*, pp. 43-45; Long, 1995, *op. cit.*, pp. 60-61.
8 Benton, M. 1993. "The Rise of the Fishes," in *Life*, S. J. Gould, ed., *op. cit.*, p. 73.
9 Stebbins, 1982, *op. cit.*, pp. 275-276.
10 Long, 1995, *op. cit.*, pp. 100-125.
11 Benton, 1993, *op. cit.*, pp. 73-74.
12 Stebbins, 1982, *op. cit.*, p. 276; Long, 1995, *op. cit.*, pp. 90-95.
13 Long, 1995, *op. cit.*. Press, pp. 66-67.
14 Long, 1995, *op. cit.*, p. 105.
15 Long, 1995, *op. cit.*, pp. 128-131.
16 Radinsky, L. 1987. *The Evolution of Vertebrate Design*, Chicago: The University of Chicago Press, pp. 83-84.
17 Radinsky, 1987, *op. cit.*, p. 84.
18 *Ibid.*
19 Radinsky, 1987, *op. cit.*, p. 56.
20 Stebbins, 1982, *op. cit.*, pp. 276-277.
21 Stebbins, 1982, *op. cit.*, pp. 281-282.
22 Long, 1995, *op. cit.*, p. 135.
23 Long, 1995, *op. cit.*, pp. 134-135, 186.
24 Long, 1995, *op. cit.*, p. 102.
25 de Duve, Christian. 1995. *Vital Dust*, N.Y.: Basic Books, p. 205.
26 Professor Kenneth Hellman, Smith College, personal communication, October 16, 1997.
27 Long, 1995, *op. cit.*, p. 31; Benton, 1993, *op. cit.*, pp. 66-67.
28 Stebbins, 1982, *op. cit.*, p. 279.
29 Benton, 1993, *op. cit.*, p. 32;; Eldredge, N. 1991. *The Miner's Canary*, Englewood Cliffs, N. J.: Prentice Hall.
30 Carroll, R. L. 1996. "Revealing the Patterns of Macroevolution," in *Nature*, 2 May 1996, 381:19-20.
31 Long, 1995, *op. cit.*, p. 138*ff.*
32 Long, 1995, *op. cit.*, p. 42.
33 Zimmer, Carl. 1995. "Coming Onto The Land," in *Discover*, June 1995, p.9.
34 Long, 1995, *op. cit.*, pp. 203-204.
35 Long,. 1995, *op. cit.*, p. 207.
36 Long, 1995, *op. cit.*, pp. 208-209.
37 Nisbet, E. G. 1991. *Living Earth*, N.Y.: Harper Collins, p. 157.
38 Stebbins, 1982, *op. cit.*, pp. 282-285.

6

Transitions: Land, Brain, Extinction

- 1 -
Land

Plants and Animals

The expansion of metazoan eukaryotic animal life in the period after 1bya was linked to the development of photosynthetic plant life in the algae, seaweed, and other protozoa floating in the oceans, and after the final oxidation of water-dissolved iron. The release of enormous amounts of molecular oxygen into the seas exploded the opportunities for the growth and proliferation of animal forms.

So, too, plants later led the way onto land. By about the late Ordovician, 470mya, there is evidence that the now most primitive spore-reproducing mosses and liverworts, which had probably flourished for long millennia in the shallow interface shores of the inland seas, began to develop hard external seed-like shells. These shells would then be discharged onto the moist adjoining swamps, then to reap the dividend of more direct access to the metabolic power of the sun and the light of the open atmosphere.[1]

The first tentative greening of the land surfaces by mosses and liverworts was contemporaneous with the fossil appearance of agnathan jawless fish, some 470mya. By 400mya, approximately 20my after the estimated development of vascular plant life, spider-like trigonotarbids—mites, springtails, even some shrimp-like creatures— all relatively tiny invertebrate forms, are associated with these plants (found in the Rhynie Chert in Scotland.

In Australia, at about the same time frame, the late Silurian, large sea scorpions, eurypterids, some several feet in length, multi-segmented arthropods, ancestors of the earliest insects, were associated with perhaps 15 other animal types, judging from land burrow and feeding traces, and various imprints.[2] Clearly the invertebrates had begun to find their own solutions for earning a living outside of water. The development of systems of ducts, tracheae, in arthropods, for instance, created passages throughout the interior of their external hard carapace coverings. These passageways allowed oxygen to diffuse into all parts of the body and carbon dioxide to diffuse out. This general body plan seemed to serve all invertebrates that gradually ventured onto the lands.[3]

By the time the first amphibians were experimenting with the land, 375-365mya, either hurtling from one water hole to another, or lying about the shores of inland swamps or lagoons for food, there existed on the lands great forests of spore-reproducing trees and assorted flora, plus a rich ecology of invertebrates on which to feed, as well as fish in the shallows. What was needed was time for the variable genetic heritage of these lines to present morphogenic variations that could be acted upon by natural selection to provide these creatures with a longer leash so that they could move away from their dependence on water—new skin coverings, stronger interlocking vertebrae to support the spine, a gradual reduction of the atavistic fish-like fin and tail structures, modifications toward heavier skull bones. Perhaps most important, sensory organs were restructured, the brain and head coordinated for a more sensorially diverse awareness of the environment, light, sound, and smell.[4]

The late Devonian and early Carboniferous period, 375-345mya, was an era of wet, half-submerged continents, inland seas, swamps. Such conditions were highly conducive to the radiation of the amphibians. It was empty of competitive challenge from animal or plant life. Once the basic morphological and physiological requirements had been found in these evolving creatures to meet the basic selective conditions of land life, the future, whatever the possibly defensive reasons for leaving life in the water behind, was open-ended. Still the bond with the waters remained, for example in the fish-like mode of reproduction, the laying down of a cloud of sperm in the water in the general direction of the previously laid eggs. The larval young, the tadpoles of the frogs, with their gill slits and waving tails testify to a bondedness that defines amphibian taxonomy.

A variant creature—it will be called "reptile"— was soon to emerge in the explosive radiation of the air breathers. Heretofore it has been thought that the earliest reptiles radiated from the amphibian expansion in the mid-Carboniferous, about 300mya. However, recent discoveries in the East Kirkton excavations in Scotland identify a reptile from the early Carboniferous, 350mya.[5]

This reptile arrived on the scene quite early in comparison with the usual timetable for the amphibian invasion of the land, c.375-365mya. It denotes the development of hard bone-like scales, protection in a life away from the water. Another development was internal sexual copulation, the intromission of sperm into the cloaca, similar to reproduction in the sharks and other fish, and thus constituting an interesting retention or reintroduction of an ancient pattern. The sharks themselves have characteristics in skull structure that are reminiscent of even more ancient agnathan jawless fish; indeed they may be related to this stem.[6]

Above all was the water-emancipated, but "breathing," cleidoic egg. The fact that various lizard-like reptiles, turtles, and snakes lay leathery-coated eggs argues for the variability of the external sheathing of the vertebrate egg, in terms of the possible genetic alternatives available to a "somewhat" amphibian. These first reptiles were small, 6-8 inches long, as compared with such early amphibians as *Acanthostega* and *Ichthyostega*, which were about 40 inches long. The basic creation, in Romer's phrase: "...[I]t was the egg which came ashore first, the adult followed later"—of such a complex and seemingly advanced innovation for adapting to the uplands, the egg, argues for time.[7]

Did this process of creating the amniotic egg occur simultaneously with the movement of the fish to the land? Or did the amphibians make their move well before the time of *Acanthostega*, some 365mya? Again the question of linearity of descent proves a puzzle to the seeming sharply creative macro-evolutionary events to which the fossil record points.

The very structure of what Long calls the "greatest single advancement in the evolution of vertebrates from fish to human" was a highly specialized innovation, one that was articulated and perfected in the contemporary birds, merely refined in the development of mammal reproduction.[8]

We should not omit to reiterate the hypothetical possibility that placental mammals were the inheritors of an heretofore undiscovered evolutionary route of adaptively successful reproduction that avoided the oviparous egg state of most of the amphibians, reptiles, and failed mammal lines.

The reptile egg: first an external calcareous but porous coating. Internally, the amnion, which protects the embryo and its yolk sac food supply, shunts waste into a sac called the allantois for expulsion as gas. The inner development of the embryo is further secured by the membranous sheath called the chorion. The structural capacity to retain water within the cleidoic egg was later passed to the birds in their conversion of urine to a near solid waste.[9]

- 2 -

A Brain That Moves

Air and Oxygen

It is probable that the earliest metazoan eukaryotes were surface feeders in the oceans, seas, lakes. The gradual buildup of oxygen in water and atmosphere that stimulated this trend was the increase in photosynthetic life. Protozoa and eubacterial forms likewise prospered in that interface of water and sun.

Andrew Knoll's hypothesis is that the first increase in dissolved oxygen, and the possibilities for aerobic respiration could go back before 2bya. The mechanisms of eukaryote metabolization and reproduction of mitochondria, organelles needed much time. For multicellular animal and plant life, the more efficient metabolic energy production given in photosynthesis, symbolized by the final development of chloroplasts in plant eukaryotes, would be crucial.[10]

Plant food and abundant microscopic animal and bacterial sustenance could be expected to be found in the interface of air and water by swarming metazoan animals in the era around 1bya. So, too, the osmotic link with the air and oxygen was probably never fully severed. McMenamin and McMenamin refer to this process as diffusion across the cell surface membrane in which higher concentrations of oxygen outside the organism will tend to migrate into the cell body.[11] The bottoms, where we today find the wealth of well-adapted fossil remains had to have been an attractive magnet in the search for adaptive stability by all life forms. The gravitational fall of dead but nourishing protein, the buildup of resources in and around ground level, especially in the shallow seas and lakes, was continuously being reshaped as an inviting destiny for the always evolving and competing animal forms in the long Pre-Cambrian.

The existence of cilia, flagella, and undulipodia in a great variety of unicellular and multicellular forms argues for the perdurance of motility as the ancient goad for the eukaryote cell's carnivorous profile. It is at the water surfaces where molecular tensions would allow for both stability and rapid movement. We see the fossil remains at the gravitational climax of life in the sea bottoms. But life must have most dynamically competed in pursuit of its destiny in the upper and mid-waters.

Where there is a flagellum or undulipodium there eventually will be directionality. Life propelled from one part of the body—as in a motor boat with the propeller at the stern—will thence have a front. Unfortunately we have no record of the most primitive free-swimming bilateral, elongated representative of this line of evolutionary advance that is contemporary with the seemingly earliest and most primitive forms of rooted sessile feeding forms.

Neurological Pathways

The earliest observed forms of metazoan animal life, the Porifera, the sponges, are still with us. They were ubiquitous and powerfully adapted filter feeders that siphoned residues from presumably ancient and teeming seas. Their nerve tissue enveloped the external orifices and pore sphincters through which the seawater carrying food particles would circulate. This sensory surface was barely differentiated without specialized receptors, nerve tissue, or neurons. There is movement, but it is reflexive motor action in direct response to external stimulation.

Sponges do contain neurotransmitters such as those found in the human brain—serotonin, acetylcholinesterase, adrenalin, noradrenalin. Severing a portion of a sponge will automatically induce a contraction of tissue in further regions of the sponge. There is, therefore, a form of protoplasmic information transmission that many hundreds of millions of years later was transformed in animal behavior to movement, memory, emotions.[12]

It is possible that the planaria flatworms, perhaps the first triploblast animals, in advance of the coelenterate jellyfish and corals, were also first to represent this frontal/lateral structure, and in consequence the development of the first true neuron.[13] Flatworms, one of the simplest bilateral forms, are differentiated into about 50 different kinds of cells, equal to the maximum number in highly evolved plants.[14] Yet their mouth is also their anus. This compares with jellyfish, which have both muscle and nerve cells diffusely extended over their radial symmetry. The jellyfish body plan, contrasted with flatworms, cannot be coordinated for directional neuronic movement. Thus, except for their capacity for movement, flatworms are much like the sponges..[15]

Flatworms are today restricted to a mostly parasitic existence—tapeworms and flukes—residing in mammal digestive systems and becoming agents for a number of serious tropical diseases.[16] They do, however, have three sets of nerve cells: sensory, motor, and ganglion cells. Without a brain, their nerve cells cluster in the anterior head region. Planaria are sensitive to light, having retinal cells with long axons that connect with motor neurons. They seem to be responsive to temperature changes and other external stimuli.[17]

Joseph hypothesizes that the first neurons were without axons and dendrites. Only later could they secrete the electrical and chemical substances, first operative on the organism in a generalized manner, through the axons and dendrites to other neurons through selective receptor surfaces at the terminal junction. It is through the gradual differentiation of these neuronal passageways, especially assisted by the development of myelin coating along the axons and dendrites, that bilateral communication was made possible. And it is in the selective shaping of a bilateral, slimly elongated worm-like creature either free swimming or ground adapted, as in the various worms phyla, that we gradually obtain a concentration of neuronic material in the anterior or frontal part of the animal where reception of information could be integrated into behavior.[18]

In general, the more primitive bilateral worms and presumably other similarly structured creatures had these neuronal sensitizers externally distributed around their bodies. The earliest collectivization in the frontal areas triggers sensitivity to smell, chemical, and sexual information. Eventually it was concentrated in the nose, which remained as an external neuronal receptor. Other neurons realigned to integrate these messages with sensory information received by different neuronal networks, light, vibrations, food, danger, were gradually concentrated in the olfactory lobe of the forebrain. In time, with the gradual expansion of the importance of visual information collected and integrated in the optic lobe—the tectum or colliculi—the mid-brain became an important source of information.[19]

The nerve tissue structure in invertebrates, especially including the most successful and widespread phyla, the arthropods/insects, and the mollusks/shellfish, reflects a very different body plan, one in which the latter are somewhat restrictive but seemingly secure at the sea bottoms, the former widely adaptive to life in the seas, on land, and in the air. But in general, the mollusk body plan restricts the growth of the brain, trading it off for stereotyped instinctual and thus pre-programmed behaviors. Here the central ganglion is built as a ring of tissue that surrounds the gut. The growth of this tissue would have the probability of strangling the food-ingesting capacity of this organ. Thus it has struck an evolutionary agreement to follow behavioral avenues other than braininess in its adaptive destiny.

Vertebrate Brain

Defining the vertebrate sub-phylum is the nerve cord that runs front to back just above the notochord, later to become a fully evolved spinal column. This elastic rod functioned primarily to protect the major neuronic communication link between head and tail. However, neural arches roofing the nerve cord and connected to the musculature, called myomeres which functioned by way of nerve relays from the spinal cord and the sensory organs, act as propelling contractions for propulsive force—for movement forward, sideways, and for braking. A series of first, cartilaginous, then inverted bone arches under the nerve cord were to become, with the neural arch above, the protective vertebrae, which would serve also as anchor for the musculature of the fish.

The spinal cord connected to the nervous center at the front of the fish. A variety of sensory messages would be received from all the surfaces of the animal. Three systems clustered, in addition: a) The olfactory system, with receptor cells in the nasal capsule, through which water flowed. These messages were transmitted to the olfactory bulbs at the front of what would become the brain (the forebrain). b) Light sensitive cells arranged in a sheet (retina), located in two lateral eyes and one pineal eye at the top of the head, later to be lost. These messages were received in the brain by the optic tectum located in the roof of the midbrain. c) The acoustic system, which received messages through hair cells that were located in grooves of the head and down the sides of the animal, the lateral line system. These latter signaled vibrations in the immediate vicinity of the fish. In addition, another set of acoustic receptors on either side of the rear portion of the brain detected distant sounds. Other detectors sending messages to the hind brain noted turning motions and other bodily adjustments. These served to transmit this information via fluids in semicircular tubes that were connected to the hind brain.

The beginnings of cerebral integration of all sensory information were located on the upper surfaces of the olfactory centers in the forebrain. A cerebellum on the roof of the hind brain controlled motor coordination.[20] It is suggested that the olfactory system in the basic vertebrate design early gave rise to the amygdala and hippocampus, indeed, then still primitive components of the rhinencephalon, the nose brain. Modern descendants of these ancient jawless fish, the so-called cyclostomes, possess a well-developed hypothalamus, thalamus, rudimentary hippocampus, and almost mammalian amygdala. These are all part of the so-called limbic system memory structures, critical to the basic responsive survival functions working in the brain.[21]

Recent work by Philippe Janvier, in Paris, on an advanced agnathan, Benneviaspis, an osteostracan, (ostracoderm), and not a true vertebrate, has confirmed the rich and complex brain structure already existing in this first line of fish.[22]

Brain and Intelligence

Too many confused relationships still exist between the various classes and subclasses of fish as we first discover them in the fossil record from c.470mya to construct a sure phylogenetic tree back to the Cambrian. The sharks are seen to have similarities to the early agnathans, especially in their lack of swim bladder. The fossil Antiarch placoderms, 420mya, Radinsky hypothesizes, hint at a primitive lung, thus linking them to the crossopterygians and dipnoan lungfish, 410-400mya, all of these being relative contemporaries.[23]

Back in the Cambrian are *Pikaia,* a possible lancelet ancestor, the enigmatic conodont fossils, and the tunicates, sea squirts, whose larval state fascinates John Long. Long places them as a hypothetical ancestor, possibly the root chordate.[24] Considering that the protochordates all cashed in their chips for possible vertebrate immortality when they opted for the plenitude and economic security at the sea bottoms, as did the other blastospores, the echinoderms before them, indeed as most of the fossil animals yet discovered, from the Ediacarans on, it stands to reason that some if not most of the agnathans and placoderms would in their own competitive rush for survival eventually gravitate down-ward similarly to make their economy from the richer and less dynamically competed for resources, both animal and plant, at the sea bottom.

Since life is always opportunistic, and since a presumptive case can be made for the possibilities for eking out a living in relatively shallow waters or close to the surface, where oxygen was plentiful and a light-sensitive eye would early come in handy, the sudden appearance in the fossil record of true vertebrates between 470-420mya should not fool us into erring on the side of a macro-evolutionary creationism. The enormous time spans that are now estimated for the evolution and development into modern fungi, plants, and animals of the large eukaryote cell ought to warn us about the necessity for "time," in which molecular, genetic, and then selective processes created not only the evolved vertebrate body plan, albeit in constant process of modification and specializa-tion, but also an already highly-articulated brain and neural structure.

So decided was this evolutionary innovation, the vertebrate brain, that by the time we meet it in the Ordovician, c.470mya, it is clear that an adaptive breakthrough had already been made. Not only the mere carving out of an ecological niche by an organ that allowed for the successful and mobile exploration of the environment, then the exploita-tion of the inert and vulnerable prey at the sea bottom, but an organ that would not sig-nificantly change either in structure or size for over 250 million years.[25]

Harry Jerison's basic argument, as set forth in his various writings, is that the lower vertebrate brain, which encompasses the fish, all classes except the Chondrichyes—the sharks and their kin—was maintained as a basic adaptive model during this long time period, 250my. The amphibians and reptiles share a very similar brain and intelligence profile with the fish. This relational profile Jerison established through a mathematical and geometrical set of correlations, a series of convex polygons in which body weight is related to brain weight.[26]

This brain/body relationship in all the so-called lower vertebrates remains the same up and until the development of the more recent mammals and the birds. The exception as noted above lies in the sub-class representing the sharks, and its brain, at the least in their modern descendants. The brain of the shark is larger than would be expected from its size. It lies intermediate between other fish, amphibians, reptiles, and the bird/mammal range.[27]

The larger the body, the larger concomitantly is the brain. Jerison's argument is that the changes that do take place in the relationships of structure and function during these many millions of years do not essentially change the model ratios in the relationship of brain and body weights. Thus from the placoderm to *Tyrannosaurus* the brain grows correlatively with gross size and weight, in terms of its general information processing abilities, intelligence.

One additional caveat to this principle is noted by Jerison, the special adaptations in the bony ray-finned fish, the *Actinopterygii*. They reveal a specialized enlargement of the facial, acoustic, vagal lobes of the medulla, the optic lobe of the midbrain, the valvula cerebelli, and the forebrain structures associated with olfaction.[28] In general these adap-tations, which are probably traceable to their ancient precursors, the paleonscids, do not appreciably change this brain/body relationship. Yet the restructuring is significant. The adaptation is primarily a visual one, arguing for specialized rapid mid-water movement. It was probably a critically decisive morphological innovation that allowed the *Actinopterygii* to conquer the waters, perhaps drive most of the other classes of fish, with the exception of the sharks, into either extinction or into peripheral adaptive niches.[29]

> If fish, amphibians, and reptiles can all be subsumed under a single function relating brain to body size, the first guess would be that no special evolution of the brain was favored within or between any of these groups. Put more conservatively, this points to the proposition that the niches invaded by these lower vertebrates did not demand sufficiently new or different behavioral adaptations to be reflected in expansion of enough of the brain to appear in the gross brain:body analysis. In addition, this implies that most present adaptations are probably of great antiquity, since a 300my-old fossil presents as specialized a picture of the brain as does a modern fish.[30]

With the fish, Jerison thus argues, the vertebrates had now firmly left their earlier phyletic connectivities behind, entering a totally new ecological adaptive space for animal life.

Vertebrates are swimmers first, having a phosphatic bone structure within their bodies as well as a cartilaginous notochord. The basic body plan of bilateral frontal and lateral organization, and the adaptive circumstances of living in the water for sustenance rather than fixed at the bottoms, or under the ground itself like the worms, was perhaps forced upon protovertebrates by circumstance. Their complex evolutionary unraveling is hinted at by the deuterstome embryological development shared only with the modestly successful echinoderms, the latter finally choosing the safe life, on the ground floor.

Clearly, the neurological structure developing in these protovertebrate creatures as they struggled to secure their oxygen supplies either close to the surface or in deep water environments, demanded as part of their adaptive passage, and made possible in their basic body plan, more interconnected neurons in the anterior regions of the body permanently cementing the frontal/posterior organization of the animal. Whether from the basic requirements of securing food in this niche, given the basic body structure available to them, else through some kind of "red queen" to keep up with the competition of similar forms in the lee of the continents, free-swimming arthropods, or perhaps intraspecific competition with other fish, the selective demands, in contrast to the many Cambrian bottom dwellers, were shaped not to acquire, for example, massive defensive calcite shields, but rather a brain sufficient to move as a predatory master of the ecology.[31]

Once the vertebrates attained a generalized capacity for information processing to meet the demands of their mid-water ecological niche, and attaining a size and predatory capacity that clearly made them masters of their domain, further mutation in terms of accommodation to specialized morphologies, behavior, for environmental exploitation, whether once more to the bottoms and feeding on equally, if defensively competitive mollusks, worms, and echinoderms, or in the more oxygenated surface ecologies, was unnecessary. At the water bottoms they were not filtering microbes and organic detritus. Rather, they were now uprooting and crumbling into food morsels the defensive morphological bastions of the echinoderms, arthropods and mollusks.

The early vertebrates had mysteriously attained an adaptive Rubicon of behavioral competence that did not require more than the shifting around of these various brain structures and sensory and muscular connections to meet micro-needs, rather than a more expansive macro-growth of the brain. That this growth was still theoretically possible is evidenced by the relatively empty and beckoning cranial cavity. Some 250my later, significant growth of the brain would begin again in two widely dispersed successor "reptile" lines, birds and mammals.

One wonders why a process of orthoselection for continued brain expansion did not earlier occur. Here, growth in this set of organs, sensory inputs, and muscular and behavioral outputs, leading to successively more adaptive behaviors, and therefore issuing in positive selection, did not continue beyond a mere radiation of the three classes of early fish. Could further growth of the brain have then been maladaptive, causing internal physiological dysfunction? Or would a larger brain have been dysfunctional in a competitive and mechanical sense, precipitating a shift to a new and precarious adaptive plane? Apparently, the aqueous and earthly world of the early vertebrates, into which they successively penetrated, did not as yet require greater sensory integration. What seems to have been necessitated was raw body restructuring, ever more streamlined for immediate competition, movement, biting, breeding.

- 3 -
Extinction

Causal Conditions

"...[T]he most plausible causes of extinction are interactions between continental fusion and climatic change."[32] While Michael Benton refers here to the late Permian extinction, perhaps the greatest that our fossil and geological records permit us to postulate, other causes—declining sea levels, cooling climates, catastrophic impacts—are all possibilities in this and other apparent decimations of the living flora and fauna on our planet at any one moment of history.

Donovan argues that mass extinctions should be seen as mainly paleozoological events that rarely have significantly long-term effects on the composition of the flora.[33] Donovan defines a mass extinction "...where there has been a (geologically) rapid reduction in biological abundance and diversity on a global scale."[34][35]

Mass extinctions are real in the sense that they are taking place among our historically identifiable fauna and flora, in a sense before our eyes. Going back from 15,000 B.P. to the beginning of the Pleistocene, some 1.9mya, we have a good record of animal life that existed on Earth in this hardly remote period of prehistory. We know what was here and what is here no longer. We also accept the fact that the recent large-scale decimation of many large mammal fauna goes beyond the usual and expected succession of animal life presented to us by the evolution of life.

It must be that the trends in climate change symbolized by the Milankovich cycles that describe the successive tiltings of the earth's axis, its inclination toward the sun, also the unpredictable geological shiftings of the earth's mantle and the positions of the land masses relative to the equator and the poles, had to have occurred many times over in this ancient 3by span of time. Therefore, significant and stressful physical changes affecting living forms must be assumed.

6.1 Permian (250mya) land masses.

Rhythms of Change

The so-called Varengian glaciation that took place some time after 1bya has been thought to have been a possible product of the explosive infusion of free oxygen into the seas and atmosphere of the earth, a biologically caused physical event attributed to the development of photosynthesis in the evolving eukaryote plant kingdom. The consequent return to what are thought to be normal temperature and living Gaia balances on our earthly environment paralleled the evolution of the animal metazoa.

The logic is that somewhere on our earth the drop in temperatures during this great oxygen-caused glaciation still allowed for the survival of heterotrophic life, which began to flourish in the bonanza of plant protein. This latter released into the atmosphere enough CO_2 as a byproduct of their metabolic orgy to bring the oxygen balance back down to a temperature range in the waters and in the atmosphere such that life broke through in the metazoan explosion that we see exemplified in the later Rhipean and Vendian faunal expansions.[36]

The various mass extinctions that seem to punctuate the fossil and geological record are further exemplifications of these more general pulsations in the physical world that affect life. Occasional extra-planetary intrusions, such as the very controversial bolide collision, have also been proposed. This collision is thought to have taken place around 65mya and caused as consequence the deformation of climatic and environmental circumstances that made the dinosaurs extinct.[37]

Important, too, is the general competitive struggle in life forms for sustenance. It is quite possible, as for example in the case of the Ediacaran fauna, that the development of wholly new forms of predatory life, new morphologies and behaviors could have rendered them easy and susceptible prey for more mobile heterotrophic forms. Here, however, important differences exist between the raw physical changes that can affect a wide range of floras and faunas and more limited biological successions. The former constitute mass extinctions that go beyond the traditional and limited biological decimations and transitions—what we have seen among the vertebrates, including the fish. These latter seem to point more clearly to the so-called "progressivity" in the evolution of life into the present.

Whereas the 50my of the Cambrian may have seen five different extinctions, the basic fauna remained plentiful and diverse until the great Ordovician extinction of c.438mya. One can hypothesize here a period of perhaps 150my of evolutionary development and proliferation with apparently only one significant milestone, the appearance of the vertebrates, or the protochordates, the jawless fish, agnathans.[38]

These post-Cambrian fauna, which consisted of a plentiful number of trilobites (early arthropods, relatives of the crabs, barnacles, and insects), brachiopods (ancestors of the lamp shells—now heavily reduced in number), various families of mollusks (clams, snails, octopi), and echinoderms (sea lilies, sea urchins, crinoids). They dominated the seas of this period of evolutionary time. At the time of the Ordovician mass extinctions, many of the lesser seen families of sea animals seem to have lurched forward in number and diversity, even as the Cambrian fauna edged gradually into the background. Sepkoski's argument, using the great Permian cataclysm as the final pre-modern disturbance of the internal intracompetitive adaptive cycle, argues that these successions would have happened anyway. The extinctions just jarred the timetable of events somewhat.[39]

Nevertheless, with almost 70% of the extant water-dwelling species made extinct, (in the Ordovician), the oceans were emptied. Jablonski agrees with the consensus that extreme glaciation had its impact over a wide swath of the earth.[40] The subsequent expansion of the various classes and families of the jawed fishes subsequent to this event, which ushered in new and richly varied fauna in the seas, may be related to the seemingly explosive radiation of predator fish during this Paleozoic faunal period. This is not an implausible correlation. The Ordovician extinctions involved mostly brachiopods and predatory trilobites (arthropods), the latter class of creatures began their slow descent into complete extinction. Brachiopod, shelled filter feeders, are found today only in a few Southern Hemisphere ecologies.

One hundred thirty million years later, c.367mya, the so-called late Devonian extinction occurred.[41] Jablonski states that the consensus as to cause by glacier-related events, as with the more powerful Ordovician extinction, is clear, and that the decimation of the coral reefs, as in the Ordovician was critical. [42] But oddly, fresh water fish and flora might not have been significantly affected.[43] Again, large groups of invertebrates were eliminated, trilobites, ammonoids, and fish such as the advanced if jawless Osteostraci, were gone.[44]

The super-continent christened Rodinia by McMenamin and McMenamin broke up sometime before the Vendian/Cambrian boundary, c.600-550mya. It had been in existence since before 1bya, and probably was the most extensive and compact of all the super-continents. Thus the total amount of shoreline or coastal waters conducive to the development of highly nutritive environments and the progression of metazoan life was not extensive. The Vendian, similar to the Cambrian, saw four major glacial episodes.[45]

The breakup or rifting of Rodinia brought into being a less extensive super-continent, Gondwana, in the Southern Hemisphere, consisting of South America, Africa, India, Antarctica, Australia, parts of the Mid-East, Southeast Asia. North of Gondwana was Laurasia, consisting of North America, Europe, the Russian and Siberian platforms, Kazakastan. China seems to have been scattered into the seas of the East. These super-continents, which existed since the Cambrian c.560-510mya, began to move to the North, colliding about 300mya.[46]

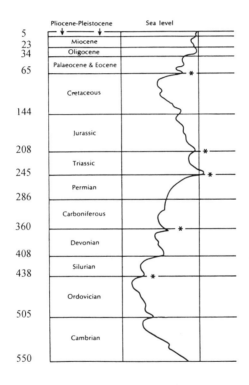

6.2 Five mass extinctions (*) seem to occur at times of rapidly dropping sea level.

Mother of Extinctions

The result was a short-lived, but important geological entity. Pangea, the combined super-continent of the continental collisions, with a great enclosed sea, Tethys, product of an important geological fault, one that existed earlier between Gondwana and Laurasia. By 250mya Pangea was well formed. At this point, a period of massive worldwide extinctions begins. This was an approximately 20my period during which it is estimated that 95% of the extant animal species, and 50% of the animal families of the planet disappeared. Also many plant lines became extinct.[47] By the late Triassic, some 200mya, Pangea began its breakup toward the modern continental pattern. By then wholly new evolutionary dynamics on land and in the seas were on the way. As had been typical over the historic geological and paleontological record, it is estimated that within a five to ten million year period after any traditional extinction event, not necessarily including the late Pleistocene destruction of large mammals, the record would show the repopulation of emptied ecologies by new families of old classes and phyla.

The most obvious explanation for this massive Permian extinction—which included many reptilian lines, a number of "mammal-like" synapsid reptiles, vast numbers of amphibians, the always susceptible invertebrates and corals—was the drying up of these coastal water as the continents joined.[48] Into this calculation is a hypothesis of colder continental climatic conditions. This change in climate weakened many groups that had flourished in the warm Gondwanian/Carboniferous period.[49]

Douglas Erwin's assessment: "The terrestrial extinction was not insignificant, but does not appear to be as extensive as the marine extinctions. Here global warming, increased seasonality, and a possible reduction in habitat diversity associated with harsh environmental conditions in the interior of Pangea seem sufficient to cause the extinction..."[50] But in addition, Erwin argues that the main marine extinctions began first with habitat reduction as the earlier continents united, leading to a reduction in shelf area. Then came dramatic increases in CO_2 and methane from the oxidation of organic material, gas hydrates, and massive volcanic activities (in Siberia).[51] This triggered global warming, the "greenhouse effect," and the possibilities of oceanic anoxia, not enough oxygen in the coastal waters.[52]

Note here the hypothesized simultaneous occurrence of colder climatic, continental seasonality, along with a greenhouse effect indicating general global warming, both contributing to the Permian catastrophe. Earlier, we commented upon a similar controversy. Might it have been the transition into the Holocene, a generally warmer period for the entire planet than the Pleistocene Ice Ages, yet now with sharp continental temperature and rainfall transitions, along with real seasonal north and south temperate zone shifts in climate, that led to the great extinction of the large mammals of the Pleistocene, 1.9-0.012mya?

> The Earth and its tenants have come to seem more vulnerable than they once appeared. Persuasive evidence of repeated mass extinctions has compelled science to recognize that they could happen again, and to investigate their history and possible causes.[53]

Endnotes, Chapter 6

[1] Long, John A. 1995. *The Rise of Fishes*, Baltimore: Johns Hopkins Univ. Press, p. 201.

[2] Long, 1995, *op. cit.*, p. 201.

[3] de Duve, Christian. 1995. *Vital Dust*. N.Y.: Basic Books, pp. 203-204.

[4] Benton, M. 1993. "Four Feet on the Ground," in *Life*, S. J. Gould, ed., N.Y.: W. W. Norton, pp. 80-81.

[5] Nisbet, E. G. 1991. *Living Earth*, N.Y.: Harper Collins, p. 159; Benton, 1993., *op. cit.*, p. 89.

[6] Long, 1995, *op. cit.*, pp. 67, 69-70.

[7] Smith, Homer. 1961. *From Fish To Philosopher*, N.Y.: Anchor-Doubleday, pp. 120-121.

[8] Long, 1995, *op. cit.*, p. 209.

[9] Benton, 1993, *op. cit.*, p. 88+ *diagram*.

[10] Knoll, A. 1992. "The Early Evolution of Eukaryotes: A Geological Perspective, *Science*, 1 May 1992, 256:622-627.

[11] McMenamin, Mark A. S., and McMenamin, Dianna L. S. 1990. *The Emergence of Animals, the Cambrian Breakthrough*, N.Y.: Columbia Univ. Press, p. 27.

[12] Papez, J. W. 1967. *Comparative Neurology*, N.Y.: Hafner; Lentz, T. L. 1968. *Primitive Nervous Systems*, New Haven: Yale Univ Press; Emson, R. H. 1966. "The Reaction of the sponge to applied stimuli," *Comparative Biochemistry and Physiology*, 18:805-827; Joseph, R. 1993. *The Naked Neuron*, N.Y.: Plenum.

[13] Joseph, 1993, *op. cit.*, p. 15.

[14] Stebbins, G. Ledyard. 1982. *Darwin to DNA, Molecules to Humanity*, *op. cit.*, p. 210.

[15] Stebbins, 1982, *op. cit.*, p. 250.

[16] de Duve, Christian. 1995. *Vital Dust*, *op. cit.*, p. 191.

[17] Jacobson, A. L. 1963. "Learning in Flatworms and Annelids," *Psychological Bulletin*, 60:74-94.

[18] Joseph, 1993, *op. cit.*, pp. 15-18.

[19] Joseph, 1993, *op. cit.*, pp. 18-20.

[20] Radinsky, L. 1987. *The Evolution of Vertebrate Design*, Chicago: Univ. of Chicago Press, pp. 25-27.

[21] Joseph, R. 1993. *The Naked Neuron*, *op. cit.*, pp. 54-56.

[22] Janvier, P. 1984. "The relationship of the Osteostraci and the Galeaspida," *Journal of Vertebrate Paleontology*, 4:344-358.

[23] Radinsky, 1987, *op. cit.*, pp. 50-52.

[24] Long, 1995, *op. cit.*, pp. 30, 32, 34.

[25] Jerison, H. J. 1973. *Evolution of the Brain and Intelligence*, N.Y.: Academic Press; Jerison, H. J. 1982. "The Evolution of Biological Intelligence," in *Handbook of Human Intelligence*, Robert J. Sternberg, ed., Cambridge: Cambridge Univ. Press, pp. 723-791; Jerison, H. J. 1977. "The Theory of Encephalization," *Annals of the New York Academy of Sciences*, Vol. 299, 146-160; Jerison, H. J. 1983. "The Evolution of The Mammalian Brain As An Information Processing System," in *Advances In The Study Of Mammalian Behavior*, J. F. Eisenberg and D. G. Kleinman, eds. Special Publication No. 7, March 11, 1983, Shippensburg, PA: The American Society of Mammalogists.

[26] Jerison, 1973, *op. cit.*, pp. 44, 48; also Jerison, 1977, *op. cit.*, Vol. 299, *passim*, for extended mathematical and neurobiological elaboration of basic brain/body allometry argument.

[27] Jerison, 1973, *op. cit.*, p. 100.

[28] Jerison, 1973, *op. cit.*, pp. 122-123.

[29] Jerison, 1973, *op. cit.*, p. 115.

[30] Jerison, 1973, *op. cit.*, p. 115.

[31] Jerison, 1982, *op. cit.*, pp. 746-748; Van Valen, L. 1973. "A New Evolutionary Law," *Evolutionary Theory*, 1:1-30; Van Valen, L. 1974. "Two Modes of Evolution," *Nature*, 252:298-300.

[32] Benton, 1993, *op. cit.*, p. 108.

[33] Donovan, S. K., ed. 1989. "Paleontological Criteria for the Recognition of Mass Extinctions," in *Mass Extinctions: Process and Evidence*, N.Y.: Columbia Univ. Press, p. 26.

[34] Donovan, 1989, *op. cit.*, p. 20.

[35] Sepkoski, J. J., Jr. 1990. "The taxonomic structure of periodic extinctions," in *Global Catastrophes in Earth History*, V. L. Sharpton and P. D. Ward, eds., Boulder Colo.: Geological Society of America, Geological Society of America Special Paper 247, pp. 33-44; Sepkoski, J. J., Jr., and Raup, D. M. 1986. "Periodicity in marine extinction events," in *Dynamics of Extinction*, D. K. Elliott, ed., N.Y.: John Wiley, pp. 3-36; Raup, D. M. 1991. *Extinction: Bad Genes or Bad Luck?*, N.Y.: Norton; Raup, D. M. and Boyagian, G. E. 1988. "Patterns of generic extinction in the fossil record," *Paleobiology*, 14:109-125; Erwin, Douglas H. 1993. *The Great Paleozoic Crisis: Life and Death in the Permian*, N.Y.: Columbia Univ. Press; Jablonski, D. 1989. "The biology of mass extinction: a paleontological view," *Philosophical Transactions of the Royal Society*, Ser. B.: 325:357-368; Jablonski, D., and Bottjer, D. J. 1990. "The origin and diversification of major groups: environmental patterns and evolutionary lags," in *Major Evolutionary Radiations*, P. D. Taylor and G. P. Larwood, eds., Oxford: Clarendon Press, pp. 17-57.

[36] Brasier, 1989. *op. cit.*, pp. 73-88.

[37] Alvarez, L. W., Alvarez, W., Asaro, F., and Michel, H. V. 1980. "Extraterrestrial cause for the Cretaceous-tertiary extinction, *Science*, 208 (4448):1095-1108; Alvarez, L. W. 1983. "Experimental evidence that an asteroid impact led to the extinction of many species 65 million years ago," *Proceedings of the National Academy of Sciences U.S.A.*, 80 (2):627-642.

[38] Sepkoski, J. J., Jr. 1993. "Foundations: Life in the Oceans," in *Life*, S. J. Gould, ed., *op. cit.*, p. 59.

[39] Sepkoski, J. J., Jr. 1984. "A kinetic model of Phanerozoic taxonomic diversity: Post Paleozoic families and mass extinctions," *Paleobiology*, 10:246-267; Erwin, Douglas H. 1993. *The Great Paleozoic Crisis: Life and Death in the Permian*, N.Y.: Columbia Univ. Press, pp. 18-30.

[40] Jablonski, D. 1986. "Causes and Consequences of Mass Extinctions: A Comparative Approach," in *Dynamics of Extinction*, David K. Elliott, ed., N.Y.: John Wiley, pp. 183-229; McLaren, D. J. 1986. "Abrupt Extinctions," in *Dynamics of Extinction*, David K. Elliott, ed., *op. cit.*, pp. 37-46, esp. p. 42.

[41] Benton, 1993, *op. cit.*, p. 109.

[42] Jablonski, 1986, *op. cit.*, p. 191.

[43] Jablonski, 1986, *op. cit.*, p. 186.

[44] Benton, 1993, *op. cit.*, p. 109.

[45] McMenamin, Mark A. S., and McMenamin, Dianna L. S. 1990. *The Emergence of Animals, op. cit.*, pp. 92-105, esp. 96-97, 104-105.

[46] Erwin, D. H. 1993. *The Great Paleozoic Crisis: Life and Death in the Permian*, N.Y.: Columbia Univ. Press, pp. 38-41.

[47] J. John Sepkoski, Jr., quoted in Michael Benton, 1993, *op. cit.*, p. 107. Douglas Erwin labels it as "The Mother of Mass Extinctions" (Erwin, 1993, *op. cit.*, pp. 223-258).

[48] Benton, 1993, *op. cit.*, pp. 106-109.

[49] Stanley, S. M. 1988. "Paleozoic mass extinctions: shared patterns suggest global cooling as common cause," *American Journal of Science*, 288:334-352.

[50] Erwin, 1993, *op. cit.*, p. 257.

[51] Benton, 1993, *op. cit.*, p. 106.

[52] Erwin, 1993, *op. cit.*, pp. 255-257.

[53] Benton, 1993, *op. cit.*, p. 109.

7

Mammals:
Creation, Transformation, and Dominance

- 1 -
Creation and Transformation

Timeline Reprise
1. Amniotes Arrive

> During the Upper Carboniferous period, some 300 million years ago, the climate of
> what is now Nova Scotia was warm and moist, and great forests dominated by giant lyco-
> pods occurred. These lycopods were related to the modern club mosses but grew to 100 feet
> in height. The hard, woody part lay at the periphery of the trunk, and after the death of the
> plant they remained as hollow stumps. Numerous small tetrapods appear to have sheltered
> within the stumps and in due course died in them, eventually to be covered by sediments
> and fossilized. Today a number of such trees have been discovered containing fossil re-
> mains of the animals. Various kinds of amphibians are present, along with the earliest
> known reptiles.[1]

Close to the time of the arrival of amphibian-like osteolepiformes/crossopterygians
on the shore and land interface of the Devonian-Carboniferous border, some 375-
350mya, a group of transitional amphibians, soon to be reptiles, experimented with more
permanent land adaptations. Perhaps their air-breathing equipment, their ability to hold
their heads high, or their locomotor facility allowed for a deeper penetration of the land
surfaces. In process, the reproductive dangers of laying eggs in ecological settings where
desiccation was possible were tested.

Possibly because of a tradition in the crossopterygian line for thicker, less permeable surface coverings of their eggs, some of these reptile "experiments" with leather-like
external membranes were successful. The young survived and an adaptive tradition
leading toward a fully cleidoic egg was established.

We observe from the fossil record only a minute proportion of the possible scenarios for the ascent from the seas to the land, thence proceeding toward the long-awaited appearance of the mammals as a class. Consider the outside possibility of a more direct, if at this time still hidden process of evolution of transitional creatures—placentally nurtured, live-born young, akin to some ancient and modern sharks. Could there have been another, different kind of adaptive shift onto the land from that described through traditional reptile egg-laying patterns?

2. Synapsid Reptiles

The establishment of the reptiles in a fully land-inhabiting life probably took another 25my, and was surely established by 325mya, if not before, given the East Kirkton, Scotland, discovery of "*Westlothiana lizziae*," which seems to date back to about 350mya.[2] The pelycosaur, the ancestral synapsid, mammal-like reptile, line was also quickly differentiated from the stem reptiles.[3] The latter, quite crocodilian in structure and behavior, lagged behind. However, they eventually, especially after the late Permian decimations, began to radiate into the Triassic, 245-208mya, producing the thecodonts, and their increasingly successful successors throughout the Triassic, the dinosaurs.

3. Therapsids

By 300mya, the therapsids, themselves successors to the pelycosaurs, became the dominant representatives of the synapsid lineage. In fact, they clearly spread over Gondwana throughout the Permian, 286-245mya. The Permian was a period of eruptive radiation and the consequent populating of practically every available and possible ecological niche for both the synapsid as well as diapsid reptiles. In addition to the multiplying and dominating therapsid reptiles on land, the diapsids had created "*Hovasaurus*," an animal that had returned to the seas, used its tail for propulsion in water, "*Mesosaurus*" apparently a fully aquatic reptile that likewise did not leave descendants into the Triassic. Finally, there was the diapsid "*Coelurosauravus*," a late Permian glider, our first experiment with life on high.[4]

As with later radiations of both reptiles and mammals into the seas and air, and unlike the water committed amphibians, the more adaptable land living forms could muster enough genetic variability so that when under pressure, these incipient and often genetically recessive physical and behavioral potentialities could appear in the phenotype and allow for egress from this selective pressure into now relatively uncontested ecological niches in the water and air. Though the therapsids were relatively dominant on land, it is clear that many other lines of reptiles were sifting their genetic potential and awaiting a selective opening for the full realization of their nascent adaptive skills. The 50my of the late Carboniferous and the Permian were time enough for this rush of occupation over the land, seas, and air. Stebbins places the flourishing of the therapsid reptiles to have taken place over a duration of 60my.[5]

4. Cynodonts Dominate

At the end of the Permian [250-245mya] there was a massive upheaval in the land faunas....81% of amphibian families died out. Altogether 75% of all amphibian and reptile families disappeared. Similar drastic extinctions seem to have happened in the ocean: one half of all marine families, four-fifths of all genera. By all estimates the end-Permian extinctions amount to the most catastrophic event, or closely compacted series of events that life has ever suffered—whether in terms of sheer numbers of species lost, or of the traumatic effects on subsequent evolution.[6]

Within five to ten million years these ecologies were once more filled. The next selective phase, now in the lower Triassic, would reveal the cynodonts as the dominant therapsid line, competition coming from the developing thecodont/archosaur line leading to the first phase of dinosaurian evolution. The archosaurs were now represented by *Proterosuchus* and *Euparkeria*, respectively 5ft. and 2ft. carnivores, the herbivorous rhynchosaurs, 3-6 ft.[7]

This process of phyletic advance would continue until the end of the Triassic, about 208mya, during which the division of the archosaur line into the Ornithosuchia and the Crocodylotarsi, the former evolving into the dinosaurs, also pterosaurs, soon the birds, the latter group (Crocodylotarsi) evolving into the crocodiles and alligators. A side line of aquatic reptiles was represented by the ichthyosaurs, plesiosaurs, mososaurs. The latter, only secondarily aquatic, continued a trend of adaptive opportunism inherent in the vertebrate genetic heritage.[8]

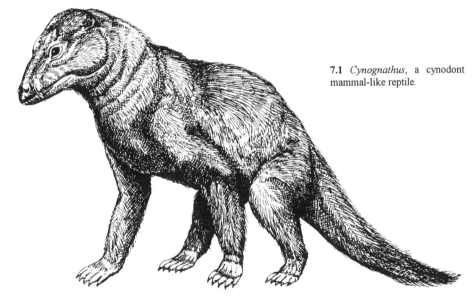

7.1 *Cynognathus*, a cynodont mammal-like reptile.

A Restructured Reptile

The cynodonts emerge from the Permian crisis, some 245mya as one of the few therapsid survivors. They have characteristics that are widely separated from the ancestral lines of archosaurs, then relatively restricted by the therapsids to their ancient adaptations to a wetland way of life. The cynodonts may have been upland creatures in the Permian, and therefore relatively invisible in that period to archeological scrutiny. In the Triassic they appear with already developed adaptations that herald their unique destiny. They survived the Permian climatic and ecological crisis by developing more than purely inertial mass—endothermal tendencies, large body size to buffer against heat loss, dehydration, and to protect against rapid cooling.[9]

1. For the cynodonts to maintain the kind of internal temperature that would allow them to survive variable climates, they would need much more food and in steady supply to maintain their metabolic processes. For this, they needed improved masticatory skills, as well as the sensory equipment that would allow both for predation and defense. As the Triassic ecologies filled up with competing forms, the refining of the various cynodont adaptations continued. Stebbins sees the cynodonts as inefficiently homeothermic, similar to the later mammal monotremes. In contrast, bone structure in the various classical therapsid lines argues persuasively for traditional reptilian "cold-blooded" metabolism.[10]

2. The dentary bone in the jaw gradually took over the role of anchoring the various muscles needed for mastication. Instead of a jaw joint as in the reptiles and early synapsids where the articular and the quadrate bones meet, the dentary increasingly takes over the lower jaw and the quadrate and articular bones migrate to a position between the ear drum and the stapes, now in the middle ear cavity as the incus (quadrate) and malleus (articular). In the final stages of cynodont evolution and the early-defined mammals, two joints did exist in the jaw, with the lower jaw housing the inner ear.[11]

The adaptive importance of this enormous structural transformation was great. "The functional significance of these remarkable changes was two-fold. First, the jaw was strengthened, because it was now composed of a single bone rather than several. Second, with three ear ossicles rather than one, mammals had the benefit of better amplification of sound vibrations from the tympanic membrane, since there were two additional joints and levers in the sound-transmitting system between ear-drum and inner ear."[12]

It has also recently been argued that there was a reciprocality in the posterior shift of the quadrate and articular bones to a position between the stapes and the ear drum. This involved the concomitant growth of the bones surrounding an expanding brain, itself integrating the increased sensory information provided by the auditory as well as the olfactory pathways. A skull-protected brain is characteristic of mammal morphology.[13]

3. The fact that a secondary palate had developed in the therapsids, once again arguing for a longer evolutionary and genetic history for such an adaptation that allows for simultaneous mastication of food and breathing, gave the cynodonts a necessary advantage in the active search and immediate utilization of nourishment. In the crocodiles, this evolved later independently. The continuous development throughout the Triassic of more complex tooth structure and vertical alignment of the teeth, which allowed for finer chewing and grinding down of food, improved the efficiency and rapidity with which food substances could become metabolically available. This was providing for a creature that would be active in the cool of day and night and not, as with the ectomorphic archosaurs/dinosaurs incredibly active at high noon and lethargic in the cool of evening, presumably digesting the day's "haul."

4. Both lines of reptiles, archosaurs and therapsids, the latter including the cynodonts, present a more erect, feet-under-the-body stance as the Triassic advances 245-208mya. The dinosaurs had a more triangulated arrangement in which their rear feet and tail were used for balance and propulsion, similar to the marsupials (mammal), kangaroos, who stand upright, using their feet and tail both as observational balance and pro-

pulsive structures. Kangaroos can use their front limbs for defense, even as they are basically vegetarians. In the long run this balance, especially for rapid predatory attacks, won the day for the dinosaurs, especially as they were able to mobilize enormous amounts of daylight energy for growth, energy that could be conserved at night.

5. Kemp asserts the probability that olfaction was highly developed in the cynodonts, given the large size of the nasal cavity and the various supporting bone structures that are part of the maxillary in the nasal capsule.[14] In all, the cynodonts represent a line with a tendency toward high metabolic needs at all times of the day/night cycle, therefore somewhat restricted in size, early on wolf- or dog-like, and specializing in hearing-smelling as primary sensory inputs. The dinosaurs, by contrast, were extremely visual creatures that thrived in the daylight. Since the Triassic was in general quite warm and relatively dry, the archosaur/dinosaur line was not disadvantaged.

6. In his early studies of the cynodont skull and brain, Olsen had argued that these creatures reveal a lateral expansion, a flocculus on the cerebellum. This analysis was obtained through serial sections and not through casting.[15] Jerison argues that there may have been much cartilage between the brain and the inner border of the skull bones in the region of the cerebellum. The evidence is clearer with regard to the supposed expansion of the forebrain, as claimed by Olsen. Jerisen argues that available evidence through complete endocasts show that the cynodont forebrain is typical of the lower vertebrate model.[16]

In a more recent analysis Kemp argues that the depth of the anterior parts of the cynodont brain, as expressed in the fossil imprint on the inner skull surface, is unknown, especially as regards the cerebral hemispheres. He argues that in *Procynosuchus,* a brain much more deeply embedded in the skull would reveal a brain volume approaching mammal size. He follows Olsen in seeing the expansion of the cerebellum as close to mammalian size, given that "this part of the brain is almost completely impressed on the roof, sides, and floor of the braincase."[17]

Jerison concedes the possibility of the enlargement of the of the cynodont cerebellum. However, his basic model of brain/body size in lower vertebrate is not undermined by this one structural deviation. "Although there may have been some expansion of the cerebellum, as suggested by Olsen, in 1944, such expansion could not have been large enough to produce the order-of-magnitude change in brain size to affect the quantitative analysis. The mammal-like reptiles, in short, were reptilian and not mammalian with respect to the evolution of their brains. In that respect the quantitative analysis is in agreement with the conclusion of most workers who have limited themselves to the examination of the form rather than the size of the brain and endocast of reptiles."[18]

Paul MacLean, in his monumental study, *The Triune Brain in Evolution,* discusses the therapsid reptiles in terms of their mysterious evolutionary position between traditional reptilian forms and true evolved mammals.[19] He is agnostic, noting that Olsen had to rely on an endocast of a cynodont brain made 80 years ago.[20] In this he tends to support Jerison. Against Jerison and arguing for the possibility of greater cortical development in the depth of these fossil impressions is Quiroga, whose work led to the view that the cynodonts had a very mammal-like brain.[21]

Mammal Challenges and Solutions

Three critical problems of terrestrial life that all land animals, mammals in particular, in terms of their adaptive potentialities, had to be solved: 1. Temperature variation, both diurnal and seasonal. 2. The tendency to lose water because of the huge water gradient between the air and the animal's tissues; difficulties related to maintaining osmotic and ionic balances. 3.Gravitational problems arising from the absence of buoyancy in the air.[22]

1. Temperature control. The metabolic rate in maintaining a constant high internal temperature is sometimes 7X that of similar-sized ectothermic reptiles. This is regulated by hair at body surface, variable blood flow, sweat glands, involuntary heat production by muscles. The purpose of endothermy is to keep the internal body temperature within fine limits under a wide range of environmental conditions. The adaptive function of high constant body temperature allows for the working of the larger enzymatic system to coordinate the multiple adaptive functions of the mammals. This requires a high intake of food, 10X that required by reptiles. Locomotor adaptations for the search for food, then the need to break down food in digestion is more demanding than that performed by intestinal processes alone. Here mastication and the digestive function of saliva are crucial. There is also need for hair, sweat glands, specialized skin blood vessels. A diaphragm is needed for greater exchange of external gases, kidneys are necessary to regulate water loss from a higher temperature and greater breathing rate. Finally, the sense organs and central nervous system must organize and control all these various activities.

2. Chemical control. In all animals there is a tendency to lose water from the tissues, which alter osmotic pressure and ionic balances. Here the mammal kidney is critical to the ultrafiltration rate of blood, the production of a concentrated, hypertonic urine that conserves water. Hypertonic urine allows the animal to excrete liquid while conserving water, the plasma level of ions are thus conserved. Environmentally, these regulatory mechanisms free the animal from dependency upon excessive needs for external water supplies or specialized diets. The heart and circulatory system must therefore produce the high blood pressure needed by the kidneys. Also needed is a complex endocrine system to detect levels of enzymes, initiate appropriate rates of secretion and reabsorption in the kidney tubules. The production of concentrated urine, in addition to allowing the inner body to adjust to extremes of warm and cold, also allowed mammals to invade variably dry environments and climates.[23]

3. Spatial Control. Mammalian limbs have a wide range of amplitudes and angles by which they can be moved. They thus can cope with irregular ground and obstacles. Their muscles are capable of sustained aerobic activity of a high rate. Mammals are not faster than reptiles, but can maintain rapid movement for a longer period than equivalent-sized reptiles. Therefore, the adaptive need was for increased food and oxygen supply, a complex sensory and central nervous system for overall behavioral control and a higher metabolic rate to support sustained efforts.

4. Homeostasis and Reproduction. Juveniles of mammals are sensitive to more environmental variation because of their small size and greater surface area ratio to total volume. They are also subject to temperature fluctuation and water loss. The complexity of mammal homeostatic regulatory structures requires time to develop, ontogenetically.

Parents need to maintain for the young a relatively constant external environment in which to develop. Parental care became important early on in the monotremes' burrows and nests. Viviparity and lactation for the provision of nutritious fluids in the therians (marsupials and placentals) made parental care that much more important. Protection by parents requires of the young little in the way of early locomotor skills. All these dimensions of mammalian internal regulation are subsumed under their general homeostatic morphology and physiology. Mammals are thus buffered in their spatial and temporal environmental experiences and experimentation. Geography, night and day, seasons, no longer absolutely inhibit. New niches and habitats are opened up. Cost: high metabolic structure requires intense food availability, else low population density.

5. Time and Evolutionary Pressure: Features of mammalian evolution conditioned by high degree of complexity and internal integration of structures and functional processes.

    a). Only small advances in any one part of the mammalian system could occur without awaiting small changes in other systems, highly integrated assemblage of structures and functions.

    b). Mammalian structures make all forms of adaptive life suitable: carnivores, insectivores, herbivores. Not correlated with any particular environment, terrestrial, aqueous, air.

    c). Mammals represent only one solution to the homeostatic equation of control and environmental independence.[24]

Keys To Survival

The fossil evidence for the first appearance of the three primary groups of mammals, morganucodontids, *Khuneotherium*, haramayids, has seemingly shifted further back into the mid-Triassic, c. 225-230mya, parallel to the wide-ranging dispersion of the many cynodont lines. It is quite possible that the separation and derivation of the early mammals from the advanced eucynodont line of Tritylodontidae proposed by Rowe and from the Tritheledontidae put forth by Kemp and Rowe may require revision.[25]

Both Colbert/Morales and Kemp view the great diversity of late-Triassic eucynodonts, evolving with the various mammal lines now being uncovered still earlier into the Triassic, as reflective of a wide-ranging dispersion of the eucynodonts as well as "sister lines." True mammals had early evolved the critical prismatic enamel and tooth shape characteristic of the Tritheledontidae (*Diarthrognathus*), as well as a rib and jaw structure that allowed them to dominate into the Jurassic.[26]

Today we receive a steady revision of evolutionary time tables. Origins and separations edge toward an always more ancient dating, thus implying slower rates of change. This could well argue for a position of the earliest mammal groups not as linear successors, but as unseen and parallel escapees from the Permian extinctions, c.245mya, along with the more successful and observed cynodont line.

How does one conceptualize this process of cynodont emergence, diversification, and dominance, quickly followed by the desiccation of the line, its gradual shrinkage in average size, and then disappearance? It could have been the archosaur/dinosaur advance and proliferation. It could also have been the new survivors, the mammals becoming plentiful in the late mid-Triassic, some 15-20 my after the appearance and efflorescence of the cynodonts. Most lines of cynodonts disappeared before the Jurassic boundary c.208mya. The exceptions were the insectivorous Tritheledontidae, extinct in the early Jurassic, c.200mya, and the Tritylodontidae, herbivorous creatures that survived into the mid-Jurassic, c.175mya.[27]

If we think of these cynodont/mammals as survival machines, perhaps shaped to their particular internal adaptations by the Permian crisis, we must accept their momentary dominance as attributable to their having inherited a relatively unoccupied ecological niche. Recall the estimated elimination of over 73% of the land-living tetrapod families and perhaps as many as 98-99% of the tetrapod species inhabiting our planet before the Permian crisis.[28] The cynodonts must have had in their pre-adaptive mix the sensory, metabolic, and behavioral requirements to have secured a living during the various episodes of environmental change, as relatively small sized, perpetual day-and-night energy-using machines. But now, in the Triassic, they seemed to have thrived within a relatively equable temperature and environmental gradient.

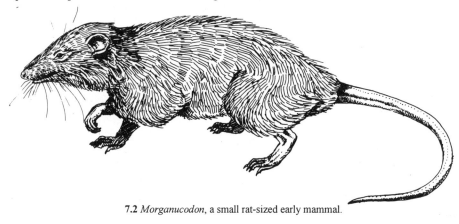

7.2 *Morganucodon*, a small rat-sized early mammal.

The competitor reptiles, endowed with a visual, rather than an auditory/olfactory mode of sensing and behaving, and given their high-energy daylight domination, gradually inherited that world in which the cynodont/mammal line was not then primarily dominant, given the changing climatic patterns from those that challenged and created them during the Permian crisis. The ceding of high-energy herbivorous and carnivorous opportunities to the archosaurs and then the dinosaurs ought not be thought of as a defeat for the seemingly fading late synapsid/therapsid line. The eucynodonts produced ever more compact descendants leading to the production of rabbit-sized late-Triassic, early-Jurassic forms. Almost simultaneously there is then revealed a more radically redesigned mouse-sized creature, now termed "Mammal," and in larger numbers and diversification as time goes on. Clearly a rich ecological niche still existed in the netherworld below the archosaurian visual perspective.

The mammals would not have prospered and diversified had they not over a significantly long time span perfected the wide-ranging set of adaptations for a life below the gaze of the dinosaurs, and achieved this in a manner far beyond the cynodont frame-work of adaptive and selective success. Strongly implied is that over a period of some 40 million Triassic years, largely small in numbers, and even smaller in size, a more specialized representative of the cynodont radiation, the protomammals exemplifying an old pattern of hidden evolution as they worked through their unique "cynodont" morphology, had become fitted for this world of smelling and hearing, of evasive scampering, in constant need of food, an ability to simultaneously eat, breathe and digest. This adaptive pattern must have been long in process from the time of the terminal Permian, 245mya, to their first appearance between 225-210mya.

Who Are the Mammals?

The taxonomic class, Mammals, whose surviving representatives from the Cenozoic, after 65mya, are the sub-class Multituberculates, *Allotheria*, extinct some 35-30mya; sub-class Monotremes, *Prototheria*, now represented only by the echidna and the platypus; sub-class *Theria*, composed of infra-class *Metatheria*, Marsupials: opossums, kangaroos, wombats; infra-class *Eutheria*, Placentals: humans, bats, whales, gorillas, dogs, etc.[29]

As described in the previous section, three different evolved mammal representatives of the upper and late Triassic, 218-208mya, existed—the morganucodontids, the kuehneotheriids, the haramiyids. Good fossil skeletal evidence has been identified with regard to the former, much less in the way of skeletal material from the latter two.

Megazostrodon, a morganucodontid from about 210mya, terminal Triassic, with an abundant fossil record, was a mouse-sized creature. It probably laid eggs, its immature young were probably without teeth, (only two sets per lifetime), it likely lapped milk from its mother's glands. The mature mother had no nipples or ears in her 1 oz. body. "The fossils show a streamlined shoulder and pelvic girdle and a more flexible type of backbone and ankle joint. The backbone of early mammals allowed them to move with bounding gait, flexing the spine up and down, in contrast to the sideways-curving reptilian walk...Morganucodontids evolved larger jaw muscles and precisely interlocking teeth (molars and premolars) that would shear food more rapidly, so that the gut could work faster and make room for more food."[30]

Kemp and most researchers (early 1980s) viewed these three exemplar categories as true ancestors of all subsequent mammalian sub-classes. They were viewed as well as being derived from the late cynodonts (now termed eucynodonts) during the middle Triassic, 230-220mya.[31] The one exception is Kermack, who believes that the morganucodontids could not have been derived from the same line of cynodont ancestors as the later mammals, which must have come from another sister line on the basis of tooth and partial skull structure. The kuehneotheriids, Kermack argues, could have been ancestral to the modern therians, the marsupials, and the placentals. He sees a more ancient non-cynodont, perhaps Permian, 250mya, therapsid ancestor for the morganucodontids.[32] As Kemp notes, given the similarity of both lines in so many characteristics, this would have involved "an incredible degree of parallel evolution between the two respective groups."[33]

According to Miao, writing in 1993, late 1980s discoveries in France of haramiyids, the third line of primeval mammals, by Sigogneau-Russell, as well as other Triassic
discoveries of *Kuehneotherium*, discussed by Fraser and then Clemens, argue for a relationship with the multituberculates in the haramyids.[34]

The general consensus of scientific opinion now supports an early separation of the
multituberculates from the other mammal taxa (late Triassic, c.220mya), then tracing the
monotremes' later separation from the therian line, at the so-called pre-tribosphenid
phase of therian molar dental development, about 110mya (late/early Cretaceous, 144-
65mya), in the Southern Hemisphere, Gondwana: Australia, South America, Antarctica.[35]

Stebbins, in supporting this majority perspective, sketches in the time line for a
separation of the monotremes from the mainline therian evolutionary process, dating it
earlier, back to about 140mya. He dates it from a line of root mammals (early Cretaceous, 144-65mya), before the final development both of the modern mammalian jaw
and skull structure.[36]

Both Timothy Rowe and Nancy Simmons argue against this perspective, even in
the face of the new findings and conclusions of Hahn and Sigogneau-Russell.[37] Rowe
and Simmons propose that the monotremes form the more fundamental outgroup of
mammal phylogeny and that the multituberculates are closer to the mainline mammal
radiation. "Although this phylogenetic position for multituberculates (i.e. more closely
related to therian mammals than are monotremes) is still controversial, these relationships are accepted in this study for purposes of outgroup comparisons."[38] Col-
bert/Morales, agreeing with Rowe and Simmons, see the monotremes as extremely
primitive, reptile-like creatures. Their presumption is that this line may be a relic from
the earliest period of mammal evolution.

Christine Janis takes a conservative view of this evolutionary process of the multituberculates, seeing them as originating about 190mya, at least 30my earlier than Miao
and Sigogneau-Russell, and perhaps 70my before Rowe and Simmons' estimate.[39]

Out of the mists of a vast diversification of the mammals in the Jurassic period,
208-144mya, there occurred, either in the late Jurassic or the successor early Cretaceous,
144-65mya, *i.e.*, 150-125mya, during which time the "great beasts," the dinosaurs seem
to have dominated, an ancestral separation, probably in Eupantotheres. The separation
eventually led toward the two "modern" mammal infra-classes. The marsupial specializations and first flourishing apparently originated in North America with a possible subsequent South American radiation.[40]

Conclusion

What is supportable is a position that places the origins of primeval mammal morphology to the late Permian, c.250mya, a hidden breakaway from the mainline and successful cynodont pathways. By the terminal Triassic, c.210mya, at least three distinct and
decidedly mammal lines appeared on the evolutionary scene. Parallel with the cynodont
shrinkage in size over these c.40 million years, from wolf- or dog-like size to that of a
rabbit, except for the insectivorous Tritheledontidae, extinct from the early Jurassic,
about 200mya, and the herbivorous Tritylodontidae, who survive into the mid-Jurassic,
c.175mya, the earliest mammals seem never to have been larger than mouse size.

Mammals had found a permanent, if peripheral niche under the dinosaur canopy. For approximately 150 million years, they would undergo their own phylogenetic, morphological, and behavioral selective dynamics. In the end a cataclysm, geological or biological, which ended the age of the reptiles, would spew forth a proliferating and dominating inheritor of the vertebrate mantle.

- 2 -
Preparation for Dominance

Evolutionary Stages

The general consensus on mammalian evolution is of an adaptive radiation in three phases or stages.[41] The radiation of the Mammals from the late Triassic, c.220mya, had produced eight separate orders of early and true mammals, all sharply distinct from therapsid reptiles and modern mammals.

> Six [new] orders are contemporaneous with each other in the Upper Jurassic and lower Cretaceous, (160-130mya), [by the time of Evolutionary Stage 2]...But the earliest of the six new orders are separated by about 20 million years from the very early mammals, 8 orders of the Upper Triassic and Lower Jurassic period (220-190mya) [Evolutionary Stage 1]...
>
> The latest of the orders in Stage 2 are separated from the even later marsupials and placentals [Evolutionary Stage 3], 130-100mya, by an equal or greater time span, 20-40my, except for an anomalous side line (Multituberculata).[42]

These are serious gaps in the fossil record.

Stage 1. a) The breakout from general advance eucynodont evolution of the so-called triconodonts, of which *Morganucodon* was a representative, so, too Borealestes, a member of a successor order of docodonts, reveal teeth of a more frugivorous/omnivorous diet. These two orders, triconodont and docodont seem not to have left any descendants and thus became extinct, excepting the views of Colbert/Morales, see below. b) Major views, Rowe and Simmons excepted, confirm Miao's contention that the haramyids were early Triassic deviants from the mainline mammal radiation. They are seen as ancestral to the multituberculates.[43] c) The Kuehneotheriidae continued on their mainline path (toward the therian grade) producing the symmetrodonts, known by their special molar cusp arrangements, *e.g.*, *Spalocotherium*. The lower jaw continues its evolution toward the full mammal articulation of the dentary/squamosal hinge.

Stage one finale of the first, Triassic/Jurassic diversification of the mammals reveals the Eupantotheres, the final stage of the Kuehneotheriidae line, a group evolving toward the therian grade, and one stage in their tooth evolution beyond the symmetrodonts. Colbert/Morales see the Eupantotheres as providing the common ancestry, if independent evolutionary pathway for the therians, the marsupials, and placentals.[44]

Stage 2. Early mammals of the Triassic, after 220mya, [Stage 1] radiated throughout Pangaea, the super-continent. After this, during the Jurassic, the continents separated and different forms of mammalian life evolved independently. Jurassic lineages of true mammals in Stage 2 did not outlast the advent of the Cretaceous. Here the beginning of flowering plants, new insect species, presumably had an impact both on the mammal economy and subsequent opportunities for further adaptive development and radiations.[45] In each of the three early mammal lines, noted above as: a, b, and c, many representative examples disappear from the fossil record in higher geological strata, other perhaps unknown examples continuing on their passage into the Cretaceous, 144-65mya.

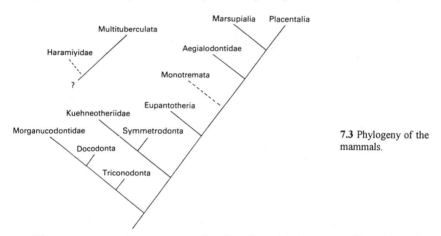

7.3 Phylogeny of the mammals.

The monotremes are now considered to have broken away from the main therian line sometime in the early Cretaceous.[46] However, in contrast, Colbert/Morales view them as an early offshoot from the docodonts of the late Triassic/early Jurassic, c.200mya, noting the resemblance in the monotremes of the shoulder girdle of *Morganucodons*, the triconodont predecessors of the docodonts of the late Triassic; Rowe and Simmons agree with this minority position.[47] Thus in this view *Morganucodon*, from group "a" above, one of the earliest mammals of the Triassic, did *not* disappear without leaving descendants.

Stage 3. Late Mesozoic evolution of recent mammals, after the extinction of many early Cretaceous lines, c.100-65mya. Monotremes are now to be found in Australia, but probably radiated early out of the southern super-continent into South America. Multituberculates appeared in both Asia and North America, (northern part of the super-continent). They are possible descendants of Stage 1 haramyids.

Marsupials originated in South (possibly North) America (see also Cifelli).[48] Placentals probably originated in Asia. Both infra-classes were independent and morphologically articulated by the beginning of the Cretaceous, 140mya.[49] Placentals and marsupials crossed paths in North America by the late Cretaceous. Marsupials dispersed to Australia by way of Antarctica in the late Cretaceous or early Tertiary. Antarctica in Paleocene, 65-53mya, was subtropical. Placentals also came to Australia, but then became extinct, until modern placental bats and rodents appeared in the late Miocene, 10mya.[50]

The final phase of Stage 3 takes place sometime in the mid-Cretaceous, between 110-80mya.[51] Here, long after the presumed monotreme branching, viviparity had been developing in a Prototherian, soon to split into two infra-classes: a) Metatherians-

marsupials; and b) Eutherians-placentals. The multituberculates continued their separate herbivorous adaptations into the Cenozoic, end Eocene period, some 35mya. It is thought that they were finally eradicated by newly evolving placental rodent lines competing for the same general ecology.

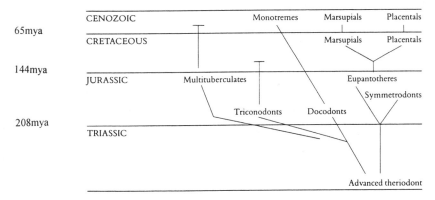

7.4 Radiation of the mammals.

Origin of Cenozoic Mammals

1. Multituberculates lasted from c.195mya to the end Eocene, 35mya. Modern therian mammals, 130mya into the present. The fall of the multituberculates was due to the rise of early placental rodents, primates and ungulates, competing with similar lifestyles. Most multituberculates were small mouse to squirrel sized and lived in trees. Omnivorous/ frugivorous and mostly nocturnal in habits, their narrow pelvis argues for live birth probably to very immature, marsupial-like young. Their pelvis is thought to be too narrow for eggs or large, live newborns.[52]

2. Monotremes found also in South America as well as Australia, a radiation from Mesozoic and early Tertiary Gondwana. Moles have similar monotreme characteristics, heavily built limbs with reptilian sprawl. Janis does not believe this adaptation to be an original monotreme characteristic, rather a modern specialization of the echidna and platypus (with webbed feet and duck bill in the platypus).[53] Monotremes are not fully homeothermic; during warm weather they have a lower and fluctuating internal temperature in contrast to most placentals. During cold weather they hibernate, their internal body temperature very little higher than the outside environment.[54]

And, of course, monotremes lay eggs, which are hatched in burrows, the young thence lap milk from modified sweat glands, homologous to the mammae of therian mammals.[55] Colbert/Morales: "The skeleton and soft anatomy show the persistence of various reptile characters. For instance, the shoulder girdle is very primitive with a persistent interclavicle, large coracoids, and no true scapular spine. The cervical ribs are unfused. Various reptilian characters persist in the skull. The rectum and urinogenital system open into a common cloaca as in reptiles, not separately as in mammals. There are no external ears or pinnae as in most other mammals."[56] Clearly Colbert/Morales believe the monotremes to have been directly descended from docodont and triconodont, (morganucodont), ancestry of some 200mya. It is thus a member of one of the three sister taxa of the original mammals of the earliest mammal radiation in the late Triassic.[57]

W. K. Gregory once argued that the monotremes were not really a throwback to an early mammalian transitional stage. He saw them as a paedomorphic product of mammal marsupials. This particular retention of ancient phylogenetic characteristics of the line came about as the ancestors of the duck-billed platypus and the echidna retained certain infantile characteristics into maturity. In their case, Gregory noted, the pressures that produced a clearly marginal and peripheral member of the evolving marsupial line still allowed it to survive into modern times. Its genetics did not produce the fortuitous forward-looking adaptations that led toward the great therian breakthrough.[58]

3. Therians probably evolved in the north, around the Jurassic/Cretaceous boundary, c.140mya, at a time when the continents were beginning to drift away from each other (at the time of the dissolution of Pangea). Placentals are located in Asiatic Cretaceous deposits. Marsupials are found in North American and South American locales. Separation brought about a long period of independent evolution, as with the monotremes, the latter seemingly restricted to the Southern latitudes.

This separation seems to suggest that the placentals—Eutheria—may have been the outlier line. Earlier forms of mammals all seem to have had epipubic bones, the pair of struts that now grow forward from the pubic bone of the marsupials to support their pouches. Other research has related the epipubic bones to the support of the litter mass of lactating young for suspension while the mother is in motion.

Janis believes that the loss of epipubic bones allowed the abdomen to continue its expansion in the final periods of pregnancy, thus allowing for the birth of a less immature neonate in this line as compared with the maruspials. She cites the work of John Kirsch of University of Wisconsin and Jason Lillegraven of University of Wyoming who theorize that even earlier therian mammals developed from a pouchless form, apparently still retaining the epipubic bones, and whose young were born very immature, then to mature while fastened on the nipples.[59]

Michael Novacek has reported on a rat-sized eutherian (placental) mammal from the dinosaurian Cretaceous with epipubic bones. More recently Novacek et al. have reported other late Cretaceous, 90-65mya, eutherian (placental) mammals with such epipubic struts, indicating significant variability as well as again intimating an earlier time of origination in the placental line.[60] These discoveries hint at the as yet undiscovered progenitors of the modern placentals who lost these struts as part of a process of lengthening gestation. It also hints at a process of intramammalian selection that eliminated this presumptive archaic line of Eutheria.

4. Therian Reproduction. Renfree, following Colbert/Morales, emphasizes the reproductive organization of the marsupials as differentiating them from the eutherian (placental) mammals, differences that are established early in the embryonic development of the marsupials:

> In the marsupials the ureters pass between the oviducts; in the eutherians the oviducts pass between the ureters....Since the ureters pass between, and hence separate, the oviducts of the marsupials, these ducts cannot meet in the midline and form a large single median uterus with a wide median vagina opening to the exterior. This may be one of the

reasons that marsupial young are so remarkably small at birth, at the "larval" stage when compared with the size of the parent.[61]

The so-called "bush" kangaroo, the wallaby, a marsupial form that achieves a mature length of about 2.5 feet, not including the tail, has a gestation period of about 30 days. The young are born at two centimeters in size, thence to climb into the mother's pouch for an extended stay.

Almost 90 years ago H. F. Gadow of Cambridge University noted that "...many lizards, some chameleons and many snakes...retain their, in these cases very thin-shelled, eggs in the oviducts until the embryo is ready to burst the egg-membrane during the act of parturition or immediately after it. Such species are usually called ovoviviparous, although there is no difference between them and other viviparous creatures, for instance, the marsupials."[62]

This reproductive resemblance both to reptile and fish live bearing in the maruspials, as well as the existence of true placental-like reproduction in ancient and modern sharks argues for a protomammal line of air-breathing fish-amphibian-synapsid reptiles that might eventually be traced to the earliest stages of the tetrapod invasion of the land surfaces.

Important adaptive strategies of marsupial and placental therians: In times of extreme danger placentals would have to abort, whereas marsupials could eject their young from the pouch, implying for the latter a less threatening adaptive pattern to the life of the mother. Once born, however, placental young grow faster; also placentals have a quicker reproductive cycle. There is also a better nutritional advantage for the young to receive nutrients across the placenta. Again, forelimbs of placentals can evolve in numerous ways, while marsupial young must be early specialized to climb into the mother's pouch and at an undeveloped stage.[63]

The innovations inherent in placental reproduction should not be thought of as a unique evolutionary development. In all likelihood it was experimented with in the tetrapods at some early point in their transition from the water. Viviparity, the intimate circulation of nourishment from the mother's placenta to the embryo within her body, occurs in various fishes, a number of cyprinodonts, the four-eyed fish, Anableps, and a wide variety of hammerhead and carcharhinid sharks.[64] Ovoviviparous rays, which lack placenta, the young at first depending on their yolk sac, produce a "milk" rich in protein and lipids, quite similar to mammalian breast milk. This they channel from the uterine wall into the mouths and gill chambers of the embryos.[65]

What is additionally interesting about the placental mode of viviparous reproduction in sharks is that, as Jerison notes, a Permian shark fossil similar to the contemporary living horned shark, Heterodontus, is reported to show a brain size similar to modern sharks, which are at the mammal-placental rodent level of brain/body encephalization.[66] Early in the Silurian, as the jawed fishes expanded, some 420mya, the sharks radiated into their own tenaciously-held ecological niche and with this move seem to have developed an unusually large fish brain, viewed by Jerison as intermediate in size between most lines of fish (except the visual teleosts) and the amphibians-reptiles in terms of their brain/body encephalization quotient.[67]

The reproductive adaptive strategy of placental development allows more nutrients to be directly passed through the placenta. Placental young are thus born larger and later in development, protected in the womb, even if this strategy is more dangerous for the mother, *i.e.*, abortion. The result is that the larger young will be born with a bigger brain, the product of greater nourishment in the womb. Hoofed placentals and whales bear young that are independently mobile almost immediately after birth. The generally shorter period of total foetal development allows the placental mother to become pregnant sooner than the marsupial mother.

The evolutionary message here is that placental reproduction represents a continuation of an ancient pattern, perhaps hidden as yet in the evolutionary record of the transition to life on land.

Marsupials seem to have evolved in and are dependent on more consistently benign external environmental conditions. Under conditions of extreme danger they can ditch their young from the protectiveness of their pouches, and escape. But they have slower reproductive patterns, the Australian marsupial mouse, for example, once or twice in a lifetime. Placental mothers, however, can usually act to protect themselves without aborting their young until the very last stages of pregnancy.

5. Therian Morphology and Behavior. Therian mammals have modern tribosphenic molars that are adapted to crushing foods. The coracoid bone in the shoulder, jointed to the breastbone in reptiles and early mammals differs in therians. Now a collarbone, also scapula and shoulder muscles, allow creatures to move limbs so as to cushion jumps or falls when they land on their front legs, also facilitates bounding movements. All marsupials except wombats and anteaters are nocturnal. Janis believes that early marsupials were tree living, with grasping tail and forepaws to hold food. Their metabolism was slower than that of the placentals. Placentals were more terrestrial in the earlier stages, burrow dwellers that buried their feces.[68] The internal carriage of the unborn young over a relatively long period of pregnancy probably allowed for more behavioral flexibility, and thus an ability to move from ground to tree living, as the need arose.

The clue to the unique future dominance of the placental morphology lies in the presumed ancient connection with viviparity in the fish (sharks). It is thus highly suggestive that the contrast between the marsupial benign adaptive morphology, the marsupials' similarity to many extant reptile lines, and the placental patterns of true viviparity and birth could lie in the paedomorphic retention of an ancient fish/shark/tetrapod adaptation for the protection and nourishment of the unborn young. Further, this argues for the hidden evolution of the placentals, which protected their way of life by nurturing the ostensibly defensive morphological adaptations, until these morphologies had played out their latent selective power.

Mammal Brain
The radiation of the eucynodont line of advanced mammal-like reptiles took place, in all probability not long after the first fossil appearance of the cynodonts in the late Permian, or the early Triassic, c.245-240mya. Fossil remains which are now dated to between 225-220mya represent animals that are tilted over the mammal morphological Rubicon. And they already reflect an existing radiation within the mammal cohort, again

arguing plausibly for a participation in the original cynodont breakout from the afflicted therapsid lineage at the terminal Permian.[69]

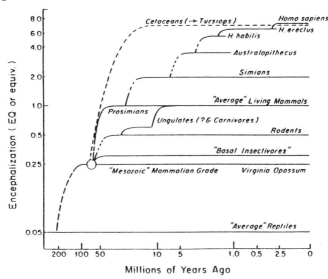

7.5 The course of encephalization.

The evolving jaw structure, a more ossified and thus bone-enclosed brain, is characteristic of the morganucodontids of the final Triassic, c.210-200mya. With it came an increase in brain size over the trithelodontids, their closest cynodont cousins.[70] As to the question whether significant brain growth can also be attributed to the earlier transitional mammal-like reptiles, there is a difference of opinion.

Jerison, who has made the most detailed study of the evolution of the brain, is very clear. He argues that no significant expansion of the brain over the traditional reptilian relationship of brain/body size can here be found in the early mammal. The one possible exception, and here he partially cedes to Olson's earlier analysis that the early synapsids were at an intermediate grade between the reptiles and the mammals, namely a lateral expansion of the cerebellum, is the caveat that the increase in size of this organ in *Thrinaxodon* might be superficial, and that part of the space ostensibly reserved for the cerebellum could have been taken up by cartilage. Such an expansion, Jerison argues, even if true, could not have been on "an order of magnitude" that could have changed the basic brain size of these animals.[71]

Kuhne, on the basis of a close examination of the skull of a herbivorous, late Triassic cynodont, a tritylodont, inferred that its brain "was not much larger than in undoubted reptiles."[72] Here he supports Jerison's general position.

Timothy Rowe sees the growth of the brain taking place in a continuum throughout eucynodont and subsequent mammalian history.

> [It]...involves a major reorganization of the skull involving repackaging of a greatly inflated brain and special sensory organs. This trend was manifested throughout eucynodont history, and during the Mesozoic it resulted in the complete and intimate osseus enclosure of the brain along with some of its associated vessels. The brain expanded to nearly one-half the length of the skull and greatly increased in width. This was associated with ontogenetic fusions among bones that primitively remained separate throughout life, a great increase in the extent of both membranous and endochondral bone, and profound remodeling of inherited structures. The nasal capsule and associated structures also expanded enormously, extending backward to a sub-cerebral position, displacing the choana backward as well. The orbit, lying between the inflated nasal capsule and brain, became enclosed medially and was extensively reorganized in other respects.[73]

MacLean discusses the therapsid *Probainognathus jenseni*, studied by Quiroga, in terms of the speculatively possible location and development of its neocortex. This is an animal that Colbert/Morales consider to be on the direct line that leads to the early mammals. MacLean does not agree with Quiroga that a true neocortex existed in this animal. His conclusions concerning *Probainognathus*: "....[T]he widening of the brain seen in the therapsid-mammal transition...might be interpreted as a reflection of the development of limbic parahippocampal, cingulate, and entorhinal [olfactory] cortex, rather than that of the neocortex."[74] Here again we encounter doubts as to the possibility that the closest anticipator eucynodonts participated in the brain expansion and reconstruction exhibited in defined true mammals. In addition, the earliest mammals seem to appear in the fossil record as contemporaries of their supposedly ancestral forms.

Both MacLean and Jerison discuss G. G. Simpson's well-known comparison of the therapsid, *Nythrosaurus,* with the Upper Jurassic mammal, triconodont. Whereas in the therapsid, the olfactory bulbs seem quite enlarged relative to the elongated cerebral structures, the mammal's brain hemispheres are widened and enlarged relative to its smaller body size. In addition, the cerebral structures and the cerebellum of triconodont seem to overlap the midbrain giving its brain a three-dimensional aspect. Here, too, the mammal-like reptiles, unlike mammals, have brains that are smaller than their endocranial cavities. As Rowe describes these structures, the diminution of the olfactory bulbs might be only apparent; other amplifying olfactory connections could have extended beneath the cerebral and midbrain portions.[75]

The question of brain structure and size within mammal phylogeny itself has been raised. We may have to concede that in all probability a larger span of time existed between the separation of the protomammals from their closest cynodont relations, the ictidosaurs or as Kemp describes them, tritheledontids, *Diarthrognathus*, or *Probainognathus*, (protomammals). An even greater time may have elapsed in splitting from a not quite as advanced cynodont, chiniquodont. The particular mystery of the "whens," and "hows" of mammal origins from a cynodont radiation remain unanswered for now.[76]

The question then shifts to the evolutionary process within the class of mammals itself. The upper Jurassic mammal triconodont has already been compared with a therapsid cynodont, *Nythrosaurus*.[77] Patterson and Olson analyzed the brain structure of a late Triassic mammal, (Luo says lower Jurassic), thus an early example, *Sinoconodon* (a possible morganucodontid, states Kemp) and compared it with *Triconodon*, which could have lived 50my later. These are probably on the line to the monotremes. Their interpretation, about which Jerison is hesitant, is that the brain of *Triconodon* is relatively no larger than *Sinoconodon*.[78] Clearly the evolution of the mammal brain was not in selective play at the early stages of their separation from the reptiles.

Comparative Brain Dynamics

Pursuing this seemingly surprising fact of slow mammal evolution, even while they were presumably under the survival gun of the dinosaurs, thus supposedly under some form of selective pressure from above, we come to *Didelphis virginiana*. This is the common opossum. Colbert/Morales compare this living marsupial with the dawn opossum, *Eodelphis*. They find little difference in the brain, skull, and body structure in these two examples of one line of mammals, some 100my apart.[79]

A nocturnal prowler, the modern form feeds on insects, vegetation, and small animals, worms, grubs, insects, and slightly larger vertebrates. Its threat posture is much like that of reptiles, up-tilted snout, and mouth opened wide. It also attacks with a reptile-like downward slashing movement of the teeth.[80]

This modern opossum is "at first strangely similar to that of one of the mammals-like reptiles of the far-off Triassic."[81] Jerison confirms this odd bit of evolutionary stagnancy in a table comparing the body/brain weight and volume of endocranial "olfactory bulbs" of animals that he believes to have inhabited similar ecologies in the Mesozoic and in more recent times. They are a) *Triconodon mordax* from the upper Jurassic, early Cretaceous, 140mya; b) *Ptilodus montanus,* an extinct multituberculate from the Paleocene, some 60mya; c) *Didelphis marsupialis*, the contemporary Virginia opossum; d) *Rattus norvegicus*, the contemporary wild rat.

Jerison's encephalization quotient, the relative level of brain to body size in these creatures, given the average fossil and living mammal to be at Encephalization Quotient, or EQ, of 1.0, is as follows: a) 0.28; b) 0.26; c) 0.22; d) 0.42, (average of many singulars). This means that it is possible that triconodont," one of the final representatives of the extinct morganucodontid line, (monotremes?) itself relatively unchanged from the upper Triassic, c.210mya, and its successor form from the upper Jurassic, lower Cretaceous, c.140mya, had more brain power (0.28) than a Cenozoic multituberculate (0.26), and a contemporary marsupial opossum (0.22). The clear winner in brain power, and apparent adaptive survivability, is the contemporary and ubiquitous wild rat (0.42), almost double the opossum's encephalization quotient. [82]

It is thus possible, if not likely, that once precipitated into dominance from the generalized post-Permian cynodont radiation, brain size and relative encephalization of the early mammals remained static for at least 100my, from c.220mya to 120mya.[83] "...[T]he expansion of the brain event in 'Triconodon' [c. 140mya] had probably occurred as part of the transition between mammal like reptiles, cynodonts, and the true mammals, [even] before the appearance of the [earlier] 'Sinoconodon' [c.210-195mya]."[84]

The two ends of the mammal evolutionary continuum first reveal a 5X to 10X increase in average mammal brain size over the reptiles.[85] At the other end of the comparative evolutionary spectrum is the small relative size of this average Mesozoic mammal brain, 10-30% as compared with modern mammals, given similar body size.[86]

The typical retinotectal visual dominance that is hypothesized for the basic sensory orientation of the stem reptile line was thus redirected in the post-Permian therapsid/cynodonts. Having survived a period of great climatic temperature instability, their evolving homeothermy created metabolic requirements 7X that of the equivalent-sized reptile. This necessitated change in sensory dominance. Here, also, is the clue to the steady reduction in size of the eucynodonts and the tiny mammals that inherited the late Triassic, early Jurassic landscapes, 220-200mya.

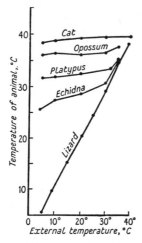

7.6 The evolution of homeo-thermy.

Leonard Radinsky stipulates that in going from reptiles to mammals there was first a five to tenfold increase in brain size relative to body size. The cerebellum was relatively enlarged, reflecting greater motor coordination. Unlike birds, early mammals, as stated above, had a fairly small visual system, and the olfactory bulbs were relatively large. Mammals also expanded the outer layer of the cerebral hemispheres of the forebrain into a major higher information-coordinating center, the neo-cortex.

> Many groups of later mammals experienced a further increase in relative brain size that was correlated with the increased size of the neo-cortex, compared with the early mammal condition. Most workers consider the increased brain size an indication of increased "intelligence." However, while such a conclusion may seem to be intuitively correct, there are virtually no scientific data to support it, and the functional significance of increased relative brain size remains an unsolved puzzle. The puzzle is particularly intriguing because increased brain size occurred dozens of times independently among various groups of birds and mammals. [87]

Radinsky, in discussing the slow evolution of the mammals from their first appearance, 220-190mya, to their radiation at the end of the Cretaceous, and thus their relatively slow evolution into dominance, cites the following reasons: a) endothermy was only advantageous in relatively cold climates or in climates of great variation. Most of this period was quite warm and less seasonal. One could ask of Radinsky, why the protomammals did seem to develop endothermy as an adaptive characteristic? It was a fairly early adaptation, with internal viviparity the final placental adaptation. Possible reply:

the Permian, from which the cynodonts radiated, may have been colder than we now generally concede.   b) It is costly to be endothermic and maintain a constant internal metabolic rate. Mammals require ten to thirteen times as much food energy as reptiles and amphibians to maintain the same body mass, less energy available for growth and reproduction—they were small. Radinsky argues that it was more advantageous for mammals and birds to be endothermic rather than ectothermic for the past 65my than for the 160my of the age of reptiles.[88]

Reptile and Mammal Adaptive Patterns

The largely equable climate of the Triassic, 245-208mya, on the other hand, enabled the ectothermic and still highly visual archosaur line to make the most of its demanding daylight and visual energies, gradually taking over the mainline land adaptive niches, where size and food bulk reinforced each other.[89] The gradual redirection of therapsid-eucynodont evolution was toward the diurnal way of life. Endothermy demands a steady supply of food at all hours in the day, 10X more than similar-sized reptiles. It also allowed the latter in the cool of the evening to slowly digest the vast amount of daytime food in their gut. Endothermy in the mammals was in all likelihood a preadaptation stimulated by the Permian (250mya) variability of climate, not a later accommodation away from a reptile dependence on the warmth of the sun for energy renewal. It was a pre-adaptation for life in the cool of the night.

The adaptive split was further heightened by the morphology of the palate that the mammal-like reptiles were evolving, a palate that allowed for simultaneous chewing and breathing, on the run, as it were, and the development of increased audition, as the jaw bones were gradually rearticulated. Too, there was an increase in olfactory sensitivity and organization in the brain, vibrissae in the nose area for additional tactile sensitivity.[90]

The brain is metabolically demanding. Natural selection tended, over many millions of years, to link brain and behavior metabolically. Along with an additional adaptive direction toward feeding on smaller animal and insect forms, the incipient mammals thus carved out a new division of land adaptations, negotiating an adaptive balance with competing reptiles.

The reptile neural retina contains millions of neurons. The auditory system plays a much smaller role, with a few hundred neurons in the area of the middle ear. By contrast, mammals have about 35,000 neurons in the spiral ganglion of the inner ear. Processing this new information source, the product of the reconstruction of the various bone ossicles of the jaws, was gradually taken up by the brain itself, in contrast to the reptile information processing system, in the neural retina. "Encephalization in the earliest mammals was probably an adaptation in response to a packing problem: where to put the neurons from non-visual systems that had evolved to do the kind of processing that is done by retinal neurons in 'normal reptiles."[91]

On the other hand, ectothermic regulation probably demands more neural tissue than endothermic. Endothermy involves autonomic control of blood and sweat glands, kidney function, muscle heat production. Ectothermy demands of the animal structure a complex of neural regulation of the skeletal musculature for the behavioral orientation of the animal, toward heat and the land surfaces (away from cool), and slow toward the evening. But reptile behavioral regulation, as with mammal endothermy, took place outside of the brain.

What the brain required for the mammals, and which was not involved in simpler retinal visual behavior in reptiles, was the integration of the various sense organs, the newly specializing auditory, tactile, and olfactory inputs, as well as a restructured scotopic, rod-based retinal visual system that was useful in dim light, as compared to the cone structures of the lower vertebrates. Cone system vision responds rapidly to light with high photic energies, often 1,000X as strong as that required for the activation of the rod system. Later, according to Walls, the cone system that modern mammals utilized, "redeveloped" in a homologous manner to the reptile system, when most mammals began to invade diurnal ecological niches.[92] The adaptive response from the information provided from these variously located sensory input systems would have had to be integrated.

The first step would be the recognition within the brain that the information was, for instance, visual or tactile. Since information came in momentarily from these various sources as well as from the body's more autonomic emotional and physiological markers, there thence came the beginnings of a hierarchical marking and organization of this information for adaptive behavioral responses. Here began the recognition of an outside world in which the sensory and integrative dimensions of experience created images of "objects" outside of the body, none of which were without impact on the internal valences of the mammal's semi-spontaneous behavior system: fear, flight, appetite, desire. Both information systems, the sensory and the emotional/physiological, required their integration in a larger brain. A number of researchers view the earlier creation of the vertebrate brain itself as having the capability for "chunking" such information from the senses into an object-rendered "real world of experience."[93]

Evolutionary Hints for Future Understanding

1. The significant gaps in the fossil record both at the beginning of mammal evolution, Upper Triassic/Lower Jurassic, 220-190mya, and later in the Upper Jurassic/Lower Cretaceous, 160-130mya. There is always the temptation to fill in such blanks with pre-existing candidates. Such speculative temptations ought to be resisted.

2. Comparative brain size of mammals: A) *Triconodon mordax,* c.140mya, had a larger brain than the contemporary *Didelphis marsupialis* (Virginia opossum). B) *Sinoconodon*, c.220mya, and *Triconodon*, c.140mya, the latter a probable descendant of the former, had equal brain size, even after 100-80my of evolutionary change. Evolution takes time.

3. Contemporary monotremes reveal many reptilian features, not the least egg laying, which places them on an evolutionary grade close to the earliest stages of mammal morphology, c.220-190mya.

4. Placentals with marsupial-like epipubic struts, present hints about the earliest stages of therian evolution and separation. These recidivistic placentals were still extant toward the end of the Cretaceous, 90-65mya. This suggests both the branching character of the evolutionary process, as well as the probably recessed time origins of many seemingly suddenly modern forms.[94]

Endnotes, Chapter 7

[1] Kemp, T. S. 1982. *Mammal-like Reptiles and the Origin of Mammals*, N.Y.: Academic Press, p. 18.

[2] Benton, M. 1993. "Four Feet on the Ground," in *Life*, S. J. Gould, ed., N.Y.: W. W. Norton, p. 89.

[3] Stebbins, G. Ledyard. 1982. *Darwin to DNA, Molecules to Humanity, op. cit.*, p. 289.

[4] Benton, 1993. *op. cit.*, pp. 97-98, 112.

[5] Stebbins, 1982, *op. cit.*, p. 288.

[6] Benton, 1993, *op. cit.*, pp. 98-99.

[7] Benton, 1993, *op. cit.*, pp. 116-117.

[8] Radinsky, L. 1987. *The Evolution of Vertebrate Design, op. cit.*, pp. 125-129.

[9] Hillenius, Willem J. 1994. "Turbonates in therapsids: Evidence for late Permian origins of mammalian endothermy (with appendix)," *Evolution*, April, 1994, 48:207-229.

[10] Stebbins, 1982, *op. cit.*, p. 293.

[11] Janis, Christine. 1993. "Victors by Default," in *Life*, S. J. Gould, ed., *op. cit.*, p. 172.

[12] Radinsky, 1987, *op. cit.*, pp. 144-145.

[13] Padian, K., Professor of Integrative Biology, Univ. of California, Berkeley. *The New York Times*, 11/3/96, #4, p. 14.

[14] Kemp, 1982, *op. cit.*, p. 250.

[15] Olsen, E. C. 1944. "Origin of mammals based on the cranial morphology of therapsid suborders," *Geol. Soc. of America. Spec. Papers*, 55:1-136.

[16] Jerison, H. J. 1973. *Evolution of the Brain and Intelligence*, N.Y.: Academic Press, pp. 152-154.

[17] Kemp, 1982, *op. cit.*, p. 250.

[18] Jerison, 1973, *op. cit.*, p. 154.

[19] MacLean, Paul. 1990. *The Triune Brain in Evolution*, N.Y.: Plenum., pp. 80-98.

[20] Watson, D. M. S. 1913. "Further notes on the skull, brain, and organs of special sense in Diademodon," *Ann. Magaz. Nat. Hist.*, 12:217-228.

[21] Quiroga, J. C. 1979. "The brain of two mammal-like reptiles (Cynodontia-Therapsida)," *J. Hirnforsch*, 20:341-350; Quiroga, J. C. 1980. "The brain of the mammal-like reptile Probainognathus jenseni (Therapsida-Cynodonta). A correlative paleo-neoneurological approach to the neocortex at the reptile-mammal transition," *J. Hirnforsch*, 21:299-336.

[22] Kemp, 1982, *op. cit.*, pp. 306-307.

[23] Smith, Homer W. 1961. *From Fish To Philosopher*, N.Y.: Anchor-Doubleday, pp. 138-140.

[24] Kemp, 1982, *op. cit.*, pp. 307-313.

[25] Kemp, 1982, *op. cit.*, p. 316; Rowe, T. 1993. "Phylogenetic Systematics and the Early History of the Mammals," in *Mammal Phylogeny*, F. S. Szalay, M. J. Novacek, M. C. McKenna, eds., N.Y.: Springer-Verlag, pp. 132, 142.

[26] Colbert, E. H., and Morales, M. 1991. *Evolution of the Vertebrates*, 4th ed., N.Y.: Wiley-Liss, pp. 127-128; Kemp, 1982, *op. cit.*, pp. 271-273.

[27] Luo, Z. 1996. "Relationship and Morphological Evolution of Early Mammals," in *Carnegie Museum of Natural History Home Page*, Pittsburgh, PA.

[28] Benton, 1993, *op. cit.*, p. 103.

[29] Szalay, F. S. 1993. "Metatherian Taxon Phylogeny: Evidence and Interpretation from the Cranioskeletal System," in Szalay *et al.*, eds., N.Y.: Springer-Verlag, pp. 234-240.

[30] Janis, 1993, *op. cit.*, p. 172.

[31] Kemp, 1982, *op. cit.*, pp. 266-270.

[32] Kermack, K. A., Mussett, F., Rigney, H. W. 1981. "The skull of Morganucodonton," *Jnl. Zool. J. Linn. Soc.*, 71:1-58.

[33] Kemp, 1982, *op. cit.*, p. 270.

[34] Miao, D. 1993. "Cranial Morphology and Multituberculate Relationships," in Szalay *et al.*, eds, pp. 63-74; Sigogneau-Russell, D. 1989. "Haramyidae (Mammalia Allotheria) en provenance du Tria superior de Lorraine (France)," *Paleontographica Abt.*, A 206:137-198; Clemens, W. A., Jr. 1986. "On Triassic and Jurassic Mammals," in *The Beginning of the Age of Dinosaurs*, K. Padian, ed., Cambridge: Cam-

bridge Univ. Press, pp. 237-246; Fraser, N. C., Walkden, G. M., Stewart, V. 1985. "The first pre-Rhaetic therian mammals," *Nature*, 314:161-163.

[35] Wible, J. R. 1991. "Origin of Mammalia: The craniodental evidence reexamined," *Jnl. Vert. Paleontol*, 11:1-28; Kielan-Joworowska, Z., Crompton, A. W., Jenkins, F. A., Jr. 1987. "The origin of egg laying mammals," *Nature*, 326:871-873; Archer, M. *et al.* 1993. "Reconsideration of Monotreme Relationships Based on the Skull and Dentition of the Miocene `Obdurodon dicksoni,'" in Szalay *et al.*, eds., *op. cit.*, pp. 75-94; Colbert and Morales, 1991, *op. cit.*, pp. 234-242; Kemp, 1982, *op. cit.*, pp. 287-293.

[36] Stebbins, 1982, *op. cit.*, p. 295.

[37] Hahn, G., Sigogneau-Russell, D., Wouters, G. 1989. "New data on `Theroteinadae'--Their relations with `Paulschoffatiidae' and `Haramiyidae,'" *Geol. et Paleontol*, 23:205-215.

[38] Simmons, N. 1993. "Phylogeny of Multituberculata," in Szalay *et al.*, eds., *op. cit.*, p. 148 (pp. 146-164); Rowe, 1993, *op. cit.*, pp. 129-145.

[39] Janis, 1993, *op. cit.*, p. 172.

[40] Cifelli, R. L. 1993. "Theria of Metatherian-Eutherian Grade and the Origin of Marsupials," in Szalay *et al.*, eds. *op. cit.*, pp. 204-215.

[41] Colbert and Morales, 1991, *op. cit.*, p. 242.

[42] Stebbins, 1982, *op. cit.*, p. 293.

[43] see Kemp, 1982, *op. cit.*; Colbert and Morales, 1991, *op. cit.*; Miao, 1993, in Szalay, *et al.*, eds., *op. cit.*; Rowe, 1993, *op. cit.*; Simmons, 1993, in Szalay, *et al.*, eds., *op. cit.*; infra above.

[44] Colbert and Morales, 1991, *op. cit.*, p. 252.

[45] Janis, 1993, *op. cit.*, p. 176.

[46] Janis, 1993, *op. cit.*, p. 172; Wible, J. R. 1991. "Origin of Mammalia: The craniodental evidence reexamined," *Jnl. Vert. Paleontol.*, 11:1-28; Kielan-Joworowska, Z., Crompton, A. W., Jenkins, F. A., Jr. 1987. "The origin of egg laying mammals," *Nature*, 326:871-873; Archer, M., *et al.* 1993. "Reconsideration of Monotreme Relationships Based on the Skull and Dentition of the Miocene `Obdurodon dicksoni,'" in Szalay *et al.*, eds., *op. cit.*, pp. 75-94; Stebbins, 1982, *op. cit.*, p. 295.

[47] Colbert and Morales, 1991, *op. cit.*, pp. 240-242; Rowe, 1993, *op. cit.*; Simmons, 1993, in. Szalay *et al.*, eds., *op. cit.*

[48] Cifelli, 1993 in Szalay *et al.*, eds., *op. cit.*, pp. 205-215.

[49] Colbert and Morales, 1991, *op. cit.*, p. 252.

[50] Janis, 1993, *op. cit.*, p. 177.

[51] Stebbins, 1982, *op. cit.*, p. 294; Colbert and Morales, 1991, *op. cit.*, pp. 241-242.

[52] Janis, 1993, *op. cit.*, p. 174.

[53] Janis, 1993, *op. cit.*, pp. 174-176.

[54] Smith, Homer W. 1961, *op. cit.*, p. 134.

[55] Stebbins, 1982, *op. cit.*, p. 193.

[56] Colbert and Morales, 1991, *op. cit.*, p. 241.

[57] Nisbet, E. G. 1991. *Living Earth*, N.Y.: Harper Collins, p. 195.

[58] Gregory, W. K. 1936. "On the Meaning and Limits of Irreversibility in Evolution," *American Naturalist*, 70:517; Gregory, W. K. 1937. "Supra-specific Variation in Nature and in Classification: A Few Examples from Mammalian Paleontology," *American Naturalist*, 71:268-276.

[59] Janis, 1993, *op. cit.*, p. 176.

[60] Novacek, M. J. 1997. "Ukhaatherium nessovi," *Nature*, Vol. 390, #6650, Oct.2, reported by Browne, M. 1997. "Old Bones From Gobi Desert Spur a New Look at Evolution," *The New York Times*, Oct. 5, p. 14; Novacek, M. J., *et al.* 1997. "Epipubic Bones in Eutherian Mammals from the Late Cretaceous of Mongolia," *Nature*, 10/2/97, 389:483-486.

[61] Renfree, M. B. 1993. "Ontogeny, Genetic Control, and Phylogeny of Female Reproduction in Monotreme and Therian Mammals," in Szalay *et al.*, eds., *op. cit.*, p. 5; Colbert and Morales, 1991, *op. cit.*, pp. 241, 245.

[62] Gadow, H. F. 1911. "Reptiles-Anatomy," *Encyclopaedia Britannica* 11th Ed., N.Y.: Cambridge Univ. Press, Vol. 23, p. 170.

[63] Nisbet, 1991, *op. cit.*, pp. 198-199; Janis, 1993, *op. cit.*, pp. 174-176.

[64] Bone, Q., Marshall, N. B., Blaxter, J. H. S. 1995. *Biology of Fishes*. London: Blackie Academic & Professional, p. 178.

[65] Bone *et al.*, 1995, *op. cit.*, pp. 180-182.

[66] Jerison, H. J. 1982. "The evolution of biological intelligence," in *Handbook of Human Intelligence*, Robert J. Sternberg, ed., Cambridge, England: Cambridge University Press, p. 775; Deacon, T. W. 1990. "Rethinking Mammalian Brain Evolution," *Amer. Zool.*, 30:629-705, esp. p. 652.

[67] Jerison, 1973, *op. cit.*, p. 100.

[68] Janis, 1993, *op. cit.*, p. 176.

[69] Jerison, 1973, *op. cit.*, p. 226, Fig. 11.1.

[70] Janis, 1993, *op. cit.*, p. 172; Kemp, 1982, *op. cit.*, p. 255.

[71] Jerison, 1973, *op. cit.*, pp. 152-154; Olson, E. C. 1944. "Origin of mammals based on the cranial morphology of therapsid sub-orders," *Geol. Soc. of America Special Papers*, 55:1-136.

[72] Quoted in Van Valen, L. 1960. "Therapsids as mammals," *Evolution*, 14:304-313.

[73] Rowe, 1993, *op. cit.*, p. 142.

[74] MacLean, 1990, *op. cit.*, pp. 256-257; Quiroga, 1979, *op. cit.*, *Jnl. Hirnforsch*, 20:341-350; Quiroga, 1980, *op. cit.*, *Jnl. Hirnforsch*, 21:299-336; Colbert and Morales, 1991, *op. cit.*, pp. 238-240.

[75] Jerison, 1973. *op. cit.*, pp. 203-205; MacLean, 1990, *op. cit.*, p. 94; Rowe, 1993, *op. cit.*, p. 142; Simpson, G. G. 1927. "Mesozoic Mammals IX. The brain of Jurassic Mammals," *Am. Jrnl. of Science*, 214:259-268.

[76] Kemp, 1982, *op. cit.*, pp. 211-215; MacLean, 1990, *op. cit.*, pp. 256-257; Quiroga, 1979, *op. cit.*, *Jnl. Hirnforsch*, 20:341-350; Quiroga, 1980, *op. cit.*, *Jnl. Hirnforsch*, 21:299-336; Colbert and Morales, 1991, *op. cit.*, pp. 238-240.

[77] Jerison, 1973, *op. cit.*, pp. 203-205; MacLean, 1990, *op. cit.*, p. 94; Rowe, 1993, *op. cit.*, p. 142; Simpson, 1927, *Am. Jrnl. of Science*, 214:259-268.

[78] Jerison, 1973, *op. cit.*, p. 205, Fig. 10.1, pp. 213-214; Patterson, B., and Olson, E. C. 1961. "A triconodontid mammal from the Triassic of Yunnan," in *Int. Colloq. of Lower and Non-specialized Mammals*, G. Vanderbroeh, ed., Brussels: KonVlaamse Acad. Wetensch Lett. Sch. Kunsten, pp. 129-191; Romer, A. S. 1966. *Vertebrate Paleontology*, 3rd. ed., Chicago: Univ. of Chicago Press; Kemp, 1982, *op. cit.*, p. 255; Luo, Z. 1996. "Relationship and Morphological Evolution of Early Mammals," in *Carnegie Museum of Natural History Home Page*, Pittsburgh, PA.

[79] Colbert and Morales, 1991, *op. cit.*, pp. 245-247.

[80] Evans, L. T. 1958. "Fighting in young and mature opossums," *Anat. Rec.*, 131:549.

[81] Gregory, W. K. 1967. *Our Face from Fish to Man*, N.Y.: Hafner, p. 48; MacLean, 1990, pp. 251-252.

[82] Jerison, 1973, *op. cit.*, p. 212, Table 10.2; Jerison, H. J. 1977. "The Theory of Encephalization," in *Annals of the New York Academy of Sciences*, 299:156-157.

[83] Jerison, 1983. "The evolution of the Mammalian brain as an information-processing system," in *Advances in the Study of Mammalian Behavior*, Spec. Publ. #7, March 11, 1983, J. F. Eisenberg and D. G. Kleiman, eds., Shippensburg, PA: The American Society of Mammalogists," p. 131.

[84] Jerison, 1973, *op. cit.*, p. 214.

[85] Radinsky, 1987, *op. cit.*, p. 148.

[86] Jerison, 1973, *op. cit.*, p. 216.

[87] Radinsky, 1987, *op. cit.*, p. 148.

[88] Radinsky, 1987, *op. cit.*, pp. 148-149.

[89] Crompton, A. W., Taylor, C. R., and Jagger, J. A. 1978. "Evolution of Homeothermy in Mammals," *Nature*, 272:333-336.

[90] Jerison, 1982, *op. cit.*, p. 777.

[91] *Ibid.*

[92] Jerison, 1973, *op. cit.*, pp. 272-273; Walls, G. 1942. *The Vertebrate Eye and its Adaptive Radiation*, Bloomfield Hills, Michigan: Cranbrook Press.

[93] Griffin, D. R. 1976. *The Question of Animal Awareness*, N.Y.: Rockefeller Univ. Press; Humphrey, N. K. 1978. "Nature's psychologists," *New Scientist*, 78, 900-903.

[94] Kumar, S., and Hedges, S. B. 1998. "A molecular timescale for vertebrate evolution," *Nature*, 392:917-920.

8

Origin and Radiation of the Primates

- 1 -
Origins

Mammal Progress

The course of mammalian evolution can be characterized, following Stebbins, Janis, and Kemp, as a series of step-like breaks in the evolutionary pathway. First is the break from the late Permian/early Triassic eucynodont tradition by a new and highly specialized mammal line related to the eucynodont Tritylodontidae (herbivorous), and the Tritheledontidae (insectivorous) lines. The three main mammal lines, the Morganu-codontidae, Kuehneotheriidae, Haramiyidae, seem to have been well differentiated by the end of the Triassic, 210mya.[1]

They all reveal an increase in brain size over the advanced eucynodont lines of 4-5x. This level of brain/body size continues on for between 100-125my.[2] It reveals an important fact of mammal adaptive stability, even while the major land domination by the dinosaurs continues. It should be noted that another reptile transition, in the air, takes place, with a new class of animals, birds, beginning their evolutionary sojourn, at about 150mya, with *Archaeopteryx*. It should be remembered that the first flying reptiles, the pterosaurs, were contemporary to the first mammals, c.225-210mya.

These lines of late Triassic-early Jurassic mammals underwent the expected radia-tion of successful lines into the early Cretaceous, about 140mya. The line of morganu-codontids, which include *Sinoconodon* (late Triassic-early Jurassic), c.210-190mya, tricinodont, mid-Jurassic, c.170mya, and the successor docodontids, all disappear in the early Cretaceous.[3]

Janis describes the early Cretaceous botanical explosion of flowering plants and the concomitant evolution of a wide variety of new insects. A turnover in many dinosaur lines can be traced back to this period, 145-130mya. In mammal evolution, the gap of 20 million years between the extinction of several older core lines, the morganucodon-tids/docodonts, the Kuehneotheridae/*Symmetrodonta*, and the appearance and disappearance of lines clearly in the therian vanguard, the *Eupantotheria*, seems to reflect a selective reassortment within the class.[4]

Perhaps these events are related to environmental changes that initiated the proliferation of flowering plants and insects. It should be noted that the evidence for these changes, no less an actual explanation or even interpretation of adaptive/selective pressures has to be considered extremely speculative, as the evidence for patterns of mammal evolution is found largely in widely dispersed tooth discoveries.

Now traced back to the late/early Cretaceous, c.120mya, fossils have been found that clearly reflect the distinction between marsupial and placental lines. These are now, including the monotremes, and some new multituberculate forms, the dominating morphologies amongst the mammals for the remainder of the Cretaceous, until c.65mya. Yet, the variety of forms is great, perhaps reflecting the fact that the continents were now well on their way of separation from Pangea, thus erecting a geographical bar to casual migratory enfiladation, and probably intensifying the specialization and infracompetition between closely related mammal groups.[5]

The events of the K/T boundary, Mesozoic/Cenozoic, 65mya, during which the dinosaurs became extinct and seemingly simultaneously allowed for the egress and explosive growth in a wide variety of mammal lines, are controversial. Up to this point the mammals had at most grown from early Jurassic, 195mya, mice-sized creatures to rabbit or domestic cat-sized animals, in the Cretaceous, c.140mya. The disappearance of the dinosaurs and the expansion of the modern lines of mammals have been perceived as a cause and effect set of events. Yet at the same time that the dinosaurs became extinct large proportions of mammals as well as some fish were also hard hit.

By the K/T boundary marsupials had lost 75% of their genera, (90% of species) and shrank to the present four orders consisting of only a few species, described by Szalay.[6] Multituberculates lost four of eight genera (close to 80% of the species) at the end of the Cretaceous. They multiplied somewhat in the North American Paleocene, only to become extinct in the Eocene, possible victims of highly competitive rodent and primate placentals. The placentals lost only one of nine existing genera, (about 18% of the species) thence to explode in both variety of taxonomic lines, as well as adaptive niches, and of course in relative numbers. But in addition, in the waters, rays and sharks seem also to have been reduced by 60% of their genera, (about 85% of their species) thus pointing to complex climatic-geological interactions.[7]

One can hypothetically sum up the Cretaceous as heralding the arrival of modern mammal forms, 140-120mya, especially a widely divergent set of therians, clearly in competition with each other in their basic reproductive efficiency, as well as ability to adapt to the special nocturnal, sometimes diurnal ground and tree environments. They were ever more evading the efficient and intelligent dinosaurian carnivores. An enormous turnover of mammal as well as reptilian lines seems to have occurred as the continents moved away from each other and the land (uplift during the latter Cretaceous, 100-65mya) and seas took on wholly new configurations from what had existed when most of these lines burst into affluence in the late Triassic, 210mya.[8]

Dinosaur Extinction

The most popular and controversial explanation of the great K/T extinction event which as noted above, affected a wide diversity of animal, plant, plankton, coral reefs throughout the planet, is the so-called boloid impact of one or more giant asteroids, perhaps 10km (7 miles) in diameter. The resulting cloud of dust would have suppressed photosynthesis production for many months, producing enormous impacts on the food chain, directly or indirectly causing the loss of animals, especially large species, through starvation, else deteriorating reproductive vitality. This hypothesis presented by Walter Alvarez and his father, Nobel Prize winner in physics, Luis Alvarez, focused on the extremely high iridium deposits (anomalies) throughout the world at geological levels corresponding to the K/T transition, about 65mya. The element iridium is found in high concentrations in meteor fragments. In addition, the possible location of an impact zone off the Caribbean coast of Mexico, when it was land, has given additional credence to this possibility.[9]

There are, of course, other explanations, perhaps in synchronization with the asteroid impact theory, climatic changes toward traditional continental temperature extremes, shrinking levels of the inland seas, as, for example, those in North America, volcanic activity which exuded large amounts of iridium, geological shifts in the eruption of mountain ranges, themselves causing changes in biotic relations.[10] Even the evolving maturation of certain lines of animal life could have affected the destiny of these tetrapod families. Some were already "going downhill."[11] Most likely the K/T boundary was a period of several million years in which a confluence of processes and singularities conspired to cause this epochal set of evolutionary events.[12]

The growing consensus that sees these transitions as having complex, probably multidimensional causes, is given in this summary review:

> ....Bony fishes, amphibians, turtles and crocodilians show far less extinction at the level of genus and family than lizards, snakes, dinosaurs and mammals....The strong difference in extinction magnitude between freshwater aquatic and terrestrial food chains is wholly consistent with extinction by one or more catastrophic events. This is because the time needed to reestablish three-dimensional ecosystem architecture and maximum levels of primary productivity/biomass after a major disruption is much faster in the aquatic realm, especially considering evidence for abundant precipitation following a terminal Cretaceous mass-kill event.[13]

Climatic jolts have a long evolutionary precedent for precipitating nature's relatively rapid sorting process of available genetic, morphological, and behavioral variability, with which to begin again. It had presumably happened many times in the billions of years before the Cambrian. It clearly was significant in bringing the tetrapods ashore in the late Devonian, some 375mya. Something "big" happened in the climate and geology of our Earth during the terminal Permian, 245mya, to destroy the vast range of life in all phyla, and also to weaken the synapsid/therapsid reptiles, bringing forth the modestly homeothermic cynodont/therapsids. So, too, the upper Triassic, from about 225-208mya reveals the elimination of many reptile lines, paving the way for the archosaurs/dinosaurs, but also decimating the many proliferating cynodont lines, giving us in their stead the tiny mammals of the end Triassic and early Jurassic, 210-190mya.

It is not irresponsibly speculative to argue that the process of evolutionary change on land was determined by a set of inner biological genetic and environmental interactions, in which environmental change and the ability of animals both to survive successive alterations in the world's ecological balances, as well as to produce those genetic, morphological, and behavioral guidance systems that could "predict" such alterations, and thus come through the extinction sieve, constitutes the core selective and thus Darwinian dynamic of terrestrial evolution on the planet.

Origin of Primates

Stebbins gives us a hint at a model of mammal and primate evolution leading out of the Cretaceous into the Tertiary/Paleocene, from around 100-65mya. Given the agreed-upon early to mid-Cretaceous appearance of placental and marsupial forms, mostly in the Northern Hemisphere, there subsequently seems to have been a gap of about 20-30my before their reappearance in the earliest Paleocene.[14] It is this gap in the fossil record that reveals the disappearance of the large number of marsupial families at the K/T boundary, noted above.

During this final phase of the Cretaceous, the sea reptiles, including the icthyosaurs, had already become extinct.[15] Clemens argues that of the two main lines of dinosaurs, there may have been significant declines in both the saurischians (*Tyrannosaurus*, *Brontosaurus*, etc.) and ornithischians (*Stegosaurus*, *Tricerotops*) lines between the mid-late and terminal Cretaceous, 77-67mya.[16] He calls the decrease in ornithischian genera, from 20-14 during this 10my period, "profound." In one particular formation, the "Western Interior" study area, he notes that 50% of the saurischian genera and 75% of the ornithischians, have disappeared from the last 2-3my levels of the K/T boundary. He believes, citing the work of Alvarez, that this could represent the waning of a line of animals even before the final extinction.[17]

Harry Jerison surmised that the first increase in relative encephalization above the basal mammalian grade probably took place in *Plesiadapis* in the Paleocene, 65-55mya.[18] Colbert/Morales report the discovery in Upper Cretaceous sediments of a tooth belonging to a primate, *Purgatorius*, possibly a plesiadapid, known also from numerous specimens assigned to the Paleocene. Colbert/Morales compare these creatures to *Tupaia*, a contemporary oriental tree shrew that may be a primate, an insectivore, or something in-between. This squirrel-sized animal, in addition to feeding on insects, is also to a large extent frugivorous. Andrews and Stringer see these creatures' brain structure as not highly developed, and with claws instead of nails, eyes that faced sideways and not forward. Their conclusion is that these creatures were a side branch not leading directly to the evolution of more modern primate forms, and therefore, in all likelihood part of that supposed lineage that could be traced back to the original insectivore radiation and branching, possibly as early as the middle to late Cretaceous, 100-75mya. But this is still obscured by that cloud of uncertainty provided in Stebbins 20-30my blackout before the K/T boundary.[19]

The plesiadapids, being both frugivorous and insectivorous, imply the shifting of a way of life from a more ground-dwelling nocturnal existence to a life both in the trees and on the ground. This versatility almost surely heralds a change in the brain structures for behavior, the return to the cone system of vision, (and possibly derived from another, more ancient mammalian line), from the earlier rod vision developed for life in the dark. It reflects the changing adaptations of the earliest insectivores/primates as they began to move around an environment that now allowed for more day as well as night exploration and feeding.[20]

The late Cretaceous saw a general uplifting of land masses, the creation of new mountain ranges, likely continental climate alteration ranges, desiccating inland seas. The discovery and reporting of Cretaceous dinosaurs in Mongolian strata seemingly dying in the midst of a possible sandstorm—bellies up, heads held high against the on-coming winds and sand—hint at the kinds of challenges that this great climatic change must have presented to the dinosaur line. Thus supported are the surprising statistics reported by Clemens concerning the "profound" disappearance of many dinosaur genera in the final 10-12my of the Cretaceous.[21]

The lone Cretaceous tooth of *Purgatorius*, the primate or plesiadapiform, also ought not surprise us for its presumed dating, considering recent molecular evidence arguing for a much earlier Cretaceous separation of placental mammal lines, still hidden from archeological eyes.[22]

This sequence is implied in the mitochondrial data developed in Munich by Axel Janke and Svante Paabo *et al.*, in which the rodents are viewed as an early divergence from the placental evolutionary line, the primates and ungulates/artiodactyls grouped as a sister taxon. In addition, Janke and Paabo view the ungulates and carnivores as derived from a common ancestor (*Oxyclaenus*—arctocyonids), placing whales, seals, with the cows. Their divergence schema for the placentals is: A) rodents, ungulates, and primates, c.114mya; B) primates, ungulates, c.93mya; C) carnivores, artiodactyls, c.55mya; D) cow, hippopotamus, whale, c.41mya; E) mouse, rat, c.35mya. Their schema of phylogenetic relationships based on mitochondrial data jibes significantly with those of G. G. Simpson, made over 50 years earlier on the basis his paleontological analysis.[23]

A team of molecular geneticists headed by S. Blair Hedges of Pennsylvania State University has recently postulated the early (115-90mya) separation of three widespread placental orders.[24] 1. The artiodactyls, (camels, deer, bison, hippos, boars), heretofore thought to have appeared in the Eocene, after c.50mya.[25] 2. The rodents, (beavers, rabbits, mice, squirrels) supposedly appeared early in the Paleocene, c.60mya.[26] 3. The primates, also universally thought to have shown up on the world scene as exemplified by the transitional plesiadapids, in the Paleocene, c.65-55mya.

The separation of the three groups was calibrated by the molecular changes in a number of reliable nuclear and mitochondrial gene sequences. Hedges and his team estimate that these three highly articulated groups and in their own individual ways, had already become specialized mammals, and separated from each other from between 115-90mya, with the rodents breaking away from the primate/artiodactyl group about 104mya. Naturally there are difficulties with such an estimate, since there may be other groups, insectivores—shrews; edentates—anteaters; perissodactyls—horses; carnivores—leopards, etc. which could show a closer relationship to the primates.

The diversification implied in the molecular data argues for a different explanation for the extinction of so many animal lines, including the dinosaurs:

....We suggest that the fragmentation of emergent land areas during the Cretaceous, not the sudden availability of ecological niches following the K/T extinction event, was the mechanism responsible for avian and mammalian orders. When plate tectonics and sea levels are considered together, all the major continental breakup events during the last 250myr occurred in the Mesozoic and mainly during the Cretaceous. The timing of these events corresponds closely to the molecular time estimates for divergences of the orders.[27]

Michael Novacek, curator of vertebrate paleontology at the American Museum of Natural History, New York City, commenting on the work of the Hedges team, noted that an evolutionary link to the breakup of continents made sense. Yet, he was skeptical about the use of genetic analysis to estimate the time of evolutionary splits. Further, he now doubts whether gene changes at supposed constant rates must still be taken seriously. However, Novacek did not doubt that mammals and birds diversified before dinosaurs died out.[28]

Dynamic Structures

Placentals were identifiable by about the late-early Cretaceous, 120mya. Part of the evolutionary selective machinery adaptively stimulating the development of both the placental and the marsupial strategy, both morphological possibilities part of the existing genetic repertoire derived from more ancient vertebrate (fish) traditions, was, of course, the increased probability of more young surviving into the next generation.

The allantois, part of the old reptilian amniotic egg, in placentals, remains in contact with the uterus, within which is the embryo. The placenta acts as contact point and conduit by which nourishment and oxygen are transmitted to the developing embryo. In turn foetal waste is eliminated through the mother.[29] Marsupials, without the placental separation of embryo and mother, must deliver externally the undeveloped, literally larval, young. Any longer stay within the mother and contact between the two biological systems would result in an auto-immune form of rejection as the different genetic composition of the embryo is attacked by the mother's biological defenses.

Let us recall the adaptive value of the internal incubation of the fertilized egg-embryo. The dinosaurs, controlling the major land adaptive and therefore food zones, ceded the more marginal nocturnal and ground ecologies to the relatively tiny and dynamically competing mammals at the peripheries. Internal gestation of the young had as a primary selective value to give to the parents of the young more mobility. Away from the nest or burrow, they could move about in search of food, escape from predatory competitors without losing a breeding season's young.

Given the ongoing separation of the continents during this early-mid Cretaceous period, the various fundamental experiments in mammal reproductive adaptive patterns were allowed to continue along a number of separate pathways. The monotremes clearly were secured in a relatively non-competitive niche both against non-mammals, as well as between other orders of the class. Janis believes the multituberculates to have then been a live-bearing line, somewhat between the marsupial "larval" birth and the clinging and lapping feeding strategy that is observed in monotremes after their hatching from externally laid eggs. The multituberculates, apparently largely frugivorous and seemingly adapted to arboreal life, must have early taken that particular pathway away from strict insectivorous patterns. They never seemed to have deviated until their extinction sometime in the Eocene, c.40mya.[30]

A product of placental diversification had to have been the early expression of different adaptive plans in carving out stable niches made possible by the advantages given in placental reproduction. Here, mobility, internal safety of the foetal young, the relatively advanced state of development and survivability, upon birth, a restriction in number of young in each birth season, were all positive selective elements. Concomitantly, greater possibility for intense maternal care through lactation/nursing and protection, ultimately resulting in a larger proportion of young being sustained through to their reproductive maturity were additional factors leading to placental domination in a time of rapid environmental change.

Given the variable pathways of behavior seemingly remaindered to the earliest tree shrew-primate progenitors—living on the ground as well as in the trees, bearing fewer young, having early on fewer specialized adaptive morphological patterns, especially as compared to the arteriodactyls and rodents—it is appropriate to see them as having gradually made an adaptive virtue out of their relative versatility of behavior and elusiveness. This defensive profile was clearly successful against the ruling reptilian host, on land and in the air (pterosaurs), as well as the strongly active competing lines of diversifying mammals, c.120-90mya.

An important conceptual component of a model of placental and then primate evolution perceives the separation and radiation of the various observed Paleocene fossils occurring much earlier than their ostensible fossil appearance. This model is supported by the implacable fact that diversification takes time in the basic chromosomal and genetic sense. First, variant genes must find their phenotypic expression. This often requires rearrangements intra- and interchromosomally in the individual genomes and through sexual reproduction. Second, time and generations are needed, in this case longer mammalian generations by which to sort out those basic genetic patterns that will work at the core selective levels of survivability. Consider the fact that by the time the mammals had made their basic adaptive play in the early Jurassic, 200-180mya, a fully modern and complex number of chromosomes had come to reside within the Class. In the words of Qumsiyeh,

> ...There is a lack of any chromosomal evolution in mammals. It appears that mammalian chromosomal evolution occurred by both increases and decreases of different numbers in different lineages....To date, there are no studies unequivocally documenting a phenotypically beneficial effect of a chromosome rearrangement in either the heterozygous or the homozygous state.[31]

Certainly in the earliest period of primate diversification, and probably located in but one of a number of shrew-like insectivore variants, the carriers of these chromosomal and genetic rearrangements had become the unwitting servant transmitter of an ultimate evolutionary revolution.

The Primate Brain

One of these deviant specializations had to be the particular visual-brain system that would be selected for in an animal line that was probably left on the margins of early placental radiations. As the protomammals entered a more nocturnal life, the older visual-tactile system, the optic-tectum (retino-tectal) had become reduced, c.240-210mya. The thalamus, receiving direct retinal projections and already in contact with the cerebral cortex through the olfactory system, reinforced a newer association of visual stimuli (rod system) with the older reptilian olfactory-cortical system. Later, 110-80mya, as the mammals reentered a diurnal mode of life the most efficient structural readaptation was to reassociate the visual (now a newly-appearing cone system) and the motor pathways with the cortical system rather than to redirect it to the older mid-brain (optic tectum or superior colliculus) visual brain centers. The reciprocal growth of the cortex in organizing and integrating this visual information as part of the new adaptive arboreal life of the primates continued to further incorporate the diverse sensory inputs and modalities as part of cortico-cortical connectivity.[32]

The primate precursors, without evolving hoofs, or gnawing teeth, without the long-nosed insect, burrowing specializations represented in the Edentates, made do with a classical outlander mammalian set of defensive adaptations. This is the traditional selective role of the animal line represented in the adaptive valences represented by the early vertebrates, the Crossopterygians/tetrapods, the cynodonts, the mammals themselves. To survive and evolve in such a peripheral, if versatile adaptive ecology, the primates needed the typically extended phylogenetic neurological growth time frame required by brain tissue, c.110-70mya, to develop those primal mammalian sensory and sensorimotor areas of the neocortex.[33] These areas were gradually built upon, as stated above, to sustain an adaptive life under high cover.

We must recall that among the reptiles, it was the deviant birds that developed a brain that was extraordinarily large in comparison to their body size, and for surviving on high. This brain was a visual instrument, gradually selected out for its efficiency in avoiding tree branches and other objects at high speed, being able to identify insects on the fly, and to be quickly alerted to dangers from ground animals and other predatory birds.[34]

Evidence is that even today frugivorous arboreal forms tend to have larger brains than ground-living forms. "Brain size depends on the habits of a mammal: it is larger in arboreal species and in species that feed on vertebrates, seeds, or fruit, and it is smaller in terrestrial species that feed on grass or the leaves of woody plants."[35] This relationship holds as well for primate species that are frugivorous, as compared with their folivorous relatives.[36] It should be noted that in terms of tooth structure, none of the Cretaceous or early Paleocene mammals were folivorous in their diet.[37]

Other synchronous restructuring was taking place in the protoprimate placental mammals during the mid-Cretaceous, c.110-100mya. The greater adaptive choice of life styles provided by viviparity, including a mixed ground- and tree-living pattern gave a greater selective premium to those lines that could bring a larger proportion of young to viability at and after birth. The need to nurse and still move around within a relatively precarious set of variable adaptive niches could make large and very altricial (undeveloped) litters vulnerable. Inevitably those lines developing visual brains requiring alertness and anticipation of danger, gave birth to smaller and more phenotypically developed litters of young. As primates became adaptable climbers, their limbs gradually differentiating in function, the thumb and large toe, set apart for grasping, as compared to rodents and ungulates, the need to hold and carry nursing young put a greater premium on the care and nurturing of only one or two fairly well-developed neonates.[38]

> Allometric and energetic explanations for variation in neonatal brain size in mammals lack a theoretical foundation for explaining why some species show systematic deviations from the trends they predict. Our adaptive explanation based on the life history theory suggests that the increased gestation lengths and larger neonatal brain sizes of some mammals function to reduce the risk of mortality during the juvenile period.[39]

Tupaia, the modern oriental tree shrew, a creature the size of a squirrel, is described by both Colbert/Morales and Andrews/Stringer as similar in size to the early plesiadapids, a large rat- or squirrel-sized animal of the early Paleocene, 65-57mya. *Tupaia* and its ancestors may be on the same line as *Plesiadapis*, and not directly ancestral to the later primates which radiated in the early Eocene period, c.57-45mya.[40] Most probably, since Colbert/Morales view *Plesiadapis* as already having a relatively enlarged brain, and given Jerison's view that the post-Cretaceous mammals evolved brains 4-5x as large as the stasis mammals had achieved by the early Cretaceous, *Tupaia* is a creature already endowed with a growing brain and therefore higher information-processing abilities.[41]

Recent research into the evolution of the mammalian brain has concerned itself with issues of allometric growth as well as the reorganization of the brain from basal mammalian architectonics. This research focuses on the development of more recent isocortical structures, some of which are associated with visual/cortical reassociations.[42] According to the principle of neurogenesis, the most recent brain structures developed in the evolution of an animal, were those most likely to be increased out of proportion to the whole, during the growth of the entire organ:

> The order of neurogenesis was found to be highly conserved across a wide range of mammals and to correlate with the relative enlargement of structures as brain size increases, with disproportionately large growth in late-generated structures. Because the order of neurogenesis is conserved, the most likely brain alteration resulting from selection for any behavioral ability may be a coordinated enlargement of the entire nonolfactory brain.[43]

This general approach is consonant with Deacon's above view of the competitive displacement theory of neural connections in the evolution of the mammal brain. In this theory, he explains what was likely a long-continued process during which the older connections between cortex and sensory pathways were displaced through the influence of "...differential allometry, cell death or axon-target affinity changes. The `displacement hypothesis' is used to propose speculative accounts for the differential enlargement and multiplication of cortical areas, the origins of mammalian isocortex...."[44]

Evolutionary Success and Failure

As the mid- to late-Cretaceous mammals began to integrate their internal placental or marsupial morphologies, they increasingly found secure adaptive niches. What we see bursting forth in the Paleocene in terms of mammals being ostensibly freed of dinosaurian domination after the K/T transition and extinctions, certainly was rooted in prior Cretaceous dynamics, as the molecular evidence set forth by Hedges clearly implies.[45]

Along with the various radiating adaptations to the several ecologies that modern placentals were exploring, the defensive tree shrew/primate adaptations were one of an expanding circle of opportunity. Part of this seeming success paralleled the dinosaurian decline.[46]

Success implies expansion in numbers, probably size also, since increased body bulk provides a measure of purely physical insurance and caloric/metabolic reserves for the animal, as well as constituting a passive defense against larger animals. The growth of tiny mouse-like mammals to the size of a squirrel or large rat, accompanying a significant modernization and corticalization of sensory inputs would have given the newer integrating functions of the brain a boost in relative size. Selectively, it would provide the protoprimates more information-processing power, extrovertish energies, all that a somewhat larger animal would be able to muster. Finally, it would be well-prepared to defend its arboreal niche in the wave of expansion opportunity beyond the K/T boundary.

The beginning Paleocene, 65mya, saw the appearance of apparent holdovers from the upper Cretaceous, expanding multituberculates that replaced a number of extinct lines, surviving possum-like marsupials, raccoon-like ungulates, numerous shrew and hedgehog-like insectivores, and the semi-carnivore ungulate condylarth, *Oxyclaenus*. Janis pictures *Oxyclaenus* as predating on the P*lesiadapis*, *Purgatorius*, the early insectivore/primate, discussed above.[47] In fact the ungulate condylarth *Protungulatum*, whose fossils appear in the late Cretaceous, had both herbivorous and carnivorous features, which at first seem to relate them to the carnivorous creodonts. It is quite unclear what their specialized diet was. All indications are that the differentiations between herbivores and carnivores were, early on in modern mammalian history, still unclear.[48] If omnivorous capacities can be attributed to these evolving Cretaceous mammals, it is hardly likely that small reptiles, amphibians, and birds were not also part of the diet, along with less lucky mammals. Then, why not dinosaur eggs?

Most authorities view the K/T boundary as marked by the intrusion into the planet of an extra-terrestrial asteroid, causing sudden and enormous climatic alteration around the planet, affecting those animals over approximately 25kg-55lb., and thus extinguishing the dinosaurs as a group. Other views postulate that a combination of climatic changes, geological upheavals leading to alterations in water levels, desiccating land masses, and continental alterations of cold and warm could have had an impact on the larger ectothermic creatures. But, the K/T boundary also decimated many marsupial lines, wreaked havoc on many lines of plants, reefs in the seas and plankton varieties. No question but that the mammals were the beneficiaries of the complete disappearance of the dinosaurs, plesiosaurs and pterosaurs. But the turtles, snakes, crocodiles, lizards and other reptiles perdured. Why, as Colbert/Morales wonder, did none of the many kinds of *small* dinosaurs survive?[49] The relatively unpopular conjecture often put forth by George Gaylord Simpson must still be considered: "Among the many developments within this potent reptile-mammal line, care of the young must be given high place. Eggs were no longer deposited and left at the mercy of an egg hungry world, nor even given such lesser care as external (as in birds) or internal (as in some reptiles) incubation."[50]

- 2 -
Primate Radiation

Primate Time-Line:
   a) Plesiadapidforms (sub-order)—Late Cretaceous, c.75-70mya—to Middle Eocene—c.45-40mya = c.30my tenure, before extinction.
   b) Strepsirhini and Haplorhini prosimians, (sub-orders), lemur-like adapids and tarsier-like omomyids. Flourished from early Eocene c.55mya to 30mya=dominance of c.25my. Remnant forms are still extant. Also evolving were modern monkeys, apes, and protohominids.
   c) Catarrhines and Platyrrhines infra-order, Old and New World Monkeys, established by c 35mya, originated earlier. Flourished for c.34my.
   d) Hominoidea : super-family. Apes and Hominids, at the latest from c.40mya, late Eocene.

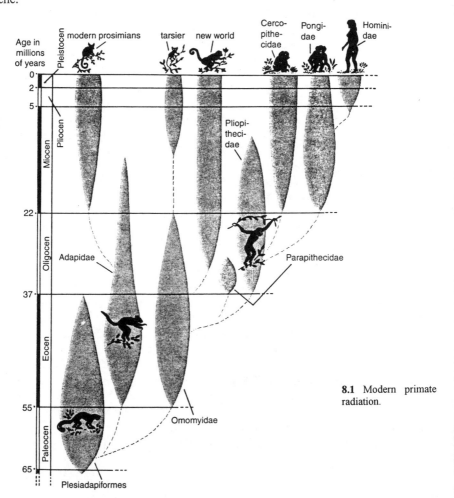

8.1 Modern primate radiation.

Contexts

Evolutionary periods: Eocene: 55-34mya; Oligocene: 34-23mya; Miocene: 23-5mya.

A gap exists in the fossil record between the Fayum (Egypt) primate fossils (c.35-30mya) and the definite establishment of a fossil record of apes, the super-family Hominoidea, out of which the various transitional and true apes derive. This taxonomic category includes some of the questionable Fayum fossils, as well as the related and later East African Catarrhine, *Dendropithecus*, which has hinted to some researchers of a distant relationship to the gibbon.[51]

The super-family Hominoidea includes the definitive ape and hominid fossils, including *Proconsul* and *Australopithecus*.[52] If the well-established Oligocene coolings, early, c.34mya, and the more extreme late-early, c.30mya Oligocene coolings did not affect the evolutionary interactions in the Fayum-North African geographies, the final extinction of the multituberculates, possibly remnant plesiadapiforms, "Ignacius," c.39mya, plus many other early mammal lines, could point us to a new evolutionary boundary, and thus new evolutionary dynamics within the primate clade.[53]

The Fayum evidence is but one small sample of what was going on in the world at the end of the Eocene and early Oligocene. The assumption must be that the early radiation of Paleocene primates contained a number of covert evolving forms, which, with each environmental, ecological, or climatic lurch, extruded new specializations and potencies in some heretofore peripheral forms, and in turn relegated others to the historical archives. Our fossil record in general is a reflection of raw numbers where opportune paleontological excavation is possible. It does not yet illuminate the evolving character of the extant lines (hidden and evident) at any one temporal slice of evolutionary history.

Stebbins sees anatomical changes in primates being stimulated selectively by adaptation to a diurnal life requiring vision more than smell (nocturnal), also, vision was required for arboreal existence. He views the mid-Oligocene frost and subsequent development of savannahs that replaced the heavy jungle like tropical canopy, as conducive for the split toward human/ape divergence. Mosaic environments precipitated the mosaic evolution of many experiments. These pathways were now exploited through an adaptive exploratory trend rather than being driven, ecologically, from the trees.[54]

Proconsul in Kenya

A series of fossils, hominoid, dated between 27.5-19mya. This time frame seems to have seen the rise of several species, small siamang to large female gorilla size: lack of brow ridges, thin tooth enamel, broadening incisors, large surface area molars, larger brain. Post-cranial: shoulder gave arm all round mobility, as in modern apes, arm could not straighten fully at elbow. Opposable thumb, hand proportions like humans, no thumb reduction as in modern apes. Hip and knee structure similar to primitive catarrhine, also omomyids (tarsiers), but ankles and feet are great-ape-like. Andrews and Stringer see an opposable thumb, large brain as heralding possible tool use in *Proconsul*.[55]

Andrews and Stringer discuss the mosaic qualities of *Proconsul*, a "confection" of anatomical relationships. Shoulders and elbows like apes. Hand and arm bones like monkeys. Hips not ape-like, but lower legs and foot bones much like modern apes. Running on all fours, and climbing trees, too.[56]

The relative length of arms and legs in *Proconsul* was similar, unlike great apes and humans, the latter two having very differing proportions. *Proconsul* had strongly gripping hands and feet, a short muzzled face, not projecting (prognathous), no large canines, nor knuckle walking, and a lighter build than modern apes.[57]

Proconsul's brain is estimated by Stebbins to have been only 7-10% smaller than that of the chimpanzee, the skull of same general shape. However it lacked the latter's massive brow ridges, and *Proconsul*'s face and jaws protruded somewhat less, finally as noted above, its limbs were shorter than the chimpanzee "*Pan troglodytes*." Probably *Proconsul* was a less agile brachiator. Foot structure intimates that *Proconsul* stood on its hind legs more often than the chimpanzee and gorilla. Intermediate between apes and monkeys—some characteristics foreshadow those of hominids and humans. Stebbins argues that it fulfills the expectations of a common ancestor of all hominoids, apes and humans. A supporting assessment even places the similarity of *Proconsul* with *Pan* a notch further up the evolutionary line to a resemblance with the Australopithecines.[58]

If, as Nisbet argues, *Proconsul* was baboon-sized, then the relative brain size of this creature is impressive, as compared to the chimpanzee. Nisbet sees a similarity between the two forms in their elbows, feet, and shoulder joints. However, the back of *Proconsul* is seen as similar to the gibbon, with monkey-like wrist.[59]

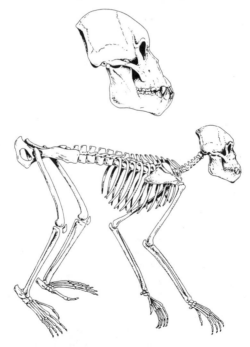

8.2 *Proconsul*, Miocene primate, c.23mya.

Szalay and Delson view *Proconsul* and its affiliates as a derived species from the dryopithecine clade. Included in the taxonomy of this group was one genus, four sub-genera, eight species. Szalay and Delson exclude *Ramapithecus, Sivapithecus, Gigantopithecus* from this clade. The line, *Proconsul*, or "*Dryopithecus africanus*" constitutes a characterological mosaic of New World monkey, Old World monkey, gibbon, and great ape, in its post cranial morphology, especially locomotion and brachiation.[60]

Considering the long time span, perhaps throughout the Miocene, that *Proconsul* and its African ape affiliates roamed the mixed tropical forest-savannah ecology from East Africa to Arabia, and then in several subsequent genera, into Europe and West Asia, all related to the *Proconsul* clade, from 28-27mya to 14mya, we here have an important evolutionary reality to be dealt with.[61] Foremost is the taxonomic question. Clearly Szalay and Delson are "lumpers" rather than "splitters." They tend to underrate the differences in these dryopithecine apes, (one genus, four sub-genera, and eight species), spread over a timespan of over 10my, and throughout an extremely large geographical swath. But it does coincide with the primate dominance of the hominoid apes. This then was still a strongly adaptive and relatively non-specialized group of primates.[62]

Proconsul (c.27-19mya) will inevitably prove to be a yardstick of comparison when we move on in evolutionary time to probe the further differentiation and specialization of the line, clearly an exemplar that has leapt far beyond the parameters of primate evolution indicated in the Fayum deposits, 35-30mya. It is important to note that the first Old World Monkey to appear in the fossil record dates to about 18mya. After c.14mya, Africa is joined to Eur-Asia allowing for the radiation of both Infra-orders of Catarrhines into that vast, still largely subtropical-temperate land mass.

This time frame invites comparison with the appearance 25mya of the extremely successful and adaptively stable New World monkeys in the Western Hemisphere. The prehensile tail of the New World Monkey is unique; it serves as a fifth arm. In addition, since the first fossil indications of these monkeys date to the Oligocene, 30-25mya, these monkeys seem to have remained completely and efficiently arboreal, even though their brain size and presumed intelligence, and relative lack of ground competitors, arguably should have opened up additional ground-living adaptations (Darwin's finches?), and, as it did for the Old World primates, to the New World monkeys.

> Whatever their early history, the development of the New World primates offers a cautionary example to theories of hominoid evolution. They need to explain what special causes may have drawn or driven the biped venture of the Old World, but tied these New World cousins to the trees, even when they had an entire continent to explore and be changed by, and more than 35my to evolve in.[63]

Miocene Ape Fragmentation
1. Afropithecines

Heliopithecus, 17-16mya, beginning of thick enamel teeth, leads to *Kenyapithecus africanus* and *K. wickeri*, 16-14mya, also recently found, *Afropithecus* and *Otavopithecus*, (Glen Conroy). Climate more temperate and seasonal.[64]

> The molars in the early Afropithecines show the beginning of one of the most important adaptations in later fossils and recent hominoids, the thickening of the molar tooth enamel. This was a key change because it would enable its makers to live in less friendly conditions. The function of the enamel is to armor the teeth against wear caused by chew-

ing. A mammal's life expectancy can often be measured in terms of the length of time its teeth stay functional. Some animals with course or abrasive diets may starve to death when their teeth wear out and they can no longer process food. A whole series of changes in later hominoids would not have been possible without this key survival factor, and the longer life span it allowed.[65]

Not only did the Afropithecines have the thick enamel molar equipment requisite to a more open-country nuts, roots, and fruit economy. Their jaw structure and the associated ability to use their incisors and canines for biting reveal a more versatile set of tooth and jaw adaptations for living in a world, 16-14mya, that was rapidly drying out from its previous tropical rain forest characteristics. These Afropithecines seem also to have been the derived descendants of *Proconsul*, and the possible ancestors of *Sivapithecus*, possibly the contemporary African apes, even of the hominids.[66]

The multituberculates, the mammal Sub-class, *Allotheria*, which had existed from the late Triassic, c.220mya, into the early Eocene, c.50mya, was then probably competing with the rapidly-expanding placental rodents and primates. These multituberculates had small enamel tips on their teeth which limited them in both their diet and thus ecological flexibility. The placentals, however, had fully-enameled teeth, if thinly layered, facilitating a more omnivorous diet, and opening up a wider range of ecologies to pursue their food getting, probably indirectly pressuring the multituberculates into extinction, rather than through direct aggressive contact.[67]

"Thickening the enamel may seem to be an obvious adaptation, but it takes radical improvements in physiology to absorb and deliver the minerals it requires, which are needed early in life while the teeth are forming. Most mammals have relatively thin enamel." Harder, thicker enamel teeth and the flourishing of these primates in such an environment argue for a diet that goes beyond soft fruit, flowers, and insects, to acorns and nuts, needing to be stored for seasonal use in a drying and cooling Miocene climate, c.15mya.[68]

2. Dryopithecines: Ape Evolution—Europe.

These apes moved into Europe subsequent to the joining with Africa in mid-Miocene, c.15-11mya, also possibly into Asia, even China. Their post-cranial bones are more advanced, than Afropithecines, yet with robust ridges over eyes, unlike *Proconsul*. Lightly-built jaws contrast with heavier brow ridges which buttressed the lower jaws, implying a coarser diet of seeds, nuts, roots.[69] Thinly-enameled teeth seem to make *Dryopithecus* more primitive than *Kenyapithecus*.[70] The morphology of *Dryopithecus*, an emigrant from Africa, suggests to us that it is "more closely related to the great apes and humans, than, for instance, the living gibbons are. However, in several important characters it is less advanced than *Kenyapithecus* and *Heliopithecus*...[Afropithecines]...so that even though these lived earlier in time they are thought to be closer to the ancestry of the living apes and humans than is '*Dryopithecus*.'"[71] M. Koehler and S. Moya-Sola report on a dryopithecine ape, 9.5mya, a 75-lb. male who could stand partially upright on ground, having a semi-erect posture. This fossil was found in 1994 near Barcelona.

3. *Oreopithecus*

Italy, 9-7mya, a specialized tree dweller with long arms, hook like hands. There is controversy over its monkey like teeth and presumed ape like post cranial structure.

Martin sees the relatively small molars as a human like reduction in size in relation to body weight, since "[T]he overall bodily dimensions of '*Oreopithecus*' indicate that it was at least as big as a modern chimpanzee, it was a large ape."[72] It probably branched off from the hominoid lineage before the orangutans, African apes, and humans, diverged.[73] *Oreopithecus* possibly migrated to Europe and evolved separately after Europe/Africa made their connection, c.14mya.

    4. *Sivapithecus, Ramapithecus* and Descendants

Africa, Europe, Western Asia, India 13-7mya. All have a shared ancestry with *Ramapithecus* leading to the orangutan line. Very thickly-enameled teeth, partially ground living because of size, significant sexual dimorphism.[74] Simons and Andrews have respectively reviewed the general ecological and selective requirements of life in a mixed woodland, savannah. The latter were conducive to developing heavy enamel and large molars, heavy chewing and crushing of foods by posterior teeth. All seem characteristic of the adaptive position of the various forms of *Ramapithecus*.[75]

    At one time many scientists, including Simons and David Pilbeam, viewed *Ramapithecus* as a hominid precursor along the lines leading to *Homo* and *Australopithecus*. There has been a general retreat from this earlier position, of *Ramapithecus* as a hominine. This was precipitated by the discoveries by Walker and Andrews in 1973 of *R. wickeri*, which unlike *R. punjabicus*, the once classic representative, has a more typical parallel arrangement of teeth on either side of jaw, not the parabolic human-like dental arcade of *R. punjabicus*. New discoveries from Hungary, Turkey, and Pakistan have tended to support the Walker and Andrews reconstruction.[76] *Ramapithecus* is now incorporated within the genus *Sivapithecus*.[77]

    The line of thick molar enamel ground apes, *Sivapithecus, Ramapithecus*, and more recently, the extremely large *Gigantopithecus* species, of Pakistan, India, and China, c.8-1mya, were associated on the basis of this tooth enamel morphology, and the seeming similarity in the parabolic dental arcade of *Homo* and *R. punjabicus* thought to be part of the same clade.[78] *Gigantopithecus* teeth have been found in China, c.1.9mya, associated with the remains of *Homo*.[79]

    The Sivapithecines are now thought to have earlier broken off from the mainline of pongid-hominid evolution and to have produced the modern orangutan, instead.[80] Andrews and Stringer note that thick enameled teeth have been found in cercopithecid monkeys, and thus the thick enameled teeth found in orangutan, *Australopithecus* and *Homo*, in contradistinction to thin enameled teeth in Pan and Gorilla are not to be considered crucial in terms of phylogenetic relationships.[81]

    Pickford reports on the earlier association of *Kenyapithecus africanus* as ancestor of the Ramapithecines. This is no longer tenable in spite of shared characteristic of thickly-enameled teeth between *Kenyapithecus africanus*, *K. wickeri*, and *Ramapithecus*. *K. africanus'* mandible arcade is U-shaped not parabolic. In both lines teeth are highly dimorphic. *K. wickeri* the younger species, is also dimorphic. Pickford believes that *K. africanus* could have predated the split between the pongines—*Ramapithecus*, the African apes, and then *Homo*: "*K. africanus* does however recall to some extent the morphology seen in 'Pongo' [Orangutan] and some of the Hadar [Australopithecines] hominids."[82]

Pongid Relationships

The recent discovery in the Valles Penedes region of Spain, of post-cranial bones of the European *Dryopithecus*, "*D. laietans*," dated to 9.5mya, reveals an animal that has certain orangutan-like affinities in its below the branch arboreal locomotion, albeit with some additional ground-walking propensities. These postcranial bones underline the current puzzlement over pongid phylogenetic relationships, as well as temporal evolutionary processes.[83]

Oreopithecus is unique in all dimensions, cranially, jaws and teeth, as well as postcranially. It was probably a migrant into Europe sometime after 14mya when the continents, Africa and Eur-Asia, were joined. How long it survived after its appearance in an Italian swamp, approximately 9mya, we do not know?

Sivapithecus, which along with the ramapithecine species can be traced back to about 14mya, has definite cranial affinities with the contemporary orangutan. Its fossils can be traced to about 8mya. At that point the *Gigantopithecus* genus appears in the fossil record, clearly a member of the *Sivapithecus* clade and making a geographic connection toward the Southeast Asian homeland of the orangutan, whose postcranial structure seems to depart from *Sivapithecus*, yet could be related to the Dryopithecines. The Dryopithecines appear in the fossil record in Europe about 14mya, to disappear during the late Miocene, c.8mya.

As noted above, *Sivapithecus*, in terms of thickly-enameled molars and postcranial bones, appears related to earlier Afropithecines such as *Kenyapithecus* that date back to c.22mya. The Afropithecines disappear from the fossil record about the time that *Sivapithecus* appears. *Sivapithecus*, however, is a more northerly anthropoid, found from Hungary and Turkey to Pakistan.

No fossil record exists yet that would indicate a direct phylogenetic relationship of any of these fossil apes with the contemporary African, two chimpanzee species and the one gorilla species, and the latter's two varieties, or races, the mountain and lowland types. The arm bones of the chimpanzee and its thinly-enameled teeth contrast with humans. The knuckle-walking structure of the arms of both species reveal them to be more highly specialized anthropoids than practically any of the fossil apes, now extinct, except for very different *Gigantopithecus*, and seemingly for at least the past 5 or 6my.

Old World monkeys begin to appear in the African fossil record about 20-17mya. At that time the fossil record reveals an 80/20% split between the more numerous apes and the fewer monkeys. In the mid-Miocene, 15-10mya, their percentages begin to equalize. The Eur-Asian apes appear about 14mya. By the time we reach a period after 8mya, this ratio is reversed. The apes have practically disappeared from the evolutionary horizon, especially in Europe and Africa.

One questionable explanation is that the monkeys were able to eat and digest unripe fruit, had a wider adaptability to variable food sources than the apes.[84] Today, gorillas and bonobos, (apes!) are noted as being able to eat leaves and shoots, having a folivorous diet like many monkeys, which allows them to utilize a broader variety of food substances for their massive needs.

There is a mystery here.

The first hominid fossils fragments, in Africa, probably *Ardipithecus* or *Australopithecus*, are now dated to between 6 and 5mya.[85]

Endnotes, Chapter 8

[1] Janis, Christine. 1993. "Victors by Default," in *Life*, S. J. Gould, ed., N.Y.: W. W. Norton, pp. 172-173; Kemp, T. S. 1982. *Mammal-like Reptiles and the Origin of Mammals*, N.Y.: Academic Press, pp. 272-273; Stebbins, G. Ledyard. 1982. *Darwin to DNA, Molecules to Humanity*, San Francisco: W. H. Freeman, pp. 293-294.

[2] Jerison, Harry J. 1973. *Evolution of the Brain and Intelligence*, N.Y.: Academic Press, pp. 253-255.

[3] Jerison, 1973, *op. cit.*, pp. 200-205.

[4] Kemp, 1982, *op. cit.*, pp. 293; Janis, 1993, in Gould, ed., *op. cit.*, p. 173.

[5] Colbert, E. H. 1986. "Mesozoic Tetrapod Extinctions: A Review," in *Dynamics of Extinction*, David K. Elliott, ed., N.Y.: John Wiley, pp. 57-61.

[6] Szalay, F. S., Novacek, M. J., McKenna, M. C., eds. 1993. *Mammal Phylogeny*, N.Y.: Springer-Verlag, p. 240; Janis, 1993, in Gould, ed., *op. cit.*, p. 178.

[7] Clemens, W. A. 1986. "Evolution of the Terrestrial Vertebrate Fauna During the Cretaceous-Tertiary Transition," in Elliott, ed., *op. cit.*, pp. 63-85; Raup, D. 1991. *Extinction: Bad Luck or Bad Genes?*, N.Y.: W. W. Norton, p. 73 ("Reverse Rarefaction").

[8] McKinney, M. L. 1993. *Evolution of Life*, Englewood Cliffs, N.J.: Prentice Hall, pp. 170-171.

[9] Alvarez. L. W. 1983. "Experimental evidence that an asteroid impact led to the extinction of many species 65 million years ago," *Proceedings of the National Academy of Sciences U.S.A.*, 80(2):627-42; Alvarez, L. W., Alvarez, W., Asaro, F., and Michel, H. V. 1980. "Extraterrestrial cause for the Cretaceous-Tertiary extinction," *Science*, 208(4448):1095-1108.

[10] Jablonski, D. 1986. "Causes and Consequences of Mass Extinctions: A Comparative Approach," in Elliott, ed., *op. cit.*, pp. 183-229; Colbert, E. H., and Morales, M. 1991. *Evolution of the Vertebrates*, 4th ed., N.Y.: Wiley-Liss, p. 211.

[11] Colbert and Morales, 1991, *op. cit.*, p. 214.

[12] Raup, 1991, *op. cit.*; Eldredge, N. 1991. *The Miner's Canary*, Englewood Cliffs, N.J.: Prentice-Hall.

[13] Upchurch, G. R. 1989. "Terrestrial Environmental Changes and Extinction Patterns at the Cretaceous-Tertiary Boundary, North America," in *Mass Extinctions: Process and Evidence*, S. K. Donovan, ed., N.Y.: Columbia Univ. Press, p. 212; Colbert, and Morales, 1991, *op. cit.*, p. 214.

[14] Janis, 1993, in Gould, ed., *op. cit.*, pp. 173-174,; Stebbins, 1982, *op. cit.*, pp. 293-294.

[15] Colbert and Morales, 1991, *op. cit.*, p. 211.

[16] Clemens, 1986, in Elliott, ed., *op. cit.*, p. 65.

[17] Clemens, 1986, in Elliott, ed., *op. cit.*, p. 75, Appendix 1, pp. 79-81; Alvarez, 1983, *op. cit.*; Colbert and Morales, 1991, *op. cit.*, Fig. 12. 1, p. 151.

[18] Jerison, H. J. 1983. "The Evolution of the Mammalian Brain as an Information Processing System," in *Advances in the Study of Mammalian Behavior*, J. F. Eisenberg and D. G. Kleinman, eds. Special Publication No. 7, March 11, 1983, Shippensburg, PA: The American Society of Mammalogists, pp. 132-133.

[19] Andrews, P., and Stringer, C. 1993. "The Primates' Progress," in Gould, ed., *op. cit.*, pp. 222-223.

[20] Jerison, 1973, *op. cit.*, pp. 272-273.

[21] Novacek, M. 1996. *Dinosaurs of the Flaming Cliffs*, N.Y.: Anchor-Doubleday; Clemens, 1986, in Elliott, ed., *op. cit.*, p. 75.

[22] Janis, 1993, in Gould, ed., *op. cit.*, p. 184.

[23] Janke, A., *et al.* 1994. "The Marsupial Mitochondrial Genome and the Evolution of Placental Mammals," *Genetics*, May, 1994, 137:243-256; Simpson, G. G. 1945. "The principles of classification and a classification of mammals," *Bull. Am. Mus. Nat. Hist.*, 85:1-350.

[24] Hedges, S. Blair, *et al.* 1996. "Continental breakup and the ordinal diversification of birds and mammals," *Nature*, May 16, 1996, 381:226-229.

[25] Colbert and Morales, 1991, *op. cit.*, p. 379.

[26] Colbert and Morales, 1991, *op. cit.*, p. 297.

[27] Hedges, *et al.*, 1996, *Nature*, May 16, 1996, *op. cit.*, 381:228; Padian, K., and Clemens, W. A., 1985, in *Phanerozoic Diversity Patterns*, J. W. Valentine, ed., pp. 41-96, Princeton: Princeton Univ. Press.

[28] Novacek, M. 1996. Commentary on Hedges, quoted by Associated Press in *The New York Times*, May 16, 1996, p. 228.

[29] Colbert and Morales, 1991, *op. cit.*, p. 254.

[30] Janis, 1993, in Gould, ed., *op. cit.*, p. 174.

[31] Qumsiyeh, M. B. 1994. "Evolution of Number and Morphology of Mammalian Chromosomes," in *Jnl. of Heredity*, 85:459.

[32] Aboitiz F. 1993. "Further Comments on the Evolutionary Origin of the Mammalian Brain," *Medical Hypotheses*, 41:409-418.

[33] Kaas, J. H. 1989. "The Evolution of Complex Sensory Systems in Mammals," *Jnl. Exp. Biol.*, 146:170.

[34] Jerison, 1973, *op. cit.*, pp. 156-199.

[35] McNab, B. K., and Eisenberg, J. F. 1989. "Brain Size and its Relation to the Rate of Metabolism in Mammals," *The American Naturalist*, Feb., 1989, 132:2:166.

[36] Pagel, M. D., and Harvey, P. H. 1989. "The Taxon-Level Problem in the Evolution of Mammalian Brain Size: Facts and Artifacts," *The American Naturalist*, Sep., 132:3:355; Clutton-Brock, T. H., and Harvey, P. H. 1980. "Primates, Brains, and Ecology," *Jnl. Zool. (London)*, 190:309-324.

[37] Schwartz, Jeffrey. 1987. *The Red Ape*, London: Elm Tree Books.

[38] Pagel, M. D., and Harvey, P. H. 1988. "How Mammals Produce Large-Brained Offspring," *Evolution*, 42(5):948-957.

[39] Pagel, M. D., and Harvey, P. H. 1990. "Diversity in the Brain Sizes of Newborn Mammals, Allometry, Energetics, or Life History Tactics," *BioScience*, Feb., 1990, 40:2:121-122.

[40] Colbert and Morales, 1991, *op. cit.*, pp. 274-275; Andrews and Stringer, 1993, in Gould, ed., *op. cit.*, pp. 222-223.

[41] Colbert and Morales, 1991, *op. cit.*, pp. 276-277; Jerison, 1973, *op. cit.*, p. 255.

[42] Aboitiz F. 1993. *Medical Hypotheses*, 41:409-418.

[43] Finlay and Darlington, 1995, *op. cit.*, *Science*, 268:1578.

[44] Deacon, T. W. 1990. "Rethinking Mammalian Brain Evolution," *Amer. Zool*, 30:629-705, "Synopsis."

[45] Hedges *et al.*, 1996, *Nature*, May 16, 1996, *op. cit.*, 381:226-229.

[46] Clemens, 1986, in Elliott, ed., *op. cit.*

[47] Janis, 1993, in. Gould, ed., *op. cit.*, pp. 182-184.

[48] Colbert and Morales, 1991, *op. cit.*, pp. 330-333.

[49] Colbert and Morales, 1991, *op. cit.*, p. 214.

[50] Simpson, G. G. 1952. *The Meaning of Evolution*, New Haven: Yale Univ. Press, pp. 62-63.

[51] Szalay, F. S., and Delson, E. 1979. *Evolutionary History of the Primates*, N.Y.: Academic Press, pp. x-xii, 454-460; Andrews, P., and Stringer, C. 1989. *Human Evolution, an Illustrated Guide* Cambridge: Cambridge Univ. Press, pp. 14-17.

[52] Szalay and Delson, 1979, *op. cit.*, pp. xi-xii.

[53] Prothero, D. R. 1994. *The Eocene-Oligocene Transition*, N.Y.: Columbia Univ. Press, pp. 204-219; Szalay and Delson, 1979, *op. cit.*, p. 36, Fig. 11.

[54] Hooton, E. 1946. *Up From the Ape*, N.Y.: Macmillan; Stebbins, 1982, *op. cit.*, pp. 316-318.

[55] Andrews and Stringer, 1993, in Gould, ed., *op. cit.*, pp. 227-229.

[56] Andrews, and Stringer, 1993, in Gould, ed., *op. cit.*, p. 221.

[57] Andrews and Stringer, 1989, *op. cit.*, pp. 18-19.

[58] Walker, A. C., and Pickford, M. 1983. "New postcranial fossils of `Proconsul africanus' and `Proconsul nyanzae,'" in *New Interpretations of Ape and Human Ancestry*, R. L. Ciochon, and R. S. Corruccini, eds., N.Y.: Plenum Press, p. 325.

[59] Nisbet, E. G. 1991. *Living Earth*, *op. cit.*, p. 209.

[60] Szalay and Delson, 1979, *op. cit.*, pp. 470-485.

[61] Andrews and Stringer, 1989, *op. cit.*, p. Fig. 1, p. 8.

[62] Szalay and Delson, 1979, *op. cit.*, pp. 470-485.

[63] Andrews and Stringer, 1993, in. Gould, ed., *op. cit.*, pp. 223-224.

[64] Andrews and Stringer, 1989, *op. cit.*, pp. 20-21; Pickford, M. 1985. "Kenyapithecus: A Review of its Status Based on Newly Discovered Fossils from Kenya," in *Hominid Evolution: Past, Present, and Future*, P. V. Tobias, ed., N.Y.: Alan R. Liss, pp. 107-112.

[65] Andrews and Stringer, 1993, in Gould, ed., *op. cit.*, p. 229.

[66] McCrossin, M. L., and Benefit, B. R. 1993. "Recently recovered Kenyapithecus mandible and its implications for great ape and human origins," *Proc. Natl. Acad. Sci. U.S.A.*, Mar. 1993, 90:1962-1966; Ward, S., *et al.* 1999. "*Equatorius*: A New Hominoid Genus from the Middle Miocene of Kenya," *Science*, 8/27, 285:1382-1386.

[67] Miao, 1993, in Szalay, *et al*, eds., *op. cit.*, p. 72; Prothero, 1994, *op. cit.*, pp. 13-14; Janke *et al.*, 1994, *Genetics*, May, 1994, 137:243-256.

[68] Andrews and Stringer, 1993, in Gould, ed., *op. cit.*, p. 233.

[69] *Ibid.*

[70] Andrews and Stringer, 1989, *op. cit.*, pp. 22-23.

[71] Andrews and Stringer, 1989, *op. cit.*, p. 22.

[72] Martin, R. D. 1990. *Primate origins and Evolution, a Phylogenetic Reconstruction*, Princeton, N.J.: Princeton Univ. Press, p. 77.

[73] Andrews and Stringer, 1989, *op. cit.*, pp. 24-25.

[74] Andrews and Stringer, 1989, *op. cit.*, pp. 26-27.

[75] Szalay and Delson, 1979, *op. cit.*, p. 502 (also see Figures 252, 253, 254, pp. 499-501, on R. punjabicus and R. wickeri); Simons, E. L. 1976. "The nature of the transition in the dental mechanism from pongids to hominids," *Jnl. Human Evol.*, 5:500-528; Andrews, P. 1976. "Taxonomy and Relationship of Fossil Apes," *Abstract and Manuscript, VI Intern. Primatological Congress*, Cambridge: Abstracts, p. 80.

[76] Pilbeam, D., *et al.* 1977. "New hominoid primates from the Siwaliks of Pakistan and their bearing on hominoid evolution," *Nature*, 270:689-695; Walker, A. C., and Andrews, P. 1973. "Reconstruction of the dental arcades of `Ramapithecus wickeri,' *Nature*, 244:313-314; Szalay and Delson, 1979, *op. cit.*, pp. 500-502.

[77] Andrews and Stringer, 1993, in Gould, ed., *op. cit.*, p. 221.

[78] Hsu, C-h, Han, K.-x and Wang, L.-h. 1974. "Discovery of 'Gigantopithecus' teeth and associated fauna in western Hopei," *Vert. palasiat.*, 12:293-309.

[79] Szalay and Delson, 1979, *op. cit.*, pp. 494-498; Wood, B. A., and Turner, A. 1995. "Out of Africa and into Asia," *Nature*, 11/16/95, 378:239-240.

[80] Szalay and Delson, 1979, *op. cit.*, pp. 494-498.

[81] See J. Schwartz, 1987, 1993, on unique Sivapithecus, Orang-utan relationship with hominid clade, pp. 176-177, 191-194. Premaxilla-Maxilla, nasal region, as contrasted with the African apes. Schwartz, 1987, *op. cit.*; Schwartz, Jeffrey. 1993. *What the Bones Tell Us*, N.Y.: Henry Holt.

[82] Pickford, 1985, in Tobias, ed., *op. cit.*, p. 110.

[83] Andrews, P., and Pilbeam, D. 1996. "The Nature of the Evidence," *Nature*, Jan. 11, 379:123-124; Moya-Sola, S., and Koehler, M. 1993. *Nature*, 365:543-545; Moya-Sola, S. 1995, *Jnl Hum. Evol.*, 29:101-139; Moya-Sola, S., and Koehler, M. 1996. *Nature*, Jan. 11, 379:156-159.

[84] Andrews and Stringer, 1993, in Gould, ed., *op. cit.*, p. 233.

[85] Tobias, P. V. 1994. "The Evolution of the Early Hominids," in T. Ingold, ed., *Companion Encyclopedia of Anthropology*, London: Routledge, p. 53.

9

The Outlanders

Fitness and the Earth Environment

Lawrence J. Henderson, 1878-1942, as a young professor of biochemistry at Harvard, wrote these words in 1912:

> From the materialistic and the energetic standpoint alike, carbon, hydrogen, and oxygen, each by itself, and all taken together, possess unique and preeminent chemical fitness for the organic mechanism. They alone are best fitted to form it and to set it in motion; and their stable compounds, water and carbonic acid, which make up the changeless environment, protect it and renew it, forever drawing fresh energy from the sunshine.[1]
>
> ...Life must be highly complex in structure and function; that the conditions of the environment must be regulated, and that there must be very exact regulations of conditions, both structural and functional within the organism...while life is active, there must be exchange of both matter and energy with the environment. Complexity, regulation, and food are essential to life as we know it, and in truth we cannot otherwise conceive of life....[T]hese postulates are quite as true of the world of our senses as are the fundamental laws of matter and energy, space and time.[2]
>
> ...The properties of matter and the course of cosmic evolution are now seen to be intimately related to the structure of the living being and to its activities; they become, therefore, far more important in biology than has been previously suspected.[3]

The conditions for the evolution of life on Earth in its earliest prokaryote forms did lead over subsequent billions of years of planetary evolution to the development of complex and energetically stable organic metabolisms. The fabrication of ever larger and more complex eukaryote cells and their varied morphological and physiological adaptations for survival in the Earthly environs, constitutes the circle of argumentation with regard to the fitness of our unique and primeval biochemical setting. How chemically and energetically unique the role of the Sun is, in the context of other sidereal environments, is still unknown to us.

Time, Stability, Change

The origin of life on this planet is augured by the cataclysmic thermal processes that precipitated the wandering chemical atoms into materialistic tangibility within the Earth's gravitational embrace. Hundreds of millions of years went by as the Earth and its seething atmospheric coating literally exploded with underground upheavals of magmas, gases, volcanic eruptions, and the hurtling explosiveness of meteorites rupturing and erupting its boiling surfaces.

The energies were there externally to bring together the available chemical compounds. Higher energy coacervates were formed out of strings of molecules interacting in the waters with each other and adjoining metallic deposits. Eventually the Earth cooled, but not that much, as a growing Sun and the heat it poured out into our opaque atmosphere maintained a steady infusion of thermal stability. And the water bathed our planet with life.

The conceptual theme of the billions of years that followed—complex molecules enveloped within a single-celled boundary, exchange energies with the available external world—was homeostasis. Equilibrium was achieved in which the most efficient forms of "counterentropic" metabolic processes dominated in their reproductive and thus selective efficiency. The key to eukaryote complexity and largeness of structural and thus energetic efficiency must lie in the pulsating changes in the Earthly environment amid the basic stability and fitness of those universal elements retained gravitationally within its boundaries.

Efficiency as emblematic with growth argues for plenitude—the test of stability affording variability within the environment. This variability of external circumstance could not have been a mere passing occasion. It had to have happened often enough with deleterious selective consequences for the majority of life forms. The paradigmatic eukaryote cell mustered the chance of good fortune and those available symbiotic molecular elements to surmount the challenge. What may have been part of an earlier random assemblage of variable, if homeostatic prokaryote forms, over time and change, established itself as a viable fixture within the inevitabilities of a constantly changing environment. The eukaryote cell was one step up on the metabolic energy reserves ladder to maintain itself and proliferate within those basic boundaries of fitness earlier established for life possibilities on Earth.

So, too, archaebacteria, perhaps at one time co-sponsors of the original prokaryote single-celled experiment in the counterentropic sweepstakes, eventually established themselves in a simpler, more basic and probably in the long-term more secure adaptive niche, anaerobic, living off of inorganic food substances, usually deep in the interior of the earth, sometimes under enormous temperature gradients. In the competition for food and security, they were forced, or chose, to opt for stability and longevity, basically unchanging, themselves simple in molecular structure and insured against mutational chance taking, probably the ultimate consequences of unfailing failure.

Time and the gentlest rhythms of planetary change were needed to precipitate eukaryote and then animal life from its hidden, slow experiments in fabrication, fallibility, and redesign, to outlast time and change. Finally, it was nested within relatively certain, undefined, yet bounded sureties of existence, *e.g.*, reproduction and generational survival.

It is therefore not surprising that the molecular time clock of Schopf and others argues for a two-billion-year+ heritage for the eukaryote cell, even while it reveals its tangible existence only little more than one billion years ago.[4] The same is true for the eukaryote photosynthesizing plant cell which provided seemingly explosive amounts of organic nutrients and energies through the aegis of plastids and chlorophyll released in chemical interaction with the Sun.

The stromatolites, prokaryote eubacteria, represent the earliest metabolic use of sunlight. They date back to the 4.1by boundaries of a still tentatively stabilizing earth surface. Yet, for all the billions of years of stromatolite flourishing there was no sign of the massive release of molecular oxygen that the later eukaryote plant cell would make available to the scavenging heterotrophs. Time for this to happen was needed amidst experimentally stimulating environmental change. Change and time are the key factors for the ultimate complexities that make up life. But always these processes took place within the context of the broader fitness rules that had been laid down for the basic fabrication of life on Earth.

Evolutionary Theory: Knowns and Unknowns

In April 1996 Christopher Beard of the Carnegie Museum of Natural History, Pittsburgh, reported on his continuing research into primate origins in China: fossilized jaw and teeth of *Eosimias centennicus*, discovered in May 1995 along the banks of the Yellow River in Shanxi Province. Weighing, 3.5 oz., *Eosimias* had many monkey-like traits, deep chin and dagger-like canine teeth, but small-sized, blunt molars suggesting a fruit and insect diet. However, Beard suggested that this primate, at c.55mya, (late Paleocene-early Eocene), still resembled a rodent-like lemur more than a modern monkey.[5]

The discovery of primates seemingly different from other forms yet discovered, both ancient and extinct as well as early modern forms, suggests the depth of evolutionary levels from which this radiation of human placental mammal ancestors derives.[6]

Yoder has also reported on the fact, heretofore unrecorded, of prosimian, strepsirhine lemurs originating in Africa at an even earlier Paleocene level, c.62mya. Heretofore the prosimians were thought to have radiated to Africa from Northern Hemisphere origins. In her phrase, "...early primate evolution was characterized by rapid divergence and diversification that nearly simultaneously (in geological terms) produced both the fossil and the living lineages, sometime before the late Paleocene."[7]

When we include the molecular genetic research of Hedges and Janke, which places the divergence of the placental mammals and their incipient modern families well back into the Cretaceous, prior to the total K/T extinctions of the dinosaurs and the disappearance of many marsupial lines, we realize that what we know today about evolutionary origins and separations leads almost unfailingly ever back in time.[8] This is true of the origin of eukaryote metazoan animals, probably true also of the origin of the phylum Chordata and the vertebrates, and as recently argued by Wray *et. al.*, the amphibian invasions of the land, the discovery of the earliest reptiles.[9] It underlines the fragility of datings, especially those based on the existing paleontological record, what we have up to now dug up from the ground. Molecular analysis although still fraught with ever newly discovered and modifying variables—for example, the real possibility that rate changes over time in mitochondrial DNA, ribosomal RNA, and in other parts of the genome—can skew interpretation, constitutes a sobering check on both phylogenetic as well as chronological sureties.

The cytogenetic evidence seems to indicate that the modern genetic and chromosomal structure of animals has been in place for at least 500 million years. This means that the number of chromosomes and genes has remained stable, the kind of rapid phenotypic impact of mutations on structure and activity to be found in bacteria was no longer possible in metazoa. The buffering against rapid genetic change in animal forms by the preponderance of non-coding genes within the chromosomes has acted to slow down mutational changes that have an impact on the adaptive behavior of animals. In addition, the great heterogeneity in the number of chromosomes within a variety of animal lines argues against seeing, at least in contemporary forms, a pattern in which supposedly more recent animal lines have more chromosomes and genes than supposedly atavistic forms that have not changed over many hundreds of millions of years.

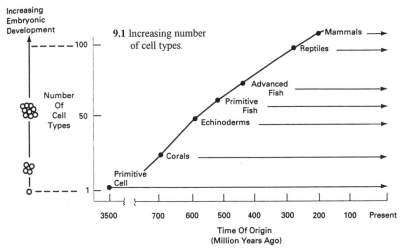

9.1 Increasing number of cell types.

Genetic variability is indeed the stuff of evolutionary change. The question then is how do we understand the process of change in the lines of animals of greatest interest to us, namely the placental mammals, the primates, and indeed the particular evolutionary forms that led to *Homo*? What probably strikes the mind with ever greater force as we observe the constant readjustment in scientifically established chronological patterns of evolutionary origins and diversification, ever toward more ancient derivations, is the contrast between observable fact and those hidden evolutionary processes yet waiting to be discovered, *i.e.*, covert evolution.

The theory of punctuated equilibrium, proposed by Eldredge and Gould,[10] inspired earlier by Richard Goldschmidt's "hopeful monsters," attempts to account for the seeming contrast between gradual evolutionary processes of speciation, even stasis within species, then the seemingly explosive creation of higher taxonomic categories.[11] Punctuationists argue that the genes within any one species are so highly integrated that small changes cannot occur without the entire genome being subject to a higher order overhaul.[12]

This perspective has been proposed to contrast with more traditional neo-Darwinian principles, for example, as enunciated by Julian Huxley, Ernst Mayr, Bernhard Rensch and others, several decades ago, which combined modern genetic theory with the basic Darwinian presumption of small, regular changes in the variability of lines of animals.[13] These small changes were constantly subject to the sifting processes involved in subsequent adaptation to the external environment, itself suffused with variable changes, and thence processed by natural selection, as Raup and Sepkoski have expressed it, bad or good luck, as much as bad or good genes.[14]

In an ordinary evolutionary situation, it is persuasive that the kinds of macro-chromosomal reconstructions that can theoretically take place during meiosis, the diploid form of the chromosome being reduced to the haploid pattern, else gametic reproduction and mitosis, in which major chromosomal rearrangements become possible as genes are shunted up and down the chromosome, can rarely conclude with the production of a revolutionary departure from the adaptive status quo, that which is shunted into selective acceptance by the external environment.

Indeed most of animal life, major phyla such as Porifera, sponges; *Cnidaria*, corals and jellyfish; nematoda, round worms; mollusks, snails, clams; echinoderms, starfish, sea urchins; even ancient Hemichordata, acorn worms; and chordates, lancelets, have remained unchanged adaptively and morphologically for hundreds of millions of years. Nestled in the security of their working adaptive niche, mutations that could alter the security of this adaptive pattern have been ruthlessly suppressed by a variety of genetic strategies selectively established within the respective chromosomal structure. As a result, these forms have been subject to successive and major extinction events when the security of their adaptive niche has been threatened by external events. They had heretofore secured their adaptive niche, genetic variability had been selectively discouraged over the eons, they had surrendered their reservoir of genetic, morphological, and behavior plasticity for efficiency within the niche.

On the other hand, the vertebrates have long taken an evolutionary road premised on the selective reality of ecological and environmental variability, having made their living out of an adaptive fitness predicated on modest external changes, and in turn constant genetic change and much intraspecific variability to maintain the possibility for selective "good luck," even in the face of major external catastrophes.

What we are not observing as we dig deeply into the geological record of physical as well as organic evolution is the full range of variability that exists at any one slice of time within any clade. Much of this variability cannot be observed in the limited available fossilized exemplifications of these ancient forms. Taxonomic categories are an imposed classificatory device helping to organize the concreteness of what we observe at any one time. Too often we reify these categories and miss the relevant concreteness of unknowability in the fossil exemplars.

Ernst Mayr has long emphasized the evolutionary importance of peripheral outlier populations for the future fortunes of a line:

> Evolution progresses rather slowly in large, populous species, while most rapid evolutionary changes occur in small, peripherally isolated founder populations.15

The more populous a species is, the more epistatic interactions occur and the longer it
will take for a new mutation or recombination to spread through the entire species and there-
for the slower evolution will proceed. A founder population, with less concealed variation
because of having fewer individuals, can more readily shift to another genotype, or to use
another metaphor, to another adaptive peak.16
    The genetic reorganization of peripherally isolated populations permits evolutionary
changes that are many times more rapid than the changes within populations that are part of
a continuous system. Here, then, is a mechanism that would permit the rapid emergence of
macroevolutionary novelties without any conflict with the observed facts of genetics.17

Fossils should tell us as much about what we do not know as what we think we do
know. What we need looking over our interpretive shoulders is an evolutionary historian
constantly at work critiquing our conclusions on the basis of what we have learned since
the setting down of earlier erroneous evolutionary conclusions. In a sense, all sciences
require a metatheoretical chronicle of the patterns of our evaluative and intellectualized
errors. Such a principle of scientific accounting ought always to allow us here to factor
in hidden, unobservable sets of taxonomic categories and phylogenetic relationships—in
a sense, a structure of ongoing ignorance, yet theoretically principled. It could constitute
a separate division of our bio-physical knowledge, yet still be an integral part of the
study of the vast unknowability of the totality of actors on the evolutionary scene.

The Meaning of Innovation
The evolutionary puzzle that needs to be addressed is the relationship between an
apparent adaptive stasis with the environment and then the seemingly momentary explosion of evolutionary "progress," punctuated equilibrium, that radiates new forms into
dominance, others into oblivion. What are the inner dynamics, what is happening both
before our retrospective vision and covertly, out of observational range?
    A good example is the seeming appearance out of nowhere of the mammals in the
late Triassic, some 225mya, literally under the noses of the cynodont and archosaur.
Partially this is a taxonomic issue, one of categorization, for it is clear, as we have explained above, that the cynodont line was producing a number of close approximations
to the defined mammalian taxon, and as is usual with these evolutionary transitions, almost simultaneously in a synchronous pattern of replacement. Most probably the mammals were not transformed momentarily from the existing cynodont lines.
    A more traditional explanation was demonstrated with regard to the recent discov-
eries of *Acanthostega*, a transitional osteolepiform/amphibian that pushed this evolutionary transition back another several million years. Recent purported discoveries of
early reptiles, only several tens of millions of years after the beginning of the amphibian
radiation, also requires that we argue for a wider variability in what is defined as an amphibian, even at its very earliest taxonomic uncovering.
    The prototype mammal line, as we will probably discover eventually, will be seen
not as a direct descendant of mid- to late-Triassic cynodonts, but probably from an outlier line of cynodonts that survived the macro-extinctions of the terminal Permian,
c.250mya. The morphological innovations that saved the cynodonts from the fate of the
general therapsid extinction was probably a measure of internal homeothermy, perhaps a
more developed auditory/olfactory sensory system that allowed it to adapt to a needed
nocturnal feeding system. This reorganization of the brain/sensory system became pre-

adaptive for competitive life alongside the more ectothermic and visual archo-
saur/dinosaur line that would dominate the thermally benign Triassic/Jurassic environment.

The radiation of a wide variety of cynodonts probably included a number of less-
adapted groups that encompassed what in the future would become the salvation of the
declining synapsid-therapsid-cynodont line. The radiant line of future mammals was
there, working out its adaptive profile, under external pressures, climatic as well as those
imposed by momentarily better-adapted cynodonts and archosaurs. The post-Permian
protomammalian cynodonts were finding their ever more specialized niches, which
seems to have required an extreme reduction in size along with powerful metabolic
drives to obtain the necessary energy resources. These adaptive and selective pressures
pushed them away from a diurnal pattern of living. It also intensified their furry warm-
bloodedness, omnivorous tooth/feeding patterns, gradually reshaping into functionality a
very different sort of "reptile" brain/sensory system, all to underlay and drive the adaptive machinery.

The above theoretical hypothesis concerning the origin of the mammals under the
nose of a collapsing therapsid/cynodont line is predicated on our not discovering additional placental newcomers on the waters edge alongside more traditional amphibians
and reptiles, 375-360mya.

Within the major portion of vertebrate history observable to us from the evolutionary record, no "pure" or monophyletic lines of vertebrates exist. Each species (our own
definition of evolutionary consanguinity) constitutes a mosaic of variability.[18] The adaptive niche may seem to require a delimited range of behaviors and aptitudes. However,
the broad fitness encompassed in the vertebrate body plan requires a versatility of behavioral and morphological response that needs to be reflected in all lines. There does
exist from the dawn of eukaryote sexual reproduction the selective imprint for genetic
variability as well as in its phenotypic, day-to-day embodiments. In a sense the "selfish
gene" operates, because it has become part of the selective legacy, and on the sub-
species and racial levels as well, of the particular line of animals.

The reason "why" of rapid evolutionary "progress," the supposed lifting of evolutionary change above the species and generic taxonomic categories, lies in the preceding
history of the involved line. It is rare that a line of mollusks or echinoderms will suddenly spurt forward in a frenzy of genetic change, after having been somnolent, in terms
of morphology and thus its adaptive patterns, for over hundreds of millions of years.

The mammals that seemed to have spurted ahead at the end of the Triassic, or
across the Tertiary, at the K/T boundary, were there before, and in some force. If they
were hidden, it was a matter of relative numbers, and probably because of their diminutive size, since small animals tend to leave fewer discoverable fossils. It is inconceivable
that the crossopterygian lungfish, the mammal-like cynodonts, the Cretaceous evolving
marsupials, and the placental mammals were not in vigorous competitive dynamic with
each other over a long time line, the latter under the probably indifferent dinosaurian
canopy and its ecological boundary lines.

It is hardly conceivable that we would have by now discovered masses of such
originating fossils in this latter time frame, some 110-65mya. The enormous existing
variability, the dynamic, selective honing of mammalian forms raises natural skepticism

of ever finding these exemplars. A few prospered, many became extinct, and some hung on desperately at the fringes of this diminutive but admittedly rich and extensive nocturnal, sometimes diurnal environmental/ecological niche.

The evidence as we go forward to understand human evolution, as in the placental form of gestation, is that all vertebrate lines carry with them a rich genetic memory of ancient phenotypic possibilities. Along with the sharks and rays, someday in the fossil record a hint of viviparity in some obscure reptilian line will probably be discovered. Within the basic placental body plan, as laid down in the early Cretaceous, some 130-110mya, this core mosaicism was expressing itself in an extreme of micro-variability as the placentals, along with marsupials and multituberculates, mined every possible micro-niche. The molecular research indicates separations of some of the basic placental lines, rodents, primates, artiodactyls, insectivores, somewhere between 115-100mya. Does this mean that had we been able to observe these little creatures in the earliest phase of this diversification it would have been easy to discern the phenotypic morphological/behavioral correlates of this genetic fragmentation? It is doubtful. The fact that certain carnivore/ungulate ancestors (mesonychids and arctocyonids) had their evolutionary "feet" in both worlds in the late Cretaceous or early Paleocene argues for this hypothesis of micro-variability.

The explosion of mammal diversification and seeming taxonomic restructuring in the early Cenozoic was surely brought about by the demise of the dinosaurs and opening up of their diverse and mainline ecological niches. The preconditions for this later explosion in numbers, size, and variability were presumably established much earlier in those covert evolutionary movements that do not yet meet the paleontological eye.

Gregory and de Beer early noted that in evolutionary processes, rate gene developmental changes (heterochrony) more often than not secure the survival of a threatened animal type. It has resulted in behavioral adaptive shifts, often covert, by moving the particular phenotype out of the ongoing selective crucible, often as an adult behaving and looking like a juvenile. And because this genetic tradition of variability has given a new lease on life to many different phenotypes it has been a mainstay dimension of evolutionary dynamics for hundreds of millions of years.[19]

Larval echinoderms hint at an incipient notochord before they bury their roots into the sea bottom. Indications are that developmental retention of the larval state into the mature animal could have been a key to the creation of the chordates.[20] The earliest amphibians hint at the paedomorphic retention of juvenile crossopterygian physical features, giving them the plasticity to adapt to a mixed water and wetland environment.

So, too, the diminutive modeling of the mammals, both in their first mouse-like realization in the late Triassic, early Jurassic, c.225-200mya, and then again in the late Cretaceous, could have involved sequences of developmental gene mutations which dredged up a heritage of such successful options from their evolutionary history. Summoning the genetic resources involved in producing highly variable adaptive patterns, both structural and behavioral, was made possible by a hundreds-of-millions-of-years-old heritage that is largely unknown to us today. The subjects of this fortuitous reservoir of variability were tiny, furtive, diverse in behavior and location, and small in number. The subsequent explosion in the Paleocene became the phenotypic expression of an adaptively repressed genetic heritage of evolutionary change, heretofore under overt

selective restraint. The distinction to be made here lies in the fact that new external ecological opportunities suddenly presented themselves for the existing evolutionary potential to express itself, now in expanding demographics and widening geographic expression. Not only could the mammals now grow larger; they could take their micro-
variability of phenotypic potential into an exploding diversity of ecological opportunity.

Land: The Inevitable Fitness of the Brain

Stages: 1. The sensory line system of the fish. 2. The primary mammalian 4X (average reptile) growth of the brain as a nocturnal auditory/olfactory sensory machine supporting a demanding metabolism amidst a circumscribed adaptive ecology, c.200mya. 3.
The second mammalian 4-5X expansion of the brain starting at end Cretaceous (75-
65mya) in competition with evolving placental mammals as they begin to displace
waning dinosaurs. 4. The defensive brain of the primates—back to the trees. Highly visual anthropoids *versus* nocturnal prosimians, the visual system as a key element in the
triangulation of the three distance sensory (olfactory, auditory, visual) systems by the
brain. Long distance sensors as a defensive aid in supporting variability of ecological
adaptation and behavior.

1. The lateral line system in fish is the major sensory information-gathering system
that detects vibrations in the water surrounding the body of the fish. It is adaptive because of the higher density of water, as compared with air. Because the acoustic imped-
ance of water and the body of the fish are low, sound can travel from water through the
body of the fish as if the fish were transparent. Hair cells located inside the otic capsule,
inner ear, of the fish pick up the vibrations. These vibrations are recognized in the brain
of the fish and reflected outward to the entire organism as reflexive behavior.

Land animals, because of the thinness of air as a transmitter of sound, reflect rather
than transmit the sound to the animal's body. Sensory organs, now highly articulated are
needed to pick up sound messages. A liquid-filled perilymphatic system in the inner ear
substitutes for an external transmission medium, and the hyomandibula, a strut between
the inner ear and the side of the skull, called the stapes, and then the middle ear, act as
transmission systems for sound. The focus of sound reception to the head area is more
directly involved in the brain in land animals. This was an important development in
preparing the way for the triangulation of information processing of the three major information sources in the tetrapod brain.[21]

The greater importance of vision in the more illuminated environment of land life,
the sensitization of smell as distinct from the frontal tactile tendrils above the snout
which also provided for olfactory information for the fish, were important in stimulating
new brain structures, if yet within basic vertebrate size and design.

2. The linkage in the early mammals of a new pattern of internal heat regulation,
responsive to the drift of continents in Gondwana during the end Permian climatic crisis,
was added to a required sensory shift brought on by competition exemplified in dynamic
reptile trends during the successor Triassic. These comprised the critical selective elements leading to the "stage one" explosion in brain growth. The final extinction of the
synapsid-therapsid-cynodont line brought forth a hidden group of survivors, seeming
outlanders, honed by the 40-50my of competition with regnant cynodont forms as well

as the dominating archosaur line, the latter having a strong visual brain, animals violently mobile and predatory.

The first stage mammalian brain was a sensory survival machine. It served to organize the higher metabolic requirements with the newer sensory necessities of life in the dark, often in trees or burrows, opting for an insectivorous or omnivorous feeding regimen. The price was diminution in size, but always the focus was on a rich food ecology, a domain to which the larger reptiles were largely indifferent.

3. The therian mammalian solution to the challenges of reproductive survival brought to the eutherian placentals an additional bonus in brain and behavior. It allowed for an automatic structural means by which brain growth was facilitated within the mother's womb. The larval metatherian marsupials crawling out of the womb into their mother's pouch were relatively fixed in their brain development to the basic physical survival needs of an earlier ontogenetic stage in development. The latters' need for early developmental specialization in the use of their forelimbs to climb from the birth canal to the pouch subsequently limited the adaptive options of this line in terms of general morphological/behavioral development and diversification.

The loss in the modern placentals of the epipubic bones, which act as struts to support the pouch in the marsupials, gave the placental foetus more room to develop, probably allowing for the birth of a larger neonate, and indeed provided the growth ingredients, including a higher and protective metabolic rate, for the development of a bigger brain.

Growth of this brain by an additional 4-5X to its existing on-average size during the Paleocene and Eocene, c.67-35mya, and thence into the future, reflects the increasing competitive conditions attending the expansion of the placentals into all the existing ecologies on land, sea, and in the air. During the early Cenozoic, there is only a narrow spread of brain size between ungulates and carnivores. "Both average and maximum brain size increases through time in both groups, with carnivores being generally smarter."[22] The probability is that this increase in brain size and competitive potency of the mammals, especially the revolutionary structures and behaviors provided in placental reproductive strategies, may have had as much to do with the decline of the dinosaurs during the late Cretaceous, 75-65mya, as did the highly vaunted and hypothetical meteorite that may have caused the iridium deposits around the world. Thence the speculated ensuing blackout of the Sun, followed by a presumed photosynthetic starvation, finally, dinosaurian extinction.

4. Janis considers the placentals to have been predominantly ground living, given their patterns of burial of feces.[23] The fact that numerous early prosimian primate stocks became secondarily nocturnal argues for the oncoming wave of competition from rodents, lagomorphs, insectivores, edentates, not to speak of carnivorous creodonts. All were equipped with a good mammalian brain and the expansive reproductive and energetic food supplying adaptations that allowed them to expand over the Paleocene and Eocene landscapes, c.65-35mya. The return to the waters of a number of carnivorous, seals, walruses, and herbivorous types, *e.g.*, whales, further exemplifies the level of infra-class competition among the mammals.

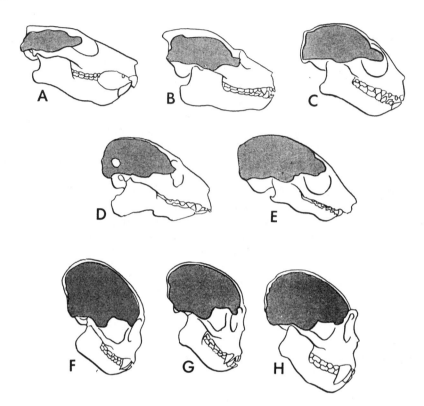

9.2 Diversity of skull shape and brain size in Primates. *A. Plesiadapis*, a plesiadapid (after Szalay and Delson, 1979). *B. Adapis*, an adapid (after Szalay and Delson, 1979). *C. Tetonius*, an omoyiid (after Szalay and Delson, 1979). *D. Indri*, a prosimian. *E. Microcebus*, a prosimian. *F. Cebus*, a ceboid. *G. Cercopithecus*, a cercopithecoid. *H. Hylobates*, a hominoid.

The primate adaptive route was behavioral non-specialization, a pathway having classic mammalian antecedents, defensive, alert, omnivorous. The various routes taken by the catarrhine branch merely exemplify the adaptive breadth provided by life in the trees as well as on the ground, adaptability to a wide range of behavioral profiles, as well as foods, a specialization of the unspecialized, in which a larger brain primed for alert anonymity became the key to survival. Consider the fact that the anthropoids of Africa during the Miocene, c.25-5mya, the survivors of the Oligocene climatic shift, c.30mya, had been able to proliferate and stabilize their adaptive zone. They were now growing in size and dominance. It is a wonder that by the end of the Miocene, some 10-5mya the apes were ceding their ecology throughout the world to an oncoming wave of Old World monkeys, and then hominids, c.6-2mya.

Considering that chimpanzees often attack and eat ground-dwelling cercopithecine baboons, it is doubtful that monkeys competed strongly with the ground-dwelling apes. More probably, as with the baboon, they moved into a vacated ecological niche. The oncoming hominids were certainly constrained in their diet to nuts, roots, fruit, as well as animal sustenance, as exemplified in their tooth structure. Yet they came onto the scene.

The modern African apes, two chimpanzee species and one gorilla, seem to have only one possible morphological antecedent in the fossil Miocene apes. Hominids, in all likelihood Australopithecines, give notice of their presence via dental evidence some 6mya, at the terminal Miocene. Where did they come from, to whom are they related? What is the evolutionary significance of these late-Miocene primate transitions?

Endnotes, Chapter 9

[1] Henderson, Lawrence J. 1913. *The Fitness of the Environment*, N.Y.: Macmillan, p. 248 Boston: Beacon Press, 1958.

[2] Henderson, 1913, *op. cit.*, pp. 33-34.

[3] Henderson, 1913, *op. cit.*, p. 312.

[4] Brock, J. J., *et al.* 1999. "Archaean Molecular Fossils and the Early Rise of Eukaryotes," *Science*, 8/13/99, 285:1033-1036; Schopf, J. W. 1999. *Cradle of Life*, Princeton: Princeton Univ. Press.

[5] Beard, Christopher. 1996. "Fossil May Fill a Gap in Early Primate Evolution," *The New York Times*, 4/9/96 (*Reuters*, 4/8/96).

[6] Beard, K. C., *et al.* 1994. "A Diverse New Primate Fauna from Middle Eocene Fissure-fillings in southeastern China," *Nature* (London), 368:604-609.

[7] Yoder, A. D., *et al.* 1996. "Ancient single origin for Malagasy primates," *Proc. Natl. Acad. Sci. U.S.A.*, (May) l93:5122-5126.

[8] Hedges, S. Blair, *et al.* 1996. "Continental breakup and the ordinal diversification of birds and mammals," *Nature*, May 16, 1996, 381:226-229; Janke, A., *et al.* 1994. "The Marsupial Mitochondrial Genome and the Evolution of Placental Mammals," *Genetics*, May, 1994, 137:243-256.

[9] Wray, G. A., *et al.* 1996. "Molecular Evidence for Deep Precambrian Divergences among Metazoan Phyla," *Science*, Oct. 25, pp. 568-573.

[10] Gould, S. J., and Eldredge, S. 1977. "Punctuated Equilibria: tempo and mode of evolution reconsidered," *Paleobiology*, 3:115-151.

[11] McKinney, M. L. 1993. *Evolution of Life*, Englewood Cliffs, N.J.: Prentice Hall, pp. 247-249.

[12] *Ibid.*

[13] Huxley, J. 1943. *Evolution: The Modern Synthesis*, N.Y.: Harper; Rensch, B. 1959. *Evolution Above the Species Level*, N.Y.: Columbia Univ. Press; Wright, S. 1963. "Adaptation and Selection," in *Genetics, Paleontology, and Evolution*, G. L. Jepson, G. G. Simpson, E. Mayr, E., eds., N.Y.: Atheneum, pp. 365-391.

[14] Raup, D. 1991. *Extinction: Bad Genes or Bad Luck?*, N.Y.: Norton.

[15] Mayr, E. 1997. *This Is Biology, The Science of the Living World*, Cambridge. Mass: The Belknap Press-Harvard Univ. Press, p. 172; also Mayr. E. 1963. *Animal Species and Evolution* Cambridge, Mass: The Belknap Press of Harvard Univ. Press.

[16] Mayr, 1997, *op. cit.*, p.173.

[17] Mayr, 1997, *op. cit.*, p. 195; Mayr, E. 1954. "Change of genetic environment and evolution," in *Evolution as a Process*, J. Huxley, A. C. Hardy, E. B. Ford, eds., London: Allen and Unwin, pp. 206-207.

[18] McKinney, 1993, *op. cit.*, pp. 38-43, 247-248.

[19] Gregory, W. K. 1937. "Supra-specific Variation in Nature and in Classification: A Few Examples from Mammalian Paleontology," *American Naturalist*, 71:268-276; de Beer, G. 1958. *Embryos and Ancestors*, London: Oxford Univ. Press, 3rd revised edition.

[20] Garstang, W. 1928. "The Origin and Evolution of Larval Forms," *Report of the British Association for the Advancement of Science for 1928*, p.77.

[21] Radinsky, Leonard. 1987. *The Evolution of Vertebrate Design*, Chicago: The Univ. of Chicago Press, pp. 83-85.

---

[22] McKinney, 1993, *op. cit.*, p. 274, Fig. 4-32; see also McNamara, K. 1990. *Evolutionary Trends*, Tucson, AR: Univ. of Arizona Press, p. 39.

[23] Janis, Christine. "Victors by Default," in *Life*, S. J. Gould, ed., N.Y.: W. W. Norton, p. 176.

10

Human Ancestors

- 1 -
Molecular Mystifications: Disappearing Apes

Disappearing Apes

Lurking behind the controversies regarding the nature of the first hominids are the Australopithecines. Were they one variable species, or several? Did their evolution constitute a line separate from *Homo*, or, as with the formerly majority view, were they antecedents on the direct phylogenetic pathway leading to modern humans? Beyond these problems always intruded a more shadowy question. Where did the hominids, including "Lucy," come from?

A gap in evolutionary time existed between the last disappearing African fossil apes and the first hominids and modern apes, surely their African descendants. The time lapse is significant. As we have chronicled earlier, it is estimated that some 12-7my of protohominid African evolution was unaccounted for in the fossil record, Andrews and Stringer place this gap at between 12-5mya.[1]

At the time that these issues were being thrashed out, in the 1970s, it was thought that the earliest hominids were somewhere between 2-3 million years old. The first true human, *Homo habilis,* was dated at less than 2mya. Today with the proliferating *Australopithecus* clade, new and older exemplars, beyond *Australopithecus afarensis* (still a controversial entity) were being uncovered. As summarized by Tobias and Itzkoff, the teeth and bones of a non-pongid primate, seemingly *Australopithecus* or *Homo,* are turning up in a variety of places in Africa, and are being dated back to at least 6mya.[2]

In the 1970s, however, it seemed that the connection between the modern hominids and the Miocene primates in Africa some 14mya may have been bridged. Elwyn Simons had uncovered a jaw of *Ramapithecus* when reconstructed showed a parabolic tooth arc similar to humans and quite different both from contemporary and fossil apes, whose teeth were lined up parallel inside the jaw. In addition, these teeth, especially the molars, were thickly enameled, again like the Australopithecines and humans, and similar to the orangutans, but different from the thinly-enameled teeth of the chimpanzees and gorilla.

Szalay and Delson in their 1979 opus on the evolution of the primates still referred to the Ramapithecines as hominids, as had David Pilbeam, a student and close associate of Simons, in an earlier 1972 book. However, by 1979, Pilbeam had studied new finds from Pakistan, Turkey, and Hungary, labeled *Ramapithecus wickerii*. These examples revealed a tooth structure within the jaw that was very similar to that of the traditional apes, plus postcranial bones that were definitely simian.[3] Simons may have erred in his reconstruction.[4] In fact Szalay and Delson included a concession in their 1979 book that this new reevaluation of *Ramapithecus* was under way, and that it was dissolving all claims that *Ramapithecus* was on the direct line to *Homo*.[5] Today *Ramapithecus* is included in the genus *Sivapithecus*, whose skull structure definitely aligns it with the orangutans.[6] The latter seem also to be related to the Indian, Tibetan, and Chinese *Gigantopithecus* genus, large ground-dwelling apes with thickly-enameled teeth. They were related both to the Sivapithecines and orangutan, yet without the latter's relatively recent and specialized postcranial locomotor and arboreal adaptations.[7]

Considering the specialized locomotor structure both of the African apes and the hominids, including the extreme brachiating adaptations of the Asiatic apes (the gibbons), it is clear that the apes took a variety of pathways as the remnants of a once-numerous African clade disappeared into various narrow survival niches toward the end of the Miocene, only to have the most specialized appear again in the Pleistocene, after a gap of 12-7my. The European Dryopithecines, who apparently were widespread throughout Eur-Asia as generalized quadruped great apes, and as recently as 9mya, have disappeared without a trace.[8]

Molecular Clocks and Phylogenies

"[M]olecules appear to change regularly during the process of evolution...may serve as an evolutionary clock to date the points of divergence from the evolutionary tree."[9]

The debate over ape-hominid affiliations took a radically different turn in the mid-to-late 1960s. Emile Zuckerkandl and Linus Pauling, as well as Morris Goodman, began reporting on their methods of tracing both evolutionary relationships and temporal sequences in the branching of various lines of animals through an analysis of the sequences of gene coding for blood proteins, globins.[10]

G. Ledyard Stebbins, himself a distinguished genetics researcher, reported on some of the significant successes of this method. This tedious study of the amino acid sequences, usually between 100-160, in these protein chains, produced in the work of Margoliash and Fitch with the protein, cytochrome "*c*", the realization that fungi are more closely related in their molecular structure to animals than to plants. They also argued that turtles were more closely related to birds than either was related to snakes, though birds had evolved into their own taxonomic class.[11]

At the same time, Sarich and Wilson were reporting on their hybridization research with serum albumin proteins sampled from a number of primate lines. Hybridization combined the albumin of both species and compared the antiserum reactivity of the two albumin samples. This research showed that the African apes were more closely aligned with humans than were the orangutans with humans. In fact it showed humans as closer to chimpanzees than chimpanzees were to the gorilla. In addition, Sarich and Wilson placed the time of human and chimpanzee separation at 5 mya.[12]

The DNA hybridization work of Charles Sibley (Professor of Ornithology and Director of Yale University Peabody Museum of Natural History) and Jon Ahlquist was the next step in the advancing tide of molecular studies attempting to trace phylogenetic relationships and their time lines. Sibley and Ahlquist first worked to trace bird relationships before they turned their method to primates and humans.

Their method consisted of combining the single strands of DNA of two different species, first calculating the temperature at which the DNA helixes unraveled—melted—in the original species, then calculating how much below the DNA temperature of the single species was the temperature of the mixed species DNA when it melted, or unravels. Melting point lowered by one degree centigrade meant that the DNA of the two species differed by one percent. Seventeen hundred bird species were subjected to DNA hybridization studies.

In 1984 after ten years of bird DNA studies, Sibley and Ahlquist published their research on primates: humans, chimpanzees—common and pygmy—gorilla, orangutan, two species of gibbon, and seven species of Old World monkeys. Chimpanzee species DNA differed from each other by 0.7%; humans from either chimpanzee species by 1.6%; gorillas differed from both chimpanzees and humans by 2.3%. Sibley and Ahlquist concluded that human-chimpanzee binding in DNA hybridization experiments is 20% stronger than either human-gorilla or chimpanzee-gorilla binding.[13]

Other molecular approaches attempted a more direct inspection of the genetic structure and sequences than the more global analysis of proteins and DNA involved in hybridization research: nucleotide DNA sequencing and mitochondrial DNA analysis. The more laborious method of sequencing portions of the nuclear DNA involved a much smaller picture of the total genome variation.[14]

Of the approximately 3 billion DNA bases in nuclear DNA, only 1-5% encode proteins. Thus there is about 100X more information in the genome as a whole than in that part of DNA which codes for proteins, the individual genes.[15] Zihlman prefers the use of the entire DNA genome in terms of the larger informational base upon which evolutionary conclusions must be based.[16] Humans and chimpanzees still differ with respect to 2500 gene pairs in respective genomes. The small percentage difference, therefore, does still add up to much internal genetic variation that may not reveal itself in more limited sections of the nuclear DNA.[17]

Mitochondrial DNA, the third of the basic DNA methods of analysis, and which is found in all of our cells, contains only 15,000 base pairs in humans. In mammals it evolves at about five to ten times the average rate of nuclear DNA. Sequencing data shows a similar family tree to other methods.[18]

A more recent summarizing assessment of these molecular sequences based on the rates of random DNA mutations show orangutans to have more missing DNA sequences in their genomes than African apes, when compared to DNA in humans. Andrews and Stringer state that changes in proteins, amino acids, and directly in DNA, show that humans differ from chimpanzee at 1.2%; from orangutan at 1.8%; from gorilla at 1.4%;

gorilla from-orangutan, 2.4%; orangutan from chimpanzee, 1.8%; chimpanzee from gorilla, 1.2%—*equal* to humans and chimpanzees![19]

The counterintuitive evidence, that humans are thus more closely related to chimpanzees than gorillas are to chimpanzees, has inevitably raised eyebrows. Immunological differences: lysozyme showed differences between gorilla and humans, taxonomically separate families, that compared similarly to the species differences between dog and coyote, cat and bobcat, Drosophila species, all of the latter having quite small phylogenetic evolutionary distances as compared with the large family differences, *e.g.*, those between apes and humans.[20] Difference between humans and chimpanzees, 1.2 or 1.6%, was smaller than between two gibbon species, 2.2%, or between two bird species, North American red-eyed and white-eyed vireo, which was 2.9%. Another puzzle: human blood hemoglobin is identical in all its 287 units with both chimpanzee species.[21]

Molecules versus Morphology

Allan Wilson has concluded that in different groups of organisms three kinds of evolutionary changes proceed at different rates relative to each other: 1) changes in protein molecular structure; 2) organization of the chromosomes; 3) anatomical structure of the body. Because of the inherent variability of anatomical changes and even restructurings of the genetic material within the chromosome the temporal invariance of molecular change gives us a more reliable dating frame for evolutionary change.[22]

However, early in their research, Sarich and Wilson also stated that they "...aligned African apes more closely than the orangutan with humans not only because the albumin of the African apes reacted more strongly with human antiserum, but because they saw data as in qualitative agreement with anatomical relationships."[23]

Bernard Campbell,[24] in the first edition of his classic text on the structural adaptations of humans, still saw humans as a composite of monkey and ape morphologies, with *Ramapithecus* closely related to the hominids.[25] However, by the third edition, 1985, Campbell would write in his Preface: "The taxonomy of the Hominidae themselves has been greatly simplified by the discovery of further remains of *Ramapithecus*, (Pilbeam, Andrews, and Cronin) which has turned out to be much closer to an ancestral orangutan (*Pongo*). It is included here within *Sivapithecus*."[26]

Campbell's earlier, 1966, edition argued from morphologically-induced views, of the closeness of humans and Old World monkeys. It is an even more interesting observation.

> In certain characters man seems to resemble most closely the living semibrachiating monkeys, and we have noted in particular the high index of cephalization of these primates. Man's hand and penis show close similarities to certain Old World monkeys. In contrast, the apes have hands that have undergone specialization for brachiation, so they have to a great extent lost their manipulative power.
> The situation is typical of many characters of man when they are compared with the apes; we find that man is less specialized in many of his brachiating features and shares, instead, more generalized features with the Old World monkeys. The generalized nature of modern man was stressed in an important paper by Straus and is of the most utmost importance.[27]

Campbell is highly influenced in his reevaluation of human origins, relative to the great apes by the new research into protein structure as composed of the 20 amino acids, all proteins being left optical isomers. In 1985 he recognized, in addition, the importance of nucleic acids and mitochondrial evidence as part of the general DNA complement in animal molecular genetics.[28] His conclusions give assent to these recent views. Protein hemoglobins show more and more amino acid differences as we move away from our own species. Accepting the existing estimates that show both chimpanzee species and humans being 98.5% similar in their respective DNA, he presents a wide variety of other biochemical relationships as exemplified in proteins: cytochrome "c", myoglobins, fibrinopeptides.[29] Listing the many methodologies being used to measure molecular differences: amino acid immunodiffusion, microcomplement fixation, radioimmuno-assay, electrophoresis, nucleotide sequence and restriction endonuclease mapping, Campbell in effect withdraws any morphological input as to the possibility of another phylogenetic route to the hominids, except through the great apes, especially the chimpanzee.[30][31][32][33]

Molecular Comparisons among the Great Apes and *Homo*[a]

Molecular comparisons	Homo-Pongo	Pan/Gorilla-Pongo	Homo-Pan/Gorilla
lsopeptide sequence (no. of amino acid differences)	2	2	0
hybridization (% base pair mismatch)	2.4	2.0	1.1
hybridization (% base pair mismatch)	—	4.5	2.4
anological distance (ID units)	37	39	14
unodiffusion distance (antigenic distance)	1.6	1.6	0.8
ophoresis			
sma proteins	>>2	>>2	~1.6
hanges at 23 loci	8	9	7
netic distance value based on 23 loci	0.349	0.300	0.367
chondrial DNA comparisons using endonuclease restriction	1*	2†	7‡
enzyme maps of site shared			

rom Andrews and Cronin, 1982. *Homo* shares a specific site with *Pongo* but others do not; †*Pan* and *Gorilla* share a site in non with *Pongo* but *Homo* does not; ‡*Homo* shares this number of sites with at least one of the species of *Pan* or *Gorilla* but not *Pongo* (or *Hylobates*).

Immunological Distances between Albumins of Various Old World Primates[d]

Species tested	Antiserum to		
	Homo	Pan troglodytes	Hylobates
Homo sapiens	0	3.7	11.1
Pan troglodytes	5.7	0	14.6
Pan paniscus	5.7	0	14.6
Pan gorilla	3.7	6.8	11.7
Pongo pygmaeus	8.6	9.3	11.1
Symphalangus syndactylus (siamang)	11.4	9.7	2.9
Hylobates lar	10.7	9.7	0
Old World monkeys (average of six species)	38.6	34.6	36.0

[d]Calculated from data in Sarich and Wilson, 1967.

10.1 Primate/human molecular relationships.

Contemporary with Campbell's conversion to the molecular clock phylogenies is the research of Jerold Lowenstein of the University of California Medical School, San Francisco. Lowenstein used radioimmunoassay, one of the techniques Campbell refers to as crucial evidence in solidifying the molecular position.

Radioimmunoassay: "DNA encodes RNA which encodes proteins, so that comparisons of organisms on the most fundamental level involves comparisons of their DNA, RNA, or proteins, not their bones or teeth."[34] RIA, radioimmunoassay solid-phase double-antibody technique: "First extracts of the fossil or other material are placed in the cups of plastic microtiter plates, where some of the protein binds to the plastic. Second, rabbit antisera to various proteins are placed in cups, where some of the antibodies bind to the already-bound protein. Third, radioactive (I-125 labeled) goat anti-rabbit gamma globulin (GARGG) is added to the cups and binds to the rabbit antibody. Finally, the radioactivity in each cup, which reflects the affinity of the antisera for the fossil protein, is measured. If the fossil is human, for example, antisera to human proteins will bind better than those to monkey proteins (Lowenstein, 1980b). In this way, the relations of the fossil proteins to those of living species can be estimated."[35]

Relating to the issue of ape-human ancestry, Lowenstein cites his research into the phylogeny of *Ramapithecus/Sivapithecus*.

> Fragments of 5 different specimens, combined and injected into a single rabbit, yielded antisera which reacted strongly with sera of orangutan, gibbon, and gorilla, less strongly with sera of humans and chimpanzees, and weakly or not at all with sera of monkeys and other mammals (Lowenstein, 1983). These results suggest that *Ramapithecus/Sivapithecus* was hominoid but not hominid and more or less equally distant from living Asian and African hominoids.[36]

Molecular Reaction

A scholar at the University of Pittsburgh, Jeffrey Schwartz, has been one of the lone anthropological voices to oppose the conclusion that the African apes, especially the chimpanzee, are the closest contemporary descendants of an African ancestor that was also at the root of our own genus, and that lived 5mya.

He also has attempted to draw from the molecular genetic literature as many dissenting caveats as possible. Clearly he is limited here as a physical anthropologist, however versed in morphology and evolutionary cladistics he himself must be. In discussing the problem of human-ape relations, and skeptical of the definitive nature of majority conclusions on the basis of molecular studies that place the chimpanzee as a sister taxon to the hominids, the orangutan an outlier form, Schwartz' cites Lowenstein's earlier, 1982, research on the molecular relationship of extant apes: Immunological analysis of collagen shows that the maximum binding (MB) averages of relationships of humans with apes and the monkey place the orangutan closer to humans than humans are to the chimpanzee.[37]

Schwartz goes forward to cite a series of authors and studies that seem to support close orangutan and human phylogenetic relationship.[38] He further quotes Sarich and Wilson's 1967 article on protein albumin serum reactions between ape and human DNA, to the effect that what was revealed in this research was not merely the greater reactivity of orangutan albumin with human, but also that these conclusions were reached because their data was in qualitative agreement with the anatomical evidence.[39] Schwartz notes that thermal stability/immunological reactivity can suggest homology, but cannot distinguish between primitive and derived state of homology.[40]

Further, the work of Goodman, *et al.*, 1983, that myoglobin and carbonic anhydrase reactions supported a grouping with African apes, but also revealed that nucleotide replacement sequences were lacking for all hominoids, and that, therefore, the most parsimonious myoglobin grouping was with the orangutan, which differed only at positions 23 and 110. In such a situation, Schwartz argues, various phylogenies are available for choice and the fossil record or comparative anatomy must be invoked.[41]

Bruce and Ayala, in 1979, using electrophoresis, obtained calculations of genetic identity and genetic distance that places chimpanzees and orangutans equally distant from humans with, gorillas the outliers.[42] Hasegawa *et al.* are sarcastically cited for their conclusions based on molecular and chromosomal studies, especially their recalibration of the mtDNA clock, that views humans and chimpanzees as separating c.2.5mya. Schwartz laments the implication that such a dating would abandon a hominid-australopithecine ancestry for *Homo*![43]

Schwartz believes that "...there must be a melding of theory applicable to both the molecular and the organismal. Sophisticated technology does not produce more accurate phylogenies than conventional means. Phylogenetic interpretation is ultimately a reflection of the theoretical predisposition of the investigator."[44]

A "Conference Report: Molecular Anthropology: Toward a New Evolutionary Paradigm," March 12-14, 1995, Wayne State University School of Medicine, Detroit, honored Morris Goodman. In 1961 Goodman introduced the idea that evolution, measured by mutation rates was slower in humans than in other primates and mammals. Early on this research seemed to fly in the face of those, such as A. C. Wilson, who argued for a steady state molecular clock in the hominoids.[45]

Population geneticist Wen-Hsing Li, University of Texas, Houston, presented new evidence from the DNA sequences of humans, apes, monkeys, and rodents to show that humans undergo fewer changes in their DNA each year. Roy Britten a molecular biologist at the California Institute of Technology, and Walter Fitch, a molecular evolutionist at the University of California, Irvine, both enthusiastically agree.[46] Goodman had earlier noted that blood protein albumin in chimpanzees, gorillas, and humans were almost the same. This was odd because antelopes and cows, also closely related in phylogenetic evolution, have very different blood albumin proteins. Sarich and Wilson disagreed with Goodman's interpretation; they continued to argue for a steady clock.

Li's research, noted above, examined a large number of noncoding stretches of DNA, eight different introns—pseudo genes—flanking sequences from humans, squirrel monkeys, and baboons. Noncoding DNA, because it is not expressed as protein products, is immune to selective pressure. Li after relating these three primate forms concluded that Old World monkeys had undergone 1.5X more numerous mutations within their sequence than had humans. In earlier studies he used rats, mice, and chickens. He found that the rodents had accumulated about twice as many mutations as had humans. This was explained through generational life span differences. Mutations arise in these species usually when DNA in sperm is being copied, also to a lesser degree when the DNA is being copied for female egg cells.[47] Britten agreed with this primate slowdown commenting that longer-lived animals can repair their DNA more easily than can animals with shorter spans, thus building up fewer mutations.[48]

The interspecies molecular clock was first put forth by Linus Pauling of Stanford and Emile Zuckerkandl in 1965.[49] They thought that the rate of change was regular regardless of the species. Thus they thought that rats and mice separated 40mya, on the basis of their molecular differences.[50] Today, the split is assumed to have taken place 15mya. Sarich cites the 1985 hybridization study by Raoul Beneviste of the National Cancer Institute that showed no slowdown between humans and baboons as regard such molecular changes.[51] Li, however, does see a slowdown in all parts of the noncoding DNA sequences. Goodman, too, now agrees, using DNA sequence studies and his own DNA hybridization data.

Li's conference data compares base pairs studied in species: Rats—4038; New World monkeys—8478; Old World monkeys—8478; humans—8478. Changes in nucleotide site per billion years: rats—4.8; New World monkeys—2.1; Old World monkeys—1.8; humans—1.2. He also uses the fossil record to approximate the date of splitting from a common ancestor. Mutation rates in DNA sequences were then calculated to show that humans have the slowest rate of mutations.[52]

No anatomical analysis in Li's study was made of the physical differences undergone by each line from its primitive forms at the estimated time of branching. This would have underscored Allan Wilson's claim of the independence of change in protein structure, chromosomal organization, and anatomical changes in animal lines over equal spans of evolutionary time.[53]

Molecular Complexities—Evolutionary Puzzles

Highlighting the complexity and inconclusiveness of the present state of molecular genetics when applied to evolutionary phylogenies is a report on recent studies authored by Svante Paabo of the Institute of Zoology, the University of Munich.[54] Paabo discusses recent advances and complexities of DNA sequencing in the gene nucleus and in mitochondrial DNA. He reflects on the apparent rooting of human mtDNA sequences in populations around the world, in Africans, when compared to deviations with chimpanzee sequences.[55] Paabo: "...[R]eanalyses of the data indicated that there is very little information in the sequences to justify this conclusion, [the roots of chimpanzee/human genetic relationship lie in African human populations] mainly because the chimpanzee sequence is so distantly related to that of humans that most of the information on its relation to human sequences has been erased by substitutions occurring multiple times at the same position."[56]

Humans around the world seem to be more highly related to each other than are chimpanzees genetically related to each other in their relatively circumscribed West African homeland. Great genetic changes and consequent increases in variation can occur in the DNA genome or nucleotide sequences by an expansion in the species population, the "effective population size."[57] Reduction and thence expansion of a population would cause a shrinkage of the nucleotide diversity. A variant in one gene can become selectively favored. Thence, it can sweep through a population dragging all linked genes on chromosomes with it.

Mitochondrial DNA evolves faster than nuclear DNA. Thus a reasonable amount of sequencing can here reveal more evolutionary information. Mitochondrial DNA also is seemingly inherited through the female line without recombination. Schwartz[58] argues that to use mitochondrial (mt) DNA cleavage map data would reveal an orangutan/human group as easily as an African ape/human nested set.[59] Brown *et al.* choose an orangutan/human group as the pair most closely related, though one must first decide which species are most closely affiliated in the first place. This is so for subsequent analysis, because mtDNA evolves 5-10 times more rapidly than nuclear DNA. The presumption here is that phylogenetic analysis precedes mtDNA sequence data. [60]

Dorit *et al.* report on sequencing the ZFY intron on a non-recombining part of Y chromosome which revealed no nucleotide differences in human males from 38 nations around the world. By contrast when the same sequences are contrasted between humans and the various great apes, also between the great apes themselves, significant differences can be identified.[61] Goodfellow *et al.* studied the SRY gene on the Y chromosome, which directly induces human maleness. This gene evolves very rapidly, and as such could drag the rest of the chromosome with it, a "gigantic selective sweep" with the possibility for homogenizing the gene pool within a species, "yet allow for rapid evolution between species" [Hominids-pongids?][62]

A larger perspective, from the standpoint of the chromosome itself, is taken by Brunetto Chiarelli. Chiarelli states that the introduction of chromosomal banding (cytogenetics—the study of the form of chromosomes) and gene mapping have allowed for comparisons in chromosomes of humans and related forms. Similarity of chromosome 2 in humans and 12 and 13 in chimpanzees leads him to believe that translocation could have taken place after the 6-8mya separation of chimpanzees and humans. First to leave the line, was the conservative orangutan, second humans, *Pan* and gorilla (most closely related), last.[63]

Schwartz, using the same basic form of chromosomal analysis, uses Yunis and Prakash, (1982) data on homologous chromosomes. These seem to show, contra Chiarelli, humans and orangutans sharing the greatest number of chromosomes over other apes.[64] Also, Schwartz quotes Mai, who "concluded that there are five equally likely chromosomal phylogenies, of which three unite humans with the Orangutan."[65]

Philip Gingerich, a paleontologist at the University of Michigan, was unhappy with the linear molecular clock calibration: "Some studies use a linear and others a non-linear scale, some a single, well dated paleontological divergence and others several divergences, in order to calibrate the clock. (Gingerich, 1985). There is no consensus on the right approach to adopt in molecular evolutionary studies; nor is there any agreement as to which nucleotide sequences, or which combinations of them, provide the most reliable results."[66]

Compared to the fossil record, Gingerich argues, molecular evolution is simple. It is based on the 1965, Zuckerkandl/Pauling, Poisson metric for blood proteins, (globulins). Paleontological estimates had first to be made in order to calibrate the rate of molecular differentiation.[67] Gingerich questions Sarich's linear clock method,[68] in which prosimian/anthropoid divergence is placed at 75mya—too far back—and the recent divergence of humans/chimpanzees at 4.2mya—too recent.[69] Gingerich suggests a power function mathematical model, in which the rate of molecular change would have decreased over time, and which would result in a 8.9 or 9.2mya divergence time between the ancestors of the hominids and the chimpanzee, 9.8mya between the gorilla and hominids, and 16my B.P. and 18.7my B.P. for the orangutan and gibbon respectively. Gingerich strongly supports Goodman's 1963 suggestion of a slowing of molecular change in the primates.[70]

Problematic Molecular Timetables

Robert Martin has raised a number of issues with regard to the usefulness of the concept of the "molecular clock" for solving some of the existing mysteries regarding recent primate evolution:[71]

Calibration of any phylogenetic tree through an analysis of molecular change and distance between existing species must be calibrated with paleontological evidence and the dates that attach thereby. The view following Zuckerkandl and Pauling is that the sequence data changes for proteins and/or DNA prescribed by individual genes accumulate at an approximately constant rate, and thus it is possible to interpret the number of sequence distances in terms of relative times of origin.[72] Arguing that rates of change in genes and proteins are similar in the various lineages thus followed, it can be possible to infer dates for a variety of branching points. But one needs at least one well-established fossil time base to calibrate the molecular clock.

Sarich and Wilson in their various writings on human/ape phylogenies used one seriously questioned date, the 30mya separation point between the Old World monkeys and the hominoids, based on the now-acknowledged limited perspectives of the Fayum, Egypt, primates of the Oligocene. Recent discoveries reported by Beard, for example, that may push back the monkey/ape/prosimian divisions to the deep Eocene, c.55mya, could undermine the basic timetable of human/ape separation.[73] See also the early Paleocene date that Yoder advances for the African appearance of prosimian lemurs.[74] As Martin phrases it: "There is certainly an element of circularity involved if inferred paleontological dates are used to determine a formula relating immunological dissimilarity to time, and values determined from the formula are subsequently used to question paleontological dates."[75]

Constant rate change in the molecular clock is dependent to a great extent on the neutrality of mutational changes in DNA and protein sequences, that they do not imply high selective values. Martin sees a recent empirical challenge to the principle of balanced polymorphism in a population, whereby the different forms of the allele at each genetic locus are held more or less in balance with each other by "gentle" selective factors.[76] Recent electrophoretic surveys of protein polymorphism for a variety of animal species show far more genetic variability and change than heretofore postulated by Haldane.[77] "It is necessary to examine with a critical eye to determine whether rates of change at the molecular level are in practice relatively constant in accordance with the prediction from neutral mutation theory."[78] Clearly the recent evidence presented by Paabo in 1995 argues for a more rapid rate of change in larger portions of the human genome than that predicted by the neutral DNA molecular clock advocates.[79]

This is why, Martin argues, much of the research has been with more global use of protein albumin immunological comparison. Ninety-seven to ninety-nine percent of the mammalian genome does not code for protein. These non-coding areas, introns, further complicate the study of nuclear DNA when it comes to assessing rates of molecular change as unaffected by natural selection. In sum, Martin argues, given the probability that natural selection does exert an influence on the fixation of nucleotide substitutions in the genome, then the possibility of reliable phylogenetic relationships must be dealt with skeptically.[80] In fact DNA hybridization studies of single-copy DNA nucleotide base replacement in lemurs was shown to be about one half as divergent as that in other primates. Something beyond merely neutral evolutionary processes must be operating to cause such seemingly special case molecular changes.[81]

Adding to these problems is the issue of generational variance which may cause the evolutionary process of molecular change to slow down or to speed up depending on the length of the reproductive generation of the species in questions as well as its presumptive ancestors, were their generations longer or shorter. Martin does support Gingerich's use of a power function in the analysis of molecular change.[82] Here, too, Martin follows Goodman's view that the change is not strictly linear, as Sarich and

Wilson have argued; rather it decreases in the primates in line with their lengthening generations.[83]

Martin's concluding caveats:

1. "Only in the very broadest sense can it be claimed that rates of evolution of a particular protein, or of the sequence of DNA coding for that protein, remain approximately constant over long periods of geological time....[It] seems likely that natural selection and other factors have also played a part."

2. The rate of change of individual proteins has been shown to decrease systematically over time. It seems probable that no linear relationship exists between the number of fixed mutations and time.

3. Individual proteins evolve in different patterns of change. In addition they exhibit different rates of change over equal amounts of time.

4. At particular genetic sites there can exist both superimposed changes as well as reversals. These "hidden" mutations must be accounted for in any attempt to calculate rates of change over fixed quantities of time. Otherwise, there could be taking place a hidden evolutionary process, unbeknownst to the simplified theoretical "eye."[84]

- 2 -
Cousins: The Morphological Connection

Consensus

> The numerous fossil "apes" from the early-middle Miocene of east Africa are generally very primitive compared with modern hominoids with only a few taxa showing potential derived features linking them with the living radiation....The origin of the other hominoids, gibbons, the other African apes, humans is largely unknown. *Pliopithecus*, considered a gibbon ancestor for most of the past 150 years, is known generally as a primitive Catarrhine with a primitive ear morphology, robust limbs, and a tail. There are no fossils from Africa that show similarities to chimpanzees or gorillas from the Miocene, Pliocene, or Pleistocene...
>
> In contrast with the African fossil apes, many of the generally younger fossil apes from Eurasia are probably members of the great ape and human clade...less diverse and until recently more poorly known, seem to sample an extensive radiation of forest apes with a modern hominoid dental, cranial, and postcranial anatomy that is related more directly to living great apes and humans. Orangutans seem to be a remnant of some of these Asian apes.[85]

This recent quotation represents a confirmation of the long-held position of Jeffrey Schwartz, even in the face of nearly unanimous rejection during the 1980s by his colleagues. This was despite the molecular evidence ostensibly linking the chimpanzee with humans as part of an evolutionary sequence that could have been joined as recently as the Pliocene, some 5mya. This earlier perspective argued, again from the DNA evidence, that the orangutan was a distant outlier form.

One can understand the persuasiveness of a largely office/laboratory theoretical and deductive evolutionary model. It leaps over the nitty-gritty field controversies dealing with geological strata, physical-morphological affiliations, the leaps and gaps of the fossil record, to give us a clean linear molecular evolutionary sequence, universal in its biological affinities and affiliations. Such a chronology suggests its predictive power by affiliation with *a priori* physicalist and astronomical theoretical pivots, such as the speed of light, the red shift expanding universe, and other deductive scientific keystones.

Unfortunately, complexities begin to show up, even as they have in the seemingly well-established astronomical estimates of the age of our universe. Here, we again must question the patently linear deductivity of the so-called chimpanzee-human molecular dyad—humans as "third chimpanzees." Such deductive datings are now being called into question by an increasingly large chorus of qualifiers. Philip Gingerich's proposed non-linear, power DNA progression, which pushes back in time the starting point of the hominid-African ape separation, is but one example.[86] Many new molecular elements from other segments of the primate genome, new methods of analyzing the constituent genetic data, have dissipated the surety of scientists with the earlier "simple and beautiful" theory.

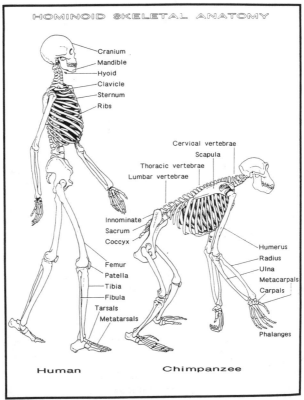

10.2 Human—chimpanzee morphology compared. Is it possible that these two very different primates, despite an "apparent" close molecular relationship, had the same ancestor 5-6mya? What genetic principles would have to be invoked to explain this enormous structural recreation?

In the end, the weight of molecular evidence still seems to suggest that we are more closely related to the chimpanzee and the gorilla than we are to the orangutan. But then, the chimpanzee, on this evidence, seems also to be more closely related to humans than to the gorilla. The molecular data must be seen as an early and still tentative assay of a deeply mysterious set of genetic relationships. Ultimately, any purely molecular hypothesis will be evaluated, like all scientific theories, by its heuristic value in predicting and bringing together into the symbolic web of theory and practice, as surely-to-be-discovered fossils, as well other tangible factors and relationships.[87]

Ape/Morphological Relationships

In his several books and articles, Jeffrey Schwartz has presented and argued for the evidence that places the orangutan closer in morphology to the hominids than are the contemporary African apes. As we have noted in the previous section, he has also attempted to "throw some sand" into the seemingly immovable certainty given by the molecular data that indicate the closeness of the chimpanzees and the hominids.

What follows, with some critical exceptions, is the morphological case for a close relationship between the hominids and the *Sivapithecus* clade, of which the orangutan has long been considered to be a modern affiliate, if not a direct descendant.

Locomotor Patterns

Russell Tuttle has been one of the more vocal exponents of the view that the knuckle-walking gait of the gorilla and the chimpanzee are unique in the locomotor patterns of the primates. Monkeys, orangutans, and young humans, when they use a four-limbed mode of locomotion, walk palms extended, with no hint of knuckle-walking tendencies. In addition the unique length of the arms of chimpanzees and gorillas in relation to their legs, as compared with humans, gibbons, orangutans and monkeys also argues for a separate evolutionary heritage of as-yet unknown length.[88] Orangutans in captivity, when on wet surfaces, occasionally have been noticed curving their fingers under their hands in a seemingly knuckle-walking pattern so as to gain stability.[89] Such patterns may also be observed in certain contexts in young humans.

Tuttle argues that the pattern of knuckle-walking in the African apes is supported by a wide series of morphological adjustments in the anatomy of these apes. These included many muscular and bone articulations in the hands, wrists, arm bones, joints and attachments to the shoulders, which, as Schwartz notes, make the evolutionary relationship of these two animals a close and compelling one.[90]

Going back in the historical tradition, Schwartz cites the more traditional scientific view by Thomas Huxley, G. Elliot Smith, and William. Gregory that the gorilla was more closely related to humans than chimpanzees. Gregory, saw the gorilla hand and foot as most closely related to man than to other great apes.[91] Schwartz further cites the more recent research of Colin Groves, Australian National University, on his comprehensive comparison of the morphological features of anthropoids, 200 in all. Humans and chimpanzees shared only 3-5 elements.[92]

Philip Tobias, summarizing the morphological characteristics of man as compared to the gorilla and chimpanzee obliquely quadrupedal posture and bone structure, compares the ilium of chimpanzee and hominids, raising the question of how fast such mutations for each restructuring could have come for each of these species to diverge so greatly?[93]

Limb Structure

One of great comparative anatomists, Adolph Schultz, working on developmental rates in primates, especially of the ossification of the epiphyses of the arm bone, hardening attachment to the long bones of the head sections of these bones, noted that orangutan and humans had the slowest rate of ossification.[94] Also, Schultz saw the scapula, the shoulder blade, of orangutan and humans quite similar in comparison with African apes and gibbon.[95]

Schultz is cited as opposing Weinert in associating the supposedly unique slow fusion of the carpal scaphoid and centrale bones of the wrist, late in development in the orangutan, as showing our human relatedness to the African apes. Rather Schultz sees this uniqueness of the orangutan as associating early fusion in humans with all the apes, including the gibbon.[96]

Elizabeth Vrba of Yale University noted that a Sterkfontein *Australopithecus* scapular (shoulder bone) fragment was most similar to the gorilla and orangutan; she also noted that the humerus head, part of the scapular fragment, was close to *Homo* and the orangutan pattern.[97] Similarly, Henry McHenry at the American Association of Physical Anthropology is quoted on the similar reduction of the tubercle-talus on the ankle bone in humans and orangutan.[98]

More recently an article by R. Thiranagama, A. T. Chamberlain, and B. Wood on the superficial vein in the forelimb of a number of mammals and primates and which described 12 character states, argued forcefully for a relationship or convergence between *Pongo* and *Homo*. "....[The] presence of this vein would constitute strong evidence supporting a sister group relationship between "*Pongo*" and "*Homo*."[99]

Facial Structure

The structure of the cranio-dental areas of the face seems to have provoked the most controversial morphological debate concerning human/ape relationships.

Taking into account both morphological and molecular data, Andrews and Cronin in an important article published in *Nature,* showed that on a study of cranio-dental features, the development of frontal sinuses in humans is similar to the African apes and dissimilar to the orangutan.[100]

Schwartz countered that the only major morphological linkage of humans with African apes, against orangutan linkage, lies in the development of the etmoidal air cells, citing Adolph Schultz on the variation in the frontal sinus development in all the hominoids, especially humans and the pigmy chimpanzee.[101] Schwartz also admits to the fact of the unique confining of the palatine ridge to the front of the palate in African apes and humans.[102] However, in Schwartz' view, an analysis of the snout of hominoids, union of premaxilla, with teeth, and maxilla, and configuration of the nasal and oral cavities does argue for a *Sivapithecus*/orangutan/hominid relationship.[103]

Further, argues Schwartz, the anterior palatine fenestrae, the windows in the palate between the oral cavity and the nasal cavity, are different from humans in the African apes. There is here a similarity in the orangutan and humans.[104] In 1993 Schwartz responded to Andrews' and Tekkaya's refuting analysis of the relationship of humans to *Sivapithecus* and orangutan. Along with Steve Ward, Schwartz reanalyzed the bony palate, premaxilla and maxilla, floor of nasal cavity, to re-ascertain such relationships in

African apes as compared to humans and orangutans. Ward's conclusions were to separate the African apes along with *Australopithecus* from orangutans and humans, with *Homo* seeming to reflect an ancestral condition.[105]

Brow Ridges

Peter Andrews and J. Cronin in *Nature* argued that the thickening and enlarging of the supraorbital (torus) region as well as above the bridge of the nose in African apes and prehistoric humans unite them.[106] Schwartz argued in turn that these ridges disappear in truly modern humans. Also Old World monkeys have them, they therefore could be ancestral. Orangutans are gracile in these regions of the skull and face. They are also underdeveloped in gibbons and siamangs.[107] Certainly, it is possible that the gracile structure of the skull of *Homo sapiens sapiens* is a modern and thus derived feature, similar to the independent development of these features in the orangutan. However, recall that the Miocene apes of Africa were to a great extent gracile in these supraorbital skull areas.

Teeth

There was a time when the thick molar tooth enamel of the Sivapithecines, especially *Ramapithecus*, who was also thought to have had a remarkably human-like parabolic tooth arcade, was seen as a defining characteristic in the march of the anthropoids toward humanity. After all, were not humans, orangutans, and the Australopithecines, in contrast to African apes with their thinly-enameled teeth, endowed with a similar tooth structure?

Subsequent disillusioning fossil remains of *Ramapithecus*, as well as the molecular revolution, disabused many anthropologists of this enthusiasm. Today we read comments such as: "Thick tooth enamel was not unique to hominids, but was acquired by several different lineages."[108] Schwartz noted that the Miocene African apes—*Kenyapithecus* is an example—some 20-15mya, had developed teeth with thick enamel. Thick molar enamel can be found in one New World monkey species and in one Old World monkey species.[109]

Schwartz also argued that molar-thick enamel and reduced tooth cusp height are characteristics of humans and orangutans.[110] By contrast, David Pilbeam saw in *Sivapithecus*' upper canine rotation of crown and root a morphology unlike the aligned canines in *Proconsul* and the African apes.[111] But, as Schwartz enthusiastically trumps, such a rotational pattern between the root and the crown of the upper canine in *Sivapithecus* is similar to that of the Australopithecines.[112]

E. Delson and Peter Andrews in articles and a co-authored book comment on the phylogeny of the third molars, or wisdom teeth. They are smaller in orangutan and modern humans, larger in robust australopithecine and African apes.[113] However, Schwartz elaborates—no cingulum, a ridge of enamel around the upper inner surface of each molar—can be found in the teeth of humans and orangutans, but are to be found in *Proconsul* and the gibbon, somewhat in gorilla and chimpanzee.[114]

Further, Schwartz argues, the cusps of the large molars in the gorilla are tall, while in the orangutan and humans they are low.[115] One can trace a line of canine reduction back from *Homo*, to the robust Australopithecines, then to *Ramapithecus* and its presumptive descendant, *Gigantopithecus*, along with the concomitant articulation of the canines with incisors in an anterior tooth complex. However, "Lucy"—*A. afarensis*—had large canines.[116]

Molar Dilemmas

The issue of the meaning of thick or thin molar tooth enamel in primates is an example of the complexities that need to be unraveled in the mysterious origin of humans. There is much discussion in the literature of the relationship of food preferences and the resultant tooth structures, or *vice versa*, in the lineages of the several primates.

Why, for example, as has been suggested, did the African apes, presumable derived from the Miocene Dryopithecines, who were developing thick molar enamel in an ecology rapidly going from tropical to mixed savannah, quickly revert to a thin molar enamel tooth structure in their West African jungle redoubt? Was the tropical West African jungle any less demanding of their tooth enamel in terms of the roots, fruits, vegetation on which they survived, than the diet of the thick molar enamel orangutans in their own Indonesian tropical jungle habitat? And why was thick and thin tooth enamel so variably dispersed among the several Old and New World monkeys?

Evidence is that the enamel ultrastructure of human and chimpanzee molars is similar, but variably layered in thickness, although Schwartz attempts to question this claim.[117] Still, the lack of clear adaptive correlation between those animals having thick or thin tooth enamel suggest that it is an ancient and perhaps primitive condition that has been preserved. It could be similar to the long-maintained thin enamel tooth tips of the multituberculates, here within the various lines regardless of the particular adaptive or ecological setting in which primates found themselves.

The implication is that more decisive morphological and behavioral factors set the different lines on their respective evolutionary encounters than thick or thin tooth enamel. That being the case, the respective carriers of this trait could indeed be reflecting a trace evolutionary record that points to real phylogenetic relationships over time. Still, given the existence of thick molar enamel lines of apes that subsequently became extinct, the carrying of this trait into recent evolutionary history could be a parallelism that has very ancient but perhaps coincidental origins.

It is difficult to reconcile the African ape patterns, so different from the Asiatic apes as well as the hominids in this and other morphological traits, to indicate other than a distant cladistic relationship with the hominids.

Miscellaneous

Schwartz does concede that humans and African apes both have ear lobes.[118] Schultz is cited as noting that humans and orangutan alone have long hair, but also as observing that of all the large anthropoids, humans and chimpanzees have the fewest number of hairs per square centimeter on their backs.[119]

Ischial callosities: very pronounced in baboons, somewhat in chimpanzees, patches of furrowed skin in orangutan, but not true callosities, none on humans.[120] On widely-spaced breasts in female orangutans, noted earlier by Schultz: Schwartz says they are not primitive but a derived novelty, very different from African apes, and very similar to human females.[121]

Reproduction

The gestation period of the orangutan, noted by Schultz as being the longest of the great apes, has now been confirmed in detail by Martin and Kingsley in England: chimpanzees, 245 days; gorillas, 260 days; humans and orangutans, 270 days. No swelling has been observed in the genital areas during ovulation in the female orangutan or in humans, unlike chimpanzees and gorillas.[122] Mating by orangutans and humans is not periodic during the estrus cycle, but continuous (Ron Nadler, Charles Graham, of Yerkes Primate Center in Atlanta). Orangutans, up to 7 years between offspring; however, they do form a partnership for several weeks during which they engage in long sexual bouts. They rejoin the same male-female relationship years later for the next sexual mating relationship.[123]

Jared Diamond notes that pygmy chimpanzees differ from common chimpanzees, they have longer legs, copulate frontally and in other ways. Copulation is initiated by either sex; females are sexually receptive for much of the month. Stronger bonds exist between females, and between males and females in the pygmy chimpanzee, not merely between males. Diamond puts the molecular differences between humans and chimpanzees ate 1.6%, Andrews and Stringer at 1.2%.[124] This molecular distance, as noted in Part 1, is smaller than between two gibbon species, 2.2%, or between two bird species, North American red-eyed and white-eyed vireo, 2.9%. Human blood hemoglobin is identical in all its 287 units in both chimpanzee species: common *chimpanzee (Pan troglodytes)*; pygmy chimpanzee (*Pan paniscus*).[125]

Michael McKinney argues, on the other hand, that gorillas and chimpanzees are very closely related. The greater growth of the gorillas is caused by change in the growth hormone during the juvenile stage. Gorillas prefer to eat leaves, chimpanzees, fruit. Gorillas tend to form stable harem-like groups with one male, several females, with young. Chimpanzees have a much looser social relationship, groups forming and breaking up much more often.[126]

Diamond notes that a 200-lb. gorilla bears a much smaller neonate, in weight and size, than a 100-lb. female human.[127] However, pigmy chimpanzees, like humans, do engage in frequent sexual bouts during estrus cycle, and enact face-to-face copulation. Also, the male chimpanzee penis is twice as large as the orangutan penis, and at 3 inches in size approaches the male *sapiens* at 5 inches.[128]

Brain Structure

In the deflection of the left/right sylvan sulcus, Geschwind and Lemay found that the gorilla had some occipital asymmetry, but the orangutan had far more asymmetry in the sylvan sulcus as with humans.[129] Bresard and Bresson tested the larger apes and found that orangutans are right handed while chimpanzees are ambidextrous.[130] The basicranial region shows a greater similarity between *Australopithecus afarensis* (Lucy), and the orangutans than the chimpanzees. This resemblance was first illustrated by D. Johanson, the discoverer of "Lucy."[131]

Schwartz reports on the research of Lasley, Czekela, and Shideler, with regard to estrio excretion, adrenal gland development, and fetal steroid secretions. Estrio secretion was four to five times higher in humans and orangutans than in gorillas and chimpanzees. Lasley associates humans and orangutans with one of two types of fetal-placental interactive units, the other being the African apes. Schwartz states that this latter factor directly affects brain development, thus the orangutan/human similarity in asymmetrical brain structure.[132]

Morphological Perspective

Twenty-five years since its original 1974 publication in *Current Anthropology*, Russell H. Tuttle's article "Darwin's Apes, Dental Apes, and the Descent of Man: Normal Science in Evolutionary Anthropology," still is an important contribution. It considers purely morphological factors in evaluating the sources in primate history for *Homo*'s specialized morphological structure. Specifically, it considers a variety of theories of brachiation and knuckle walking as related to human bipedalism.[133]

Especially interesting is his use of D. J. Morton's 1920s research at the American Museum of Natural History. Morton, an orthopedic surgeon, worked with the distinguished paleontologist W. K. Gregory at that institution. Their views on the evolutionary origins of humans, however, turned out to be quite different. Gregory, following the ideas of Sir Arthur Keith, believed that human ancestry could be traced to a line of giant, brachiating apes that eventually came down to the ground and evolved toward bipedality through adaptive changes in their lower limbs.

Morton by contrast, and more modestly in his writing and in regard to his subsequent scientific reputation followed his independent pathway based in part on his orthopedic training. This background made him sensitive to the evolutionary possibilities given in the basic structure of all four limbs to the hypothetical ancestor of the hominids. He postulated that the protohominid ape had the following characteristics: size of a modern gibbon; all four limbs equal in length; brachiating as in the modern chimpanzee, not the gibbon; erect posture and bipedal, both in the trees and on the ground, the latter as in modern gibbons; cranium like the modern gibbon; no ischial pads (similar to the orangutan); no tail.[134]

Morton believed that the modern gibbon diverged from this line of catarrhine primates before the protohominids and the great apes. The protohominid line early on adopted a bipedal posture as part of a largely terrestrial habitat.[135] Today, we would probably take into consideration the seeming retention of arboreal features in the Australopithecines, implying that this line of protohominids early diversified in their habitats from the main line of proto-*Homo*, some Australopithecines continuing or retaining arboreal patterns and morphologies.

Naturally, this type of thinking seems to argue for an ancient protohominid separation from the great apes. But it also supplies evidence for a relatively early parting of the ways from the proto-Australopithecines.

Schultz also believed in an early protohominid branching from the root ape stock, but probably later than the departure of the gibbon line, the hylobatids.

I incline to the view that gibbons have retained a greater number of primitive characters which may have been the property of the "missing link" than any of the living apes.[136]

The Hylobatidae and man have evolved in opposite directions from a common early stock, yet in a number of important features they have retained a closer similarity than exists in regard to the same features between man and the great apes.[137]

In assessing the basic morphology of man as it contrasts to the knuckle-walking arboreal troglodytian chimpanzee model, Tuttle inclines to a version of Morton's hylobatian position with greater emphasis on an arboreal component that continues longer into recent evolutionary time.[138]

Vertebrae Clues

Recently Latimer and Ward analyzed the phylogenetic heritage of the so-called Nariokotome boy, KNM-WT-15000, an early African *H. erectus*, c.1.6mya. This fossil had 6 lumbar vertebrae; (96% of modern humans have 5, the rest 6). Citing the example in a South African *Australopithecus africanus*, ST-14, which also had 6 lumbar vertebrae, they concur with Adolf Schultz' long-held position that 6 lumbar and 13 thoracic vertebrae constituted the primitive hominoid condition.*[139]*

Modern African apes and the orangutan have 3-4 lumbar and 13 thoracic vertebrae elements. The Miocene ape, *Proconsul nyanzae*, KNM-MW-13142, had 5-7 lumbar vertebrae. The conclusion of these authorities is that the modern African apes and the orangutan are highly specialized and convergent, as compared with the Miocene apes, in their thoracic/lumbar vertebral count, and that the gibbon, with 5 lumbar and 13 thoracic vertebrae, also approaches the more unspecialized primitive state.

Modern humans with their 12 thoracic and mostly 5 lumbar vertebrae seem to stand apart. Latimer and Ward see the Australopithecines and *H. erectus* as related in the overall character of vertebral morphology.[140]

- 3 -
Origin of the Hominids: A Discussion

In 1983, 1985, and 1991, Itzkoff, on the basis of accepted comparative evolutionary timetables and the associated morphological evidence, adduced into the early 1980s, but not yet persuaded by the early presentation of DNA and human and ape protein comparisons, argued for a separation of the protohominids from the lines that eventually resulted in the contemporary great apes going back, at the most recent, to the late-Oligocene, 30-25mya.[141]

Tobias, in 1994[142], placed the earliest verified hominid remains at between 5-6mya. A. Hill and S. Ward had earlier given a ball-park estimate of the origin of the hominids at between 4-14mya. The newer if fragmentary fossil evidence as well as even more recent discoveries of newly identified australopithecine-like species, *Ardipithecus ramidus* and *Australopithecus anamensis*, all between 4-5mya, possibly predating *A. afarensis*, seem to suggest an ever earlier hominid originating point. [143]

Most molecular advocates for a chimpanzee/hominid association have now pushed back their original time frames for the separation of the two lines from 5mya to about 10mya. For this more recent theoretical, even deductive estimate to find empirical fruit in the fossil record, given the weight of morphological evidence, certain theoretical hypotheses would have to be sustained. The rate of morphological change, especially in the African apes, would have to be extremely intensified and speeded up. This means that the mutational and thus the molecular changes underlying these alterations in what seems to be traditional African ape patterns would have to have proceeded far more rapidly than appears in the prior fossil record.

10.3 Left to right: modern African chimpanzee; *Sivapithecus* (GSP-15000) from Pakistan, c.9mya; modern orangutan from the East Indies. Nine million years and many thousand miles in distance, yet the similarity of the latter two primates is striking. To find a chimpanzee-human ancestor so close in form, we likely will have to go back at least 25my.

For example, the pathway from the mainline sivapithecine line toward *Gigantopithecus* and then to the contemporary orangutan, an evolutionary sequence of some 10-15 million years, seems reasonably consonant with traditional evolutionary morphological and behavioral rates of change within the primate evolutionary sequence going back to the Paleocene, some 55 million years ago and probably beyond into the Cretaceous. The orangutan may have gradually evolved from the earlier sivapithecine and ramapithecine forms of living in a mixed forest and plains ecology in southern Asia to being pushed into the tropical forest environment of the Indonesian Islands. Yet, one is hard pressed to identify the presumably sharp morphological changes that should have accompanied this shift to a completely arboreal tropical life style.

Jerrold Lowenstein has reported on his experiments in the radioimmunoassay of extinct and extant species. His method is to grind up the bones and teeth, which are placed in plastic containers—which binds the protein—whereupon rabbit anti-serum is added. The antibodies produce a radioactive reaction that reflects a degree of affinity, both measurable comparatively, then calibrated to equate with divergence sequences.

Lowenstein's results, while occasionally surprisingly informative, reveal that the mainline equids and other mammals have divergence rates that established recognizable lines of descent that reflect a slow and steady evolutionary progression from the late Eocene on, some 40mya.[144]

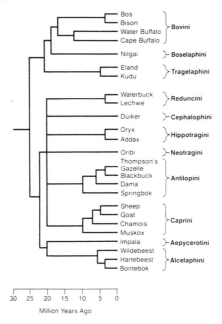

10.4 Radio-Immuno-Assay phylogeny of the bovids. The time scale created by Lowenstein's experiments is reasonable from a morphological standpoint. It constitutes a striking contrast with the molecular time scale estimates for hominoid divergence.

Yet, we are expected to concur in the revolutionary reshaping of the chimpanzee and the gorilla into highly specialized knuckle-walking semi-brachiating apes from what had to be a relatively unspecialized post-Miocene ape living in a mixed forest, savannah type of environment. At the same time this evolutionary scenario has it that another relatively unspecialized pongid having both hylobatinoid and sivapithecine morphological characteristics was comet-like, evolving into a true biped.

What were the selective conditions that so radically reshaped these creatures away from the common pathway, while at the same time maintaining their molecular affinity? The extensive variability in the genetic character of these indigenous West African jungle apes seems to argue for a long and relatively separate existence for their different family troops. It persuades rather, for a picture of a long placid evolutionary history in the jungles, one that has not undergone the sharp selective pressures that might have put their DNA through a tightening uniformatory sieve.

In sum, the molecular relationship of humans with the African apes as compared with the surviving member of the sivapithecine/ramapithecine clade is a puzzle. Until we find the fossil that binds together hominid and African ape in a concrete and empirical relationship, the molecular affinities must remain interesting theoretical speculations that still carry the experimental burden of proof, obligatory for all deductive hypotheses. Most probably we can predict the eventual discovery of a Miocene, c.15mya, knuckle-walking fossil ape that is a relatively unspecialized precursor, a blend of the three extant African species.

By contrast, there is much evolutionary support for a view that sees the origin of the protohominids, as Bernard Campbell once surmised it in 1966, before the intimidating force of mtDNA and blood albumin protein theory. Campbell saw in the human morphology so many hints of a cercopithecine, Old World monkey heritage, along with the dominant hominoid morphology, that he placed the origin of the protohominids back in the Oligocene, c.35mya, contemporary with what most anthropologists view as the breakout and diversification period of the hominoids and also the Cercopithecines from the then-existing mixed and undefined heritage of primates, prosimians, and apes and monkeys.

Klein, summarizing recent views on the evolution of these primate forms, sees a two-fold development in the Oligocene. The first phase, reflecting the confusing mixture of forms in the Fayum deposits in Egypt, exemplifies the jockeying for position by these extremely varied, still more intelligent and adaptable primates than those in the first phases of primate evolution, the plesiadapiforms—adapids, omomyids, and other sprinters from the Cretaceous boundary. By the end of the Oligocene, which also corresponds to a sharp climatic change toward cooler temperatures and drier terrestrial conditions, the separation of the Catarrhines and Haplorrhines had taken place.[145]

Some of these early ape/monkeys had tails. The ape line reflective of *Proconsul* definitely revealed a semi-arboreal quadruped, moving in a monkey-like manner, if without a tail. We ought not put limits on the range of variation in these primates, only partially exemplified in the Fayum fossils. Presumably they varied freely between what we consider today to be the model of the Old and New World monkeys. The taxonomic distinctions that we make today between monkey and ape clades was then probably more fluid in the morphologies and presumably behaviors of these variable evolving ape lines.

It is reasonably possible for a creature, small in size, carrying with it features we now recognize as relating to the gibbon, orangutan, Old World monkey, even the chimpanzee and gorilla, to have gradually separated itself out adaptively for a long and at first unheralded venture into a more terrestrial, partially arboreal slice of this rich adaptive mosaic of anthropoid evolution. Only time and natural selection would groove the multiplicity of possibilities into narrower linear progressions that today, some 30 million years later appear distinct and separate.

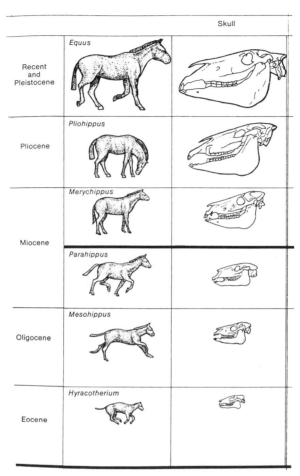

		Skull
Recent and Pleistocene	*Equus*	
Pliocene	*Pliohippus*	
Miocene	*Merychippus*	
	Parahippus	
Oligocene	*Mesohippus*	
Eocene	*Hyracotherium*	

10.5 Horse evolution. Over a forty-million-year period, horses developed diverse foot structures, and have grown larger. But the basic morphological body plan and their adaptive specializations are remarkably recognizable.

Anthropologists have found fossil New World monkeys on the islands of the West Indies, some tens of thousands of years old, that seem extremely different in structure from the surviving forms of this super-family, Ceboideia. And yet the consensus has been that the extraordinary variability contained in the Fayum fossils, which do not reveal the sharp differentiation in structure between the cercopithecoids and the ceboids at that stage, the mid-Oligocene, 30mya, leads to a seemingly stagnant evolutionary pattern in the New World monkeys when in place in the Western Hemisphere from the early Miocene, 25mya. Perhaps primate evolution in the New World slowed down to a halt upon separation from Old World primate dynamics and selection. Else, the survivors were the least innovative and experimental lines of New World monkeys. The New World adventurers, all the genetic experiments, the ecological opportunists, may have fallen victim to a placid and relatively unchanging faunal, climatic, and environmental setting in which conservative forms perdured selectively, at least until historical times.

One of the persistent errors that evolutionary theorists have made is in jumping to conclusions, eager to hypothetically fill in the existing gaps in the fossil record. Some of these errors are time sequence blanks, in the sense that, "if we do not yet find them, therefore they did not exist." Because we find fully-formed members of a group, say the vertebrates, in the Ordovician, some 476mya, but not in the Cambrian, 530mya, we assume that the vertebrates were not yet formed. Inevitably, as new discoveries have filled in these gaps in the evolutionary map we have had to extend our dating into more remote time frames. We continue to discover more of the iceberg that lies beneath.

Another error is to postulate macro-evolutionary processes, such as punctuated equilibrium theory, to explain the seeming jumps in the fossil record. In reality, as we more often discover, no special molecular or chromosomal revolutions in the process over time from "known" to "unknown" have occurred. Rather, the gaps were of our own conceptual making, assumptions about times of origins, never accounting for the mosaic evolutionary patterns that shape great cladistic diversity. Thus we create "hopeful monsters" composed of linearly extrusive theoretical leaps from one visible fossil point to the next.[146]

In the evolution of the hominid precursors too, the wisely restrained will not exclude the possible existence of more truly antecedent forms, even if they have not as yet been uncovered.

Endnotes, Chapter 10

[1] Andrews, P., and Stringer, C. 1993. "The Primates' Progress," in *Life*, S. J. Gould, ed., N.Y.: W. W. Norton, p. 234.

[2] Tobias, P. V. 1994. "The Evolution of Early Hominids," in *Companion Encyclopedia of Anthropology*, T. Ingold, N.Y.: Routledge, pp. 33-78; Itzkoff, S. W. 1991. "The Evolution of Human Intelligence: A Reply," *Evolutionary Theory*, Jan., 10:63-64.

[3] Szalay, F. S., and Delson, E. 1979. *Evolutionary History of the Primates*, N.Y.: Academic Press; Pilbeam, D. 1972. *The Ascent of Man*, N.Y.: Macmillan.

[4] Schwartz, Jeffrey. 1987. *The Red Ape*, London: Elm Tree Books; Schwartz, Jeffrey. 1993. *What the Bones Tell Us*, N.Y.: Henry Holt.

[5] Szalay and Delson, 1979, *op. cit.*

[6] Andrews, P., and Cronin, J. E. 1982. "The relationship of *Sivapithecus* and *Ramapithecus* and the evolution of the Orangutan," *Nature*, 297:541-546; Pilbeam, D. 1982. "New hominoid skull material from the Miocene of Pakistan," *Nature*, 295:232-234.

[7] Koenigswald, G. H. R., von. 1952. "'Gigantopithecus blacki' von Koenigswald, a giant fossil hominoid from the Pleistocene of southern China, " *Anthrop. Papers. Amer. Mus.*

[8] Begun, D. R. 1991. "European Catarrhine Diversity," *Jnl. Hum. Evol.*, 20:521-526.

[9] Campbell, Bernard. 1985. *Human Evolution*, N.Y.: Aldine De Gruyter, p. 370, cites V. Sarich and J. E. Cronin, 1977, "Generation lengths and rates of hominid molecular evolution," *Nature*, 269:354-355.

[10] Zuckerkandl, E., and Pauling, L. 1965. "Evolutionary divergence and convergence in proteins," in *Evolving Genes and Proteins*, V. Bryson, H. J. Vogel, eds., N.Y.: Academic Press, p. 97; Goodman, M. 1963.

"Man's place in the phylogeny of the primates as reflected in serum proteins," in *Classification and Human Evolution*, S. L. Washburn, ed., Chicago: Aldine, pp. 204-234.

[11] Stebbins, G. L. 1982. *Darwin to DNA, Molecules to Humanity*, San Francisco: W. H. Freeman, pp. 124-129; Dobzhansky, T., Ayala, F. J., Stebbins, G. L., Valentine, J. W. 1977. *Evolution*, San Francisco: Freeman; Campbell, Bernard. 1985., *op. cit.*, Table 12.1, p. 371.

[12] Sarich, V., and Wilson, A. C. 1966. "Quantitative immunochemistry and the evolution of primate albumins: micro-complement fixation," *Science*, 154:1563-1565; Campbell, Bernard. 1985. "Immunological Distances between Albumins of Various Old World Primates, *Human Evolution, op. cit.*, Table 12.2, p. 371 (calculated from data in Sarich and Wilson, 1967, *op. cit., Proc. Nat. Acad. Sci. U.S.*

[13] Sibley, C. G., and Ahlquist, J. E. 1984. "The phylogeny of the hominoid primates, as indicated by DNA-DNA hybridization," *Jnl. Mol. Evol.*, 20:2-15; Sibley, C. G., Comstock, J. A., Ahlquist, J. E. 1990. "DNA hybridization evidence of hominoid phylogeny: a reanalysis of the data," *Jnl. Mol. Evol.*, 30:202-236; Diamond, Jared. 1992. *The Third Chimpanzee*, N.Y.: Harper/Collins, pp. 19-21.

[14] Miyamoto, M. M., *et al.* 1988. "Molecular systematics of higher primates: genealogical relations and classification," *Proceed. Nat. Acad. Sci.*, 85:7627-7631; Goodman, M. *et al,.* 1990. "Primate evolution at the DNA level and a classification of hominoids," *Jnl. Mol. Evol.*, 30:260-266; Ueda, S., *et al.* 1988. "Multiple recombinational events in primate immunoglobulin epsilon and alpha genes suggest closer relationship of humans to chimpanzees than to gorillas, *Jnl. Mol. Evol.*, 27:77-83.

[15] Nei, M. 1987. *Molecular Evolutionary Genetics*, N.Y.: Columbia Univ. Press; also, see the work of R. J. Britten (late 1960s), work of, cited in. Stebbins, 1982, *op. cit.*, p. 169.

[16] Zihlman, Adrienne. 1990. "Knuckling Under," in *From Apes to Angels, Essays in Honor of Philip Tobias*, G. H. Sperber, ed., N.Y.: Wiley-Liss, pp. 1870-188.

[17] Stebbins, 1982, *op. cit.*, p. 320.

[18] Hasegawa, M., *et al.* 1984. "A new molecular clock of mitochondrial DNA and the evolution of the hominoids," *Proceed. Japan. Acad.*, 60B:95-98; Hayasaka, K., *et al.* 1988. "Molecular phylogeny and evolution of primate mitochondrial DNA," *Mol. Biol. Evol.*, 5(6):626-644.

[19] Andrews and Stringer, 1993, in Gould, ed., *op. cit.*, pp. 225-226.

[20] Stebbins, 1982, *op. cit.*, p. 319.

[21] Diamond, 1992, *op. cit.*, p. 23.

[22] Wilson, A. C., *et al.* 1977. "Biochemical Evolution," *Ann. Rev. Biochem.*, 46:573-639.

[23] Sarich and Wilson, 1966, *op. cit., Science*, 154:1564-1565.

[24] Campbell, Bernard. 1966. *Human Evolution: An Introduction to Man's Adaptations*, 1st ed., Chicago: Aldine, pp. 326-328.

[25] Campbell, Bernard. 1966. *Human Evolution: An Introduction to Man's Adaptations*, 1st ed., *op. cit.*, pp. 80-85.

[26] Andrews and Cronin, 1982, *op. cit., Nature*, 297:541-546; Pilbeam, 1982, *op. cit., Nature*, 295:232-234.

[27] Campbell, Bernard. 1966. *Human Evolution: An Introduction to Man's Adaptations*, 1st ed., *op. cit.*, pp. 326-327; Straus, W. L. 1949. "The riddle of man's ancestry," *Quart. Rev. Biol.*, 24:200-223; Itzkoff, S. W. 1983. *The Form of Man*, Ashfield, MA: Paideia, p. 16.

[28] Campbell, Bernard. 1985. *Human Evolution, op. cit.*, p. 368.

[29] Campbell, Bernard. 1985. *Human Evolution, op. cit.*, p. 369.

[30] *Ibid.*

[31] Campbell, Bernard. 1985. *Human Evolution, op. cit.*, Table 12.1, p. 371, from Dobzhansky *et al.,* 1977, *op. cit.*

[32] Campbell, Bernard. 1985. "Immunological Distances between Albumins of Various Old World Primates," *Human Evolution, op. cit.*, p. 371, Table 12.2, calculated from data in Sarich and Wilson, 1967, *op. cit., Proc. Nat. Acad. Sci. U.S.*, shows humans closer to chimpanzees than chimpanzees are to gorillas; see also Wilson, A. C., and Sarich, V. M. 1969. "A molecular time scale for human evolution," *Proc. Nat. Acad. Sci. U.S.*, 63:1088-1093.

[33] Campbell, Bernard. 1985. "Molecular Comparisons among the Great Apes and *Homo*," *Human Evolution, op. cit.*, p. 372, Table 12.3, from Andrews and Cronin, 1982, *op. cit., Nature*, 297:541-546.

[34] Lowenstein, J. 1980a. "Immunospecificity of Fossil Proteins," in *Biogeochemistry of Amino Acids*, P. E. Hare, ed., N.Y.: John Wiley, p. 401.

[35] Lowenstein, J. 1985. "Radioimmunoassay of Extinct and Extant Species," in *Hominid Evolution: Past, Present, and Future*, Tobias, P. V., ed., N.Y.: Alan R. Liss, pp. 401-410 (esp. p. 402); Lowenstein,

1980a, " in Hare, P. E., ed., *op. cit.*; Lowenstein, J. 1980b. "Species-specific proteins in fossils," *Naturwissenschaften*, 67:343.

[36] Lowenstein, 1985, in Tobias, ed., *op. cit.*, p. 405; Lowenstein, J. 1983. "Fossil proteins and evolutionary time," *Pontif. Acad. Sci. Scripta. Varia.*, 50:151.

[37] Lowenstein, J., *et al.* 1982. "Piltdown jaw confirmed as orang," *Nature*, 299:294; Schwartz, Jeffrey. 1985. "Toward a Synthetic Analysis of Hominoid Phylogeny," in Tobias, ed., *op. cit.*, pp. 265-269 (esp. pp. 267-268).

[38] Andrews and Cronin, 1982, *op. cit., Nature*, 297:541; Schwartz, Jeffrey. 1984a. "The evolutionary relationship of man and orang-utans," *Nature*, 308:501; Schwartz, Jeffrey. 1984b. "Hominoid evolution: a review and a reassessment," *Current Anthropology*, 25:655.

[39] Sarich and Wilson, 1967, *op. cit., Proc. Nat. Acad. Sci. U.S.*

[40] Schwartz, 1985, in Tobias, ed., *op. cit.*, pp. 266-267.

[41] Schwartz, 1985, in Tobias, ed., *op. cit.*, p. 267; Goodman, M., *et al.* 1983. "Evidence of human origins from haemoglobins of African apes," *Nature*, 303:546.

[42] Schwartz, 1985, in Tobias, ed., *op. cit.*, p. 268; Bruce, E. J., and Ayala, F. J. 1979. Phylogenetic relationships between man and the apes: electrophoretic evidence," *Evolution*, 33:1040.

[43] Hasegawa *et al.*, 1984, *op. cit., Proceed. Japan. Acad.*, 60B:95-98.

[44] Schwartz, 1985, in Tobias, ed., *op. cit.*, p. 268.

[45] Gibbons, Ann. 1995. "When It Comes to Evolution, Humans Are in a Slow Class," *Science*, 3/31/95, 267:1907-1908 (Research News, Molecular Anthropology).

[46] Fitch, Walter, and Roy Britten referred to in Stebbins, 1982, *op. cit.*, pp. 124-131, 169, see above.

[47] Li, Wen Hsing, *et al.* 1993. *Nature*, 362:745-747-1993; Gibbons, 1995, *op. cit., Science*, 3/31/95, 267:1908.

[48] Britten, R. J. 1986. *Science*, 231:1393-1398.

[49] Zuckerkandl and Pauling, 1965, in Bryson and Vogel, eds., *op. cit.*, p. 97.

[50] Stebbins, 1982, *op. cit.*, Fig. 10.1, p. 320.

[51] Gibbons, 1995, *op. cit., Science*, 3/31/95, 267:1908.

[52] Gibbons, 1995, *op. cit., Science*, 3/31/95, 267:1907-1908; Li, Wen Hsing, *et al.*, 1993, *op. cit., Nature*, 362:745-747.

[53] Wilson *et al.*, 1977, *op. cit., Ann. Rev. Biochem.*, 46:573-639.

[54] Paabo, Svante. 1995. "The Y Chromosome and the Origin of All of Us (Men)," *Science*, May 26, 1995, 268:1141-42.

[55] See J. Mountain and L. L. Cavalli-Sforza on this methodology: Mountain, J., and Cavalli-Sforza, L. L. 1993. "Evolution of Modern Humans: Evidence from Nuclear DNA Polymorphosis," in *The Origin of Modern Humans and the Impact of Chronometric Dating*, Aitken, M. J., Stringer, C. B., and Mellars, P. A., eds., Princeton, N.J.: Princeton Univ. Press.

[56] Paabo, 1995, *op. cit., Science*, May 26, 1995, 268:1141; see also Hedges, S. B., and Stoneking, M. 1992. *Science*, 255:737.

[57] Paabo, 1995, *op. cit., Science*, May 26, 1995, 268:1141.

[58] Tobias, ed., 1985, *op. cit.*, p. 267.

[59] Schwartz, 1984a, *op. cit., Nature*, 308:501.

[60] Brown, W., *et al.* 1982. "Mitochondrial sequences of primates: tempo and mode of evolution," *Jnl. Mol. Evolution*, 18:225.

[61] Dorit, R. L., *et al.* 1995. *Science*, 268:1183.

[62] Paabo, 1995, *op. cit., Science*, May 26, 1995, 268:1142; see also Whitfield, L. S., and Goodfellow, P. N. 1993. *Nature*, 364:713.

[63] Chiarelli, B. 1985. "Chromosomes and the Origin of Man," in Tobias, ed., *op. cit.*, pp. 397-400.

[64] Schwartz, 1985, in Tobias, ed., *op. cit.*, p. 268; Schwartz, 1984b, *op. cit., Current Anthropology*, 25:655; Yunis, J., and Prakash, O. 1982. "The origin of man: a chromosomal pictorial legacy," *Science*, 215:1525.

[65] Schwartz, 1985, in Tobias, ed., *op. cit.*, p. 268; Mai, L. 1983. " A model of chromosome evolution and its bearing on cladogenesis in the hominoideia," in *New Interpretations of Ape and Human Ancestry*, R. L. Ciochon, R. and R. Coruccini, R., eds., N.Y.: Plenum, pp. 87-114.

[66] Gingerich, P. 1985. "Nonlinear Molecular Clocks and Ape-Human Divergence Times," in Tobias, ed., *op. cit.*, pp. 411-416.

[67] Gingerich, P. 1985. "Nonlinear Molecular Clocks and Ape-Human Divergence Times," in Tobias, ed., *op. cit.*, p. 412.

[68] Sarich, V. 1970. "Primate systematics with special reference to Old World monkeys, a protein perspective," in *Old World Monkeys*, J. Napier and P. Napier, eds., N.Y.: Academic Press, p. 194.

[69] *Ibid.*

[70] Goodman, 1963, in Washburn, ed., *op. cit.*, pp. 204-234.

[71] Martin, R. D. 1990. *Primate Origins and Evolution, a phylogenetic reconstruction*, Princeton N.J.: Princeton Univ. Press, pp. 690-709.

[72] Zuckerkandl, E., and Pauling, L. 1962. "Molecular disease, evolution, and genetic heterogeneity," in *Horizons in Biochemistry*, M. Kasha and N. Pullman, eds., N.Y.: Academic Press.

[73] Beard, K. C. 1996. "Fossil May Fill a Gap in Early Primate Evolution," *The New York Times*, 4/9/96 (*Reuters*, 4/8/96); Beard, K. C., *et al.* 1994. "A Diverse New Primate Fauna from Middle Eocene Fissure-fillings in southeastern China," *Nature* (London), 368:604-609.

[74] Yoder, A. D., *et al.* 1996. "Ancient single origin for Malagasy primates," *Proc. Natl. Acad. Sci. U.S.A.*, May, 1996, 193:5122-5126.

[75] Martin, 1990, *op. cit.*, p. 693.

[76] Haldane, J. B. 1957. "The cost of natural selection," *Jnl. Genet.*, 55:511-524.

[77] Martin, 1990, *op. cit.*, p. 694.

[78] Martin, 1990, *op. cit.*, p. 695.

[79] Paabo, 1995, *op. cit., Science*, May 26, 1995, 268:1141-42.

[80] Martin, 1990, *op. cit.*, pp. 697-698.

[81] Martin, 1990, *op. cit.*, p. 700.

[82] Gingerich, 1985, in Tobias, ed., *op. cit.*, pp. 411-416.

[83] Goodman, 1963, in Washburn, ed., *op. cit.*, pp. 204-234.

[84] Martin, 1990, *op. cit.*, p. 709.

[85] Fleagle, J. G. 1995. "Origin and Radiation of Anthropoid Primates," in *Biological Anthropology, The State of the Science*, N. T. Boaz and L. D. Wolfe, eds., Bend, Oregon: International Institute for Human Evolutionary Research, Central Oregon University Center, pp. 1-21, (esp. pp. 1, 16).

[86] Gingerich, 1985, in Tobias, ed., *op. cit.*

[87] See Schwartz, 1987, *op. cit.*, pp. 276-277, on J. Desmond Clark's views of J. Lowenstein's "Radio-Immunoassay chronologies and taxonomic affinities.

[88] Klein, R. G. 1989. *The Human Career*, Chicago: Univ. of Chicago Press, p. 48.

[89] Tuttle, R. H. 1985. "Darwin's Apes, Dental Apes, and the Descent of Man: Normal Science in Evolutionary Anthropology," in *Primate Evolution and Human Origins*, R. L. Ciochon and J. G. Fleagle, eds., Menlo Park, CA: Benjamin/Cummings Publishing, pp. 333-342.

[90] Schwartz, 1987, *op. cit.*, pp. 94-95.

[91] Schwartz, 1987, *op. cit.*, pp. 113-115, Fig. 4f.

[92] Schwartz, 1993, *op. cit.*, pp. 261, 265.

[93] Tobias, 1994, in Ingold, ed., *op. cit.*, p. 39*ff*, esp. figs. 1-3, pp. 41-43. See also Campbell, Bernard. 1985. *Human Evolution, op. cit.*, pp.146-148, for illustrations of comparative pelvic structure in chimpanzee, *Australopithecus, H. sapiens.*

[94] Schwartz, 1987, *op. cit.*, pp. 161-163.

[95] Schultz, A. H. 1968. "The recent hominoid primates," in *Classification and Human Evolution*, S. L. Washburn, ed., *op. cit.*, pp. 85-115; Schwartz, 1987, *op. cit.*, pp. 196-197.

[96] Schwartz, 1987, *op. cit.*, fig. 7C, p. 188; Schultz, A. H. 1936. "Characters Common to Higher Primates and Characters Specific for Man," *Quarterly Review of Biology*, 11:259-283, 425-455.

[97] Vrba, E. S. 1979. "A new study of the scapula of *Australopithecus africanus* from Sterkfontein," *American Journal of Physical Anthropology*, 51:117-130.

[98] Schwartz, 1987, *op. cit.*, p. 198.

[99] Schwartz, 1993, *op. cit.*, p. 268; Thiranagama, R., et al. 1991. "Character Phylogeny of the Primate Forelimb Superficial Venous System," *Folia Primatologica*, 57:181-190.

[100] Andrews, and Cronin, 1982, *op. cit., Nature*, 297:541-546; Schwartz, 1987, *op. cit.*, pp. 181-183, also fig, 7A, p. 182.

[101] Schwartz, 1987, *op. cit.*, pp. 183-184; Schultz, 1936, *op. cit., Quarterly Review of Biology*, 11:259-283, 425-455.

[102] Schwartz, 1987, *op. cit.*, fig. 7B, p.186, also pp. 186-187.

[103] Schwartz, 1987, *op. cit.*, fig. 7D, p. 192.

[104] Schwartz, 1987, *op. cit.*, pp. 168-169; also see fig. 6B, p. 170.

[105] Schwartz, 1993, *op. cit.*, pp. 251-254.

[106] Andrews and Cronin, 1982, *op. cit., Nature*, 297:541-546.

[107] Schwartz, 1987, *op. cit.*, p. 195.

[108] Andrews and Stringer, 1993, in Gould, ed., *op. cit.*, p. 221.

[109] Schwartz, 1987, *op. cit.*, p. 38.

[110] Schwartz, 1987, *op. cit.*, pp. 199-200.

[111] Pilbeam, 1982, *op. cit., Nature*, 295:232-234; see also Pilbeam, D. 1996. "Genetic and Morphological Records of the Hominoidea and Hominid Origins: A Synthesis," *Molecular Phylogenetics and Evolution*, Feb., 5:1:155-168.

[112] Schwartz, 1987, *op. cit.*, p. 201.

[113] Delson, E., and Andrews, P. 1975. "Evolution and Interrelationships of the Catarrhine Primates," in *Phylogeny of the Primates*, W. P. Luckett and F. S. Szalay, eds., N.Y.: Plenum Press, pp.405-406; Schwartz, 1987, *op. cit.*, pp. 202-203.

[114] Schwartz, 1987, *op. cit.*, fig. 7F, p. 204.

[115] Schwartz, 1987, *op. cit.*, p. 166.

[116] Schwartz, 1987, *op. cit.*, pp. 95-97.

[117] Klein, 1989, *op. cit.*, p. 92; Martin, L. 1985. "Significance of enamel thickness in hominoid evolution," *Nature*, 314:260-263; Schwartz, 1987, *op. cit.*, pp. 284-289.

[118] Schwartz, 1987, *op. cit.*, p. 187.

[119] Schultz, A. H. 1938. "The Recent Hominoid Primates," in *Perspectives on Human Evolution*, Vol. 1, S. L. Washburn and P. C. Jay, eds., N.Y.: Holt, Rinehart and Winston, pp. 122-195; Schwartz, 1987, *op. cit.*, pp. 194-196.

[120] Schwartz, 1987, *op. cit.*, pp. 209-210.

[121] Schultz, A. H. 1936. "Characters Common to Higher Primates and Characters Specific for Man," *Quarterly Review of Biology*, 11:259-283, 425-455; Schwartz, 1987, *op. cit.*, p. 210.

[122] Martin, R. D. 1968. "Toward a New Definition of Primates," *Man*, 3:377-401.

[123] Schwartz, 1987, *op. cit.*, pp. 211-212.

[124] Andrews, and Stringer, 1993, in. Gould, ed., *op. cit.*, p. 226.

[125] Diamond, 1992, *op. cit.,*, p. 23; Zihlman, A. L., *et al.* 1978. "Pygmy Chimpanzee as a Possible Prototype for the Common Ancestor of Humans, Chimpanzees and Gorillas," *Nature*, 275:744-746.

[126] McKinney, M. L. 1993. *Evolution of Life*, Englewood Cliffs, N.J.: Prentice Hall, p. 205.

[127] Diamond, 1992, *op. cit.*, pp. 81-82.

[128] Diamond, 1992, *op. cit.*, p. 75; Kano, Takayoshi. 1991. *The Last Ape: Pygmy Chimpanzee Behavior and Ecology*, Stanford: Stanford Univ. Press; Nishida, T., *et al.* 1992. "Meat sharing as a coalition strategy by an alpha male chimpanzee?" in *Topics in Primatology, Vol. 1: Human Origins*, T. Nishida *et al.*, eds., Tokyo: Univ. of Tokyo Press, pp.159-174; see also, on the Bonobo, de Waal, Franz. 1989. *Peacemaking Among Primates*, Cambridge, MA: Harvard Univ. Press; de Waal, Franz. 1996. *Good Natured*, Cambridge, MA: Harvard Univ. Press.

[129] Schwartz, 1987, *op. cit.*, fig. 7I, p. 213.

[130] Schwartz, 1987, *op. cit.*, p. 215.

[131] Schwartz, 1987, *op. cit.*, pp. 205-208.

[132] Schwartz, 1987, *op. cit.*, p. 216.

[133] Tuttle, R. H. 1974. "Darwin's Apes, Dental Apes, and the Descent of Man: Normal Science in Evolutionary Anthropology," *Current Anthropology*, 15:389-398.

[134] Morton, D. J. 1924. "Evolution of the Human Foot, 2," *Am. Jnl. Phys. Anthr.*, 7:1-52, esp. p. 39.

[135] Morton, D. J. 1924. "Evolution of the Longitudinal Arch of the Human Foot," *Jnl. Bone and Joint Surg.*, 6:56-90, esp. p. 88.

[136] Schultz, A. H. 1927. "Observations on a gorilla fetus," *Eugenical News*, 12:37-40, esp. p. 40.

[137] Schultz, A. H. 1936. "Characters Common to Higher Primates and Characters Specific for Man," *Quarterly Review of Biology*, 11:259-283, 425-455, p. 452; Schultz, A. H. 1969. *The Life of Primates*, N.Y.: Universe Books, p. 251.

[138] Tuttle, 1985, in Ciochon and Fleagle, eds., *op. cit.*, pp. 333-342.

[139] Shultz, A. H. 1930. "The Skeleton of the Trunk and Limbs of Higher Primates," *Human Biology*, 2:203-438; Ward, C. V. 1993. "Torso morphology and locomotion in Proconsul nyanzae," *Am. Jrnl Phys. Anthr,* 92:291-328; Pilbeam, D. 1997. "Research on Miocene Hominoids and Hominid Origins: The Last Three Decades," in *Function, Phylogeny and Fossils*, D. R. Begun, ed., *et al.*, N.Y.: Plenum Press.

[140] Latimer, B., and Ward, C. 1993. "The Thoracic and Lumbar Vertebrae," in *The Nariokotome `Homo erectus' Skeleton*, A. Walker and R. Leakey, eds., Cambridge, Mass.: Harvard University Press, pp. 266-293, esp. 292-293.

[141] Itzkoff, 1983 *op. cit.*, pp. 81-82; Itzkoff, S. W. 1985. *Triumph of the Intelligent*, N.Y.: Peter Lang, Diagrams 4, 5; Itzkoff, *op. cit., Evolutionary Theory*, January, 10:63-64.

[142] Tobias, 1994, in Ingold, ed., *op. cit.*, p. 53.

[143] Hill, A., and Ward, S. 1988. *Yearbook Of Physical Anthropology*, 31:49-83; 1990. The original taxonomic classification emphasized an australopithecine derivation. But the thinly-enameled teeth may have changed the genus attribution to *Ardipithecus*. (See White, T. D., *et al.* 1994. "*Australopithecus ramidus*, a new species of early hominid from Aramis, Ethiopia," *Nature*, 22 Sept., 371:306-312.

[144] Lowenstein, 1985, in Tobias, ed., *op. cit.*, also Illustrations.

[145] Klein, 1989, *op. cit.*, pp. 68-77.

[146] Goldschmidt, R. 1940. *The Material Basis of Evolution*, New Haven: Yale Univ. Press.

11

Transition: From Pongid to Hominid

"Physics Envy"[1]

The "general theory of relativity," as put forward by Albert Einstein early in the 20th century, followed on his "special theory," which established the speed of light as the fulcrum by which all physical laws describe the motion of objects, in all coordinate systems and moving uniformly, relative to each other. "Mass is energy and energy has mass" leads to the conservation law of mass-energy. The geometry of objects and their energic equivalence was thus subject to a mathematical equivalence in recording their movement relative to a hypothetical observer.

It was clear that this theoretical postulation of Einstein's, the "special theory," published in 1905, explained and integrated a number empirical as well as theoretical anomalies reflecting the tension between classical Newtonian mechanics and the newer electromagnetic equations of Faraday, Maxwell, and Hertz. Early on there was empirical confirmation of these first of Einstein's equations.

The "general theory" was even more abstract since it related the geometry of space and time (coordinate systems) to the movement of objects, "The geometrical nature of our world is shaped by masses and their velocities."[2] Einstein was arguing that, contra-Newton, there was no absolutely objective geometrical and gravitational reality in the universe that inextricably shaped our knowledge of physical reality, and that the movement of objects themselves created the gravitational forces within our universe of planetary and galactic attractions and repulsions. These laws, the "general theory," even defined the movement of objects in space and time within the atmosphere of our Earth.

It was an extraordinarily elegant theoretical proposition, one that is changing our entire perspective on the macro-structure of physical and cosmological knowledge. Still, it was just a theory, overarching, abstract, and beautiful in its simplicity. In 1919, an expedition headed by Eddington and Crommelin of the Royal Astronomical Society went to Brazil and West Africa to observe simultaneously an eclipse of the sun. The purpose was for each to measure the angle of distortion of light from the sun as it was altered by the gravitational mass of the planet Mercury. Through the results of this experiment, the theory finally received universal acceptance. Factual, concrete, sensory information had been obtained to test the theory objectively. The "general theory" could have been falsified were the light from the Sun observed differently as it passed close to Mercury.[3]

In the 1950s Cesare Emiliani, analyzing the rate of organic sedimentation on the ocean floor under different temperature and climatic conditions, arrived at a new and radically reduced estimate of the duration of the Pleistocene Ice Ages. He estimated a length of 400,000 years as compared to the 1-2 my period, the general consensus at that time.[4]

The anthropologist Loren Eiseley lent great notoriety to Emiliani's work when he incorporated it as a basis for the evolutionary hypotheses in his best selling, *The Immense Journey*.[5] The well-known geophysicist Rhodes Fairbridge of Columbia University was publicly reported as supporting this fore-shortened time frame for the Pleistocene.[6] In the end an unconsidered variable in this deductive theoretical model rendered it factually unsupportable. We now have gone back to the approximate surety of a time span of about 1.9my for the Pleistocene.

So, too, other theories will be subject to skepticism and judgment. An example is the molecular analysis of the relationship of living primates, and the presumed time of separation into their respective lineages, calculated from a deductive theoretical model as to the extent and rapidity of these stochastic molecular changes. The vindication or the falsification of this model is yet to come from the fossil (empirical) record. All that we presently have in the concrete are formulae that analyze relationships between living taxa. How well they predict will define the scientific status of these theoretical models.

J. Clark is reported to have refused a request by Jerold Lowenstein, both of the University of California, for samples of australopithecine fossils so that the latter might attempt to ascertain their molecular affinities. As reported earlier, Lowenstein has developed a method of radioimmunoassay analysis of fossil materials by which he has attempted to clarify phylogenetic relationships of various lines of mammals.[7]

The reason given by Clark for this refusal was his apparent skepticism of the maturity of this science and the probable usefulness of any protein-reactivity results worth the sacrifice of the fossil australopithecine material. His challenge was that, first he would like to see what the molecular systematists and biochemists could do "with a set of samples of unknown origin." In other words, the level of knowledge about the relationships of molecular protein or DNA structure in various animals was as yet too superficial for such an investment of rare fossils. In fact, the theory used known fossil relationships as a "crutch" or fulcrum for shaping the supposed deduction.

Gerard Schwartz goes on to note that the method used by Lowenstein to identify the relationship of the Piltdown hoax materials with an orangutan, as well as other identified mammal relationships—baby mammoth tissue with living elephant species; remnant muscle tissue of an extinct 19th-century Tasmanian wolf to the various living lines of marsupials—has helped to clarify a number of affinities between living and extinct forms.

Importantly to Schwartz, Lowenstein's albumin reactivity experiments have resulted in placing the orangutan closer to humans than to either of the two chimpanzee species.[8] The controversies and the mystery continue as to the origin of the hominids and their phyletic relationship to the other extant and extinct anthropoid lines.

Anthropoid Affinities: An Hypothesis

A Look Back: Our base line is the Oligocene period, 35-30mya.

The origin of the primates, as noted earlier, can now be traced back to the Cretaceous, at least 70mya, and probably more, the splitting of the various ungulate, carnivore, insectivore, and rodent lines of therian placentals. One source of debate involves the two lines of prosimians, the adapoid lemurs, and the seemingly more evolved omomyids, tarsiers, the latters' skull and tooth structure more approaching the evolved primate patterns. Can these lines be traced back to an original ancestral form, perhaps to the extinct plesiadapiforms, animals with claws, and thus perhaps only peripheral primates, or were they already separate lines in the Paleocene, 60mya?

The discoveries of Beard, of *Eosimia*, seem to argue that the two surviving lines were probably but two of many branchings of an early protoprimate opportunistic fragmentation, expansion and radiation, then selection and extinction of most of these forms in the competitions of the Paleocene and Eocene, 65-40mya. In all probability we will eventually conclude that the higher apes—anthropoids, monkeys and hominids—existed simultaneously with other cousins of this host. In other words, the anthropoids, even though not yet represented for the early phases of the Cenozoic, from 65mya, were still an evolving but hidden evolutionary line. This seems to be the preliminary lesson of *Eosimia*, whose collateral affiliations seem yet to be in doubt.

Our model is that which we have learned from mammal evolution as well as ear-lier.evolutionary transitions. While the mammals first appear at the very end of the Triassic, c.220-210mya, seeming evolutionary outgrowths of the then-contemporary therapsid cynodonts, it should be clear that their revolutionary morphology, including their diminution in size relative to the cynodonts, is reasonably traceable to the earliest stages of the latter's evolution, a product of the vast Permian extinctions, c.250mya. Indications are that the cynodonts had some internal homeothermic control of their metabolic processes. They became increasingly specialized over this period, c.250-210mya. If we have not officially found a direct ancestral form to the earliest mammals, which seem to have rapidly radiated into a variety of forms, mostly extinct today, further indicating a well-established genetic diversity, they were probably being selectively honed into a quiet but competitive niche throughout the 40 my or so of cynodont evolution under the noses of the proliferating dinosaurs.

Bear in mind that we are dealing with vertebrates that for several hundred million years have had full complements of chromosomes. These chromosomes were apparently subject to the same level of molecular genetic instability as were the more recent primate vertebrates. There were no superior "gods" that were able to speed up or slow down a process of genetic change and stability merely because recent sea- and land-living environments had impacted the primates. The Darwinian processes of adaptation and selection first must be presented with genetic "facts." Our hypothesis is that it took at least 40 to 50my to shape the first mammalian prototype from its supposed ancient reptilian model. Then came a subsequent 150-million-year process of mammalian evolution. The results, at the border of the Cenozoic, some 65mya, were numerous preadapted primate placentals.

The Oligocene, c.35mya, some 40-50my after our conservatively presumed primate differentiation from herbivore, insectivore, rodent, and carnivore placental forms, seems to be the time of confluence. Then, a sharply-selective competitive scene was set for the future of the primates. In the Miocene, from c.25mya, the primates flourished in a broad niche of mixed arboreal/ground dwelling life styles that were made possible by a heritage that by-passed morphological and behavioral specialization. A somewhat larger defensive brain, the ability to move through modestly varied environmental and ecological settings, reveals in the Fayum, Egypt, fossils, real differentiation of form, plus fossils in plenitude.

Fayum, south of Cairo: A small number of what are now believed to be disappearing prosimians. Four fossils: two tarsier species, an adapoid or loris.[9] But, there were literally thousands of other anthropoid fossils, at least 7 genera. In the early stages of analysis, scientists attempted to relate them to later monkey or hominoid forms. Today they are viewed, including the seemingly protoape-like *Aegyptopithecus* into two great but extinct super-families of anthropoids: A. Parapithecoidea: *Qatrania*, *Apidium*, *Parapithecus*, *Simonsius*. B. Propliopithecoidea, *Aegyptopithecus*. The former may be precursor monkey types, both New World and Old World possibilities. The latter might perhaps be viewed as existing somewhat later in time, 30mya in contrast to the "A" group at 35mya. The "B" group is still considered to be unrelated to any subsequent ape-human fossil forms.[10]

Because New World monkey fossils have been found in Bolivia, dated to 25mya, fossils that seem to combine elements of the various Fayum fossils, it is not impossible that the range of variation among the anthropoids of Africa, perhaps even North America and Europe, mostly in the earlier Eocene, of adapoids, too, was quite extensive. Here, as usual, our sampling is of veritable the tip of the iceberg, only now one-thousandth of the possibilities of fossil knowledge. Hopefully time and circumstance will allow us to reduce these possibilities with further scientific research.

Outside of the semi-tropical Fayum environment, the Oligocene constitutes one of the many climatic and thus environmental turning points in evolutionary history.[11] One hypothesis is that the turn to a cooler, drier climate, and thus a less jungle-like environment throughout the world, placed the highly specialized prosimians under strong competitive and selective pressures from both anthropoids and rodents. The latter had presumably eliminated the multituberculate mammals by the end of the Eocene, c.40mya. The multituberculates had thinly-enameled and small-cusped teeth as well as a more specialized and less developed non-placental intelligence. They marked the end of a long and competitive mammalian line.

Going Forward

There is an admitted gap in the fossil record from the time of the Fayum primates, at about 30mya, to close to 25-20mya, now mostly in East Africa. Here we find *Proconsul,* and subsequently a wide variety of apes. Names such as *Dendropithecus, Heliopithecus, Afropithecus, Kenyapithecus,* leading to *Sivapithecus, Ramapithecus, Oreopith-*

ecus, and D*ryopithecus* as the Eurasian continent joined with Africa to allow migratory egress from about 17-14mya.

The perspective is that the period from 30mya saw the full differentiation of the two mainline catarrhine forms, the Old World cercopithecine monkeys and the apes, leading eventually to a splitting of the line into the recent and modern great apes and humans. The apes of the Miocene, from *Proconsul* to the European Dryopithecines, were quite different both from the recent great apes and the hominids. They were by and large gracile creatures, smallish like, gibbons, mixed arboreal and ground dwelling, still showing signs of the original Oligocene anthropoid heritage of monkey-like behaviors and morphologies, while in their tooth and skull formation, and in their somewhat larger size, they reflected a unique and successful way of life.

J. G. Fleagle believes that *Proconsul africanus* was an arboreal quadruped with suspending and climbing abilities, but no obvious adaptations for brachiating, as did the gibbons, or knuckle-walking, as did the gorillas and chimpanzees. Neither of these specializations nor full climbing adaptation was yet fully developed in the mid-Miocene.[12]

The monkeys were relatively sparse during this time period. Their spurt of development and radiation came during the late Miocene, after 15mya, coinciding with the African disappearance of all but one line of Miocene apes. The Old World monkey morphology, exemplified in the bilophodont molars, two pairs of cusps linked by shearing crests, are today seen as derived, more recent Miocene modernizations and specializations for a successful life of leaf-eating in the trees, and in relatively warm and subtropical settings. It should be noted that apes with differently structured teeth, such as the European Miocene O*reopithecus* and the modern gorilla and bonobo, flourished on a diet of leaves.[13]

The veritable disappearance of the African apes after about 12mya, then in Europe after about 9mya lends an element of mystery as the Old World monkeys proliferated and spread throughout the continents. The Sivapithecines with their heritage of thick-enamel molars, perhaps derived from the mid-Miocene *Kenyapithecus* forms, spread throughout Asia, G*igantopithecus* perhaps surviving to about 0.5mya, and the ancestors of the orangutans gradually pushed into the deep jungles of Southeast Asia and the islands. The gibbon ancestors probably were pushed out of Africa in the earliest phases of the land bridge connection. In all probability they were then, 17mya, well on their way toward a specialization of extreme brachiation in the upper forest ecology.

As earlier noted, the first hominid fossil fragments appear in the record about 6mya, and identifiable skeletal remains shortly after 5mya. No fossil remains of the ancestors of the contemporary great apes have been found beyond reasonably contemporary times. Is there a hypothetical explanation for the DNA genetic connection of these apes—and yet their sharp morphological separateness from the hominids—at the same time accepting the close sivapithecine/hominid morphological affinity, along with the seeming distant molecular connection between the orangutan and contemporary humans?

Hypothesis

Let us establish a line of evolutionary descent starting in the late Oligocene-early Miocene, c.30-25mya. Along this hypothetical "Oklahoma Land Rush" starting line of putative apes are many diverse forms, including the two that are thought to have disappeared: the Parapithecoideia and the Propliopithecoideia. Undoubtedly there were many others. Along this line of diverse protoapes are the protohominid precursors. Positioned to the genetic/morphological near right are other protoapes carrying with them many of the same morphological features later identified with the Sivapithecines. At the extreme right of this array is positioned the ancestral line of the orangutan, most distantly related of the future Sivapithecines to the future hominids.

To the immediate left of the protohominids are ape forms one day to evolve into the chimpanzees and the gorillas, sharing some physical features with the protohominids, and, of course, as with those apes to the immediate right, a close molecular relationship. To the further left of this latter grouping would be the protogibbons, also sharing a number of morphological characteristics with the future hominid line.

It is hypothesized that the gibbon proceeded rapidly on its own way, as the preadapted ape forms swarmed into the ecologically beckoning African Miocene. But, the gibbon was able to retain certain morphological characteristics—arm structure, some remnant bipedal skills as it moved into a secure and fixed ecology, early to specialize, stabilize, eventually migrate at a distance from the other related ape forms. The Sivapithecines, on the other hand, including the future R*amapithecus,* may have shared more molecular and morphological factors with the protohominids (perhaps a greater molecular affinity than the protochimpanzees and gorillas), they did eventually fail and disappear.

The argument is that, of the extant apes, the African survivors early on were pressed for survival into a specialized African jungle niche. Their current diverse within-species DNA profile argues for a long heritage of life in the West African jungles. The overall morphological specializations of these apes, in their knuckle walking, hip and torso structure, testify to a long shaping for survival in a peripheral and highly specialized ecology. That the gorilla is now a grass and leaf eater, and that all three of these apes are thinly enameled in their molar structure, adds weight to their probable long separation from the protohominids.

On the other hand, the only remnant of the extensive and diverse Afro/Euro/Asiatic sivapithecine clade is the orangutan, whose preadaptations for a life in the southeast Asian jungles could also carry with it the greatest molecular distance of this group from the hominids. Still, the orangutans retained over a much longer period of evolutionary history the ancient morphological affinities. These ancient retentions may have been possible because this long migrating clade of apes never had to undergo the competitive pressures as did the last surviving African apes, the chimpanzees and the gorilla.

Hominid Origins: Probabilities

In certain characters man seems to resemble most closely the living semibrachiating monkeys, and we have noted in particular the high index of cephalization of these primates. Man's hand and penis show close similarities to those of certain Old World monkeys. In contrast, the apes have hands that have undergone specialization for brachiation, so they have to a great extent lost their manipulative power. This situation is typical of many characters of man when they are compared with apes; we find that man is less specialized in many of his brachiating features and shares, instead, more generalized features with the Old World monkeys.[14]

> Though we bear the marks of the apes in our bodies, we are profoundly different from any of them. As noted earlier, we actually share more of our locomotor morphology with *Alouatta* [New World Howler monkey] than with any living ape. This demonstrates with some force how far both we and the African apes have evolved from the condition of our ancestors.[15]

Oxnard and Stern both see the human shoulder as most functionally similar to the orangutan, noting also that the human ancestor used its forelimb as much as the orangutan, but was probably smaller in size.[16] Morton, Schultz, and Tuttle see characteristics of the brachiating structure of the gibbon as related to the human arm and shoulder, as well as the gibbon's similar, if occasional bipedal excursions.[17]

It is evident that Campbell's reference to a New World monkey as having locomotor morphological similarities closest to humans is further support for an Oligocene, 35-30mya distilling of the various monkey and ape lines, including the protohominids. We must recall the great climatic transition that occurred in the Oligocene, cooling, drying, falling of sea levels, Antarctica now covered by ice, the northern latitudes composed of a mixed coniferous and deciduous temperate woodland.[18]

Primates had been honing their mix of arboreal and land surface adaptations for at least another 35-40my, before the Oligocene, since the late Cretaceous, the end of the dinosaurian hegemony. The extreme heterogeneous mosaicism implied in the mix of primate heritages as part of the human morphological composite should not surprise.

It should be possible to hypothesize that the brachiating heritage still reflected in human morphology need not be one constructed in the Oligocene or afterward. What we are today as humans could reflect that more ancient tradition of anthropoid evolution before the Oligocene. In sum, at the core of any hypothesis concerning human origins three preadaptive factors must stand as preeminent:

1. Bipedalism. Of all the anthropoid lines, one line with predominantly ape, but also bipedal characteristics, had to have already been on the scene. A more conservative creature in structure than other apes, with a valence not sharply defined toward the platyrrhine or the catarrhine prototype would not have been atypical of the Oligocene anthropoids. In the special case of the protohominids, this particular anthropoid was a bit more catarrhine, and, of course, remaining in Africa, reflects this dimension of its heritage. Clearly it was more ape than monkey, but either it must have been forced earlier by more successful arboreal forms to specialize on the ground, or else by the time of the Oligocene was established as at least as ground oriented as was *Aegyptopithecus*, c.32mya.

2. Brain and Intelligence. Together with bipedal preadaptations, this particular anthropoid probably had a larger than average defensive brain, typical of mammalian regressives. Together with its bipedalism, its large brain enabled it to evade the real predators, probably rodents or true carnivores. It could make a diversified living on the ground and also if necessary climb up a tree, even swinging a bit. Animals, in general, especially under changing ecological conditions make a virtue of necessity. Higher intelligence, and minimal specialization, allowed the protohominid to survive on the land surfaces where there were more ecological opportunities for sustenance and reproduction.

3. Size. During the Oligocene and into the early Miocene 25-20mya, the high probability is that the protohominids were quite small, smaller than gibbons, in the 5-10 lb. range. Small animals, like the early mammals, need relatively small amounts of food to survive. Small, highly intelligent semibipeds could maneuver through their environment relying on their efficient, large brains to fend off their expansionary anthropoid competitors, those having more specialized physical attributes. Losers, at most stages of an evolutionary transition tend to be on the small side.

Of all vertebrate adaptations, particularly in the early stages, intelligence tends to be the most environmentally malleable defense. It was originally the preeminent primate adaptation, to be gradually refined first in the omomyids in a more frontal binocular visual orientation, and then in a gradually expanding brain in the modern primates (anthropoids).

By the middle Miocene, when *Proconsul* and the East African apes begin to dominate in the fossil record, 22-15mya, this hypothesis would propose the as-yet unobserved presence of the protohominids evolving at the periphery of these still gracile and universally acknowledged monkey-like apes. The true evolving into specialization, cercopithecoids, Old World monkeys, likewise were surviving at the periphery of the African ape clade.

The Miocene seems overall to have had a drier, climate. What we should bear in mind is the inevitable increase in competitive pressures by the ape clade as it carved out the parameters of its adaptive niche. The gibbons were probably evolving their specialized brachiations, perhaps as defense against the Old World monkeys. At any rate the protogibbon survivors left for the Euro-Asian land masses within that super-continent's tropical forest zone.

The ape line seemed to lead, from thick-molared *Kenyapithecus* to *Sivapithecus*, then *Ramapithecus*, *Gigantopithecus*, and finally in fragile survivorship, to the East Asian orangutan, with its suite of associated adaptations. There were migrants, too, the so-called European Dryopithecines, *Oreopithecus, et.al.* This does not mean that few apes were left in Africa, merely that the Eurasians survived into the fossil record for longer into the present than did the African apes, who disappear from our fossil searches at about the 10mya level.

The Old World monkeys in general did not displace these apes in this mixed forest-plains economy. Only the baboon has reentered the savannahs of Africa to take up a position that was widely held by the hominoids during most of the Oligocene and Miocene. Indeed, there had to be apes, because there are chimpanzees and gorillas in Africa today, living side by side with Old World monkeys, and nowhere else in the fossil record. The most obvious assumption is that they had chosen or had been driven into the West African jungles and remained long and securely ensconced, adapting to the special ecological requirements of jungle life, along with a wide assortment of monkeys.

Why no apes on the African savannahs? Was it as Andrews and Stringer surmise, characteristic of the result of the drying up of the landscape and the inability of the apes to eat unripe fruit, an adaptation available to monkey physiology?[19] Certainly the long-existing thick enamel on the molars of *Kenyapithecus* and the various Sivapithecines was an adaptation that meshed efficiently with the requirements of temperate, seasonal, ecological conditions. They ate nuts, roots, tubers, grittier foods, even as the thin-enameled-toothed gorillas eat silicon-rich roughage grasses and leaves. Why then the disappearance? Certainly not because of lions, leopards, hyenas, dogs. They were much too warily intelligent to fear the specialized prey-predator relationships that the carnivores had negotiated with the various ungulates.

Richard Klein suggestively phrases the answer to this mystery: "In the very late-Miocene, between 10mya and 5mya, in response to an ever more open, nonwooded environment in eastern Africa, one of the more terrestrial forms began to alter its habitual pattern of ground locomotion to emphasize an energetically efficient form of bipedalism, and the hominid lineage emerged. More or less simultaneously, the monkeys burgeoned, probably in response to the same late-Miocene vegetational change. Under pressure from the protohominids and the proliferating monkeys, many thick-enameled apes became extinct in the late Miocene, but some readapted to more forested conditions. Such readaptation could explain the secondary dental and locomotor specializations that the chimpanzees and gorillas exhibit today."[20]

Where the present writer's views diverge from those of Richard Klein's, is in the latter's assumption of the convenient and rapid malleability of the anthropoid gene structure. It seems doubtful that such clearly specialized morphologies as exhibited severally by the hominids or the African apes could have come about through normal selective evolutionary processes in such a blink of evolutionary time, i.e., from 15-10mya. Note: in 25my of evolution none of the New World monkeys has descended from the trees. Why not? Most probably, when they arrived in the New World, they were already well-articulated and adapted to an arboreal style of life for which there were no further genetic possibilities, morphologically and or selectively, to return to the ground. The protohominids, at this period of evolutionary history (the earliest Miocene) were doubtless already well adapted into a bifurcated life style of walking and climbing.

Further, as noted above, the singular move of a lone baboon species down into the savannahs does not argue strongly enough for a competitive surge against apes by the Old World monkey. More likely it was the relative emptying out by formerly dominating ape forms of the various ecologies, forest and savannah, that allowed the monkeys to proliferate in the forests of Africa and Asia. They were, in the late Miocene undisturbed by the *new competitor,* which had eliminated all but several highly specialized apes, these long-departed from the mainline evolutionary expansion of the hominoids, *viz.,* the chimpanzees and the gorillas.

The above hypothesis, which argues for a more distant point of separation between the ancestors of the modern African apes and the protohominid ancestors than that implied by the DNA time-clock is given potential confirmation in a recently-reported discovery. This is a 90-110-pound animal, *Morotopithecus*, discovered in the Moroto area of Uganda in Africa. It had shoulders that would allow it to swing from tree branches as well as act as a quadruped when it was aground. Dr. Laura MacLatchy of the State University of New York, Stony Brook, a member of the research team that studied *Morotopithecus,* stated that it anticipated similar forms of apes by about 10 million years. *Morotopithecus* dates from about 20mya, and thus could have been an ancestor or a contemporary of an already evolved chimpanzee-like creature. [21] This dating would also tend to strengthen the argument for a more distant point of departure of modern apes and humans than is generally held today by the scientific consensus.[22]

Dominating Hominids

The principle of allometry relates the growth of one morphological trait to the accompanied growth of another. This process is rooted in the linkages existing on the chromosomal and gene level. Here complexes of genes associated both within and between chromosomes and subject to the strong positive selection of one phenotype, act to carry another linked feature to phenotypic expression even when it itself is not under direct positive selection. The formerly neutral feature can subsequently cross an adaptive Rubicon and become an element in the selective success or failure of the organism.[23]

The positive external element, which fitted the preadapted structure of the protohominids, was bipedality. The drying of the Miocene, the mixed woodland-savannah environment put a premium on walking or running, standing above the grasses, as opposed to being fixed in a tree, else climbing down and moving quadrupedally to the next tree. The ability to find more nourishment in such a setting, abetting reproductive efficiency, gradually led to growth in size. These larger, more efficient "information-processors" were now able to move efficiently over longer distances, find more food both vegetative and animal.

Larger size pulled along with it a larger than average anthropoid brain, defensive at first, but with increasingly sensory and neural energies, which gave rise to a more active and dynamic animal. At some point in the later Miocene, 15-10mya, these protohominids, once timid, furtive outlanders, began to compete actively with previously well-adapted and comfortably-ensconced ape forms, the ecology ever stranger, for large, traditionally arboreal quadrupeds.

The protohominids probably did not actively kill off the various Miocene apes that had dominated this ecology for so long. They out-reproduced them, forcing them into strange ecologies where they had to struggle to maintain their old life-styles.[24] Such geographical shifts and the pressure to maintain the food-reproductive chain clearly cut down on adaptive viability. The apes had been generalized arborealists with some ground-dwelling abilities. Africa was becoming alien to their mixed economy. As the ground-roaming bipedal protohominids, still equipped with vestigial arboreal skills, pushed them out, the Old World monkeys multiplied into the now-vacant forest areas.

Only in the deep West African jungles, not penetrated as yet by protohominids, did apes, the gorilla and the chimpanzees, continue their specialized adaptive tack. Interestingly, several million years later, the ancestors of the orangutan must have felt such pressures from early invasions by true *Homo* into the Asian continent. The orangutans also found refuge in the East Asian jungles. Their morphological adjustments included an increase in the length of their arms, reduction of the legs, great wrist and shoulder flexibility, very small hallux (big toe) and thumb.[25] Yet they retained much of their ancient sivapithecine morphology, as well as that which links them from an even earlier time period with the hominids.[26]

Klein, citing Matsuda's dating of a fragmentary upper jaw, maxilla, from the Samburu hills of Kenya, notes the gorilla-like molars, yet with thick enamel, (as in an orangutan or hominid), embedded in a possibly hominid maxilla that could be between 10.5 and 6.7mya.[27]

The mandible at Lothagam, with molars and roots intact, is the first clearly recognizable identifiable hominid (australopithecine) structure. It dates from between 5.5 and

5.mya. Hill and Ward have identified fragmentary hominid fossils at between 8-6mya.[28] The Lothagam jaw, discovered in 1967, southwest of Lake Turkana, in Kenya, has a mandible with first molar and roots of second and third molars.[29] More recently, and almost as old, fossils from this area have been identified as *Ardipithecus ramidus* and *Australopithecus anamensis*.

The next oldest, from Lake Baringo in Kenya, the Tabarin jaw fragments, found in 1984, date between 4.9-4.15mya. Both examples from this site seem to be *A. afarensis*, the earlier, possibly *A. anamensis*.[30] Here begins the tangible, concrete fossil mystery of the evolution of the hominids. These were not creatures that were suddenly reshaped, like clay pots, from some typical existing Miocene ape prototype. Because we have not as yet found the long-evolving ancestors of the sub-family, Homininae does not mean that they were not out there slowly evolving, gradually inheriting a changing climatic and ecological landscape. Eventually these altered evolutionary conditions, external to the animals' prior destiny, provided that final dynamic impetus toward the present.

The discovery in 1924 by Raymond Dart, in South Africa, of the so-called Taung Australopithecine, (southern ape), *A. africanus* set off a gradually awakened awareness of the possible time depth of evolutionary history involved in the evolution of the sub-family, the hominids, now generally divided into two taxonomic genera: *Australopithecus* and *Homo*.

Eventually, a whole new clade of Australopithecines came to our attention, especially through the archaeology of Lewis Leakey in East Africa. It was clear that some kind of human history was in the making far beyond the time zone of earlier-discovered fossils, the Neanderthals, in the 100,000 B.P. time frame. In addition, we must note the work of Dubois in Java at the turn of the century—his discovery of *Homo erectus pithecanthropus*, then dated to c.750,000 B.P.—the work of Weidenreich and Black in China in the 1930s with so-called Peijing Man, now *Homo erectus*, dated from about 500,000 B.P.

The Australopithecines were then dated back to 2-3mya. Now, through ever new discoveries, their fossil heritage is being pushed back toward and beyond the Pliocene, c.5mya. Up until the 1970s the perspective was represented by two main lines, a small gracile type, *Australopithecus africanus*, and a larger, seemingly more ape-like vegetarian form, labeled variously *Zinjanthropus*, *Paranthropus*, *A. robustus,* and *A. boisei*.

In the 1970s Donald Johanson and a large group of associates discovered a massive number of fossil remains at Hadar in Ethiopia. Controversial reconstructions of what turned out to be the most complete skeletal fossil remains of any group of Australopithecines seem to point to a more primitive form, either extremely dimorphic sexually, or else two different races or species. Given the moniker "Lucy," *Australopithecus afarensis* seemed in its primitivity to lead us back in time toward the 3mya level of the splitting point between *Australopithecus* and *Homo*. At least, this was the claim of Johanson and his associates.

It is natural that scientists claim special conceptual status for their discoveries. And in the study of evolutionary remains the proudest discoveries inevitably point to linear splits and derivations of lines of animals that become "missing links." In this case "Lucy" was deemed the direct lineal ancestor of *Homo sapiens sapiens*, as well as of *Australopithecus boisei*. The latter, seemingly from the final stage in the evolution of the genus. *A. boisei*, in morphological terms, is the most specialized large, herbivorous form. It is, as well, the surviving Australopithecine, hypothesized to have survived into the mid-Pleistocene, 500,000 years ago, and perhaps into the eve more recent past.

The same sort of "special origination" claim, as we have discussed in earlier chapters, has been made by the molecular systematists with regard to a 5-6mya split between the ancestor of the chimpanzee, as yet undiscovered, and that of the earliest hominids, now viewed to be a form of the Australopithecines. There is little glory in noting vague relationships and affinities, as yet muddled, that still require far more clarifying empirical evidence. Eventually these facts do arise and the once glorious moment of decisive discovery is obscured in a cloud of controversy, even new and disquieting fossil evidence!

Australopithecine Data:

Richard Klein presents the following comparative weight and size statistics of the Australopithecines: *A. africanus* 72-142lb. Average 101lb. Height 1.45m (4ft. 9in.).

Andrews and Stringer place *A. africanus* at 65-90 pounds, less than 4ft. 6in; orangutans 155lb., gorillas far in excess; chimpanzees up to 5ft. in height; gorillas up to 6ft.

Klein puts *A. robustus* and *A. boisei* at 101-136lb., height 4ft. 11in.to 5ft. 4in.; *A. afarensis,* 73-150lb., height 3ft. 3in. to 5ft 7in. Is this great variance in *A. afarensis* sexual dimorphism or does it represent two species?[31] Also note that the orangutan weighs about 155lb.; gorillas weigh well over 200lb. and are up to 6ft. in height/length; chimpanzees are between 4-5ft in height/length.[32]

The following presents the mean cranial capacities in cubic centimeters in primates: *Pan*, Chimpanzee—383-385; Gorilla—505; Orangutan—405. The size of the brain is measured in proportion to the size of the animal, when comparing relative intellectual levels.[33] Repeat fact: Stebbins notes that the early Miocene, c.25mya, quadruped ape, *Proconsul*, though quite a bit smaller than the chimpanzee, had a brain case only 7-10% smaller than the chimpanzee, and thus roughly proportional intelligence.[34]

Philip Tobias sees ape and A*ustralopithecus* brain size at 2-3mya similar. Lake Turkana *A.. robustus*, WT17000—410cm^3; Al333-105 Hadar, *A. robustus*—343-413cm^3; adult Taung, *A. africanus*—412cm^3 (Falk, 1987) to 440cm^3; *A. robustus-A. boisei*, 7 examples with great variation—463-530cm^3; chimpanzee—average 385cm^3.[35]

Klein summarizes the literature on the australopithecine endocranial capacity roughly as between 400-550cm^3; *A. afarensis*—380-450cm^3; *A. africanus*—430-520cm^3 (about 10% more than *A. afarensis*); *A. robustus* and *A. boisei*—500-530cm^3. The following australopithecine fossil, KNM-WT17000—410cm^3, West Turkana, *A. aethiopicus,* is a robust form, possibly a descendant of *A. afarensis*, 2.5mya.[36]

Chronological Sequence of Australopithecines

Most anthropologists viewed the sequence of Australopithecines as having East African *afarensis* as the earliest form, the South African, gracile *A africanus* possibly being a sister or derived line. The time line for the various robust forms of Australopithecus seems to post-date both *A. afarensis* and *A. africanus*. In addition, for morphological reasons, these robust forms were seen as evolving both later in time and were perhaps linearly derived from the smaller and lighter Australopithecines. "One line of Australopithecines exploited their niche through extreme specialization of the masticating system [robust *Australopithecus/Paranthropus*]."[37]

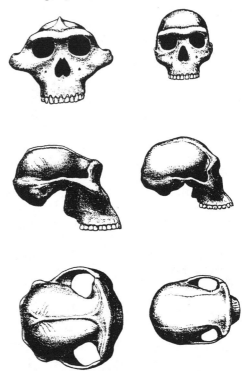

11.1 Contemporary species? *A boisei–H. habilis*. At 1.6mya, KNMER 406, *Australopithecus boisei* (left) and KNMER 1813, *Homo habilis* (right) were contemporaries in East Africa. Other *H. habilis* types found in the area hint at a sagittal crest, as in *H. boisei*. Probably the above represent different genera, certainly different species. The variability within all these lines and their shaded differences reflects a widely diversified and a well-established and adapted clade. To where did they disappear?

With regard to *A. robustus* and *A. boisei*. Andrews and Skinner now name them *Paranthropus*, formerly Lewis Leakey's East African *Zinjanthropus*. In general, these robust forms date from 2.1 to 1.5mya. Both species were described as follows: females 70lb. (32kg) 3ft. 6in (1.1m); males c.90lb. (40kg) 4ft. 4in. (1.35m), (less than Klein's estimates). They had bony crests on top and back of skull. This design and size of brain showed some resemblance to the gorilla, but the flattened face, tiny front teeth, huge back teeth with thick enamel were hominid. The "Black" skull found in 1985, West Turkana, Kenya, "*A.* or *P. aethiopicus*," at 2.5mya is a primitive robustus, small brain, projecting face. Together with a 1968 fragment, *P. aethiopicus* could either be predecessor to later robust Australopithecines or descendant of *A. afarensis*. Andrews and Skinner do say, as with Rak, in *The Australopithecine Face*, that *A. afarensis* is up until now, the root Australopithecine and that along with *A. africanus* leads us to the robust Australopithecines.[38]

As to the question of the place of the highly controversial *A. afarensis* discoveries in the lineage of the Australopithecines, the past 20 years since Johanson's original 1976 publication have produced many new fossils.[39] *Ardipithecus ramidus*, discovered in 1994 and described by Tim White of the University of California at Berkeley, as at

4.4mya, antedates "Lucy."[40] Its primitive hominid fragments seem to reveal a skull and thin enamel teeth that are very chimpanzee-like. *A. ramidus* lived in a densely wooded habitat with monkeys and "kudu" antelope. One hundred fragments of dozens of bones—hand, wrist, foot, enough eventually to reveal its level of bipedality—are still encased in sediment. *Ardipithecus ramidus*, its still tentative taxonomic designation, was found in Aramis, Ethiopia, south of Hadar.[41]

Also discovered in 1994 was *Australopithecus anamensis*, found south of Lake Turkana, Kenya (Kanapoi and Allia Bay), tentatively dated at 4.2mya. Its environment at that time would have been lakeside forests within an arid region. Discovered by Meave Leakey, Alan Walker, of Pennsylvania State University, Craig Feibel, National Museum of Kenya, and Ian McDougall of Australian National University, Canberra, the fossils consist of a primitive jaw with a shallow palate, large canines, a "U"-shaped dental arch similar to the average ape, small ear openings similar to a chimpanzee and *A. ardipithecus*. *A. anamensis* is the product of a long series of excavations going back to the discovery in 1965 of a hominid humerus, a shin bone in 1994, two skulls in 1995, all at Kanapoi. Because there were no associated datable rocks, the time estimate of 3.9-4.2mya is approximate. Also, the evaluation of the fossils seems to indicate a very large creature of c.55 kilograms (c.120lb.).

The shin and arm bones of *A. anamensis* indicate to their discoverers that it walked upright, but that it also may have foraged in trees. Bernard Wood of University of Liverpool agrees. Tim White, uncoverer of *A. ramidus,* believed *anamensis* to be a descendant of *ardipithecus*—single lineage. M. Leakey opined that it probably led to *afarensis*. Peter Andrews of the Natural History Museum in London disagreed. The human-like shin bone and humerus could put *anamensis* on the road to *Homo*, not Lucy.[42]

Australopithecus (bahrelghazalia) afarensis—Chad—found by M. Brunet, University of Poitiers, is the latest of the australopithecine-like fossil to be uncovered and reported in the scientific press. But this example was discovered in a wholly new African location, neither South African, nor East African, rather in the North and West of Africa, Bar El Ghazal, Chad. Here in a dry, grassy woodland, with accompanying fossils of rhinoceros, giraffe, hipparion, pigs, elephant, a hominid partial mandible, (lower jaw), was discovered and dated to an estimated 3-3.5my old, therefore contemporary with the Ethiopian *A. afarensis*.[43]

Summary Timeline of African Hominids
1. Hominid fossil fragments, East Africa—c.10-5mya.
2. *Ardipithecus ramidus*, Ethiopia—c.4.4mya.
3. *Australopithecus anamensis*, Kenya—c.4.0mya.
4. *Australopithecus afarensis*, Ethiopia, Chad—c.3.4-3mya.
5. *Australopithecus africanus*, South Africa—c.3-2.5mya!
6. Robust Australopithecine*s*, South Africa-East Africa, c.2.-.5mya.[44] Using cladistic analysis Bernard Wood puts *A. africanus* in a sister group with the robust Australopithecines.[45] Klein places the demise of the robust Australopithecine*s* at sometime between 1.2- 0.7mya.[46]
7. *Homo habilis; Homo rudolfensis; Homo ergaster*; East Africa, (Central China, Longgupo)—c.2.2-1.5mya.[47]

Early Homo

By 1985 fossils at East Turkana, Northern Kenya, and elsewhere showed too much variation for one species, in brain size, teeth, facial shape. Three different species were now hypothesized.

1. *Homo rudolfensis,* found at Olduvai and Koobi Fora. At Koobi Fora, 1470 man (*Homo rudolfensis*) with 750cm^3 capacity, transversally flat but projecting face, big upper jaw. a large human being, 5ft., 115lb., dated 2.2-1.9mya

2. KNMER-1813, *H. habilis,* whose upper jaw and teeth seem more human—brain 510cm^3. 3ft 3inches, 70lb., at 1.6mya. Another human skull has more teeth, brain, 580cm^3, and crests on skull, like ape or *Paranthropus* (*A. robustus*), dated to about 2mya.[48]

3. KNMER-3733, *H. ergaster.* Andrews and Stringer suggest that *H. ergaster* might be a precursor to *H. erectus. H. ergaster*, as with *H. rudolfensis*, seems to have had a Broca's area in the frontal cortex, indicating language abilities. *H. rudolfensis* is the first hominid with whom tool making is definitely associated, (Oldowan industry).[49] Both R. Ciochon and I. Tattersall describe KNMER-3733 as having a lightly-built, high-vaulted skull with a large endocranial capacity, 850cm^3, at 1.8mya.[50]

Most mysteriously of all, as we shall see in later chapters, is Christopher Stringer's recent conclusion that of all the intermediate fossils of *Homo*, the closest antecedent form of *Homo sapiens* is *Homo rudolfensis*, 1470 man, and not the generic group of intermediate in time, fossils, *Homo erectus.*[51]

What we are to be entertaining in this hypothesis is that a time and species gap exists between the respective and presumed appearance of the two forms of man, (a) early humans—*H. rudolfensis/H. ergaster* and/or *H. erectus*—and, (b) anatomically and culturally modern humans: between c.2mya and c.50,000 B.P. What happened to all the viable human types during this interval, *and*, where and when will we find the true and ancient ancestors of modern humans?

Endnotes, Chapter 11

[1] Kauffman, S. A. 1993. *The Origins of Order: Self-organization and Selection in Evolution*, New York: Oxford Univ. Press, p. 643.

[2] Einstein, A., and Infeld, Leopold. 1938. *The Evolution of Physics*, N.Y.: Simon & Schuster, p. 251.

[3] Einstein, A. 1931. *Relativity: The Special and the General Theory*, Chicago: Regnery, pp. 102-104.

[4] Emiliani, C. 1956. "Notes on absolute chronology of human evolution," *Science*, 23:24-26; Emiliani, C. 1960. "Dating Human Evolution," in *The Evolution of Man*, Sol Tax, ed., Chicago: Univ. of Chicago Press, pp. 57-66.

[5] Eiseley, Loren. 1957. *The Immense Journey*, N.Y.: Random House, p. 113.

[6] Fairbridge, Rhodes. 1959. *The New York Times*, Sept. 8, 1959.

[7] Schwartz, Jeffrey. 1987. *The Red Ape*, London: Elm Tree Books, pp. 277-278.

[8] Schwartz, 1987, *op. cit.*, pp. 278-282.

[9] Fleagle, J. G. 1986. "The fossil record in early catarrhine evolution," in *Major Topics in Primate and Human Evolution*, B. A. Wood, L. Martin, and P. Andrews, eds., Cambridge: Cambridge Univ. Press, pp. 130-149; Simons, E. L. 1986. "'Parapithecus grangeri' of the African Oligocene: an archaic catarrhine without lower incisors," *Jrnl. of Hum. Evol.*, 15:205-213; Simons, E. L. 1987. "New faces of 'Aegyptopithecus'"

from the Oligocene of Egypt," *Jrnl. of Hum. Evol.*, 16:273-289; Klein, R. G. 1989. *The Human Career*, Chicago: Univ. of Chicago Press. p. 69.

[10] Klein, 1989, *op. cit.,* pp. 71-73.

[11] Prothero, D. R. 1994. *The Eocene-Oligocene Transition*, N.Y.: Columbia Univ. Press.

[12] Campbell, Bernard. 1985. *Human Evolution*, N.Y: Aldine De Gruyter, p. 368, quotes J. G. Fleagle, 1983, in *New Interpretations of Ape and Human Ancestry*, R. L. Ciochon and R. S. Coruccini, eds., N.Y.: Plenum, pp. 301-324.

[13] Szalay, F. S., and Delson, E. 1979. *Evolutionary History of the Primates*, N.Y.: Academic Press, p. 434; actually, Szalay and Delson place *Oreopithecus* in its own family under the super-family of *Cercopithecoidea*, Old World monkeys, but without bilophodonty in their molar cuspal morphology, unlike most monkeys, p. 426.

[14] Campbell, Bernard. 1966. *Human Evolution*, 1st ed., Chicago: Aldine, pp. 326-327; Straus, W. L. 1949. "The riddle of man's ancestry," *Quart. Rev. Biol.*, 24:200-223.

[15] Campbell, Bernard. 1985. *Human Evolution*, 3rd ed., N.Y.: Aldine De Gruyter, p. 202.

[16] Oxnard, C. E. 1969. "Evolution of the human shoulder; some possible pathways," *Amer. Jrnl. Phys. Anthrop.*, 30:319-322; Stern, J. T. 1975. "Before bipedality," *Yearbook of Phys. Anthropol.*, 19:59-68.

[17] Morton, D. J. 1924. "Evolution of the Human Foot, 2," *Am. Jnl. Phys. Anthr.*, 7:1-52, esp. 39; Morton, D. J. 1924. "Evolution of the Longitudinal Arch of the Human Foot," *Jrnl. Bone and Joint Surg.*, 6:56-90, esp. 88; Schultz, A. H. 1927. "Observations on a gorilla fetus," *Eugenical News*, 12:37-40, esp. 40; Schultz, A. H. 1936. "Characters Common to Higher Primates and Characters Specific for Man," *Quarterly Review of Biology*, 11:259-283, 425-455, esp. 452; Schultz, A. H. 1969. *The Life of Primates*, N.Y.: Universe Books, p. 251; Tuttle, R. H. 1985. "Darwin's Apes, Dental Apes, and the Descent of Man: Normal Science in Evolutionary Anthropology," in *Primate Evolution and Human Origins*, R. L. Ciochon and J. G. Fleagle, eds., Menlo Park, CA: Benjamin/Cummings Publishing, pp. 333-342.

[18] Janis, Christine. "Victors by Default," in *Life*, S. J. Gould, ed., N.Y.: W. W. Norton, pp. 192-196; Prothero, 1994, *op. cit.,* pp. 167-222.

[19] Andrews, P., and Stringer, C. 1993. "The Primates' Progress," in *Life*, S. J. Gould, ed., N.Y.: W. W. Norton, p. 234.

[20] Klein, 1989, p. 98.

[21] MacLatchy, Laura. 1997. "Fossil Shows Apes Emerged Far Earlier," *The New York Times*, (AP), 4/17/97. David Pilbeam sees no great evolutionary significance in this creature. He views the missing link ancestor of man and chimpanzee as a knuckle-walking, long-armed, short-legged arboreal swinger/climber. Pilbeam, D. 1989. "Human Fossil History and Evolutionary Paradigms," in M. K. Hecht, ed., *Evolutionary Biology at the Crossroads*, N.Y.: Queens College Press, pp. 117-138.

[22] Recent interesting reports of interbreeding of related species: Macaque and Baboon (J.-J. Hublin—personal communication) and an Arabian camel with a South American llama (*The New York Times*, 1/20/98) raise questions about the seeming inability to interbreed humans and chimpanzees, considering the supposed recent 5-6my separation of the two lines, and their close mtDNA affinities.

[23] Pagel, M. D., and Harvey, P. H. 1990. "Diversity in the Brain Size of Newborn Mammals, Allometry, Energetics, or Life History Tactics," *BioScience*, Feb. 1990, 40:2:121-122.

[24] Itzkoff, S. W. 1983. *The Form Man*, N.Y.: Peter Lang, p. 87.

[25] Campbell, Bernard. 1985. *Human Evolution, op. cit.*, p. 76; Tuttle, R. H. 1985, in Ciochon and Fleagle, eds., *op. cit.*, pp. 333-342.

[26] Schwartz, 1987, *op. cit.*; Oxnard, C. E. (University Professor of Anatomy and Biology, Univ. of Southern California). 1985. "Hominids and Hominoids, Lineages and Radiations," in *Human Evolution: Past, Present, and Future*, P. V. Tobias, ed., N.Y.: Alan Liss, pp. 271-278.

[27] Klein, 1989, *op. cit.*, p. 93; Ishida, H., *et al.* 1984. "Fossil anthropoids from Nichola and Samburu Hills, Samburu District, Kenya, *African Studies Monographs (Kyoto), Supplemental Issue* 2:73-85; Matsuda, T., *et al.* 1986. "Geochronology of Miocene Hominids East of the Kenya Rift Valley," in *Primate Evolution*, J. G. Else and P. C. Lee, eds., Cambridge: Cambridge Univ. Press.

[28] Tobias, P. V. 1994. "The Evolution of Early Hominids," in *Companion Encyclopedia of Anthropology*, T. Ingold, ed., N.Y.: Routledge, pp. 33-78, esp. pp. 53-55.

[29] Kramer, A. 1986. "Hominid-pongid Distinctiveness in the Miocene-Pliocene Fossil Record: the Lothagam mandible," *Amer. Jrnl. of Phys. Anthrop.*, 31:49-83; Hill, A., and Ward, S. 1988. "Origin of the Homini-

dae: the record of African large hominoid evolution between 14My and 4My," *Yearbook of Physical Anthropology*, 31:49-83; Conroy, G. C. 1990. *Primate Evolution*, N.Y.: W. W. Norton.

[30] Tobias, 1994, in Ingold, ed., *op. cit.*, pp. 53-55.

[31] Klein, 1989, *op. cit.*, pp. 146-155; Andrews and Stringer, in Gould, ed., *op. cit.*, p. 237.

[32] Andrews and Stringer, 1993, in Gould, ed., *op. cit.*, p. 237.

[33] Campbell, Bernard. 1985. *Human Evolution*, 3rd ed., *op. cit.*, Table 8.2, p. 233; Tobias, P. V. 1971. *The Brain in Hominid Evolution*, N.Y.: Columbia Univ. Press; Cronin J. E., Boaz, N. T., Stringer, C., and Rak, Y. 1981. "Tempo and Mode in Hominid Evolution," *Nature*, 292:113-122; Zihlman, Adrienne L. 1990. "Knuckling Under: Controversy Over Hominid Origins," in *From Apes to Angels, Essays in Anthropology in Honor of Philip Tobias*, G. H. Sperber, ed., N.Y.: Wiley-Liss, pp. 185-196, esp. p. 191.

[34] Stebbins, G. Ledyard. 1982. *Darwin to DNA, Molecules to Humanity*, San Francisco: W. H. Freeman, p. 315.

[35] Tobias, P. V. 1975. "Long or short hominid phylogenies? Paleontological and Molecular Evidences," in *The Role of Natural Selection in Human Evolution*, Salzano, F. M., ed., Amsterdam: North Holland; Tobias, 1994, in Ingold, ed., *op. cit.*, pp. 45-46; Falk, D. 1987. "Hominid Paleoneurology," *Annual Review of Anthropology*, 16:13-30.

[36] Klein, 1989, *op. cit.*, pp. 139-154.

[37] Rak, Y. 1983. *The Australopithecine Face*, N.Y.: Academic Press, p. 122.

[38] Andrews and Stringer, 1993, in Gould, ed., *op. cit.*, pp. 238-239; Rak, 1983, *op. cit.*, p. 120. The discovery of a new and quite large *Paranthropus boisei* type skull at Konso in Ethiopia, dated to 1.4mya, and quite different from the normal *P. boisei* type continues to raise questions about the polytypic character of this line of hominids: Suwa, G., *et al.* 1997. "The first skull of *Australopithecus boisei*," *Nature*, October 2, 389:489-492; Delson, E. 1997. "One skull does not a species make," *Nature*, 10/2/97, 389:445-446.

[39] Johanson, D. C. 1976. "Plio-Pleistocene Hominid Discoveries in Hadar, Ethiopia," *Nature*, March, 25, pp. 293-297.

[40] White, Tim (University of California, Berkeley), 1995. *Science,* 8/18/95, 269:918; also discussed in Shreeve article, E.20

[41] Culotta, Elizabeth. 1995. "New Hominid Crowds the Field," *Science*, 8/18/95, Vol. 269.

[42] Reported in *Nature*, week of 8/18/95.

[43] Simons, Marlise, 1996. *The New York Times*, 5/23/96; Morell, Virginia, 1995. "African Origins: West Side Story," *Nature*, 11/16/95; and *Science*, 11/17/95, p. 1117.

[44] Vrba, Elizabeth. 1985. "Early Hominids in South Africa...," in Tobias, ed., *op. cit.*, pp. 195-200; Vogel, J. C. 1985. "Further Attempts at Dating the Taung Tufas," in Tobias, ed. op cit. pp. 189-194.; Partridge, T. C. 1985. "Spring Flow and Tufa Accretion at Taung," in Tobias, ed., *op. cit.*, pp. 171-187; Vogel, J. C., and Partridge, T. 1984. "Preliminary Radiometric Ages of the Taung Tufas," in *Late Cenozoic Paleoclimates of the Southern Hemisphere*, J. C. Vogel, ed., Rotterdam: A. A. Balkema, pp. 507-514 (both see Taung *africanus* juvenile as between C.1.5-1mya).

[45] Wood, B. A. 1985. In Tobias, ed., *op. cit.*, pp. 227-232, esp. p. 231; Wood, B. A. 1992. "Evolution of Australopithecines," in *The Cambridge Encyclopedia of Human Evolution*, S. Jones, R. Martin, D. Pilbeam, eds., *op. cit.*, pp. 231-240.

[46] Klein, 1989, *op. cit.*, p. 182.

[47] Schwartz, Jeffrey, *et al.*, and Wanpo, H., *et al.* 1996. "Whose Teeth?" *Science*, 5/16/96, Vol. 381. Letters debating the status of Longgupo fossils. Schwartz *et al.* express certain doubts over the question of hominid affinities. Wanpo, *et al.* attempt to consolidate their claims of *H. ergaster* (WT 15000, Nariokotome boy) and *H. habilis*, (ER 1813).

[48] Andrews, P., and Stringer, C. 1989. *Human Evolution, an Illustrated Guide*, Cambridge: Cambridge Univ. Press, p. 34.

[49] Andrews and Stringer, 1993, in Gould, ed., *op. cit.*, pp. 240-241.

[50] Ciochon, R. L. 1995. "Dragon Hill Cave, China: The Earliest Asian Yet," *Natural History*, December, pp., 51-54; Tattersall, I. 1995. *The Last Neanderthal*, N.Y.: Macmillan, pp. 52-62.

[51] Stringer, C. 1990. "The Emergence of Modern Humans," *Scientific American*, 262:98-104.

12

Australopithecus: Sister, not Mother

Australopithecus: Ape-Man or Man-Ape?

To understand and place in perspective our cumulative knowledge of the Australopithecines is to be able to evaluate the various claims and counterclaims concerning the origin, heritage, and relationship of the forms of the genus *Australopithecus*. What follows is a topical examination of the current understanding of the status of the various Australopithecines, both their relationship to the acknowledged ape heritage, as well as a searchlight from the past looking forward to the human future.

1. Dimorphism

Charles Oxnard and Adrienne Zihlman both were concerned with the mixed message sent out in terms of evolutionary significance as to the seemingly extreme sexual dimorphism reflected in the accepted analysis of the Afar Australopithecines.

As late as 1985 Oxnard was still impressed by the morphological affinities of the Sivapithecines, especially *Ramapithecus*, to *Homo*, at a time when there was an almost universal allying of the chimpanzee with *Homo*, based on the molecular relationship.

By contrast Bernard Campbell had reversed himself by the 1985, 3rd edition of his *Human Evolution*, as compared with his 1966 views about the closeness of humans to *Ramapithecus*, the Sivapithecines. Then, his inconclusiveness with regard to *Homo*'s mixed monkey and ape morphology was suggestive, as contrasted with *Homo sapiens'* supposedly definitive molecular DNA affinities to the chimpanzee.

To Oxnard, it was incomprehensible for evolution to reverse itself in terms of sexual dimorphism as many times as it would have to have done, were we forced to accept the road from *Pan* to *Australopithecus* to *Homo*, as the majority view was inclined to do.[1]

Oxnard argued: Is it possible to postulate that, before *Ramapithecus*, large ape-like sexual dimorphisms existed, then an evolutionary shift to hominid-like proportions in *Ramapithecus*, back again to ape-like in the Australopithecines, then, finally back to modest human-like differences in fossil and living *Homo*? Interestingly, Oxnard argued that the generic sivapithecine form falls into an orangutan mode, while *Ramapithecus* falls into the human. *Gigantopithecus*, a descendant of Sivapithecines is odd in that it had no sexual dimorphism in teeth.[2] "The age old idea that 'human' sexual dimorphism was much larger in relatively recent progenitors, resembling that in the African apes of today, seems to be incorrect."[3]

To Adrienne Zihlman, incredulity with the so-called sexual dimorphism of the "Lucy" fossil remains.[4] Were the fossils to be sustained as reflecting the same species, but dimorphic forms, then the Hadar (Ethiopia) Australopithecines would show more dimorphism than any other hominoid, including the gorilla and orangutan![5] She notes, however, that, the pigmy chimpanzee, *Pan paniscus* shows much less sexual dimorphism than *Pan troglodytes*, the ordinary chimpanzee.[6]

This controversy has in part been answered by the discovery by the Johanson team near Hadar, Ethiopia, of skulls attributed to "Lucy," *Australopithecus afarensis*. They are approximately 200,000 years younger than the original postcranial fossil material, at c.3mya. Again, the debate will revolve around the issue of sexual dimorphism, else different varieties of Australopithecines. One skull is described as "massive with a projecting face and large canines." The other has a face that is similar, if smaller, and presumed by the team to be a female.

Critics such as Todd Olson, of the Albert Einstein College of Medicine, and Pat Shipman, of the Johns Hopkins School of Medicine, view the new skull as too large to be accommodated as a dimorphic exemplar of traditional smaller-sized fossils, this despite the above new smaller skull discovered in the same area, described above.[7]

It is important to note that in apes, the size of the canines is a ubiquitous distinction between male and female dental structures. Also significant is the so-called diastema between the lateral incisor and the canine, a space that is found in the chimpanzee and other apes, and in *Australopithecus afarensis*, but not in the other well studied forms, *A. africanus* and the robust Australopithecines. In fact in the robust Australopithecines the size of the incisors and canines are sharply reduced, the cheek teeth expanded in size, the pre-molars "molarized."[8]

Comparisons of dental enamel thickness show that the enamel of the molars of *A. robustus* was thicker than *africanus*; both had enamel thicker than that of *Homo* which is thicker than orangutan, described as the thickest enamel of all the living apes. "The hypotauradont pulp chambers of *Pongo pygmaeus*—orangutan—resemble those of the australopithecines."[9]

The Taung child, the first discovered australopithecine fossil, *A. africanus*, found in South Africa by Raymond Dart in 1924, has been the subject of much speculation and analysis over the decades. Recent studies of its dental profile has revealed that it was 3.3 years of age when presumed killed by an animal. Its permanent molars were erupting. This is the same age that chimpanzee molars emerge. Its rates of development—tooth, face, bipedality—were similar to that of the chimpanzee.[10]

The probability that *A. afarensis* stands as the stem, unspecialized Australopithecine, is supported by Yoel Rak, even though there is now general agreement that *A. africanus* does overlap the East African form, (*A. afarensis*) in time. In fact Timothy Partridge and John Vogel independently confirm, through thermoluminescence and U234 methods of dating, that the Taung infant in particular died between 1.5-1mya, an astoundingly recent date. If this was the case, it could have been part of an isolated and relic population of Australopithecines. Baboon fauna associated with this fossil make a date any earlier than 2mya impossible. Springs from the plateau, a very dry area, around which these hominids existed, could have maintained them. The adjoining Kalahari could have prevented migration, allowing for the existence of a "relic" population so late in evolutionary history. Philip Tobias now reiterates the correctness of the earlier dates, 3.5-2.5mya.[11]

While accepting the taxonomy of the Taung juvenile as *A. africanus*, Rak entertains the possibility that other *A. africanus* types may be female or juvenile *robustus* types.[12] Rak's minute study of the australopithecine face persuades him that *A. africanus* is a distinct form as compared to the East African Australopithecines. Agreeing with the consensus opinion, Rak states that *A. africanus* is related both to *A. robustus* and *A. boisei* (*Paranthropus*). *A. africanus* is on the evolutionary road leading to both robust species. He views *A. afarensis* as a perfect ancestor to other Australopithecines and *Homo*, one later group, the australopithecine robust form, undergoing highly specialized masticatory development, the other, *Homo*, specializing in brain growth.[13]

This linear evolutionary conclusion by Rak draws a linear connection between existing fossils. However, such a conclusion is inconsistent with the evolutionary message indicated by the fossil evidence. Rak's questionable evolutionary derivations are fixed on the immediacy of the fossil material and the need to be authoritative, to "fill in the gaps." Why?

Consensus dating procedures now place gracile Australopithecines as contemporaries of the robust forms. It is quite possible that there were genetic tendencies in some of the earlier forms, *A. afarensis* and/or *A. africanus*, toward robusticity and the extensive dental and skull remodeling that occurred in the seemingly more recent vegetarian forms of *A. robustus* and *A. boisei* (*Paranthropus*).

It is also possible that we will yet discover fossils that are more truly antecedent to the two robust australopithecine lines, and that what we have thus far discovered in the australopithecine fossil museum is an only minimal rendering of the full picture of this line of evolution. The consensus claim that the unspecialized "root" Australopithecine, *A. afarensis*, was mother both to the robust forms of *Australopithecus* as well as *Homo* who appears on the scene well within the time range for the existence of both the gracile and robust australopithecine lines, *e.g.*, 2mya, requires explanatory evolutionary, genetic, and morphological elaboration.

2. Bipedality

Science writer James Shreeve has noted the growing skepticism among paleoarcheologists that human upright bipedality evolved as a response to climatic drying and consequent spreading savannah conditions. Evidence now suggests that the important fossil localities of early australopithecine fossils were mixed woodland, brush, open savannahs and, often, heavily-wooded closed canopy forests. One theory of upright stance is that it arose as an adaptation to reduce evaporation of body fluids (Peter Wheeler, of Liverpool, John Moores University), another, as the need to stand in order to feed (Kevin Hunt of Indiana University). A third hypothesis argues that it was sexual relations and the male need to forage for the female that stimulated upright stance (Owen Lovejoy of Kent State University).[14]

What such arguments seem to have in common is the view, that as fundamental a human adaptation as bipedality, carrying with it a vast complex of genetically-rooted morphological, physiological and behavioral characteristics, came into being as a recent and singular adaptive response to a concrete selective challenge, ecological and environmental. One is reminded of the now legendary explanation by the 19th-century Lamarckists of the length of the giraffe neck: how better to eat the higher leaves on the tree branches!

Charles Oxnard of the University of Southern California has held firm in his non-orthodox anatomical perspective on the evolutionary relationships between fossil and living apes, the hominids, both Australopithecines and *Homo*:[15]

> Australopithecines possessed orangutan features and features different from all living forms. [Conclusions: 1]...Australopithecine post crania are uniquely different from both apes and humans. [2] While bi-pedal they were also accomplished in the trees. [3] If a different morphology reflects a different locomotion...creatures that display them arose independently of humans, otherwise we can only interpret the Australopithecine hominid relationship as expressing an odd and curious mosaicism.[16]

Oxnard, a distinguished and venerable scholar, agrees with J. Schwartz on the morphological affinities between the orangutan, *Australopithecus*, and *Homo*, affinities that he implies cannot be effaced by theoretically based molecular chronologies. But, in addition, he seems to place the Australopithecines and *Homo* farther apart in the evolutionary spectrum. Clearly he is hinting at an undiscovered "extra-Uranian" fossil form that might connect *Homo* with the Sivapithecines, relatives of the orangutan and *Ramapithecus*.

The large number of *A. afarensis* fossil fragments, perhaps more than one species of australopithecine fossils, plus the consensus that up until recently it was, at 3.3mya, the oldest and most primitive member of the clade, has given rise to great controversy as to its status as a hominid. Also raised is the question of its relation to other Australopithecines, and thus its imputed position in evolutionary history as the Ur-hominid, ultimate ancestor of *Homo*.

Zihlman summarizes the debate up to 1990 by placing the disputants over the issue of bipedality in *A. afarensis* into three divisions.[17]

1. *A. afarensis* is to be considered a well-adapted biped. Owen Lovejoy, for one, implies an ancient descent from the trees for australopithecine precursors, with plenty of time to perfect the bipedal adaptation before the full emergence of *Australopithecus*.[18]

2. The Australopithecines climbed trees. Tuttle has argued that our ancestor must have been small-bodied and an arboreal climber. Further, Tuttle rejected a knuckle-walking chimpanzee and gorilla ancestry, noting that orangutans—here he agrees with Schwartz—were not knuckle walkers. The latter are, to Tuttle, as close to *Homo* as the African apes. To Tuttle, Prost, as well as Stern and Sussman, the Hadar (*A. afarensis*) post-cranial fossils and the Laetoli footprints—with curved phalanges, robust hallux, shortened and lateral orientation of the iliac blades—are evidence that is compatible with the idea that the "Hadar"

blades—are evidence that is compatible with the idea that the "Hadar" hominids derived rather recently from arboreal bipeds engaged in notable tree climbing.[19]

3. J. G. Fleagle, who has studied the evolution of the catarrhine anthropoids in great morphological detail, argues that vertical climbing appears "to be preadaptive for human bi-pedalism." Of course, the fact that humans still are modest climbers and swingers in the trees and elsewhere must be factored into the equation of Fleagle's evolutionary conclusions. Here, too, we must note that the prosimians, lemurs and tarsiers, are adept vertical tree-trunk climbers.[20]

Perhaps the most unsettling fact in the postcranial anatomy controversy that undergirds the ostensible bipedalism of *Australopithecus* is the seeming closeness in structure of the Hadar *A. afarensis* fossils to the pongids rather than *Homo*. Summarizing the research of numerous specialists, Zihlman lists them as follows:

1. The nearly complete humerus and femur of *Australopithecus*-Hadar-AL288. It presents a thorax shape based on a rib morphology that is reminiscent of the chimpanzee rather than a human.[21]

2. Pelvic and limb bone features such as the less curved iliac crest, small and more laterally-oriented acetabulum, and longer ischium were, in South African Australopithecines, ape-like or unique.[22]

3. The australopithecine hip joint is within range of the chimpanzee and of the same size.[23]

4. The femoral head is small, the neck long, shaft is robust, the distal femur is more oblique, and very different from humans.[24]

5. The Hadar pelvic and limb bones confirm the South African material: less curved ilium, long ischium, long femoral neck, and lack of torsion in femur, *i.e.*, pongid affinities.[25]

6. Foot and ankle are viewed by some as ape-like, others compatible with human. Hand bones, fossil hand phalanges from Hadar, 3mya, are still quite curved similar to African apes. Robust *Australopithecus*, from Swartkrans, South Africa, C. 1.8mya had relatively short, uncurved hand bones, thumb also adapted to use tools, grasp objects.[26]

Zihlman quotes N. Boaz as stating in 1988 that there is no evidence in fossil or extant hominid hands for knuckle-walking ancestry. Zihlman, on the basis of persuasive molecular evidence for a chimpanzee-hominid separation some 5mya, believes, in contrast to Boaz' telling cumulative empirical evidence, that such diverse walking adaptations could have independently and *recently* developed in each line.

Homo would have consequently shed the various ape-like adaptations of *Australopithecus* in a million years or so, c.3-2mya, when *Homo* appears on the fossil scene. The recent naming of *Australopithecus garhi*, at 2.5mya, showing derived *A. afarensis*, c.3.5mya, characteristics, but with large teeth, casts further doubt on a supposed gracile *Australopithecus-Homo* lineage.[27] And, of course, *Australopithecus* should have separated from an Ur-chimpanzee ancestor, at earliest 3my earlier, *i.e.*, 6mya, this on the basis of accepted molecular chronologies. Is there an evolutionary inconsistency in Zihlman's logic?

Klein and Andrews and Stringer diagrammatically summarize these various hypothetical lineal transformations of *Australopithecus* into *Homo ergaster* and *Homo habi-*

lis. The two vegetarian Australopithecines, *A. robustus and A. boisei* (*Paranthropus*) who themselves were from 2mya, still evolving into their culminating ape-like morphologies, survived until approximately 500,00 B.P. (Klein says 700,000 years B.P.).[28]

In the late 1980s, Mary Leakey was leading an expedition at Laetoli in Tanzania, when she discovered hardened volcanic ash footprints of a hominid. The dating, universally agreed upon, was from between 3.7-3.5mya, which predates the *A. afarensis* fossils. The controversy hinged around which hominid made those footprints, apparently a family profile. Stern and Sussman argued that *A. afarensis* made them, as they were ape-like. Tuttle argued vigorously against this view, seeing them as completely human, and that only an *H. habilis* could have made them. Andrews and Stringer seem to take an intermediate position, noting that they were "human" but probably made by *A. afarensis*. If indeed they were *Homo*, this would constitute an extremely early appearance of our ancestor, some 1.3my before the dating of its fossil bones. The weight of evidence with regard to these footprints is that they are completely human without evidence for the apparent curved digitals that are attributed to the early gracile Australopithecines.[29]

Most recently, a set of 4 footbones of *A. africanus* excavated in the early 1980s at Sterkfontein in South Africa, and dated to 3.5mya, but only recently subject to close analysis by Philip Tobias and Ronald Clarke, University of Wittwatersrand Medical School, has provided additional information on this question of bipedality and the level humanness in the early Australopithecines. Tobias claimed the reconstructed foot shows a weight bearing heel adapted to bipedalism, plus, a long flexible big toe which "...is perfect for grabbing onto tree limbs and along with some other traits, it 'virtually settles the argument' that our ancestors at that time were partly in the trees." Recently, the cranium and some post-cranial bones of this specimen have been found and partially uncovered from the matrix. It reveals an *A. Africanus* with heavy jaws, a sagittal crest, yet *africanus*-like teeth.

Randall Susman of the State University of New York at Stony Brook agreed. Elwyn Simons of Duke University, long experienced in the analysis of primate morphology, who saw the bones, stated that they revealed a climbing ability. Owen Lovejoy of Kent State University, Ohio, strongly disagreed. Absurd, he commented, reiterating his long-held views that *Australopithecus*' bipedal postcranial morphological, clearly well-established in its structure and behavior, more than overrode what could be, in the flexible toe, a primitive, and largely non-functional retention from the past. Tobias tends to see this creature as partially tree climbing.[30]

3. Brain and Language

The 4.5 to 5ft. chimpanzee has an average endocranial capacity of about 385cm^3. Zihlman claims that ape and australopithecine endocranial capacities, at 2-3mya, were similar. She gives the Lake Turkana *robustus* (WT17000) 410cm^3; Al333-105 Hadar, 343cm3; adult Taung, *A. africanus*, 412cm^3.[31]

Note: There are only six examples of the *A. africanus* skull for which to estimate endocranial capacity. An important specimen from Makapansgat, MLD 37/38 , is now thought to be a young adult female. Earlier estimates on Sts 5, from Sterkfontein, *A. africanus*, were estimated at 482cm^3. New methods reveal MLD37/38 now at 425cm^3, 10% less than Dart originally estimated. Earlier assumptions may have overstated endocranial capacity; average *A. africanus* endocranial capacity is now estimated at 440.3cm^3.[32]

chimpanzee, *Pan troglodytes*

temporal line
nuchal line
subnasal prognathism
diastema
broad (heavily pneumatized) cranial base

Australopithecus afarensis
(left: AL 333-1 + 333-45; right: AL 333-45)

12.1 Australopithecine exemplars. Chimpanzee face and back of skull compared with a roughly contemporary group of Australopithecines, c.3-1.5mya, and a contemporary member of the genus *Homo*.

Australopithecus africanus
(left: STS 5 + 7; right: STS 5)

left: *Australopithecus robustus*
(SK 46 + 47)

right: *Australopithecus boisei*
(KNM-ER 406)

Homo habilis
(KNM-ER 1813)

Pound for pound and inch for inch, it is probable that the Australopithecines had a slightly larger proportionate endocranial capacity (contra Zihlman and Tobias, see below), and a higher corticalization or encephalization quotient (Jerison) than all the great apes.[33]

Ralph Holloway of Columbia University has long specialized in the technique of making endocasts of fossil skulls to ascertain how subtle impressions made by the brain on the inner skull reveal its inner structure. Not only did Holloway concede the relative enlargement in the brain of *A. afarensis* over the apes, but stated that "endocast of morphology...suggests enlargement of the association area in the parietal areas of the cerebral cortex." In general, Holloway argues that some brain reorganization may have occurred in the early hominids along lines leading from the pongid to human patterns.[34]

Falk has vigorously challenged this view, arguing that brain enlargement preceded cortical reorganization in hominid evolution.[35] He uses the East African "Hadar AL-162-

28" endocast as his evidence.[36] Falk argues that an analysis of 7 natural endocasts of South African Taung skulls leads to the conclusion that the sulcal patterns (the fissures between the convolutions in the cortex) are ape-like and not human.[37]

The study of the imputed brain structure of the Australopithecines has not merely been concentrated on the Australopithecines' relative position ape/human, but, in addition, has attempted to clarify their position relative to each other. Adrienne Zihlman has argued that two or more species are represented in the suite of fossil parts of *A. afarensis* (Lucy), an argument echoed ten years later by Pat Shipman and Todd Olson as we have noted above with regard to the discovery of two new purportedly associated skulls of "Lucy" and her brethren.[38] Falk and Conroy, for example, in their comparative brain structure research on the Australopithecines have concluded that the *A. afarensis* fossils in their basic morphologies represent two distinct species that exhibit the same venous drainage patterns of the robust Australopithecines from East and South Africa![39] In contradistinction to Y. Rak, who views *A. afarensis* and *A. africanus* as part of an evolutionary tradition that splits, the latter going toward the robust Australopithecines, the former toward *Homo*, Zihlman argues that the split between the gracile and robust lines of *Australopithecus*, began early, before 2-2.5mya.[40]

In 1990, Conroy, Vannier, and Tobias published a paper based on new 2D and 3D Computed Tomography imaging that enabled them more clearly to follow the admittedly indistinct brain patterns embossed in stone on the inner skull fossils. In addition to more clearly estimating the endocranial capacity of these skulls, the cranial venous outflow patterns revealed some interesting, if puzzling, new relationships. The authors placed *A. africanus* with humans. *A. afarensis*, as in their 1983 study, is placed with the two robust australopithecine lines. Note that this analysis reaches conclusions the exact opposite of those mentioned in the paragraph above. They attributed these differing blood outflow patterns in the brain as an adaptive response to different bipedal postures.

12.2 Incapacity of *Australopithecus* for language. Reconstruction of the upper respiratory tract of an Australopithecine during normal respiration. Note the high position of larynx, which provides a direct airway from the nose to the lungs.

The assumption had to be that the two gracile forms had long histories of separation, and that since recent discoveries had placed the South African gracile form, *A. africanus*, further back in time toward the 3mya boundary of *A. afarensis*, their research implied that neither of these forms could be seen as recently derivative from the other. Whether *A. africanus* was truly antecedent to *Homo*, else the venous outflow patterns merely parallel evolutionary coincidents is unclear. The fact that the Taung infant has been placed hypothetically in the 2.5-1.5mya time frame suggests a more incidental, parallel similarity between *Homo* and *A. africanus*.[41]

4. Language

Jeffrey Laitman argues that an analysis of the flexion-basicranium (the respiratory tract) in the Australopithecines shows a great similarity to that of the apes.[42] "As with the living non-human primates, the early hominids exhibited a larynx positioned high in the neck. This...would have allowed them to breathe and swallow liquids simultaneously."[43]

A high larynx would have made it impossible to produce some of the universal vowel sounds found in modern human speech patterns. This view is similar to Philip Lieberman's views on the Neanderthal vocal tract, in which he sees significant structural problems that would probably have prevented this human from producing a full repertoire of vowel sounds.[44] Australopithecines, Laitman argues, had a radically restricted vocal repertoire, unlike *H. erectus/H. ergaster*, exemplified in KNMER 3733, where the basicranial flexion is more modern, showing a lower position for the larynx.[45]

Lieberman has confirmed Laitman's analysis with regard to the similarity of the australopithecine/ape vocal tracts. So, too, there is some progressive hominization, in the flexure of the basicranium of the above-noted KNMER-3733, Lake Turkana, Kenya, 1.8-1.6mya. This increase in the flexure of the vocal tract is greater than in apes or Australopithecines, indicating a lowering of the larynx to facilitate mouth breathing.

The sequence in this process of shifting morphologies to allow for articulated speech, along with restrictions in the ability of hominids to breathe and eat at the same time, is presented as follows by Lieberman: a) Broken Hill, *H. erectus*, c.150,000 B.P.—a longer palate than moderns, with some presumed difficulty in pronouncing vowels, such as "i" and "u"; b) Qafzeh 6, *Homo sapiens*, c.92,000 B.P.; c) Skhul 5, *Homo sapiens*, c.85,000—b) and c) have completely modern supralaryngeal vocal tracts; d) Tabun, Shanidar, Kebara, are Neanderthals, c.80,000-50,000 B.P. They lack a truly modern supralaryngeal vocal tract, but the tract is more advanced than *Australopithecus* and *H. erectus*. The Neanderthals are contemporary or even more recent in time than b) and c), two *sapiens* with modern vocal morphologies.[46]

New techniques of studying the inner parts of fossilized skulls and thus the physical impression of brain structures have thrown clarifying light on the differences between the brains of *Homo* and *Australopithecus*. Tobias has summarized these in a recent overview of the early phases of hominid evolution: *H. habilis* shows both Broca's bulge and Wernicke's area protrusions indicating language abilities closely resembling modern sapiens.[47] Broca's area does show on endocasts of *A. africanus;* Wernicke's bulge does not.

Holloway has stated that Broca's bulge does show on the endocasts of chimpanzee skulls.[48] In addition, Raichle and Peterson, using positron emission techniques, have shown that blood flow patterns during human speech activate the left inferior frontal lobes, not the Broca's area directly. Broca's cap area seems to activate higher motor programming, casting into doubt the actual speech controls with which Broca's cap is involved.[49]

Falk has argued that the sulcal patterns of the frontal lobes in apes and humans are very different, especially in Broca's area.[50] The brains of *A. africanus* resemble ape brains more than human in respect to the frontal lobes, or Wernicke's area.[51]

Summing up the general comparison between the australopithecine endocranial capacities of c.425-475cm^3, and *Homo*, Tobias concludes that the australopithecine endocranial capacity is comparable to that of the great apes, chimpanzee—c.385cm^3—here he agrees with A. Zihlman. *H. habilis*, from 2.3-2.mya, (c.560-750cm^3), shows a 40% increase in brain size over *A. africanus*. Tobias claims both an absolute and relative increase in brain size, compared with body size, in *Homo* over contemporary *Australopithecus*.[52]

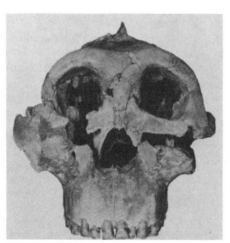 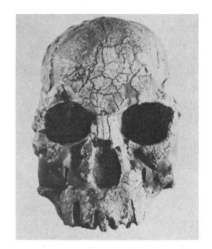

12.3 *A. boisei—H. rudolfensis:* the adaptive power of the brain. These contemporaries, at about 1.8mya-1.5mya, reveal the portent of "*rudolfensis*—1470," endocranial capacity, c.760cm^3, as compared with "*boisei*," c.480cm^3.

Genealogy of Australopithecines: Issues

1. The Australopithecines.

It should be clear from the above evidence that there is almost total overlap of the once fairly distinct australopithecine lines. It is difficult to believe even with the evidence for morphological affinities between the face of *A. africanus* and *A. robustus* that the former is linearly related to the latter. Evidence is for a temporal overlap of the two forms, *i.e.*, they both were living at the same time. The teeth of the robust forms are certainly, in their reduction, incisors and canines, and extreme molar enlargements, highly specialized departures from that of the gracile Australopithecines. It is difficult to accept the hypothesis that in a breath of genetic time, at most 1.-1.5my, Darwinian processes could have produced the requisite genetic and selective alterations. It is wholly within possibility that the enlargement in size of the robust forms as well as their general survivability into the mid-Pleistocene can be attributed to the opening up of an ecology—similar in circumstance to that of the great apes—wherein they both were protected from outside faunal pressures, as well as able quickly to adapt and perfect existing incipient and also divergent morphological tendencies, *e.g.*, teeth and size. Apparently they were momentarily succeeding in a quasi-ape like ecology.

If we draw a line connecting the various fossil discoveries of the past 25 years, it will show more clearly that the Australopithecines represented a clade that was both widespread and extremely variable, as well as one that had existed in a time frame that increasingly intersected the supposed juncture of a common ancestor of the knuckle-walking apes and the hominids, c.5-6mya. The newly-discovered robust Australopithecine, *A. boisei*, at Konso in Ethiopia, 1.4mya, reveals affinities with a wide variety of hominids: cheek bones similar to the South African robust Australopithecines, *A. robustus*; back of cranium similar to the primitive robust Australopithecine, *A. aethiopicus* (in the same general geography of the Konso specimen); similar to the general robust Australopithecine's refined anterior teeth, its short and broad palate, all resembling that of *Homo*.[53]

Christopher Wills, approving Skelton's and McHenry's views on these puzzling similarities between *H. habilis* and the robust Australopithecines (*Paranthropus*) supports the hypothesis that by 2mya, a widely diverse group of hominids was making its adaptive push into evolutionary history. The most prudent hypothesis is to predict earlier and always more diverse forms of the genus *Australopithecus* coming to light, then gradually disappearing in the time frame of 2-0.5mya.[54]

2. Relationship to *Homo*:

Although the models of hominid affinities still almost unanimously assume a lineal descent between *Homo* and the australopithecine cousins, the debate involving which particular form of *Australopithecus* hominid is closer both in morphology and in reasonable temporal association with *Homo* breaks apart this unanimity. Simply, the morphological evidence of difference between the earliest fossils of *Homo*, now at about 2+mya, the heyday of the Australopithecines, would necessitate a "creationist miracle" of genetic reconstruction, adaptive integration into existing environments and ecologies, then a selective sieve of extraordinary precision and decisiveness. Thus, we have had some fantastic explanations as to why humans are so different in their dental, cranial, dimorphic sexual differences, bipedal patterns, finally brain and linguistic structures, from those of the various Australopithecines.

If one accepts the possibilities that the chimpanzee and hominid ancestors went their own ways about 5mya, the old molecular hypothesis, even 10mya, the ever-newer accommodation to factual evidence, then the reconstruction in a mere 2 or 3 million years between *A. afarensis'* clearly ape-like morphology and early *Homo* types appears to be eminently reasonable. The difficulty lies in conceptually accepting the verisimilitude of a process that radically breaks with the "tempo and mode" of parallel mammal evolutionary patterns since the Oligocene. Practically all of the lines that survived into the Pleistocene were there clearly defined in their morphology and behavior. Their evolutionary successions reveal only increasing specialization and encephalization.

Truly, we have an adaptive directionality here that was well established by 25mya. By that time, the primates and other mammal lines had undergone at least 50my of prior evolutionary experiments with their genetic and phenotypic possibilities. As Charles Oxnard has argued, a reversal over time, to turn an incipient chimpanzee into an incipient *A. afarensis* and then into *H. ergaster,* even in 10my, is inconceivable, on the prior evolutionary evidence that we have with regard to vertebrate evolutionary trends in morphology and dynamics, these at least 600my in the making. The maturity of our genetic structure, given the evidence of the science of cytogenetics, argues against a unique transmammalian individuality for our primate chromosomal and gene processes.

We are therefore obliged to invoke more mainline time frames in evaluating the question of hominid origins, the relationship between the Australopithecines and *Homo*. A useful comparative quibble in this regard might raise the difference between the highly specialized and peripheral orangutan and its 15mya ancestor *Sivapithecus* or *Ramapithecus*. The morphological affinities are clearly recognizable, hinting at a more typical, gentle mammalian adaptive movement into specialization.

Using the same yardstick for humans, going back in time, we certainly do not arrive at the chimpanzee or gorilla morphology. We might well see *A. afarensis* as a generalized mixed tree-living and bipedal ape of the mid-Miocene, c.15mya. Some kind of ancestral "Lucy" type might have turned into *A. boisei* or *A. africanus*. But, certainly it would not subsequently, at about 1.9-1.6mya have been reshaped into the various intermediate forms of early *Homo*. In fact, it would not even be unreasonable to argue that the ancestors of *A. afarensis* and *H. ergaster*, as with other examples of the plethora of hominid (*Australopithecus, Homo*) forms, some of which seem increasingly to shade into each other, are all part of a mosaic of cercopithecine-like anthropoids that emerged as a result of climatic revolutions in the Oligocene, 35-30mya. Partial bipedality was merely one of a number of adaptive orientations within this great wave of primate expansion that thence took place in the Miocene, 25-7mya.

Implicit confirmation of this mosaicism is given in the recent research of Henry McHenry and Lee Berger concerning the seemingly more ape-like limb structure of *A. africanus* as compared with the apparently earlier *A. afarensis*: "Based on discoveries in Sterkfontein in South Africa Henry McHenry and Lee Berger have found evidence to suggest that the skeleton of *Australopithecus africanus* is more ape-like and primitive than any earlier species of *Australopithecus*. Similar to apes and in contrast to humans, the limb proportions of the new South African discoveries indicate relatively large forelimbs and short hind limbs. This seems to contradict craniodental evidence which links *A. africanus* more closely with early *Homo*, compared with other early hominid species such as *Australopithecus afarensis* and *Australopithecus anamensis,* which have more primitive-looking crania and are found earlier in time."[55]

And, for *Homo*, why not the possibility, as part of this preadaptive bipedal, bigger-brained, but smaller-bodied animal's profile, a bit of the trunk-hopping pro-simian postural uprightness, as residue of a hybrid heritage? The key element in this perspective is the recognition that all-important evolutionary transitions need time. The protomammals were invisible for the 40-50my of their parallel evolutionary transformation among the cynodonts, before their sudden appearance at the end of the Triassic c.210mya. Subsequently, the therian placental restructuring evolved over a time frame of close to 150my. Certainly, the primates inherited an evolved genetic/chromosomal structure far more stabilized than the rapid malleability experienced by the eubacteria, then and now.

We need to exercise caution in being intellectually seduced by seemingly decisive abstract theories. Abstractions become flesh and blood by virtue of their predictive and concrete explanatory power. In this, respect the DNA and protein molecular chronologies and affinities have clearly failed to produce. In fact, the paradoxical perspective on the evolutionary process that they engender with respect to the evolution of the anthropoids verges on *creationism*.

3. Genocide of the Australopithecines.

What happened to the Australopithecines? One view, argued by D. Johanson with regard to *A. Afarensis* is that they were transformed into *Homo* much as osteolepiforms came ashore to become amphibians, and thence reptiles, finally to evolve into mammals. But here we make note of extremely broad and inclusive taxonomic categories—classes—of which the primates constitute one order, the hominids, a sub-family.[56]

A rejection of this model certainly leaves out in the cold many who have made solid pronouncements that an in-hand Australopithecine is the root mother of all subsequent hominids. However, all the evidence precludes such views, especially since careful and recent morphological analysis of early *H. habilis* and *H. rudolfensis* fossils, by Bernard Wood and Mark Collard, reveal more pongid characteristics, closer even to the Australopithecines than to proto-sapiens. The two genera were clearly contemporaries for many millions of years on the African mixed woodland-plains ecology. They evolved into competitive dominance, within the sight of our fossil explorations. Then the Australopithecines disappeared along with the earliest *Homo*.[57]

Johanson, rumor has it, faced with an avalanche of disconfirming evidence, has finally abandoned his theory.

The Australopithecines, given their extremely dispersed geography and plentiful fossil remains, were an extraordinarily well-adapted clade. But so were the extremely diverse Miocene apes. Then the chasm, which begins at about 12mya in Africa, c.8mya in Europe. Subsequently, we discover a plethora of Old World monkey species throughout Africa, as well as on the Eur-Asian land mass. In Asia the Sivapithecines seem to have had a wide radiation during this period, 12-0.5mya. A noteworthy large-sized, open-country living group of Sivapithecines, *Gigantopithecus,* in its various specific forms, was quite successful in establishing itself alongside the expanding monkeys.

In fact, we find the fossil bones of *Gigantopithecus* associated with early human fossils in East Asia at the 1.8-1.5mya level. Evidence argues for the extinction of *Gigantopithecus* no later than 0.5mya. However there is a mythological tradition in that part of the world about the existence in historical times of an Himalayan ape, entitled "Big Foot," now a possible relic survivor of the Gigantopithecines. One suggestive hypothesis is that the relatively unspecialized Miocene apes in their adaptive life-style, ground and tree dwelling, without brachiation or knuckle walking, could have been pressured by oncoming proto-Australopithecines. The latter, slightly more intelligent, incipiently bipedal, and even less specialized in their adaptive orientation, together with a branching group of small but restless protohominids, pushed these Miocene apes, *Kenyapithecus*, *Dryopithecus*, *Ramapithecus* into oblivion. Even indirect competition for life-space, food, and reproductive efficiency could have exerted the requisite selective pressure on these apes either to leave or die. Only the Sivapithecines escaped, to Asia, as that continent connected with Africa about 17-14mya. Note again, several million years later, it was a highly specialized monkey, the baboon, despite its monkey-awkward ground adaptations, that has moved back into the woodland-savannahs ecology, which had been vacated both by the older Miocene apes and then too, the seeming australopithecine victors. The probability is that *Homo* rendered the same kind of *coup-de-grace* to the Australopithecines as to *Gigantopithecus*, and probably, soon, to the orangutan, except in well-patrolled preserves and zoos. It need not be actual warfare or intrapersonal conflict that destroyed first the gracile forms of *Australopithecus* that more directly competed with *Homo*, then finally reaching the more isolated and specialized robust forms in their forested redoubt.[58]

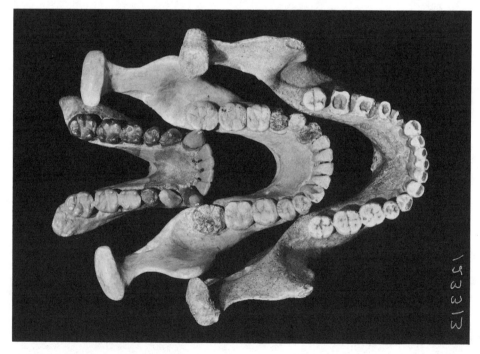

12.4 Upper jaw comparison: *Sivapithecus*, c.15-9mya; robust *Australopithecus*, c.1.8mya; *H. Heidelbergensis*, c..5mya. Robust Australopithecines had a more human-like tooth structure than did their gracile *A. afarensis* and *africanus* contemporaries.

Homo's Place

How did proto-*Homo* position itself in this evolutionary flux? According to evolutionary perspective, the *almost* losers in any one stage of evolutionary dynamics can become winners, unless they are subject to extreme ecological or biological displacement. They could, and did, exist on the periphery of an evolutionary movement, perfecting, in this case a suite of defensive adaptations, *e.g.*, brain growth and intelligence, morphological and behavioral non-specialization, the ability to move in and about a variegated ecological setting. Then they awaited their destiny.

This destiny followed the gradual desiccation of the African continent throughout the Oligocene/Miocene transition. Gradually, a small, alert omnivore, perfecting the above and as yet "non"-specialized bipedal morphology, carved out an increasingly functional, then positively selective adaptive valence. Perhaps the Australopithecines swept ahead at the end of the Miocene to clear the playing field for the as yet obscure, smart but timid protohominids. And probably by this time, 5.0mya, several different non-australopithecine hominid lines experimented with their given morphologies. Crossing beyond a size Rubicon, they became increasingly aggressive, behaviorally. The brain, long different in structure from the Australopithecines, grew allometrically, with the language and cortical areas now especially expanding.

Recent research by Finlay and Darlington highlights the reality of the expansion of the cortex, now a seemingly gratuitous hypertrophic growth. Their analysis of data on 131 species of primates, bats, and insectivores showed the size of brain components highly predictable on the basis of absolute brain size. The order of neurogenesis was highly conserved with the relative enlargement of other structures as brain size increased. The evolutionary conclusion was that selection for any late-originating brain-related behavior would result in the enlargement of the entire nonolfactory brain. In primates, relatively minor positive selection for one ability might cause, in parallel, greater processing capacity for all others.[59]

This research strengthens the case for the isocortex as a general purpose integrator that allows the organism to take advantage of the extra brain structures in ways not directly selected for during evolution. In other words, the correlation of gross body size to a highly adaptive brain size/structure would cause the brain to grow as the body grew, without there necessarily being any immediate adaptive need for this increased growth in brain size, what G. G. Simpson called "orthoselection." This view is buttressed by the work of Harry Jerison, *i.e.*, body/brain size, encephalization quotient.[60]

It was this nonspecialized planning, foreseeing brain, plus the flexible mobility that the long bipedal heritage gave humans that allowed them to move successfully about in search of sustenance. The nervous energy, vocalizations, organized social coordination, more than any weaponry, must have exerted pressure on the the-ape like rigidities of the australopithecine behavioral repertoire. As *Homo* expanded in numbers, variety, and geographic extant, the adaptive paralysis and hysteria that come from being suddenly outclassed, where formerly, they were securely ensconced, must have had a sharp impact on the reproductive viability of the Australopithecines, first gracile, then robust.

The land masses of the world in the early Pleistocene, 2-1.5mya, were being ceded to a once tiny defensive primate, which in physical growth and adaptive competence was gradually being transformed into the planet's premier vertebrate of aggression and dominance. This transformation could hardly have been predicted from the standpoint of that ostensible struggling mid-water heterotroph of the early Vendian, some 650mya.

Endnotes, Chapter 12

[1] Oxnard, C. E. (University Professor of Anatomy and Biology, Univ. of Southern California). 1985. "Hominids and Hominoids, Lineages and Radiations," in *Hominid Evolution: Past, Present, and Future,* P. V. Tobias, ed., N.Y.: Alan Liss, pp. 271-278.

[2] Oxnard, 1985, in Tobias, ed., *op. cit.,* p. 276.

[3] Oxnard, 1985, in Tobias, ed., *op. cit.,* p.277.

[4] Zihlman, Adrienne L. 1985. "A. afarensis: Two Sexes or Two Species," in Tobias, ed., *op. cit.,* pp. 213-220.

[5] Zihlman, 1985, in Tobias, ed., *op. cit.,* p. 216.

[6] Zihlman, 1985, in Tobias, ed., *op. cit.,* p. 215.

[7] Shreeve, J. 1994. "Lucy, Crucial Human Ancestor, Finally Gets a Head," *Science,* 4/1/94, 264:34-35, D. Johanson, William Kimball, Yoel Rak, of IHO in Berkeley, and Sackler School of Medicine, Tel Aviv.

[8] Klein, R. G. 1989. *The Human Career,* Chicago: Univ. of Chicago Press, pp. 146-153.

[9] Sperber, G. H. 1985. "Comparative primate dental enamel thickness: radiodontological study," in Tobias, ed., *op. cit.,* pp. 443-454, esp. p. 449; also Sperber, G. H., ed. 1990. "The phylogeny and Ontogeny of Dental Morphology," in *From Apes to Angel, Essays in Honor of Philip Tobias,* N.Y.: Wiley-Liss, pp. 215-219.

[10] Zihlman, Adrienne L. 1990. "Knuckling Under, Controversy Over Hominid Origins," in Sperber, ed., *op. cit.,* pp. 185-196, p. 191; see also: Bromage, T. G. 1985. "Taung Facial Remodeling," in Tobias, ed., *op. cit.,* pp. 239-245; Bromage, T. G., and Dean, M. C. 1985. "Re-evaluation of the Age at Death of Immature Fossil Hominids," *Nature,* 317:525-527; Conroy, G. C., and Vannier, M. W. 1987. "Dental Development of the Taung Skull from Computerized Tomography," *Nature,* 329:625-627; Beynon, A. D., and Wood, B. A. 1987. "Patterns and Rates of Enamel Growth in the Molar Teeth of Early Hominids," *Nature,* 326:493-496.

[11] Partridge, T. C. 1985. "Spring Flow and Tufa Accretion at Taung," in Tobias, ed., *op. cit.,* pp. 171-187 esp., p. 185; Vogel, J. C. 1985. "Further Attempts at Dating the Taung Tufas," in *Hominid Evolution: Past, Present, and Future,* P. V. Tobias, ed., *op. cit.,* pp. 189-194; personal communication, P. V. Tobias, 4/11/99.

[12] Rak, Y. 1985. In Tobias, ed., *op. cit.,* pp. 233-237. Rak's hypothesis concerning the possibility of some of the *africanus* types being *robustus* may be confirmed by Ronald Clarke's uncovering at Sterkfontein of an *"africanus"* at 3.3-3.0mya with a sagittal crest. Tobias, P. V. 1999. "3.0 mya australopithecine skeleton at Sterkfontein" (lecture), *Foundation for the Future,* Blaine, WA, 4/13/99.

[13] Rak, Y. 1983. *The Australopithecine Face,* N.Y.: Academic Press, p. 120.

[14] Shreeve, J. 1996. "Sunset on the Savanna," *Discover,* July 1996, pp. 116-125.

[15] Oxnard, 1985, in Tobias, ed., *op. cit.,* pp. 271-278.

[16] Oxnard, 1985, in Tobias, ed., *op. cit.,* pp. 271-272; Oxnard, 1975; Ashton, 1981; also see Stern, J. T., and Susman, R. L. 1983. "The Locomotor Anatomy of *Australopithecus afarensis,*" *Am. Jrnl. Phys. Anthrop.,* 60:279-318.

[17] Zihlman, Adrienne L. 1990. "Knuckling Under, Controversy Over Hominid Origins," in *From Apes to Angels, Essays in Honor of Philip Tobias,* G. H. Sperber, ed., *op. cit.,* pp. 185-196.

[18] Zihlman, 1990, in Sperber, ed., *op. cit.,* pp. 189-190; Latimer B., *et al.* 1987. "Talocrural Joint in African Hominoids: Implications for Australopithecus afarensis," *Amer. Jrnl. Phys. Anthrop.,* 74:2:155-175; Lovejoy, C. O. 1974. "The Gait of Australopithecus," *Yearbook of Physical Anthropology*; Lovejoy, C. O. 1978. "A Biomechanical View of the Locomotor Diversity of Early Hominids," in *Early Hominids in Africa,* C. Jolly, ed., London: Duckworth, pp. 403-429.

[19] Tuttle, R. H. 1981. "Evolution of Hominid Bipedalism and Prehensile Capabilities," *Phil. Transact. R. Soc. London,* B292, pp. 89-94, esp. p. 92; Prost, H. 1980. "Origin of Bipedalism," *Am. Jrnl. Phys. Anthrop.,* 52:175-189; Stern and Susman, 1983, *op. cit., Am. Jrnl. Phys. Anthrop.,* 60:279-318 (311); Tuttle, R. H. 1975. "Parallelism, Brachiation and Hominoid Phylogeny," in *Phylogeny of the Primates,* W. P. Luckett and F. S. Szalay, eds., N.Y.: Plenum Press, pp. 447-480; Prost, H. 1985. "Chimpanzee Behavior and Models of Hominization," in *Primate Morphophysiology, Locomotor Analyses, and Hominid Bipedalism,* S. Kondo, ed., Tokyo: University of Tokyo Press.

[20] Zihlman, 1990, in Sperber, ed., *op. cit.*, p. 190; Fleagle, J. G., *et al.*, 1981. "Climbing: A Biomechanical Link with Brachiation and with Bipedalism," *Sympos. Zool. Soc. London*, 48:359-375; Fleagle, J. G. 1988. *Primate Adaptation and Evolution*, London: Academic Press.

[21] Zihlman, 1990, in Sperber, ed., *op. cit.*, pp. 191-192; Schmid, P. 1983. "Ein Rekonstruction des Skelletes von A. L. 286-1 (Hadar) und deren Konsequenzen," *Folia primat*, 40:283-306.

[22] Washburn, S. L., ed. 1963. "Behavior and Human Evolution," in *Classification and Human Evolution*, S. L. Washburn, ed., Chicago: Aldine; Le Gros Clark, W. E. 1947. "Observations on the Anatomy of the Fossil Australopithecinae," *Anatomy*, 81:300-334.

[23] Zihlman, Adrienne, and Brunker, L. 1979. "Hominid Bipedalism: Then and Now," *Yearbook Phys. Anthrop.*, 22:132-162.

[24] Lovejoy, 1974, *op. cit., Yearbook of Physical Anthropology*.

[25] Stern and Susman, 1983, *op. cit., Am. Jrnl. Phys. Anthrop.*, 60:279-318.

[26] Susman, R. L. 1984. In *The Pygmy Chimpanzees*, R. L. Sussman, ed., N.Y.: Plenum; Zihlman, 1990, in Sperber, ed., *op. cit.*, p. 192.

[27] Astaw, B., *op. cit.* 1999. "Australopithecus garhi: A New Species of Early Hominid from Ethiopia," *Science*, 23 Apr., 629-635; de Heinzelin, J., *et al.* 1999. "Environment and Behavior of 2.5-Million-Year-Old Bouri Hominids, *Science*, 23 Apr., 625-629; Zihlman, 1990, in Sperber, ed., *op. cit.*, pp. 193-194; Boaz, N. T., and Wolfe, L. D., eds. 1995. "Calibration and Extension of the Record of Plio-Pleistocene Hominidae," in *Biological Anthropology, The State of the Science*, Bend, Oregon: International Institute for Human Evolutionary Research, Central Oregon University Center, pp. 23-48.

[28] Klein, 1989, *op. cit.*, fig. 3.30, p. 159; Andrews, P., and Stringer, C. 1993. "The Primates' Progress," in *Life*, S. J. Gould, ed., N.Y.: W. W. Norton, pp. 230-231.

[29] Tuttle, R. H. 1985. "Ape Footprints and Laetoli Impressions," in Tobias, ed., *op. cit.*, pp. 129-133; Stern and Susman, 1983, *op. cit., Am. Jrnl. Phys. Anthrop.*, 60:279-318; Andrews and Stringer, 1993, in Gould, ed., *op. cit.*, p. 236.

[30] Tobias, P. V., and Clarke, R. 1995. "New Foot Steps into Walking Debate," *Science*, 7/28/95, 269:476, 521; Tobias, P. V. 1999. "3.3my A. *africanus* Skeleton Revealed," Blaine, WA: *Foundation for the Future*, 13 Apr., lecture: "3.3mya Australopithecine Skeleton at Sterkfontein."

[31] Falk, D. 1987. "Hominid Paleoneurology," *Annual Review of Anthropology*, 16:13-30; Zihlman, 1990, in Sperber, ed., *op. cit.*, pp. 185-196; Tobias, P. V. 1975. "Brain Evolution in the Hominoidae," in *Primate functional Morphology and Evolution*, R. H. Tuttle, ed., The Hague: Mouton.

[32] Conroy, G. C., Vannier, M. V., Tobias, P. V. 1990. "Endocranial Features of A. africanus Revealed by 2- and 3-D Computed Tomography," *Science*, 2/16/90, 247:838-841.

[33] Klein, 1989, *op. cit.*, pp. 146-155.

[34] Klein quotes Holloway, R. L. 1983. "Cerebral Brain Endocast Pattern of `Australopithecus afarensis' Hominid," *Nature*, 303:420-422; and Holloway and Kimball 1986; Holloway, R. L. 1978. "Problems of Brain Endocast Interpretation and African Hominid Evolution," in *Early Hominids of Africa*, C. J. Jolly, ed., London: Duckworth.

[35] Falk, D. 1985. *Nature*, 313:45-47.

[36] Falk, D. 1986a; Falk, 1987, *op. cit., Annual Review of Anthropology*, 16:13-30; citation in Klein.

[37] Falk, D. 1980. "Language, Handedness and Primate Brains: Did the Australopithecines Sign?" *American Anthropologist*, 82:72-78; Falk, D. 1983. "Cerebral Cortices of East African Early Hominids," *Science*, 222:1072-1074.

[38] Zihlman, 1985, in Tobias, ed., *op. cit.*, pp. 213-220; Shreeve, 1994, *op. cit., Science*, 4/1/94, 264:34-35, D. Johanson, William Kimball, Yoel Rak, of IHO in Berkeley, and Sackler School of Medicine, Tel Aviv.

[39] Falk, D., and Conroy, G. C. 1983. "The Cranial Venous Sinus System in `Australopithecus afarensis,'" *Science*, 306:779.

[40] Zihlman, 1985, in Tobias, ed., *op. cit.*, pp. 213-22; Rak, , *op. cit.*, p. 120.

[41] Conroy *et al.*, 1990, *op. cit., Science*, 2/16/90, 247:838-841.

[42] Laitman, J. T. 1985. "Evolution of the Hominid Upper Respiratory Tract: The Fossil Evidence," in Tobias, ed., *op. cit.*, pp. 281-286.

[43] Laitman, 1985, in Tobias, ed., *op. cit.*, p. 284.

[44] Lieberman, P. 1984. *The Biology and Evolution of Language*, Cambridge, Mass: Harvard University Press.

[45] Laitman, 1985, in Tobias, ed., *op. cit.*, p. 285.

[46] Lieberman, P. 1994. "The Origin and Evolution of Language," in *Companion Encyclopedia of Anthropology*, T. Ingold, ed., N.Y.: Routledge, pp. 108-132.

[47] Tobias, P. V. 1994. "The Evolution of Early Hominids," in Ingold, ed., *op. cit.*, pp. 62-63.

[48] Holloway, R. L. 1983. "Human Paleontological Evidence Relevant to Language Behavior," *Human Neurobiology*, 2:105-114.

[49] Peterson, S. E., *et al.* 1989. "Positron Emission Tomographic Studies of the Processing of Single Words," *Journal of Cognitive Neuroscience*, 1:163-170.

[50] Falk, 1983, *op. cit. Science*, 222:1072-1074.

[51] Geschwind, N. 1965. "Disconnexion Syndromes in Animals and Man," *Brain*, 88:237-294, 585-644.

[52] Tobias, 1994, in Ingold, ed., *op. cit.*, p. 61.

[53] Suwa, G., *et al.* 1997. "Robust Australopithecine Skull from Konso, Ethiopia," *Nature*, 10/2/97, Vol. 389, No. 6650; Wilford, J. N. 1997. "African Skull Suggests Diversity of Early Human Relatives," *New York Times* 10/7/97, p. C9. Wilford quotes E. Delson in same *Nature* issue: Delson, E. 1997. "The Robust Australopithecine Skull of Konso, Ethiopia," *Nature*, 10/2/97, Vol. 389, No. 6650. Delson, of the American Museum of Natural History, comments on the diversity of the australopithecine clade and includes himself in the category of a taxonomic lumper, rather than a splitter.

[54] Wills, C. 1993. *The Runaway Brain*, N.Y.: Basic Books, pp. 137-138; Skelton, R., and McHenry, H. 1992. "Evolutionary relationships among early hominids," *Journal of Human Evolution*, 23:309-349.

[55] Harrison, T. 1998. "How Australopithecines Measure Up," from *Journal of Human Evolution* July (Web site); Wilford, J. N. 1998. "New Analysis of Fossils May Muddy Accepted Path of Human Evolution," *The New York Times*, July 28.; McHenry, H., and Berger, L. 1998. *National Geographic*, August.

[56] Szalay, F. S., and Delson, E. 1979. *Evolutionary History of the Primates*, N.Y.: Academic Press, pp. v-xii.

[57] Andrews, P., and Stringer, C. 1989. *Human Evolution, an Illustrated Guide*, Cambridge: Cambridge Univ. Press, pp. 36-37; Wood, B., and Collard, M. 1999. "The Human Genus," *Science*, 2 Apr., 284:65-71.

[58] Tobias, P. V. 1999. Philip Tobias places the extinction of the Australopithecines at 1.2mya, contemporary with the first evidence of the use of fire by *H. erectus,* personal communication, 12 Apr.; Stanley, S. 1996. *Children of the Ice Age,* N.Y.: W. H. Freeman, pp. 112-123.

[59] Finlay, B. I., and Darlington, R. B. 1995. "Linked Regularities in the Development and Evolution of Mammalian Brains," *Science*, 268:1578.

[60] Simpson, G. G. 1953. *The Major Features of Evolution*, N.Y.: Columbia Univ. Press; Itzkoff, S. W. 1983. *The Form of Man*, N.Y.: Peter Lang; Jerison, H. J. 1982. "The Evolution of Biological Intelligence," in *Handbook of Human Intelligence*, R. Sternberg, ed., Cambridge: Cambridge Univ. Press, pp. 723-791.

13

Toward Sapiency

Introduction.
The general perspective on the evolution of *Homo* has altered, sometimes radically, over the years. However, even into the 1990s the same basic taxonomic categories have been retained, even though as we make the transition into a new century, we see evidence of the pushing and pulling at our earlier categories and relationships. Certainly the division into *Homo habilis, Homo erectus, Homo sapiens,* though still utilized in recent writings, no longer seems as comfortable a fit.[1]

Early *Homo*, epitomized by KNMER 1470; 3733; 1813; 3883; 15,000; OH-62, (their official appellations), all of East Africa and contemporaries of the Australopithecines, was apparently on the road toward modern humanity, even at a remove of c.2my. Then there was the intermediary form, *Homo erectus*, a catch-all category into which fossils as far removed as Broken Hill (Kabwe), from northern South Africa, others from Beijing, Java, and Europe, (Swanscombe, England, and Heidelberg, Germany) were included, indicating a general migration out of Africa of evolving humans at the 1+mya level. Today, *H. erectus* as a taxonomic category is reserved for the South East Asian and East Asian hominids.[2]

The Neanderthals, c.125,000-35,000BP (to 27,000 B.P.—according to I. Tattersall) were included in *Homo sapiens* because of their great endocranial capacity, and also because their geography, Europe and West Asia, argued, to many, a lineal ancestry that linked them with the Cro-Magnon fossils, *Homo sapiens sapiens,* also in the same geographies but later in time, 45,000 B.P. to present.[3] The situation is far more complex now. Present-day finds are routinely subject to careful morphological and anatomical analysis, mitochondrial DNA studies that have seemingly thrown a revolutionary spin on the geographical origin of modern humans, now in the 200,00 B.P. range, but also migrating in a unique manner out of Africa. Finally, there has been a maturing of an old debate between a multiregional evolutionary progression into modern humans, as opposed to a single "Garden-of-Eden" scenario. The former argument, begun by Franz Weidenreich, was continued in great empirical detail by Carleton Coon, and most recently by Milford Wolpoff and his allies, Wu Xinzhi from China, and Alan Thorne from Australia.[4]

Whereas one can describe the debates over australopithecine origins and destiny as secularly scientific in nature, the issue of the evolution of modern humans is fraught with powerful political, ideological, emotional resonance. Simply, we confront the impact of this evolutionary question daily in our national and international debates. No living human can be without an interest in the shape and outcome of these controversies. They involve the obtaining of monies for research for the scientists, often from governmental and thus from political sources. It is not without possibility that financial and professional success could be dependent upon the particular conclusions that scientists might arrive at. Also, and very important, is access to the sources of the fossils, often crucial for a scholar's career. Finally, these research geographies are governed by nations and peoples who may have an interest in the answers that scientists appear to put forward. The reader must be warned that many of the positions taken by individual scholars, even whole groups of scientists, may have an ideological political, as well as a purely dispassionate and secular scientific agenda. Sadly, Christopher Stringer of the British Museum has recently fallen into that trap.[5]

First African Diaspora

1. The period in human evolution from the time frame of *Homo habilis, H. ergaster, H. rudolfensis,* 2.2-1mya is a time both of mysterious transformation as well as migration. It is no longer questioned that humans early were established in the Eur-Asian land mass and in the islands of Southeast Asia. The fossil evidence is increasingly compelling that humans early on, in the great primate tradition, migrated in force, given the geographical and climatic opportunity.

Again, in the primate tradition, these humans were relatively unspecialized creatures regarding their dietary and interspecific relationships, *i.e.*, predator/prey. They could adapt to a wide variety of climates, ecologies, or they could give in to the mental temptation inherent in "biological curiosity" to explore for the imagined possible, the "garden of plenty" that lay beyond the horizon:

> In Xanadu did Kubla Khan
> A stately pleasure dome decree:
> Where Alph, the sacred river, ran
> Through caverns measureless to man
> Down to a sunless sea
> So twice five miles of fertile ground
> With walls and towers were girdled round.
> *Kubla Khan*, Samuel Taylor Coleridge, 1798

2. In Sichuan Province, Central China, at Longgupo Cave, were discovered a lower jaw, mandible, of a hominid with a premolar plus an upper incisor. They were dated at about 1.9-1.77mya through the magnetic resonance technique. This involves the tracing of the polarity of the field, which reverses itself periodically and is in turn stored in the dated sediments. We may have here the earliest and most primitive hominid outside of Africa. These discoveries were made in the early 1980s and published in an obscure

Chinese scientific journal by Huang Wanpo of the Institute of Vertebrate Paleontology and Paleoanthropology in Beijing and Russell Ciochon of the University of Iowa. Only in 1995 were they revealed to the larger scientific community. Tools associated with the fossils consisted of rounded pieces of igneous rocks that show signs of repeated battering, similar to the basic choppers at Olduvai Gorge in East Africa that were associated with *H. habilis* types. Ciochon stated that the Longgupo hominid looked more primitive than recently redated Java hominids, both at same time level.[6]

Bernard Wood and Alan Turner saw this fossil as a more primitive human than *H. erectus*, positing that it possibly *H. ergaster*. The date of 1.9mya fits the associated extinct fauna, *Nestoritherium*, an extinct perissodactyl, like a tapir or rhinoceros.[7] Also fossils of *Gigantopithecus*, a relic Sivapithecine, were found in the cave, as in several other associated finds of human fossil material in China and Northern Vietnam, in this case not necessarily thought to have been killed by *H. ergaster*, but subject to hyena storage and foraging.[8] Wood and Turner feel that the lithic material, much larger stones than the surrounding gravel, as likely to be stone tools from that period of time as anything could be.

A note of caution: Milford Wolpoff of the University of Michigan who saw the Longgupo jaw premolar opined that it looked more orangutan than hominid, questioning whether the tooth wear pattern on the premolar from the adjoining teeth might not be hominid.[9] Subsequent analysis by Wolpoff and his colleagues has led him to argue that the mandibular fragment should be associated with *Lufengpithecus,* a Pliocene ape from China, c.5mya. The hominid incisor found associated with it is seen by Wolpoff *et al.*, as well as by Schwartz and Tattersall to be characteristic of modern human populations, and thus possibly intrusive from a higher and more recent geological layer. They claim that it also shows affinities with orangutan and other hominoid teeth.[10]

3. What gives a measure of verisimilitude to the hominid character of the Longgupo fossil is the independent research of Alan Walker, a colleague of Richard Leakey, who is an anatomist on the faculty of Pennsylvania State University. In a recent book written with Pat Shipman, he summarizes years of analysis of the various hominid fossils accumulated in East Africa. He also describes in detail the discovery of the tall so-called "Nariokotome boy," KNMWT 15000, a very complete *H. erectus* fossil that dates back to c.1.8-1.6mya.

With regard to the relationship between the Longgupo *H. ergaster* fossil, Walker describes the various *A. boisei, H. habilis* and *H. erectus* fossils as all coming from an approximately similar chronological stratigraphy.[11] It is thus possible, considering the broad slice of chronology involved in such dating at a distance, that there was time aplenty for some lines of hominids at the given grade level of the Longgupo and the East African "*Homo*" forms to have migrated, a time span of 10,000 years seems not too short.

Walker and Shipman discuss a variety of supposed *H. habilis* or *H. ergaster* fossil elements, all small, some having more human-like faces and small brains, others quite ape-like in morphology.[12] Larger *H. habilis*, have a larger brain but oddly australopithecine faces.[13] Walker and Shipman also discuss a variety of excavated and human-like limb bones, seemingly far more human than ostensible *H. habilis* post-cranial fossils, all in a time frame of 2.2-1.8mya. "...[E]ither...these long-armed, partial skeletons weren't *habilis* at all, or if they were, then *habilis* wasn't an intermediate between the Australopithecines and *Homo erectus*."[14] Walker & Shipman believe that these are large, presumably male limb bones, far more human than the fuller skeletal materials labeled *H. habilis*. Walker asserts that the taxonomic category *H. habilis* is probably wrong in the sense that the distinction between Lucy, other *Australopithecus* and the so-called *H. habilis-H. ergaster* clade is not that clear, except for the specialized uniqueness of the robust *Australopithecus* species, now having been shifted taxonomically to the *Paranthropus* genus.[15]

Finally, with regard to the increasing mystery of *H. habilis* Walker & Shipman argue that, at the least, the smaller habilines are dead ends of hominid evolution.[16] They believe that large habilines might be part of the process going forward, possibly leading to *H. erectus*: Nariokotome, Dimanisi, Georgia, and the Mojokerto and Sangiran, Java finds.[17] Ian Tattersall seems to agree with this general picture, noting that OH-62 and KNMER 1813 seem to have been accepted into the new *H. habilis* taxonomy, closer to the Australopithecines than *Homo*, a seeming dead end of evolutionary development.[18]

In their earlier technical analysis of the Nariokotome skeleton, Walker and Richard Leakey left the unmistakable impression that they thought the East African erectines were related to the East Asian *Sinanthropus* erectines described by Weidenreich:[19] comparable thickness of the skull bones of East African erectines, 8.6-8.75mm; Zhoukoudian erectines, c.500ka B.P., 8.78mm.[20]

Especially noteworthy was the uniformly modern estimated height and weight of these erectines: mean weight 58kg, height 170cm, within the averages for the tallest 17% of modern human populations.[21]

4. Indonesian cast of ancient characters: a) Mojokerto 1; formerly 750,000 B.P. now 1.81mya. b) Sangiran S27; now 1.65mya. c) *H. erectus pithecanthropus* (Trinil) still c.850,000 B.P.

It is the Java time frame revision that has set off the most debate, perhaps to cause a tidal revision in the picture of a wandering and evolving dispersion of humans at a far earlier evolutionary level. The Mojokerto 1, a juvenile calvaria, (the neurocranium without the facial bones), found near Perning, has been newly redated by Swisher and Curtis to 1.81mya (about 1my older than earlier thought when found in 1936. Likewise, the Sangiran S27, S31, fossils found in 1974, are now redated at 1.65mya. Swisher was utilizing a recently developed method that involved 40Ar/39Ar laser incremental heating of hornblende method, in order to date the associated material near the fossil site.[22]

We note that the classic Trinil, 1891, Dubois discovery of *Pithecanthropus erectus*—Java Man—is still dated so as to be .6 to .8my younger than the above fossils. The above fossils thus seem to be older than Koobi Fora KNMER 3733, the oldest African *H. erectus* (also designated taxonomically as *H. ergaster*, a form parallel to *H. habilis* and *H. rudolfensis*, KNMER 1470), at 1.77-1.8mya. Note that KNMER 406, *A. boisei* (*Paranthropus*) was found at the same stratigraphy as the above *H. erectus*, KNMER 3733.[23]

The so-called Acheulian culture dates back to Africa at about 1.4mya. This stone tool culture is characterized by increasingly sophisticated faceting of tools, in which so-called Levallois technology was used. This involved the development of different uses for these carefully fabricated instruments—axes, knives, pounders.[24] The explanation for the simplicity of all Asiatic erectine tools, in the style of the Oldowan flakes, which show little human fabrication facility, is that the Asian hominids left Africa before the invention of the Acheulian. Itzkoff, in 1983, suggested the possibility of an early hominid migration from Africa to Asia, as explaining the technological differences, Oldowan-Acheulian, in the *H. erectus* tool assemblages.[25]

Andrews and Stringer view the stone tools at Zhoukoudian, Beijing Man, c.0.5mya and implicitly throughout other Chinese and Southeast Asian sites as showing "little advance over the Oldowan industry of *Homo habilis*." They, along with others believe that *H. erectus* in Asia may have made greater use of bamboo and other perishable materials.[26] This fact was early noted by Davidson Black and his associates in the first publication of the Zhoukoudian excavations in 1933. Despite the fact that a number of artificially broken bones showed evidence of conscious and deep incisions drawn through them, the views of Black *et al.* of the culture of *Sinanthropus*, at "zone C" of their excavations, could be summed up as follows: no bifaces, indifferent use of entire pebbles or boulders, at most only rudimentary preparation of the stone tool quartz pieces, right-handed use of tools, a Paleolithic technology with little resemblance to other Asiatic or European tool industries known at that time, 0.5mya.[27]

The dating of the Java material has generated much debate, not only because of the method utilized, as Swisher and Curtis are part of a specialized team from the Berkeley, University of California, Geochronology Center. Francis Brown, Alan Walker, and Ernst Mayr, for example, expressed hesitancy about the reliability of these dates, skepticism based more on association of the fossils with the tested stratigraphy.[28]

A debate in the pages of *Science* between J. de Vos of the National Museum of Natural History, Leiden, Netherlands, and Swisher about Swisher's surety of the site stratigraphy and his dating techniques' usefulness for establishing the time frame of these fossils raised further questions.[29] Swisher tried to assure de Vos that all was well, the fauna discovered with fossils all go back in Asia to over 1.7my. More paleomagnetic studies were under way.

Walker and Shipman, more recently, continued to express skepticism of Swisher's and Curtis' conclusions on Mojokerto because of the fact that sediments were not conclusively located— the skull being found 40 years before a careful search for the location was begun, also because the point of origin sites indicated by an earlier Japanese-Indonesian team were different from those indicated by Swisher-Curtis.[30]

5. Whatever the exact dates for the Indonesian fossils, it is agreed that they can be broadly subsumed into *H. erectus*. Wood and Turner noted that the Dimanisi, Georgia fossil is an *H. erectus*, dated at about 2mya, or 1.8-1.6mya.[31] In addition, hominid fossils found at Ubeidiya, Israel, have now been dated back to 1.4mya.[32] Wood and Turner believe migration was possible across the Bab-el-Mandab straits, Africa to Arabia, else via the Levant—Sinai—both open in the late Pliocene/early Pleistocene.[33]

Walker and Shipman have compared Gabunia's (Gabunia was the discoverer) Dimanisi mandible with that of KNMWT 15000, the Nariokotome boy erectine, and found it extraordinarily similar. Both fossils date to the same era, 1.8-1.6mya, but were located several thousand miles apart.[34] It is important to lay out the facts as Walker studied them in the African erectine: Nariokotome boy, KNMWT 15000, 11 years old, skeletal bones, indicated height of 5'3," c.106lb.—at maturity, c.5'11"-6'1," 132lb.[35] Brain size of KNMWT 15000 at death, 880cm³—if alive to maturity, 909cm³—respectably average erectine.[36] Note that a contemporary of "15,000," KNMER 3733, often designated *H. ergaster*, also East Africa, had an endocranial capacity of 850cm³, at 1.7mya.

Fred Spoor's and Frans Zonneveld's research on the inner ear vestibular system, which helps humans in balance, movement (jumping), bipedality, is cited by Walker and Shipman to underlie the evolutionary position of "15K." According to these researchers' use of 3D-Tomography analysis, all australopithecine balance systems from *A. africanus* on were ape-like=chimpanzee. Not even the transitional South African *H. habilis*, StW53, which resembles the East African *Homo habilis/ergaster* fossils, had sapient-like inner ear vestibular systems. The South African *H. habilis* fossil had an inner ear vestibular system more like a gibbon or monkey than either an ape or hominid. However, a South African *H. erectus* that Spoor and Zonneveld had studied had a human-like vestibular system. They did not study the Nariokotome fossil.[37]

Most interesting, and perhaps crucial: "15K," as earlier noted, did have 6 lumbar vertebrae, similar to the basal Miocene ape, *Proconsul*, at 22-20mya, as well as *A. africanus*. Most *Homo sapiens* have 5 lumbar, vertebrae; 4% have 6 lumbar vertebrae. A basic morphological oddity such as this cannot readily be altered in the genetic evolutionary sense in a scant million or so years.[38] Jeffrey Schwartz in referring to Walker's work with *H. erectus* in East Africa, states that the *H. erectus* that Walker has worked with (15K) may be unique, erectine-like, but different from the other erectines of Asia and Africa.[39]

On the other hand, Walker, in summing up his and others' technical analysis of the 15K, Nariokotome fossil, by comparing its brain/body weight ratio in the broader context of the evolution of the hominoids:

> A line through *H. habilis* and *H. erectus* has a slope very close to regression lines calculated for the apes and Australopithecines....[T]he average body weight of early *H. erectus* is as big as those found in some modern populations with very big people, but the average cranial capacity of early *H. erectus* is much smaller than modern human cranial capacities.[40]

Walker concludes that there is little change in human morphology from c.1.8mya to 500,000 years ago, somewhat similar to Carleton Coon's observation concerning the Olduvai hominid 9, now, 1.2mya, compared to the Broken Hill (Kabwe), Zambian skull, which Coon finally dated to about 65,000-25,000 B.P., today c. 200,000 B.P. David Pilbeam also has noted this extremely slow pace of evolution in the erectine line.[41]

Considerations: First Phase

The evidence of a widespread hominid radiation, starting perhaps as early as the late Miocene, c.8.0mya, is highly suggestive. More and different varieties of *Australopithecus*, perhaps new generic taxonomic categories such *Ardipithecus* (*ramidus*) and

Paranthropus (*robustus* and *boisei*), seem to be discovered almost yearly, and in always more remote sedimentary layers of time.

13.1 Slow African *erectus* evolution: Olduvai (Kenya) Hominid 9, c.1.2mya (above); Kabwe (Zambia-Rhodesia), c.200ka B.P. (below). All time estimates have been revised back in time. Coon, in 1982, estimated Kabwe to date to 62-25ka B.P.

The disappearance of the great apes from Africa, then from Europe, except for the specialized knuckle walkers in the West African jungles, constitutes indirect and inferential buttressing for this hypothesis. The land masses of Africa, with their mixture of plains, woodlands, swamps, jungles, provided ample ecological variety and at the same time a not overwhelming challenge to a mainly bipedal ground ape/protohominid with a more aggressive and enterprising brain.

Behind and among the various australopithecine-type bipeds were the hominid types, laggard perhaps in size and morphological specialization as compared with those in the mainline "australopithecine" expansion, but out there nevertheless, probably in equal variety. And, why not? Both forms, as we now understand the fossil record, were by the late Miocene part of a long-expanding clade of primates, the branches of an ancient trunk, perhaps better to be conceived more as from a clump of birches, rather than from a great oak pillar.

Inevitably, to attempt to understand the root source of these animals, we will still one day return to the Oligocene, some 35-30mya, or even earlier. This kind of march into modernity represented in a relatively contemporary time frame, the late Miocene, is still reflective of an ancient vertebrate tradition of evolutionary succession. It would not surprise to view the human surge into dominance as typical of all evolutionary patterns through time. Indeed, the next phase of the struggle of the several branches of the tree was to be for the light of the sun and the eventual domination of one major leading vertical branch and its ecology, the domain of adaptation.

The picture of *Homo* has been fast-changing from its very inception. Much depends on how well the large skulls of East African "1470" (*H. rudolfensis*) and "3733" (*H. ergaster*) hold up as real and typical representatives of early *Homo* at 2.-.7mya, the former with a primitive australopithecine/ape-like maxilla, and post-cranial bones still in a transitional australopithecine/hominid morphological profile. If Alan Walker is correct, our linear projection of the *H. habilis*/*H. erectus* evolutionary progression may have to be radically revised. Evidence now clearly demands that the linear derivation between *Australopithecus* and *Homo* be re-conceptualized.

At any rate, what seems to be emerging from the mists of human evolution is a set of creatures, mostly in Africa, between 2.2-1.8mya, that are extremely variable in size and form, now representing at least several species, even genera, of *Homo* (*habilis, ergaster, rudolfensis*) all intermediate to *Australopithecus* and *H. erectus*. It should not surprise if non-australopithecine hominid fossils are found that belong to an even earlier time, perhaps in geographies beyond the African genesis time line of the hominoids. For example, in January of 1997, a report appeared in *Nature* that described the discovery, between 1992-1994 at Gona in Ethiopia, by Dr. Sileshi Semaw, of approximately 3,000 fist size, rounded as well as small, sharp flake tools. The tools were made apparently by *Homo* and date back to 2.6-2.5mya. This, along with Boaz' recent reporting of a similar time frame for other toolmaking sites in Africa, pushes further back the horizons claimed for hominid tool making.[42]

Clive Gamble would place the West Turkana, Kenya, KNMWT 15000, at 1.6mya, as the earliest erectine fossil. Further, he placed the various extra-African erectines at time levels more recent than 1mya.[43] The weight of evidence, in contrast, now points to a widely-dispersed panorama of morphologically and cladistically variable humanity contemporary with the earliest *H. habilis* specimens, 2.2-1.8mya, probably including the Australopithecines. If not altering our African "Garden-of-Eden" scenario, this places the origin and dispersal of *Homo* much further back in time.

The hint that Alan Walker gives us, that his Nariokotome boy, KNMER 15,000, is different from the majority of modern humans, along with other early *Homo* types that are similar morphologically to the apes, should underscore the probability that even the more advanced erectines, in their bipedality, brain size, and presumably culture, were part of a long, fragmenting evolutionary radiation. Perhaps they were derived from some early form of *H. habilis*, else from an as-yet unknown branch of this long dividing and wandering hominid clade.

Evidence and Considerations—Second Phase
1. Post-erectine gap

A leader in the list of current mysteries in this evolutionary process, is the seeming gap in the fossil record from around 700,000 B.P., a time still reflecting the erectine morphology, to about 300,000 B.P., when forms with somewhat more gracile structures and larger endocranial capacities seem to herald a group of fossils now lumped into the category of "anatomically archaic sapients."

Jeffrey Schwartz quotes Philip Rightmire of SUNY, Binghampton, as suggesting, tentatively, that after 1.5mya, contemporaneous with or after the flourishing of *H. erectus* types, 4 different species of *Homo* existed. Rightmire saw the Asiatic *H. erectus* and the grouping of humans under *H. heidelbergensis* as a fundamental splitting of the line in which the latter produced *H. neanderthalensis* and *H. sapiens*. Kabwe, (Broken Hill), and Chinese erectine exemplars might be unique species. Then he backed off, describing the entire group—non East Asiatic and African erectines—as *Homo sapiens*.[44] Interestingly, as we will note below, Noel Boaz has Rightmire arguing that the African and Asiatic erectines at about this same time frame, are all part of one worldwide, if variable species. This is similar to Philip Tobias' reported unwillingness to remove the various *H. habilis* variants, *e.g., ergaster, rudolfensis*, etc. from the *H. habilis* taxonomy.[45]

Ian Tattersall suggested that anatomically archaic sapiens were composed of the descendants of Asian erectines, e.g. Beijing, Java. These were the earlier, 500,000-200,000 B.P., *H. heidelbergensis*: Kabwe (Zambia), Petralona (Greece), Bodo (Ethiopia), Arago (France), *H. steinheimensis* (Steinheim-Germany, Swanscombe-England):

> Any mammalian paleontologist seeing morphological differences on the order of those separating modern humans from their various precursors, and the latter from each other, would have no difficulty in recognizing a number of separate species. And in this decision there is no special pleading even when it is our own closest relatives that are involved.[46]

Schwartz further argued that Steinheim and Swanscombe might be ancestral to the Neanderthals. Considering the Neanderthal domination of Europe and West Asia after 150,000 B.P., the *H. heidelbergensis* group may have been related to the successor Neanderthals.[47] Finally, in this wide-ranging interpretive sweepstakes, Carleton Coon saw in Petralona (Greece), Vertessolos (Hungary), Mauer (Germany)—[*H. heidelbergensis?*]—then in the range of 300,000-200,000 B.P., possible ancestors of the Neanderthals. The above *H. heidelbergensis* types are now dated back to c.500ka B.P[48]

2. Carleton Coon

Final conclusions on early African erectines. Coon's views were as usual, independent and controversial[49]:

    a) KNMER 1470, 2.0-1.8mya (now *H. rudolfensis*), cranial capacity 755cm³ resembles *H. erectus*, while its "brain/palate ratio indicates affinities with Australopithecus." 1470, narrow nasal skeleton=Caucasoid?[50]

b) KNMER 3733 (now *H. ergaster*)—1.7-1.6mya—Bushman-like female, flat face, steep slope of forehead above brow ridges, *H erectus* cranial capacity, c.850cm³.

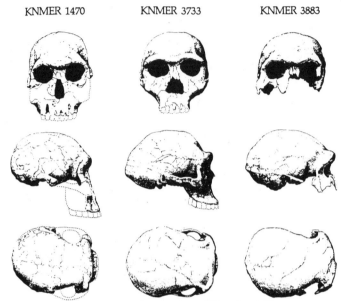

KNMER 1470   KNMER 3733   KNMER 3883

13.2 Early African *erectus:* Carleton Coon, in 1982, saw these African hominids as precursor members of modern races. "1470"—Caucasoid; "3733"—Capoid/Bushman; "3883"—Negroid. All date c.1.8-1.4mya, probably still contemporary with the disappearing Australopithecines.

c) KNMER 3883—a bit later, 1.6-1.4mya, than KNMER 3733, same cranial capacity; instead of braincase rising and then curving above its brow ridges, its forehead slopes more flatly back, its facial bones and mastoids more massive=Negro. This latter example is a quite fragmentary fossil.

Coon:
> Note the narrow nasal bones of 1470, its relatively high cranial vault, its moderate brow ridge, and its lack of alveolar prognathism; also note the higher forehead of 3733, the marked notches over its brow ridges, its sloping malar bones lacking a notch under the eye sockets, and its extreme alveolar prognathism. The third, 3883, has the most sloping forehead and nasal profile, and its brow ridges have the most curved profile when viewed from above; it is convex. That of 3733 is concave, and that of 1470 is straight above both eye sockets and the nasal bones between them. The tentative interpretations are the authors. The discoverer [R. Leakey] and the anatomist [A. Walker] are more cautious.[51]

In 1993, Leakey and Walker would confirm Coon's analysis in a comparison between KNMWT 15000, KNMER 3733, KNMER 3883, as follows: "In comparison with KNMWT 15000, this specimen [KNMER 3883] seems closest to what we imagine its adult state to have been. The brow ridges are 13.5[mm] thick and form a continuous torus rather than being interrupted by a strong supra-glabellar groove as in KNMER 3733."[52]

It is also possible, since we are dealing with time parameters adjustable at least, in clumps of 100,000 or so years, that some of the erectines and other primitive humans, e.g., those of Longgupo Cave, similar to contemporary East African KNMER 3733 (*H. ergaster*), may have continued to evolve in Asia for a time, then spread back into Europe and Africa. Carleton Coon, in 1965 on the basis of a number of physical similarities between the Bushman and modern Asiatics, hypothesized an ancient *Sinanthropus* counterintrusion into both Africa and Europe. It would not have taken more than a small band to have made its genetic impact on existing African populations. See Itzkoff's 1983 analysis of Coon's conjecture.[53] Note, however, Coon's later placing of KNMER 3773, c.1.6mya, as an incipient Capoid/Bushman. This could, as he does state in his 1982 book, preclude any relationship between the *Sinanthropus*, Chinese erectines, and the Bushman-like erectine of East Africa.[54] Else it could make the *Sinanthropus* line in Northeast Asia a wandering branch of the early Capoids, and KNMER 3773.

3. Variable mid-Pleistocene *Homo*—continued.

Jeffrey Schwartz on the puzzle: *Homo erectus*, (800,000-500,000 B.P.) consisting of Java, Beijing, even Olduvai Gorge; primitive *H. erectus*, Leakey's sites in Kenya— KNMER 15000.

Homo neanderthalensis ancestors: primitively Neanderthal (500,000-200,000 B.P.)—Steinheim, possibly Swanscombe (at 225,000 B.P.). This group of Neanderthal precursors is now assigned the taxonomic status: *Homo heidelbergensis*—Arago (France), Petralona (Greece) Kabwe (Zambia), and Bodo (Ethiopia), especially in the face. "Now is the *neanderthalensis-steinheimensis-heidelbergensis* group more closely related to a *Homo erectus* group (based for example, on thickened cranial and post cranial bone; and enlarged, protruding brow ridges) than it is to *Homo sapiens* (based on what)? And what about *Homo habilis*"?[55] Note, Coon disagreed with the recent consensus placing Arago with the Neanderthals. He stated that Arago had no relationship to the Neanderthals.[56]

Schwartz, in 1990:

...Alan Thorne criticized Chris Stringer's attempt to delineate uniquenesses of *Homo sapiens* (anatomically modern humans). Alan suggested that some of the characters Chris cited as being uniquely *Homo sapiens*—such as the vaulted skull with tall forehead and round occipital bone—were relevant only to European specimens. If Chris had looked at some Australian Aborigines, for instance, [argues Thorne], [he] would have come to a different conclusion—such as seeing the continuity."[57] Continuity here meaning—with in situ Southeast Asian *H. erectus*.

4. Who were the Neanderthals?

Early discoveries in Belgium, 1829-1830, then in 1848 on the Rock of Gibraltar, finally recognized in 1856 in the Neander Valley near Düsseldorf in Germany, the Neanderthals have always exercised a fascination. Partly because of their European origins, and their temporal priority of discovery, they early raised the question of the evolutionary origins of modern humans.[58] One of the earliest publications reporting the discovery in Germany, by G. Busk in England, appeared but 2 years after Darwin's *On the Origin of Species* [59]

The question in recent decades has concerned the Neanderthals' admittedly close relation to modern Europeans and Cro-Magnon. Were the Neanderthals the direct precursors of the Upper Paleolithic peoples, and through internal mutational and selective processes gradually transformed into modern forms, else were they a unique race of big-brained Caucasoids, with clearly primitive facial, skull, post-cranial morphologies, and a simple and stagnant Mousterian culture? By the early 1980s, it was clear that the Neanderthals had too many morphological differences, despite their seeming human behaviors—conscious burials (perhaps with flowers), care of the handicapped—to be viewed as a transitional phase in European-West Asian, late-Pleistocene human evolution.[60]

Mellars and Tattersall have attempted to bring this race of humans to life, the former in a detailed monograph on their technology, culture, way of life, the latter in a more popularized and evocative account of their humanity. Mellars' review of the research literature on their hunting techniques reveals them to be quite competent quasi-industrialized hunters as to types of species hunted, the modes of preparing the meat, settlement patterns. The picture is not too different from the traditional view of the Cro-Magnids trapping, driving herds over cliffs, stampeding by fire.[61]

Scientific opinion has increasingly turned toward the view that we are witnessing in Eur-Asia the evolution of two discrete taxa of human beings, at the very least two races, one the apparent successor of the more primitive, erectine-like form; perhaps, in terms of morphology, two species. Research into the morphology, culture, inevitably the evolutionary destiny of the Neanderthals has led to many scholars accepting the distinct species position, yet possibly not intersterile with the Cro-Magnons, now clearly contemporaries in time and space with the Neanderthals.

Crucial was Bernard Vandermeersch's work on the morphology of the Neanderthals, *viz.* the mastoid process (bony projection behind the ear), the styloid process (a projection of bone that juts down from the auditory tube). Vandermeersch argued that the Neanderthal styloid process is in a completely different position at the base of the skull as compared with modern humans, intimating that the swallowing function would be quite different. Vandermeersch's conclusion: Neanderthals have different morphology as compared with modern sapiens.[62]

Also important was Albert Santa Luca's research on Neanderthal uniquenesses: 1) Styloid process—as with Vandermeersch. 1) Occipital torus—a uniformly thick horizontally-oriented strut of bone that runs across and is confined to the occipital bone, plus an elliptical depression rimmed by an elevation of bone above the torus (brow ridges). None of the following *H. erectus* and/or transitional, archaic, *H. sapiens* had these unique Neanderthal morphologies: Kabwe (Broken Hill-Zambia), Ngandong (Java), Skhul, Qafzeh, (Israel), Omo 2 (Ethiopia), Jebel Irhoud (Morocco). Yes—possibly Steinheim and Swanscombe.[63]

The position that the Neanderthal-Cro-Magnon transition showed little admixture, a seeming sudden and clearly defined taxonomic difference, was put forward by Ernst Mayr of Harvard in a 1963 analysis.[64] Recent mtDNA analysis of organic material procured from the original 1856 Neander Valley, Neanderthal, by Svante Paabo of Munich

University, argues for no genetic association between the two lines, as evidence by a study of mtDNA in modern populations around the world.[65]

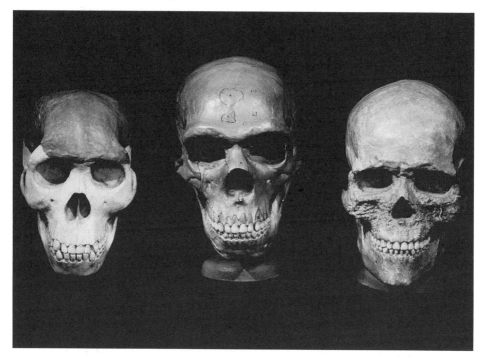

13.3 Pathways to sapiency. The original *H. erectus pithecanthropus* from Java, c.1mya; Neanderthal Man, Eur-Asia, c.100-30ka B.P; Cro-Magnon, Eur-Asia, c.35ka B. P.

The other view, that the transition between Neanderthal and Cro-Magnon populations was gradual and probably involved the transformation of at least the Central European populations of Neanderthal into modern Upper Paleolithic, Cro-Magnon populations, if indeed it did not include Western European populations whose replacement seems to have been more abrupt, was reiterated by Smith *et al.* in 1989.[66]

Milford Wolpoff, who has long viewed the Neanderthals as genetic ancestors of the Cro-Magnons, has recently argued for this position from the morphology of the mandibular foramen, a nerve opening into the lower jaw teeth from the neck. He illustrates the manner in which earlier modern Europeans share the particular morphology with the Neanderthals.[67] The morphology disappears in later Europeans, becoming the dominant and contemporary form, possibly confirming Paabo's inability to find Neanderthal genes in modern humans. But this morphology is also not to be found in the Qafzeh or Skhul specimens, either in early Cro-Magnon types or Neanderthal hybrids.[68]

Zubrow has presented a theoretical analysis of a modestly interactive but still competitive ecological relationship, if not necessarily open warfare, between two adjoining populations of relatively equal numbers of Neanderthals and Cro-Magnons. He uses existing evidence derived from fossil analysis in terms of life expectancies, and based on the statistical advantage of bringing more individuals of successive generations into the reproductive cycle, finally assuming a success advantage over the Neanderthals of as little as 1-2% per year by the Cro-Magnons. The result is a picture of the full extinction of the Neanderthals in 300 generations, or about 1,000 years.[69] At least in Western Europe, there seems to have been a full replacement of the Neanderthals by the Cro-Magnons in no more than 5,000 years, between c.35,000-30,000 B.P. Tattersall places the final extinction of the Neanderthals in southern Spain near the Mediterranean at the Zaffaraya Cave, at c.27,000 B.P.

5. Recent Australasian cast of characters

Australia: Kow Swamp, 13,000-4,000 B.P.; Willandra Lakes Hominid, 50,000-30,000 B.P.; Lake Mungo graciles, 30,000 B.P.

Indonesia: Ngandong, formerly 300,000-200,000 B.P, now 53,000-27,000 B.P.; Sangiran 17, formerly 400,000-200,000 B.P, now 53,000-27,000 B.P.

The Australasian hominid evolutionary scene has recently centered on the more recent time frames, in addition to those earliest discoveries of human-like fossils, described above, at the beginning of the Pleistocene, some 1.9-1.7mya.

Alan Thorne is a proponent of the so-called multiregional view of recent hominid evolution. He believes in the semi-independent evolution of *Homo* in the various regions of their habitat throughout most of the Pleistocene and into the near present. Thorne has analyzed the Australian Kow Swamp skull, dated at between 13,000-4,000 B.P. Morphologically primitive, if recent, it has a flat, sloping forehead, thick bones and brow ridges, a distended occipital with a bony strut. Quite different from the Neanderthals, it is similar to Sangiran 17, *Homo erectus* in Java, once dated at 400,000-200,000 B.P. There is in the Kow Swamp skull the possibility of an intentional cultural deformation of the forehead, as if by compression of the head with boards, as with contemporary Melanesian tribespeople.[70]

Newly-found Willandra Lakes Hominid, WLH50, is dated as older than 30,000BP. Similar to Kow Swamp: robust bone, brow ridge, and distended occipital, also sloping forehead, thus not cultural deformation, and similar to contemporaries. Also WLH-50 is very similar to Ngandong *H. erectus*, which formerly was dated back to 300,000-200,000 B.P. Recent redating estimates would place the Ngandong fossil as a contemporary with WL-50, at 53,000-27,000 B.P. However WLH-50 is unique in having a thick layer of spongy bone sandwiched between a thin layer of hard outer and inner skull bone.[71]

C. C. Swisher and Susan Anton, along with Teuku Jacob, curator at Gadja Mada University, Indonesia, reporting on 12 Ngandong skulls, without faces, that were discovered in 1930s, have redated the Ngandong site after using their new dating technique, which was developed at the University of California, Berkeley Geochronology Laboratory. They undertook a reexamination of the Ngandong fossil fauna, also at Sambungmacan (Sangiran 17, *H erectus*), another well-known and nearby erectine fossil site. Both sites, dated now at 53,000-27,000 B.P., earlier were thought to be c.300,000 B.P.[72] This new dating implies that *H. erectus*, the Ngandong skull "people," coexisted with *H. sapiens*. Fossils representing early gracile *sapiens* at Lake Mungo, in Australia, could be dated to 30,000 B.P. It is possible that the gracile Lake Mungo sapients, as distinct from

Willandra Lake, WL50, hominids, and the Kow Swamp fossils were all Australian contemporaries of the Indonesian erectines at Ngandong and Sangiran. J. Desmond Clark, citing Rightmire, sees Ngandong as Archaic *Homo sapiens*.[73]

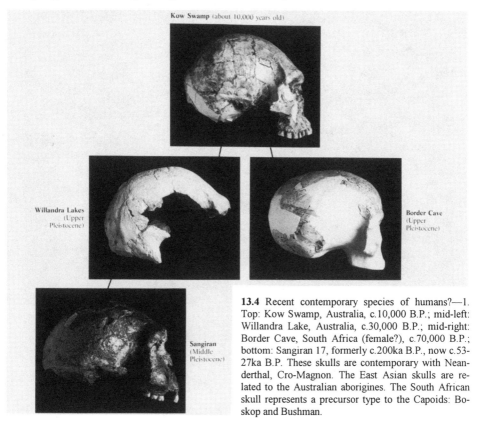

13.4 Recent contemporary species of humans?—1. Top: Kow Swamp, Australia, c.10,000 B.P.; mid-left: Willandra Lake, Australia, c.30,000 B.P.; mid-right: Border Cave, South Africa (female?), c.70,000 B.P.; bottom: Sangiran 17, formerly c.200ka B.P., now c.53-27ka B.P. These skulls are contemporary with Neanderthal, Cro-Magnon. The East Asian skulls are related to the Australian aborigines. The South African skull represents a precursor type to the Capoids: Boskop and Bushman.

Peter Brown, writing at the same time, and in the same scientific anthology as Clark, associates the Ngandong crania with the Australian examples. He is persuaded that the Ngandong fossil crania, 53,000-27,000 B.P., may be *H. erectus*.[74] Milford Wolpoff, viewing these interpretations of the new dating of the Ngandong and Sambungmacan as threatening to his "regional continuity" interpretation, especially as restated in a recent 1997 book, argues that the above fossil specimens should be viewed as *H. sapiens* and not as *H. erectus*. He argues that the variety of Australasian forms should be considered one variable population without the presumption of intrusive populations living at different taxonomic and evolutionary grades.[75]

Habgood, writing in 1985 and 1989, confirms Thorne's views on the similarity of Willandra Lake, WL-50, to Ngandong, the latter possibly *H. erectus*. Habgood feels that Lake Mungo graciles, c.30,000 B.P., and Willandra Lake, 50,000-30,000 B.P are representatives of a highly variable Australian population.[76] What would Habgood believe in

1996, given the new datings of Ngandong, not 300,000 B.P., but 53,000-27,000 B.P., and its previous acknowledged similarity to WL-50, 30,000-50,000 B.P.?

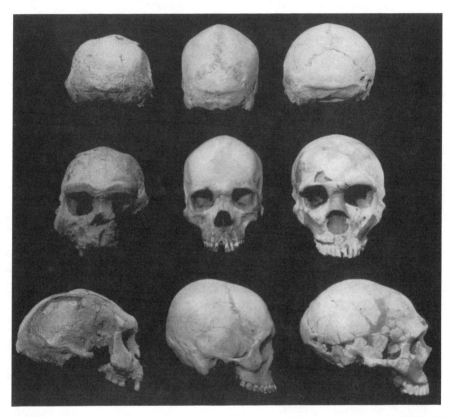

13.5 Recent contemporary species of humans?—2. Left to right: Sangiran 17, Indonesia, now 53-27ka B.P.; Modern Indonesian; La Ferrasse, Neanderthal, France, c.+50ka B.P. What evolutionary process could have turned, so recently, the transitional human fossil into a contemporary Indonesian or European? Possible answers: genes, highly selective, unleashed from within the respective ethnicities, or, genes traveling from afar?

The weight of evidence for the Australasian late-Pleistocene, early-Holocene context has shifted. It seems clear that rather than a smooth transition from *H. erectus* to recent borderline sapient forms among the aboriginal peoples of the region, there were a number of morphologically and taxonomically distinct populations during the period from c.50,000-10,000 B.P. The distinct grades leading in real time from ancient *H. erectus*, *H. sapiens*, and the typical *Homo sapiens sapiens* European, Cro-Magnon types, c.30,000 B.P., cannot be upheld in Australasia. The acknowledged borderline sapient morphologies and culture of the historical aboriginal peoples noted and discussed by Coon, Baker, Pilbeam, Itzkoff, and more recently argued for by Thorne, Wolpoff, Wu, have substantial chronometric support, given the continued verification of the new chronology for the fossil material. If not as distinct species, they now seem to have existed in Southeast Asia, a very blurred set of transitional erectine and sapient populations, almost into the historical horizon.[77]

6. How many contemporary human species?

That there were at least three species of humans, or at least 5 distinct racial types throughout the late-Pleistocene world, is underscored by the near unanimous agreement within the paleoanthropological community that the Neanderthals were a distinct clade as compared with Cro-Magon. Both lived contemporaneously, but may have had morphological differences verging on the species level, without necessarily exhibiting the traditional taxonomic interfertility that characterizes species differentiation. This scenario is not too different from the three species model that Carleton Coon was hinting at between 1962 and 1982 when he proposed that the Kabwe/Broken Hill (Zambia) skull, which he then dated to 26,000-62,000 B.P.—thus contemporary with the other two species of humans—was at that time viewed as Neanderthal/Cro-Magnon. Coon interpreted Kabwe to be a large-skulled erectine. Today it is viewed as *H. heidelbergensis* or Archaic *Homo sapiens*, along with Petralona, Bodo, Arago, and at c.250,000-150,000 B.P. What about the status of the Australasian clade of humans? Coon saw them as borderline erectines/sapients.[78]

7. Complicating discoveries

In a recent publication Noel Boaz, discusses the systematics and phylogeny of the genus *Homo*: Wood, along with Tattersall, sees *Homo habilis*, *Homo ergaster*, *Homo rudolfensis*, and *Homo erectus*, KNMER 1813, KNMER 15000 as all being contemporaries in Africa.[79] Philip Tobias includes all of these taxa within *Homo habilis*. Also, Boaz raises the question about the supposed taxonomic relationship of African *H. erectus, e.g.*, KNMER 3733, (*H. ergaster*), and KNMER 15000, (Nariokotome), and Asiatic forms of "*H. erectus.*" Philip Rightmire, however, argues that the Asiatic and African erectines are of the same species. Wood, as well as Groves and Mazek, see the African "*H. erectus*" as really *H. ergaster*.[80]

Boaz: "In phylogenetic terms the major result of this interpretation [Wood; Groves and Mazek] is that *H. erectus* is moved off the lineage leading to *H. sapiens*."[81] Tattersall agrees: "...*Homo erectus* seems to be a specialized Asian offshoot—one that eventually became extinct—from the human lineage."[82] Boaz has also noted some complicating discoveries in terms of relationships within the mid-to late Pleistocene hominids:

a) In China, a discovery made ten years ago at Jinniushan of an archaic *Homo sapiens* skull was dated by ESR (Electro-spin resonance) and uranium series to the unexpectedly early date of approximately 200,000 B.P.[83] "The authors suggest that its early age, almost as old as some Chinese *Homo erectus* finds, raises the possibility of the co-existence of the two species."[84] Geoffrey Pope has been quoted as expressing astonishment that this human combines heavy brow ridges with a large endocranial capacity of 1400cm^3, and extremely thin cranial bones.[85]

b) Recent controversy over the time of the first human colonization of Australia has developed over a number of early dates for this set of events. Traditional colonization dates of c.40,000-30,000 B.P. (radio carbon dating) have been pushed back to 60,000-50,000 B.P. using "thermoluminescent" dating methods.[86] Most recently, the latter method has produced, from discovered stone artifacts in sediments, a date back to C. 116,000 B.P.! [87]

c) "Sussex, U.K. whose last widely known contribution to paleoanthropology was the fraudulent Piltdown fossils, has now yielded a real hominid partial tibia [shin bone] dating to some 500,000 B.P. on the basis of faunal zonation."[88] "This is by far the oldest hominid record in Britain and equals the Heidelberg mandible in age. The authors ascribe the specimen to *Homo,* cf. *heidelbergensis.* Others would assign it to archaic *Homo sapiens.*"[89]

How long ago was there a *Homo sapiens* on our planet?

Questions/Issues

It is not necessarily the facts surrounding the ever-increasing variety of human fossils that raise the deepest questions. Issues of chronology and morphological grade and affinity are real, and always subject to differences of opinion, especially as many of the "facts" of discovery—where the fossils were found and with what associated fauna are the stuff of continued controversy.

But more, it is interpretation. The sweeping changes in taxonomic association, only part of which we have recounted in this and earlier chapters, raise important questions of clarity of relationships, grades of evolutionary development, inevitably the contemporary implications for a humanity still subdivided into races and ethnicities.

There are even deeper and, again, more global theoretical concerns that have an impact on how the rational scientific mind views the concrete artifacts of evolution, the fauna, the fossils, the geological strata, the chronometric dating techniques. Two major issues to be discussed in the next chapter:

1. The mitochondrial DNA "African Eve" scenario, which has had a crucial influence on the taxonomic definitions as to which fossils to place in the category "Archaic *Homo sapiens*, AHS," and "Morphologically Modern Humans, MMS." It is an example of how larger abstract theoretical models influence our perceptions of the concrete.

2. The ongoing debate between advocates of the a) multiregional view of the evolution of *Homo*, a perspective that purports to identify a number of parallel *in situ* internal evolutionary processes leading to modern forms of *Homo*, and b) a replacement scenario. The latter "Garden-of-Eden" point of view postulates one relatively recent geographical locus for the origin and evolution of *Homo sapiens* and the five modern races. The more ancient forms of *Homo* have in this latter interpretation disappeared, leaving no contemporary trace of their genetic existence.

Inevitably, the molecular data once more will have an enormous influence in shaping this particular dimension of the debate over the final evolutionary thrust toward modern sapiency.

Endnotes, Chapter 13

[1] Andrews, P., and Stringer, C. 1993. "The Primates' Progress," in *Life*, S. J. Gould, ed., N.Y.: W. W. Norton, pp. 219-251; Gamble, C. 1994. "Human Evolution: The Last One Million Years," in *Companion Encyclopedia of Anthropology*, T. Ingold, ed., London: Routledge, pp. 79-107.

[2] Tattersall, I. 1995. *The Last Neanderthal*, N.Y.: Macmillan, pp. 59-61.

[3] Tattersall, 1995, *op. cit.*

[4] Weidenreich, F. 1946. *Apes, Giants, and Man*, Chicago: Univ. of Chicago Press; Coon, C. S. 1962. *The Origin of Races*, N.Y.: Knopf; Coon, C. S., and Hunt, E. E., Jr. 1965. *The Living Races of Man*, N.Y.: Knopf; Coon, C. S. 1982. *Racial Adaptations*, Chicago: Nelson-Hall; Wolpoff, M. H., Xinzhi, Wu, Thorne, A. G. 1984. "Modern *Homo Sapiens* Origins: A General Theory of Hominid Evolution Involving the Fossil Evidence from East Asia," in *The Origins of Modern Humans: A World Survey of the Fossil Evidence*, F. H. Smith and F. Spencer, eds., N.Y.: Alan Liss, pp. 411-483; Wu, Xinzhi, and Wu, Maolin. 1985. "Early Homo Sapiens in China," in *Paleoanthropology and palaeolithic archaeology in the People's Republic of China*, Wi Rukang and J. W. Olsen, eds. N.Y.: Academic Press, pp. 91-106; Wolpoff, M. H. 1992. "Theories of Modern Human Origins," In *Continuity or Replacement: Controversies in Homo Sapiens Evolution*, G. Brauer and F. H. Smith, eds., Rotterdam: Balkema, pp. 25-63.

[5] Stringer, C., & McKie, R. 1997. *African Exodus*, N.Y.: Henry Holt, p. 185.

[6] Culotta, Elizabeth. 1995. "Asian Hominids Grow Older," *Science*, 11/17/95, 270:1116-1117; Ciochon, R. L. 1995. "Dragon Hill Cave, China: The Earliest Asians Yet," *Natural history*, December, pp. 51-54; Wills, C. 1998. *Children of Prometheus*, Boston: Perseus Books. Wills hypothesizes a migration of hominids out of Africa as early as 2.6mya (pp. 197-207).

[7] Wood, B. A., and Turner, A. 1995. "Out of Africa and into Asia" *Nature*, 11/16/95, 378:239-240.

[8] Klein, R. G. 1989. *The Human Career*, Chicago: Univ. of Chicago Press, p. 188.

[9] Culotta, 1995, *op. cit., Science*, 11/17/95, 270:1116-1117.

[10] Etler, D. A., Crummett, T. I., and Wolpoff, M. H. 1997. "Earliest Chinese Hominid Mandible Is An Ape," *Human Origins News*, 1/30/97, 8pp; Schwartz, Jeffrey, and Tattersall, I. 1996. "Whose Teeth?" *Nature*, 5/16/96, 381:201-202; Wanpo, Huang, and Ciochon, R. L., *et al.* 1996. "Whose Teeth?: Reply to Schwartz & Tattersall," *Nature*, 5/16/96, 381:202.

[11] Walker, A. C., and Shipman, P. 1996. *The Wisdom of the Bones*, N.Y.: Knopf, pp. 122-134 (KNM-ER3733, KNM-ER 1808, both erectines, as with KNMWT-15000, found at same levels as KNMER-406 (A. boisei)).

[12] Walker and Shipman, 1996, *op. cit.*, p. 133: as follows: OH-62-ape like (1.8mya), KNM-ER 3735-ape like (1.88-1.91mya), OH24-ape like, small, KNM-ER1813, OH13 (Cindy).

[13] Walker and Shipman, 1996, *op. cit.*, pp. 122-133, #1590 +#1470.

[14] Walker and Shipman, 1996, *op. cit.*, p. 133.

[15] Andrews and Stringer, 1993, in Gould, ed., *op. cit.*, p. 240.

[16] Walker and Shipman, 1996, *op. cit.*, p. 259; smaller *H. habilis* types: 1813, OH13, OH24, StW53 (Southern Africa).

[17] Walker and Shipman, 1996, *op. cit.*, p. 259; larger *habilis*: 1470, 1509; Wood, B., and Collard, M. 1999. "The Human Genus," *Science*, 2 Apr., 284:65-71; Strait, D. S., *et al.* 1997. *Jrnl of Human Evol.*, 32, 17.

[18] Tattersall 1995, *op. cit.*, pp. 52-62.

[19] Weidenreich, F. 1942. "The Skull of `Sinanthropus pekinensis,'" *Paleontologia Sinica*, new series D., 10:1-291; Leakey, R., and Walker, A. C. 1993. "The Skull," in *The Nariokotome Homo erectus Skeleton*, A. Walker, and R. Leakey, eds., Cambridge, Mass.: Harvard University Press, pp. 64-96, p.76.

[20] Walker, A. C. 1993. "Perspectives on the Nariokotome Discovery," in Walker and Leakey, *op. cit.*, p. 420.

[21] Walker, 1993, in Walker and Leakey, *op. cit.*, p. 412.

[22] Swisher, C. C., *et al.* 1994. "Age of the Earliest Known Hominids in Java, Indonesia," *Science*, 2/25/94, 263:1118-1121.

[23] Walker and Shipman, 1996, *op. cit.*, pp. 122-134.

[24] Dibble, H. L., and Bar-Yosef, O., eds. 1995. *The Definition and Interpretation of Levallois Technology*, Madison, WI: Prehistory Press.

[25] Itzkoff, S. W. 1983. *The Form of Man*, N.Y.: Peter Lang, p. 165.

[26] Andrews and Stringer, 1993, in Gould, ed., *op. cit.*, p. 242.

[27] Black, Davidson, de Chardin, Teilhard, Young, C. C., Pei, W. C. 1933. *Fossil Man In China: The Choukoutien Cave Deposits....*, Peiping: The Geological Survey of China--National Academy of Peiping, May, 1933, pp. 130-136.

[28] Holloway, M. 1994. "Family Matters," *Scientific American*, May, pp. 31-32; Mayr, E. 1998. Personal conversation, 27.

[29] de Vos, J., and Swisher, C. C. "Dating Hominid Sites in Indonesia," *Science*, 12/9/ 266:1726-1727.

[30] Walker and Shipman, 1996, *op. cit.*, pp. 234-240.

[31] Gabunia L., and Vekua, A. 1995. *Nature*, 373:509-512.

[32] Tchernov, E. 1992. "Mammalian Migration and Dispersal Events in the European Quaternary," W. von Koenigswald, and L. Werdelin, eds., *Cour. Forschungsinst. Senckenberg*, 153, pp. 103-123.

[33] Wood and Turner, 1995, *op. cit., Nature*, 11/16/95, 378:239-240.

[34] Walker and Shipman, 1996, *op. cit.*, pp. 232-234.

[35] Walker and Shipman, 1996, *op. cit.*, pp. 178-201.

[36] Walker and Shipman, 1996, *op. cit.*, pp. 202-229.

[37] Walker and Shipman, 1996, *op. cit.*, pp. 252-258; South African: StW53; East African: OH 13, OH 24, OH 62.

[38] Walker and Shipman, 1996, *op. cit.*, pp. 248-252.

[39] Schwartz, Jeffrey. 1993. *What the Bones Tell Us*, N.Y.: Henry Holt, pp. 229-230.

[40] Walker, 1993, in Walker and Leakey, *op. cit.*, pp. 411-430, esp. p. 417.

[41] Walker, 1993, in Walker and Leakey, *op. cit.*, pp. 415-416; Coon, 1962, *op. cit.*, p. 616; Pilbeam, D. 1972. *The Ascent of Man* N.Y.: Macmillan, p. 183.

[42] 1997. *New York Times*, 1/23/97; Boaz, N. T. 1995. "Calibration and Extension of the Record of Plio-Pleistocene Hominidae," in *Biological Anthropology: The State of the Science*, N. T. Boaz and L. D. Wolfe, eds., Bend, Oregon: International Institute for Human Evolutionary Research, Central Oregon University Center, p. 32.

[43] Gamble, 1994, in Ingold, ed., *op. cit.*, pp. 81-82.

[44] Rightmire, C. P. 1985. "The Tempo of Change in the Evolution of Mid-Pleistocene Homo," in *Ancestors: The Hard Evidence*, E. Delson ed., N.Y.: Alan R. Liss, pp. 255-264; Schwartz, 1993, *op. cit.*, p. 228.

[45] Boaz, 1995, in Boaz and Wolfe, eds., *op. cit.*, pp. 23-41, esp. p. 40.

[46] Tattersall, I. 1986. "Species Recognition in Human Paleontology," *Journal of Human Evolution*, 15:165-175.

[47] Schwartz, 1993, *op. cit.*, pp. 227-231.

[48] Coon, 1982, *op. cit.*, pp. 158-161.

[49] Coon, 1982, *op. cit.*, pp. 125-127.

[50] Coon, 1982, *op. cit.*, p. 124.

[51] Coon, 1982, *op. cit.*, p. 127, under Fig. 6.4.

[52] Leakey, R., and Walker, A. C. 1993. "The Skull," in. Walker, and Leakey, eds., *op. cit.*, p. 74.

[53] Coon and Hunt, 1965, *op. cit.*; Itzkoff, 1983, *op. cit.*, p. 172.

[54] Coon, 1982, *op. cit.*, p. 127.

[55] Schwartz, 1993, *op. cit.*, p. 231.

[56] Coon, C. S. 1982, *op. cit.*, pp. 158-159.

[57] Schwartz, 1993, *op. cit.*, p. 231.

[58] Klein, 1989, *op. cit.*, pp. 264-265.

[59] Busk, G. 1861. "On the Crania of the Most Ancient Races of Man--by Professor H. Schaaffhausen of Bonn. With Remarks and Original Figures, Taken from a Cast of the Neanderthal Cranium," *Natural History Review*, 2:155-176; Huxley, T. 1863. *Zoological Evidences as to Man's Place in Nature*, London: Williams and Norgate.

[60] Trinkaus, E., and Howells, W. W. 1979. "The Neanderthals," *Scientific American*, 241(6):118-133; Trinkaus, E. 1983. *The Shanidar Neanderthals*, N.Y.: Academic Press; Mellars, P. 1996. *The Neanderthal Legacy*, Princeton, N.J.: Princeton Univ. Press; Trinkaus, E., and Shipman, P. 1993. *The Neanderthals*, N.Y.: Knopf; Tattersall, 1995. *op. cit.,*.

[61] Tattersall, 1995, *op. cit.*; Mellars, 1996, *op. cit.*, esp. Chap. 7, "Middle Paleolithic Subsistence"; Farizy, C. 1994. "Behavioral and Cultural Changes at the Middle to Upper Paleolithic Transition in Western Europe," in *Origins of Anatomically Modern Humans*, M. H. Nitecki and D. V. Nitecki, eds., N.Y.: Plenum Press, pp. 93-100.

[62] Vandermeersch, B. 1978. "Le Crane Pre-Wurmien de Biache-Saint Vaast (Pas de Calais)," in D. J. Chivers and K. A. Jousey, eds., London: Academic Press, pp. 345-418; Schwartz, 1993, *op. cit.*, pp. 223-225.

[63] Santa Luca, A. P. "A Reexamination of Presumed Neandertal-Like Fossils," *Journal of Human Evolution*, 7:619-636; Schwartz, 1993, *op. cit.*, pp. 220-223.

[64] Mayr, E. 1963. "The Taxonomic Evolution of Fossil Hominids," *Classification and Human Evolution*, in S. L. Washburn, ed., Chicago: Aldine, pp. 332-346.

[65] Svante Paabo, 1997, in "Neanderthal DNA Sheds New Light On Human Origins," N. Wade, *New York Times*, 7/11/97, in *Cell*, issue of 7/11/97.

[66] Smith, F. H., *et al.* 1989. "Geographical Variation in Supraorbital Torus Reduction during the Later Pleistocene (c. 80,000-15,000BP)" in *The Human Revolution*, P. Mellars and C. Stringer, eds., Princeton, N.J.: Princeton Univ. Press, pp. 172-193.

[67] Wolpoff, M. H., and Caspari, R. 1997. *Race and Human Evolution*, N.Y.: Simon and Schuster, p. 297.

[68] Wolpoff and Caspari, 1997, *op. cit.*,, pp. 296-297; Frayer, D. W. 1993. "Evolution at the European Edge: Neanderthal and Upper Paleolithic Relationships," *Prehistoire Europeenne*, 2:9-69. Recent analysis has further emphasized the possibility of interbreeding by the mid-Eastern Neanderthal with a Cro-Magnon type of *Homo sapiens sapiens*. In addition, there is a continuing possibility that many Neanderthal dates will have to be pushed back in time. Grun, R., and Stringer, C. 1991. "Electron spin resonance dating and the evolution of modern humans," *Archeometry*, 33: 153-159.

[69] Zubrow, E. 1989. "The Demographic Modeling of Neanderthal Extinction," in Mellars and Stringer, eds., *op. cit.*, pp. 212-231.

[70] Schwartz, 1993, *op. cit.*, pp. 206-209.

[71] Thorne, A. G., and Macumber, P. G. 1972. "Discoveries of Late Pleistocene Man at Kow Swamp Australia," *Nature*, 238:316-319; Santa Luca, A. P. 1980. *The Ngandong Fossil Hominids: A Comparative Study of a Far Eastern Homo Erectus Group*, New Haven, CT: Yale Univ. Publications in Anthropology, no. 78; Swisher, C. C., and Anton S. 1996. "Ngandong, Solo River H. Erectus Sites Redated," *Science*, 12/13/96, 274:1870.

[72] Swisher, C. C., and Anton S. 1996. "Ngandong, Solo River H. Erectus Sites Redated," *Science*, 12/13/96, 274:1870; Gibbons, Ann. 1996. "Homo Erectus in Java: A 250,000-Year Anachronism," *Science*, 12/13/96, 274:1841-1842; Wilford, J. N. 1996. "3 Human Species Coexisted on Earth, New Data Suggest," *The New York Times*, 12/13/96.

[73] Rightmire, C. P. 1990. *The Evolution of Homo erectus*, Cambridge Univ Press, pp. 34-52; Clark, J. D. 1993. "African and Asian perspectives on the origin of modern humans," in *The Origin of Modern Humans and the Impact of Chronometric Dating*, M. J. Aitken, C. P. Stringer, and P. A. Mellars, eds., Princeton, N. J.: Princeton Univ. Press, p. 148.

[74] Aitken, M. J., Stringer, C. B., and Mellars, P. A., eds. 1993. "Recent Human Evolution in East Asia and Australasia," in *Aitken et al.*, *op. cit.*, pp. 218-219; Stringer, C., and Andrews, P. 1988. "Genetic and Fossil Evidence for the Origin of Modern Humans," *Science*, 239:1263-1268.

[75] Wolpoff, M. 1997. "No `Homo erectus' at Ngandong," in *Human Origins News*, 1/4/97, 6pp, esp. p. 4; Wolpoff and Caspari, 1997, *op. cit.*

[76] Habgood, Philip. 1985. "The Origin of the Australian Aborigines: An Alternative Approach and View," in *Hominid Evolution: Past, Present, and Future*, P. V. Tobias, ed., *op. cit.*, pp. 367-380, esp p. 376; Habgood, P. J. 1989. "The Origin of Anatomically-Modern Humans in Australasia," in Mellars and Stringer, eds., *op. cit.*, pp. 245-273.

[77] Coon, 1962, *op. cit.*, pp. 410-411; Pilbeam, 1972, *op. cit.*, p. 175; Baker, J. 1974. *Race*. N.Y.: Oxford Univ. Press; Itzkoff, 1983, *op. cit.*, pp. 162-164, Pl.7, Fig.17.

[78] Coon, 1962, *op. cit.*; Coon, 1982, *op. cit.*

[79] Wood, B. A. 1992. *Nature*, 355:783-790; Tattersall, 1995, *op. cit.*, pp. 58-62.

[80] Groves, C. P., and Mazek, V. 1975. "An Approach to the Taxonomy of the Hominidae: Gracile Villefranchian Hominids of Africa," *Cas. Miner Geol.*, 20:225-247.

[81] Boaz, 1995, in Boaz and Wolfe, eds., *op. cit.,*, p. 40.

[82] Tattersall, I. 1995. *The Last Neanderthal, op. cit.*, p. 60.

[83] Timei, C., *et al.* 1994. "Antiquity of Homo sapiens in China," *Nature*, 368:55-56.

[84] Boaz, 1995, in Boaz and Wolfe, eds., *op. cit.*, p. 37.

[85] Brown, M. H. 1990. *The Search For Eve*, N.Y.: Harper & Row, pp. 287-288.

[86] Roberts, R. G., and Jones, R. 1994. "Luminescent Dating of Sediments: New Light on the Human Coloni-zation of Australia," *Australian Aboriginal Studies*, 1994/2:2-17.

[87] Fullagar, R. L. K., Price, D. M., and Head, L. M. 1996. "Early Human Occupation of Northern Australia: Archeology and Thermoluminescent Dating of Jinmium Rock-shelter, Northern Territory," *Antiquity*, 70:751-773.

[88] Roberts, M. B., Stringer, C. B., Parfitt, S. A. 1994. "A Hominid Tibia from Middle Pleistocene Sediments at Boxgrove UK., *Nature*, 369:311-313.

[89] Boaz, 1995, in Boaz and Wolfe, eds., *op. cit.*, pp. 23-41, esp. 37-38.

14

Modern Humans=African Eve?

"In appealing to the Out of Africa model [a scholar] seems to me a victim of the fashion inspired by the gurus of the golden sixties, whose only ability was to impose "politically correct" false truths on a credulous world. It is regrettable that members of the new generation are wasting intellectual energy trying to escape from them, since their conclusions do not favor such a model."

Marcel Otte, 1998[1]

"African Eve" and mtDNA

In the late 1980s research led by Allan Wilson, the University of California, Berkeley, Rebecca Cann, and Mark Stoneking, made a comparative analysis of the mtDNA in 148 individuals from all over the world, (elsewhere stated by Dawkins and de Duve to be 135 or 157). This was done by extracting and subjecting to molecular separation the relatively small amounts of DNA to be found in the mitochondria. Their results created a revolution in the evolutionary perspective concerning the origin of morphologically modern human beings.[2]

As noted in earlier chapters, the mitochondria are to be found in all cells of the human organism as well as the nuclear ones. They now constitute the respiratory cell organelles, and are ultimately derived from the era, several billion years ago, as a part of the process of fabrication of the large, complex eukaryote cell. The mitochondria may have been absorbed (phagocytosis) as part of an endosymbiotic adaptive, and then positively selective process that made possible the metabolic viability of the primeval eukaryotic cell, then its expansion in the metazoa. The few genes that these early bacterial cells contributed as mitochondria have been retained in modern heterotrophic and autotrophic complex forms of life.

Mitochondria are seemingly inherited from the female line. Sperm cells in the fertilization process do not contain them. The female egg cell passes on its mitochondria to the progeny of both sexes. The DNA in mitochondria also seems to mutate more rapidly than the DNA in the nucleus, approximately 2-4% per million years in the vertebrates.

Therefore, a shorter evolutionary time frame will still reveal changes in the mtDNA.[3] Also, these mutations do not seem to carry with them any special selective valence that would influence their retention within the mitochondrial organelle. The rate of mutations, when one compares the differences between these 148 individuals from all over the world, is arrived at by comparative mtDNA mutation rates estimated for a variety of animal groups.[4]

The results of this computer analysis of the differences in mtDNA in this population—creating a family tree that filtered out coincidental differences and similarities was that all of these individuals seem to have been descended from a female who lived in Africa approximately 200,000 years ago. Further, the computer simulation of relationships required that these populations of humans not have bred, and thus would not have shared genetic material, with any indigenous populations of humans in the territories that they invaded subsequent to their migration out of Africa. Finally, it was required that there be no "feedback" return of populations into Africa during the subsequent millennia.[5]

As Dawkins recently phrased it, "...some Africans are more distantly related to other Africans than to anybody in the whole of the rest of the world. The whole of the rest of the world—Europeans, Native Americans, Australian aboriginals, Chinese, New Guineans, Inuits, and all [others]—form one relatively close group of cousins. Some Africans belong to this close group. But other Africans don't."[6]

Critique of "African Eve"

Dawkins and de Duve argue that other scientists have claimed to be able to construct equally parsimonious trees in which the innermost branches occur outside of Africa. Other critiques make the point that the Berkeley group obtained its results because of the order in which the computer looked at the possible trees.[7]

> One point is clear. The method used to construct the original tree was flawed. Other trees rooted at different times and in different geographical locations can be constructed from the same data....It is highly unlikely that Eve could be more than 500,000 years old, 200,000 is a possibility....It certainly does not mean that the whole of humankind is derived from a single couple or even that there may have been something special about Eve....If Eve lived 200,000 years ago, she may have had 4,999 female cogeners, in which case the survival of her line was due to chance and has no special meaning....Perhaps a more probably alternative is that the present human race originates from a highly inbred population.[8]

This outcome could also result from a mutation in "Adam's" nuclear DNA. The theory rules out any admixture with Neanderthal females, which is highly unlikely considering the historical behavior of males.

The branch point, argues Dawkins, which unites the tree of womankind based on the divergence rates established for MDT, is between 250,000 and 150,000 years ago. Considering the existence of humans both within Africa and outside at dates far more remote, this would constitute at least a second Diaspora. These earlier migrations have left no surviving genetic descendants, according to the Berkeley theory.[9] "The correct claim is only that Mitochondrial Eve is the most recent woman of whom it can be said that all modern humans are descended from her in the female only line."[10] Question: Did

she live here or there, at this time rather than that time? Dawkins' answer: There are numerous other Eves and Adams from whom we are descended.

> The number of possible pathways to set alongside the female-only pathway is so
> large that it is mathematically highly unlikely that Mitochondrial Eve is the most recent of
> these many Eves and Adams. It is special among pathways in one way (being female-only).
> It would be a remarkable coincidence if it were special among pathways in another way
> (being the most recent). An additional point of mild interest is that our most recent common
> ancestor is somewhat more likely to have been an Adam than an Eve.[11]

One of the earliest criticisms of the Wilson, Cann, Stoneking method of analysis
was given in Alan Templeton's reanalysis of the mitochondrial DNA computer program
that generated the "Out of Africa Eve" scenario. Simply, as Dawkins and de Duve phrase
this criticism of Wilson's phylogenetic "tree," it "was not appropriate."[12]

Modifications to the "African Eve" Hypothesis

Under this persuasive criticism, the authors of the mtDNA, African Eve theory have
in one way or another retracted or modified their position.[13] Stoneking responded to the
critiques and corrected earlier data. He now feels that mtDNA data imply a modern-hu-
man-origins, mtDNA ancestor, at 63-356ka or 63-416ka years ago.[14]

Stoneking: "...although mtDNA analyses are valuable for the insights they yield
into human evolutionary history, many more genes need to be analyzed in similar fashion
for a statistically accurate picture of the history of human populations to emerge."
Stoneking et al. conclude by backing off: It is still very complicated to predict dates and
place of modern human origins on the basis of one gene's variation over time, despite its
supposed isolation from the rest of the genome.[15]

Discussing the debate as it appeared in 1992, in the journal *Science*, from an apparently neutral theoretical perspective, paleoanthropologists Trinkaus and Shipman state:
"All three papers concurred that there were errors in the procedures being used to build
genetic trees from the mtDNA data."[16]

Responding to Wolpoff's and others' critiques as to how securely this "African
Eve" hypothesis stands atop an unstable mountain of other possibly variable chronological and systematic estimates, Mellars et al. concur that a revision in the date of a chim-
panzee/hominid divergence points further back than 5-6mya could alter the "Out-of-
Africa" scenario. This would be because of the implied difference in mutation rates in
mtDNA that could result in the recalibration of the origin of modern humans from
200,000 B.P. to well over one million years.[17] Recent research by Harris and Hey sees
the separation of African and non-Africans as being much earlier than the 200ka B.P.
orthodox view, yet still assuming a 5mya chimpanzee/hominid split.[18] Here an unstable
set of chronological assumptions, pongid/hominid time of separation, leads further down
the time line to even more controversial assertions, "African Eve" origins and migration.

Male Perspectives

The use of mtDNA and the analysis through the female line of human evolutionary
inheritance has been expanded into inquiries into the question as to what information can

be derived from the male side of things when it comes to evolutionary knowledge via molecular pathways. A 1991 article in *Nature* argued suggestively for the inheritance of mitochondrial DNA in mice through the paternal line.[19] More recently, Svante Paabo of the Institute of Zoology, University of Munich, discussed his own research and that of the reported research of Dorit *et al.*, who sequenced an intron on a gene, ZFY, on the nonrecombining part of the male Y chromosome.[20]

Paabo uses this perspective and his own research to launch into a discussion of its evolutionary meaning, seeing that Dorit's estimate of a branching of the line leading to modern humans wandering out of Africa, some 270,000 B.P. harmonizes with the work of Wilson and Stoneking *et al.* Paabo adds that "...when the root of such trees was sought by connecting them to chimpanzee sequences, the root seem to fall among African sequences."[21] Quoting Nachman and Aquadro, who argue that not enough information is available because the chimpanzee sequence is too distantly related to humans, and because information has probably been erased by gene substitutions occurring multiple times in the same position, Paabo notes that humans are much more closely related to each other than are chimpanzees to each other.[22]

If a mtDNA mutation could have conferred "some substantial advantage in reproductive success or survival [that] occurred some 100,000 years ago, then this substitution could have swept around the Old World and could be presenting us with a picture today which is true for mtDNA but not for the genome in general." Paabo's explanation for the mtDNA mystery: 1) Africans have much more mitochondrial sequence diversity among them than do other populations; 2) the diversity between Africans (some) and others is much smaller than that found within Africa.

One answer, in addition, to the theme that "we are all Africans" is the possibility of much larger populations having existed in Africa over a longer period of time. Such populations would contain more molecular diversity. Jonathan Kingdom notes, for example, that a sample of Japanese women had a divergence in their mtDNA of .26 whereas San/Capoid, women from the Kalahari in South Africa, had the largest divergence ever recorded, .59.[23] This view would also point to the so-called "bottleneck" explanation, which views the similarity in mtDNA throughout the rest of the world as a product of a small population concentration—or simply as a product of mtDNA African Eve—the latter perspective now seriously questioned as a valid explanation.[24]

Nuclear DNA Diversity

1. An important parallel molecular research effort has been carried out by Cavalli-Sforza and his associates. They have collected samples of blood from 42 different populations from around the world—Mbuti Pygmies, Melanesians, Europeans, Eskimos. They analyzed 120 genetic alleles to ascertain their relative frequency in each of these populations to ascertain the genetic resemblance or dissimilarity between the human populations. Using a set of statistical techniques, they constructed a series of phylogenetic trees that would reflect these relationships as well as the probable branching points between the different groups. The latter would reflect the sequence of diversification from a theoretical point of origination of the modern human nuclear genotype.[25]

Their 1988 conclusions: "The first split in the phylogenetic tree separates Africans from non-Africans—and the second separates two major clusters, one corresponding to Caucasoids, East Asian, Arctic populations, and American natives, and the other to southeast Asians (mainland and insular), Pacific islanders, New Guineans and Australians."[26]

More recent publications have brought their research to completion.[27] It stands as an important contrast and supplement to the mtDNA work of the team represented by the late Allan Wilson. The focus is now on the sharing of alleles with primates in search of ancestral alleles. Subsequent genetic trees are constructed from classical marker allele frequencies. A condensed version of a genetic tree for the 42 aboriginal populations consisting of nine populations, represents many samples. It is based on frequencies of 120 alleles associated with 44 classical markers (blood groups, HLA, and protein polymorphisms). First separation signifying a relative ratio of genetic distance—African/non-African populations—has genetic distance = 0.21; second separation—Australian, South East Asian-Pacific Islanders/North East Asian, Arctic, European, Amerindian—genetic distance = 0.12.[28] The genetic distance between modern humans and chimpanzees, given in percentages, is 1.2%; between the two chimpanzee species, 0.7%.[29]

population	mean frequency ± s.e.
Zaire Pygmies	0.648 ± 0.038
C.A.R. Pygmies	0.618 ± 0.039
Melanesians	0.578 ± 0.046
New Guineans	0.564 ± 0.046
Europeans	0.563 ± 0.035
Australians	0.560 ± 0.042
Japanese	0.545 ± 0.042
Chinese	0.534 ± 0.039

14.1 Ancestral alleles: Pygmies and East Asians compared: Pygmy populations of Africa have much higher frequencies of ancestral chimpanzee alleles than do Chinese and Japanese. It could mean that Pygmies are not the genetic source of a recent "out-of-Africa" migration of modern humans, else that these geographically separated populations are only distantly related in time. (Cavalli-Sforza)

Cavalli-Sforza recognizes that this genetic tree has a remarkable similarity to, and is comparable with that given by classical linguistic analysis of the differentiation and distance of the various human languages spoken around the world.[30]

In their analysis of the source of human genetic similarity, Cavalli-Sforza and his group see humans generally sharing, out of 71 polymorphisms, one with chimpanzees in 57 cases, sharing one allele with the gorilla in 39 cases, and sharing one allele with the orangutan in 41 cases.[31] With regard to ancestral alleles presumably shared with chimpanzees at the time of the separation of the two lines, and still embedded in the genotype of each primate species, (*Pan* and *Homo*), for 60 out of 80 polymorphisms studied for 8 human populations, the chimpanzees shared a single allele with humans. "The frequency of ancestral alleles differ significantly from population to population. [Zaire and Central African Republic. Pygmies = 0.618-0.648; Chinese-Japanese = 0.534-0.545]. This implies at the very least, that the two Pygmy populations [Zaire and C.A.R.—the latter admixed with non-Pygmy native Africans] have significantly higher frequencies of ancestral alleles than do the two Asian populations [Japanese, Chinese]."[32] The two African, (plus) New Guinean and Melanesian populations both have very high ancestral alleles. Authors postulate that the equatorial populations may have been influenced by natural selection—"close ecological neighbors"—to retain these shared chimpanzee alleles.[33]

2. A Yale University research group headed by Sarah Tishkoff studied the genetic pattern in a single chromosome from 1600 individuals in 42 populations around the world.[34] It found an extensive variety in the DNA of groups in sub-Saharan Africa, but very few differences among those in Asia, Europe, the Americas, and the Pacific Islands. "This pattern of variation suggests that all non-Africans derive from a single common ancestral population which migrated out of northeast Africa."[35]

Tishkoff and her group studied the DNA sequences on human chromosome 12. Out of 24 possible variations of DNA sequence, 21 of them are found in sub-Saharan Africa, from Nigeria to Kenya and south. In European and the Middle East, three variants were found; only two were found in specimens from Asia, the Pacific Islands, and the Americas. Tishkoff estimated that the migration out of Africa could be as recently as 70,000 years, and could have constituted a migrant population of no more than 1,000 persons. Mark Stoneking of Pennsylvania State University is reported to have agreed: "Those findings are most easily explained by an African origin." However, Tishkoff's and Stoneking's migration conclusions do not follow necessarily from the DNA data. It is their own *ad hoc* interpretation of the purely molecular statistics.

Kenneth Kidd of Yale University is quoted on the DNA profile of Pygmy tribes in the Central African Republic and the Democratic Republic of the Congo (Zaire):

> I would say, without a doubt, that in almost any single African population—a tribe or however you want to define it—there is more genetic variation than in all the rest of the world put together....In a sample of fifty Pygmies, for example, you might find nine variants in one stretch of DNA. In a sample of hundreds of people from around the rest of the world, you might find only a total of six variants in that same stretch of DNA—and probably every one of those six variants would also be in the Pygmies.[36]

Clearly, these populations seem to be unique in the possible relationship that exists between mtDNA and nuclear DNA variability and long-existing phenotypic homogeneity. The external morphological/ecological homogeneity of an inbreeding tribal population still does not preclude the buildup over time in the communal genome of an enormous non-selective/coding genetic variability.

3. Recent research of Naoyuki Takahata, of The Graduate University for Advanced Studies in Japan, further probes the mystery of the large molecular distance between African human populations and all others throughout the world, especially focusing, as does the Yale Tishkoff group, on the reconciliation of this research with the "Out-of-Africa" model of human evolution and dispersion.[37] Takahata traces in wonderment the seeming human genetic squeeze (bottleneck) from an indigenous African population of at least 100,000 down to a molecular population of about 10,000 as part of the emigration out of Africa, sometime during the past 400,000 years.

Maryellen Ruvolo, anthropologist from Harvard University, supports this perspective. She sees more genetic similarity within our species than within species of the common chimpanzees and lowland gorillas, these respective pongids from the same forest in West Africa. Henry Harpending, anthropologist from Pennsylvania State University agrees with Takahata. However, Jan Klein of the Max Planck Institute for Biology, Tübingen, Germany, a collaborator with Takahata, disagrees: 10,000 people is too large a population to be considered a bottleneck. Some monkey, seal, and ape species have as few members. M. Nei, of Pennsylvania State University, and F. Ayala of the University of California, Irvine, are also quoted as saying that a population of 10,000 is no bottleneck. The mtDNA studies of John Maynard Smith, the University of Sussex, as well as of H. Harpending, Pennsylvania. State, and Alan Rodgers, the University of Utah, likewise point to a population of 10,000, Harris and Hay estimate a founder population of 18,000, somewhere in the world.[38]

Takahata and Klein compared the variation within 50 pairs of neutral genes and then calculated the mean from all 50 pairs. Then they looked at the most diverse part of the human genome, the histocompatibility complex, MHC. These MHC or HLA alleles are of great antiquity, older than our species.[39] Takahata came to the conclusion that over the past one million years human populations fluctuated at around 100,000 persons. The explanation of the current genetic similarity in human populations is attributed to the vast growth of contemporary populations to 6 billion people. Rapid demographic growth mixes genes up in a large population far more than they would in small populations.

Considerations

Both the Tishkoff and Takahata groups imply that the long-term stagnancy of the indigenous African populations, below the Sahara—like the long-term stagnancy among our ape cousins—was the cause for the enormous genetic diversity of the African populations. There was plenty of time for this diversity to build up in a random non-selective manner. This presumably contrasts with the dynamics reflected in modern humans suddenly exiting, presumably from Africa and migrating rapidly around the world.

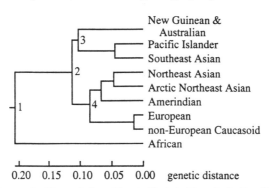

14.2 Condensed genetic tree for 42 populations. Here is illustrated how L. L. Cavalli-Sforza's nuclear DNA research echoes the seeming results of mtDNA "out-of-Africa" conclusions in terms of a non-participating African population. It does not explain the genetic distances of the indigenous African populations relative to the rest of humankind. Should they not be closer?

Cavalli-Sforza's group in addition to further buttressing the seeming unity in diversity of the African groups reveals the successive differentiations of human groups following some of their members primeval migration out of Africa. The Cavalli-Sforza group does not put an absolute time-frame on the departure from Africa, as the nuclear DNA research does not, as contrasted to the mtDNA research, lend itself to a chronometric analysis. However, the Cavalli-Sforza data are consistent within the mtDNA hypothesis of between 500-100ka for the "Out-of-Africa" migration.[40]

Given the Cavalli-Sforza analysis of the genetic closeness of the Central African and Zairian Pygmy and other sub-Saharan African populations to the genetics of the original pivotal presumed ancestral chimpanzee, (or Schwartz-Fleagle-Oxnard orangutan hypothesis), and then a human split, the question is inevitably raised as to the specific sub-Saharan African population that is being invoked as part of this "Out-of-Africa" model. We must bear in mind that de Duve, Dawkins, Wolpoff and others are quite skeptical that the various mtDNA phylogenetic trees, all equally compatible with the data necessarily rule out a non-"Out-of-Africa" population that would encompass and explain the genetic similarity reflected in the non-African populations of the world.

There is, for example, mtDNA evidence cited by Clark and Linley that throws a wholly different light on the "Out-of-Africa" scenario and mtDNA relationships to an ostensibly African primate heritage.[41] They cite the work of Wallace, whose study of the mtDNA of 700 subjects, in order to understand Amerindian mtDNA origins, found that the human mtDNA most similar to the African apes was located in Southeast China Mongoloids![42] Clearly the issue of molecular genetic roots and branches in human evolution is still up a tree.

Persuasive Power of Theory

The mtDNA model presenting the chronological as well as the geographical contexts within which we should consider the evolution of modern human beings has proved to be extraordinarily persuasive. Unlike the analysis of the DNA of humans and primates, which hypothesized a temporal and phylogenetic relationship, a point of origin between a common human and chimpanzee ancestor, mtDNA analysis sampled contemporary humans, and pointed to a time in Africa, not 5-6mya, as the earlier research seemed to indicate, but a mere 200,000 years before the present, on average. A wide range of dates was presented for this migration out of Africa, partially influenced by the fact that an enormous fund of living human mtDNA existed to test the theory, unlike what was available to test the more hypothetical chimpanzee/hominid ancestor.

Two assertions/implications seemed to be at the core of the mtDNA African "Eden" model. 1) Anatomically modern humans were created in or evolved in Africa at an advanced *Homo sapiens* grade, subsequently spreading over the Eur-Asiatic land masses and the islands of Southeast Australasia. 2) The model demands that contemporary populations be representatives "only" of this sudden outswelling of African migrants. This is despite the fact that contemporary genetic analysis argues for a so-called "bottleneck" population of from 10,000 to 100,000—the "founder effect" population—subsequently and recently spreading over the Earth and diversifying into the racial and ethnic profiles that existed at the beginning of historical memory.

Crucial in all of this was that there be no admixture with pre-existing populations, and, indeed, as Milford Wolpoff, the contemporary theoretical heir to the multiregional continuity model has pointed out, the sudden replacement model has overtones of genocide. No anthropologist today would argue against the view that prior to 400,000-200,000 B.P., there were significant human populations throughout the world, at the least, *Homo erectus*. [43]

Indeed, it must be stated that a measure of the enthusiasm with which most scientists involved in the study of human evolution gave to the "Out-of-Africa" mtDNA hypothesis can be attributed to the clear rebuff it seemed to give to the older Weidenreich-Coon view of the independent and semi-autonomous evolution of the various racial groups found in the modern world. [44] The acknowledged modernity of the European Upper-Paleolithic fossil remains, associated with their extraordinary cultural sophistication, could now be explained differently. It was a product of a recent out-migration of fully modern human beings, of which the contemporary Africans were a part, and not the "bypassed" residue, as Coon argued, of a more ancient human hegira.

In addition, the "Out-of-Africa" scenario gave confirmation to that more traditional view of the modern origin of the races, made famous in the United Nations manifesto authored by anthropologist, M. F. Ashley-Montagu.[45] What we now accept about the five major races of *Homo sapiens* is that they were formed in relatively recent times, from the evolutionary standpoint, and have their roots in an African Eden.[46]

Most important, the evidence from mtDNA underscores the manner in which the human mind strives first for generalized philosophical and theoretical parameters within which to organize more concrete empirical material, material that never speaks for itself, buried as it is in a vast continuum of facts. Facts always seem to cry out for the sorting procedures of theory. The late 1980s saw a number of anthologies of research and texts on human evolution that reflects the two themes, that modern humans had recently originated and migrated out of Africa, and that they had rapidly replaced original human populations.[47]

The 1990s have seen, under the press of new fossil discoveries and their associated chronologies, much more skepticism concerning the invariability of the mtDNA evidence. A recent book by Stringer and Gamble, which used the Neanderthal/Cro-Magnon question of derivation or replacement as an opportunity once more to develop the "Out-of-Africa" mtDNA theme, came under the fire of a number of critics, including Milford Wolpoff, who asserted that the mtDNA evidence for an "Out-of-Africa" scenario for modern humans had been refuted by the recent work of Templeton and Stoneking (referred to above). This elicited an interesting defense by the authors:[48]

Stringer and Gamble cite the research of Hasegawa, Ruvolo, Nei, and Roychoudhury, among others, who argue that estimates of a common mtDNA ancestor of modern humans range from *536,000 to 52,000 B.P.*, as determined by using molecular data. They state that such an analysis is more consistent with a replacement model of evolution than a multiregional perspective. However, Stringer and Gamble do *not* now commit themselves to a purely "Out-of-Africa" scenario.[49]

Coming into an even more recent time frame (1997), Stephen O'Brien of the National Cancer Institute states: "...the clock calculation is something we have to take with a grain of salt." Richard Klein, of Stanford University, sums it up: "...If the genetic evidence were more secure, I would accept it...It is not something I would want to put a lot of faith in."[50] Indeed, even Stringer and Gamble now hesitate in their confidence in a theory that hinges on the clarity of the "Out-of-Africa"—full replacement—position.

> Recent developments, however, show that the original concept of an African origin and single dispersal/replacement event is too simplistic...The evidence points to a more intricate pattern where the full modern package of genes, anatomy, and behavior came together by degrees rather than being built in a single African "factory" and then transported entire to the rest of the world.[51]

Intellectual Farrago

Reflective of the theoretical chaos emanating from the now worldwide search into the human genome to discover these molecular affinities and timetables in contemporary populations of humans was a 1997 symposium held at Cold Spring Harbor Laboratory in New York. A variety of papers came up with interesting as well as odd contributions and contradictions to the contemporary picture.

Much of the research concentrated on the male "Y" chromosome. Attempts were made to find DNA polymorphisms in those parts of this chromosome that do not code for proteins. Stanford University researchers, led by Peter Underhill and L. L. Cavalli-Sforza, found male populations of Ethiopians, Sudanese (both of these groups today are hybrid Negroid-Caucasoid peoples) and Khoisans (Bushman and Hottentots) to have inherited an ancient marker shared with primates, M42 (adenine). Subsequently, after migration out of Africa (estimated at between 200,000-100,000 B.P.), it mutated to T, or thymine, found in all non-Africans and most Africans.

Other research by M. Hammer of the University. of Arizona located an ancestral site common in chimpanzees to be located only in Africans, most notably in some Khoisan males. It, too, seems to have mutated to a form found throughout the world and in most Africans. But Hammer also sees a subsequent infusion into Africa of an ancient Asian nuclear DNA marker, as well as an unreported mutation on the "Y" chromosome that originated in Asia, but somehow returned to Africa.[52]

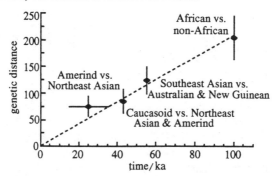

14.3 Genetic distance and migration. A hypothetical chronology that places the first point of arrival, "out-of-Africa," in Southeast Asia, thence settlement in Northeast Asia, Europe, finally to the New World. This theoretical chronology is not buttressed by the fossil/geological evidence. (Cavalli-Sforza.)

Neither of these research groups consider the possibility that the newer supposedly mutant forms on the "Y" chromosome could have originated out of Africa, and been spread back into Africa, to become the majority form of the marker, to coexist with the more ancient ancestral polymorphism.

Furthering the puzzle is M. Stoneking's continuing research at Pennsylvania State University into the nuclear DNA of a worldwide sample of 1500 people. Stoneking's research into the hypothesized migration some 140,000 years ago out of Africa of presumably modern humans, shows indigenous Africans closest to Melanesians and Australians (stipulated aboriginals). Thus the assumed migration of "modern" humans went not to Europe to become Cro-Magnon, but to Southeast Asia.

But as noted earlier, the most recent redating of ancestral fossils in Australia-Indonesia puts these borderline erectine/sapiens into a time frame of 53,000-27,000 B.P., which certainly would not imply modern humans in the morphological sense. Interestingly, Cavalli-Sforza has also noted the similarity between the nuclear DNA of African and Southeast Asian populations as regards their retention of ancient primate alleles.

The work of D. Wallace, Emory University, is reported on the mtDNA profiles of the Western and Eastern Pygmies of the Central African Republic. These populations reveal a "remarkable dissimilarity, despite the close physical similarity of the two groups." The conclusions of Kenneth Kidd about this issue of genetic variability in pigmy populations are upheld. As Bernard Wood notes with regard to the various hypothesized chronologies, geographical dispersions, subsequent genetic relationships, of the "Out-of-Africa" migration, all of the papers do not necessarily contradict the thesis; neither have these papers added to the precision of the timing.[53] Nor, we should add, have they in any way allowed for subsequent predictive testing.

Beliefs and Doubts
1. We are all South Africans?

Scholars such as J. Desmond Clark and G. Brauer focused on a suite of African fossils as fitting the criteria of modern humans.[54] Clark believed that anatomically modern humans appeared 100ka B.P. Klasies River Mouth and Border Cave humans living in South Africa at that time were anatomically modern humans.[55] In North Africa we encounter Dar-es-Soltan, Tamara, as modern hominid fossils.[56] These all lead to Mechta-Afalou, at 20ka B.P., which spread over all of North Africa and are related to European Cro-Magnon.[57]

Brauer views Omo in Kenya, again, the Klasies River, Border Cave, South African skulls, as anatomically modern.[58] He quotes W. W. Howells: "Thus one may argue...that Africa south of the Sahara was one scene of the direct evolution of modern man."[59] Richard Klein, in a well-accepted textbook agrees as to the priority of Klasies River and Border Cave fossils being the earliest anatomically modern humans, at 130,000-50,000 B.P.[60]

G. Philip Rightmire approvingly reviewed the general current position that the African Elandsfontein, Broken Hill (Kabwe), Ndutu, "are usually referred to as *Homo sapiens*."[61] In other contexts, the African fossils have been placed, taxonomically, within

H. heidelbergensis and Archaic *Homo sapiens*, and thus not with anatomically modern humans.

Christopher Stringer of the British Museum: "...from Klasies River Mouth Caves, Border Cave, Equus Cave, Mumba Cave, Omo Kibishi 1, and East Turkana (KNM-ER 3884) we may have the oldest known fossils approximating the modern human anatomical pattern." Stringer notes the Mousterian Qafzeh fossil, in Israel, at about 92,000 B.P., to be competitive. Also, Stringer argues that a close relationship between Qafzeh and African samples can be adduced from various analyses, including those conducted in his own work. Limb proportion shows a tropical/subtropical derivation.[62]

The above "crural" index of ratios contrasts modern humans with Neanderthals and modern Lapps. The modern human has a long tibia, like contemporary Africans. "The earliest modern skeletons in Europe and Israel are unlike the Neanderthals and look as though they came from a hot climate, possibly African."[63] These above conclusions of an African origin of modern humans must be evaluated in the context of Stringer's strongly-asserted political beliefs.[64]

2. Neanderthals Hang Around:

By the late 1980s, early 1990s, it was clear that the Neanderthals of Europe and West Asia, dated in their classical morphological realization to at least 125,000 B.P., if not as a fully distinct species, were unrelated to modern humans, and, as Stringer notes, they were a clearly separate clade. However, Smith, along with Wolpoff, has outlined an argument of the gradual absorption of Neanderthal characteristics into the Upper Paleolithic populations of Central Europe during the late Pleistocene, c.45,000-12,000 B.P.[65]

Vandermeersch, who undertook the detailed analysis of Neanderthal morphology that led to the view of their separateness from the category of "modern humans" despite their large endocranial capacity, sees the Qafzeh and Skhul fossils in Israel, both from the 80,000-90,000 B.P. range, as possible products of hybridization. Similar to Stringer's description of them as Mousterian, *i.e.*, Neanderthal, Vandermeersch, in a 1989 article, cites the following scholars who believe that Skhul and Qafzeh represent a proto-Cro-Magnon and Neanderthal hybrid: Coon, 1939; Ashley-Montagu, 1940; Dobzhansky, 1944; A. Thoma, 1957-58, 1962, 1963; also McCown and Keith, 1939,[66] and as distinct from Tabun, from the same locality, but clearly Neanderthal in morphology.[67]

Vandermeersch saw Zuttiyeh, from Wadi Amud, northwest of Tiberias, as crucial, a creature that seems to be pre-proto-Cro-Magnon and pre-Neanderthal, before 100,000 B.P.—similar to Djebel Irhoud I in Morocco.[68] O. Bar-Yosef, in 1993, reported that new dating for Zuttiyeh should be placed back to 250-350ka B.P., similar to Bodo, Petralona, and other Archaic *Homo sapiens*, else *H. heidelbergensis*.[69] An even more recent chronological analysis reported by H. P. Schwarcz in 1994 gives two possible time frames. One, in accordance with the "Acheulo-Yabroudian" artifacts, is from 148,000-97,000 B.P. Other more persuasive dating materials go back to 164,000-95,000 B.P. This time span is not contradicted by Bar-Yosef in his introductory remarks to the edited volume.[70] Vandermeersch says mosaic features of Neanderthals can be observed only in earliest forms—Arago (France) and Petralona (Greece).[71] This is not the currently-held view in which Swanscombe and Steinheim are held to be the only early European *Homo* with Neanderthal possibilities, Arago and Petralona possibly being *H. heidelbergensis*.

Coon rejected Arago as a Neanderthal possibility, accepted Petralona[72] as an *H. erectus cum neanderthalensis* along with Mauer (Heidelberg) and Vertesszollos. Trinkaus, with whom Vandermeersch takes issue, earlier viewed the Zuttiyeh fossil as close to the Shanidar Neanderthals.[73]

What is clear is that the sharp chronological time line separating more morphologically and culturally primitive indigenous forms of *Homo* both in Europe and West Asia, from those of more modern morphologies cannot be sustained. They coexisted within a long time span. Recent studies of newly-analyzed Neanderthal remains associated with proto-Cro-Magnon Chatelperronian cultural artifacts highlight the enigmatic interplay of morphology and culture.

From Arcy-sur-Cure in France, 35km. southeast of Auxerre, at a long-discovered early Chatelperronian cultural site, the remains of a one-year-old child have now been subject to careful analysis.[74] The remains include a treasure trove of ivory and bone personal ornaments, pierced or grooved animal teeth, and ivory rings. Part of the discovery included a hominid temporal bone fragment, parts of the petrous, tympanic and mastoid portions. Study of the morphology of the bony labyrinth within the temporal bone revealed that it was typically Neanderthal, and at a very late date for survival, 34,000 B.P. It differed from then contemporary Cro-Magnons even more so than do average modern humans differ from Neanderthals. The differences between the Neanderthal and Cro-Magnon morphology now exist on a possible species level, hinting at a reproductive barrier.

The investigators wonder at the seeming association of the Cro-Magnon-like cultural objects with so different and specialized a human, as indicated by this Neanderthal fossil.

> The association of the Arcy Neanderthal with personal ornaments so similar to those found in contemporary and nearby Aurignacian [true Cro-Magnon] layers questions the nature of the cultural interactions with modern humans. At least in the case of these specific objects, we may be facing evidence of a trading process rather than the result of technical imitation of modern human technology by Neanderthals.[75]

Other, and recent genetically-rooted mtDNA studies, Svaabo, 1997, and Torroni, 1994, continue to argue for the long-separated Eur-Asian residency of the Upper Paleolithic Cro-Magnons (c.80,000 B.P.—Torroni; c.135,000 B.P.—Svaabo) and the Neanderthals, who lived as a species in Eur-Asia, from between 600,000-300,000 B.P. and c.30,000 B.P. Thus both species of northerly Caucasoids coexisted providing no evidence of Neanderthal genetics in the surviving European descendants of the Cro-Magnons, for at least 100,000 years.[76]

Arensberg discusses the Mt. Carmel find of Kebara Man, dated through thermoluminescence burnt flint samples, to 60,000 B.P.—no skull, but a mandible and part of the upper body skeleton. It exhibited a mosaic of features, some Mousterian, some even earlier, yet the mandible and hyoid bone argue for full speech ability as in modern humans—contra Philip Lieberman's view of the inability of the Neanderthals to enunciate a variety of vowels.[77] Arensberg sees an extreme overall robusticity in Kebara; the Shanidar Neanderthals (Iraq) seem gracile by contrast. Clearly, here is a more primitive human type morphologically than the Skhul or Qafzeh proto-Cro-Magnids. The latter two date between 25,000-30,000 years *earlier* than Kebara. Thus exists a variety of diverse morphological types—in the Middle Paleolithic of the Middle East.[78]

Mellar's recent systematic study of the Neanderthals supports the general perspective presented above, especially as it focuses on the impact of language on the technological and cultural power of its users:

> ....The emergence of essentially modern language must by its nature have been a relatively sudden, "catastrophic" event, rather than a gradual process of mental and linguistic evolution...we must presumably expect to see a fairly dramatic reflection of this transition in the available behavioral records of human development, and arguably in the whole spectrum of behavior ranging from technology, through subsistence and social patterns, to the more overtly symbolic domains of the human groups...where in the available archaeological records of Europe, might we identify such a watershed, if not over the period of the Middle- to Upper-Paleolithic transition? [Neanderthal to Cro-Magnon].[79]

3. Old and New in Australasia:

In dealing with the Australasia materials, both Philip Habgood and Colin Groves are moderately inclined to bend with the theoretical imperatives of the rapid replacement position on the evolution toward modern forms of *Homo sapiens*. From the distance of the Australasian sphere, they, it goes without saying cannot comment on the ultimate "Out-of-Africa" questions of sources for this steady movement toward modern human form.

Habgood, while admitting the modernity of the Lake Mungo fossil, as compared with that of younger contemporary Willandra Lake 50, yet demurs that for all its (Lake Mungo) gracile and thus modern characteristics, it still carries with it the "architecture" of many other older Australasian fossils throughout the region.[80] Earlier, Habgood quoted Alan Thorne, a multiregionalist, approvingly, that the Lake Mungo fossil is part of a gracile group, in contrast to a robust pithecanthropine, erectine type in Australia that came in later.[81] Thorne sees the gracile Lake Mungo type as representing a Chinese intrusion similar to the Liujiang fossil in South East China. Habgood confirms Thorne on the Ngandong (*H. erectus*?) similarity to Willandra Lake Hominid 50, primitive, also dated about 30,000+ B.P.[82] In 1985 Habgood concluded that the two seemingly quite different populations are really "a variable population derived from a single homeland."[83] By 1989, Habgood hesitates; certainly there are changes toward modernity, yet he sees at "at least four morphological features that seem to be indicating a relatively high degree of morphological continuity within the region."[84]

GENETIC TREE   POPULATIONS   LANGUAGE GROUPS

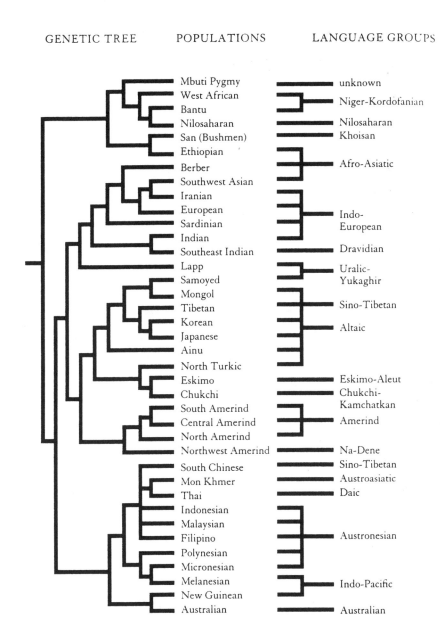

14.4 Concordance of genetic and linguistic evidence. The factual question relates to the time when these relationships developed. Clearly, the above model argues against any contemporary African groups having close ties with any group that participated in the supposed recent "Out-of-Africa" migration of modern humans. (Adapted from Cavalli-Sforza.)

Colin Groves perceived a general clinal overtaking of the indigenous populations in the late Pleistocene, 50,000-20,000 B.P., by new elements, perhaps Malay-Chinese—an overall if gradually diminishing gracilization-brachycephalization (broad faced), shifting southward and southeastward toward the Wallacean open water barrier.[85] The Negritos seem unique, not Australoid as posited by Coon, and thus perhaps an intrusion, yet probably an ancient people considering their wide dispersion on the islands of the Indian and Pacific Oceans. While Groves sees replacement in Australasia as more probable, continuity can be explained in other ways, yet "...a Replacement model within anatomically modern *Homo sapiens* in the region seems increasingly hard to maintain as Late Pleistocene and Early Holocene fossil remains become better known."[86]

4. Recent Contemporary Human Species:

The Indonesian Ngandong skulls, calvaria (skull without the facial bones), and the Sangiran 17 fossils, since 1996, are seen as contemporaries (53,000-27,000 B.P.) of the Kow Swamp and Lake Mungo Australian sapiens, also affiliated with fossil 200,000 B.P. "*Homo* erectines" at Sangiran (S.27) in Indonesia. Can any commentator on Southeast Asian hominid evolution not conclude that we are in the presence of at least several taxonomically distinct and contemporaneous human populations? Even Milford Wolpoff, who argues for regional continuity concedes and confirms the above conclusions that the seemingly recent, if primitive Ngandong fossils relate to recent humans in Australasia as "...one of several ancestral populations."[87] This coinciding of taxonomically unique ancient populations, alongside seemingly modern intruders is not unlike the situation that seems to present itself in Southwest Asia, as well as in Western Europe.

Conclusion: As we have noted in the first part of this chapter, the theoretical mtDNA genetic trees constructed by the advocates of the "Out-of-Africa Eve" model of a migration of moderns has been subject to definitive criticism, and, consequently, inconclusive revision. And recently, "inferences that will have to be reconsidered."[88]

Given the real evidence of a relatively recent movement of modern humans throughout the globe from some "presumptive" center, there is yet strong empirical data that reject any "full replacement" model. The indigenous worldwide survivors of the most ancient "Out-of-Africa" Diaspora, c.2-1mya, seem not to have disappeared in a mtDNA flash.

Endnotes, Chapter 14

[1] Otte, M. 1998. *Current Anthropology*, June Supplement, Vol. 39.

[2] Cann, R. L., Stoneking, M., and Wilson, A. 1987. "Mitochondrial DNA and Human Evolution," *Nature*, 325:31-36; Stoneking, M., Cann, R. L. 1989. "African Origin of Mitochondrial DNA," in *The Human Revolution—Behavioral and Biological Perspectives on the Origins of Modern Humans*, P. Mellars and C. Stringer, eds., Princeton, N.J.: Princeton Univ. Press, pp. 17-30; Stoneking, M., Sherry, S. T., Vigilant, L. 1992. "Geographic Origin of Human Mitochondrial DNA Revisited," *Syst. Biol*, n.d.; Stoneking, M., *et al*. 1993. "New Approaches to Dating Suggest a Recent Age for the Human mtDNA

Ancestor," in *The Origin of Modern Humans and the Impact of Chronometric Dating*, M. J. Aitken, C. Stringer, P. A. Mellars, eds., Princeton, N.J.: Princeton Univ. Press, pp. 84-103.

[3] Kingdom J. 1993. *Self-Made Man*, N.Y.: John Wiley, p. 258.

[4] Mellars *et al.*, 1993. "Outlining the Problem," in Aitken *et al.*, eds., *op. cit.*, pp. 5-6.

[5] Dawkins, R. 1995. *River Out of Eden* , N.Y.: Basic Books, pp. 48-49.

[6] Dawkins, 1995, *op. cit.*, p. 52.

[7] Dawkins, 1995, *op. cit.*, p. 53.

[8] De Duve, C. 1995. *Vital Dust*. N.Y.: Basic Books, pp. 232-234.

[9] Dawkins, 1995, *op. cit.*, p. 53.

[10] Dawkins, 1995, *op. cit.*, p. 54.

[11] Dawkins, 1995. *River, op. cit.*, p. 55.

[12] Templeton, A. 1983. "Phylogenetic Inference from Restriction Endonuclease Cleavage Site Maps with Particular Reference to the Evolution of Humans and Apes," *Evolution*, 37:221-244; Templeton, A. 1992. "Technical Comments: Human Origins and Analysis of Mitochondrial DNA Sequences," *Science*, 255:737.

[13] Hedges, S. B., and Stoneking, M. 1992. "Technical Comments: Human Origins and Analysis of Mitochondrial DNA Sequences," *Science*, 255:737; Schwartz, Jeffrey. 1993. *What the Bones Tell Us*, N.Y.: Henry Holt, p. 265.

[14] Vigilant, L., Stoneking, M., Wilson, A., Harpenden, H., and Hawkes, K. 1991. "African Populations and the Evolution of Mitochondrial DNA," *Science*, 253:1503-1507; Wilson, A. C., and Cann, R. L. 1992. "The Recent African Genesis of Humans," *Scientific American*, April, 266:4, 22-27.

[15] Stoneking, M., *et al.* 1993. "New Approaches to Dating Suggest a Recent Age for the Human mtDNA Ancestor," in Aitken *et al.*, eds., *op. cit.*, pp. 84-103, esp. p. 101.

[16] Trinkaus, E., and Shipman, P. 1993. *The Neanderthals*, N.Y.: Knopf, pp.394-396.

[17] Maddison, D. R. 1991. "African Origin of Human Mitochondrial DNA Reexamined," *Syst. Zool.*, 40:355-363; Templeton, A. 1992. "Technical Comments: Human Origins and Analysis of Mitochondrial DNA Sequences," *Science*, 255:737; Wolpoff, M. H. 1989. "Multiregional Evolution: The Fossil Alternative to Eden," in *The Human Revolution—Behavioral and Biological Perspectives on the Origins of Modern Humans*, P. Mellars and C. Stringer, eds., *op. cit.*, pp. 62-108; Aitken, M. J., Stringer, C. B., and Mellars, P. A., eds. 1993. "Outlining the problem," in Aitken *et al.*, eds., *op. cit.*, p. 6.

[18] Wade, N. 1999. "Study Gives New Time Line for Human Population Split," *The New York Times*, 16 Mar., A-14; Harris, E. E., and Hey, J. 1999, *Proceedings of the National Academy of Sciences*, 16 Mar.

[19] Gyllensten, U., Wilson, A., *et al.* 1991. "Paternal Inheritance of Mitochondrial DNA in Mice," *Nature*, 352:255-257.

[20] Dorit, R. L., *et al.* 1995. *Science*, 268:1183.

[21] Paabo, Svante. 1995. "The Y Chromosome and the Origin of All of Us (Men)," *Science*, 5/26/95, 268:1141-42.

[22] Nachman, M. W., and C. F. Aquadro in *Mol. Biol. Evol.* 11. 539 (1995).

[23] Kingdom J. 1993. *Self-Made Man*, N.Y.: John Wiley, p. 258.

[24] Paabo, 1995, *op. cit.*, 268:1141.

[25] Walker, A. C., and Shipman, P. 1996. *The Wisdom of the Bones*, N.Y.: Knopf, pp. 290-291.

[26] Cavalli-Sforza, L. L., *et al.* 1988. "Reconstruction of Human Evolution: Bringing Together Genetic, Archaeological and Linguistic Data," *Proc. National Acad. of Science*, Aug. 1988, 85:6002-6006, esp. 6002.

[27] Mountain, J. L. (Genetics, Stanford), Lin, A. A. (Genetics, Stanford), Bowcock, A. M. (Pediatrics, Univ. of Texas Med. Ctr., Dallas), Cavalli-Sforza, L. L. (Genetics-Stanford). 1993. "Evolution of Modern Humans: Evidence From Nuclear DNA Polymorphisms," in Aitken *et al.*, eds., *op. cit.*, pp. 60-83; Cavalli-Sforza, L. L., *et al.* 1993. *History and Geography of Human Genes*, Princeton, N.J.: Princeton Univ. Press.

[28] Cavalli-Sforza, L. L. 1993. Fig.1, in Aitken *et al.*, eds., *op. cit.*, p. 71.

[29] Andrews, P., and Stringer, C. 1993. "The Primates' Progress," in *Life*, S. J. Gould, ed., N.Y.: W. W. Norton, p. 232.

[30] Cavalli-Sforza, L. L., *et al.* 1992. "Coevolution of Genes and Languages Revisited," *Proceed. National Acad. Sciences*, 89:5620-5624; Kaiser, M., and Shevoroshkin, V. 1988. "Nostratic," *Ann. Rev. Anthropology*, 17:309-329; Itzkoff, S. W. 1991. "The Evolution of Human Intelligence: A Reply," in *Evolutionary Theory*, Jan., 10:63-64.

[31] Mountain and Cavalli-Sforza, 1993, Aitken *et al.*, eds., *op. cit.*, Table I, p. 76.

[32] Mountain and Cavalli-Sforza, 1993, Aitken *et al.*, eds., *op. cit.*, Table 1, p. 77.

[33] Mountain and Cavalli-Sforza, 1993, Aitken *et al.*, eds., Princeton, *op. cit.*, p. 81.

[34] Tishkoff, Sarah. 1996. *Science*, as reported in *The New York Times*, 3/8/96 (via the Associated Press).

[35] *Ibid.*

[36] Gladwell, M. 1997. "The Sports Taboo," *The New Yorker* 5/19/97, pp. 49-55.

[37] Takahata, N., Satta, Y., Klein, J. 1995. "Divergence Time and Population Size in the Lineage Leading to Modern Humans," *Theoretical and Population Biology*, quoted in "The Mystery of Humanity's Missing Mutations," Ann Gibbons, *Science*, 1/6/95, 267:35-36.

[38] *Science*, 10/1/93, p. 27; Wade, N. 1999. "Study Gives New Time Line for Human Population Split," *The New York Times*, 16 Mar., A-14; Harris, E. E., and Hey, J. 1999, *Proceedings of the National Academy of Sciences*, 16 Mar..

[39] Takahata *et al.*, 1995, quoted in "The Mystery of Humanity's Missing Mutations," Ann Gibbons, *Science*, 1/6/95, 267:36.

[40] Mountain and Cavalli-Sforza, 1993, Aitken *et al.*, eds., *op. cit.*, pp. 79-80.

[41] Clark, G. A., and Lindley, J. M. 1989. "Modern Human Origins in the Levant and Western Asia: The Fossil and Archeological Evidence," *American Anthropologist*, 91:962-985.

[42] Clark and Lindley, 1989, *op. cit., American Anthropologist*, 91:962-985, esp. 976, 978, footnote 5; Wallace, D., *et al.* 1985. "Dramatic Founder Effects in Amerindian Mitochondrial DNAs," *American Journal of Physical Anthropology*, 68:149-155.

[43] Wolpoff, 1989, in Mellars and Stringer, eds., *op. cit.*, pp. 62-108, esp. p. 98.

[44] Stringer, C., and McKie, R. 1997. *African Exodus*, N.Y.: Henry Holt.

[45] Ashley-Montagu, M. F. 1951. *Statement on Race*, N.Y.: Henry Schuman.

[46] Kingdom, 1993, *op. cit.*, pp. 99-101.

[47] Trinkaus, E., ed. 1989. *The Emergence of Modern Humans*, Cambridge, Eng.: Cambridge University Press; Mellars, P. A., and Stringer, C., eds. 1989. *The Human Revolution—Behavioral and Biological Perspectives on the Origins of Modern Humans, op. cit.*; Klein, R. G. 1989. *The Human Career*, Chicago: Univ. of Chicago Press.

[48] Stringer, C. B., and Gamble, C. 1993 *In Search of the Neanderthals: Solving the Puzzle of Human Origins*, London: Thames and Hudson; Wolpoff, M. H. 1994. "The Calm Before the Storm," *Cambridge Archaeological Journal*, 4:1:97-103.

[49] Stringer, C. B., and Gamble, C. 1994. "Reply: Confronting the Neanderthals," *Cambridge Archaeological Journal*, 4:1:112-119; Hasegawa, M., *et al.* 1993. "Toward a more accurate time scale for the human mitochondrial DNA tree," *Journal of Molecular Evolution*, 37:347-354; Ruvolo, M., *et al.* 1993. "Mitochondrial COII sequences and modern human origins," *Molecular Biology and Evolution*, 10:1115-1135; Nei, M.. and Roychoudhury, A. K. 1993. "Evolutionary relationships of human populations on a global scale," *Molecular Biology and Evolution*, 10:927-943.

[50] Wade, N. 1997. "Man Has Older Friend Than Thought," quoted in *The New York Times*, 6/13/97, p. A-12. See, however, Klein's slightly earlier modest support for the "Out-of-Africa" scenario for modern humans: Klein, R. G. 1995. "Anatomy, Behavior, and Modern Human Origins," *Journal of World Prehistory*, 9:2:167-197, esp. p. 191; in 1999, Klein is still skeptical as to where and when modern humans originated. "In the end the genetics will have to accommodate the fossil and archeological records, not the reverse." Wade, N. 1999. "Study Gives New Time Line for Human Population Split," *The New York Times*, 16 Mar., A-14; Harris and Hey, 1999, *op. cit., Proceedings of the National Academy of Sciences*, 16 Mar.

[51] Stringer, C. B., and Gamble, C. 1994. "The Neanderthal World: Flat Earth or New Horizons," *Cambridge Archaeological Journal*, 4:1:96.

[52] Gibbons, A. 1997. "Y Chromosome Shows that Adam Was an African," *Science*, 10/31/97, 278:804-805.

[53] Wood, B. A. 1997. "Ecce Homo—behold mankind," *Nature*, 11/13/97, 390:120-121.

[54] Clark, J. D. 1993. "African and Asian Perspectives on the Origin of Modern Humans," in *The Origin of Modern Humans and the Impact of Chronometric Dating*, M. J. Aitken, C. P. Stringer, and P. A. Mellars, eds., *op. cit.*, pp. 148-178.

[55] Clark, 1993, Aitken *et al.*, eds., *op. cit.*, p. 153

[56] Clark, 1993, Aitken *et al.*, eds., *op. cit.*, p. 154.

[57] Clark, 1993, Aitken *et al.*, eds., *op. cit.*, pp. 159-160.

[58] Brauer, G. 1989. "The Evolution of Modern Humans: A Comparison of the African and Non-African Evidence," in Mellars and Stringer, eds., *op. cit.*, pp. 123-154, esp. 125.

[59] Howells, W. W. 1988. "The Meaning of the Neanderthals in Human Evolution," in *L'Evolution dans sa Realite et ses Diverses Modalites*, Fondation Singer-Polignac, ed., Paris: Masson, pp. 221-239, esp. 225.

[60] Klein, 1989, op. cit., pp. 353-354.

[61] Rightmire, C. P. 1989. "Middle-Stone Age Humans from Eastern and Southern Africa," in Mellars and Stringer, eds., *op. cit.*, pp. 109-122, esp. p. 109.

[62] Stringer, C. 1989. "The Origin of Early Modern Humans: A Comparison of the European and non-European Evidence," in Mellars and Stringer, eds., *op. cit.*, pp. 232-244, esp. p. 242; Trinkaus, E. 1981. "Neanderthal Limb Proportions and Cold Adaptation," in *Aspects of Human Evolution*, Stringer, C., ed., London: Taylor and Francis, pp. 187-224.

[63] Andrews and Stringer, 1993, in Gould, ed., *op. cit.*, p. 251, fig. and diagram.

[64] Stringer, and McKie, 1997, *op. cit.* See the review of this book by R. R. Richards of the University of Chicago: Richards, R. R. 1997. "Neanderthals Need Not Reply," in *New York Times Sunday Book Review*, 8/17/97, 10.

[65] Smith, F. H., *et al.* 1989. "Geographical Variation in Supraorbital Torus Reduction during the Later Pleistocene (c. 80,000-15,000BP)" in Mellars and Stringer, eds., *op. cit.*, pp. 172-193; Wolpoff, M. H., and Caspari, R. 1997. *Race and Human Evolution*, N.Y.: Simon and Schuster, pp. 270-313.

[66] Coon, C. S. 1939. *The Races of Europe*, N.Y.: Macmillan; Ashley-Montagu, M. F. 1940. Review of T. D. McCowan and A. Keith: *The Stone Age of Mount Carmel*, Vol.2, *The Fossil Remains of Levalloiso-Mousterian, American Anthropologist*, 42:518-522; Dobzhansky, T. 1944. "On the Species and Races of Living and Fossil Man," *American Journal of Physical Anthropology*, 2:251-265; McCowen, T. D., and Keith, A. 1939. *The Stone Age of Mount Carmel* Vol.2, *The Fossil Remains from the Levalloiso-Mousterian*, Oxford: Clarendon Press; Thoma, A. 1957-58. "Essai sur les Hommes Fossiles de Palestine," *L'Anthropologie*, 61:470-502, 62:30-52; Thoma, A. 1962. "Le Deploiement Evolutif de l'Homo Sapiens" *Anthropologia Hungarica*, 5:1-179; Thoma, A. 1963. "La Definition des Neandertaliens et la Position des Hommes Fossiles de Palestine," *L`Anthropologie*, 69:519-534.

[67] Vandermeersch, B. 1989. "The Evolution of Modern Humans: Recent Evidence from Southwest Asia," in Mellars and Stringer, eds., *op. cit.*, pp. 155-164, esp. p. 156.

[68] Vandermeersch, 1989, in Mellars and C. Stringer, eds., *op. cit.*, pp. 161-162.

[69] Bar-Yosef, O. 1993. "The Role of Western Asia in Modern Human Origins," in Aitken *et al.*, eds., *op. cit.*, p. 138.

[70] Schwarcz, H. P. 1994. "Chronology of Modern Humans in the Levant," in *Late Quaternary Chronology and Paleoclimates of the Eastern Mediterranean*, O. Bar-Yosef and R. S. Kra, eds., Tucson, AZ: Radiocarbon, University of Arizona, pp. 21-32, esp. 27, also "Introduction," above volume, p. 12.

[71] Vandermeersch, 1989, Mellars and Stringer, eds., *op. cit.*, p. 162.

[72] Coon, C. S. 1982. *Racial Adaptations*, Chicago: Nelson-Hall, pp. 132-133, 159.

[73] Trinkaus, E. 1983. *The Shanidar Neanderthals*, N.Y.: Academic Press.

[74] Hublin, J.-J., *et al.* 1996. "A Late Neanderthal Associated with Upper Paleolithic Artifacts," *Nature*, 5/16/96, 381:224-226 (*The New York Times* 5/16/96, (AP)).

[75] *Ibid.*

[76] Torroni, A., *et al.* 1994. "mtDNA and the Origin of the Caucasians: Identification of Ancient Caucasian-specific Haplogroups, One of Which Is Prone to a Recurrent Somatic Duplication in the D-Loop Region," *Am. Jnl. Hum. Gen.*, 55:760-766; Wade, N. 1997. "Neanderthal DNA Sheds New Light On Human Origins," *The New York Times*, 7/11/97.

[77] Lieberman, P. 1994. "The Origin and Evolution of Language," in *Companion Encyclopedia of Anthropology*, T. Ingold, ed., N.Y.: Routledge, pp. 108-132.

[78] Arensberg, B. 1989. "New Skeletal Evidence Concerning the Anatomy of Middle Paleolithic Populations in the Middle East: The Kebara Skeleton," in Mellars and Stringer, eds., *op. cit.*, pp. 164-171, esp. p. 170.

[79] Mellars, P. A. 1996. *The Neanderthal Legacy*, Princeton, N.J.: Princeton Univ. Press, p. 391.

[80] Habgood, P. J. 1989. "The Origin of Anatomically-Modern Humans in Australasia," in Mellars and Stringer, eds., *op. cit.*, pp. 245-273.

[81] Habgood, P. J. 1985. "The Origin of the Australian Aborigines: An Alternative Approach and View," in *Hominid Evolution: Past, Present, and Future*, P. V. Tobias, ed., N.Y.: Alan Liss, pp. 367-380.

[82] Habgood, 1985, in Tobias, ed., *op. cit.*, p. 376.

[83] Habgood, 1985, in Tobias, ed., *op. cit.*, p. 377.

[84] Habgood, 1989, in Mellars and Stringer, eds., *op. cit.*, p. 268.

[85] Groves, C. P. 1989. "A Regional Approach to the Problem of the Origin of Modern Humans in Australasia," in Mellars and Stringer, eds., *op. cit.*, pp. 274-285.

[86] Groves, 1989, in Mellars and Stringer, eds., *op. cit.*, p. 283.

[87] Wolpoff, M. 1997. "No `Homo erectus' at Ngandong," in *Human Origins News*, 1/4/97, 6pp, esp. p. 4.

[88] Awadalla, P., *et al.* 1999. "Linkage Disequilibrium and Recombination in Hominid Mitochondrial DNA," *Science*, 268:2524-2525, Dec. 24. Research into rate of specific mutations in mtDNA indicates possible mixing of paternal and maternal influences in studies of four out of five tested groups of humans and one group of chimpanzees.

15

Homo sapiens sapiens: Eur-Asian Origins

In this chapter we review the controversies and evidence that divide scientific opinion on the origins of truly modern *Homo sapiens sapiens*, peoples represented in Eur-Asia by the Cro-Magnids. Did they or their immediate precursors migrate from Africa as the "Out-of-Africa Eden" mtDNA hypothesis first predicted? Or did humans around the world evolve in place, exemplifying the multiregional hypothesis, all gradually becoming members of the recent races of humankind? But, what about *Homo sapiens sapiens*, Cro-Magnon, and its unique Eur-Asian civilization?

What are the alternative scenarios for the origin of modern humans, other than Eur-Asia? To answer this question, the empirical evidence must be reviewed.

Australasia:

Colin Grove concluded that, as more fossils become better known in the Australasian research area, both through discovery and analysis, a purely replacement theory becomes more difficult to reconcile with the evidence of morphological continuity. These views, enunciated in 1989, have proved to be prescient, given the radical redating of the Javanese Ngandong and Sangiran 17 fossils, from c.400,000-200,000 B.P. to c.53,000-27,000B.P. The impact, however, has not been alone on the so-called "Out-of-Africa" replacement model. It has challenged the multiregional continuity views, as well. For now, we have two distinct populations, one clearly ancient *Homo erectus* in form, others clearly on the road to full sapiency, all living within the Australasian context.[1]

In his most recent (1997) writing, Milford Wolpoff was still vigorously defending his evolutionary association of the recent Kow Swamp fossil skull, 13,000-4,000 B.P. (Alan Thorne of Australia), with the Middle Pleistocene Indonesian example, Sangiran 17 (then, 300,000-200,000 B.P.), arguing that the latter was directly ancestral to the former.[2] Wolpoff could not have known, as his book was about to be published, that the dates for Sangiran 17, the special focus of his most recent analysis, were being revised upward to coincide with the new dating of the Ngandong skulls, 53,000-27,000 B.P.[3]

R. G. Roberts is reported by J. Desmond Clark, himself an advocate of the sudden replacement theory and the "Out-of-Africa Eve" model, as stating that anatomically modern humans entered Australia 60-40ka B.P. with a tool kit that had been used in China since the days of *Homo erectus*. If not an argument for complete regional continuity in Australasia, it certainly did not signify a perspective of modern human replacement that evolved lately in Africa.[4]

Citing Franz Weidenreich with approval, Philip Habgood has hypothesized that the origin of the modern Australian aborigines could be traced to a time from about 53,000 B.P., when the sea level was much lower. "The most probable ancestors are represented by the Ngandong fossils from Java which are, on the whole, surprisingly alike."[5] Today, the Ngandong would be considered contemporaries, if more primitive.

On the status of the Lake Mungo fossil material, Habgood cites A. Thorne's earlier analysis of these crania, noting their gracile seemingly non-Australasian morphology. Thorne sees the Lake Mungo "gracile crania as displaying the `stamp of ancient China.'"[6] The genetics of modernization apparently came from outside the immediate Australasian region, from the Chinese north. But certainly, not from Africa.

15.1 Map of late-Pleistocene Australian sites. Ancient continental land masses of Sunda and Sahul were separated by a deep-water trench called "Wallace's Line." Indonesian hybrid peoples and Asian wildlife predominated west of this line. Australasian, mainly marsupial mammals and Australian aboriginal-type humans, predominated to the east.

Peter Brown sees the late-Pleistocene hominids in both areas of Asia as ancestral to modern inhabitants.[7] Going back further in time would be to create additional controversy; for example, the Ngandong crania, now redated to 53,000-27,000 B. P., may still be *H. erectus*.[8] The Dali, Archaic *H. sapiens*, 230,000-180,000 B.P., in China, one of the more transitional fossil examples of a modern East Asian *H. sapiens* morphologically, is not at all represented in the Indonesian sequences. No replacement here. Thus the earliest truly modern *H. sapiens* in East Asia and Australasia is Lake Mungo 1 (Australia), dated to c.24,000 B.P.[9]

Likewise, Fred Smith is persuaded that the Australasian transitionals reflect a morphological continuity from *Homo erectus* to Archaic *H. sapiens* to modern *Homo sapiens sapiens*.[10] Smith believes that the weight of scholarly opinion has shifted toward these continuity perspectives. However, he does concede that there are still many gaps in the fossil record. In China, the Dali *sapiens* at 230,000-180,000 B.P., is similar in time frame to the African transitional group, Kabwe, Bodo, etc. (*H. heidelbergensis*, Archaic *H. sapiens*, or what?).[11] The implication was that semi-modern humans were already in China at the purported mtDNA time frame that modernizing African *sapiens* should have been emigrating, c.200,000-150,000 B.P.

China

Chris Stringer, the steadfast advocate of the "Out-of-Africa" rapid replacement model, agrees with J. Desmond Clark, who argues that early modern fossils from eastern Europe are closer morphologically to each other than are modern fossils from eastern Asia to the antecedent hominid fossils of the region. Clark suggests that a unique migration into China may have catapulted the borderline *H. sapiens* such as Dali, Maba, Yinkou, Jinnushan, Xujiayao, Yunxian into modernity, else completely replaced them.[12] Stringer argues that gene flow between regions seems to be observable in all parts of East Asia and Australasia.[13]

On the other hand, Richard Klein has concluded that the Chinese fossils are quite different from the fossils of the same age from Africa and Europe. Whereas the "later mid-Quaternary people in Africa and Europe were generally distinguished from *Homo erectus* by larger cranial capacities, more expanded parietals, and less angulated occipitals, the later mid-quaternary occupants of Java and China remained remarkably similar to classic *H. erectus* in virtually all significant cranial features and proportions."[14] Clearly, Klein implies a continuity with the past throughout East Asia, at the very least, that the in-migration and replacement of the indigenous populations was slow and gradual, if indeed it was ever a complete displacement from without.

Milford Wolpoff: *"With regard to the Garden of Eden hypothesis, it is ominous that none of these earlier specimens [China] possess features which resemble archaic or modern Africans..."* Wolpoff discusses Maba and Dali, plus other examples of Chinese fossils stretching back to famous Zhoukoudian Cave casts, now estimated to date to 500,000 B.P.[15] Klein has estimated the dates for Maba, Southeast China, at 140,000-120,000 B.P.; Dali, Northeast China, 230,000-180,000 B.P.[16]

More recently, Milford Wolpoff has focused again on Maba and Dali.[17] He illustrates the Maba skull (140,000-120,000 B.P.) to compare it with its presumed contemporary, the Neanderthal LaChapelle—Maba has typically Mongoloid facial morphology— smaller and less projecting nose, forward facing cheek rather than to the side as in Europeans.[18] Dali, 230,000-180,000 B.P., is compared with its once supposed contemporary Sangiran 17 as a similarly long and low skull with thick brow ridges. However, it differs from Sangiran. Dali has facial flatness, and differs in the angle between the face and cranial vault. (It is a typical Mongoloid.)[19]

Carleton Coon, in 1962: "The Mapa [sic] skull [140,000-120,000 B.P.] seems to stand at the threshold between two grades of *Homo*. If it was not *sapiens*, it was very close to being so. In any case, it represents a higher stage of human evolution than *Sinanthropus* [earliest level at Zhoukoudian—Beijing Man] himself, which is the most important conclusion we can reach. As to its race, it seems to be mostly if not entirely Mongoloid; and in ways in which it differs from *Sinanthropus*, as in the shape of the orbits [ring of bone that protects the eye], it is a link between *Sinanthropus* and the modern Mongoloid peoples."[20]

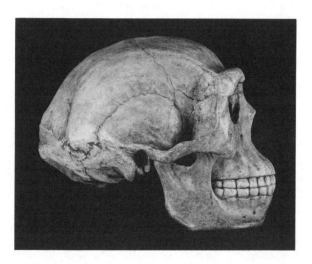

15.2 "Beijing Man," *Sinanthropus pekinensis* (reconstruction), c.5mya. This classic East Asian exemplar carries the unique suite of racial identifiers first described by Weidenreich in the 1930s that link this fossil to contemporary Chinese. Such evidence is used by the multiregionalists to argue their case for independent human evolutionary pathways toward sapiency.

Peter Brown, of the University of New England, Australia, accepts the existing mid-Pleistocene affiliations of various skeletal materials with a Mongoloid morphology.[21] His questions relate to the terminal Zhoukoudian Upper Cave skeletons, dated reliably to the terminal Pleistocene, 20-12ka B.P. He focuses on the Upper Cave skeletons, especially the so-called "101" cranium, which even Weidenreich, its discoverer, questioned as to its Mongoloid affinities. Brown sees it as looking more like its Mongoloid descendants than do other terminal Pleistocene skulls, and, throughout the world, look like their geographical descendants. "Whatever has been selecting for 'Mongoloid' facial characteristics appears to have been doing so for a long period of time."[22] The controversy to Brown, regarding the late-Pleistocene humans in China, focuses on the Southeast China Liujiang skull, c.70ka B.P. "'Mongoloid characteristics' include a shovel shaped central incisor, shallow prenasal fossa, congenitally absent third molars and an arteriolateral surface of the frontal process which is rotated forwards."[23] The problem with the Liujiang fossil is its surprising morphological modernity, especially if it turns out to be a male, given its 70ka B.P. dating. This is because of its "relatively small facial height, minimal alveolar and tooth dimensions, low orbits, and a supra-orbital and occipital torus development which would be slight for a late Pleistocene *female* [emphasis added]."[24]

As with the Australasian fossils, the Chinese materials reveal no wider relationships beyond their geographical provenance. African morphologies, either of the Kabwe, Bodo, or Klasies River Mouth patterns, are not evident. Clearly there is an infusion of genes from without, else why the seeming fits and starts of archaism and modernity, as well as the overlaying and underlying fossils that confuse the researching mind about both the grade of evolutionary direction and the taxonomic predictivity in differing layers of time? This latter situation has also become particularly vexing with regard to the Eur-Asian Neanderthal-Cro-Magnon interactions.

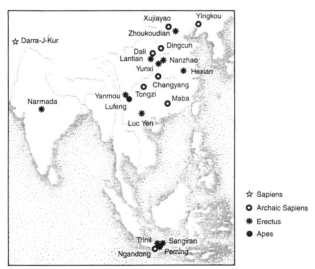

15.3 Map of Asian primate fossil finds in the Ice Age.

It is the Jinniu Shan fossil, supposedly an Archaic *H. sapiens*, and dated to about 200,000 B.P. that seems to precipitate doubts for Leslie Aiello about the "Out-of-Africa" scenario of fully modern humans. While Aiello rejects Wolpoff's multiregional perspective, mainly for its incompatibility with the mtDNA evidence, but also for its inability to explain so many contemporaneous, yet quite different affiliated forms of *Homo*, this North Asiatic fossil raises important issues. How does a creature such as the Archaic *sapiens* from Jinniu Shan, within the Chinese clade of fossils, morphologically, fit in with an "Out-of-Africa" migration of humans scenario, an event that seems to be contemporary with this racially very Chinese example?[25]

We recall Noel Boaz' report on Jinniu Shan, with its ESR (electro-spin-resonance) and uranium series datings of this skull, to 200,000 B.P. This skull would presumably pre-date the Chinese Maba and be contemporary with the archaic Dali fossils.[26] "The authors suggest that its early age, almost as old as some Chinese *Homo erectus* finds, raises the possibility of the coexistence of the two species."[27]

North Africa

Carleton Coon's final analysis (1982), based on his earlier two books on the evolution of the races, views the ancient Ternefine, Algeria, fossil material, a mandible, parietal, perhaps as old as 700,000 B.P., as related to the Capoid racial clade.[28] Molar and premolar teeth seemed reminiscent of *Sinanthropus*. "Ternefine anticipated a number of North African crania which follow the same line after crossing the threshold to *Homo sapiens*."[29] Coon believed that Ternefine, an *H. erectus*, follows in line of *H. erectus*, (or *H. ergaster*) in Kenya, KNMER 3733, which he believed to be then part of a Capoid racial line, traceable back to about 1.6mya. Concerning Jebel Irhoud 1, c.100,000 B.P., an adult male, endocranial capacity at 1480cm³, from between Safi and Marakeesh in Morocco, and Jebel Irhoud 2, same time frame, an adolescent with endocranial capacity of c.1500cm³, Coon argues that Jebel Irhoud 1 has similar straight-across brow ridges as does KNMER 3733. He believed them to be, as in the Ternefine fossils, Capoids.[30]

J.-J. Hublin, Director of Research, Musée de l'Homme, Paris, more recently has made his specialty the general context of human evolution in North Africa.[31] Hublin labels the Aterian industry beginning about 40ka B.P., as seemingly a product of morphologically modern people (see the discussion below by O. Bar-Yosef). Preceding were the Jebel Irhoud fossils first discovered by Coon, in 1939. Hublin believes that they can be traced back to between 120,000 and 70,000 B.P., corresponding with oxygen isotope stage 5, 75ka+ B.P, or possibly 6, 190-130ka B.P.[32] These fossils have some primitive features reminiscent of the Neanderthals, but are not part of the Neanderthal clade, no apomorphies, derivative morphologies paralleling the Neanderthals. Hublin does not comment upon the supposed Capoid affinities that Coon thought to exist.

The Jebel Irhoud fossils strike Hublin as similar to Qafzeh and Skhul, (somewhere between the Neanderthals and Cro-Magnon, but more primitive than the latter).[33] Generally he sees an accretion of Neanderthal features in Europe and West Asia from about 400-300ka B.P. (Steinheim/Swanscombe).[34] Clearly, the Northwest Africans are different. Hublin accepts the theoretical imperatives of the "Out-of-Africa"scenario as including Northwest Africa to South Africa, but also, as of necessity, including the Middle East.[35] The great difficulty with the "Out-of-Africa" theory, he argues, is its postulation of a quick and clear displacement of previous human types, thence the emergence of an "Adamic," anatomically modern man. The empirical evidence as evinced in the fossil record, Hublin notes, informs us of the gradual modernization of humans in the North African and Middle Eastern sequence. "To remain with the North African record, how can we classify together as `Archaic *Homo sapiens*,' such a primitive specimen as Sale' which indeed already displays some `*sapiens*'-derived features [Morocco—400,000 B.P.] together with the very different Irhoud specimens, which are already phenetically very near to the Middle-Eastern forerunners of modern Europeans?"[36]

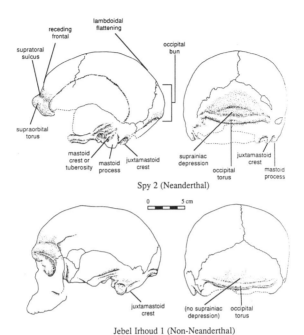

15.4 Jebel-Irhoud 1 (North Africa) and Spy 2 (European Neanderthal) compared. Consensus is that the two contemporary lines are not related. Evolutionary affinities of the North African hominids are unclear. The Neanderthals were Caucasoids that became extinct as an independent group consequent to their contact with Cro-Magnon. It is doubtful that the genes of either line have disappeared.

Fred Smith of Northern Illinois University has a somewhat different perspective on the North African fossils.[37] He sees Jebel Irhoud 1, in North Africa, Florisbad, in South Africa, Ngaloba (Laetoli 18), Tanzania, contemporaries at about 100ka B.P. He is quite uncertain as to their all being included in an African sapient transitional group. However, J. Irhoud 1 and 2 do resemble European types in the shape of supraorbital torus.[38] J. Irhoud 1-3 were found "in association with Mousterian artifacts."[39] Smith does not commit himself either to a North African-Neanderthal relationship, despite the apparently Mousterian stone artifacts associated with the Jebel Irhoud fossils, nor either to challenge or agree with Coon's association of these fossils with the Capoids, and then to the Southern African Klasies River Mouth, Border Cave fossils, which as we will note below are now seen to be Capoid in racial heritage.

In North Africa, from Ternefine, c.700,000 B.P., to Sale', c.400,000 B.P., to Jebel Irhoud, c.190,000-100,000 B.P., to Tamara, c.120,000 B.P., Dar es Sultan, c.65,000 B.P., there seems to have been a fairly direct line of morphological continuity, hinting of an *in situ* evolutionary process upwardly graded toward the *sapiens* level, finally reflecting, in the Aterian culture, c.40,000 B.P., the arrival, yet without human morphological evidence, of a new "Out-of-Africa" presence, perhaps from Europe.

Hublin, as noted above, sees only a North African connection with the Middle Eastern skeletal material, especially Qafzeh 9 and Skhul 5, which date from about

95,000-85,000 B.P., and which, as we shall note below, were discovered, like the Jebel Irhoud fossils, with associated Mousterian artifacts, these usually denoting Neanderthal fabrication. Given Hublin's estimate of a 400-300,000-year-old origin for the Neanderthal morphology, possibly represented by the English Swanscombe and the German Steinheim fossil materials, at a grade well below sapiency, perhaps, *Homo heidelbergensis*, any postulated originating point south of the Sahara in Africa, must remain highly conjectural for this evolving clade of modern humans.

Africa, South of the Sahara

Turn to Africa, south of the Sahara, the touted source of modern human beings, at an advanced sapiency grade. These are not Archaic *Homo sapiens,* and certainly not *Homo heidelbergensis* into which taxonomic category both Kabwe (Broken Hill) in Zambia, 350,000-200,000 B.P. (Coon, c.62,000 B.P.) and Bodo, near Hadar in Ethiopia, 400,000-300,000 B.P., have been tentatively placed along with the Arago, France, and the Petralona, Greece, skulls. These latter European skulls are in the same general time frame as the above Africans. Schwartz hypothesizes that they may be seen as Archaic *Homo sapiens*.[40]

Klein considers Kabwe a mosaic of erectine/*sapiens* characteristics, tilted toward the *sapiens* grade by its 1280cm^3 endocranial capacity, but also with puzzling modernistic dental caries. Bodo is viewed by Klein as definitely *H. erectus*, at a similar time frame.[41] Carleton Coon in his final book argued for a date of the Kabwe (Broken Hill) fossil as no earlier than 62,000 B.P., along with Saldanha. Klein places an approximate period of from 500,000-200,000 B.P. for Saldanha, which despite its large endocranial capacity, c.1250cm^3, he views as borderline *H. erectus*.[42] Coon adduced considerable evidence for his time frame thesis including the unusual tooth decay of Kabwe considering its presumed ancient origins. This was an additional argument for his viewing both fossils, Kabwe and Saldanha as recent, late-Pleistocene (Coon, 1962: 26,000 B.P) *H. erectus* types.[43]

Klein's more general worldwide perspective on these African transitionals: Whereas the "later mid-quaternary people in Africa and Europe were generally distinguished from *Homo erectus* by larger cranial capacities, more expanded parietals, and less angulated occipitals, the later mid-quaternary occupants of Java and China remained remarkably similar to classic *H. erectus* in virtually all significant cranial features and proportions."[44]

Two seemingly modern fossils have been found in South Africa that have lent great credence to the "African Eve" hypothesis. The Klasies River Mouth and Border Cave crania show unequivocal signs of modernity in their large endocranial capacity and seemingly modern morphology. Coon, in the 1962 *The Origin of Races*, discussed several primitive South African fossils, Cave of Hearths and Cape Flats, which he felt to be quite ancient, erectine, and also Negroid, in character. Beyond that he did offer the supposition that the Capoids had entered South Africa from the north, Jebel Irhoud, toward the end of the Pleistocene, gradually being transformed into the prehistoric, but modern Boskopoids, tall, with a large endocranial capacity, the immediate ancestors of the Bushmen and the Hottentots.[45]

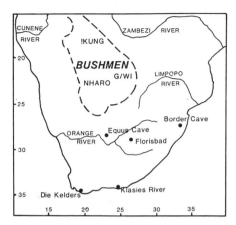

15.5 Map of South African fossil sites.

H. J. Deacon, of the University of Stellenbosch in South Africa, has probably done the most specialized and technical analysis of these fossils.[46] Deacon sees them as highly dimorphic, admittedly a retrogressive characteristic. The Klasies River Mouth fossils, also, are placed into the Bushman clade, tacitly confirming Coon, but Deacon pushes back their presence in South Africa by tens of millennia, and possibly locating South Africa as an original homeland. However, Deacon, does concede that though southern Africa reveals a regional human continuity, there is the possibility of an intrusion from the north, from sub-Saharan Africa in the Middle Pleistocene, c.800,000-500,000 B.P.[47]

"....the branching of this clade occurred before the beginning of the late Pleistocene. Genetic evidence is that the Bushmen are a long separated African population."[48] Deacon suggests a date of c.90ka B.P. for the Klasies Rivers Mouth fossils and c.70ka B.P. for the Border Cave fossils. With large modern crania, short, slender postcranial bones similar to present-day San people, these humans seem to fit the bill for a fully modern *Homo sapiens*, in Africa, and at a time level far enough removed to be a candidate for a correlation with the mtDNA predictions of a branching out from Africa.[49]

Deacon: "This provides clear support for the "Out-of-Africa" hypothesis for the origins of anatomically-modern people....The conclusion is that not only were people in the southern Cape some 100,000 years ago anatomically modern, but that they were also behaviorally modern."[50]

One of the tests of modernity in human behavior has been the issue of cannibalism. At the *Homo erectus* level, at the least, a number of skulls have been found throughout the world with the foramen magnum (the point of entrance of the spinal chord to the skull) having been torn apart, presumably to gain food access to the brain matter within the skull. In the case of the Klasies River Mouth fossils, Klein and Wolpoff, following White, note that a number of bones show fractures, marks of tool scraping, even burning of the bones, implying cannibalism.[51]

As with L. Binford, and Churchill *et al.*, Klein seems skeptical of the true behavioral modernity, hunting procedure, technology of the South African sapiens. "...The artifacts and animal remains associated with early modern or near modern fossils in Southern Africa suggest non-modern behavior, perhaps broadly on a par with that of the contemporary European Neanderthals."[52]

Deacon replies: "Contrary to the argument offered here...a number of researchers ...have reasoned that the behavior of later Pleistocene Middle Stone Age people was not modern because they did not exploit their environment as efficiently as the Later Stone Age Holocene hunter-gatherers did. It assumed that they were not capable of doing so because of inferior intelligence. However, arguments of this kind imply an innate motivation to optimize use of resources rather than to satisfy needs."[53]

Deacon's argument could just as well be placed at the feet of the chimpanzee: The chimpanzee does not optimize use of and exploit its environment because it can satisfy its needs without so doing. All animals utilize their intincts to satisfy their needs, and they do so to the maximum of their adaptations. The question goes to the core of human behavioral differences and inner motivations. What does it mean in human behavior to satisfy or optimize one's needs?

Fred Smith, in his survey of the African *sapiens* material cites a number of geographic sources that seem to argue for the regional continuity of humans from *H. erectus* through Archaic *sapiens*, to modern human beings. In his view one of the Klasies River Mouth hominids could be an adolescent or female, that at a distance of 100-60ka B.P., the fossils might not be telling us enough about the possible robusticity of an adult male. His view, confirmed in recent analysis by Churchill *et al.*, is that they were probably not fully modern humans, anatomically. However, Smith also does not confront their Capoid racial status.[54]

Smith's conclusion: The transition in Africa was taking place when the Neanderthals were ensconced in Europe and Western Asia, but in China a transition was also taking place—and the African fossil dates are uncertain progenitors.[55] Smith believes, on the basis of careful analysis, that Klasies River Mouth specimens are not modern, even at the 100-60ka B.P. dates set for them, but are more like the Bodo, Kabwe (Rhodesian-Broken Hill)—borderline erectine/*H. heidelbergensis*/Archaic *Homo sapiens*—groups.[56] In his view the oldest specimens of early modern humans are the Levant Qafzeh and Skhul, 95-85ka B.P., and like Rightmire, he does not see them as having any morphological relationship to the transitional South African samples. Qafzeh and Skhul may be intrusive into the Levant, but probably not from Africa.[57]

The strongest advocate of the "Out-of-Africa" scenario, along with Guenter Brauer, of Hamburg University, is Christopher Stringer of the British Museum. A specialist in the statistical techniques involving comparative morphology, he has been at pains in his various writings to show that many of the apparent regional morphological continuities and supposed racial affiliations are more apparent than real, and that other people outside the specific geographies or racial centers share similar derived metrical patterns.

In the case of the African fossils, and throughout the continent, he has been a strong advocate of the view that the mtDNA evidence is strongly supported by the concrete evolutionary evidence, both chronological sequencing as well as the morphological ascent leading toward modernity of structure and behavior.[58]

Stringer, 1989:

> This does not mean that these specimens, drawn from various parts of Africa, must represent the ancestral population for early modern *Homo sapiens*. However, they appear morphologically and metrically close to the hypothesized common ancestor. Further, and independent, data which support the model of an African origin for modern humans can also be added. First, Africa has plausible (and fairly complete) morphological intermediates between "archaic" and "modern" morphologies (such as Irhoud 2 and Omo Kibish). Second, from Klasies River Mouth Caves, Border Cave, Equus Cave, Mumba Cave, Omo Kibish 1, and East Turkana (KNM-ER3884) we may have the oldest known fossils approximating the modern human anatomical pattern...[59]

Since 1989, perhaps the apogee of the support for the "Out-of-Africa" model, this perspective, as noted above, has been under pressure by an increasing number of scientists who, with every new uncovered bone or human artifact, are troubled with the empirical foundations of the theory, increasingly wobbly, in terms of what it should predict, and what it has not been able to predict. Some of these have been chronicled above.[60] Yet Stringer continues to hold to his views.

Stringer, 1993: "Thus a model of universal multiregionalism is not supported by these analyses. If *Homo sapiens* originated in one region, that region was probably Africa....It seems unlikely that Dali [230-180ka B.P., China] represents a late Asian form of *Homo heidelbergensis,* as other analyses...show African (*e.g.*, Bodo, Broken Hill), and European (*e.g.*, Arago, Petralona) earlier middle Pleistocene fossils to be more similar to Neanderthals...Neither does Dali appear close to the Zhoukoudian [Beijing-China] *Homo erectus* sample in shape from other more limited analyses."[61]

African Negroids: No discussion of the role of Africa in the creation and then racial dispersion of anatomically and behaviorally modern humans would be complete without at least a reference to the modern African Negro and heritage. Coon was of the opinion that there were no fossils of modern Negroids earlier than 8,000 B.P., mainly because of the generally acidic conditions of the West African tropical soil, the presumed origin of modern Negroids.[62]

Milford Wolpoff, in his recent discussion of the evolution of the races, in a defense of his multiregional theory of human evolution, briefly alludes to the still-existing paucity of modern Negroid fossils in the African record, at a time frame similar to the Capoid Bushman and Hottentot, as evidenced in the South African fossils discussed above.[63]

The only possible exception to the gap in early Negroid fossils is the South African Tuinplaas skeleton on which Alun Hughes of the University of Wittwatersrand Medical School has recently reported.[64] He dates it to about 15,000 B.P., does reflect on its affinities to a number of fossil Capoid remains—Border Cave, Boskop, Matjes River, Cape Flats. However he does state that a number of authorities see in the skeleton both proto-Negroid as well as proto-Khoisanoid (Capoid) features.[65]

Summary African Evidence: It is clear that the anatomically modern Africans predicted by the mtDNA could only be the southern African Capoids, of about 90,000-65,000 B.P. Yet their modernity is in serious dispute. More difficult for an "Out-of-Africa" model is Coon's evidence and argument for a Capoid presence in North Africa, prior to the presumed invasion by Aterian, perhaps hybrid, Neanderthal Caucasoids toward the final Pleistocene, c.40,000 B.P. This evidence lies in the evident migration of the remnant Capoids south, first as Boskopoids, then as Khoisanoids. Their artistic trademark was left on the outer cave walls and other protected sites throughout the Sahara and south. More, the recent advance of Negroids from West Africa into the Khoisanoid lands, and not without conflict, continued the latter's pattern of retreat and dwarfing. It seems evident that these Capoid people did not egress Africa, at the least within the guidelines laid down by mtDNA theory, within the last 400a, and on an Archaic or Modern *sapiens* morphological grade.

What is additionally persuasive about their great presumed antiquity as a people of Africa is the additional mtDNA evidence reported earlier, and research by Linda Vigilant that Capoid women had the greatest mtDNA variance of any population group throughout the world, 0.59, as compared with a Japanese comparison group variance of 0.26.[66]

The source of the African mtDNA genetic diversity now appears to have been located in the modern Capoids, as well as the African Pygmy populations, related to, as described by Coon, the probable ancestral Negroid population. Cavalli-Sforza, *et al.*, describes both the Pygmies of Africa and the Bushmen as being the most distinctive and primeval nuclear genetic populations of humans. This relationship is additionally buttressed by the research of comparative linguistics. Now we can further understand the so-called mtDNA genetic bottleneck, which lumps together the non-African populations around the world, in the second great human division.[67]

The bottleneck refers to the close genetic ties of non-African populations around the world, as compared with most of the African mtDNA data. The presumption is that the source of this bottleneck derives from a population leaving Africa behind. Stoneking, one of the authors of the basic mtDNA "African Eve" theory, as noted earlier, has recently corrected his earlier data. He now feels that mtDNA data imply a modern-human origins, an mtDNA ancestor, at 63-356ka, or 63-416ka years ago![68]

Clearly there is a great measure of indefiniteness in these massively expanded temporal parameters from which to make any predictive estimates. Still there is no empirical evidence for an African source to the mtDNA bottleneck, that is, a relatively small population of Africans leaving within a genetically homogeneous time frame, subsequently becoming the displacing modern human population throughout the world.[69]

Europe and West Asia

Both Dawkins and de Duve pointed to the fatal problem in the "African Eve" mtDNA model. The computer program used to construct the original tree was flawed. Other trees rooted at different times and in different geographical locations can be constructed from the same data.[70]

Modern humans did not leave Africa for other parts of the world, given the empirical evidence available to us, during this recent time frame, c.350,000-150,000 B.P. The South African fossils are also questionably modern. The evidence of their ancient African origins may lie in Coon's ascription of KNMER 3733 in East Africa as a proto-Capoid erectine, c.1.6mya, Ternefine in Algeria, c.700,000 B.P., the Jebel Irhoud fossils of Morocco, c.150,000-100,000 B.P. and thence into South Africa. Neither they nor modern Negroids nor their presumed ancestors in Africa, *e.g.*, Kabwe and Bodo, are seen as candidates for an "Out-of-Africa-Eden" migration by the majority of paleoanthropologists and archaeologists now studying these matters. The latter Africans seem not to be morphologically related to any modern non-African fossils.[71]

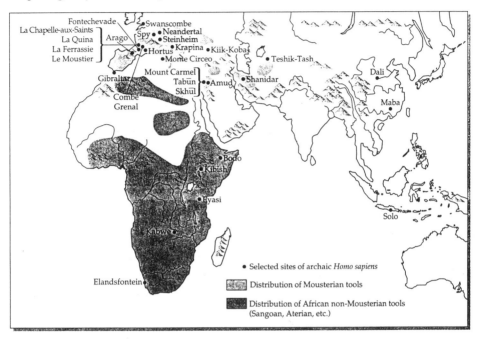

15.6 Map of Old World late-Pleistocene sites. Upper Paleolithic Cro-Magnon and other modern human fossil sites are not shown.

Yet, in truth, a purely multiregional theory of long and parallel evolutionary lines of humans, without Wolpoff's important and continuous addendum, of genetic interchange at the periphery of these geographical populations, also can not be sustained. That there is a rapid evolutionary, and thus taxonomic jump into *Homo sapiens sapiens*, seems most persuasive. It also appears to have been a discrete event in time.

The relationship of the Neanderthals to the Cro-Magnons in Europe and West Asia has been debated. Almost universally, now that the distinctive Neanderthal morphology has been explored in detail, it is seen as a unique ethnicity. Both large-brained humans, the Neanderthals still may be declared to be a different species from Cro-Magnon, as Svante Paabo has recently argued, analyzing the DNA of the original 1856 Neanderthal fossil.[72]

Certainly they were Caucasoids, as Coon details at great length, and others support implicitly by distinguishing the Neanderthals from any other contemporary population of humans.[73] It is universally accepted that the Cro-Magnons, Upper-Paleolithic ancestors of modern Europeans and West Asians, were on a fast track into modernity and domination. This pathway was not merely a morphological one, thus the great emphasis on the South African fossils' supposed modern behavior.

The big, gracile-brained Cro-Magnons independently created one of humanity's most breathtaking cultural environments, and with extremely rudimentary material resources, *i.e.*, stone tools, starting at c.45,000 B.P. These technological materials were no different from those that had been available for all humans, and used by them for almost two million years. The key to the cultural leap lies in the evolving internal mental processes that goaded them to take these self-same materials and transform them and other naturally occurring products—bone, ivory, clay, natural dyes—into their earliest Aurignacian civilizational settings.

Contra H. J. Deacon, to understand the course of human evolution, the pathway of progress must be understood, from the evolutionary standpoint, as not lying in the minimal satisfaction of "basic needs": *e.g.*, any animal's fulfillment of its gross adaptive requirements through the automatic invocation of genetically-rooted instinct. Rather, it lies in the progressive and spontaneous mental reconceptualization of needs, as reflected in differential human cultural behaviors. A basic example can be found in the evolving esthetic and practical design of *Homo*'s tools from the *Homo* erectine, Acheulian, some 1.5mya, to the present day.

The Harvard anthropologist, O. Bar-Yosef, has most fully appreciated both the theoretical and factual dilemmas posed by the collapse of the "Out-of-Africa-Eve" model for understanding the extrapolation of modern humans from the complex array of borderline and transitional forms, found throughout the world, and dating from about c.300,000 B.P.[74] A specialist in the Near East, and Western Asia, he has made detailed analyses of the tools and fossils found in this area.

Bar-Yosef sees a long fossil and tool history from Zuttiyeh, (inland Israel), possibly as old as Petralona (Greece), and Bodo (Hadar-Ethiopia), 400,000-200,000 B.P. Where the seemingly modern, proto-Cro Magnon fossils of Qafzeh 9 and Skhul 5 from about 95-85ka B.P. were increasingly touted as the first true modern humans, and as Klasies River Mouth and Border Cave were now theoretically abandoned as models of modern humans, Bar-Yosef held off. The reason was the associated and typically Mousterian, Neanderthal-like tools found along with the above Levant fossils. They were similar to the Aterian, North African tools, and to other African Middle Stone Age assemblages. These fossils of Skhul and Qafzeh are followed chronologically and in the same geography by a wide variety of Mousterian and typically Neanderthal fossils, Amud, Kebara, Tabun, from about 80,000 B.P. to c.47-46ka B.P.

Upper Paleolithic industries then, rapidly appear at Boker Tachtit, southern Levant (Negev), perhaps similar to the Chatelperronian industry.[75] The Upper Paleolithic (Cro-Magnon?) Ahmarian bladelet tradition can be dated from 38-35ka to 22-20ka B.P., with an intrusive Aurignacian-like industry in central Levant dated from 35-28ka B.P.[76] Bar-Yosef describes the behavioral changes which seem to be evident in the remnants of this temporally ancient, yet culturally modern way of life.

> The main behavioral differences between the Middle [Neanderthal] and Upper Paleolithic assemblages (as reflected in the latter) are as follows: production of bone and antler objects, use of worked marine shells (possibly for body decorations), very rare art objects,

frequent use of red ochre, systematic presence of a few grinding tools, stone encircled hearths and use of rocks for warmth banking. Observable differences between the two sets of sites include the appearance of clear occupational horizons in the Upper Paleolithic that indicate less frequent re-occupation of the same locale and therefore are interpreted as greater mobility, possibly within larger territories.[77]

Bar-Yosef sees the Middle East as a refuge during times of climatic danger, as it was then endowed with good resources. No fossils indicating migration from Africa into the Middle East exist. There seem to be no parallel African cultural hints except recently-discovered barbed and unbarbed bone points of a Middle Stone Age character, with which, however, no associated human fossils were found. These were found in Katanda, Zaire (Democratic Republic of the Congo).[78] Bar-Yosef perceives the Levant as an attractive refuge during times of diminishing resources or social stress in the North both for Neanderthals and Upper Paleolithic peoples, presumably from the Anatolian Plateau, the Balkans, the Taurus-Zagros ranges. P. E. Smith also hypothesizes that the Upper Paleolithic peoples might be derived from the Zagros Mountains, also home of the Neanderthal of Iraq and Iran.[79]

Bar-Yosef sees the peoples of the Caucasus area, during the recurrent advances and retreats of the glaciers, as having their own refuge in the lowlands adjoining the Caspian and Black Seas. His analysis of the interactions of the Neanderthals and the Cro-Magnons seeming to result in the sudden disappearance and permanent replacement of the former by the latter, invokes, rather than conscious genocide, the reproductive attrition of the Neanderthals. Bar-Yosef cites Zubrow for giving a persuasive demographic analysis of comparative reproductive patterns that could have led to the rapid extinction of the Neanderthals.[80]

To highlight his skepticism about the possible relationship between Africa and even the borderline hybrid modernity of Qafzeh and Skhul, no less the Upper Paleolithic Cro-Magnon, *Homo sapiens sapiens* morphology and cultural behavior, Bar-Yosef presents a chronologically more recent example. He notes the widely accepted sequences, such as the radiocarbon dating of J. D. Clark, and the more recent genetic analysis of Ammerman and Cavalli-Sforza, which indicated the spread of advanced Neolithic, agricultural, metal and pottery cultures.[81] These led to the first great demographic explosions that produced urban civilizational life—from the Levant, c.11-10ka B.P.—(Ammerman and Cavalli-Sforza give earliest priority to the Euphrates River Valley), north to Anatolia, then to the Balkans, thence East to Pakistan, all within 1500 radiocarbon years, 11-9.5ka B.P. These civilizational patterns took another 2,000 years to get to the Nile River Valley. The Nile River Valley is a one-week walk from the Jordan Valley—Jericho, one of the originating foci of the Neolithic.[82]

What Bar-Yosef is pointing to is his considered view that the geographical origins of anatomically modern humans, the Upper Paleolithic Cro-Magnons, will be found in the North, perhaps in a wide swath of geographies bounded by the Zagros Mountains of Iraq and Iran, the Caucasus, the Anatolian Plateau, and other points in the Eur-Asian borderlands. Coon, earlier agreed with this view.[83] He cited the Hotu Cave on the Caspian shore of Iran as producing from "the penultimate millennium of the Pleistocene, three Cro-Magnon skeletons."[84] This is one of the most easterly geographic recordings of Cro-Magnid habitation.

Beyond the facts of the origin of the Upper Paleolithic Cro-Magnons, and their culture, out of indigenous European-West Asian roots, is the recent research of Martin Richards, *et al.* He agrees that the transmission of the Neolithic patterns referred to above in the research of Cavalli-Sforza and Ammerman, as well as Bar-Yosef, was a basically indigenous phenomenon. Thus the skills, knowledge, organizational "know-how," were internally communicated, rapidly learned by the existing post-Cro-Magnid residents of Europe. The "Neolithic," therefore, as a cultural tradition, as with the Upper Paleolithic, was *not* disseminated by supposedly oncoming immigrants, for whom there is little or no genetic and archaeological evidence.[85]

Endnotes, Chapter 15

[1] Groves, C. P. 1989. "A Regional Approach to the Problem of the Origin of Modern Humans in Australasia," in *The Human Revolution — Behavioral and Biological Perspectives on the Origins of Modern Humans*, P. Mellars & C. Stringer, eds., Princeton, N.J.: Princeton Univ. Press, pp. 274-285; Swisher, C. C., and Anton S. 1996. "Ngandong, Solo River H. Erectus Sites Redated," *Science*, 12/13/96, 274:1870.

[2] Wolpoff, M., and Caspari, R. 1997. *Race and Human Evolution*, N.Y.: Simon and Schuster, pp. 24-25, 321; Wolpoff, M. 1997. "No 'Homo erectus' at Ngandong," in *Human Origins News*, 1/4/97, 6pp, esp. p. 4.

[3] Schwartz, Jeffrey. 1993. *What the Bones Tell Us*, N.Y.: Henry Holt, pp. 205-206.

[4] Clark, J. D. 1993. "African and Asian perspectives on the origin of modern humans," in *The Origin of Modern Humans and the Impact of Chronometric Dating*, M. J. Aitken, C. P. Stringer, and P. A. Mellars, eds., Princeton, N. J.: Princeton Univ. Press, pp. 148-178, esp. pp. 172-173; Roberts, R. G., *et al.* 1990. "Thermoluminescence Dating of a 50,000 Year Old Human Occupation Site in Northern Australia," *Nature*, 345:153-156

[5] Habgood, P. J. 1985. "The Origin of the Australian Aborigines: An Alternative Approach and View," in *Hominid Evolution: Past, Present, and Future*, P. V. Tobias, ed., N.Y.: Alan Liss, pp. 367-380, esp. p. 376.

[6] Habgood, 1985, in Tobias, ed., *op. cit.*, pp. 369; Thorne, A. G. 1980. "The Longest Link: Human Evolution in Southeast Asia," in *Indonesia: Australian Perspectives*, J. J. Fox, *et al.*, Canberra: Australian National University Press, p. 35.

[7] Brown, Peter (Univ. of New England, Australia). 1993. "Recent Human Evolution in East Asia and Australia," in Aitken *et al.*, eds., *op. cit.*, pp. 217-233.

[8] Brown, Peter, 1993, in Aitken *et al.*, eds., *op. cit.*, p. 218; Santa Luca, A. P. 1980. *The Ngandong Fossil Hominids: A Comparative Study of a Far Eastern Homo Erectus Group*, New Haven, CT: Yale Univ. Publications in Anthropology, no. 78.

[9] Stringer, C., and Andrews, P. 1988. "Genetic and Fossil Evidence for the Origin of Modern Humans," *Science*, 239:1263-1268.

[10] Smith, F. H. (Northern Illinois University). 1993. "Models and Realities in Modern Human Origins: The African Evidence," in Aitken *et al.,* eds., *op. cit.*, pp. 234-248.

[11] Smith, F. H., 1993, in Aitken *et al.*, eds., *op. cit.*, p. 239.

[12] Clark, J. D. 1993. "African and Asian perspectives on the origin of modern humans," in Aitken *et al.*, eds., *op. cit.*, p. 172.

[13] Stringer, C. 1990. "The Emergence of Modern Humans," *Scientific American*, 262:98-104; Rightmire, C. P. 1990. *The Evolution of Homo erectus*, Cambridge Univ. Press, pp. 34-52; Rukang, W., and Olsen, J. W., eds. 1985. *Paleoanthropology and Palaeolithic Archaeology in the People's Republic of China*, N.Y.: Academic Press, pp. 79-165.

[14] Klein, R. G. 1989. *The Human Career*, Chicago: Univ. of Chicago Press, p. 250.

[15] Wolpoff, M. H. 1989. "Multiregional Evolution: The Fossil Alternative to Eden," in *The Human Revolution — Behavioral and Biological Perspectives on the Origins of Modern Humans*, P. Mellars and C. Stringer, eds., *op. cit.*, pp. 62-108, esp. 83.

[16] Klein, 1989, *op. cit.*, pp. 247, 249.

[17] Wolpoff and Caspari, 1997, *op. cit.*, pp. 29, 298.

[18] Wolpoff and Caspari, 1997, *op. cit.*, p. 298.

[19] Wolpoff and Caspari, 1997, *op. cit.*, p. 29.

[20] Coon, C. S. 1962. *The Origin of Races*, N.Y.: Knopf, p. 464.

[21] Brown, Peter, 1993. "Recent Human Evolution in East Asia and Australia," in *The Origin of Modern Humans and the Impact of Chronometric Dating*, M. J. Aitken, C. B. Stringer, and P. A. Mellars, eds., *op. cit.*, pp. 217-233.

[22] Brown, Peter, 1993, in Aitken *et al.*, eds., *op. cit.*, p. 226.

[23] Brown, Peter, 1993, in Aitken *et al.*, eds., *op. cit.*, p. 226; Wu, X., and Zhang, Z. 1985. "Homo Sapiens Remains from the Late Paleolithic and Neolithic China," in *Paleoanthropology and Paleolithic Archaeology in the People's Republic of China*, R. Wu and J. W. Olsen, eds., London: Academic Press, pp. 107-133.

[24] Brown, Peter, 1993, in Aitken *et al.*, eds., *op. cit.*, p. 228, **Fig. 2**.

[25] Aiello, L. 1993. "The Fossil Evidence for Modern Human Origins in Africa: A Revised View," *American Anthropologist*, 95:1:73-96; see also Ch. 42, Timei, C. *et al.* 1994. "Antiquity of `Homo sapiens' in China," *Nature*, 368:55-56.

[26] Timei, C., *et al.* 1994. "Antiquity of Homo sapiens in China," *Nature*, 368:55-56.

[27] Boaz, N. T. 1995. "Calibration and Extension of the Record of Plio-Pleistocene Hominidae," in *Biological Anthropology: The State of the Science*, N. T. Boaz and L. D. Wolfe, eds., Bend, Oregon: International Institute for Human Evolutionary Research, Central Oregon University Center, p. 37.

[28] Coon, C. S. 1982. *Racial Adaptations*, Chicago: Nelson-Hall; Coon, C. S., and Hunt, E. E., Jr. 1965. *The Living Races of Man*, N.Y.: Knopf; Coon, C. S. 1962. *The Origin of Races, op. cit.*

[29] Coon, 1982, *op. cit.*, p. 131.

[30] Coon, 1982, *op. cit.*, p. 153; Coon, 1962, *op. cit.*, p. 592.

[31] Hublin, J.-J. 1993. "Recent Human Evolution in Northwestern Africa," in Aitken *et al.*, eds., *op. cit.*, pp. 118-131.

[32] Mellars, P. A., Aitkin, M. J., Stringer, C. P. 1993. "Outlining the Problem," in Aitken *et al.*, eds., *op. cit.*, p. 8, fig. 1.

[33] Hublin, 1993, in Aitken *et al.*, eds., *op. cit.*, p. 118.

[34] Hublin, 1993, in Aitken *et al.*, eds., *op. cit.*, p. 127; also, personal communication 12/2/1997.

[35] Hublin, 1993, in Aitken *et al.*, eds., *op. cit.*, pp. 127-128.

[36] Hublin, 1993, in Aitken *et al.*, eds., *op. cit.*, p. 128.

[37] Smith, F. H., 1993, in Aitken *et al.*, eds., *op. cit.*, pp. 234-248.

[38] Smith, F. H., 1993, in Aitken *et al.*, eds., *op. cit.*, p. 239.

[39] Smith, F. H., 1993, in Aitken *et al.*, eds., *op. cit.*, p. 236; Wolpoff and Caspari, 1997, *op. cit.*, p. 353; Stringer, C. 1994. "Out of Africa — A Personal History," in *Origins of Anatomically Modern Humans*, M. H. Nitecki and D. V. Nitecki, eds., N.Y.: Plenum pp. 149-172.

[40] Schwartz, 1993, *op. cit.*, p. 203.

[41] Klein, 1989, *op. cit.*, pp. 229-233.

[42] Klein, 1989, *op. cit.*, pp. 228-229.

[43] Coon, 1982, *op. cit.*, pp. 129-131.

[44] Klein, 1989, *op. cit.*, p. 250.

[45] Coon, 1962, *op. cit.*, pp. 628-641.

[46] Deacon, H. J. 1993. "Southern Africa and Modern Human Origins," in Aitken *et al,*. eds., *op. cit.*, pp. 104-117; Deacon, H. J. 1989. "Late Pleistocene Palaeoecology and Archaeology in the Southern Cape, South Africa," in Mellars and Stringer, eds., *op. cit.*, pp. 547-564.

[47] Deacon, 1993, in Aitken *et al.*, eds., *op. cit.*, p. 114; Wolpoff, and Caspari, 1997, *op. cit.*, pp. 267-268.

[48] Deacon, 1993, in Aitken *et al.,* eds., *op. cit.*, p. 114; Nurse, G. T., *et al.* 1985. *The Peoples of Southern Africa and their Affinities*, Oxford: Clarendon Press; Vigilant, L., *et al.* 1989. Mitochondrial DNA Sequences in Single Hairs from a Southern African Population," *Proc. Nation. Acad. of Sciences*, 86:9350-9354.

[49] Deacon, 1993, in Aitken *et al.*, eds., *op. cit.*, pp. 107-109; Wolpoff and Caspari, 1997, *op. cit.*, pp. 267-268.

[50] Deacon, 1989, in Mellars and Stringer, eds., *op. cit.*, p. 561.

[51] Klein, 1989, *op. cit.*, pp. 383-385; White, T. D. 1987. "Cannibals at Klasies?" *Sagittarius*, 2:1:6-9; Klein, R. G. 1992. "The archaeology of Modern Human Origins," *Evolut. Anthr.*, 1:5-14; Wolpoff and Caspari, 1997, *op. cit.*, pp. 267-268.

[52] Klein, R. G. 1989. "Perspectives on Modern Human Origins in Southern Africa," in Mellars and Stringer, eds., *op. cit.*, pp. 529-546, esp. p. 543; Binford, L. R. 1984. *Faunal Remains from Klasies River Mouth*, Orlando: Academic Press; Churchill, S. E., *et al.* 1996. "Morphological Affinities of the Proximal Ulna from Klasies River Main Site: Archaic or Modern?" *Jrnl. of Human Evolution*, 31:3:213-237.

[53] Deacon, 1993, in Aitken *et al.*, eds., *op. cit.*, p. 113.

[54] Smith, F. H., 1993, in Aitken *et al.*, eds., *op. cit.*, pp. 234-248, esp. p. 239; Churchill *et al.* 1996, *op. cit.*, *Jrnl. of Human Evolution*, 31:3:213-237. See also: Thackery, J. F., and Kieser, J. A. 1993. "Variability in shape of dental arcade of *Homo sapiens* in Late Pleistocene and modern samples from southern Africa," *Paleontologia africana*, in *The Runaway Brain*, C. Wills, N.Y.: Basic Books, p. 302. Thackery sees significant primitivisms in the Late Pleistocene southern African examples, Klasies River Mouth, Border Cave, etc.

[55] Smith, F. H., 1993, in Aitken *et al.*, eds., *op. cit.*, p. 240.

[56] Smith, F. H., 1993, in Aitken *et al.*, eds., *op. cit.*, pp. 241-244.

[57] Smith, F. H., 1993, in Aitken *et al.*, eds., *op. cit.*, pp. 244-245; Rightmire, C. P. 1978. "Human Skeletal Remains from the Southern Cape Province and Their Bearing on the Stone Age Prehistory of South Africa," *Quaternary Research*, 9:219-230.

[58] Stringer, C. 1989. "The Origin of Early Modern Humans: A Comparison of the European and non-European Evidence," in Mellars and Stringer, eds., *op. cit.*, pp. 231-244.

[59] Stringer, 1989, in Mellars and C. Stringer, eds., *op. cit.*, p. 242.

[60] Also see, Frayer, D. W., *et al.* 1993. "The Fossil Evidence for Modern Human Origins," *American Anthropologist*, 95:1:14-50.

[61] Stringer, C. B. 1993. "Reconstructing Recent Human Evolution," in Aitken *et al.*, eds., *op. cit.*, pp. 179-195, esp. p. 194; Stringer, C., and McKie, R. 1996. *African Exodus: the Origins of Modern Humanity*, London: Jonathan Cape.

[62] Coon, 1962, *op. cit.*, pp. 649-657; Coon, 1982, *op. cit.*, pp. 149, 154.

[63] Wolpoff and Caspari, 1997, *op. cit.*, pp. 267-268.

[64] Hughes, A. 1990. "The Tuinplaas Human Skeleton from the Springbok Flats, Transvaal," in *From Apes to Angels, Essays in Honor of Philip Tobias*, G. H. Sperber, ed., N.Y.: Wiley-Liss, pp. 197-214.

[65] Hughes, 1990, in Sperber, ed., *op. cit.*, pp. 211-212.

[66] Kingdom J. 1993. *Self-Made Man*, N.Y.: John Wiley, p. 258; Vigilant, L., Stoneking, M., Wilson, A., Harpenden, H., and Hawkes, K. 1991. "African Populations and the Evolution of Mitochondrial DNA," *Science*, 253:1503-1507.

[67] Cavalli-Sforza, L. L., *et al.* 1988. "Reconstruction of Human Evolution: Bringing Together Genetic, Archaeological and Linguistic Data," *Proc. National Acad. of Science*, Aug. 1988, 85:6002-6006, esp. 6002; Mountain, J. L. (Genetics, Stanford), Lin, A. A. (Genetics, Stanford), Bowcock, A. M. (Pediatrics, Univ. of Texas Med. Ctr., Dallas), Cavalli-Sforza, L. L. (Genetics-Stanford). 1993. "Evolution of Modern Humans: Evidence From Nuclear DNA Polymorphisms," in Aitken *et al.*, eds., *op. cit.*, pp. 60-83; Cavalli-Sforza, L. L., *et al.* 1993. *History and Geography of Human Genes*, Princeton, N.J.: Princeton Univ. Press.

[68] Vigilant *et al.,* 1991, *op. cit., Science,* 253:1503-1507; Wilson, A. C., and Cann, R. L. 1992. "The Recent African Genesis of Humans," *Scientific American,* April, 266:4, 22-27.

[69] Paabo, Svante. 1995. "The Y Chromosome and the Origin of All of Us (Men)," *Science,* May 26, 1995, 268:1141-42.

[70] Dawkins, R. 1995. *River Out of Eden ,* N.Y.: Basic Books, pp. 51-54; de Duve, Christian. 1995. *Vital Dust.* N.Y.: Basic Books, pp. 232-234.

[71] Frayer, D. W., *et al.* 1994. "Getting It Straight," *American Anthropologist,* 96:2:424-438.

[72] Wade, N. 1997. "Neanderthal DNA Sheds New Light On Human Origins," *The New York Times,* 7/11/97. Wade cites the work of S. Paabo, *et al.,* July 11, 1997, issue of *Cell;* see also Wilford, J. N. 1999. "Discovery Suggests Man Is a Bit Neanderthal," *The New York Times,* 25 Apr., 1, 19; Trinkaus, E., and Zilhao, J. *Proceedings of the National Academy of Sciences,* forthcoming, 1999-2000.

[73] Tattersall, I. 1995. *The Last Neanderthal,* N.Y.: Macmillan, Illustration #103, p. 149.

[74] Bar-Yosef, O. 1993. "The Role of Western Asia in Modern Human Origins," in Aitken *et al.,* eds., *op. cit..* Press, pp. 132-147.

[75] Bar-Yosef, 1993, in Aitken *et al.,* eds., *op. cit.,* p. 141.

[76] Phillips, James. 1994. "Upper Paleolithic Chronology in the Levant and Nile," in *Late Quaternary Chronology and Paleoclimates of the Eastern Mediterranean,* O. Bar-Yosef, and R. S. Kra, eds., Tucson, AZ: Radiocarbon, University of Arizona, pp. 169-176.

[77] Bar-Yosef, 1993, in Aitken *et al.,* eds., *op. cit.,* p. 141.

[78] Brooks, A., and Yellen J. (personal communication), Bar-Yosef, 1993, in Aitken *et al.,* eds., *op. cit.,* p. 143.

[79] Smith, P. E. L. 1986. *Paleolithic Archaeology in Iran,* Philadelphia: Univ. Museum, Univ. of Penn.

[80] Zubrow, E. 1989. "The Demographic Modeling of Neanderthal Extinction," in Mellars, and Stringer, eds., *op. cit.,* pp. 212-231; Bar-Yosef, 1993, in Aitken *et al.,* eds., *op. cit.,* pp. 143-144.

[81] Clark, J. D. 1965. "Radiocarbon Dating and the Expansion of Farming Culture from the Near East over Europe," *Proceedings of the Prehistoric Society,* 31:57-73; Ammerman, A. J., and Cavalli-Sforza, L. L. 1994. *The Neolithic Transition and the Genetics of Populations in Europe,* Princeton, N.J.: Princeton Univ. Press, pp. 20-30; Table 2.1, figs. 2.3, 2.4, 4.5.

[82] Bar-Yosef, 1993, in Aitken *et al.,* eds., *op. cit.,* pp. 143-144.

[83] Coon, 1962, *op. cit.,* p. 587.

[84] Angel, J. A. 1952. "The Human Skeletal Remains from Hotu Cave, Iran," *Proceed. Am. Phil. Soc.,* 96:3:258-269.

[85] Richards, M. *et al.* 1996. "Paleolithic and Neolithic Lineages in the European Mitochondrial Gene Pool," *Am. Jrnl. Hum. Genetics,* July, 59:185-203.

16

Cro-Magnon

Roots of Technology

Definition Difficulties

Debate never existed over the fact that the Cro-Magnons of West Asia and Europe were the first truly modern peoples, the indirect ancestors of all modern peoples throughout the world, and clearly the immediate precursors to historical Caucasoids of those regions. But why the rush to redefine such disparate fossils as the South African Klasies River, Border Cave peoples, the Omo, Bodo, Kabwe, and other African and non-African fossils as, at the least, Archaic *Homo sapiens*, and then the South African and Omo Kibbish fossils as the "Out-of-Africa Eve," presumptive direct ancestor of the Cro-Magnons?

The reason, of course, is the fact that mtDNA theory seemed to point to a modern human group leaving Africa and cleanly displacing all other marginal human groups around the world. Taxonomy was thus stretched to the breaking point, as we have described earlier. It did not matter that the seeming "Out-of-Africa" fossil transitionals, Qafzeh and Skhul, now residing in the Levant, were associated with Mousterian (Neanderthal/Eur-Asian) cultural artifacts, or that the Klasies River fossils were Capoid in ethnicity and were hardly modern in their cultural artifacts, and also suspect in their supposedly "modern morphology." Finally, they lived "way down South" in Africa.

Indeed, both Trinkaus and Wolpoff describe the hardly clear stratigraphic conditions under which the Omo (Ethiopia) fossils were discovered. This in turn raises questions as to their age. Such chaos of discovery leaves much room for argument.[1]

Thus little noncontroversial empirical evidence has developed to argue for a recent "Out of Africa" scenario, except Christopher Stringer's advocacy of highly interpretable tibia-femur correlation ratios between the Nariokotome-West Turkana boy, (1.6mya, archaic, 6 vertebrae, *H. erectus*), modern East Africans, and the Cro-Magnons, to

Stringer all quite similar. To make a strict connection between a fossil whose evolutionary placement is in doubt, if it ever was on a direct line to modern humans, from 1.6 mya, and then to the Cro-Magnons and modern East African humans, the latter partial northerners, given their mixed Negroid and Caucasoid heritage, (and very different bodily ratios from modern West Africans) is stretching evolutionary causality to the breaking point.

Thus it was that a number of now ephemeral taxonomic recastings of fossil humans into "modernity" were arrived at. Today, both the theory and the concretia argue strongly against a recent, 500-150ka B.P., "Out-of-Africa" migration of a modern people.

Human physical structures including skin coloration, given slowly changing population movements under prehistorical conditions, tend to change slowly. The example of the historic Amero-Indian populations of North and South America is pertinent. Only small differences in skin coloration exist presently, surprising given the 11,000-13,000 years the respective populations have been living in tropical *versus* their earlier Asian north temperate zones.

Over the past 20 years, two great controversies concerning the evolution of humans have reshaped our perceptions: 1) the splitting of our line from a presumed ancestral chimpanzee, at a very late evolutionary point, 5my B.P.; 2) the so-called "Out-of-Africa-Eve" thesis, the movement of some anatomically modern humans out of Africa, and then throughout the world. In the latter case, a displacement has occurred without any miscegenation between the incoming modern humans and the *in situ* primitives, again at a very recent evolutionary point, after c.300,000 B.P. Both theories were based on abstract laboratory models of supposedly invariant molecular changes.

As we have attempted to show in earlier chapters, the theoretical models have developed internal antinomies, while at the same time failing either to predict future discoveries or to clarify existing empirical evidence. The persuasiveness of the theoretical argument in the face of recalcitrant empirical evidence, the accompanying human "will to believe," all the while reshaping well-established evidential structures, is reminiscent of the seduction of intellectuals with abstract ideological models in politics and social thought. The above theoretical models emanate from the biochemical disciplines, where the variables are fewer, the invariants seemingly well established, the opportunities for interpretive error less likely. The bonus is that the messages embedded in the above theoretical models are both emotionally and morally assuaging.

This is not to say that all molecular and genetic models must remain tainted. But they should always be treated with a measure of sober skepticism, especially when they depart from well-established webs of factual evidence and theory. As we have pointed out, and will further elaborate on, the work of Cavalli-Sforza's group on blood protein relationships, however, does mesh with both linguistic and paleontological evidence. In the next chapter we will suggest that the mysterious genetic bottleneck that is implied in the relative genetic consanguinity of the non-African populations with each other, does lend itself to an alternative non-African Eve explanation of the origin and dispersion of these genes into the world of modern humans.

The Cro-Magnons

They seem to have arrived in Western Europe from somewhere west of the Urals. Morphologically, they represented a revolution in the form of man. These were the Cro-Magnons. They were somewhat taller than most Neanderthals and seemingly of other transitional peoples, males from 5'8" to 5'11", naturally rugged people given their Ice Age life style and necessary survival skills. (The Amud Neanderthal male, at close to 6ft. tall, and at the 40,000 B.P. terminal Mousterian level, in Israel, is exceptional.)[2] Their general physical structure, as compared with earlier, as well as contemporary humans living throughout the world, was clearly paedomorphic, child-like, in its relative delicacy. Not merely the post-cranial bones, legs and arms, but the skull itself, and the brain within were crucially different.

Skull bone thicknesses in earlier late-Pleistocene humans, including the Neanderthals, could run between 10-13mm.[3] The Cro-Magnons' skull thicknesses were usually less than the 4-5mm. of the average modern human.

Richard Klein has carefully described the Cro-Magnon morphology. An endocranial capacity greater than 1350 cm^3; frontal bone (forehead) relatively vertical; vault (brain case) relatively high, more or less parallel-sided, usually with some outward bulging (bossing) in the parietal regions; occipital contour, (back of skull), relatively rounded and lacking a prominent transverse torus (bony bulge). Brow ridge development is generally greater in males than in females and variable among populations, rarely forming a continuous bar (supra-orbital torus) as in more primitive Neanderthals and other primitive human morphologies (across the top of the orbits). Instead it consisted of two parts—a variably bulging lateral (superciliary) arch at the outer corner of each orbit, separated by a supra-orbital notch or groove from a supra-orbital (elongated) swelling along the upper inner margin (these swellings meet in a "V" between the orbits to form the so-called supraorbital trigone).

The Cro-Magnon face was relatively flat and tucked in beneath the anterior portion of the braincase, exhibited a distinct hollowing of the bone (canine fossa) below each orbit, between the nasal cavity and the cheekbone (zygomatic arch). The mandible, jaw, was variably robust, partly in keeping with significant interpopulation variation in tooth size, but almost always with a distinct chin; Rarely was there a gap, (Neanderthal-like retromolar space), between the third molar and the ascending ramus when viewed from the side, reflecting the retraction of the face under the skull.[4] Klein concludes this description with a general summary: There is "substantial variability in the expression of many features...but never sufficient to incorporate earlier forms of people."[5] (See Illustration 13.3.)

Eur-Asian Ancestors

Now that the origin of the Cro-Magnons is freed from its subservience to a non-empirical "recent and modern Out-of-Africa" model, Eur-Asia especially Europe, comes to the fore. We can focus on the evidence for early human habitation from the conjectured time of the original African hegira, that vast, enigmatic 2-1mya time frame.

The earliest site in which hominid fossils have been found thus far in Europe proper is located at the 800,000-780,000 B.P. TD6 horizon in the Atapuerca hills of northern

Spain near the city of Burgos. The fossil remains of a 10-11-year-old boy—cranium, lower jaw and teeth—plus fragments of five other individuals, have been dated back to 800,000 B.P.[6]

Earlier dated human fossils outside of Africa have been found, as noted earlier— Dminasi, in Asiatic Georgia, at about 2- 1.6mya; at Gongwangling (Lantian), and Long-gupo, 1.9-1.7mya, in China; and at Mojokerto (Perning-Java), Sangiran (Java), 1.8-1.65mya; and at Ubeidiya, Israel, c.1mya.

Also, at Boxgrove in England, 500,000 B.P., a robust tibia—probably Neander-thal—was discovered, the oldest fossil found in England since the discredited Piltdown forgery.[7] A recent report also discusses the implied existence of a Siberian Stone Age people, at 300,000 B.P. The primitive lithic materials were discovered at the Lena River, 75 miles south of Yakutsk, and 300 miles south of the Arctic Circle, by M. W. Waters, of Texas A. & M. University, S. L. Foreman, J. M. Pierson of the University of Illinois, Chicago. The site materials, "Diring Yuriakh," which consisted of crude stone tools plus flakes, were subject to thermoluminiscence dating technique. Dr. Rob Bonnischsen of Oregon State University, Corvallis, reportedly expressed "zero doubts" about the reli-ability of dating. Waters *et al.* speculated that persons moved into the Lena River area during a warm period.[8]

In the same general chronology, in Germany, three wooden spruce spears, 6 feet in length, two inches maximum diameter, were recently discovered by Dr. Hartmut Thieme, archaeologist of the Hanover-based "Institute for Historic Site Preservation" They were found in a Schoningen open-cast brown coal mine, which dates to Reinsdorf Interglacial 400,000-380,000 B.P. Comparable spear points, found in an elephant skeleton at Lehrin-gen, Germany, in 1948, had been dated to 125,000-115,000 B.P. In 1911 at Clacton, England, a tip of what might have been a spear found in deposits as old as Schoningen, have now been dated to 380,000 B.P. The center of gravity of the Schoningen spears is one-third the distance from the point. The conclusion is that they were designed to be thrown. The spears were found with stone tools and the butchered remains of 10 horses. Robin Dennell, in *Nature* stated that *H. heidelbergensis* made the spears, possibly Ar-chaic *Homo sapiens*.[9]

Also, within this general time frame, it is reported that J. L. Monnier of the Univer-sity of Rennes, discovered at Menez-Dregan on the southern coast of Brittany, a "fire-place" which, dated through ESR (electron spin resonance) techniques, could be as old as 465,000 B.P. There is natural skepticism as to whether such evidence, as paleoanthro-pologist Clive Gamble is purported to have commented, is decisive in judging whether it represents conscious fire making, else a random natural event. One would also need both quartz pebbles and charcoal to prove that an intentional human action was involved.[10]

It should be noted that there are numerous sites in Europe at long-removed time frames, 1my-700ka B.P., which as above, reveal the seeming detritus of human life. H. de Lumley's 1975 report on Le Vallonnet Cave near Nice, as well as Bonifay's 1976 re-port on the Soleihac open-air lake site in the French Massif Centrale are relevant. Both lie close to the 1mya border, the latter possibly inferring, in the 20-meter-long line of basalt blocs, a structural entity. Other sites in Isernia La Pineta (Central Italy); Prezletice (Czech Republic); Kaerlich (west-central Germany), could be slightly younger, 900,000-

730,000 B.P.[11] Clearly, there were active human cultures throughout Europe at a very early stage of the original post-African Diaspora.

The European fossil humans, in the time frame that broadly encompasses 400,000-250,000 B.P. and tentatively classified as *H. heidelbergensis,* are represented by the Steinheim (Germany), Swanscombe (England), Mauer (Germany), Petralona (Greece), Vertessolos (Hungary), and Arago (France), specimens. Ian Tattersall, regards Steinheim and Swanscombe as differing from the *H. heidelbergensis* clade, within which he also places the Kabwe (Broken Hill-Zambia) specimen. The former are included in *H. steinheimensis.*[12] The above are presumed to be part of the four independent species evolving during this period, including the East Asiatic *Sinanthropus* and the Southeast Asian post-Pithecanthropines, and possibly the remaining African types which could include the Omo Kibbish fossils. Jeffrey Schwartz places the Steinheim/Swanscombe fossils in a direct line toward the Neanderthals, while Coon earlier had placed them on the road toward Cro-Magnon. Coon saw Mauer, Petralona, and Vertessollos as the Neanderthal precursors.[13]

The most recent analysis, of the Atapuerca fossils, highly controversial because of their great age, especially since the most complete of the fossil material is that of a 10-11-year-old boy, is seen by Bermudez, the senior discoverer, as at 800,000 B.P. This would be the branching point of the two lines, Neanderthal and Cro-Magnon. In one fell swoop, Bermudez *et al.* separate themselves from all intellectual obligations to the "recent and modern "Out-of-Africa-Eve" scenario, arguing for the European origins of modern *Homo sapiens sapiens.*[14]

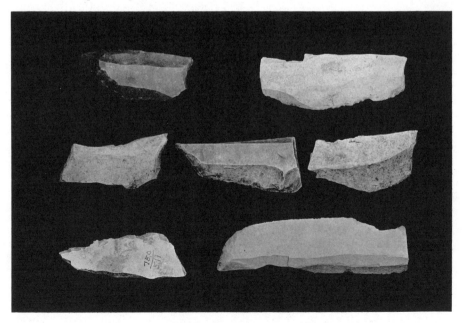

16.1 Backed knives and scrapers,Neanderthal-Mousterian, c.35-55ka B.P.

The phylogenetic relationship between the Neanderthals and the Cro-Magnons has been discussed in earlier chapters. Clearly, the evidence today points to a branching origin in the northern latitudes, and at an early stage in their respective wanderings. The splitting up must have occurred shortly after their arrival from Africa in the hypothesized 2-1mya Diaspora. Both, though evolving as members of the Eur-Asian Caucasoid clade, are highly specialized forms, perhaps even species (in the flexible hominid taxonomic sense), since they were probably interfertile.[15]

Technology's Message

Tools, consciously fabricated to create the means for next-stage survival behaviors, characterize one of the important distinctions that separate humans and animals. The conscious, freely-chosen use of various found and then shaped materials, further removed in terms of time and space, practical or esthetic behaviors, probably can be used as a taxonomic demarcation factor between *Homo* and *Australopithecus*.

The Cro-Magnons made and used tools. Their other products, art, chronometric sequencing etc., add cognitive richness and identifiability to their cultural uniqueness. It is their tools, however, fabricated for both practical as well as esthetic values, that allow for the most specific comparisons with their predecessors and contemporaries.

16..2 (A-B): Horses, Magdalenian, c.15,000 B.P. Richard Leakey, following Edouard Piette and Paul Bahn, is persuaded that A was harnessed and domesticated. The wild horse, **B**, neighing, is an esthetic evocation that, as with A, reveals the fascination of modern humans with this noble animal.

When we think of tools, we think of the practicality of the hunt. Much, however, about of the Cro-Magnons' practical life has and always will elude our awareness and consciousness. For example, do we consider the possibility that domestication of animals may have taken place as early as 20,000 B.P.? In the literature, one finds references to a shift at the end of the Pleistocene, during a period of presumed great cold, when the bones of reindeer indicate prominence in the Cro-Magnon diet. These reindeer may have been herded and preserved as objects of food, clothing, decoration, in a conscious and wholly modern manner.

Similarly, Richard Leakey has drawn attention to the research of Edouard Piette, in the early 20th century, and Paul Bahn and Henri Martin, more recently, who argue, on the basis of a number carvings and paintings in France from this period, that horses may have been domesticated as often as they were hunted. These artistic horse evocations reveal the possible existence of harnesses on these animals. An examination of horse teeth in the Musée Antiq. Nat. in St. Germain-en-Laye, near Paris, reveal numerous examples of "crib biting," a condition often seen in modern stabled and tethered horses. Pets, decoys, for riding, it is hard to know. But without revealing tools to tell us of their life, we must integrate our knowledge from both the art, as well as the paleontological remains.[16]

- 2 -
Aurignacian: First Civilization

Sudden Appearance

This is a clearly demarcated technological and cultural event. The factual reality of the break in the hominid tradition, of perhaps 5my, if we include the Australopithecines, and exclude the as yet undiscovered proto-hominid precursors of both genera, *Homo* and *Australopithecus*, is given by three decisive empirical elements.

1. The cultural remains, which show, not merely a typological uniqueness, but a stratigraphic one as well. This element of discontinuity shows itself even when earlier groups have inhabited the same shelters, caves, river sites.

2. The fossils reveal a wholly new and revolutionary morphology that is clearly linked to the new set of cultural remains.

3. New methods of chronometric dating seem to confirm the traditional geological determinants of time and event. These show a pattern of movement and deposition, which when linked geometrically to a hypothesized locus reveal a movement outward, and into worldwide occupation and dominance.

Chronology.

Bar-Yosef argues that at Kebara cave at Mt. Carmel in northern Israel, beginnings of the Upper-Paleolithic (Aurignacian) took place c.47,000-45,000 B.P. Temnata Cave in Bulgaria indicate similar TL (thermoluminescence) dates (S. Kozlowski personal communication to Bar-Yosef). Bar-Yosef, with regard to the relationship of Skhul and Qafzeh, 95,000-85,000 B.P., fossils associated with Neanderthal-type tools, to the later Cro-Magnons, *Homo sapiens sapiens*, of Europe: "While some of us view the need for an additional mutation to reach the cultural level of Upper Paleolithic technological and cultural achievements, others simply regard the shift as gradual or even rapid, but occurring within the same world population."[17]

James Phillips states that traditional Levallois techniques were used in the Nile Valley until virtually the end of the Pleistocene, c.10,000 B.P. No Upper-Paleolithic sites have been recovered in the eastern or western deserts of Egypt or Sudan—a possible result of desertification.[18] In the Negev, at Boker Tachtit, the shift from late Mousterian to Upper Paleolithic—Ahmarian-Aurignacian—took place from c.48,000-40,000 B.P. The Ahmarian site, seemingly a set of transitional camps, included backed blades, bladelets, perforators, truncators, burins, single-platform end scrapers, blade cores, cresting and core tablets. Punch technique of indirect percussion was used extensively.[19] Ahmarian culture may have existed for only 12,000 years, from 40,000-28,000 B.P. Other sites: Ein Eqev East in Negev and two sites in Jordan dated from c.20,000-16,000 B.P. are not Ahmarian but rather "... represent evolved groups with different [cultural] adaptation patterns from those typically Ahmarian."[20]

Phillips states that the Levantine Aurignacian reaches Ksar 'Akil, Lebanon, c.32,000 B.P., replaces Ahmarian in Negev, Ein Avdat, at about c.26,000 B.P. Aurignacian culture: rock-shelter habitations, retouched thick irregular blades, burins, steep end scrapers. Also, bone tools, split-based points—flakes over blades, direct percussion in tool reduction. Some possible Upper Paleolithic technology sites, dated to between 40,000-20,000 B.P., have been found in the Nile Valley. The Upper Paleolithic in the Southern Levant is here seen as a direct descendant of the Middle Paleolithic Mousterian. The Upper-Paleolithic peoples settled in open-air camps near ponds, springs, lakes. In the northern Levant forested areas, Aurignacian remains are found more often in caves.

The Upper Paleolithic thus occurred much later in the Nile Valley. The evidence consists of sparse remains with no seeming antecedents.[21] In the apparent Upper-Paleolithic sites in the Nile Valley Levallois techniques were retained after 30,000 B.P. This unique evidence seems to argue that the Nile Valley did not share a "cultural identity" with the Levant, again, "...attesting to a lack of population movement between Africa and Southwestern Asia."[22]

Olga Soffer reports on a variety of studies in Russia, those in the Dnestr Valley of Moldova having yielded the richest evidence of Middle Paleolithic, Mousterian, then Upper Paleolithic, Aurignacian habitation. She argues that in the Middle Paleolithic, humans did not construct settlements out of mammoth bones. In Moldova, the Mousterians used such bones as wind breaks. However in Upper Paleolithic Dnestr sites "...postmoulds suggest outlines of lightweight structures with one or two hearths."[23] In European Russia, the Upper Paleolithic involved qualitative changes in perception of and utilization of nature: changes in food management strategies and thus in settlement patterns, the use and reuse of settlements sites, presumably as groups moved to mesh with the available food supplies: "....[T]he change in food management strategies from opportunistic encounter to 'mapping on' foraging, permitted the successful colonization and continuous occupation of the Russian plain proper...[which] occurred irreversibly only in the Upper Paleolithic."[24] Soffer's dating of these Upper Paleolithic semi-permanent habitations: in the Dnestr, 36,000-31,000 B.P.; Kostenki-Borscevo (Don region), 36,000-32,000 B.P. Both areas had earlier, apparently Mousterian-Neanderthal occupation. At Betovo, on the Russian plain, River Don, site of Middle Paleolithic technology, the Neanderthals were contemporary with Upper Paleolithic Cro-Magnon occupation in same general region—36,000 B.P.[25]

Goebel and Aksenov report on their discoveries at Makerovo-4, a bluff overlooking the Lena River, at about longitude 107 degrees east, in Siberia, (north of Ulan Bator, Mongolia, and Chongking, China): "Thousands of artifacts, two possible hearths, a dense accumulation of bones from Wooly Rhinoceros, red deer and roe deer. Many reworked stone blades, knives, scrapers similar to the Upper Paleolithic Middle East, 45,000 years ago."

"Varvarina Gora," another site contains similar materials, bone and ivory tools and a flat disk-shaped stone that might have formed a pendant, roughly dated to 34,000 B.P. Both sites are in the Lena River area of Southeast Siberia, near Lake Baikal. More recent accelerator carbon dating 14C leads to a Makarova-4 date of earlier than 39,000 B.P.; for Varvarina Gora, earlier than 35,000 B.P.[26] It should be noted that no signs of Neanderthal people east of Uzbekistan and Afganhistan have ever been reported.

The earliest dates for the appearance of the technology of Cro-Magnon, Upper Paleolithic culture seems to derive from the Levant, c.45,000 B.P.; Bulgaria-Eastern Europe, c.45,000 B.P.; Moldova-European Russia, c. 40,000-35,000 B.P; Southeastern Siberia, c.40,000-35,000 B.P. Somewhat later, between c.35,000-33,000 B.P, the full suite of Western European Cro-Magnon culture and fossil skeletal material begins to appear.[27] Along with this movement into western Europe, especially in France, is the explosive exemplification of the civilizational palette of the Aurignacian.[28]

The points of possible early contact and mutual cultural dissemination among resident populations at this stage of migration should be mentioned. The time frame during which contacts at the social group level were presumably being made, over several thousands of years, if not preceded by tens of thousands of years of more random encounters and possible exchanges, may have produced intermediate cultural forms. The Chatelperronian and Szeletian, in Europe, the early Amudian, then, Emihran, Ahmarian and cognate forms in the Levant, the Aterian in North Africa, all seem to overlap the time frame for the appearance of the continents-spanning Aurignacian culture. These may reflect the acculturation of pre-existing or transitional peoples, but also the reality of possible mixed racial-ethnic types gradually being incorporated into a more universal scheme of the human form.

Material Culture

Paul Mellars describes the transition to the full Aurignacian from less-evolved cultures, both contemporary and more ancient:

1. A general shift was made from flake production to blades, except where poor quality of the natural raw materials made such production inefficient. Blades were fabricated under certain material and manufacturing conditions by non-Upper Paleolithic peoples as part of the Middle Paleolithic technological evolution.[29] As Campbell and Loy note with regard to the Howieson's Poort industries, mentioned earlier in connection with the Klasies River Mouth culture, blades were sandwiched between heavy layers, in this case of Mousterian deposits, also at Tabun in Israel, and at 90,000 B.P.[30]

2. End scrapers and burins were being produced, heretofore not in evidence in Middle Paleolithic (Neanderthal) cultural debris.

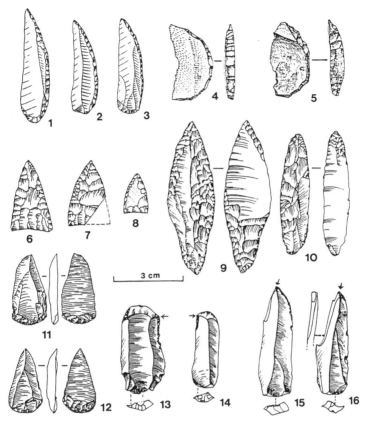

16.3 Some "type fossils" of the earliest stages of the Upper Paleolithic in Europe and West Asia: 1-3 Chatelperron points (France); 4-5 Uluzzian crescents (Italy); 6-8 hollow-based Streletskaya points (south Russia); 9-10 Jerzmanovice points (Poland/Russia); 11-12 Emireh points (Israel); 13-14 chamfered blades (Lebanon); 15-16 Ksar Akil burins (Lebanon)..

3. New artifact types: Chatelperronian tools, probably acculturated Neanderthal workmanship, points and obliquely retouched blades; crescents in Illuzian industries of Italy, which may be similarly derived from acculturated Neanderthal populations;[31] stratigraphically narrow, spatially, and in time; Howieson's Poort crescents, from Klasies River Mouth, thence overlain by less advanced industries;[32] triangular bifacially-worked points in the Streletskaya industries of southern Russia; the leaf-point Szeletian industry of Eastern Europe;[33] prior to the Ahmarian blade technology, Emireh points, chamfered blades for possible hafting, and distinctive burins in the Middle East.[34]

4. Speed with which additional new artifacts appear and replace each other constitute sharply defined, often short-lived chronological phases.

5. Use of bone, antler, and ivory artifacts, materials was adapted to new uses, unlike occasional Middle Paleolithic imitation use of these materials to mimic stone tools. Upper Paleolithic complex technology/industry: cutting, sawing, grinding, polishing, perforating, groove-and-splinter techniques.[35]

To Oakley and Clark, writing in the 1950s and 60s, this final florescence of human technology, with its wide and freely-chosen variety of materials, approaches the realm of art. They note the use of bone, but also of ivory and reindeer antler for the fabrication of spearheads with link shafts, barbed points and harpoons for spearing fish, hammers, wedges, meat-adzes, needles with eyes, often engraved.[36]

Fagan echoes the same theme. "The classic stoneworking technology used for Upper Paleolithic tools was based not only on percussion and the use of bone hammers but on punch struck blades, using a hand-held or chest impelled punch to produce parallel sided blades....These were made into a variety of tools, among them burins and scrapers, which were typical of all stages in the Upper Paleolithic. Burins...were used for grooving wood, bone, and particularly antlers, which were made into spears and harpoon points."[37]

Davidson and Noble note the bone, ivory, and antler objects, no longer stone alone. Bone projectile points were made of antlers, ivory sculptures of stylized composite creatures, such as those from Vogelherd, Geissenklosterle and Hohenstein-Stadel (lion-headed human figure).[38] Itzkoff illustrates the Venus from Dolni Vestonice: "Early Gravettian, modelled from pulverized bone and clay, then fire hardened like pottery, ca. 25,000 B.P., 11.5cm. This is the earliest known use of such advanced technology, and for the sake of art/religion."[39]

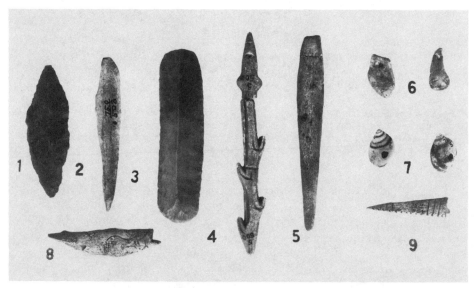

16.4 Implements and ornaments typical of the late-Paleolithic period: 1. knife blade or spear point of flint; 2. knife or etching tool of flint;. 3. end scraper or planing tool of flint; 4. harpoon point of bone; 5. lance point of bone; 6. beads or pendants of elk teeth; 7. beads of univalve shells; 8. fragment of bone with partial outline of a horse etched upon it; 9. fragment of bone with trace of geometric ornamentation.

Mellars believes that the new material culture involved symbolically-intentioned and -imposed form. Cognitive considerations interpenetrated the manufacture of the entire repertoire of Aurignacian objects. Their fabrication involved prior and formalized decisionmaking. The wide range of tool forms now being created seems to require of the mind a tighter level of standardization as part of the technology. Choice of specific materials, "sharply defined mental templates in the technological processes which lay behind the production of the tools."[40]

"By the time of the Upper Paleolithic in Europe, it was all over. Modern human beings were making tools to the shapes they decided upon, with little restriction imposed by the mechanical contraints of the technique of manufacture."[41] Upper Paleolithic culture and the technology and art that it embraced was not just a responsiveness to the unfolding contingencies of the here-and-now environment. It reveals in its creators a capacity for consciousness of what is being done—"second order intentionality...beliefs and desires about one's own beliefs and desires."[42]

Perhaps crucial to this view of the Upper Paleolithic is the contrast between an ancient human pattern of cultural existence and that which Alfred Korzybski described as the "time binding" character of human civilizational life, the capacity to act and create within temporal parameters envisioned well beyond the moment, even to a time when others will live and the participant, not.[43]

Sense of Beauty

The word "beauty" itself connotes an appreciation of an abstract idea. Yet its fulfillment both in the act of creating something that is "beautiful," and then appreciating the object or experience as an individual as well as a social entity involves more than intellectual or mental attention. The creation and apperception of beauty is suffused with emotion, powerful nervous system stimulations, our ancient and now dominating mammalian brain pulsating its energies, but always channeled through our cortex, our thinking brain. Without cognition such emotion cannot be objectively raised to what we would call "beautiful."

Randall White has studied early-Aurignacian body ornamentation, beads and pendants, made between 35,000-33,000 B.P., in southwest France, a time close to their original site occupation.[44] He argues that even at the earliest stages of arrival in this part of Eur-Asia, the Aurignacian Cro-Magnons were producing as sophisticated a level of cultural artifacts as was subsequently created in later stages of this first human civilization, the Solutrian and Magdalenian. White identifies this early French Aurignacian population through its tool assemblages, which includes split-based points, but virtually no burins and perforators.[45] Of course, it should be emphasized that even at 35,000 B.P., the Aurignacian in the Levant and Eastern Europe had apparently been well established for about 10,000 years.

His conclusions are striking:

> Aurignacian body ornamentation explodes onto the scene in southwest France during the early Aurignacian (i.e. between 35,000-33,000 B.P.). It appears to have been complex conceptually, symbolically, technically and logistically right from the very beginning. Thus, it is totally unreasonable to see Aurignacian body ornamentation as somehow formative of

or transitional to a Magdalenian florescence. This sudden, intrusive, and complex character of the earliest body ornamentation remains one of the greatest explanatory challenges in all of hominid evolution.[46]

Despite great similarities between the lithic technology of southwest France and Germany, the differences in the technology and form of beads and pendants are striking.[47]

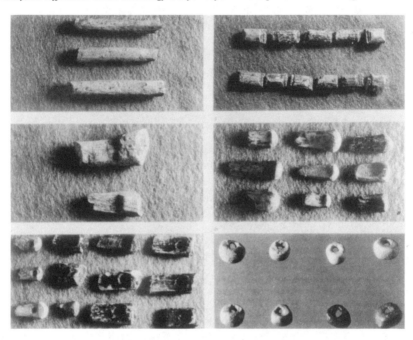

16.5 Aurignacian decorative manufacturing techniques, France, 30ka. B.P.

Ornaments were not mainly burial placements, but rather personally decorative in nature. They are not merely pierced shells or teeth, but rather formed ivory or serpentine beads, the result of complex production, piercing, grinding, polishing. Long-distance procurement of marine shells, through "trading," is linked to the fabrication of body ornaments.[48] Also ivory and steatite—mammoth bones and ivory—were imported from distances sometimes as far as 100km.[49]

Mellars has estimated that decorated shells from the early Aurignacian found in southwestern France and southern Russia had to have been imported, traded, transported over 500km from their origins along the Atlantic, Mediterranean, Black Sea coasts, implying an important interest in and value placed on these objects by the Cro-Magnons. It also implied a rich cultural setting to desire and fashion these objects into decorative, often female ornamentation, and also the trading and transportation networks between associative peoples that made such deliveries possible.[50]

Interestingly White views the incisions—meandering rows of punctuation on pendants, bone and ivory objects—as esthetic attempts to mimic the naturally occurring punctuation on exotic sea shells, a conscious stylistic appropriation of a natural pattern.[51]

Regarding these objects, White here explicitly rejects the arguments of Alexander Marshack that the incisions represent calendric lunar notation. Mellars, however, seems tentatively to accept the Marshack's general perspective.[52]

Confirming White's thesis regarding the early flowering of decorative arts among the Aurignacians was the discovery of a 28,000 B.P. burial site at Sungir, near Vladimir, northeast of Moscow, and thus several thousand miles east of the French Aurignacian sites, but also several thousand years later in time. Ian Tattersall's description reveals the universality of this cultural tradition, which implies an amazing uniformity of psychological, esthetic, and intellectual homogeneity among the Aurignacians throughout the many-thousand-year tradition that it encompasses.

16.6 "This 60 year old individual, who lived some 28 thousand years ago, was buried in garments, presumably of leather, onto which was sewn hundreds of mammoths-tusk beads. He was also wearing mammoth-tusk bracelets and pendants and necklaces of shell and animal teeth. Two juveniles in a neighboring grave were equally richly dressed and adorned."[53]

Body ornamentation, if we can generalize the phenomenon to historical times, argues for an appreciation of personal beauty and dignity, both on the part of the person wearing the beads or pendants, the jewelry, as well as the giver, the probable fabricator, and the intense emotional and cognitive symbolism involved in the entire process. Here we invoke the unique character of human sexuality, and the ubiquitous "Venus" art found throughout the range of the Cro-Magnons. Presumably, great efforts that went into the clay and bone fire-hardened fabrication of the Dolni Vestonice Venus in the early Gravettian, c.25,000 B.P., and the Venus of Willendorf, from 20,000 B.P., the latter an almost abstract evocation of fertility and sexuality; it was rubbed down with ochre for color and beauty. The latter was made of Dolomite limestone, and similar, to the Dolni Vestonice Venus, was 11 cm in height, possibly the size of a mobilary object, to be carried by a hunter away from home for a period of time.[54]

The visual representations, drawings of sexual objects, vulvas, sexual coition, the birthing process, all buttress the sense both of emotional, even passionate human feeling, sexuality and eroticism, yet seemingly under the discipline of the process of mental symbolic objectification, the desire to express these feelings both in abstract and esthetic terms.[55]

There is a seemingly unlimited number of objects, often seemingly practical, that reflect the union of deep interest and involvement with food objects and hunting equipment. They also serve to express and objectify in beautifully-crafted form this powerful emotional and intellectual immersion in the worlds of human and natural life. See, for example, the extremely miniaturized carving on a 1"-diameter piece of carved antler, of stags, salmon, ca. 12,000 B.P., late Magdalenian, from the Grotto of Lortet, Hautes-Pyrénées, France. In this carving diamond-shaped symbols are depicted at the upper right, also, the spinal chord of the salmon is indicated.[56] Another example is the "lion-headed human figure of mammoth ivory from the early Aurignacian levels in the Hohlenstein-Stadel Cave, southern Germany."[57]

Also, toward the end of the Pleistocene, spear throwers were invented. These spearthrowers were made of reindeer antler during the last and bitterest part of the Würm glaciation, 12,000-10,000 B.P. These "practical" tools were often decorated in the manner of medieval warriors. One example, colored in hematite and manganese, shows a fawn defecating, and is especially noteworthy because of its scatological humor and brilliant esthetic and technical realization. The right eye of the fawn is depicted by a tiny piece of amber, the left, of lignite. Yet another spearthrower constitutes a sensitive evocation of a ptarmigan.[58]

Art and/or Religion

By far the most impressive dimension of the Upper Paleolithic civilization, at least to the ordinary spectator from the vantage point of 35,000 years of human experience, is exemplified in the paintings, especially within the deep interior of these many caves. The vast geographic expanse wherein we locate the cave paintings, and the similarity in style—as is the case with the tools, ornaments, sculptings—are perplexing considering the at least 30,000-year duration of this cultural tradition, and the fact that it underwent much stylistic evolution throughout the period of its flourishing.

The highly dynamic and abstract rendering of animal life in these paintings, deep within the caves, and not without numerous enigmatic signs—diamond and rectangular shapes, dots, lines—that seem to guide the visitor from one vaulted chamber to another, have always evoked wonder at the virtuoistic artistic renderings. What do the paintings themselves mean? Of what significance is the fact that the paintings are so deeply regressed inside these caves?

While animal life dominates these halls, their walls and ceilings, humans do appear, giving hints as to their purpose. The Aurignacian painting at Les Trois Frères in Ariège, France, near the Pyrenées—depicts an antler-headed figure—a "sorcerer," but with a tail? Another human figure is shown as a flute playing bison; a magical bear man; chamois-pelt-covered dancing figures; other mysterious animal-like figures that reflect human involvement with the dynamic animal world, as appreciator, perhaps in ritual worship, in symbolic evocations of dance and ritual.

Lascaux, in southwestern France, a cave buried into a ridge high over the river Vézère, alongside of which the encampment of its decorators was located, is not a particularly large or spectacular cave. For approximately 75 years it was periodically visited by its decorators, their small stone lamps lit by animal fat that was deposited in cups made by carving into flat stones. They must have traveled far and wide to obtain the necessary clays and plants that provided for the paint and applicators. Lascaux, unlike other caves, such as Pech Merle, was not large enough for community-wide festivals of prayer and dance, and appears to one observer to have been a place of apartness and privacy of commitment. Was this art created as an esthetic vision of the life that its creators depended on, a fraternity of hunter-artists, a club or personal refuge, in which their inner intellective genius would bubble out in spontaneous if deliberative images, c.17,000 B.P.?

More recently, previously undiscovered caves have been announced. The written descriptions reflect today's universal sense of wonder and appreciation. "Paintings discovered last December [1994] in the Ardeche region of Southeastern France have been verified to be 30,340 years old. Chauvet cave, 300 images of animals, red hand prints of artists who drew with charcoal, red ochre, red hematite. One drawing of a bear shows the entire, muscular animal in realistic profile. Near it are profiles of bears' heads drawn by more uncertain hands trying to capture only the correct arc of the beast's snout. A simple owl any child would recognize is scratched into the wall—horns for ears, two eyes and a thin beak but only quick vertical lines for the feathers. But a reindeer is carefully drawn, with delicate strands for the white neck fur, darker shading for the shorter fur on its back and elaborate arcs and turns for the horns. A group of lions' heads is depicted, features in simple profile, in which one ear is too far back on the neck. This is under three other profiles that use elaborate shading to make them appear three dimensional."[59]

Confirming Randall White's above-stated views of the high sophistication of the early Aurignacian ornamentation, Jean Clottes, Chief Curator of the French Upper Paleolithic archaeological heritage, sees a relationship of the artists of the Ardèche with the sculptures of the Swabian Jura at Vogelherd and Geissenklosterle in Germany, also early Arignacian, 35,000-30,000 B.P, all of which he defines as "startlingly fresh and advanced." Even more recent discoveries, including a dramatic cave near Marseilles, in

1991, c.27,000 B.P., whose entrance has been covered up by a post-Ice Age rise of the Mediterranean, have evoked serious commentary.

Marlise Simons describes the archaeological analysis and writing of Jean Clottes at Niaux in the Pyrenées caves of 13,000 B.P. All of the above caves and their art are described in books by Clottes: The *Dawn of Art* and *The Cave beneath the Sea.*[60] Niaux cave:

> "'About one mile into the Niaux cave, there is a crossroad, marked by ancient geometrical signs: an orange-red dart, some stripes, a cluster of red dots. They seem to point to a great gallery where more than 60 paintings are concentrated. 'I have wondered why this hall has become the main sanctuary,' Mr Clottes says 'Is it because it is at the end of the passage, because it is round, because it has this great echo?' As his flashlight moves along the wall, bison, ibexes, horses appear. They are galloping, fleeing, charging, falling. There is no visible order, no unity of size. tests have showed the images of this panel were made 13,000 years ago.'"[61]

Some have wondered if these paintings, deep in the interiors of caves, could be the subliminal exemplification of the same human spirit that created the Sistine Chapel. The cave painting rooms, at Lascaux, Altamira, Ardèche, Niaux, Marseilles could indeed function as sacred places uniting the religious and the esthetic. Paintings and sculptures alike, deriving their sense of energy and power from the realities of animal life, the pulse of human sexuality, the unconscious sense of the beautiful are here raised to the highest level of intellectual abstractiveness and technical power, all the elements integrated to create works of art worthy of contemporary contemplation and exemplification.[62]

In the grotto of Combarelles in the French Dordogne, deep inside a winding tunnel, is a crack in the cave wall from which water drips during the wet season. Beside this crack is an ancient drawing of a reindeer reaching for water, presumably from the crack in the wall. The painting is dated at 13,000 B.P.[63] Jesper Christensen has noted the similarity between this image and the many subsequent esthetic and religious evocations of the theme of deer drinking water from a natural source: Greek geometric ceramics found in the Athenian Dyplion cemetery; late Roman mosaics exhibited in the "Galla Placidia" museum in Ravenna; the Biblical Hebrew/Christian motif of "As the hart panteth after water brooks, so panteth my soul after thee, O God," Psalms 42; innumerable medieval baptismal imagery and texts.[64]

Minds Searching

Alexander Marshack, a former magazine editor, became interested as part of a writing assignment in the odd swirls of seemingly geometric design to be found on the wall paintings of the Upper Paleolithic peoples, their stone, flint, bone, or ivory artifacts and plaques. The incisions were sometimes done on extraordinarily small pieces, often with what seemed to be different incising instruments and strokes.

At the suggestion of Hallam Movius, then director of Harvard's Peabody Museum, Marshack devoted himself, not without the assistance of many paleoanthropologists, to a study of these "notational patterns." His conclusion, published in a number of books and articles, including *The Roots of Civilization*, 1972, was that these were mnemonic markings, attempts to mentally and then physically note in a regular chronometric sequence the occurrence of events in the external world that seemed repetitive over time. Like a hunter who notches his rifle, crossing four notches with a side slash to denote five, these markings seemed to Marshack to border on an attempt to create a mathematically regular system of relational units: the phases of the moon, a woman's menstrual period, the rise and fall of the sun during the seasons, the appearance of migratory birds and the run of the salmon up the river.[65]

16.7 (A-B): Chronometric engraving? **A.** (left), engraved bone plaque with a variety of punctuations and incisions, 9.7cm long, c.25-20ka B.P.; **B.** (right), Venus of Laussel, France, Gravettian, c.27-21ka B.P., 17" high. The horn she carries and faces has 13 incisions. Thirteen days from first crescent to full moon, or, the thirteen times during the year that the crescent symbol would be visible?

Even when the notational artifacts were engraved in the same style and came from the same site and level, the specific intentional differences between them turned out to be as important in establishing the fact of notation as the similarities due to the common cultural tradition. These data are part of the evidence that what we have is not design patterns or geometric motifs but a relatively open and variable system of notation. The open variable aspect of the system is found upon every notational slate I have examined, from the Aurignacian to the terminal Magdalenian and into the Mesolithic.[66]

We have the evidence of an open, variable system of notation. In general cognitive terms we can say that the "purpose" of these notations was the sequential accumulation of sets, sub-sets, and superordinate sums. They were differentiated by a complex series of visual-kinesthetic and spatio-temporal inputs, recognition, and feedbacks...together these uses imply a sense of recurrence and periodicity as well as a sense of constancy within the open, variable system.[67]

Clearly, if we follow Randall White's analysis, not all of these incised markings were chronometric in nature, some being part of the attempt by artisans to decorate specially crafted beads or pendants.[68] However, the broad range of materials on which these incisions and notations seem to have been placed, including walls where no carving of ornaments could occur, argues for the general probability of Marshack's claims.[69]

A description of one of Marshack's exemplar bone plaques: "Inscribed Notation. Example of a tradition of markings found throughout the Cro-Magnon's peoples' range. These markings on a palm-sized piece of bone date to the mid-Aurignacian, southwestern France, c.30,000 B.P. Marshack believes that they represent a two-month span, tracing the waxing and waning of the moon."[70]

A New Brain—New Behavior

> The mind of man seeks regularities. Upper Paleolithic man must have been fascinated by the rhythm and direction of events of importance to his survival and well being. Why did the full moon appear roughly as often as the menstrual period? Why did the sun set in exactly the same spot beyond that distant hill once every 365-odd days?....Cro-Magnon's ability not only to remember but to integrate the wide variety of experiences seems to be the differentiating quality in this new culture. Innovation will not now efface the old; rather the old will be absorbed and integrated into a new web of meanings...Thus we find in the ever enlarged scope of human experience in the Upper Paleolithic a steady transformation of cultural existence.[71]

In that interlayered web of symbolically-expressed causes and their effects, integrating the past with the present, envisioning a future, *i.e.*, *meaning*, we stumble onto the sources of civilizational possibility. Following close on will come *Homo*'s domination over both man and nature.

Endnotes, Chapter 16

[1] Allsworth-Jones, P. 1993. "The archaeology of Archaic and Early Modern 'Homo sapiens': An African Perspective," *Cambridge Archaeological Journal*, 3:1:21-39; Trinkaus, E., and Shipman, P. 1993. *The Neanderthals*, N.Y.: Knopf, p. 361; Wolpoff, M., and Caspari, R. R. 1997. *Race and Human Evolution*, N.Y.: Simon and Schuster, p. 329.

[2] Tattersall, I. 1995. *The Last Neanderthal*, N.Y.: Macmillan/USA, p. 117, Illustrations 82, 83.

[3] Coon, C. S. 1962. *The Origin of Races*, N.Y.: Knopf, p. 639; Koenigswald, G. H. R., von. 1962. *The Evolution of Man*, Ann Arbor: Univ. of Michigan Press, p. 125; Baker, J. 1974. *Race*. N.Y.: Oxford Univ. Press, p. 279; Itzkoff, S. W. 1983. *The Form of Man*, N.Y.: Peter Lang, pp. 167-168.

[4] Klein, R. G. 1989. *The Human Career*, Chicago: Univ. of Chicago Press, p. 349: Cro-Magnon Cranium, figure 7.2, p. 348, fig. 7.3, p. 350.

[5] Klein, 1989, *op. cit.*, p. 349.

[6] Wilford, J. N. 1997. "Fossils Called Limb in Human Family Tree," *The New York Times*, May, 30; Bermudez, J. M., and Arsuaga, J. L. 1997. *Science*, May, 30.

[7] Dennell, R. (Univ. of Sheffield). 1997. In *Nature*, Feb. 1997, 385:27:767-768; Wilford, J. N. 1997. *The New York Times*, 3/4/97; Roberts, M. B., Stringer, C. B., Parfitt, S. A. 1994. "A Hominid Tibia from Middle Pleistocene Sediments at Boxgrove UK., *Nature*, 369:311-313.

[8] Wilford, J. N. 1997. *The New York Times*, 2/28/97, in *Science*, 2/28/97.

[9] Dennell, R. (Univ. of Sheffield). 1997. "The World's Oldest Spears," *Nature*, Feb. 1997, 385:27:767-768; Wilford, J. N. 1997. "Ancient German Spears Tell of Mighty Hunters of Stone Age," *The New York Times*, 3/4/97.

[10] Balter, M. 1995. "Did Homo erectus Tame Fire First?" *Science* 6/16/95, 268:1570.

[11] Klein, 1989, *op. cit.*, pp. 212-213.

[12] Tattersall, I. 1986. "Species Recognition in Human Paleontology," *Journal of Human Evolution*, 15:165-175.

[13] Schwartz, Jeffrey. 1993. *What the Bones Tell Us*, N.Y.: Henry Holt, pp. 227-231; Coon, C. S. 1982. *Racial Adaptations*, Chicago: Nelson-Hall, pp. 157-161, fig.8.3.

[14] Wilford, J. N. 1997. "Fossils Called Limb in Human Family Tree," *The New York Times*, May, 30; Bermudez, J. M., and Arsuaga, J. L. 1997. *Science*, May, 30.

[15] See discussion in Chapters 13, 15.

[16] Leakey, R. 1981. *The Making of Mankind*, N.Y.: Dutton, pp. 193-196.

[17] Bar-Yosef, O., and Kra, R. S., eds. 1994. Introduction: Dating Eastern Mediterranean Sequences," *Late Quaternary Chronology and Paleoclimates of the Eastern Mediterranean*, Tucson, AZ: Radiocarbon, University of Arizona, pp. 1-12, esp. p. 5.

[18] Phillips, James. 1994. "Upper Paleolithic Chronology in the Levant and Nile," in Bar-Yosef and Kra, eds., *op. cit.*, pp. 169-176, esp. p. 169.

[19] Phillips, 1994, in Bar-Yosef, and Kra, eds., *op. cit.*, p. 169.

[20] Phillips, 1994, in Bar-Yosef, and Kra, eds., *op. cit.*, pp.169-176, esp. p. 170.

[21] Phillips, 1994, in Bar-Yosef, and Kra, eds., *op. cit.*, p. 171.

[22] Phillips, 1994, in Bar-Yosef, and Kra, eds., *op. cit.*, p. 172.

[23] Soffer, Olga. 1989. "The Middle to Upper Paleolithic Transition on the Russian Plain," in *The Human Revolution—Behavioral and Biological Perspectives on the Origins of Modern Humans*, P. A. Mellars and C. Stringer, eds., Princeton, N.J.: Princeton Univ. Press, pp. 714-742, esp. p. 736.

[24] Soffer, 1989, in Mellars and Stringer, eds., *op. cit.*, pp. 736-737.

[25] Soffer, 1989, *in* Mellars and Stringer, eds., *op. cit.*, pp. 724-725.

[26] Morell, Virginia. 1995. "Siberia: Surprising Home for Early Modern Humans," *Antiquity,* June issue. Cited by Ted Goebel, Oregon State College, and M. Aksenov, Irkutsk Univ., in *Science*, 268:1279.

[27] Oakley, K. 1959. *Man the Tool-maker*, Chicago: Univ. of Chicago Press, pp. 92-105.

[28] White, Randall. 1989. "Production Complexity and Standardization in Early Aurignacian Bead and Pendant Manufacture: Evolutionary Implications," in Mellars and Stringer, eds., *op. cit.*, pp. 366-390.

[29] Bar-Yosef, O. 1997. Personal communication, 11/21/97.

[30] Campbell, B., and Loy, J. 1996. *Humankind Emerging*, 7th ed., N.Y.: Harper-Collins, p. 437.

[31] Bar-Yosef, O. 1997. Personal communication, 11/21/97.

[32] Davidson, Iain, and Noble, William. 1993. "Tools and Language in Human Evolution," in *Tools, Language And Cognition In Human Evolution*, K. R. Gibson and T. Ingold, eds., *op. cit.*, pp. 363-388, esp. 380-382; Stringer, C. B., and Gamble, C. 1993. *In Search of the Neanderthals: Solving the Puzzle of Human Origins*, London: Thames and Hudson, p. 154.

[33] Mellars, 1996, *op. cit.*, pp. 416-418.

[34] Klein, 1989, *op. cit.*, p. 303.

[35] Mellars, P. A. 1989. "Technological Changes across the Middle-Upper Paleolithic Transition: Economic, Social and Cognitive Perspectives," in Mellars and Stringer, eds., *op. cit.*, pp. 338-365; "Technological Transition," pp. 339*ff*, figs. 20.1, 20.2, 20.3, pp. 342, 344, 346.

[36] Oakley, 1959, *op. cit.*, pp. 92-105; Clark, Grahame. 1967. *The Stone Age Hunters*, N.Y.: McGraw Hill, pp. 71-74.

[37] Fagan, B. 1989. *People of the Earth. An Introduction to World Prehistory*, 6th ed. *op. cit.*, p. 174.

[38] Hahn, J. 1986. *Kraft und Aggression. Die Botschaft der Eiszeitkunst im Aurignacien Süddeutschlands?*, Tübingen: Verlag Archaeologica Venatoria, Institute für Urgeschichte der Universität Tübingen.

[39] Itzkoff, S. W. 1983. *The Form of Man*, N.Y.: Peter Lang, Plate V, (from Am. Museum of Natural History, N.Y. Public Library).

[40] Mellars, 1989, in Mellars and Stringer, eds., *op. cit.*, pp. 338-365, esp. p. 358.

[41] Davidson, Iain, and Noble, William. 1993. "Tools and Language in Human Evolution," in *Tools, Language And Cognition In Human Evolution*, K. R. Gibson & T. Ingold, eds., *op. cit.*, p. 382; Davidson, Iain, and Noble, William. 1989. "The archeology of perception: Traces of depiction and language," *Current Anthropology*, 30:125-155.

[42] Davidson and Noble, 1993, inGibson and Ingold, eds., *op. cit.*, p. 382.

[43] Korzybski, A. 1941. *Science and Sanity*, Lancaster, PA: .

[44] White, Randall. 1989. "Production Complexity and Standardization in Early Aurignacian Bead and Pendant Manufacture: Evolutionary Implications," in Mellars and Stringer, eds., *op. cit.*, pp. 366-390.

[45] White, 1989. "Production Complexity and Standardization in Early Aurignacian Bead and Pendant Manufacture: Evolutionary Implications," in *The Human Revolution—Behavioral and Biological Perspectives on the Origins of Modern Humans*, P. A. Mellars and C. B. Stringer, eds., *op. cit.*, p. 385.

[46] *Ibid.*

[47] White, 1989, in Mellars and Stringer, eds., *op. cit.*, pp. 384-385.

[48] White, 1989, in Mellars and Stringer, eds., *op. cit.*, pp. 374-375.

[49] White, 1989, in Mellars and Stringer, eds., *op. cit.*, p. 376.

[50] Mellars, P. A. 1996. *The Neanderthal Legacy*, Princeton, N.J.: Princeton Univ. Press, pp. 398-400.

[51] White, 1989, in Mellars and Stringer, eds., *op. cit.*, p. 377; fig. 21.6, p. 378.

[52] White, Randall. 1982. "The manipulation of burins and incision and notation," *Canadian Jrnl. of Anthropology*, 2:129-135; Marshack, A. 1972. *The Roots of Civilization*, London: Weidenfield and Nicolson; also see, on Upper Paleolithic art and decoration: White, Randall. 1989. "Toward a Contextual Understanding of the Earliest Body Ornaments," in *Patterns and Processes in Later Pleistocene Human Emergence*, E. Trinkaus, ed., Cambridge: Cambridge Univ. Press; Mellars, 1996, *op. cit.*, pp. 398-400.

[53] Tattersall, 1995, *op. cit.*, Illustration 129, pp. 186-187.

[54] Itzkoff, S. W. 1983. *The Form of Man*, *op. cit.*, Plate I.

[55] see Campbell, Bernard. 1985. *Human Evolution*, 3rd. ed., N.Y.: Aldine De Gruyter, fig. 10.3, p. 296.

[56] Itzkoff, 1983, *op. cit.*, Plate VI, (from Am. Museum of Natural History, N.Y. Public Library).

[57] Mellars, 1996, *op. cit.*, fig. 13.5, p. 398.

[58] Itzkoff, S. W. 1985. *Triumph of the Intelligent*, N.Y.: Peter Lang, Plate II, (Grahame Clark and Geoffrey Bibby).

[59] Cronin, Anne. 1995. "Primitive? Not the One Who Drew the Lion," *The New York Times*, 6/11/95.

[60] Clottes, Jean. *The Dawn of Art*, N.Y.: Harry Abrams; Clottes, Jean. *The Cave Beneath the Sea*, N.Y.: Harry Abrams.

[61] Simons, Marlise. 1996. "Why Ancient Images Haunt Modern Minds," *The New York Times*, 6/30/96.

[62] Itzkoff, 1985, *op. cit.*, pp. 154-155.

[63] Nougier, L. R. 1966. *L'Art Prehistorique*, Paris.

[64] Nordstrom, F. 1984. *Medieval Baptismal Fonts: An Iconographical Study*, Stockholm; Christensen, J. 1997. "Prehistoric Art—The Missing Dimension," *Mankind Quarterly*, Spring, 37:3:255-261.

[65] Marshack, 1972, *op. cit.*; Itzkoff, 1985, *op. cit.*

[66] Marshack, A. 1972. "Cognitive Aspects of Upper Paleolithic Engraving," *Current Anthropology*, June-October, 13:3-4:445-477, esp. p. 449.

[67] Marshack, 1972, *op. cit.*, *Current Anthropology*, June-October, 13:457.

[68] White, 1989, in Mellars and Stringer, eds., *op. cit.*, pp. 366-390.

[69] Marshack, A. 1974. "The Meander as a System, An Analysis in Recognition of Iconographic Units in Upper Paleolithic Composition," in Ucko, P., ed., *Biennial Conference of the Australian Institute of Aboriginal Studies*, May-June, 16, Canberra, Australia; Marshack, A. 1976. "Some Implications of the Paleolithic Evidence for the Origin of Language," *Current Anthropology*, June, 17:2:274-282; Marshack, A. 1979. "Upper Paleolithic Symbol Systems of the Russian Plain: Cognitive and Comparative analysis" *Current Anthropology*, June, 20:2:271-311.

[70] Itzkoff, 1985, *op. cit.*, Plate IV, (from A. Marshack, 1972, *The Roots of Civilization*, *op. cit.*

[71] Itzkoff, 1983, *op. cit.*, p. 201.

Modernizing the Species

- 1 -
Extinction of the Neanderthals

"One can imagine Neanderthalers watching from the edge of a cliff how the Cro-Magnons hunted in the valley. To the brutish, fear ridden Neanderthalers these almost hair-less giants with jutting chin and towering forehead must have appeared to be superhuman spirits. He saw them using a miraculous technique which was utterly unfathomable and in-comprehensible to him. He saw the animal herds from which he had for thousands of years picked what he wanted being ingeniously rounded and driven into traps, over precipices or through a narrow gorge into the fire, the clubs and spears of the hunters who jabbered excit-edly and made strange cries while they waited for the bag. As he gazed at the elaborate preparations they made for the chase, Neanderthal Man must have felt an eerie terror and sickening weariness at the futility of his own poor efforts. He must have realized that against these—what we would call God-like beings he had not the slightest chance to compete. More and more he must have drawn away from such terrifying creatures, not because they threatened his life, but simply because their miraculous powers were too much for him to contemplate and filled him with primeval panic."

A. T. S. Simeons, 1962.[1]

"His heart pounding in his chest, the Last Neanderthal collapsed behind a screen of low bushes. As his tortured breathing subsided he was dimly aware that he had lost his pur-suers, at least temporarily. When those tall, odd looking strangers had come over the hills that marked the boundary of the group's range in it isolated Iberian outpost, instinctive fear had spread amongst its members. They had seen no other humans, even of their own kind, in several months. For reasons they didn't comprehend, their Neanderthal neighbors no longer appeared at the pass through the mountains where the two groups had met and exchanged members since time immemorial. What did these strange new people represent? The Last Neanderthal and his companions were soon to learn. The strangers had immediately spotted the Neanderthals at their campsite below the rock ledge, and men had spread out and melted into the low, bushy vegetation that dotted the landscape. The Neanderthalers had sensed danger but could not understand why. The males had gathered their hunting equipment and were huddled together, uncertain what to do. Suddenly they found themselves surrounded by the strangers, who leaped into their midst with fearsome yells, spears jabbing. The sur-prised Neanderthals responded vigorously but had clearly been outwitted by the agile new-

comers. As his companions fell around him, the Last Neanderthal crept away from the fray.
A yell told him that he had been spotted, and he sprinted for the nearest cover. After a long
chase through country familiar to him but not to his pursuers, the unformed thought came to
him that he might be safe. But for how long?"

I. Tattersall, 1995[2]

Levant: Contacts and Outcomes
Ships passing in the night?

Recent changes in dating have altered earlier views. The Zuttiyeh fossil, 95,000-
164,000 B.P., is a primitive hominid cranium found near Amud and northwest of Tiberias, needs more careful dating.[3] Skhul lies at the foot of Mt. Carmel, Tabun and Kebara,
at the western slope of Mt. Carmel. Qafzeh Cave lies in a small wadi, a dry river valley
south of Nazareth.

There is now a wide range of estimates for Qafzeh, from 115,000-85,000 B.P.,
similarly for Skhul, perhaps even wider, all because of different dating techniques, including the use of C.14. Argument is that the Neanderthals, especially the Tabun remains, now dated by H. P. Schwarcz from 182,000-86,000 B.P., represents "...a robust
hominid approximately coeval with, or a little earlier than modern-looking hominids at
the nearby site of Skhul."[4]

Trinkaus and Shipman reflect on the puzzle of the two populations, true Neanderthals and seemingly morphologically modern humans coexisting in the same general
geography, yet the latter still culturally Neanderthal. "A new series of ESR dates for
Tabun, published in 1991, caused further complications. They showed Neanderthals
from Tabun to be approximately the same age as modern humans from Skhul and Qafzeh. This new twist pointed up a fundamental problem that had been there all along,
overshadowed by the problem of chronology and phylogeny. It was awkward, if not
downright contorted, to try to explain how two groups of humans occupied the same
region—either alternatively or simultaneously—using the same set of tools to exploit the
same plants and animals over a period of fifty thousand years and yet remain anatomically and genetically separate."[5] Wolpoff, in tune with his multiregional perspective on
the evolution of modern humans, suggests that they are all part of one variable population in morphology.[6]

Bar-Yosef describes the transitional Mousterian sites of Israel and Lebanon. He argues that the Mousterians came south into desertified areas only when these areas were
climatically benign. He notes the role of the barn owl, *Tyto alba*, in introducing rodent
bones into caves as being helpful for subsequent dating.[7] He argues that the expansion of
the Neanderthals south into the Levant, Southwest Asia, coincides with the expansion of
glacial conditions at about 74,000 B.P., oxygen isotope stage 4.[8]

John J. Shea's conclusion concerning the relationship between the true Neanderthals and the supposedly fully modern sapiens at Skhul and Qafzeh: no behavioral differences can be noted between the Kebara Neanderthals, at c.60,000 B.P., and the Qafzeh early moderns at c.92,000 B.P. Anatomically modern groups may have persisted in
less productive mountain and desert areas at different time levels. "If archaic and anatomically-modern hominids of the Upper Pleistocene were truly different species, then
the evidence from the Levantine archaeological record indicates that their behavior with
respect to tool use was less different than between many living populations."[9]

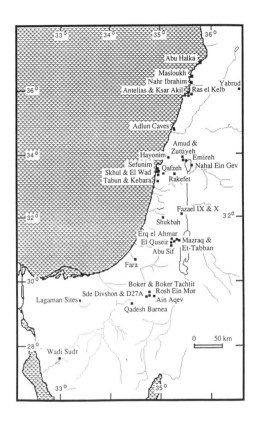

17.1 Approximate locations of the main Middle and Upper Paleolithic sites in the Levant.

Who are the Ahmarians?

The Ahmarian blade culture of the southern Levant, Boker Tachtit in the Israeli Negev, is dated to between 45,000-40,000 B.P.; it was succeeded, at about 30,000-28,000 B.P., by an Aurignacian (universal Cro-Magnon) culture already present in northern Israel, Jordan, Lebanon, and Syria, at about 40,000 B.P.[10]

Marks and Monigal describe Boker Tachtit as a terminal Early-Levantine Mousterian cultural site whose inhabitants used Levallois reduction strategies. The final transformation into the Upper Paleolithic took place, c.47,000 B.P. (Ahmarians) at Boker Tachtit.[11] Rosh Ein Mor, in the same general area as Boker Tachtit, was occupied from 85,000 B.P. The production of hard hammer single platform strategy, as in Boker Tachtit, level 4, was not invented during the Middle to Upper Paleolithic transition but was part of the technological repertoire of the Early-Levantine Mousterian (Tabun D type) from at least 80,000 B.P. Within the Early Levantine Mousterian technological strategies, many Levallois and non-Levallois production approaches existed. These techno-logical strategies reduce in number as time goes on.[12] Marks and Monigal seem to argue for increasing specialization within the Levantine Neanderthal Mousterian tradition over time.

Phillips emphasizes the early appearance and presumed priority of the Upper Pa-leolithic in the Levant by reference to an ancient and traditional technology. He states that Levallois techniques (Mousterian and earlier) were used in the Nile Valley until virtually the end of the Pleistocene. No Upper Paleolithic sites have as yet been recov-ered in the eastern or western deserts of Egypt or Sudan.[13] He views the Negev, at Boker Tachtit, as making the transition from late Mousterian to Upper Paleolithic from c.48,000-40,000 B.P. These Ahmarian sites reveal backed blades. bladelets, perforators, truncators, burins, end scrapers-single-platforms blade cores, cresting and core tablets. Punch technique of indirect percussion was used extensively.[14] The Ahmarians may have flourished for only 12,000 years, from 48-40,000 to 28,000 B.P., roughly the time modern humans have lived in the Holocene period, since the Ice Ages. Also, Ein Eqev East, in Negev, and two sites in Jordan dated from ca 20,000-16,000 B.P. are not Ah-marian but rather "... represent evolved groups with different adaptation patterns from those typically Ahmarian."[15] It is unclear what relation these cultural sites and their re-spective populations have with either the predecessor Mousterian or successor Aurignacian cultures. Perhaps they were part of the mysterious fragmentation of races and peoples that appear and disappear before the oncoming tidal wave of Aurignacian.

The Levantine Aurignacian at Ksar 'Akil, Lebanon, c.32,000 B.P., replaces the Ahmarian in the Negev, Ein Avdat, at about c.26,000 B.P., ventures Phillips. Aurignacian cultural characteristics: rock shelter habitations, retouched thick irregular blades, burins, steep end scrapers, bone tools, split-based points, flakes over blades, di-rect percussion in tool reduction. Some Upper Paleolithic technology sites between 40,000-20,000 B.P. are to be found in the Nile Valley. The Upper Paleolithic in the southern Levant seems to be a direct descendant of the Middle Paleolithic Mousterian, in terms of successor settlement patterns. They settled in open-air camps near ponds, springs, lakes. In the northern Levant forested areas, settlement occurred more in caves. The Upper Paleolithic occurred later in the Nile Valley, leaving only sparse remains and overlaying no seeming antecedents[16]

In describing the end of the era of the Neanderthals, Ian Tattersal refers to the tall, almost 6ft. Neanderthal found at Amud in Israel, now dated to about 40,000 B.P., slightly more recent than the dating of the early Ahmarian industry, after 48,000 B.P. Tattersal views the Ahmarian technology as Upper Paleolithic, but that "...their method of manufacture hints at Middle Paleolithic technology," (Mousterian).[17] They were con-temporaries.

In Egypt the process of cultural succession was much more gradual. Phillips notes that in Upper Paleolithic sites in the Nile Valley there was still a retention of Levallois techniques after 30,000 B.P. Unique evidence to argue that the Nile Valley did not share "cultural identity" with the Levant "...attesting to a lack of population movement be-tween Africa and Southwestern Asia."[18] The relationship between Levallois technology, usually ascribed to Mousterian and earlier traditions, and these presumed "Upper Paleo-lithic" sites, is unclear.

Question: who are the Ahmarians? They seem to be, in the interpretation of Bar-Yosef, the first clearly Upper Paleolithic peoples on the world scene. Dating from 43-42ka B.P in Boker Tachtit in the Negev, they hint at the possible other manifestations of Middle/Upper Paleolithic cultural fragmentation before the subsequent intrusive and seemingly conquering spread of the Aurignacians both south and west into the Levant, east or west into Asia, and certainly west into Central and Western Europe.[19] It is also possible to view the Ahmarians as part of a transitional ethnicity, perhaps associated in some manner with the more ancient Skhul/Qafzeh populations, in contact with other peripheral Cro-Magnid-like cultures including the oncoming Aurignacian.

Transition or Displacement

Bar-Yosef argues that at Kebara Cave on Mt. Carmel in northern Israel, the Upper Paleolithic took place c.47,000-45,000 B.P. Bar-Yosef, regarding the relationship of Skhul and Qafzeh to the Cro-Magnons, *Homo sapiens sapiens*, of Europe: "While some of us view the need for an additional mutation to reach the cultural level of Upper Paleolithic technological and cultural achievements, others simply regard the shift as gradual or even rapid, but occurring within the same world population."[20]

The fact that the Upper Paleolithic culture of the Aurignacian of Cro-Magnon took place in the Levant by the overlaying of the earlier Mousterian, and that the Aurignacian Upper Paleolithic culture subsequently correlates with the geographies of modern Neolithic economies, argues for a sharp cultural, if not morphological revolution. There is a time gap of at least 50,000 years between the Qafzeh and Skhul transitionals and their Neanderthal-like, Mousterian cultural remains, and thence the coming of the Aurignacian.

Something new occurred in the evolution of humans to create this sweeping transition, which first makes itself evident in the Levant between 47,000-40,000 B.P. True, Neanderthals at Kebara existed toward the end of this period. Was there a gradual cultural as well as genetic process of miscegenation and absorption? Else, was there expulsion and then rapid, if silent genocide?

The so-called transitional culture, now dated to about 47-46ka B.P in southern Levant usually has been thought to be of Mousterian derivation, designated as the Emiran.[21] Bar-Yosef and Belfer-Cohen appear recently to hesitate, noting the seeming smooth transition of the Emiran to the early Ahmarian blade transition. "Based on the sequence of Ksar Akil, Kebara, Qafzeh, Erq el Ahmar, Boker Tachtit, it seems that fully-fledged blade assemblages emerged directly from the Middle to Upper Paleolithic Transitional industry (the Emiran)....While reviewing the Levantine Upper Paleolithic we would like to stress that the so-called 'Transitional Industry' is undoubtedly an Upper Paleolithic entity by European criteria but is not necessarily `Aurignacoid.' It is dated in the Levant to about 47-46ka B.P. in Boker Tachtit."[22]

Here Bar-Yosef and Belfer-Cohen raise the question suggested above as to the identity of these clearly transitional groups. It has been suggested that a constellation of cultures, the Aterian (North Africa), Chatelperronian (France), Szetelian (Central Europe), Illuzian (Italy), Streletskaya (Western Russia), Howieson's Poort (South Africa), Emiran (Israel), perhaps even the Ahmarian (Northern Negev), were part of a non-Cro-Magnid population of either Middle Paleolithic inventors, learners, or morphologically transitional hybrid peoples who created these cultural fragments in time. In each case there seems to be no sharp boundary between the past and the future. Cultural layers were neither retrogressive nor progressive.

Carleton Coon has noted the superimposed Mousterian layers over Upper Paleolithic tool beds in Iraq. Climatic and ecological conditions changed constantly, and hunter/gatherers were constantly on the move and probably over long periods of time. The Old Man of Upper Cave Zhoukoudian, c.30,000-10,000 B.P. was buried with bone ornaments typical of Eur-Asian technologies, and ethnically he was not a classical Mongoloid.[23]

There is evidence of an early Aurignacian presence in Eastern Europe and Russia at about 45,000-40,000 B.P. Bar-Yosef argues that the Upper Paleolithic took place, c.47,000-45,000 B.P. in the Levant. Temnata Cave in Bulgaria gives similar TL dates.[24] The Aurignacians certainly were around for a long period before they burst upon the world c.45,000 B.P. Their influence throughout their long period of morphological and cultural gestation, even at a distance, at the least from their wandering cultural and genetic tendrils, could have been significant.

Contact of Races: Eur-Asian Meeting Grounds

Cro-Magnids are presumed present in France by 35,000 B.P. Here, the Chatelperronian culture, which shows elements of both the succeeding Aurignacian as well as the displaced Mousterian of the Neanderthals, has been identified with Neanderthal fossil remains. This is clearly a mystery. Is it the product of Neanderthal acculturation to the oncoming Cro-Magnid tool and cultural kit? Was it a manifestation of trade between the two groups, representing a reciprocal influence of an advanced culture on a simpler one, with a concomitant respectful imitation of a more ancient cultural technology long in place, on the part of the newly arrived interlopers?

> Near the village of Saint-Cesaire was a series of limestone quarries, lying along a cliff known as La Roche à Pierrot; they were being used to grow mushrooms. In 1979, the owner of the mushroomery decided to enlarge the turnaround area for trucks and brought in front-loaders to clear away some of the earth. Unknowingly, they dug into an archaeological site, exposing stone tools that were noticed by a local amateur who notified Leveque.... [archaeological curator of the area]....Leveque then started a salvage operation designed to retrieve the archaeological material swiftly but with appropriate care and adequate scientific documentation. On July 27, 1979, a badly crushed skeleton of an adult Neanderthal was uncovered in a layer bearing Chatelperronian tools. The skeleton was in such a tightly flexed position that it occupied an oval of only about one meter in diameter.[25]

"Francois Bordes, [archaeologist who developed the classic typology of Paleolithic tool kits] openly questioned the association of the skeleton with the Chatelperronian. Yet Bordes had long maintained that some form of pre-Sapiens had been responsible for manufacturing what he called the Mousterian of Acheulian tradition in France while Neanderthals were responsible for the other facies of the Mousterian."[26] Bordes died in 1980, also the pre-*sapiens* hypothesis, to which Carleton Coon also subscribed.

There are three possible explanations.[27] 1. The Chatelperronian represents an intrusive tradition or culture into Spain and France and was not derived from the local Mousterian. 2. The Chatelperronian developed independently from the local Mousterian.

3. The Chatelperronian represents a heavily acculturated derivation of the Mousterian. Harrold favors possibility 3.[28] "....[I]t seems most likely that the Chatelperronian represents an indigenous development of the local Mousterian under the impact of diffusion and probably migration. For reasons given above this inference is tentative, but it represents a `best fit' to the available evidence."[29] There is much continuity in flake tool production and side scrapers and denticulates. Also, there is some use of simple bone tools, coloring materials, and curios, by these supposed Neanderthals. However, discontinuities also occur: blade technologies, Chatelperronian points, new tool forms of bone working, incised stone plaques, burnt ochre, thus some implied nonutilitarian behaviors.[30]

Comparing Chatelperronian and Aurignacian, there seem to be not as many discontinuities as between Chatelperronian and Mousterian. However, Chatelperronian tools do not have the steep backing of Aurignacian tools and Aurignacian retouch. Also, as in the Aurignacian, there are no split-base bone points. Harrold concludes that the Neanderthals could learn most of the Aurignacian techniques, but lost ground over a 2,000-3,000-year period. A hesitation with his own conclusions: Harrold wonders why all the other techniques were presumably learned, but not the Aurignacian retouch.

The Aurignacian, even in its earliest exemplifications in Europe, reveals itself as fully evolved, sophisticated, implying that it was an older tradition that took its way of life into a wholly new geography, much as the European invaders of the Americas merely transferred their old way of life into a wholly new geographical and ecological setting.

Indeed, for the Amero-Indians, who like the Neanderthals felt the full weight of an advanced and alien culture thrust into their midst, there was, for the first three+ centuries of contact little of the new culture that they appropriated. Horses, introduced by the Spanish, did revolutionize the economy of the Plains Indians. Trade goods such as liquor and the rifle were utilized but never indigenously fabricated. The contact of the Neanderthals with the Cro-Magnons in Western Europe did, however, last for at least 3,000-5,000 years.

Mousterian Message

The evidence seems to argue for a greater morphological difference between the Neanderthals and the Cro-Magnids than heretofore accepted. Thus, it is believed that these were two physically and culturally separated races. Though presumably Caucasoid, these structural differences in cranial and post-cranial structure argue to many that the taxonomic level of separation might be large enough to be at the species level.[31]

That would not mean that these two species or races were inter-sterile. Mousterian culture seems to extend from Uzbekistan on the East, to Spain on the West, and then down into the Levant, at the borders of the Sinai. While the full flowering of Mousterian culture seems to extend in time from about 120,000-100,000 B.P to 35,000-30,000 B. P., the ancestral hints of Neanderthal presence in Europe in Vertesszolos (Hungary), Petralona (Greece), Swanscombe (England), Steinheim (Germany) argues for an additional 300,000-200,000-year residence in Eur-Asia, during which the specialized Neanderthal adaptations were being honed under the varying, but generally harsh glacial conditions throughout this geography.

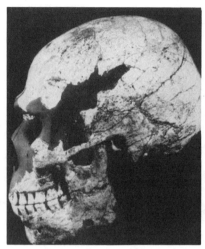 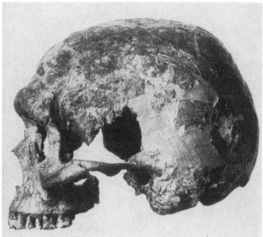

17.2 (A-B): A. Skhul 5; **B.** Qafzeh 6: How modern? Both fossils found in Israel in the context of Neanderthal-Mousterian tools. These sapiens, however, show cranial features closer to Cro-Magnon-type Europeans, with important hints of a Neanderthal heritage. Probability: both were part of mid-Eastern hybrid communities.

Toward the end of the Pleistocene, especially after 45,000 B.P., it is clear that the Neanderthals and the Cro-Magnids were, at the least, "ships passing each other in the night." We find significant and adjacent cultural layering, indicating that they utilized the same general cave and other types of home sites as they moved throughout their various and vast hunting and foraging range.

The significance of the redating of Qafzeh and Skhul in Israel to about 92,000-85,000 B.P. is that we encounter, at an early stage of this inter-species relationship, morphologies that are possibly proto-Cro-Magnid. Yet the culture associated with these clearly non-Neanderthaloid morphologies is Mousterian, the obverse of what we find associated with the later Chatelperronian in France, at c.35,000 B.P. As we have noted in earlier chapters, both of these human groups, at Qafzeh, specimen 6, and Skhul, specimen 5, still show signs of morphological robusticity, definite alveolar prognathism, super-orbital tori—heavy brow ridges.

The puzzling character of the female Qafzeh 9 fossil and the associated baby, Qafzeh 10, buried alongside her, is reflected in Ian Tattersal's description: "At this site a young [20 years of age] Mousterian woman was laid to rest over 90 thousand years ago, with an infant, possibly her child, at her feet. The deceased were, however, members of 'Homo sapiens', and this careful burial contrasts with the more casual interment typical of Neanderthals."[32]

However one views these two groups of *H. sapiens*, it is clear that some kind of Cro-Magnid was on the Eur-Asian scene at least 100,000 B.P. And this race of humans was sharing the geographies and ecologies of these domains with the Neanderthals, themselves probable inhabitants of the same territories for at least several hundred thousand years. How could they have stayed apart for so long, maintained their unique morphologies and cultures, only to meet and compete for this range of territory, after 100,000 B.P.?

It is not out of the question, as we shall later argue, that before c.100ka B.P. proto-Cro-Magnids were too few in number, and so restricted in their range of habitat as to be a hidden ethnic element at the periphery of Eur-Asian evolutionary dynamics. This appears to change radically after 100ka B.P. The intermediate cultural spirals throughout the Levant, as well as the probably hybrid Skhul and Qafzeh exemplars, can be hypothesized to be part of wandering and migrating populations miscegenating as they met with larger indigenous groups, that is, until the Aurignacian demographic and cultural tidal wave picked up full steam.

Again using the Amero-Indian analogy, in the period after 15,000 B.P. a variety of racially hybridized tribes made their way east over Beringia, bringing with them not only the genetic traces of the Cro-Magnid, Cauacasoid heritage, an east Asiatic Mongoloid remembrance, but the cultural traditions of the ancient Eur-Asian stone technology, in the Clovis points, arrow heads.

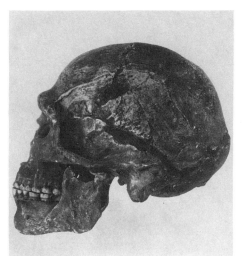 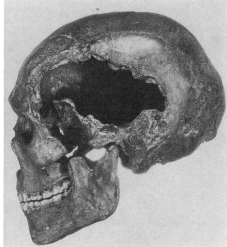

17.3 (A-B): Cro-Magnon Aurignacian skulls. **A**. Predmost (Czech Republic); **B**. Combe-Capelle (France), both c.30,000 B.P. Some observers see little difference between Predmost and Qafzeh, even at a time remove of c.60,000 years. Predmost probably shows the remains of a hybrid Neanderthal heritage, even though its tool kit was Aurignacian. Combe Capelle, a contemporary, is a classic Cro-Magnon type, in morphology and culture.

Cro-Magnon Hybrid Hints?

The argument that a number of these questionable intermediate fossil specimens are hybrids stems from the increasingly dominant views of the specialists that the classic Neanderthals and the classic Cro-Magnids are both morphologically discrete in their cranial and post cranial structure and in the cultural products that seem to define them mentally. That both Skhul and Qafzeh were found in the context of a Mousterian tool industry seems to have persuaded the majority of scientists to place them as anticipators of the Cro-Magnons, not yet part of that evolutionary clade of humans. They were not typical Neanderthals such as those found nearby, if at later time levels, such as the Amud and Kebara Neanderthals. The latter specimen, found with a hyoid bone, implies modern linguistic abilities for itself, Amud, and the earlier Neanderthaloid fossils at Tabun.[33]

In Europe, at Predmost, Mladec, and other, later Central and Eastern European sites, Cro-Magnids are found, heavy set in bone structure, with crania carrying well-developed brow ridges reminiscent of the Neanderthals, yet with skull profiles completely consonant with the Cro-Magnid, *Homo sapiens sapiens* morphology and associated Aurignacian cultural detritus.[34]

Coon purported to trace this kind of Caucasoid morphology into historical, Iron Age populations in Germany and in England:

> Cro-Magnon endocranial capacity, males with a mean 1580cm³, females 1370cm³. Most, were not prognathous except the female skull of the Proto-Magdalenian of Abri-Pataud. Brow ridges were moderate or missing, except for the Czechoslovakian, Predmost, Mladec, these of the early Aurignacian which come closest to Skhul 5 and Jebel Qafzeh 6, [Coon was not aware of the Qafzeh 9 description] but without a trace of Skhul's alveolar prognathism [upper jaw jutting forward—including nasal structures] these, Czech. skulls, also resemble a later Neolithic series from France, Iron Age skulls from Norway and Anglo-Saxon ones from the East Coast of England.[35]

Ashley-Montagu and Brace also saw these Central European skulls of Predmost *et al.*, at c.35,000-30,000 B.P., as more similar to Skhul and Qafzeh at 95,000-85,000 B.P.[36] They note that the Predmost Aurignacian skull from Czechoslovakia could be placed within the Skhul population without causing a ripple: heavy brow ridges, large teeth. Further, Mladec is even more robust, hint of bun-shaped occiput, (characteristically Neanderthal), heavy brow ridges, and powerfully-developed dentition. "What there is of reliable evidence shows that the transition from Neanderthal to modern took place gradually at the end of the Mousterian, continuing into the early Upper Paleolithic, as a response to the changes in selective factors..."[37]

Trinkaus and Shipman discuss the destiny of the Neanderthals, how they seem to have been so distinct from the modern humans in the Levant, why there is no sign of them from Uzbekistan to China during this time frame. Where did they come from to the Levant? The authors see a genetic admixture and interbreeding between resident Neanderthals and modern humans who were filtering in slowly from the Levant or elsewhere, into Central Europe.[38] "...nowhere is there evidence for violent confrontation between Neanderthals and modern humans (myths notwithstanding)."[39]

Dominique Gambier has considered and evaluated the various positions concerning the origin of modern humans in Europe during the discussed time frame, from c.45,000 B.P.:[40] 1. Brauer and Stringer argue that modern humans had a single origin in Africa. 2. Vandermeersch sees modern humans originating in Southwest Asia. Both 1 and 2 see the complete replacement of the Neanderthals. 3. Neanderthals are ancestral to modern humans. Frayer (1978); Smith (1982, 1985); Wolpoff (1980), also C. Loring Brace (1977), with M. F. Ashley-Montagu; also see P. Shipman and Trinkaus (1995) on Brace.

4. Trinkaus (1986, 1995) holds an intermediate position, *i.e.*, some absorption of Neanderthal genes. Trinkaus sees continuity in La Quina Neanderthal, and early modern humans: Hahnofersand, Mladec and Brno.[41]

Gambier acknowledges some robusticity in early modern Aurignacians, but, as with Coon, not Neanderthal-like; likewise post-cranial skeleton, more generally robust, is not considered in any way Neanderthal-like, thus agreeing with Trinkaus.[42] The occipital bun and alveolar plane on some Aurignacian specimens, were not considered specifically Neanderthal.[43] Thus they are generally primitive. Brauer, 1981, sees Hahnofersand frontal, 36,000 B.P., as possibly representing an early Neanderthal-Cro-Magnon hybrid. Gambier believes that the Chatelperronian is probably the product of early modern humans, contra Harrold above, not Neanderthal, because of cultural unity of early Aurignacian. "...[E]ven in Central Europe the paleoanthropological data supports the hypothesis of population replacement, as in Western Europe, but here [Central Europe] there is better evidence for some interbreeding during the replacement phase."[44] Thus, Gambier states that the Mladec specimens were more robust than Cro-Magnon, but like Coon, believes that the skull architecture is not different. Stringer also agrees that Mladec is not Neanderthal-like.[45]

Svante Paabo has thrown a small bombshell into the controversy concerning the relationship of the two races—or species—Neanderthal and Cro-Magnon. His mtDNA analysis, published in the July 1997 issue of *Cell*, is of the original Neanderthal fossil discovery dating from 1856. He apparently has secured uncontaminated mtDNA from the fossil remains. His conclusion is that the two lines never interbred, as there is no Neanderthal mtDNA signature in any extant contemporary human population. The recent discovery in Portugal of the skeleton of a four-year-old boy dated to 24,000 B.P. by Dr. J. Zilhao has stirred further controversy. As confirmed by Trinkaus, this child gives evidence of being a Neanderthal/Cro-Magnon hybrid. It argues for a remnant hybrid population existing several thousand years after the purported extinction of the last population of Neanderthals in Spain, c.28-27ka B.P.[46]

Any mtDNA claims must of course be taken with tentative hesitancy. The claim is radical, unless this specimen Neanderthal was unique in its genetic relationship with other Neanderthal groups. It requires that all hybridized humans (Neanderthal and Cro-Magnid) were gradually excluded from the subsequent genetic pool, first by the Cro-Magnons, then by the rest of the world, wherever such hybrid Cro-Magnon genes wandered in their various travels.

Persistent Genetic Contacts

Trinkaus and Shipman report on the decisive February, 1992, Royal Society-Ciba Foundation meeting:[47] Christopher Stringer, once the pillar supporter of the mtDNA "African Eve" scenario for the origin of modern humans here conceded that, "...there were greater possibilities for genetic admixture between African and non-African groups of late archaic humans," than he had previously accepted. At the same meeting, Fred Smith and Eric Trinkaus presented a new examination of the African fossils most often cited as the earliest anatomically modern humans. Their work challenged the supposed modernity of these remains, casting further doubts on the "Out-of-Africa" model." This would confirm Carleton Coon's long-scorned views of these early African humans as *H. erectus.*

Contrary to the "Out-of-Africa" mtDNA hypothesis, it would be a contradiction of all available evidence about the human genus to believe that miscegenation between diverse groups encountering each other would not take place, and often. Further, there is no evidence that a genetic barrier has ever existed within the genus *Homo.* Coon and Baker were the most outspoken advocates of the existence of sharply defined sub-species, *i.e.,* racial differences within the genus *Homo.* Regardless of the fluid taxonomic categorizations of the various and supposed species of *Homo,* Coon and Baker argued that there was a behavioral barrier that inhibited but did not exclude the breeding of admittedly fertile offspring of the various human ethnicities that have wandered the planet during the past two million years.[48]

In fact, Coon's description of the creation of the modern Negroids of West Africa within the past 15,000-10,000 years or earlier argued for the introduction of Caucasoid genes into the indigenous African hominids as part of the creation of both the Pygmies as well as the typical Bantu-like peoples of that region.[49]

But what do these several hints at early hybridization between Cro-Magnids and Neanderthals tell us? Recall that the association of Chatelperronian technology with Neanderthal skeletal materials, in the western range of these two Caucasoid races, in France, and at the end of the Neanderthal hegemony in Europe, c.35,000-32,000 B.P. still reveal quite orthodox Neanderthal fossil materials, no signs of intermediacy or hybridization.

In central France, 42 miles south of Auxerre, Arcy-sur-Cure, is a site in which jewelry-like bone ornaments and sophisticated stone tools were discovered (Chatellperonian?); also found was a single bone of a one-year-old Neanderthal. It revealed the opening for the left ear in which the balance canals were clearly those of a classic Neanderthal child. Fred Spoor and Frank Harrold stated that the site was younger than 33,000 B.P. J.-J. Hublin, the senior author of the report says 34,000 B.P. They argue that the Neanderthals died out without being direct ancestors of modern humans. Hublin sees the cultural artifacts as trade goods rather than Neanderthal adaptations of Aurignacian technology. The morphology of the bony labyrinth beneath the temporal bone "...is seen as an argument in support of distinguishing between Neanderthals and modern humans at the species level."[50]

Clearly, the Neanderthals have disappeared. But given their relatively late habitation in Europe, and the fact that large migratory mammals, such as humans, have the capacity for being interfertile with related forms having quite different phenotypic characteristics, could they not have left, here, too, a genetic mark upon the incoming and dominating population of Aurignacian Cro-Magnids?

- 2 -
Caucasoids: Expansion and Dominion

Dominating Genes
It has happened in evolution with regularity. A new ecological domain opens up. Opportunities for a new morphological model appear amidst the inevitable splintering mosaicism of races and forms jockeying to survive. The littering profile of hominid types, once ubiquitous, now extinct, testifies to the enormous selective competition first in Africa, then throughout the world, for a human exemplar to define this new vertebrate domain.

We can understand the dominator in terms of the genetic expression in morphology and behavior. Examining the subject now at hand, the perspective might not be clear. We gain additional understanding by visiting the results of the power and uniqueness of this paradigmatic human brain as it wreaks havoc on the less adaptive confreres that accompanied the victor along the evolutionary trail.

The Neanderthals present one exemplification of the competitive, if seemingly silent, struggle for dominance at the border of the explosion of *Homo sapiens sapiens* into our historic consciousness. But the selective story is not yet completed. These dynamics are in process to this day. And it would be instructive to follow the events as they did and are occurring, as a lesson, if yet inchoate, of the evolutionary significance of the drive of one genotype to dominate, physically and behaviorally.

A. A Most Ancient People
The great African mystery lies with the origin and ultimate fate of this ancient race. Carleton Coon claimed to be able to recognize the earliest Capoids in the Lake Turkana, Kenya, KNMER 3733, a hypothesized *H. erectus*, at 1.6mya.[51] He was also ready to go out on the limb, to relate the Capoids to the Mongoloids, and to their ancestor, *Sinanthropus*, Beijing Man. But while he ordinarily saw the later Capoids as derivative of earlier Mongoloids, chronological consistency, and his own orthodox opinion that Africa was the source of early human evolution, dictated the African priority for the Capoid-Mongoloid relationship. This would probably have persuaded Coon to see KNMER-3733 as the critical clue, and thus a *Capoid* ancestry for the Mongoloids.[52]

The earliest Capoids that Coon recognized as part of the North African assemblages and that Jean-Jacques Hublin has been investigating for a generation, is the sequence from Ternefine, c.700,000 B.P., to Sale, c.400,000 B.P., to Jebel Irhoud, c.190,000-100,000 B.P. The previously unexpected antiquity of Border Cave and Klasies River Mouth discoveries in South Africa, dating from c.90,000-60,000 B.P., and with a fairly sophisticated and distinctive tool kit, has altered somewhat the sense of priority of the North African homeland over South Africa.

Hublin's recent research into the relationship of the North African advanced hominids, the Jebel Irhoud fossils from Morocco, argues for a separate evolutionary history from the Neanderthaloids, even though Mousterian tools are associated with more recent North African exemplars.[53] He places these closer in morphological affinity to Skhul and Qafzeh, though probably they are older and more primitive. But he does not comment on their sub-species affinities, whether they are Caucasoid or Capoid. Coon placed them with the latter and thus, the successor Aterian culture. Wolpoff, like Coon and Weiden-reich, a believer in the so-called "multiregional" perspective on human evolution sees a relationship of Jebel Irhoud with Kabwe (Broken Hill) of Zambia.[54] Coon did not acknowledge such a relationship. Hublin does relate the Levantine fossils to the successor North African Aterians, and therefore places Skhul and Qafzeh in oxygen isotope stage 5 and 6, from about 180,000-70,000 B.P.

Coon argued that the Wilton tool technology of South Africa is a derivation of the Capsian of North and East Africa, also Capoid. Bushman rock paintings that extend north to Rhodesia (Zambia and Botswana today) are recent "...because they do not extend below the soil level in the caves and rock shelters in which they are found; because they have not been smoke-blackened by herdsmen's fires; because the granite on which they were painted had not exfoliated (peeled off) very much from weathering; and because the fauna depicted are all recent. The theory that the ancestral Capoids migrated southward from North Africa goes back to the discovery during the last century, of Bushman-like rock paintings in the Sahara."[55]

Coon, in 1962, claimed that there are no Bushman-like skulls of great antiquity in South Africa, thus the argument for a migration southward in near historic times. In 1905 Biasutti denoted Bushman-like traits in the earliest Egyptian skulls. The Singa skull was discovered in 1924, 200 miles south of Khartoum, on a bank of the Blue Nile. It dated from at latest 10,000-5,000 B.P., and was fully mineralized. It is a Capoid skull cap, with thick bone on the parietals (13mm.), a notch above the glabella reminiscent of *Sinanthropus*—and the Mongoloids.[56]

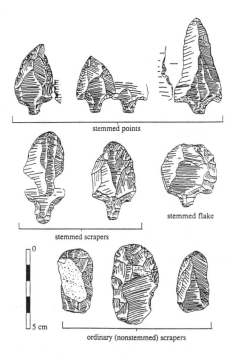

stemmed points

stemmed scrapers

stemmed flake

0

5 cm

ordinary (nonstemmed) scrapers

17.4 Aterian tanged and stemmed artifacts from North Africa. There are no fossils with which to link this type of tool kit. While contemporary with the Eur-Asian Neanderthal Mousterian culture, they differ significantly.

Unique Capoid Cultures

Davidson and Noble, writing since the early-late Pleistocene fossil discoveries in South Africa, view the Howieson's Poort Industries, c.70-50ka B.P., at Klasies River Mouth (Wilton) and the North African Aterian industries, c.40ka B.P., as the only ones, outside the Cro-Magnids that clearly argue for intentionality. The industries are narrow both in time and place. Howieson's Poort industries, at the beginning of the late Pleistocene, used microliths, small tools shaped into crescent shapes, blunting the margins of the tools, also crayons of ochre. The Aterian industries, leaf-shaped points and tangs not related to the working edge, date from the very late Pleistocene.[57] (Note our Part 1 discussion of such various pre-Aurignacian and post-Middle Paleolithic technologies, which at this point are not clarified by concrete human remains.)

No doubt Coon, today, would have to modify his view that the path of the Capoids was in only one direction, north to south, and in quite recent times. The new fossil discoveries in the south, along with their cultural debris, would not contradict his late-in-life assessment of the ancient Kenyan erectine, KNMER 3733, as a proto-Capoid. If at 1.6mya in Kenya, why not at 100,000 B.P, in both South and North Africa.

Gustave Schenck has followed this mystery:

> Henri Lhote was able to indicate that primitive military roads had crossed the region in prehistoric ages. The North-South Africa route had been a busy popular road. Caucasoids or Europeans from the last Ice Age, light-skinned Orientals and Southern Europeans pushed forward as far as the Transvaal.[58]....The remains of human skulls and limb bones that were found at Boskop in the Transvaal belong to a primitive human race that probably immigrated from the North. They may have beaten a trail before the last Ice Age—a repeatedly trodden popular road stretching from North Africa to the Cape, the length of the African Continent.[59]

Schenck describes the art of the Capoids found in the Libyan Desert by Heinrich Barth, between the years 1848-1855. It was discovered in the Hadar Massif, the highlands of Tassil-n-Ajjer, west of Egypt and South of Benghazi. Henri Lhote studied and characterized the art between 1956-57. He placed it, as did Coon, at about 8,000 B.P. Altogether Lhote described 10,000 rock paintings, from four different stylistic periods, up until the camel appears in the rock art at about 50 B.C.[60]

The dating of the quite early and sophisticated tools and cultural objects found at Howiesson's Poort, in the same general vicinity, spatial and temporal, of the fossil humans at Klasies River Mouth and Border Cave depends on the continued plausibility of the latter's early dating, to 90,000-60,000 B.P., as does the recent find along the Semlike River in the Democratic Republic of the Congo, (Zaire), of a carved bone harpoon, dated through TL and ESR methods of measurement of associated hippo teeth, to between 90,000-75,000 B.P.[61] Perhaps they were Cro-Magnid wanderers along a water course; perhaps the chronology is more recent. But clearly it is out of "place," and no human fossil remains are evident. "Why does this site stand out like a big sore thumb?"[62]

Northward Ho

The Aterians did not only go south at the end of the Pleistocene. Coon believed that the Capoids could have entered Europe during Würm 2, or oxygen isotope period 4, c.72,000 B.P.[63] Again, the typical Capoid/Bushmanoid painting style illustrated in

Schenk and Itzkoff, and found in the eastern Spanish cave at Castellan, testify to a Ca-poid/North African presence in Spain alongside the clearly Upper Paleolithic Caucasoid residents toward the end of the Pleistocene.[64]

> There is, however, a possibility that a few North Africans may have visited Europe during Würm 2 or 3. This is indicated not only by the discovery of Aterian arrowheads in Solutrian deposits in Spanish caves,...but also by the discovery of a skullcap, cut in the form of a bowl, which was found lying on the floor of a cave containing Upper Paleolithic im-plements and paintings. It has very heavy brow ridges and a receding forehead, and could hardly have belonged to an Upper Paleolithic Caucasoid. In the only available photograph, it looks, in profile, like the Florisbad skull from South Africa, an ancestral Bushman specimen of a group that probably originated in North Africa. Until the skullcap has been studied, no definitive statement about it can be made.[65]
>
> Implements of typical Aterian form (Aterian is a local African industry)—tanged and barbed pressure-flaked points—have been found in caves in Almeria and Valencia along with Solutrian points. If some North Africans could have crossed the western Mediterranean to Europe in Würm 2, others might have done so earlier.[66]

There is in the American Museum of Natural History collection a vivacious and brilliant hunting scene, in reds, yellows and browns, in typical Capoid style. It is from Castellan in eastern Spain, end of the Upper Paleolithic.[67] But this human and cultural presence disappears as the Upper Paleolithic Caucasoids move South, across the Straits into North Africa as represented by the more recent Holocene Moullian culture, still leaving hints of the ancient Capoid presence in the existing North African populations.[68] But also, remember the trail of Capoid-like art noted above and found throughout North Africa and then into South Africa, at the end of the Pleistocene, 12,000 B.P., a time when the Sahara was still passable.

17.5 Stylistically different cave painting, Spain. A copy of a late-Upper Paleolithic wall painting differs from the traditional "Cro-Magnon" esthetic. It could reflect a Capoid-Boskopoid presence in Spain toward the end of the Pleistocene, c.15,000 B.P.

Dissolution and Disappearance

One wonders whether an observer some 30,000 years hence, studying both the uni-versal Cro-Magnid and the Capoid art of Spain, North and South Africa, the Aurignacian and Solutrian and then, again, the Capsian and Aterian technologies, would raise a question with regard to the Capsian-Aterian/Aurignacian-Solutrian relationship, as we do today with regard to the relationship between the Chatelperronian and Aurignacian industries. Who influenced whom? Would they ask why the Capoids never learned to paint in three dimensions, used almost exclusively open-air sites as compared to the deep cave artwork of the Cro-Magnids? Indeed, we can ask today whether the Cro-Magnid influence here goes back much further in time, both genetically and culturally, to explain the rapid, late Pleistocene evolution of the Capoids. And, too, as with the Neanderthals, was this influence just as impotent in transforming an ancient people, its biology and culture, into a modern competitive prototype?

A late-nineteenth-century Bushman wall painting, outdoors in southern Africa, shows Bushman rustlers defending their take from Bantu pursuers.[69] The press of recently arrived European Caucasoids along the Cape, the seemingly irresistible migration of the Bantu peoples from the jungles of West Africa, herald the beginning of the final chapter of this ancient people. Much earlier, the Neanderthals, unlike the Capoids, had nowhere to flee from the oncoming invaders.

The ultimate mystery of the origins of the Northwest African humans as well as the South African Klasies River and Border Cave people, seems to center on their final retreat and evolution into the large-skulled Boskopoid peoples, in southern Africa, at the Holocene Border, some 15,000-10,000 B.P. The latter, large-skulled people, often with endocranial capacities over $1600cm^3$, are probably the remnants of Capoids pushed out of Spain and North Africa with the coming of the Cro-Magnid, Moullians.

The breaking up of the race into the Hottentot and Bushman ethnicities, the former more evidently hybridized into the oncoming Negroids from the north, heralds the eventual paedomorphic shrinking of these latter peoples to a specialized and precarious existence in the Kalahari. Today, the Bushman is no longer independent; in effect the Bushmen are captive wards of the modern national state, and are disappearing as an integral ethnic group. The hybridized Negroid Xhosa peoples of South Africa, with their Bushman-like click languages, are now represented by talented leaders of mixed blood such as Nelson Mandela. They reflect the direction of a likely inevitable process of amalgamation. As with the Neanderthals, and only a few thousand years later, an interesting, tenacious people, whose late-Pleistocene/modern hegira is still a mystery, is about to enter the annals of evolutionary extinction.

B. Eastern Impact of the Cro-Magnids

The existence of human populations in both the northeastern as well as southeastern quadrants of Asia, the *H. erectus sinanthropus* and *H. erectus pithecanthropus* traditions establish a base line of habitation at the 2.0-1.5mya level, at the latest.[70] Humans, both before this time and after, have been unendingly on the move. The appearance of the cultural detritus of Cro-Magnon at Makarova-4 in Southeastern Siberia, along the Lena River and near Lake Baikal at about 40,000 B.P., at a longitude equal to Chongking, China, should not surprise.[71]

What is puzzling is the fact that thus far no Neanderthal cultural debris or fossils have been discovered east of Uzbekistan, forty degrees longitude and 1200 miles to the southwest of the above-mentioned Cro-Magnid encampments. The Cro-Magnids make their cultural appearance at about 45,000 B.P., both in the Levant and Eastern Europe, (Bulgaria).[72] We should bear in mind that the hybridization represented by Skhul 5 and Qafzeh 9 (Israel), at about 85,000-95,000 B.P., implies the existence of the Cro-Magnons at that time level since no other people existed in any part of the world who could have contributed the genetics leading to that "almost" Cro-Magnid morphology, along with the existing Neanderthal Mousterian cultural artifacts discovered with these fossils.

17.6 Bushman, nineteenth-century external wall painting. Africa-War. Bantu attempting to retrieve their cattle from Bushman rustlers. The style is eerily similar to the Spanish wall painting of 15,000 earlier. The on-going struggle with the Bantu, advancing out of their West African homeland, and the invading Europeans up from the Cape, marks the gradual decline of the ancient Capoid race, now, their incipient extinction as a distinct ethnicity.

The implication is clear. If they were not culturally, fully-evolved Upper Paleolithic people at that time frame, c.100,000 B.P., the new survivalist behaviors presumed on the basis of this modernizing morphology had to have then at least been in process of formation. These proto-Cro-Magnid people were likely on the move, hunting and gathering, meeting other peoples, and certainly sharing their genetics with them, either through voluntary sociality or by means of physical force and cultural intimidation.[73] "...[B]y the end of the Paleolithic they had well-established territorial patterns and that summer wandering often allowed them to link up with other hunting peoples and make the usual social trading exchanges—art, wives, ideas."[74]

East Asian Population Shifts

The evidence is both direct and indirect. Australia was entered about 40,000 B.P., given the archaeological evidence, apparently by two quite different peoples. One, Kow Swamp, Coobool Creek, dated to c.14,000 B.P., is reminiscent of the populations in adjoining islands of Indonesia, evolved erectine/*sapiens* Ngandong/Sangiran descendants of the ancient "Pithecanthropines."[75] The other population, Lake Mungo, now dated to about 24,000 B.P., a far more modern population, morphologically, disappears from Australia. The contemporary aboriginal populations share more common traits with the more recent fossils, Kow Swamp.

This movement south into Australia coincides with the seeming expansion of the Chinese Mongoloids out of their northern homeland.[76] Dating from about 30,000 B.P.

this movement seems to coincide chronologically with the recent redating into several species of humans in Java.[77] The so-called Wadjak skulls found by Dubois in the 1890s, only described in 1921, are large, fully *sapiens* exemplars and date from the end of the Pleistocene, from 40,000-25,000 B.P.[78] Theunissen, believes, on the basis of associated fauna, that Wadjak should be viewed as quite recent.[79]

Today, most of the peoples of Southeast Asia are a blend of these ancient races. Clearly, the press, as with the southerly descent of the Neanderthals into the Levant, the expulsion from Europe and then North Africa of the Capoids, was from the north. New peoples were arriving, and others were leaving. Indeed, part of the answer might be climatic. However, there is no evidence of a simultaneous drying up of populations in the north, rather the dispersion of less advanced people, morphologically and culturally, into the underpopulated geographies of Southeast Asia, and into Beringia.

The present Southeast Asian languages, except for Thai and Burmese, are part of the Austranesian family of languages, traceable to the aboriginal Austranesian population of Australia, Tasmania, Papua New Guinea, and their ancestors to the North, as well as some island peoples of the Pacific, such as Fiji, possibly some of the Negrito populations of Philippines, Malasyia, India, Andaman Islands. They all are the remnants of this once widely dispersing migration from Africa, after c.2mya. Recall that many populations of Australid peoples in northeast Asia, inevitably to be hybridized with Mongoloid and Caucasoid elements, remained in Siberia and the circumpolar areas, some of which eventually migrated to North America.

It is clear here, too, that the unhybridized, but extremely variable, descendants of this once widespread morphological ethnicity, from Mojokerto 1, Sangiran 27 to Ngandong and Kow Swamp, have been pushed to the edge of survival. The Tasmanians are now extinct. The Australian aboriginal populations are largely interbred with the newly arrived Caucasoids from Europe. Except for small groups on some of the peripheral islands, we can expect these original ethnicities to be rapidly absorbed through miscegenation into the representative populations, Caucasoid and Mongoloid, of the dominant technologies and cultures of the modern era.

China

A claim can be made that the historical Mongoloid population of China, the undisputed homeland of another ancient c.2.0mya post-African Diaspora people, are themselves largely the products of a gradual Pleistocene and Holocene hybridization between oncoming Caucasoids, probably proto- or evolved Cro-Magnids, from about 50,000 B.P. The earliest fully *sapiens*, if quite robust, human fossil was found at Liujiang, in Quangxi province in southern China at the purported date of 67,000 B.P., as estimated by Wu. It is a controversial call. It may be more recent.[80] The Upper Cave specimen, #101, from Zhoukoudian, has been widely interpreted as being, Caucasoid, at least in part. It dates from c.30,000-10,000 B.P., with a seeming majority bias toward the more recent date.[81] Bar-Yosef has recently commented upon the fact that in the Upper Cave at Zhoukoudian a "rather poor flake industry is accompanied by elaborate bone tools and pendants," typical markers of Upper Paleolithic Cro-Magnon technology and art, and here well within a reasonable migratory timeframe.[82]

Coon agreed with a more recent dating for the Chinese sequences. He discussed the penetration of Middle Paleolithic peoples and their tool kits as entering the Fen Valley of North-Central China, citing the work of Bushnell and McBurney.[83] "Chinese paleontologists and archaeologists have found no clearly `sapiens' skeletons in their country which are older than the Fen Valley flints."[84]

We must recall that the dates for the migration of small and diverse groups of Amero-Indians across Bering into North America span the latter part of this period, from 13,000-11,000 B.P. The Amero-Indians are a hybrid people, combining, in various dimensions, Australoid, Mongoloid, and Caucasoid morphological features.[85] The technology of these people is clearly a derived form of the Upper Paleolithic tool kit. The discovery of a typical "Indian Arrowhead"-type spear point, slightly smaller than a house key in eastern Siberia, 25 miles north of Magadan, Uptar River, near the Sea of Okhotsk, and radiocarbon dated to c.8,300 B.P., reinforces this derivation.[86]

Most authorities believe that the overall weather patterns during long stretches of the 1.9my Pleistocene, with its various "Ice Ages," occasionally created moderate ecological conditions south of the ice packs. This allowed for the flourishing of a wide variety of mammoths, mastodons, rhinoceri, sloths, and at very high latitudes. Thus it was quite possible for populations at a more cultural modest advance, still to pursue their hunting/gathering and migratory patterns. The pathway across Siberia, as well as the so-called "Silk Road" was open. That humans camped at very northerly places, as long ago as 300,000 B.P., ought not to be very surprising.[87] Certainly, the ancestors of the Australasian and Mongoloid peoples had made their way east as long ago as 2.0mya.

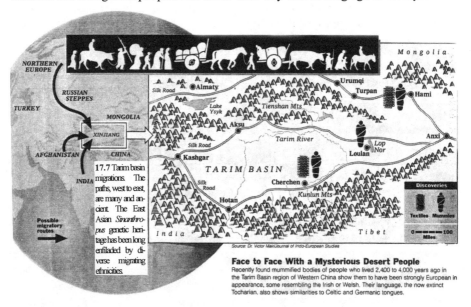

17.7 Tarim basin migrations. The paths, west to east, are many and ancient. The East Asian *Sinanthropus* genetic heritage has been long enfiladed by diverse migrating ethnicities.

Face to Face With a Mysterious Desert People
Recently found mummified bodies of people who lived 2,400 to 4,000 years ago in the Tarim Basin region of Western China show them to have been strongly European in appearance, some resembling the Irish or Welsh. Their language, the now extinct Tocharian, also shows similarities to Celtic and Germanic tongues.

Source: Dr. Victor Mair/Journal of Indo-European Studies

The closing off of this migratory route at the beginning of the Holocene, c.12,000 B.P., the coming of current continental climatic conditions, the destruction of the great herds explains the relative absence of recent migrations to North America, except possibly for the Eskimos. Today, even the hardiest sub-arctic fauna, the reindeer, are subject to the terrible cold of North Siberia. "Frightful weather in Siberia. 10,000 reindeer have died on the Chukai Peninsula in the far Northeast...could reach 30,000 deaths. Thick crust of ice over pastures, -40 below zero, Fahrenheit.. The region has about 240,000 reindeer, 60,000 have been driven off by herdsman to distant pastures not covered with ice."[88]

But such conditions did not deter more recent migrations across the central Asian plain and the subsequent amalgamation of peoples. Example, a recent widely disseminated set of discoveries: Mummies have been recovered from the Tarim Basin in Xinjiang province of China, at Hami. They have long noses and skulls, blond or brown hair, thin lips, deep-set eyes, Caucasoids, Welsh or Irish in appearance. Evidence is that they spoke a Tocharian Indo-European language, similar to Celtic or German. They are dated to 2000-1200 B.C., or up to 4,000 B.P.[89] The Tocharians linguistically controlled the Xinjiang area until about 900 A.D., then were absorbed politically by the expanding Han Chinese.

The first Chinese dynasty, the Shang, is traditionally characterized by the Chinese themselves as governed by a red-haired, green-eyed people, possibly of Persian origin, (much like characterizations of the original Mongol leadership, at 1200 A.D), who arrived on horse in the Yellow River Valley, at about 2,000 B.C.[90] Shortly after, literacy was developed, the Chinese civilization thence taking its own unique developmental route. Early dynastic iconography in China hints at the Caucasoid roots of this aristocracy, gradually to be largely effaced by a dominant modern Mongoloid phenotype.

The Japanese and Koreans, too, have a mixed ethnic heritage, like the Chinese, in effect all but effacing the ancient *Sinanthropus* heritage. These latter people crossed the great Eur-Asian plain, arriving at the Pacific Ocean about 300 B.C. They may have been related to the auburn-haired people in the frozen tomb of Pazyryk, in the Siberian Altai at 400 B.C.[91] The Koreans stayed behind on the mainland. The present Japanese ventured across the Sea of Japan to the islands. There, they found a mixed Australasian/Mongoloid people, today referred to as Malayo-Polynesian. They interbred with these peoples, as did the Koreans with the then-indigenous populations on the mainland, creating a tri-racial ethnic amalgam. The Japanese and Koreans brought with them a Central Asian Uralic/Altaic language variant, on which they later imposed a Chinese written orthography. Japanese scholars have noted that the ancient mythology of their own "*Völkerwanderung*" was similar to the traditional Indo-Germanic pantheon of gods and myths.[92] Today the similarity of Japanese with Finnish is conditioned by recent claims that the Finnish linkage to the Uralic/Altaic family of languages is spurious, and that its affinity to Persian and the other Indo-European languages is more supportable.[93]

In sum, it is fair to say that the historical and contemporary power of all three northeast Asiatic ethnicities—Korean, Chinese, Japanese—was conditioned by the absorption of those powerful and dominating genetics originating in the Cro-Magnid homeland sometime around 125,000-100,000 B.P.

In no way can it be claimed that the variety of racial and ethnic heritages that have passed through the various lines of hominids, in their own homelands and in the lands of migration, constitutes a racial blockade for this seeming outwardly expansionary and dominating behavioral profile. The Neanderthals were Caucasoids, and their genetics must be presumed to be still flowing through the blood of the Eur-Asians. Therefore, given the confirmability of the mtDNA genetic bottleneck of all extra-African populations around the world, these Neanderthal genes must have passed through practically every other ethnic group on our planet.[94]

Endnotes, Chapter 17

[1] Simeons. A. T. S. 1962. *Man's Presumptuous Brain*. N.Y.: Dutton, p 276

[2] Tattersall, I. 1995. *The Last Neanderthal*. New York: Macmillan/U.S.A., p.9.

[3] Schwarcz, H. P. 1994. "Chronology of Modern Humans in the Levant," in *Late Quaternary Chronology and Paleoclimates of the Eastern Mediterranean*, O. Bar-Yosef and R. S. Kra, eds., Tucson, AZ: Radiocarbon, University of Arizona, p. 27.

[4] Bar-Yosef, O., and Kra, R. S., eds. 1994. *Late Quaternary Chronology and Paleoclimates of the Eastern Mediterranean, op. cit.*, p. 26.

[5] Trinkaus, E., and Shipman, P. 1993. *The Neanderthals*, N.Y.: Knopf, p. 393.

[6] Trinkaus and Shipman, 1993, *op. cit.*, pp. 394-395.

[7] Bar-Yosef, O. 1989. "Geochronology of the Levantine Middle Paleolithic," in *The Human Revolution—Behavioral and Biological Perspectives on the Origins of Modern Humans*, P. A. Mellars and C. Stringer, eds., Princeton, N.J.: Princeton Univ. Press, pp. 589-610, esp. p. 604.

[8] Bar-Yosef, 1989, in Mellars and C. Stringer, eds., *op. cit.*, pp. 589-610. See fig. 30.1, p. 591; fig 30.2, p. 593.

[9] Shea, John J. 1989. "A Functional Study of the Lithic Industries Associated with Hominid Fossils in the Kebara and Qafzeh Caves, Israel," in Mellars and Stringer, eds., *op. cit.*, pp. 611-625. See fig. 31.1, p. 615, p. 622.

[10] Bar-Yosef, and Kra, eds. 1994. "Introduction: Dating Eastern Mediterranean Sequences," in Bar-Yosef and Kra *op. cit.*, pp.1-12.

[11] Marks, A. E., Monigal, Kathryn. 1995. "Modeling the Production of Elongated Blanks from the Early Levantine Mousterian at Rosh Ein Mor," in *The Definition and Interpretation of Levallois Technology*, H. L. Dibble and O. Bar-Yosef, eds., Madison, WI: Prehistory Press, pp. 267-277, esp. p. 267.

[12] Marks and Monigal, 1995, in Dibble and Bar-Yosef, eds., *op. cit.*, pp. 267-277, esp. p. 275.

[13] Phillips, James. 1994. "Upper Paleolithic Chronology in the Levant and Nile," in Bar-Yosef, and Kra, eds., *op. cit.,* pp. 169-176, esp. p. 169.

[14] Phillips, 1994, in Bar-Yosef and Kra, eds., *op. cit.*, pp. 169.

[15] Phillips, 1994, in Bar-Yosef and Kra, eds., *op. cit.*, p. 170.

[16] Phillips, 1994, in Bar-Yosef and Kra, eds., *op. cit.*, p. 171.

[17] Tattersall, 1995, *op. cit.,* p. 116.

[18] Phillips, 1994, in Bar-Yosef and Kra, eds., *op. cit.*, p. 172.

[19] Bar-Yosef, O., and Belfer-Cohen, A. 1996. "Another Look At The Levantine Aurignacian," in *XIII International Union of Prehistoric and Protohistoric Sciences*, Forli ABACO Edizioni, Coloquium XI, pp. 139-150.

[20] Bar-Yosef and Kra, eds. 1994, *op. cit.*, pp. 1-12, esp. p. 5.

[21] Marks, A. E. 1990. "The Middle Paleolithic of the Near East and the Nile Valley: The Problem of Cultural Transformations," in *The Emergence of Modern Humans*, P. A. Mellars and C. B. Stringer, eds., Edinburgh: Univ. of Edinburgh Press, pp. 56-80; Klein, R. G. 1989. *The Human Career*, Chicago: Univ. of Chicago Press, pp. 268, 303.

[22] Bar-Yosef and Belfer-Cohen, 1996, *op. cit.*, pp. 141, 145; Bar-Yosef, O., *et al.* 1996. "The Dating of the Upper Paleolithic Layers at Kebara Cave, Mt. Carmel," *Journal of Archaeological Science*, 23:297-306, esp. 304.

[23] Howells, W. W. 1989. "Skull Shapes and the Map: Craniometric Analyses in the Dispersion of Modern `Homo,'" *Papers of the Peabody Museum*, 79:1-189; Wolpoff, M. H., and Caspari, R. 1997. *Race and Human Evolution*, N.Y.: Simon and Schuster, p. 354; Brown, Peter (Univ. of New England, Australia). 1993. "Recent Human Evolution in East Asia and Australia," in *The Origin of Modern Humans and the*

Impact of Chronometric Dating, M. J. Aitken, C. B. Stringer, and P. A. Mellars, eds., Princeton, N.J.: Princeton Univ. Press, pp. 217-233, esp. pp. 221, 226; Kaminga, J., and Wright, R. V. S. 1988. "The Upper Cave at Zhoukoudian and the Origins of the Mongoloids," *Jrnl. of Human Evolution*, 17:739-767.

[24] Bar-Yosef and Kra, eds. 1994, in Bar-Yosef and Kra, *op. cit.*, pp.1-12 (S. Kozlowski, personal communication to Bar-Yosef).

[25] Trinkaus and Shipman, 1993, *op. cit.*, pp. 377-378.

[26] Trinkaus and Shipman, 1993, *op. cit.*, pp. 378-379.

[27] Harrold, Francis B. 1989. "Mousterian, Chatelperronian and Early Aurignacian in Western Europe: Continuity or Discontinuity?" in Mellars and Stringer, eds., *op. cit.*, pp. 677-713, esp. pp. 680-681.

[28] Harrold, 1989, in Mellars and Stringer, eds., *op. cit.*, pp. 696-697.

[29] Harrold, 1989, in Mellars and Stringer, eds., *op. cit.*, p. 697.

[30] Harrold, 1989, in Mellars and Stringer, eds., *op. cit.*, pp. 704-705; Wilford, J. N. 1996. "Playing of Flute May Have Graced Neanderthal Fire," *The New York Times*, 10/29/96. John Noble Wilford, Dr. Ivan Turk, Drs. Blackwell, Blicksteins (Queens College), Schwarcz (McMaster Univ. in Hamilton, Ont.). From 43,000-82,000 B.P., part of a young bear femur four holes, two aligned. Near Idrija, Northwestern, Slovenia.

[31] Hublin, J.-J. 1997. Personal communication, 12/2/97.

[32] Tattersall 1995, *op. cit.*, Illustration 115, pp. 168-169.

[33] Lieberman, P. 1993. "On the Kebara KMH 2 Hyoid and Neanderthal Speech," *Current Anthropology*, 34:2:172-177.

[34] see Klein, 1989, *op. cit.*, p. 277; Wolpoff and Caspari, 1997, *op. cit.*, p. 340.

[35] Coon, C. S. 1962. *The Origin of Races*, N.Y.: Knopf, pp. 583-584.

[36] Ashley-Montagu, M. F., and Brace, C. L. 1977. *Human Evolution*, N.Y.: Macmillan, pp. 350-352.

[37] Ashley-Montagu and Brace, 1977, *op. cit.*, fig. 153, p. 351, of Predmost skull, p. 352.

[38] Trinkaus and Shipman, 1993, *op. cit.*, pp. 414-415.

[39] Trinkaus and Shipman, 1993, *op. cit.*, p. 416.

[40] Gambier, Dominique. 1989. "Fossil Hominids from the Early Upper Paleolithic (Aurignacian) of France," in Mellars and Stringer, eds., *op. cit.*, pp. 194-211.

[41] Gambier, 1989. "Fossil Hominids from the Early Upper Paleolithic (Aurignacian) of France," in Mellars and Stringer, eds., *op. cit.*, pp. 205-206.

[42] Gambier, 1989, in Mellars and Stringer, eds., *op. cit.*, pp. 204-205.

[43] Gambier, 1989, in Mellars and Stringer, eds., *op. cit.*, p. 206.

[44] Gambier, 1989, in Mellars and Stringer, eds., *op. cit.*, pp. 207-208.

[45] Gambier, 1989, in Mellars and Stringer, eds., *op. cit.*, p. 207.

[46] Wade, N. 1997. "Neanderthal DNA Sheds New Light On Human Origins," *The New York Times*, 7/11/97; Wilford, J. N. 1999. "Discovery Suggests Man Is a Bit Neanderthal," *The New York Times*, 25 Apr., 1, 19; Trinkaus, E., and Zilhao, J. *Proceedings of the National Academy of Sciences*, forthcoming, 1999-2000.

[47] Trinkaus and Shipman, 1993, *op. cit.*, p. 396.

[48] Baker, J. 1974. *Race*. N.Y.: Oxford Univ. Press.

[49] Coon, C. S. 1962. *The Origin of Races*, *op. cit.*, p. 656.

[50] Hublin, J. J., *et al.* 1996. "A Late Neanderthal Associated with Upper Paleolithic Artifacts," *Nature*, 5/16/96, 381:224-226 (*The New York Times* 5/16/96, (AP)); see the controversial view of the "Neanderthals as Genius" and its many critics: d'Errico, F., *et al.* 1998. "Neanderthal Acculturation in Western Europe," *Current Anthropology Supplement*, June, Vol. 39.

[51] Coon, C. S. 1982. *Racial Adaptations*, Chicago: Nelson-Hall, pp. 125-129.

[52] The existence of the Capoid epicanthic fold that shields the inside corner of the eye, presumably in the Mongoloids from the cold because of the layer of fat that this fold contains, or the glare of the sun for the Capoids, is another morphological element that relates the two-widely separated peoples. See Stringer, C. B., and Gamble, C. 1993. *In Search of the Neanderthals: Solving the Puzzle of Human Origins*, London: Thames and Hudson, pp. 138-139.

[53] Hublin, J. J. 1993. "Recent Human Evolution in Northwestern Africa," in Aitken *et al.*, eds., *op. cit.*, pp. 118-131.

[54] Wolpoff and Caspari, 1997, *op. cit.*, p. 183.

[55] Coon, 1962, *op. cit.*, pp. 638-639.

[56] Coon, 1962, *op. cit.*, pp. 638-639.

[57] Davidson, Iain, and Noble, William. 1993. "Tools and Language in Human Evolution," in *Tools, Language And Cognition In Human Evolution*, K. R. Gibson and T. Ingold, eds., Cambridge: Cambridge Univ. Press, pp. 363-388, pp. 380-382; fig. 16.7, p. 381.

[58] Schenck, G. 1961. *The History of Man*, Philadelphia: Chilton Books.

[59] Schenck, 1961, *op. cit.*, p. 164.

[60] Schenck, 1961, *op. cit.*, pp. 158*ff.*

[61] Gibbons, Ann. 1995. "Old Dates for Modern Behavior," *Science*, 4/28/95, 268:495-496.

[62] R. Klein quoted in: Gibbons, Ann. 1995. "Old Dates for Modern Behavior," *Science*, 4/28/95, 268:496.

[63] Broderick, A. H. 1961. "A Newly Discovered and as yet Unexplored Treasure-House of Spanish Cave Art: The Fantastic and Beautiful Caves of Nerja--a Preliminary Note," *ILN*, 239:6366:216-219, in: Coon, C. S. 1962. *The Origin of Races*, *op. cit.*, note 8, p. 585.

[64] Schenck, 1961, *op. cit.*, pp. 155*ff*; Itzkoff, S. W. 1985. *Triumph of the Intelligent*, Plate III, N.Y.: Peter Lang.

[65] Coon, 1962, *op. cit.*, note 8, p. 585; Broderick, 1961, *op. cit.*, *ILN*, 239:6366:216-219.

[66] Coon, 1962, *op. cit.*, note 9, p. 523, Vallois and Movius: Catalogue des Hommes Fossiles.

[67] Itzkoff, 1985, *op. cit.*, Plate III: "Rock Wall Paintings."

[68] Moullians, in Coon, 1962, *op. cit.*, pp. 603*ff*; ethnic types—Capoids-Mouillians, in Coon, C. S., and Hunt, E. E., Jr. 1965. *The Living Races of Man*, N.Y.: Knopf; see Itzkoff, 1985, Plate VII.

[69] Itzkoff, 1985, *op. cit.*, Plate III, bottom, from Museum of Natural History (N.Y.C).

[70] Swisher, C. C., *et al.* 1994. "Age of the Earliest Known Hominids in Java, Indonesia," *Science*, 2/25/94, 263:1118-1121.

[71] Morell, Virginia. 1995. "Siberia: Surprising Home for Early Modern Humans," *Science* 6/2/95, 268:1279, reporting on research of Ted Goebel, Oregon State College, and M. Aksenov, Irkutsk Univ., *Antiquity*, June, 1995.

[72] Bar-Yosef and Kra, eds., 1994, *op. cit.*, pp. 1-12; Kozlowski, S. 1994, in Bar-Yosef and Kra, eds., *op. cit.*, personal communication to Bar-Yosef; Marks and Monigal, 1995, in Dibble and Bar-Yosef, eds., *op. cit.*, pp. 267-277, esp. p. 267.

[73] Itzkoff, S. W. 1983. "Culture as A Biological Activity," *The Form of Man*, N.Y.: Peter Lang, Ch. 8, pp. 194-198.

[74] Schild, R. 1976. "The Final Paleolithic Settlements of the European Plain," *Scientific American* (February), 234:2:88-99.

[75] Groves, C. P. 1989. "A Regional Approach to the Problem of the Origin of Modern Humans in Australasia," in Mellars and Stringer, eds., *op. cit.*, pp. 274-285; Swisher, C. C., and Anton, S. 1996. "Ngandong, Solo River H. Erectus Sites Redated," *Science*, 12/13/96, 274:1870.

[76] Wu, X. 1990. "The evolution of humankind in China," *Acta. Anthrop. Sin.*, 9:312-322.

[77] Swisher and Anton, 1996, *op. cit.*, *Science*, 12/13/96, 274:1870.

[78] Dubois, E. 1921. "The Proto-Australian fossil man of Wadjac, Java," *PKAW* 23:7:1013-1051; Coon, 1962, *op. cit.*, pp. 399-406.

[79] Theunissen, B., *et al.* 1990. "The establishment of a chronological framework for the hominid-bearing deposits of Java; a historical survey, in *Establishment of a Geologic Framework for Paleoanthropology*, L. F. Laporte, ed., Boulder: Geologic Society of America, pp.39-54.

[80] Wu, X. 1988. "The relationship between Upper Paleolithic fossils from China and Japan," *Acta. Anthr. Sinic.*, 7:235-238; Brown, Peter, 1993, in Aitken *et al.*, eds., *op. cit.*, pp. 217-233.

[81] Brown, Peter, 1993, in Aitken *et al.*, eds., *op. cit.*, pp. 217-233, esp. pp. 221, 226; Coon, 1962, *op. cit.*, pp. 521-522; Howells, 1989, *Papers of the Peabody Museum*, *op. cit.*, 79:1-189; Wolpoff and Caspari, 1997, *op. cit.*, p. 354; Kaminga and Wright, 1988, *op. cit.*, *Jrnl. of Human Evolution*, 17:739-767.

[82] Bar-Yosef, O. 1996. "Modern Humans, Neanderthals and the Middle/Upper Paleolithic Transition in Western Asia," in *The Origin of Modern Man*, O. Bar-Yosef and L. L. Cavalli-Sforza, *et al.*, eds., Forli: ABACO Edizioni, pp. 175-190, esp. p. 180.

[83] Bushnell, G., and McBurney, C. 1959. "New World Origins Seen from the Old World," *Antiquity*, 33:130:93-101.

[84] Coon, 1962, *op. cit.*, p. 522.

[85] Brues, A. 1977. *People and Races*, N.Y.: Macmillan.

[86] Wilford, J. N. 1996. "`American' Arrowhead Found in Siberia," *The New York Times*, 8/2/96, from article, 8/2/96, in *Science*, described by M. King and S. B. Slobodin.

[87] Wilford, J. N. 1997. *The New York Times*, 2/28/97, in *Science*, 2/28/97.

[88] *The New York Times*, 12/24/96 (AP).

[89] Wilford, J. N. 1996. "Mummies, Textiles Offer Evidence of Europeans in Far East," *The New York Times*, 5/7/96. Discusses Victor Mair's work from Univ. Of Penn. Museum written up in *The Journal of Indo-European Studies*.

[90] Linton, R. D. 1956. *The Tree of Culture*, N.Y.: Knopf, p. 527.

[91] Rudenko, S. 1970. *Frozen Tombs of Siberia*, London: J. M. Dent.

[92] Littleton, C. S. 1985. "The Indo-European Strain in Japanese Mythology," *Mankind Quarterly*, 26:152-174; Obayashi, T. 1984. "Japanese Myths of Descent from Heaven and Their Korean Parallels," *Asian Folklore Studies*, 43:171-184; Yoshida, A. 1977. "Japanese Mythology and the Indo-European Trifunctional System," *Diogenes*, 98:93-116.

[93] Kekoni, K. 1997. "Where Do Words Come From?" *Mankind Quarterly*, Spring, 37:3:283-315.

[94] Itzkoff, S. W. 1992. "Mysterious Ethnicity," *The Road To Equality, Evolution and Social Reality*, Westport, CT: Praeger Publishers, Ch. 13, pp. 139-145.

18

Explaining Modern Humans

Two Questions

1. How can we explain the revolutionary morphology that produced a creature with a brain and behavior so different from its contemporaries, and ultimately with such deadly evolutionary effect?

2. Where did this human phenomenon (sub-species) originate, and what was its immediate impact on other humans and the future morphological/behavioral profile of the larger human community?

- 1 -
Reconstruction

A Revolutionary Morphology

The most important hint as to the circumstances surrounding the origin of modern humans, the Cro-Magnons, and their genetically widely dispersed progeny, as hinted at by the presumed genetic bottleneck thought to have existed some 200,000-100,000 B.P., lies in their unique morphology. The Neanderthals clearly reflect a not-too-revolutionary expansion on the prototypical *Homo erectus* pattern. Their special northerly hunting robusticity is added to a large endocranial capacity, along with highly specialized skull and facial structures.

Cro-Magnon, by contrast, is a revolutionary "sport," unprecedented in human evolutionary history. The vertically oriented skull on which a towering cortical mass is delicately balanced, points to a radical evolutionary restructuring.

Today the term "heterochrony" is used to signify alterations in the developmental processes of a line of creatures during the ontogenetic development of the individual. The great debate now taking place is not whether or not truly modern human beings have been subject to a radical reconstruction through heterochronic genetic processes, but the actual nature of this reconstruction.

Paedomorphosis defines the slowing down of developmental time-tables so as to retain the juvenile characteristics of earlier primate forms, thus the retention in the sexually mature creature of the infantile characteristics of the ancestral type, "neoteny." The other view involves "sequential organizational hypermorphosis," late cessation of development leading to peramorphosis, the extension of development, as in a brain continuing to grow beyond the parameters of the ancestral type.

The classic work of Gavin de Beer in elaborating on the previous work of researchers, Bolk, Portmann, Griffiths, Gregory, etc., to create a synthetic evolutionary description of modern humans in comparison both with their ape as well as earlier human progenitors, first resulted in the acceptance of the view that *Homo sapiens sapiens* has been subject to radical heterochronic or "rate gene" alterations in development, productive of its radical cranial and post cranial morphology.[1] It is this radical "rate gene" (heterochronic) reconstruction that is now postulated to be the biological source of the explosive corticalization of human behavior.

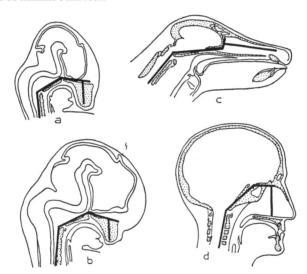

18.1 Heterochrony in humans. A series of sections showing the angle which the head makes with the trunk in A. embryo dog; B. embryo human being; C. adult dog; D. adult human being. The embryonic curvature is preserved in adult man.

Paedomorphic elements in the creation of modern humans: hairlessness, light-colored skin, slow developmental closing of the sutures of the skull over the brain, epicanthic fold over the Mongoloid and Capoid eye.[2] Most significant in humans is the adult retention of the embryonic mammal flexion curve in the spinal chord, in its connecting of the cranium and post-cranial morphology. In this new evolutionary arrangement the human skull sits directly, at a 90 degree angle, on the spinal chord. Dogs and other mammals tend toward the 180 degree pattern. The caudal flexure in the human female sexual anatomy retains the frontal embryonic pattern, whereas in other mammals, including the chimpanzee, it is positioned toward the rear.[3]

Modern humans are born after roughly the same length of gestation, consonant with the comparative adult size of other primates. They are born in a state that Gould calls, after Adolph Portmann, secondary altriciality. At birth, humans are relatively undeveloped and helpless, but with a real average weight of 3300 grams as compared to their expected relative gestational primate weight of 2200 grams. On the other hand, humans achieve the at-birth developmental state of modern apes much later in ontogeny, and only at age 21 months.[4] Schultz has noted that only in humans are the long limb bones and digits entirely cartilaginous at birth, unlike all other primates.[5]

Recently McKinney and McNamara, in a comprehensive examination of the evolutionary phenomenon of heterochrony, have argued that previous writings on the impact of paedomorphosis and neoteny on the unique evolution of modern humans are largely in error. Instead they propose that the dominant feature in modern humans that distinguishes them from early hominids and primate ancestors in general, is a process called hypermorphosis.

Instead of the slowing down of developmental processes in humans, it is rather the steady elongation or delay in the time spent during ontogeny in each stage of development that is critical. What they call "peramorphosis," the extension of development beyond the adult stages of the ancestral form, is considered to be the dominant factor that explains the unique position of *Homo* within the primate clade.[6]

Supporting this perspective, from the standpoint of developmental genetics is the writing of Raff and Deacon. They argue for the post-natal development of the human brain as being crucial. Not mere increase in size here, but significant structural realignment from the traditional primate plan. This extension in time for the development of ever-larger brain size is naturally the key element that allows for the unique behavioral restructuring of the hominid clade, as represented in *Homo sapiens sapiens*. "Humans show faster brain growth but delayed mental development...this does not mean that we have not gone through the same general stages of the ancestral or ape pattern. We have only delayed them,...not permanently "arrested" [them] as would be the case in paedomorphosis...Human behavior shows *sequential organizational hypermophosis*."[7]

One explanatory hurdle that the theory of human hypermorphosis has to face in explaining the unique morphology of *Homo sapiens sapiens* is the fact that the elongation of the developmental stages of maturity would ordinarily be thought to produce the great bony super-orbital tori, brow ridges, and other robust exemplifications of late- stage elongation and emphasis. McKinney and McNamara, for example, use the Irish Elk as "a classic example of hypermorphosis," in which allometric growth, extended ontogenetically, produced those great if ultimately weakening antler protuberances.[8]

In contrast to the Neanderthals and other borderline *sapiens*, especially exemplified in the late, very large and "bony" *Paranthropus*, Australopithecines, modern humans are very gracile and child-like in morphology—notably the delicacy of bone structure, almost as if, in certain important physical dimensions, their growth period was truncated.

Evolutionary jumps through alterations in the rate of development—the rate gene effect—are not unusual in evolution. As we have argued the origin of the vertebrates has hypothetically been attributed to a neotenous retention in the earliest chordates (proto-vertebrates) of certain larval or embryonic characteristics, the notochord. In the early protochordates this morphology disappears, as they opt for a unadventurous sedentary and rooted, sessile feeding way of life. So, too, our seemingly close Pre-Cambrian (c.1000-700mya) ancestral relatives, the invertebrate echinoderm phylum, also reveal, in their constituents' larval states, hints of a notochord. They, too, then revert to the safe patterns of sea lilies and starfish at the bottom of the seas.[9] Later in time, c.375mya, it is now hypothesized that the earliest amphibians, *Acanthostega* and *Ichthyostega*, were the products of evolutionary pressures which selected out paedomorphic forms of the existing crossopterygian air-breathing fish.

Not all paedomorphic trends turn out to be progressive. W. K. Gregory has claimed that the monotremes were not really an early mammalian phyletic retention into the modern world. He viewed them as a paedomorphic product of the evolution of a side branch of the marsupials. This particular retention of those ancient characteristics of the line came about as the ancestors of the duck-billed platypus and the echidna survived through their retention of certain infantile characteristics into maturity. In their case the pressures that produced a clearly peripheral member of the evolving marsupial line allowed them to survive into modern times, but in a distinctly marginal ecology. It did not produce the fortuitous forward-looking adaptations, and unlike the two previous examples, did not provide for a new adaptive evolutionary pathway.[10]

Covert evolution is the term often used to describe the sudden appearance of creatures seemingly successfully pre-adapted to an existing set of ecological and environmental circumstances. These forms often bring with them tangible evidence of the workings of the heterochronic process. In an earlier time frame they probably were maladapted "hangers on" at the edge, while more successful members of their clade prospered and multiplied.

The explanation must be directed to the "outlier" effect, in which one particular variant in a line of animals that contains a measure of structural and behavioral variability, is subject to strong selective pressures.[11] Those particular members that carry with them a genetic heritage of rate gene variability, and a tradition of survival on the periphery, can with the subsequent and happenstance alteration and mitigation of pre-existing and sharp external selective pressures, suddenly escape into the bright light of success. The heterochronic results of this covert, unseen, evolutionary trend usually effected by small populations of the variant (see below), could find a new adaptive and selective niche opened up for them.

As A. C. Hardy noted, this process of being a marginalized variant, often on the edge of extinction, can concomitantly carry with it a lack of the specialized adaptive grooving characteristic of opportunistic, dominant, and successful forms of the clade in question. Escape from specialization, covert or hidden evolution, necessitates that certain negative external conditions be lifted from the pressured variants, in order for there to be a second chance for adaptive dominance. How the human evolutionary scene factually fits into this model has yet to be determined.[12]

When one considers that human culture and then human behavior does not reveal clear-cut primate adaptive and selective specializations, the conclusions of McKinney and McNamara are important. They view evolution as being shaped, to a great extent, by two "non-Darwinian" processes, *i.e.*, not sharply influenced by external or internal selective conditions. One is the random "internal-developmental" trajectory of early-established metazoan body plans—-*orthoselection*. The second is random, catastrophic external selection, which has eliminated so many earlier phyla and cleared the way for more successful or "luckier" lines.

This perspective on so-called "non-Darwinian" processes, which themselves are well established within modern neo-Darwinism, does not reflect the typical work of natural selection acting on incremental variation to optimize fitness.[13] Unfortunately, much of the writing on human sociobiology suffers from such incredulous selectionism.

The questions are: What specific evolutionary circumstances occurred to stimulate the development of this heterochronic sport, *Homo sapiens sapiens*? What were the sequential events that allowed this radical alteration in structure to impact with such subsequent revolutionary effect on the external environment?

Locating the Genetic Bottleneck

As we near the close of the Pleistocene, certainly from c.200,000 B.P., the spread of a variety of big-brained human forms over the face of the planet had begun its final lap, if not the ultimate mammal/primate evolutionary stretch into the present. But in examining the morphology of body and brain in these various candidates for selective vindication, it is clear that here, too, the ancient evolutionary rhythm is manifest. Robusticity along with the presumed successful adaptive embeddedness of Middle Paleolithic life seemed to have become a worldwide theme. The evolutionary patterns of adaptive success had been imprinted upon our genes. Whether they are called post-*H. erectus, H. heidelbergensis*, even the now-awkward appellation, Archaic *H. sapiens*, they were creatures seemingly in evolutionary balance.

It is naturally an ex-post-facto generalization to consider that these creatures were, from our own standpoint, no more than dead-end manifestations of that burst of hominid expansiveness that selectively swept the Miocene/Pliocene apes and Pleistocene Australopithecines from our earthly landscape. This conclusion is increasingly assented to by more and more paleoanthropologists. One cannot genetically transform a Neanderthal, with its many hundreds of thousands of years of hard-earned adaptive morphological baggage, and in a veritable moment, into Cro-Magnon. The shared veneer of phenotypical Caucasoid characteristics, heritage of their conjoint northern incubation, fades into insignificance.

Indeed, bipedal, highly intelligent, big-brained primates had long been wandering throughout our Earth in good numbers, and with seeming impunity. But clearly, if they had remained upon this planet as they were by c.200,000 B.P., the impact on flora, fauna, even the potential for self-imposed ecological disaster would not exist. Nature would have been in balance until the next great continental shift, a tilt of the Earth's axis, another turbulent climatic episode. Who knows how far in the future danger would have presented itself to these dimly aware, yet competent hunters and gatherers who, too, struggled against entropic degradation.

As we have noted above, a new and radical morphology suddenly appeared. A new form of *Homo* emerged from the northern mists. Geographically impacting its Eur-Asian neighbors, but also, as L. L. Cavalli-Sforza has traced through his tree of genetic markers, impacting from afar the diversifying species of *Homo*. It was to *Homo sapiens sapiens* that we are now indebted for the genetic binding together of a super-species.[14]

Once the determinism implied by the "Out-of-Africa" mtDNA scenario had been effectively compromised, other evolutionary tree trunks and roots of derivation have became conceptually possible. The postulation of a "genetic bottleneck" linked with the above-mentioned work of Cavalli-Sforza, as well as the traditional Nostratic model of linguistic family affiliations, begins to add theoretical as well as empirical substance to a new "Garden of Eden," an out-of-Eurasia model of the coming of the truly modern human, Cro-Magnon.[15]

Estimates of the originating population that spread its genes around the world vary from 7,000 to 10,000 and from a time frame of origin varying from 400,000 B.P to 70,000 B.P.[16] A concurring view of the bottleneck problem is given by Rogers and Jorde.[17] These scholars view the separation of the races of man as taking place at least 100,000 years ago, with a surge in population taking place from this original breeding population that varied from 1,000-10,000 breeding individuals, some 30,000 years later.

Clearly, the attempt to use current mtDNA data to construct a hypothetical scenario for the origin of these populations, and throughout the world, is a task that often stretches empirical credulity. The interesting point that Rogers and Jorde make is that given that the mtDNA *diversity* evidence holds up, a point of current contention, as compared to all the other populations of the world taken together, "it would not follow that Africa is the point of origin."[18]

In an earlier critique of the "African Eve" scenario of A. Wilson, (University of California-Berkeley), *et al.*, especially their sampling of only 147 individuals, University of Geneva researchers L. Excoffier and A. Langaney reported on their human mitochondrial analysis of 1,064 individuals. They viewed the Berkeley group as having made serious "topological errors," undermining their "Out-of-Africa Eve" thesis. Instead the Swiss researchers offer a perspective of a molecular diversity in modern humans that has to go back at least 400,000 years. Most important, their genetic tree originates, such that the Caucasoids "could be closest to an ancestral population from which all other continental groups would have diverged." Harris and Hey's recent DNA research puts the African/non-African separation to at least 220ka B.P., "…suggesting the transformation to modern humans occurred in a sub-divided population."[19]

A. Torroni and his group concur with this view of the origination of the mtDNA sequences in present-day Caucasoids. Their date for the Caucasoid origins lies in the 100,000-80,000 B.P. range, but they propose that the mtDNA profile is unique in its origins, pointing only to this one particular human sub-species.[20]

>   …Early modern peoples everywhere tend to be most like the historic inhabitants of
>   the same region. This is clear above all for Europe, where the variability in early modern
>   (Upper Paleolithic) cranial form is completely encompassed by the variability in living

Europeans and where early modern people are set off only by a tendency toward greater robusticity.[21]

Martin Richards and his international group based at Oxford University see a complete continuity in the Caucasoid populations of Europe from the Upper Paleolithic to the
Neolithic agricultural from at least 35,000 B.P. to the Holocene, c.8,000 B.P. and beyond. From this it is clear that a genetic bottleneck based somewhere in Eur-Asia from
which the modern genes of *Homo sapiens sapiens* have spread throughout the world
along with population expansion is well within probability.[22]

The archaeological evidence in this case seems to buttress the genetic data. The
Upper Paleolithic Cro-Magnon peoples were the modernists of the late Pleistocene.
There were no other contemporary "competitors" for this appellation anywhere else in
the world, including Africa. In terms of morphology, their behavioral profile, the culture
that seemed to flow biologically from this morphology, these are the peoples whose very
unique origins in the still hypothetical bottleneck of origin, constitute the long-sought-
after human source for an incubating "Garden of Eden."

New fossil descriptions are appearing that support the model of an ancient migration out of Africa into Europe, long before the final modernization of *Homo sapiens*. In
the Atapuerca hills of northern Spain near the city of Burgos, the fossil remains were
found of a 10-11-year-old boy, cranium, lower jaw and teeth, plus fragments of five
other individuals, that have been dated back to 800,000 B.P.[23]

Whether or not these fossils prove to be the dividing point between future Neanderthals and Cro-Magnons, as claimed by the authors, remains an unresolved question.
The fact that evolving human populations existed in Eur-Asia at a very early period, c.2-
1mya, can no longer be contested. When and how one of these bands or tribes separated
themselves from the mass of heavy-boned, adaptively well-grooved humans, and underwent radical heterochronic morphological reconstruction has yet to be uncovered. One
can only propose "most probable" scenarios to be subjected, as with the "African Eden"
hypothesis, to subsequent factual confirmation or refutation.

- 2 -
Birthplace

Northerly "Garden of Eden"
The theoretical arguments adduced in favor of a northerly Eur-Asian "Garden of
Eden" for *Homo sapiens sapiens* by the most recent "mtDNA," "nuclear DNA," and "genetic bottleneck" models, coordinated with empirical linguistic and paleoarchaeological
fossil evidence, now strongly contradicts the general public representations for an "Out
of Africa—modern humans" scenario, purportedly to have occurred within the last several hundred thousand years.

The focus now is on, first, whether the immediate ancestral stock of Cro-Magnon
can be identified with any of the extant Eur-Asian fossil humans several hundred thousand years antecedent to the full-fledged appearance of Cro-Magnon and his universal

Aurignacian culture, *e.g.*: Atapuerca, Arago, Petralona, Vertessolos, Fontechevade, Steinheim, Swanscombe, Heidelberg. Else this line still remains hidden within the yet-to-be-discovered fossil record.

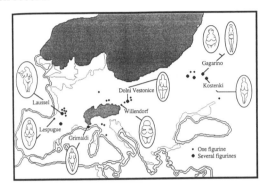

18.2 Genetic-cultural unity of the Europeans, A. Location of Gravettian Venuses, 27-20ka B.P.; B. Venus of Willendorf (Austria); C. Venus of Lespugue (France).

Second, because of its relatively gracile morphology, is it possible that *Homo sapiens sapiens* evolved under relatively more benign geographical and ecological conditions than did the Neanderthals, and then spread into the northernmost sectors of its later range of habitation?

What seems to point to a common Neanderthal and Cro-Magnon ancestry in Eur-Asia, and thus a relatively widespread distribution of the proto-Cro-Magnids over the continental land mass, is the extremely large Neanderthal endocranial capacity as compared with contemporary *Homo* erectine types in other parts of the world, both east and south. It hints at a conjoint evolutionary origin and dynamic with the proto-Cro-Magnids.

In the end it may turn out that the direct precursors to Cro-Magnon were widely distributed throughout Eur-Asia from a period after 1mya. Then, undergoing their own specialized evolutionary reconstruction, the specific line leading to the Cro-Magnids was smaller in number and thus left fewer fossil antecedents as compared with the Neanderthals.

Why the seemingly sudden extrusion of the Cro-Magnids, in contradistinction to the scientific consensus, that a number of the earlier Eur-Asian fossils give strong hints of a Neanderthal ancestry, and from about 500ka B.P., and none for Cro-Magnon, except Steinheim (Carleton Coon), and of course, Qafzeh and Skhul at 95,00-85,000 B.P. in Israel?

In the case of Cro-Magnon, the most probable hypothesis consonant with the available evidence at hand as well as the larger theoretical evolutionary perspective, points to a powerful adaptive and thus selective challenge to an isolated population of progressive *H. erectus*, more likely at the *H. heidelbergensis* stage, likely a more gracile, if as yet maladaptive group of humans. It is probable that the challenge was climatic, perhaps the tremendous cold indicated by oxygen isotope stage 6, 190,000-130,000 B.P., possibly even as far back as oxygen isotope stage 8, c. 300,000-250,000 B.P.[24]

Alternatively, was Cro-Magnon the newcomer to the North, not subject to a lengthy adaptive remodeling under the press of a glacial ecology? Throughout Eur-Asia during most of the Pleistocene, the climate immediately below the southerly extension of the ice was much less forbidding than today. The existence of the Wooly Rhinoceri, Mammoths and Mastodons, Great Cave Bear, Cave Hyena, Cave Lion, Giant Deer (Irish Elk), Primitive Bison, Auroch (Giant Ox), many large foraging animals, argues for moderately cool winters. The fossil botanical evidence seems to confirm this. The seasons were in general less continental, with a mixed temperate plains ecology. Here, over a long time period existed generally cool to temperate winter and summer temperatures, without the bitter, extended winters that we today find in the Eur-Asian continental mass away from the tempering influence of the gulf currents.

The recent views on the relatively moderate winters during the Pleistocene would of necessity exclude oxygen isotope period 6, from 190,000-130,000 B.P.[25] During this earlier and perhaps critical period for the evolution of both the Neanderthals and Cro-Magnon, the Northern Hemispheres might have experienced extremely cold temperatures, similar to those of the latest Pleistocene, 16,000-12,000 B.P., before our contemporary continental Holocene climatic experience, itself possibly an interstadial. The large, moderately cold-adapted animals of the Pleistocene, given the sites where we have discovered their bones, *i.e.*, in northern latitudes of Europe, the Ukraine, Siberia, could not have lived through some of our contemporary continental winters, especially considering the enormous amount of forage necessary for their life support over the winter months. In all probability they were primary victims of the bitter northerly cold, which obliterated their food sources for months at a time during the final Würm, and then during the Holocene continental winters.

The cold-adapted physical profiles presented by contemporary circumpolar peoples, Eskimos, Lapps, *i.e.*, short and often stocky, sharply contrasts with the Cro-Magnons' build, but confirms the highly specialized northerly Neanderthals suite of hunting and climatic adaptations—sturdy thick bones and surface joints, as well as a presumably large nasal orifice for warming the cold air.[26] Contemporary Europeans and Northeast Asiatics present interesting geographical-climatic -physically adaptive characteristics that correlate to an extent with a differing heritage of ecology and climate.

How long would it have taken a people originating in climes to the south of 40 degrees latitude North to shed their more tropical genetic adaptations and develop the seemingly specialized suite of morphological characteristics that define the northerly Caucasoids? Blonde or light-colored hair, grey, blue, green irises, light-colored skin have long been seen as correlated with life under northerly foggy, clouded skies. Roberts states: "Lack of pigmentation appears to be related to improvement of synthesis of vitamin D in conditions where its dietary supply and the availability of radiation for its conversion has been limited."

In his final and incomplete book, Carleton Coon devoted a chapter to the scientific evidence for the relationship between geography and the color of skin, hair, eyes.[27] Coon cites the research of Nobel Prize winner, George Wald, which showed "that blue and grey eyed people see more sharply over long distances than brown-eyed people do."[28] Coon stated that this includes horizons on the northern oceans, presumably arguing for the transoceanic explorations under mostly overcast conditions of such as the Vikings.[29] (How do we explain the Polynesians?) Coon also sees emotional and personality differences as correlated with hair and eye color, blue-eyed blondes being more deliberative and self-paced, darker-eyed people being more spontaneous.[30] He thus believes that the Europeans are a direct product of long-existing genetic adaptation to life in northerly, cool, cloudy, moist climates.

The research of Vrba, Savage, and Barnosky was presented earlier as documenting significant climatic and faunal changes and turnovers from about 2.5mya, toward the end of the Pliocene, and presumably anticipatory to the Ice Age sequences that dominated the successor Pleistocene, from 1.9mya.[31] deMenocal placed these sharp cycles of cold dry climate at 2.8, 1.7, and 1.0mya.[32]

Steven Stanley hypothesizes that the assumed rising from the waters of the Isthmus of Panama blocked the flow of currents between the Atlantic and Pacific at about 3mya. This time frame is wholly consonant with the above climatic/faunal alterations. The resulting blockade of currents is hypothesized to have spiraled the Gulf Stream into a more northerly direction, thence reshaping the configurations of northerly West European ecologies toward their current habitable patterns.[33]

Such a gradual restructuring of climatic conditions throughout the world probably did effect the patterns and dynamics of human evolution in Africa. But it also could have, despite the varying glaciations, invited humans into Eur-Asia to take advantage of the temperate climate and the rich faunal hunting grounds. A long-existing and long-evolving European population gradually adapting and flourishing in these moderated northerly latitudes is thus highly suggestive.

In contrast, Northeast Asiatics as well as Amerindians reveal a number of cold-adapted physiognomic characteristics. These include the face, cheek bones, upper lip, nose, lower forehead, eye lids.[34] "Mongoloid hair's thick cuticle, thick body, light packing, and straightness may like a quilted coat, be an adaptation to cold weather when needed but otherwise be an all purpose covering, like Mongoloid skin."[35] Coon does not explain the dark hair and eye coloring and the relatively darker skin of the Northeast Mongoloids, as compared with the Europeans, given their northerly cold adaptiveness. The explanation that suggests itself here is that the locus of the most ancient Mongoloids, Beijing, is itself at latitude 40 degrees north, close to Philadelphia, Thessaloniki, Istanbul, Indianapolis, Naples, clearly a latitude, given similar inclination of the Earth's orbit today, as at c.500,000 B.P., that would place these people under a strong sun and high ultraviolet radiation, making adaptive the darker skin coloration. One further confirming element is that this latitude, 40 degrees north, is not incompatible with extremes of cold and warmth, as compared to that of the Europeans, who now and possibly then, were living under relatively mild winters due to the Gulf Stream effect.[36]

An insight into the time line dimension of these ethnic and racial characteristics is given by comparing the Europeans to other groups that have migrated out of their home territories. Amero-Indians came to the New World across the Beringian land bridge sometime after 15,000 B.P. Yet throughout their recent geographical range in North and South America the physical attributes of these peoples, including their coloration, but possibly not including their genetic altitude adaptations, have remained remarkably stable throughout their range.

The estimate is that people of Melanesian heritage came to Tasmania about 38,000 B.P. Dates for human occupation of the Australian mainland have ranged from 40,000 B.P. to close to 90,000 B.P. Tasmania is at a Southern Hemisphere latitude equal to Boston, Massachusetts. In the early millennia after their arrival, at the end of the Pleistocene, the climate of Tasmania was "steppic" (cold).[37] Yet the Tasmanian natives, up until their genocide in the 19th century, maintained their black skin color.

The implication is that the skin coloration of the Caucasoids is not a recent product of a late-Pleistocene migratory people, successors to the Neanderthals, only recently insinuated into Eur-Asia from Africa. The "Out-of-Africa" hypothesis, the mtDNA data, might reflect a long and ongoing process of human miscegenation, now product of various northern incursions in and out of Africa after 500,000 B.P. Such movements are consonant with our knowledge of the primate penchant for exploratory behavior, of which *Homo* has made a specialization.

Further support for an indigenous Eur-Asian homeland of the Cro-Magnons and their descendants is presented in D. F. Roberts' diagrammatic comparison of the birth weights of various ethnic/geographical populations. The correlation shows higher birth weights with more northerly temperatures.[38] Today, the Eur-Asians are extended over a wide range of temperature clines. They also represent, especially in the South and East, much interbreeding with sub-Saharan African, and Asian populations. Yet their average birth weight is quite non-variable as compared with other groups, with the sole exception of the limited birth-weight range of Amero-Indians. This average European birth weight, from 3250-3500 grams, suggests that the original European populations may have been founded in a very delimited northerly ecology, establishing a bio-cultural homogeneity that later revealed itself in the amazing cultural parallelism, we see throughout the Cro-Magnid range first exhibited with the Aurignacian, c.45,000 B.P., and then over many subsequent thousands of years.

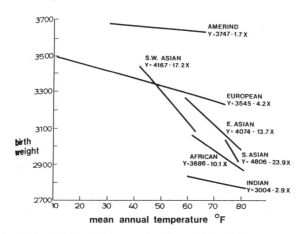

18.3 Birth weight and climate. Intravarietal regression of mean birth weight on mean annual temperature.

Consider also: a) their sudden Eur-Asian appearance, some 45,000-50,000 years ago, after a wide-ranging Neanderthal suzerainty of almost 100,000 years of expansive dominance; b) their crucible of creation, a mysterious morphogenic revolution explainable through ecological stress, then leading to heterochronic rate gene selection in this northerly incubator, possibly during Oxygen-Isotope Period 6, c.190,000-130,000 B.P.; c) after the sudden press outward, impinging on the numerous Neanderthal tribal elements, leading to the latter's inevitable genocidal obliteration, after a mere c.15,000 years of contact, 45,000-30,000 B.P. All these add up to a not-inexplicable scenario of events and temporal parameters. As E. Raymond Hall of the University of Kansas has stated,"...[T]*wo subspecies of the same species do not occur in the same geographic area*....To imagine one species of man living together on equal terms for long with another subspecies is but wishful thinking and leads only to disaster and oblivion for one or the other."[39]

The Multiregional Question
There can be no question that human populations were scattered about the Eastern Hemisphere from c.2mya onward. And there ought not to be any doubt that when they wandered, as they always did and will, they interbred, as they must, whether as an act of voluntary social and economic exchange, or as a result of violence and rapine. Some elements in hominid behavioral biology are too basic to be dismissed from consideration.

The comparative fossil, historical, morphological and physical evidence argues for the existence of relatively independent inbreeding groups of humans throughout the world, adapting to their local environmental conditions, and sharing in the inevitable genetic variability that nature regularly throws up into phenotypic visibility. Thus, we must reckon with the racial variations on which Weidenreich, Coon, and more recently Wolpoff, have concentrated. Given the relatively slow history of human morphological change, as compared to the Cro-Magnon revolution at the end of the Pleistocene, it is reasonable to view the gradual growth in endocranial capacity as an ancient hominid orthoselective trend, at all times positively adaptive, and for all groups. "The trend toward increased brain size is the most continuous, long lasting, and marked hallmark of hominization."[40]

However, considering the extreme variability in different parts of the world at the threshold of historical time, of human cultural levels of behavior and mastery, not to add the more controversial issues of relative brain size and structure that are correlated with behavioral and cultural levels, the evidence argues for the existence of differing rhythms of evolutionary change within the human clade. Indeed, this is regrettably true even 10,000 years after the retreat of the glaciers.

Given the pace of morphological change, especially brain size and structure, is it persuasive to argue for the astoundingly rapid, if irregular reconstruction into *Homo sapiens sapiens* of the various races of humans around the world *through autochthonous genetic transformations and then a very rapid and subsequent local selective filtering out of less-evolved forms*?

Both Coon and Wolpoff were at pains, when pressed by the honorable opposition to this strict multiregional perspective of independent morphological and cultural evolution, to concede the possibility of genetic intermingling at the periphery of each of the racial and ethnic homelands.[41]

Recent redatings of human fossils around the world now argue for the coexistence of two or more species of *Homo* as different as were the Neanderthals to the Cro-Magnons in Eur-Asia, and from c.100,000-30,000 B.P. But now, the taxonomy is extended to borderline erectines and sapiens living within a similar time frame in Southeast Asia.

The most parsimonious explanation for this relatively recent and existing variability, both in human form and grade, is to postulate the spasmodic and recent entrance of new genetic elements into these ancient homelands, yet not altering for one particular tribal group their general historical ethnic or racial profile, yet still acting to expand endocranial capacity and modernize other morphological elements. Small numbers of wandering individuals or bands over a period of 30,000-70,000 years can through such genetic intrusions make their presence felt on the future of the larger group.

And surely, the morphological dynamics taking place beyond the Eur-Asian homeland of *Homo sapiens sapiens* at the close of the Pleistocene, from 100ka B.P., were too rapid to be the mere rhythmic unfolding of mechanical, internally-generated genetic variation and subsequent natural selection.

The crux of the multiregional puzzle has to lie in the question: After such a long and placid adaptive grooving of human types in their respective and distantly separated homelands, from whence came the genetics of recent modernization? In evolution such phenotypic grooving, characterized especially by the "grossification" of structure—heavy-boned and relatively specialized morphologies, very similar to the final robust australopithecine adaptations, even those of the current great apes—does not suggest the existence of a genetic "bank," a recessive storehouse to be suddenly and casually unleashed and expressed in such dynamic modernizations.

The final Pleistocene fossils suggest a different scenario. Rather, these earlier Middle Paleolithic humans were well-adapted and successful forms, as A. R. Wallace long ago suggested, until, that is, truly modern humans genetically, if not behaviorally, enfiladed their previously-isolated geographical redoubts. To posit supposedly parallel multiregionally internal genetic restructurings in a mere blip of evolutionary time, c.100,000 years, is unprecedented in evolutionary processes. It is also genetically unexplained by the theory of "punctuated equilibrium" as applied to human evolution. Further, sharp heterochronic change does not here seem to apply to most of these non-Eur-Asian morphological alterations.

A parallel might again be referred to, in the European invasion of North America. The indigenous Amero-Indians were more advanced peoples than the Neanderthals and other contemporary borderline forms of *Homo sapiens*. Yet, with the exception of adopting the Spanish-introduced European horse, a related animal that they had thousands of years earlier seen become extinct, and thence taught to reinvigorate their hunting and warrior economies, their use of European technologies, as trade goods, reflects the sharp biocultural separation of the two ethnicities.

This is why the supposed adoption by the Neanderthals of Upper Paleolithic technology, the Chatelperronian, is suspect. As with the Amero-Indians, the Neanderthals could have traded the fruits of their hunting skills for Cro-Magnon tools, as did the Amero-Indians for the Amero/Europeans' rifles. Still, to modify the argument, the Neanderthals and the Cro-Magnons both fabricated stone tools, and their contact did last for several thousand years before the absorption or extinction of the former by the latter. Thus, the Neanderthals could have learned.

In sum, as regards the multiregional hypothesis, we can posit a slow and independent evolutionary hominization in the various multiregional centers from c.2.0mya on. The adaptive advantage of brain size and function for this particular primate, *Homo*, had been genetically established over a prior several-million-year period of selective grooving. The great mix of human racial and ethnic forms that seem to appear on the planet from c.200,000 B.P. could have been a product of the scatter of wandering genes emanating from the surviving populations undergoing that environmental "vale of crisis" during oxygen-isotope stage 8 or 6, 300-130ka B.P.

An examination of the various and diverse hybrid ethnic Amero-Indian variants that wandered or were pushed into North America, making their way over the glacial debris of the Bering passageway sometime between 15,000-11,000 B.P., seems to support this perspective of scattershot genetic admixing that was taking place throughout the planet before and during this interval. The discoverable cultural and morphological differences between historical racial and ethnic groups all over the world, as Europeans found them from the 15th to the 19th centuries, can be thus attributed to their relative geographical relationship with the center of the truly revolutionary Cro-Magnid genetic restructuring of the form of *Homo*.

A puzzle that merits brief discussion is the early and seemingly modern craniometry of the South African Capoids, Klasies River Mouth, and Border Cave fossils. If their ethnic relationship to the Jebel Irhoud fossils of Morocco is confirmed, and thus to the northern extension of the Capoids, as Carleton Coon has argued, then a genetic connection with Cro-Magnid Spain and Europe might be argued for the genetic sources to this large-skulled ethnicity. Note the ancient tradition of migrations spiraling along the ancient north-south African highway before the Sahara became radically desertified in the recent Holocene. But, the South African sapients appear to date back to between 90,000-60,000 B.P., long before the Cro-Magnids give evidence of having entered Spain.

Ian Tattersall has recently reported on the dating of Upper Paleolithic sites in Iberia at 40,000 B.P., as old as the previously oldest European sites at Bacho Kiro in Bulgaria.[42] The scenario for Cro-Magnid origins is thus not yet complete.

The late-Pleistocene African fossils, both in the North as well as the far South, have no affinities to the Neanderthals. Thus the puzzle and the mystery. For, the large-skulled African Boskopoid descendants of this group of humans were eventually subject to both the advance of Caucasoid Moullians from the North and Negroids from West Africa, thence subject to heterochronic, possibly paedomorphic dwarfing in the Kalahari, (unlike the tall northerly Cro-Magnids). All that can be stated is that the Klasies River, Aterian, Boskopoid Capoid cultures, despite the principals' expanded craniometry, never achieved the cultural and intellectual suzerainty of the Cro-Magnids nor the power of the aggressively-expanding Negroids. And, they have paid for this inability to compete.

Final Push

The greatest probability is that both the Neanderthaloids and the Cro-Magnids have an originating point in time and place that is roughly synchronous. Their origins in Europe and /or West Asia are from roughly the same human stem, and probably from roughly the same time of arrival on this geographical scene, from Africa, c.2mya and before 1mya.

Question: why does the present evidence point to a time of Neanderthal expansion and flourishing some 55-65ka earlier than Cro-Magnon? One could argue that such a small amount of time, from 115,000 B.P. to 45,000 B.P., could mask a simultaneous expansion, especially given the seemingly hybridized examples provided at Qafzeh 9 and Skhul 5, c.92-85ka B.P. The Chatelperronian transitional culture of Western France is still a mystery, perhaps a cultural transfer to the Neanderthals before their final disappearance in the face of the oncoming Cro-Magnon Aurignacians. But this could have been a late or final close contact of these two ethnicities. The Ahmarian culture of the southern Levant, Israel, at Boker Tachtit seems to be part of the Cro-Magnon tradition, a sudden overlaying of Neanderthal Mousterian remains, even though it precedes the intercontinental spread of the Aurignacian by about 10,000 years, c.45,000-35,000 B.P.

The probability is that, while the Neanderthals and the Cro-Magnids might have had their big-brained origins back in Oxygen-Isotope periods 6 or 8, certainly not later than 150,000 B.P., they developed their specializations independently, certainly well before 100,000 B.P, but thence, apparently meeting and hybridizing. Why are the children of this hybridizing process cultural Neanderthals at 90,000 B.P. (Qafzeh and Skhul) but Cro-Magnons at 40,000 B.P. (Predmost and Mladec)?

An explanation for the late-arriving Upper Paleolithic Cro-Magnon culture would have to take into account the radical reconstruction of the brain of *Homo* that is reflected in the Eur-Asian sector of humanity. It is not merely one of size as we compare it with comparatively enlarged skulls in a wide variety of humans and geographies from 100,000 B.P. on. Ralph Holloway has long made the point that while brain size is important, more crucial is the reconstruction reflected in the paedomorphic or peramorphic transformation of *Homo sapiens sapiens'* post-cranial long bone structure, then the face, as well as the shape and structure of skull and brain.[43]

We can appreciate the evolutionary suddenness of the appearance of the culture of high abstractness and symbolic richness in art, technology, human decoration, even possible chronometric analysis, by considering the vast difference in mental operations expressed in pre-Cro-Magnon humans, including the Neanderthals. Here existed a slowly evolving, and as far as we can perceive monochromatic culture, long stagnated, whether or not we accept the claims by Lieberman, Crelin and others that the Neanderthals were incapable of pronouncing vowels, thus limited in their speech and language production.[44]

The explosion to dominance of the cortex in Cro-Magnon, the rechanneling of emotions produced by the limbic system and the allocortex through the cortex had to require a repatterning of individual behavior and social control.[45] Some 150,000 years later, at the least, after the presumed heterochronic revolution in human morphology, we humans are still struggling to figure out methods of balancing our powerful emotional drives with the intellectual disciplines made possible by the cortex.[46]

The product evidence for this new brain supports the view that there was no external selective environmental force or stimulus that closely shaped the destiny of the new *sapiens* mind. This spilling out of inner genetic potentialities constituted a heritage of evolutionary processes beyond the ken of conscious human control or closely-honed external selection. *Homo sapiens sapiens* as well as the outside world had now to deal with this new biological sport, what Richard Goldschmidt once called "a hopeful monster."[47]

With the moderation of the oxygen/isotope 6 glacial freeze sometime after 130,000 B.P., it is possible a process began of gradual self-discovery of the inner nature and possibilities of this new brain. The fact that except for the Ahmarians of the southern Levant, there seems to be an almost simultaneous invasion of the Aurignacians into Europe, Southwest Asia, and from a variety of differing geographical loci, perhaps now including Iberia, a cultural invasion of unbelievable uniformity considering its vast range, Western Siberia, North Africa, East, Central, South, and Western Europe, in the period between 45,000-30,000 B.P., testifies to a not atypical evolutionary progression. Here is the possible expansion out of the mtDNA bottleneck of a people, at first relatively small in numbers, perhaps only a few thousand, but of uniform ethnicity and genetic heritage. Then, sometime between 100ka B.P. and 50ka B.P. came a demographic explosion of extraordinary expansiveness.

Having now finally fabricated their internal bio-social identity, able to apply a more abstract method of symbolic cultural living, disciplining their intense emotional and sexual energies, practical hunting and food gathering practices, technological envisionments, they moved out and beyond the unknown northerly "Garden of Eden."

The first impacts were on the human world of peoples. This new biological sport would rapidly challenge the very existence of vertebrate life.

Endnotes, Chapter 18

[1] de Beer, G. 1958. *Embryos and Ancestors*, 3rd ed., Oxford: Oxford University Press.

[2] Bolk, L. 1926. *Das Problem der Menschenwerdung*, Jena: G. Fischer; Stringer, C. B., and Gamble, C. 1993. *In Search of the Neanderthals: Solving the Puzzle of Human Origins*, London: Thames and Hudson, pp. 138-139; Brues, A. 1977. *People and Races*, N.Y.: Macmillan, pp. 115-117.

[3] Itzkoff, S. W. 1983. *The Form of Man*, N.Y.: Peter Lang, pp. 16, 57, 119, 129-131; diagram, p. 130, *The Form of Man*, from *Das Problem der Menschenwerdung*, L. Bolk, *op. cit.,* Jena: G. Fischer (1926).

[4] Portmann, A. 1941. "Die Tragzeiten der Primaten und die Dauer der Schwangerschaft beim Menschen: Ein Problem der Vergleichen Biologie," *Rev. Suisse. Zool.*, pp. 511-518, 516; Gould, S. J. 1977. *Ontogeny and Phylogeny*, Cambridge: Harvard Univ. Press, p. 369.

[5] Schultz, A. H. 1926. "Fetal Growth of Man and other Primates," *Quarterly Review of Biology*, 1:4:465-521.

[6] McKinney, M. L., and McNamara, K. J. 1991. *Heterochrony: The Evolution of Ontogeny*, N.Y.: Plenum, esp. pp. 291-326; also, Purves, D. 1988. *Body and Brain*, Cambridge, Mass.: Harvard Univ. Press; Shea, B. T. 1988. "Heterochrony in Primates," in *Heterochrony in Evolution: A Multidisciplinary Approach*, McKinney, M., ed., N.Y.: Plenum.

[7] McKinney and McNamara, 1991, *op. cit.*, pp. 310-311; Raff, R. A. 1996. *The Shape of Life: Genes, Development, and the Evolution of Animal Form*, Chicago: Univ. of Chicago Press; Deacon, T. W. 1997. "What Makes the Human Brain Different," *Annual Rev. Anthropology*, 26:337-357.

[8] McKinney and McNamara, 1991, *op. cit.*, pp. 227.

[9] Garstang, W. 1928. "The Origin and Evolution of Larval Forms," *Report of the British Association for the Advancement of Science for 1928*, p. 77.

[10] Gregory, W. K. 1936. "On the Meaning and Limits of Irreversibility in Evolution," *American Naturalist*, 70:517; Gregory, W. K. 1937. "Supra-specific Variation in Nature and in Classification: A Few Examples from Mammalian Paleontology," *American Naturalist*, 71:268-276.

[11] Mayr, E. 1991. *One Long Argument: Charles Darwin and the Genesis of Modern Evolutionary Thought*, Cambridge: Harvard Univ. Press, pp. 141-164.

[12] Hardy, A. C. 1954. "Escape from Specialization," in *Evolution as a Process*, London, p. 122.

[13] McKinney and McNamara, 1991, *op. cit.*, pp. 338-339; see also Waddington, C. H. 1957. *The Strategy of the Genes*, London: Allen & Unwin; Itzkoff, S. W. 1983. *The Form of Man*, *op. cit.*, Ch. 5, "Selection and Survival."

[14] Cavalli-Sforza, L. L., *et al.* 1988. "Reconstruction of Human Evolution: Bringing Together Genetic, Archaeological and Linguistic Data," *Proc. National Acad. of Science*, Aug. 1988, 85:6002-6006; Cavalli-Sforza, L. L., *et al.* 1993. *History and Geography of Human Genes*, Princeton, N.J.: Princeton Univ. Press.

[15] Mountain, J. L., and Cavalli-Sforza, L. L. 1993. "Evolution of Modern Humans: Evidence from Nuclear DNA Polymorphosis," in *The Origin of Modern Humans and the Impact of Chronometric Dating*, M. J. Aitken, C. B. Stringer, and P. A. Mellars, eds., Princeton, N.J.: Princeton Univ. Press, pp. 60-83; Kaiser, M., and Shevoroshkin, V. 1988. "Nostratic," *Ann. Rev. Anthropology*, 17:309-329.

[16] Tishkoff, S. *et al.* 1996. *Science* 3/8/96, and as reported in *The New York Times*, 3/8/96; Takahata, N., Satta, Y., Klein, J. 1995. "Divergence Time and Population Size in the Lineage Leading to Modern Humans," *Theoretical and Population Biology*, quoted in "The Mystery of Humanity's Missing Muta-

tions," Ann Gibbons, *Science*, 1/6/95, 267:35-36; Smith, J. M., *et al.* 1993. In *Science*, 10/1/93, p. 27; see Ch. 23, "Modern Humans: African Origins?"

[17] Rogers, A. R., and Jorde, L. B. 1995. "Genetic Evidence on Modern Human Origins," *Human Biology*, Feb., 67:1:1-36.

[18] Rogers and Jorde, 1995, *op. cit.*, *Human Biology*, Feb., 67:1:23.

[19] Excoffier, L., and Langaney, A. 1989. "Origin and Differentiation of Human Mitochondrial DNA," *American Journal of Human Genetics* cited in *The Search For Eve*, M. Brown, N.Y.: Harper and Row, pp. 278-279; Harris, E. E., and Hey, J. 1999. "X Chromosome evidence for ancient human histories," *PNAS*, 16 Mar., 96:6:3320-334.

[20] Torroni, A., *et al.* 1994. "mtDNA and the Origin of the Caucasians: Identification of Ancient Caucasian-specific Haplogroups, One of Which Is Prone to a Recurrent Somatic Duplication in the D-Loop Region," *Am. Jrnl. Hum. Gen.*, 55:760-766.

[21] Klein, R. G. 1989. *The Human Career*, Chicago: Univ. of Chicago Press, p. 351; see also Howells, W. W. 1973. "Cranial Variation in Man: a study by multivariate analysis," *Peabody Museum Papers*, 67:1-259; Howells, W. W. 1973. *The Evolution of the Genus `Homo'*, Reading, MA: Addison-Wesley.

[22] Richards, M., *et al.* 1996. "Paleolithic and Neolithic Lineages in the European Mitochondrial Gene Pool," *Am. Jrnl. Hum. Genetics*, July, 59:185-203.

[23] Wilford, J. N. 1997. "Fossils Called Limb in Human Family Tree," *The New York Times*, May, 30; Bermudez, J. M., and Arsuaga, J. L. 1997. *Science*, May, 30.

[24] Mellars, P. A., Aitkin, M. J., Stringer, C. P. 1993. "Outlining the Problem," in *The Origin of Modern Humans and the Impact of Chronometric Dating*, M. J. Aitken, C. P. Stringer, and P. A. Mellars, eds., *op. cit.*, p. 8.

[25] Guthrie, R. Dale. 1984. "Mosaics, Allelochemics and Nutrients," in *Quaternary Extinctions,* P. S. Martin and R. G. Klein, eds., Tucson, AZ: Univ. of Arizona Press, pp. 259-198.

[26] Coon, C. S., and Hunt, E. E., Jr. 1965. *The Living Races of Man*, N.Y.: Knopf, Photographs of peoples—Plates 1-16. Roberts, D. F. 1978. *Climate and Human Variability*, 2nd. ed., Menlo Park, CA: Cummings Publishing Co. p. 90. See the discussion of the probable origins for lactose toleration in Europeans as an element in their need for vitamin D supplementation: Deacon, T. 1997. *The Symbolic Species*, N.Y.: Norton, pp. 323-324; also, Durham, W. 1994. *Coevolution: Genes, Culture, and Human Diversity*, Stanford, CA: Stanford Univ. Press.

[27] Coon, C. S. 1982. *Racial Adaptations*, Chicago: Nelson-Hall, Ch. 5, pp. 45-82.

[28] Wald, G. 1945. "Human Vision and the Spectrum," *Science*, 101:635-658.

[29] Coon, 1982, *op. cit.*, p. 66.

[30] Coon, 1982, *op. cit.*, pp. 66-73.

[31] Vrba, Elizabeth S., cited in Eldredge, N. 1991. *The Miner's Canary*, N.Y.: Prentice Hall, pp. 183, 187; Barnosky, A. D. 1989. "The Late Pleistocene Event As a Paradigm for a Widespread Mammal Extinction," in *Mass Extinctions: Process and Evidence*, S. K. Donovan, ed., N.Y.: Columbia Univ. Press, pp. 238-239; Savage, R. J. G. 1988. "Extinction and the fossil mammal record," in *Extinction and Survival in the Fossil Record*, G. P. Larwood, ed., N.Y.: Oxford Univ. Press, p. 331.

[32] deMenocal, P. in *Columbia*, Winter, 1996, 44.

[33] Stanley, S. M. 1996. *Children of the Ice Age*, N.Y.: Harmony Books.

[34] Coon, 1982, *op. cit.*, pp. 58-59.

[35] Coon, 1982, *op. cit.*, p. 64.

[36] Brues, A. 1977. *People and Races*, *op. cit.*, pp. 93-95.

[37] Jones, R. 1995. "Tasmanian Archaeology: Establishing the Sequences," *Annual Review of Anthropology*, 24:423-446.

[38] Roberts, D. F. 1978. *Climate and Human Variability*, 2nd ed. *op. cit.,* p. 61.

[39] Hall, E. R., and Kelson, K. 1959. *Mammals of North America*, N.Y.: Ronald Press.

[40] Tobias, P. V. 1971. *The Brain in Hominid Evolution*, N.Y.: Columbia Univ. Press, p. 115.

[41] Coon, C. S. 1962. *The Origin of Races*, N.Y.: Knopf, pp. 658-664; Wolpoff, M. H., and Caspari, R. 1997. *Race and Human Evolution*, N.Y.: Simon and Schuster, pp. 283-285.

[42] Tattersall, I. 1998. *Becoming Human*, N.Y.: Harcourt Brace. P.176.

[43] Holloway, R. L. 1980. "Within Species Brain Body Weight Variability," *American Journal of Physical Anthropology*, 52:109-121; Holloway, R. L. 1983. "Human paleontological evidence relevant to language behavior," *Human Neurobiology*, 2:105-114.

[44] Lieberman, P. 1994. "The Origin and Evolution of Language," in *Companion Encyclopedia of Anthropology*, T. Ingold, ed., N.Y.: Routledge, pp. 108-131; Lieberman, P. 1991. *Uniquely Human: The Evolution of speech, Thought and Selfless Behavior*, Cambridge, MA: Harvard Univ. Press; Lieberman, P. and Crelin, E. S. 1971. "On the speech of Neanderthal man," *Linguistic Inquiry*, 2:203-222; Davidson, Iain., *et al.* 1993. "On the evolution of language," *Current Anthropology* (April), 34:2:165-170.

[45] MacLean, Paul. 1990. *The Triune Brain in Evolution*, N.Y.: Plenum, Chs. 27, 28, 29; MacLean, Paul. 1986. "Culminating developments in the evolution of the limbic system: The thalamocingulate division," in *The Limbic System: Functional Organization and clinical Disorders*, B. K. Doane and K. F. Livingston, eds., N.Y.: Raven Press, pp. 1-28.

[46] Damasio, A. R. 1994. *Descartes' Error*, N.Y.: Avon; Changeux, J. P. 1985. *Neuronal Man: The Biology of Mind*, N.Y.: Pantheon; Edelman, G. 1992. *Bright Air, Brilliant Fire*, N.Y.: Basic Books.

[47] Goldschmidt, R. 1940. *The Material Basis of Evolution*, New Haven: Yale Univ. Press.

19

Homo: Destiny Incomplete

"In effect natural selection operates *upon* the products of chance and can feed nowhere else; but it operates in a domain of very demanding conditions, and from this domain chance is barred. It is not to chance but to those conditions that evolution owes its generally progressive course, its successive conquests, and the impression it gives of a smooth and steady unfolding."

Jacques Monod

Evolutionary Roots of Domination

We have now arrived at a most probable scenario for the evolutionary extrusion of *Homo sapiens* in general, and *Homo sapiens sapiens*, the primal creator of the first universal civilization and dominating inspirator for the species, in particular. In looking back at the evolutionary processes and selective pruning that pushed this line of eukaryotes-vertebrates-primates forward we must ask at the same time, of its significance for our position in evolutionary and human history, today and tomorrow.

Certainly, changes in the environments and ecologies that incessantly impact our planet are crucial factors in reshuffling the genetic and phenotypic possibilities for life on our Earth. These changes had to take place within the boundaries of the thermodynamic, biochemical, and oxygenating conditions that have been maintained on our planet for over 4 billion years.

With oscillating change, always within limiting physical parameters, a sub-phylum such as the vertebrates could develop those morphological structures which allowed for movement, exploration, and survival first in the seas and then on land. Thus it came to be that the evolutionary products that we call humans are the paradigmatic explorers, investigators, migrators and conquerors amongst the animals first on land, and now into the seas and skies. This evolutionary process only needed time, given the above preconditions, for the inevitable appearance of an animal such as *Homo sapiens sapiens*.

We can epitomize this long-in-coming but "inevitable" extrusion of *Homo sapiens sapiens*, as a natural evolutionary process in which certain living forms, from the energy mobilizing eukaryote cell to *Homo*, were enabled to move through a series of opportune "adaptive-time deep, zones of possibility" on our life-giving planet.

It goes without saying that the evolutionary story has not ended on our planet. It is hard to predict how many more billions of years life on Earth may exist. There should be no question but that this seeming suzerainty of humans will be challenged, if not from the primeval bacterial world, then by other life forms created as products of newly-challenging alterations in the "adaptive time-deep zones of possibility" on the planet.

Our immediate concerns are, however, daunting. We need to understand the nature of *Homo sapiens sapiens*, this creature that first appeared culturally and morphologically on the historical scene some 45,000 years ago. Further, this modernizing stem on the human branch before and since has spread its genes far and wide, sending the contemporary international exemplifications of our "super-species" into an explosive demographic and amalgamating phase. We are constantly regaled with increasing examples of our suffocating impact on ever more life forms on this ecologically diminished planet.

19.1 Future: Cape Barren Island schoolchildren. Nearly all are half-caste Tasmanians—late-nineteenth century.

A Non-Adaptationist Reconstruction

What makes our task of understanding the peculiar uniqueness of the bio/social nature of *Homo sapiens sapiens* so difficult is the mix of aggressive intentionality and the seeming idealism and practical uselessness of so much in human behavior and its cultural products. Against the backdrop of some 35,000 years of Ice-Age expansion, we note a steadily diminishing profile of human diversity. The Neanderthals are the prime example. But surely there were others who were pushed into oblivion, including most of the Boskopoids and other African and Mid-Eastern borderline *Homo sapiens* forms.

Other ethnicities were shunted into sapiency by the infusion of these highly corticalized Eur-Asian *Homo sapiens sapiens* "genes." Given time the genetics of high cultural intelligence made its way inter-generationally through a variety of intermediate populations, as in the game of "telephone." We note the quiet and inexorable expansion of the Cro-Magnons. [1]

But then, the art, the delicate technology, the chronometric notations, the love of female beauty, the awe for animal life, the search for color to paint, the imaginative mind seeing in every undulating cave wall the reflection of an animal form and livingness. What adaptive survival instincts were being put into play by such behaviors? A number of years ago the geneticist Theodosius Dobzhansky attempted to explain this conundrum. His solution was to posit a biologically selective advantage for those individuals with artistic and musical talents, perhaps taking his inspiration from J. S. Bach's two wives and 20 children.[2]

This human behavioral dilemma has puzzled countless sociobiologists, most of them forced to concoct the most fantastic selectionist scenarios to create a reproductive advantage out of the complex fabric of human cultural expression, what Richard Lewontin and Ernst Mayr have called the adaptationist fallacy.[3] Countless generations of behaviorist psychologists and semanticists have attempted to reconcile what has been the perverse delight of metaphysical philosophers—glorying in the ideational character of human thought—with the reality that we are biological creatures, subject to the same laws and principles that explain the evolution and behavior of other life forms.

The clue to this intellectual conundrum is, of course, the sharp heterochronic remodeling of the ancient hominid and recent brain structure of *Homo*, to the model and form represented in the Eur-Asian Cro-Magnids. There are few today who would argue against the fact that language use is *Homo*'s unique primate adaptation. The whole complex of vocal and brain structure constructions was probably in the first place an ancient anthropoid defensive pre-adaptation which thence increasingly linked the traditional automatic signaling vocal structure in apes with greater cortical control. Small defensive proto-hominids during the Oligocene ecological breakout and expansion of the apes might well have discovered that a preexisting capability for the voluntary inhibition of sound reflexes could be turned to protective advantage.[4]

Ralph Holloway long ago noted an incipient Broca's area in the brain, one morphological source for language, in the earliest presumed members of the genus *Homo*.[5] This rudimentary indication of cultural and thus symbolic communication and behavior, along with Oldowan tools, could have already reflected a move away from the sign system of the apes. Perhaps such a behavioral level was incipient in our taxonomically variable australopithecine hominid sisters. The road upward in cognitive content of the newer sign/symbol behavior structure was probably gradual, leading our line of hominids away from traditional instinctive, *i.e.*, iconic (the shadow of a bird freezes the movements of a small mammal) and indexical referencing (repeated stimuli lead to a conditioned response), to ever more forward-looking cortical predictions on the basis of these external stimuli.[6]

This ancient alliance of our linguistic structures with the human cortex, in the final reconstruction, brought with it poetry, song, information, insult, incantation. How practical did the great reconstruction of the brain have to be in order for it to serve a positively selective function for human behavior?

Perhaps allometry was involved, the linkage of genes for the growth of one selectively important dimension of morphology with another that simply "tags along," but then, lo and behold, itself is pulled across a physiological and behavioral threshold to become a key element in the adaptive equation. There is now evidence that humans, even at the *H. erectus* stage, were already quite tall. A new brain may have even then been surging in growth in one isolated taxon.

Evolutionary theory only asks that this suddenly expanding brain not result in negative selective consequences. The term "orthoselection," selection in a straight line, has a venerable explanatory tradition. It refers to the continuous modeling of variation in a line, over time, along the most positive selective valence.[7]

For such trends to occur there must be access to the required genetic variation. Here evolutionary theory explains that genetic variation is rarely strictly random. As described by Sewall Wright and Ernst Mayr, mutation rates and direction are themselves variables. Thus certain characteristics of an ancient and stable line can be deeply grooved over long evolutionary periods, variation from the existing genetic structure proving to be maladaptive, eventually to be lost from the genetic reservoir of the particular line. In less well-adapted forms, characteristics being subject to dynamic positive and negative selection tend to appear and reappear in a variety of geno/phenotypic manifestations.[8]

No teleological metaphysical directiveness is here required, merely highly concentrated and ubiquitous selective trends. It is a rare evolutionary event for a line of complex creatures long well adapted and at peace with the external world suddenly to reactivate its genetic structure in a frenzy of variation and adaptive/selective dynamic, as the theory of "punctuated equilibrium" seems to suggest.

It should be emphasized, as we have done in the preceding chapter that there is more to the human revolution in brain morphology and behavior than the growth of the iso- (or new) cortex and its rich neurological interconnectivity. There is also a matter of reconstruction, in which the allocortex and the limbic system have also been subject to significant allometric growth, human behavior being concomitantly infused with enormous emotional affect.[9]

Symbolic Effulgence

When we contrast symbolic behavior with that of other animal systems of communication and biological survival, the differences stun and puzzle. We are still far from attaining any agreement as to the nature of the teachability of chimpanzees, whether their responsiveness to the laboratory tasks that we set for them are truly symbolic in their meaning, independently formed, and not iconic and indexically-conditioned responses into which we tend to read too much.

Symbolic thought implies the unconditioned creation of meaning from the external perceptions that *Homo*'s highly sensitized organs of sensation receive. These inputs are immediately integrated into a structure of significance rather than physical response. Symbolism appears to break with the great organic tradition. The human response is most often innovative and defies the stereotypical instinctual predictivity of animals in the wild. Let nature grant humans the wisdom to know the genetic pathways and behaviors that could deterministically lead the species toward ultimate survival over time!

The explosive reconstruction of the brain in *Homo sapiens sapiens* completed the gradual severing of human behavior with that ancient and supremely successful sign/signal system that had defined animal life over vast spans of time. Successful that is, until *Homo sapiens sapiens* appeared on the scene.

It is probably incorrect to assume that the symbol/cultural system by which humans now organize their behavior was uniquely created in *Homo sapiens sapiens*. No doubt the Neanderthals operated on the basis of an effective symbol/cultural web of meaning/behavior, if not the pulsating cognitive dynamics of the Cro-Magnids. There were probably no iconic/instinctual behavioral sureties rigidly determined by their genes. Rather, a vague sense of tradition and necessity by which an inchoately aware mind coped with the here-and-now realities that must be faced. Theirs was not rigidly programmed behavior.

Consider the classical "primitive" mind's response to nature's vagaries, magic. The ritual dance around fire. The fearful totems and taboos of superstition. Fixed symbolic cultural traditions over the centuries and millennia. Then, consider the scientific and inquiring mind's approach to these same phenomena. The former leads to embeddedness and social stagnancy over time. The latter inexorably toward the attempt to understand and control nature's power. They both reflect the breadth of possibilities in the sign/symbol system of human intelligence. How far back in human evolution did the first inchoate symbolic behaviors, including our linguistic utterances, slip the noose of instinctual directiveness?

As far as we can judge, the human symbol system of behavior operates autochthonously, far beyond any practical envisionments rooted in ancient genetic and selective traditions. Sociobiologists have pointed to many mammalian and primate reminiscences in much of human behavior, from the protection by the male of his own blood children, to a wide variety of other social/kin affinities that seem to derive from deeper levels of genetic consanguinity. However, seemingly, unlike in other mammals, human free will allows individuals and societies to violate these blood allegiances. In contrast, no animal can step back from the regulations imposed by the genes. As the psychologist Edward Thorndike once noted, all animals must say "yes" to this instinctual heritage.

What is Culture?

Historically, the human species has thus far vainly attempted to understand, no less control, its obliterating power over organic nature. We seem to be powerless to interdict *Homo*'s tendency to self-destruct in the most terrible forms of interpersonal violence, war and genocide.

These are the behavioral products of a brain that knows no proximate biological barriers. True, the enormous affect that underlies this violence and aggressive imperialism over nature is intrinsic to the miraculous growth and reconstruction of the brain. The selective feedback toward ever-greater cortical and emotional power surged the maximal growth of this organ.

And out of this brain spewed the multiplicities of symbolic expression in the richness and diversities of meaning that we call "culture." Language differences—its spontaneous and internal change—are but one dimension of the human brain's inner workings. Through the symbolic bonds that create unique languages and their cultures, individuals are bound together in social units, ever larger in number and complexity. The seeming necessity of group life to ensure the reproductive success of the minimal band as it protected the immature and vulnerable neonate, took on its own living form as greater cortical powers of objectification and predictive behavior brought under the umbrella of ethnicity larger numbers of humans into tribes, nations, and civilizations.

This richness of symbolic expression, in religion, the arts, sport, technology, science, philosophy, history, ritual festivity, represents the puzzlement in the nature and meaning of culture. The cause is a brain that is tychistic, unpredictable, in terms of the direction and nature of the symbols of meaning that will be produced within any one culture, no less the full range of human groups across the spectrum of history. Clearly, the resolution to this conundrum of meaning lies in the psychological complexity of the human brain, both intellectually and emotionally, here presented for examination on the macro-level by the symbolic products of this psychological complexity.

The so-called "universals" of culture, examples of which were noted in the above paragraph, testify to a similarity in psychological structures across the palette of human ethnicities and races. These hint at the probability that at a relatively ancient locus in the evolution of the genus *Homo* basic psychologically expressed symbolic vectors were already fixed in human brain morphology. The question remains: what content or grade of symbolic expression is represented in the particular symbolic/cultural expression?

Consider the increasing level of sophisticated symbolic objectivization exhibited by the Cro-Magnids, both in conception and external realization. Take into account the as-yet-undeveloped technological instrumentalities of these Ice Age peoples, their then-naïve and dawning awareness of their powers. One must concede the predictive, subsequent, and recent political and economic domination by their Eur-Asian Caucasoid descendants.

The door is here opened on another controversial issue. All humans are capable of symbolic communication. All cultures reflect the universality of our psychological nature, the vectors of the symbolic forms of culture. But are all cultures equal in the abstractive and cognitive power of their "symbol system" the intellectual meanings and instrumentalities that the culture brings to bear on the life experiences of its members? Is the theory of "cultural relativism," emotionally cherished by so many in the academic and political community, factually supportable?

High Intelligence: Necessary, but not Sufficient

The factual evidence, whether from a Eur-Asian "Garden of Eden" perspective or a multi-regional position, argues for the full *Homo sapiens sapiens* realization of brain growth and cortical power to have first devolved upon the Eur-Asian Cro-Magnids. The positively selective cognitive impact of this morphology was demonstrated by its rapid if often deadly diffusion amongst all the ethnicities and races of humans around the world. This revolution in morphology and behavior is ongoing.

High intelligence speaks to the issue of individuals and populations having the capacity to express themselves symbolically in abstract structures of thought, whether they be in the arts, political and legal institutions, philosophy, science and technology, religion and ethics. Here we can refer to a traditional psychological construct, the "g" factor of general intelligence, now universally applied to evaluate individual potential for higher educational training.[10]

There can be no question today but that the evidence from pre-history, as well as recorded history, argues for this general correlation in the capacity to build civilizational institutions, then expressed in powerfully aggressive and expansive genetic and cultural dynamics. Even given the examples of relatively uncouth tribal peoples, Goths, Arabs, Mongols, destroying rich if decadent civilizations, it is clear that these peoples were exemplifying their cultural potential in these military skills.

On the other hand, we have now experienced the 20th century. It has been a barbarous and clearly dysgenic century, in which hundreds of millions of the most civilized, educated, and intellectually productive humans were slaughtered in an orgy of genocidal envy and hatred. Ironically, such events occurred at the hands of the leadership of a number of our most advanced nations, in terms of education, modern civilizational institutions.

An important dimension of our evolutionary heritage of intelligence and reason was effaced by powerful and deeply irrational forces latent in our human nature. Clearly, these forces have always been precariously contained within the human psyche. Yet, mere generations after, peoples that precipitated these horrors again reveal their true civilizational potential, now at peace with the world, productive of all those rational and intellectual values that humans believe to be at the center of our hopes for the future of the species.

High intelligence itself is not enough to discipline the ongoing war of humans against life on our Earth. The need seems to be for both educated and disciplined scientific rationality, the intellectual capacity to ward off those myths and hallucinations that can propel nations, indeed international society itself, into ideological crusades both for and against phantom utopias.

What we need to understand more deeply is the nature of this orthoselective explosion of brain power and symbolic envisionment that has taken us irrevocably down a new evolutionary road, and perhaps into a totally new adaptive zone of natural selection. We have severed ourselves from the behavioral restraints established tens and hundreds of millions of years ago in the mammalian genotype. We are something new on the evolutionary scene. Indeed we have a genotype, and a biological nature within. But we do not yet understand its boundaries, variabilities, potentialities.

The tentative thought here is that only high, rational, scientifically educated intelligence can provide humankind the evidential options for decisionmaking. Such long-range planning by an intellectually and culturally diverse species depends in the first place on the disciplining of those explosively creative and expansive energies that emanate from the brain of *Homo sapiens sapiens*.

Nature will surely and eventually make known to us the boundaries for the flourishing of this now vast pan-mictic species, *Homo sapiens*. Our unique and only genetic protection lies in the intellectual capability of humans' predicting Nature's alarm bells before they actually ring.

Endnotes, Chapter 19

[1] Keeley, L. 1996. *War Before Civilization*, N.Y.: Oxford Univ. Press. Zubrow, E. 1989. "The demographic modelling of Neanderthal extinction," in *The Human Revolution: Behavioral and Biological Perspectives on the Origins of Modern Humans*, ed. P. A. Mellars and C. B. Stringer, eds., Edinburgh: Univ. of Edinburgh Press, pp. 212-231.

[2] Dobzhansky, T. 1962. *Mankind Evolving*, New Haven: Yale Univ. Press.

[3] Lewontin, R. 1979. "Sociobiology as an adaptationist program," *Behavioral Science*, 24:5-14; Mayr, E. 1983. "How to carry out the adaptationist program," *The American Naturalist*, 121:324-334; Pinker, S. 1997. *How The Mind Works*, N.Y.: W. W. Norton, pp. 163-164.

[4] Deacon, T. 1997. *The Symbolic Species, the co-evolution of language and the brain*, N.Y.: W. W. Norton, pp. 32-39

[5] Holloway, R. L. 1972. "New Australopithecine Endocasts SK 1585 from Swartkrans South Africa," *Am. Jrnl. of Physical Anthropology*, 37:173-186; Holloway, R. L. 1974. "The Casts of Fossil Hominid Brains," *Scientific American*, July, 106-115.

[6] Deacon, 1997, *op. cit.*, pp. 70-78.

[7] Simpson, G. G. 1953. *The Major Features of Evolution*, N.Y.: Columbia Univ. Press, pp. 333-376, 373, fig. 47; Simpson, G. G. 1944. *Tempo and Mode in Evolution*, N.Y.: Columbia Univ. Press; Romer, A. S. 1963. "Time Series and Trends in Animal Evolution," in *Genetics, Paleontology, and Evolution*, G. L. Jepson, *et al.*, eds., N.Y.: Atheneum, p. 107.

[8] Wright, S. 1963. "Adaptation and Selection," in *Genetics, Paleontology, and Evolution*, G. C. Jepson, *et al.*, eds., N.Y.: Atheneum, pp. 365-391; Mayr, E. 1954. "Change of Genetic Environment and Evolution," in *Evolution as a Process*, Huxley, J. C., *et al.*, eds., London: Allen & Unwin; Mayr, E. 1963. "Speciation and Systematics," in Jepson *et al.*, eds., *op. cit.*, pp. 281-298.

[9] Dimasio, A. R. 1994. *Descartes' Error*, N.Y.: Avon; Ploog, D. W. 1992. "Neuroethological Perspectives on the Human Brain: From the Expression of Emotion to Intentional Signing and Speech," in *So Human A Brain*, Anne Harrington, ed., Boston: Birkhauser, pp. 3-13; Edelman, G. 1992. *Bright Air, Brilliant Fire*, N.Y.: Basic Books; Changeux, J. P. 1985. *Neuronal Man: The Biology of Mind*, N.Y.: Pantheon; Irsigler, F. J. 1984. "Quantitative Morphogenesis and Lateralization of the Human Brain," in *Mankind Quarterly*, 25:3-46; Irsigler, F. J. 1983. "The Role of the Temporal Lobe on Morphogenesis and Lateralization of the Human Brain," *Speculations in Science and Technology*, 6:445-453; Stephan, H. 1975. "Allocortex," in *Handbuch der Mikroskopischen Anatomie des Menschen*, 4/9, Bargmann, W., ed., Berlin: Springer.

[10] Jensen, A. R. 1998. *The g Factor*, Westport, CT: Praeger.

Bibliography

Aboitiz F. 1993. "Further Comments on the Evolutionary Origin of the Mammalian Brain," *Medical Hypotheses*, 41:409-418.

Aiello, L. 1993. "The Fossil Evidence for Modern Human Origins in Africa: A Revised View," *American Anthropologist*, 95:1:73-96.

Aitken, M. J., Stringer, C. B., and Mellars, P. A., eds. 1993. *The Origin of Modern Humans and the Impact of Chronometric Dating*, Princeton, N. J.: Princeton Univ. Press.

Allin, E. F. 1975. "Evolution of the mammalian middle ear," *Jnl. Morph.*, 147:403-438.

Allsworth-Jones, P. 1993. "The archaeology of Archaic and Early Modern `Homo sapiens': An African Perspective," *Cambridge Archaeological Journal*, 3:1:21-39.

Alvarez, L. W., Alvarez, W., Asaro, F., and Michel, H. V. 1980. "Extraterrestrial cause for the Cretaceous-tertiary extinction, *Science*.

Alvarez, L. W. 1983. "Experimental evidence that an asteroid impact led to the extinction of many species 65 million years ago," *Proceedings of the National Academy of Sciences U.S.A.*, 80 (2):627-642.

Ammerman, A. J., and Cavalli-Sforza, L. L. 1994. *The Neolithic Transition and the Genetics of Populations in Europe*, Princeton, N.J.: Princeton Univ. Press, pp. 20-30; Table 2.1, figs. 2.3, 2.4, 4.5.

Anderson, A. 1984. "The Extinction of Moa in Southern New Zealand," in *Quaternary Extinctions*, P. S. Martin and R. G. Klein, eds. Tucson: Univ. of Arizona Press.

Andrews, P. 1976. "Taxonomy and Relationship of Fossil Apes," *Abstract and Manuscript, VI Intern. Primatological Congress*, Cambridge: Abstracts, p. 80.

Andrews, P., and Cronin, J. E. 1982. "The relationship of *Sivapithecus* and *Ramapithecus* and the evolution of the Orangutan," *Nature*, 297:541-546.

Andrews, P., and Pilbeam, D. 1996. "The Nature of the Evidence," *Nature*, Jan. 11, 379:123-124.

Andrews, P., and Stringer, C. 1989. *Human Evolution, an Illustrated Guide*, Cambridge: Cambridge Univ. Press.

Andrews, P., and Stringer, C. 1993. "The Primates' Progress," in *Life*, S. J. Gould, ed., N.Y.: W. W. Norton.

Angel, J. A. 1952. "The Human Skeletal Remains from Hotu Cave, Iran," *Proc. Am. Phil. Soc.*, 96:3:258-269.

Archer, M. *et al.*, 1993. "Reconsideration of Monotreme Relationships Based on the Skull and Dentition of the Miocene `Obdurodon dicksoni,'" in *Mammal Phylogeny*, F. S. Szalay, M. J. Novacek, M. C. McKenna, eds., N.Y.: Springer-Verlag, pp. 75-94.

Arensberg, B. 1989. "New Skeletal Evidence Concerning the Anatomy of Middle Paleolithic Populations in the Middle East: The Kebara Skeleton," in *The Human Revolution — Behavioral and Biological Perspectives on the Origins of Modern Humans*, P. Mellars and C. Stringer, eds., Princeton: Princeton Univ. Press.

Ashley-Montagu, M. F. 1940. Review of T. D. McCowan and A. Keith: *The Stone Age of Mount Carmel*, Vol.2, *The Fossil Remains of Levalloiso-Mousterian, American Anthropologist*, 42:518-522.

Ashley-Montagu, M. F. 1951. *Statement on Race*, N.Y.: Henry Schuman.

Ashley-Montagu, M. F., and Brace, C. L. 1977. *Human Evolution*, N.Y.: Macmillan, pp. 350-352.

Astow, B. *et al.*. 1999. *"Australopithecus garhi*: A New Species of Early Hominid from Ethiopia," *Science*, 23 Apr.:629-635.

Awadalla, P., *et al.* 1999. "Linkage Disequilibrium and Recombination in Hominid Mitochondrial DNA," *Science*, 268:2524-2525, Dec. 24.

Awramik, S. M. 1982. "The origins and early evolution of life," in *The Cambridge Encyclopedia of Earth Sciences*, D. G. Smith, ed., Cambridge: Cambridge Univ. Press, pp. 349-362.

Bailey, G. N., Callow, P., eds. 1986. *Stone Age Prehistory*, , Cambridge: Cambridge Univ. Press.

Baker, J. 1974. *Race*. N.Y.: Oxford Univ. Press.

Balter, M. 1995. "Did *Homo erectus* Tame Fire First?" *Science* 6/16/95, 268:1570.

Bargmann, W., ed. 1975. *Handbuch der Mikroskopischen Anatomie des Menschen*, Berlin: Springer.

Bar-Yosef, O. 1989. "Geochronology of the Levantine Middle Paleolithic," in *The Human Revolution Behavioral and Biological Perspectives on the Origins of Modern Humans*, P. A. Mellars and C. Stringer, eds., Princeton, N.J.: Princeton Univ. Press, pp. 589-610, esp. p. 604.

Bar-Yosef, O. 1993. "The Role of Western Asia in Modern Human Origins," in *The Origin of Modern Humans and the Impact of Chronometric Dating*, M. J. Aitken, C. Stringer, P. A. Mellars, eds., Princeton, N.J.: Princeton Univ. Press.

Bar-Yosef, O. 1996. "Modern Humans, Neanderthals and the Middle/Upper Paleolithic Transition in Western Asia," in *The Origin of Modern Man*, O. Bar-Yosef and L. L. Cavalli-Sforza, *et al.*, eds., Forli: ABACO Edizioni, pp. 175-190, esp. p. 180.

Bar-Yosef, O. 1997. Personal communication, 11/21/97.

Bar-Yosef, O., and Belfer-Cohen, A. 1996. "Another Look At The Levantine Aurignacian," in *XIII International Union of Prehistoric and Protohistoric Sciences*, Forli ABACO Edizioni, Coloquium XI, pp. 139-150.

Bar-Yosef, O., and Cavalli-Sforza, L. L., eds. 1996. *The Origin of Modern Man*, Forli: ABACO Edizioni, pp. 175-190, esp. p. 180.

Bar-Yosef, O., and Kra, R. S., eds. 1994. *Late Quaternary Chronology and Paleoclimates of the Eastern Mediterranean*, Tucson, AZ: University of Arizona.

Bar-Yosef, O., *et al.* 1996. "The Dating of the Upper Paleolithic Layers at Kebara Cave, Mt. Carmel," *Journal of Archaeological Science*, 23:297-306, esp. 304.

Barnosky, A. D. 1989. "The Late Pleistocene Event As a Paradigm for a Widespread Mammal Extinction," in *Mass Extinctions: Process and Evidence*, S. K. Donovan, ed., N.Y.: Columbia Univ. Press.

Beard, K. C. 1996. "Fossil May Fill a Gap in Early Primate Evolution," *New York Times*, 4/9/96 (*Reuters*, 4/8/96).

Beard, K. C., *et al.* 1994. "A Diverse New Primate Fauna from Middle Eocene Fissure-fillings in southeastern China," *Nature* (London), 368:604-609.

Begun, D. R. 1991. "European Catarrhine Diversity," *Jnl. Hum. Evol.*, 20:521-526.

Bengtson, S. 1993. *Early Life on Earth*, N.Y.: Columbia Univ. Press.

Bengtson, S. 1998. "Animal embryos in deep time," *Nature*, 2/5/98, 391:529-530.

Benton, M. 1993. "Four Feet on the Ground," in *Life*, S. J. Gould, ed., N.Y.: W. W. Norton.

Benton, M. 1993. "The Rise of the Fishes," in *Life*, S. J. Gould, ed., N.Y.: W. W. Norton.

Benton, M. 1993. "Life and Time," in *Life*, S. J. Gould, ed., N.Y.: W. W. Norton.

Bermudez, J. M., and Arsuaga, J. L. 1997. *Science*, 5/30/97.

Bernal, J. D., and Cairns-Smith, A. G., 1991, (in E. G. Nisbet, *Living Earth*, N.Y.: Harper Collins, pp. 30-39).

Bernard, C. Paris (1865). *Introduction a l'Etude de la Medecine Experimentale*, tr. by H. C. Greene, under the title of *Introduction to the Study of Experimental Medicine* (N.Y.: Dover, 1957).

Beynon, A. D., and Wood, B. A. 1987. "Patterns and Rates of Enamel Growth in the Molar Teeth of Early Hominids," *Nature*, 326:493-496.

Billingham, J., ed., *Life in the Universe*, Cambridge, MA.: MIT Press, pp. 259-275.

Binford, L. R. 1984. *Faunal Remains from Klasies River Mouth*, Orlando: Academic Press.

Black, Davidson, de Chardin, Teilhard, Young, C. C., Pei, W. C. 1933. *Fossil Man In China: The Choukoutien Cave Deposits....*, Peiping" The Geological Survey of China--National Academy of Peiping. May, 1933, pp. 130-136.

Blakeslee, Sandra. 1996. "Carl Woese: Microbial Life's Steadfast Champion," *The New York Times*, 10/15/96, C1, C7.

Blum, H. F. 1951. *Time's Arrow and Evolution*, Princeton, N.J.: Princeton Univ. Press.

Boaz, N. T. 1995. "Calibration and Extension of the Record of Plio-Pleistocene Hominidae," in *Biological Anthropology: The State of the Science*, N. T. Boaz and L. D. Wolfe, eds., Bend, Oregon: International Institute for Human Evolutionary Research, Central Oregon University Center.

Boaz, N. T., and Wolfe, L. D., eds. 1995. *Biological Anthropology, The State of the Science*, Bend, Oregon: International Institute for Human Evolutionary Research, Central Oregon University Center.

Bolk, L. 1926. *Das Problem der Menschenwerdung*, Jena: G. Fischer.

Bone, Q., Marshall, N. B., Blaxter, J. H. S. 1995. *Biology of Fishes*. London: Blackie Academic & Professional.

Bradley, B., and Sampson, C. G. 1986. "Analysis by Replication of Two Acheulian Artefact Assemblages," in *Stone Age Prehistory*, G. Bailey & P. Callow, eds., Cambridge: Cambridge Univ. Press, pp. 29-45.

Brasier, M. D. 1989. "On mass extinction and faunal turnover near the end of the precambrian," in "Paleontological Criteria for the Recognition of Mass Extinctions," *Mass Extinctions: Process and Evidence*, S. K. Donovan, ed., N.Y.: Columbia Univ. Press.

Brauer, G. 1989. "The Evolution of Modern Humans: A Comparison of the African and Non-African Evidence," in *The Human Revolution — Behavioral and Biological Perspectives on the Origins of Modern Humans*, P. Mellars and C. Stringer, eds., Princeton: Princeton Univ. Press, pp. 123-154, esp. 125.

Brauer, G., and Smith, F. H., eds. 1992. *Continuity or Replacement: Controversies in Homo Sapiens Evolution*, Rotterdam: Balkema.

Brink, A. S. 1955. "Note on a very tiny specimen of 'Thrinaxodon liorhinus,'" *Paleontol. Afr.*, 3:73-76.

Brink, A. S. 1958. "Note on a new skeleton of 'Thrinaxodon liorhinus,'" *Paleontol. Afr.*, 6:15-22.

Britten, R. J. (late 1960s), work of, cited in G. L. Stebbins. 1982. *Darwin to DNA, Molecules to Humanity*, San Francisco: W. H. Freeman, p. 169.

Britten, R. J. 1986. *Science*, 231:1393-1398.

Brock, T. D., *et al.* 1970. *Biology of Microorganisms*, Englewood Cliffs, N.J.: Prentice Hall.

Brocks, J. J., *et al.*, 1999. "Archean Molecular Fossils and the Early Rise of Eukaryotes," *Science*, 8/13/99, 285:1033-1036.

Broderick, A. H. 1961. "A Newly Discovered and as yet Unexplored Treasure-House of Spanish Cave Art: The Fantastic and Beautiful Caves of Nerja--a Preliminary Note," *ILN*, 239:6366:216-219, in: Coon, C. S. 1962. *The Origin of Races*, N.Y.: Knopf, note 8, p. 585.

Bromage, T. G. 1985. "Taung Facial Remodeling," in *Hominid Evolution: Past, Present, Future*, P. V. Tobias, ed., N.Y.: Alan Liss, pp. 239-245.

Bromage, T. G., and Dean, M. C. 1985. "Re-evaluation of the Age at Death of Immature Fossil Hominids," *Nature*, 317:525-527.

Brooks, A., and Yellen J. (personal communication), Bar-Yosef, O. 1993. "The Role of Western Asia in Modern Human Origins," in *The Origin of Modern Humans and the Impact of Chronometric Dating*, M. J. Aitken, C. Stringer, P. A. Mellars, eds., Princeton, N.J.: Princeton Univ. Press, p. 143.

Broom, R. 1910. "A comparison of the Permian reptiles of North America with those of South Africa," *Bull. Am. Mus. of Nat. Hist.*, 28:197-234.

Broom, R. 1932. *The Mammal-Like Reptiles of South Africa and the Origin of Mammals*, London: Witherby.

Broom, R., and Schepers, G. 1946. *The South African Fossil Ape-men, the Australopithecinae*, Transvaal Museum Mem. #2, Pretoria, South Africa.

Broom, R., Robinson, J. T., Schepers, G. W. H. 1949. *Sterkfontein Ape-Man: Plesianthropus*, Transvaal Museum Memoir #4, Pretoria, South Africa.

Brown, M. H. 1990. *The Search For Eve*, N.Y.: Harper & Row, pp. 287-288.

Brown, Peter 1993. "Recent Human Evolution in East Asia and Australia," in *The Origin of Modern Humans and the Impact of Chronometric Dating*, M. J. Aitken, C. B. Stringer, and P. A. Mellars, eds., Princeton, N.J.: Princeton Univ. Press.

Brown, W., *et al.* 1982. "Mitochondrial sequences of primates: tempo and mode of evolution," *Jnl. Mol. Evolution*, 18:225.

Browne, M. 1997. "Old Bones From Gobi Desert Spur a New Look at Evolution," *The New York Times*, Oct. 5, p. 14.

Bruce, E. J., and Ayala, F. J. 1979. "Phylogenetic relationships between man and the apes: electrophoretic evidence," *Evolution*, 33:1040.

Brues, A. 1977. *People and Races*, N.Y.: Macmillan.

Bryson, V., and Vogel, H. J. eds. 1965. *Evolving Genes and Proteins*, N.Y.: Academic Press, p. 97.

Brzezinski, Zbiegniew. 1994. *Out of Control*, N.Y.: Macmillan, p. 10.

Bushnell, G., and McBurney, C. 1959. "New World Origins Seen from the Old World," *Antiquity*, 33:130:93-101.

Busk, G. 1861. "On the Crania of the Most Ancient Races of Man--by Professor H. Schaaffhausen of Bonn. With Remarks and Original Figures, Taken from a Cast of the Neanderthal Cranium," *Natural History Review*, 2:155-176.

Campbell, Bernard. 1966. *Human Evolution: An Introduction to Man's Adaptations*, 1st ed., Chicago: Aldine, pp. 326-328.

Campbell, Bernard. 1985. *Human Evolution*, 3rd. ed., N.Y.: Aldine De Gruyter.

Campbell, Bernard. 1985. "Amino Acid Substitutions in the Hemoglobin Chains of Various Animals as Compared to Humans," *Human Evolution*, N.Y.: Aldine De Gruyter, Table 12.1, p. 371.10.

Campbell, Bernard. 1985. *Human Evolution*, N.Y.: Aldine De Gruyter, Table 12.1, p. 371, from Dobzhansky, T., Ayala, F. J., Stebbins, G. L., Valentine, J. W. 1977. "Amino Acid Substitutions in the Hemoglobin Chains of Various Animals as Compared to Humans," *Evolution*, San Francisco: Freeman.

Campbell, Bernard. 1985. "Immunological Distances between Albumins of Various Old World Primates," *Human Evolution*, N.Y.: Aldine De Gruyter, Table 12.2, p. 371, calculated from data in Sarich, V., and Wilson, A. C. 1967. "Rates of Albumin Evolution in Primates," *Proc. Nat. Acad. Sci. U.S.*11.

Campbell, Bernard. 1985. "Molecular Comparisons among the Great Apes and Homo," *Human Evolution*, N.Y.: Aldine De Gruyter, p. 372, Table 12.3, from Andrews, P., and Cronin, J. E. 1982. "The relationship of *Sivapithecus* and *Ramapithecus* and the evolution of the Orangutan," *Nature*, 297:541-546.

Campbell, B., and Loy, J. 1996. *Humankind Emerging*, 7th ed., N.Y.: Harper-Collins.

Cann, R. L., Stoneking, M., and Wilson, A. 1987. "Mitochondrial DNA and Human Evolution," *Nature*, 325:31-36.

Carcopino, J. 1940 *Daily Life in Ancient Rome*, New Haven: Yale Univ. Press, p. 230.

Carroll, R. L. 1969. "Problems of the origin of reptiles," *Biol. Rev.*, 44:393-432.

Carroll, R. L. 1996. "Revealing the Patterns of Macroevolution," in *Nature*, 2 May 1996, 381:19-20.

Cassels, R. 1984. "Faunal Extinction and Prehistoric Man in New Zealand and the Pacific Islands," in *Quaternary Extinction*, P. S. Martin and R. G. Klein, eds., Tucson: Univ. of Arizona Press.

Cassirer, E. 1944. *An Essay on Man*, New Haven: Yale Univ. Press.

Cassirer, E. 1945. *The Myth of the State*, New Haven: Yale Univ. Press.

Cassirer, E. 1923-1929. *Philosophy of Symbolic Forms*, 3 vols., tr. by R. Manheim, New Haven: Yale Univ. Press.

Cavalli-Sforza, L. L. 1993. Fig.1, in *The Origin of Modern Humans and the Impact of Chronometric Dating*, M. J. Aitken, C. P. Stringer, and P. A. Mellars, eds., Princeton, N. J.: Princeton Univ. Press, p. 71.

Cavalli-Sforza, L. L., *et al.* 1988. "Reconstruction of Human Evolution: Bringing Together Genetic, Archaeological and Linguistic Data," *Proc. National Acad. of Science*, Aug. 1988, 85:6002-6006.

Cavalli-Sforza, L. L., *et al.* 1992. "Coevolution of Genes and Languages Revisited," *Proceed. National Acad. Sciences*, 89:5620-5624.

Cavalli-Sforza, L. L., *et al.* 1993. *History and Geography of Human Genes*, Princeton, N.J.: Princeton Univ. Press.

Chaisson, E. J. 1997. "Cosmic Age Controversy Is Overstated," *Science*, 5/16/97, 276:1089-90.

Changeux, J. P. 1985. *Neuronal Man: The Biology of Mind*, N.Y.: Pantheon.

Chiarelli, B. 1985. "Chromosomes and the Origin of Man," in *Hominid Evolution: Past, present, and future*, P. V. Tobias, ed., N.Y.: Alan R. Liss.

Chivers, D. J., and Jousey, K. A., eds. 1978. London: Academic Press.

Christen, R., *et al.* 1991. *EMBO* J. 10 (1991):499-503.

Christensen, J. 1997. "Prehistoric Art: The Missing Dimension," *Mankind Quarterly*, Spring, 37:3:255-261.

Churchill, S. E., *et al.* 1996. "Morphological Affinities of the Proximal Ulna from Klasies River Main Site: Archaic or Modern?" *Jrnl. of Human Evolution*, 31:3:213-237.

Cifelli, R. L. 1993. "Theria of Metatherian-Eutherian Grade and the Origin of Marsupials," in *Mammal Phylogeny*, F. S. Szalay, M. J. Novacek, M. C. McKenna, eds., N.Y.: Springer-Verlag, pp. 204-215.

Ciochon, R. L. 1995. "Dragon Hill Cave, China: The Earliest Asian Yet," *Natural History*, December, pp., 51-54.

Ciochon, R. L., and Corruccini, R. S., eds. 1983. *New Interpretations of Ape and Human Ancestry*, N.Y.: Plenum.

Ciochon, R. L., and Fleagle, J. G., eds. 1985. *Primate Evolution and Human Origins*, Menlo Park, CA: Benjamin/Cummings Publishing.

Clark, F. N., and Synge, L. M. 1959. *The Origin of Life on Earth*, N.Y.: Pergamon Press

Clark, G. 1967. *The Stone Age Hunters*, N.Y.: McGraw Hill, pp. 71-74.

Clark, G. A., and Lindley, J. M. 1989. "Modern Human Origins in the Levant and Western Asia: The Fossil and Archeological Evidence," *American Anthropologist*, 91:962-985.

Clark, J. D. 1965. "Radiocarbon Dating and the Expansion of Farming Culture from the Near East over Europe," *Proceedings of the Prehistoric Society*, 31:57-73.

Clark, J. D. 1993. "African and Asian perspectives on the origin of modern humans," in *The Origin of Modern Humans and the Impact of Chronometric Dating*, M. J. Aitken, C. P. Stringer, and P. A. Mellars, eds., Princeton, N. J.: Princeton Univ. Press, p. 148.

Clemens, W. A., Jr. 1986. "Evolution of the Terrestrial Vertebrate Fauna During the Cretaceous-Tertiary Transition," in *Dynamics of Extinction*, David K., ed., N.Y.: Wiley, p. 65.

Clemens, W. A., Jr. 1986. "On Triassic and Jurassic Mammals," in *The Beginning of the Age of Dinosaurs*, K. Padian, ed., Cambridge: Cambridge Univ. Press, pp. 237-246.

Clottes, Jean. *The Dawn of Art*, N.Y.: Harry Abrams.

Clottes, Jean. *The Cave Beneath the Sea*, N.Y.: Harry Abrams.

Clutton-Brock, T. H., and Harvey, P. H. 1980. "Primates, Brains, and Ecology," *Jnl. Zool. (London)*, 190:309-324.

Colbert, E. H. 1972. "Antarctic fossils and the reconstruction of Gondwanaland," *Nat. Hist.*, 81:66-73.

Colbert, E. H. 1986. "Mesozoic Tetrapod Extinctions: A Review," in *Dynamics of Extinction*, David K. Elliott, ed., N.Y.: John Wiley

Colbert, E. H., and Morales, M. 1991. *Evolution of the Vertebrates*, 4th ed., N.Y.: Wiley-Liss.

Colinvaux, Paul. 1978. *Why Big Fierce Animals Are Rare*, Princeton, N.J.: Princeton Univ. Press.

Conquest, R. 1986. *The Harvest of Sorrow: Soviet Collectivization and the Terror Famine*, N.Y.: Oxford Univ. Press.

Conroy, G. C. 1976. "Primate postcranial remains from the Oligocene of Egypt," *Contr. Primatol.*, 8:1-134.

Conroy, G. C. 1990. *Primate Evolution*, N.Y.: W. W. Norton.

Conroy, G. C., and Vannier, M. W. 1987. "Dental Development of the Taung Skull from Computerized Tomography," *Nature*, 329:625-627.

Conroy, G. C., Vannier, M. V., Tobias, P. V. 1990. "Endocranial Features of A. africanus Revealed by 2- and 3-DComputed Tomography," *Science*, 2/16/90, 247:838-841.

Coon, C. S. 1939. *The Races of Europe*, N.Y.: Macmillan.

Coon, C. S. 1962. *The Origin of Races*, N.Y.: Knopf, note 9, p. 523, Vallois and Movius: *Catalogue des Hommes Fossiles*.

Coon, C. S., and Hunt, E. E., Jr. 1965. *The Living Races of Man*, N.Y.: Knopf.

Coon, C. S. 1982. *Racial Adaptations*, Chicago: Nelson-Hall.

Crompton, A. W., Taylor, C. R., and Jagger, J. A. 1978. "Evolution of Homeothermy in Mammals" *Nature*, 272:333-336.

Cronin, Anne. 1995. "Primitive? Not the One Who Drew the Lion," *The New York Times*, 6/11/95.

Cronin J. E., Boaz, N. T., Stringer, C., and Rak, Y. 1981. "Tempo and Mode in Hominid Evolution," *Nature*, 292:113-122.

Culotta, Elizabeth. 1995. "Asian Hominids Grow Older," *Science*, 11/17/95, 270:1116-1117.

Culotta, Elizabeth. 1995. "New Hominid Crowds the Field," *Science*, 8/18/95, Vol. 269.

Damasio, A. R. 1994. *Descartes' Error*, N.Y.: Avon.

Dart, R. A. 1925. "Australopithecus africanus: the man-ape of South Africa," *Nature*, 115:195-199.

Davidson, Iain, and Noble, William. 1989. "The archeology of perception: Traces of depiction and language," *Current Anthropology*, 30:125-155.

Davidson, Iain, and Noble, William. 1993. "Tools and Language in Human Evolution," in *Tools, Language And Cognition In Human Evolution*, K. R. Gibson and T. Ingold, eds., Cambridge: Cambridge Univ. Press, pp. 363-388, esp. p. 369.

Davidson, Iain., *et al.* 1993. "On the evolution of language," *Current Anthropology* (April), 34:2:165-170.

Dawkins, R. 1995. *River Out of Eden* , N.Y.: Basic Books.

Day, D. 1981. *The Doomsday Book of Animals*, N.Y.: The Viking Press, p. 13.

de Beer, G. 1958. *Embryos and Ancestors*, London: Oxford Univ. Press, 3rd revised edition.

de Duve, Christian. 1991. *Blueprint For A Cell: The Nature And Origin of Life.* Burlington, North Carolina: Neil Patterson Publishers, pp. 113-116.

de Duve, Christian. 1995. *Vital Dust.* N.Y.: Basic Books, pp. 15-16.

de Heinzelin, J., *et al..* 1999. "Environment and Behavior of 2.5-Million-Year-Old Bouri Hominids," *Science, 23 Apr.:625-629.*

de Vos, J., and Swisher, C. C. 1994. "Dating Hominid Sites in Indonesia," *Science*, 12/9/94, 266:1726-1727.

de Waal, Franz. 1989. *Peacemaking Among Primates*, Cambridge, MA: Harvard Univ. Press.

de Waal, Franz. 1996. *Good Natured*, Cambridge, MA: Harvard Univ. Press.

Deacon, H. J. 1989. "Late Pleistocene Palaeoecology and Archaeology in the Southern Cape, South Africa," in *The Human Revolution — Behavioral and Biological Perspectives on the Origins of Modern Humans*, P. A. Mellars and C. Stringer, eds., Princeton: Princeton Univ. Press, pp. 547-564.

Deacon, H. J. 1993. "Southern Africa and Modern Human Origins," in *The Origin of Modern Humans and the Impact of Chronometric Dating*, M. J. Aitken, C. Stringer, P. A. Mellars, eds., Princeton, N.J.: Princeton Univ. Press, pp. 104-117.

Deacon, T. W. 1990. "Rethinking Mammalian Brain Evolution," *Amer. Zool.*, 30:629-705; p. 652.

Deacon, T. W. 1997. *The Symbolic Species*, N.Y.: Norton.

Deacon, T. W. 1997. "What Makes the Human Brain Different," *Annual Rev. Anthropology*, 26:337-357.

Delson, E. 1997. "One skull does not a species make," *Nature*, 10/2/97, 389:445-446.

Delson, E. 1997. "The Robust Australopithecine Skull of Konso, Ethiopia," *Nature*, 10/2/97, Vol. 389, No. 6650.

Delson, E., and Andrews, P. 1975. "Evolution and Interrelationships of the Catarrhine Primates," in *Phylogeny of the Primates*, W. P. Luckett and F. S. Szalay, eds., pp.405-406. N.Y.: Plenum Press.

Delson, E., ed. 1985. *Ancestors: The Hard Evidence*, N.Y.: Alan R. Liss.

deMenocal, P., in *Columbia*. Winter, 1996, 44.

Demidenko, Yuri E., and Usik, Vitalli I. 1995. "Establishing the Potential Evolutionary Technological Possibilities of the 'Point' Levallois-Mousterian: Korolevo 1 Site-Complex 2B in the Ukranian Transcarpathians," in *The Definition and Interpretation of Levallois Technology*, H. L. Dibble and O. Bar-Yosef, eds., Madison, WI: Prehistory Press, pp. 439-454, esp. p. 447.

Dennell, R. (Univ. of Sheffield). 1997. "The World's Oldest Spears," *Nature*, Feb. 1997, 385:27:767-768.

Depew, D. J., and Weber, B. H. 1995. *Darwinism Evolving, Systems Dynamics and the Genealogy of Natural Selection*, Cambridge, MA.: MIT Press.

D'Errico, F., *et al.* 1998. "Neanderthal Acculturation in Western Europe," *Current Anthropology Supplement*, June, Vol. 39.

Dewar, R. E. 1984. "Extinctions in Madagascar: The Loss of the Subfossil Fauna," pp. 574-593, in *Quaternary Extinction*, P. S. Martin and R. G. Klein, eds., Tucson: Univ. of Arizona Press.

Dewey, J. 1927. *The Public and Its Problems*, N.Y.: Henry Holt.

Di Silvestro, Roger. 1994, in Peter Ward, *The End of Evolution*, N.Y.: Bantam Books, p. 211.

Diamond, Jared. 1992. *The Third Chimpanzee*, N.Y.: Harper Collins, p. 357.

Dibble, H. L., and Bar-Yosef, O., eds. 1995. *The Definition and Interpretation of Levallois Technology*, Madison, WI: Prehistory Press.

Dimasio, A. R. 1994. *Descartes' Error*, N.Y.: Avon.

Doane, B. K., and Livingston, K. F., eds. 1986. *The Limbic System: Functional Organization and clinical Disorders*, N.Y.: Raven Press.

Dobzhansky, T. 1944. "On the Species and Races of Living and Fossil Man," *American Journal of Physical Anthropology*, 2:251-265.

Dobzhansky, T. 1962. *Mankind Evolving*, New Haven: Yale Univ. Press.

Dobzhansky, T., Ayala, F. J., Stebbins, G. L., Valentine, J. W. 1977. *Evolution*, San Francisco: Freeman.

Donovan, S. K., ed. 1989. *Mass Extinctions: Process and Evidence*, N.Y.: Columbia Univ. Press.

Donovan, S. K., 1989. "Paleontological Criteria for the Recognition of Mass Extinctions," in *Mass Extinctions: Process and Evidence*, S. K. Donovan, ed., N.Y.: Columbia Univ. Press.

Doolittle, R. F., *et al*. 1989. *The Hierarchy of Life*, B. Fernholm *et al*., eds., Amsterdam: Excerpta Medica, pp. 73-86.

Doolittle, R. F., *et al*. 1996. *Science*, (Jan.) 271:470-477;

Dorit, R. L., *et al*. 1995. *Science*, 268:1183.

Dubois, E. 1921. "The Proto-Australian fossil man of Wadjac, Java," *PKAW* 23:7:1013-1051.

Durham, W. 1994. *Coevolution: Genes, Culture, and Human Diversity*, Stanford, CA: Stanford Univ. Press.

Dyer, B. D., and Obar, R. A. 1994. *Tracing the History of Eukaryotic Cells*, N.Y.: Columbia Univ. Press, pp. 20-22.

Dyson, Freeman. 1985. "Origins of Life," Cambridge: Cambridge Univ. Press, pp. 68-71.

Edelman, G. 1992. *Bright Air, Brilliant Fire*, N.Y.: Basic Books.

Ehrlich, Anne and Paul. 1981. *Extinction*, N.Y.: Random House.

Eigen, Manfred, *et al*. 1981. "The Origin of Genetic Information," *Scientific American*, 244,4:88-118.

Eigen, Manfred. 1992. *Steps Toward Life*, N. Y.: Oxford Univ. Press, p.48.

Einstein, A. 1931. *Relativity: The Special and the General Theory*, Chicago: Regnery, pp. 102-104.

Einstein, A., and Infeld, Leopold. 1938. *The Evolution of Physics*, N.Y.: Simon & Schuster, p. 251.

Eisenberg, J. F., and D. G. Kleinman, eds. 1983. *Advances In The Study Of Mammalian Behavior*, Special Publication No. 7, March 11, 1983, Shippensburg, PA: The American Society of Mammalogists.

Eiseley, Loren. 1957. *The Immense Journey*, N.Y.: Random House, p. 113.

Eldredge, Niles. 1991. *The Miner's Canary*, Englewood Cliffs, N.J.: Prentice Hall, p. 181.

Elliott, David, K. ed. 1986. *Dynamics of Extinction*, N.Y.: John Wiley, Table 1, p. 108.

Emiliani, C. 1956. "Notes on absolute chronology of human evolution," *Science*, 23:24-26.

Emiliani, C. 1960. "Dating Human Evolution," in *The Evolution of Man*, Sol Tax, ed., Chicago: Univ. of Chicago Press, pp. 57-66.

Emson, R. H. 1966. "The Reaction of the sponge to applied stimuli," *Comparative Biochemistry and Physiology*,

Erwin, Douglas H. 1993. *The Great Paleozoic Crisis: Life and Death in the Permian*, N.Y.: Columbia Univ. Press.

Etler, D. A., Crummett, T. I., and Wolpoff, M. H. 1997. "Earliest Chinese Hominid Mandible Is An Ape," *Human Origins News*, 1/30/97, 8pp.

Evans, L. T. 1958. "Fighting in young and mature opossums," *Anat. Rec.*, 131:549.

Excoffier, L., and Langaney, A. 1989. "Origin and Differentiation of Human Mitochondrial DNA," *American Journal of Human Genetics*.

Fagan, B. 1989. *People of the Earth. An Introduction to World Prehistory*, 6th ed. Glenview, IL: Scott Foresman, pp. 112, 115-116.

Fairbridge, Rhodes, in *New York Times*, Sept. 8, 1959.

Falk, D. 1980. "Language, Handedness and Primate Brains: Did the Australopithecines Sign?" *American Anthropologist*, 82:72-78

Falk, D. 1983. "Cerebral Cortices of East African Early Hominids," *Science*, 222:1072-1074.

Falk, D. 1985. *Nature*, 313:45-47.

Falk, D. 1987. "Hominid Paleoneurology," *Annual Review of Anthropology*, 16:13-30.

Falk, D., and Conroy, G. 1983. "The Cranial Venous Sinus System in `Australopithecus afarensis,'" *Science*, 306:779.

Finlay, B. I., and Darlington, R. B. 1995. "Linked Regularities in the Development and Evolution of Mammalian Brains," *Science*, 268:1578.

Fitch, Walter, and Roy Britten referred to in Stebbins, G. Ledyard. 1982. *Darwin to DNA, Molecules to Humanity*, San Francisco: W. H. Freeman, pp. 124-131, 169.

Fleagle, J. G. *et al*. 1981. "Climbing: A Biomechanical Link with Brachiation and with Bipedalism," *Sympos. Zool. Soc. London*, 48:359-375.

Fleagle, J. G. 1986. "The fossil record in early catarrhine evolution," in *Major Topics in Primate and Human Evolution*, B. Wood, L. Martin, and P. Andrews, eds., Cambridge: Cambridge Univ. Press. pp. 130-149.

Fleagle, J. G. 1988. *Primate Adaptation and Evolution*, London: Academic Press.

Fleagle, J. G. 1995. "Origin and Radiation of Anthropoid Primates," in, pp. 1-21, (esp. pp. 1, 16).

Florkin, Marcel. 1949. *Biochemical Evolution*, N.Y.: Academic Press.

Florkin, Marcel. 1959. "L'Extension de la Biosphere et l'Evolution Biochimique," in *The Origin of Life on the Earth*, F. N. Clark and L. M. Synge, eds., N. Y.: Pergamon Press, pp. 503-515

Fowler, C. M. R. 1990. *The Solid Earth*, N.Y.: Cambridge Univ. Press.

Fox, J. J., *et al.* 1980. *Indonesia: Australian Perspectives*, Canberra: Australian National University Press.

Fraser, N. C., Walkden, G. M., Stewart, V. 1985. "The first pre-Rhaetic therian mammals," *Nature*, 314:161-163.

Frayer, D. W. 1993. "Evolution at the European Edge: Neanderthal and Upper Paleolithic Relationships," *Prehistoire Europeene*, 2:9-69.

Frayer, D. W., *et al.* 1993. "The Fossil Evidence for Modern Human Origins," *American Anthropologist*, 95:1:14-50.

Frayer, D. W., *et al.* 1994. "Getting It Straight," *American Anthropologist*, 96:2:424-438.

Fullagar, R. L. K., Price, D. M., and Head, L. M. 1996. "Early Human Occupation of Northern Australia: Archeology and Thermoluminescent Dating of Jinmium Rock-shelter, Northern Territory," *Antiquity*, 70:751-773.

Gabunia L., and Vekua, A. 1995. *Nature*, 373:509-512.

Gadow, H. F. 1911. "Reptiles-Anatomy," *Encyclopaedia Britannica*, 11th ed., Vol. 23, N.Y.: Cambridge Univ. Press, p. 170.

Gambier, Dominique. 1989. "Fossil Hominids from the Early Upper Paleolithic (Aurignacian) of France," in *The Human Revolution — Behavioral and Biological Perspectives on the Origins of Modern Humans*, P. A. Mellars and C. Stringer, eds., Princeton, N.J.: Princeton Univ. Press, pp. 194-211.

Gamble, C. 1994. "Human Evolution: The Last One Million Years," in *Companion Encyclopedia of Anthropology*, T. Ingold, ed., London: Routledge, pp. 79-107.

Garstang, W. 1928. "The Origin and Evolution of Larval Forms," *Report of the British Association for the Advancement of Science for 1928*.

Gehling, J. G. 1987. "Earliest Known Echinoderm -- a new Ediacaran fossil from the Pound Subgroup of South Australia," *Alcheringa*, 11:337-345.

Geschwind, N. 1965. "Disconnexion Syndromes in Animals and Man," *Brain*, 88:237-294, 585-644.

Gesteland, R. R., *et al.* 1998. *The RNA World*, 2nd ed., Cold Spring Harbor, N.Y.: Cold Spring Harbor Monograph Series, 38.

Gibbons, Ann. 1995. "Old Dates for Modern Behavior," *Science*, 4/28/95, 268:495-496.

Gibbons, Ann. 1995. "When it comes to Evolution, Humans Are in a Slow Class," *Science*, 3/31/95, 267:1907-1908 (Research News, Molecular Anthropology).

Gibbons, Ann. 1996. "Homo Erectus in Java: A 250,000-Year Anachronism," *Science*, 12/13/96, 274:1841-1842.

Gibbons, A. 1997. "Y Chromosome Shows That Adam Was An African," *Science*, 10/31/97, 278:804-805.

Gibson, K. R., and Ingold, T., eds. 1993. *Tools, Language And Cognition In Human Evolution*, Cambridge: Cambridge Univ. Press.

Gingerich, P. 1985. "Nonlinear Molecular Clocks and Ape-Human Divergence Times," in *Hominid Evolution: Past, Present and Future*, P. V. Tobias, ed., N.Y.: Alan R. Liss.

Gibbons, Ann. 1995. "The Mystery of Humanity's Missing Mutations," *Science*, 1/6/95, 267:35-36.

Gingerich, P. D. 1986. "Plesiadapis and the delineation of the order Primates," in *Major topics in Primate and Human Evolution*, B. A. Wood, L. B. Martin, and P. J. Andrews, eds., Cambridge Univ. Press.

Gladwell, M. 1997. "The Sports Taboo," *The New Yorker* 5/19/97, pp. 49-55.

Goldschmidt, R. 1940. *The Material Basis of Evolution*, New Haven: Yale Univ. Press.

Gonzales, G. 1997. "Nobody Here but Us Earthlings," *The Wall Street Journal*, 7/17/97.

Goodman, M. 1963. "Man's place in the phylogeny of the primates as reflected in serum proteins," in *Classification and Human Evolution*, S. L. Washburn, ed., Chicago: Aldine, pp. 204-234.

Goodman, M., *et al.* 1983. "Evidence of human origins from haemoglobins of African apes," *Nature*, 303:546.

Goodman, M., *et al.* 1990. "Primate evolution at the DNA level and a classification of hominoids," *Jnl. Mol. Evol.*, 30:260-266.

Gould, S. J. 1977. *Ontogeny and Phylogeny*, Cambridge: Harvard Univ. Press.

Gould, S. J., ed. 1993. *Life*, N.Y.: W. W. Norton.

Gould, S. J., and Eldredge, S. 1977. "Punctuated Equilibria: tempo and mode of evolution reconsidered," *Paleobiology*, 3:115-151.

Gowlett, J. A. J. 1984. *Ascent to Civilization*, London: Collins.

Gowlett, J. A. J. 1986. "Culture and Conceptualization: The Oldowan-Acheulian Gradient," in *Stone Age Prehistory*, G. N. Bailey and P. Callow, eds., Cambridge: Cambridge Univ. Press, pp. 243-260.

Gray, M. W. *et al.* 1999. "Mitochondrial evolution. A review, *Science*, 233:1476-1481.

Gregory, W. K. 1936. "On the Meaning and Limits of Irreversibility in Evolution," *American Naturalist*, 70:517.

Gregory, W. K. 1937. "Supra-specific Variation in Nature and in Classification: A Few Examples from Mammalian Paleontology," *American Naturalist*, 71:268-276.

Gregory, W. K. 1967. *Our Face from Fish to Man*, N.Y.: Hafner.

Griffin, D. R. 1976. *The Question of Animal Awareness*, N.Y.: Rockefeller Univ. Press.

Groves, C. P. 1989. "A Regional Approach to the Problem of the Origin of Modern Humans in Australasia," in *The Human Revolution — Behavioral and Biological Perspectives on the Origins of Modern Humans*, P. Mellars & C. Stringer, eds., Princeton, N.J.: Princeton Univ. Press.

Groves, C. P., and Mazek, V. 1975. "An Approach to the Taxonomy of the Hominidae: Gracile Villefranchian Hominids of Africa," *Cas. Miner Geol.*, 20:225-247.

Grun, R., and Stringer, C. 1991. "Electron spin resonance dating and the evolution of modern humans," *Archeometry*, 33: 153-159.

Gurr, T. R., and Harff, B. 1994. *Ethnic Conflicts in World Politics*, Boulder, CO.: Westview Press, p. 8.

Guthrie, R. Dale. 1984. "Mosaics, Allelochemics and Nutrients," in *Quaternary Extinctions*, P. S. Martin and R. G. Klein, eds., Tucson, AZ: Univ. of Arizona Press.

Gyllensten, U., Wilson, A., *et al.* 1991. "Paternal Inheritance of Mitochondrial DNA in Mice," *Nature*, 352:255-257.

Habgood, P. J. 1985. "The Origin of the Australian Aborigines: An Alternative Approach and View," in *Hominid Evolution: Past, Present, Future*, P. V. Tobias, ed., N.Y.: Alan Liss, pp. 367-380, esp p. 376.

Habgood, P. J. 1989. "The Origin of Anatomically-Modern Humans in Australasia," in *The Human Revolution—Behavioral and Biological Perspectives on the Origins of Modern Humans*, P. Mellars & C. Stringer, eds., Princeton, N.J.: Princeton Univ. Press, pp. 245-273.

Hahn, G., Sigogneau-Russell, D., Wouters, G. 1989. "New data on `Theroteinadae'--Their relations with `Paulschoffatiidae' and `Haramiyidae,'" *Geol. et Paleontol.*, 23:205-215.

Hahn, J. 1986. *Kraft und Aggression. Die Botschaft der Eiszeitkunst im Aurignacien Süddeutschlands?*, Tübingen: Verlag Archaeologica Venatoria, Institute für Urgeschichte der Universität Tübingen.

Haldane, J. B. 1957. "The cost of natural selection," *Jnl. Genet.*, 55:511-524.

Hall, E. R., and Kelson, K. 1959. *Mammals of North America*, N.Y.: Ronald Press.

Hardy, A. C. 1954. "Escape from Specialization," in *Evolution as a Process*, London.

Hare, P. E., ed. 1980. *Biogeochemistry of Amino Acids*, N.Y.: John Wiley.

Harland, W. B. 1983. "The Proterozoic glacial record," in *Geological Society of America Memoir*.

Harrington, A., ed. 1992. *So Human A Brain*, Boston: Birkhauser.

Harris, E. E., and Hey, J. 1999. "X Chromosome evidence for ancient human histories," *Proceedings of the National Academy of Sciences*, 16 Mar, 96:6:3320-3324.

Harrison, T. 1998. "How Australopithecines Measure Up," from *Journal of Human Evolution* July (Web site).

Harrold, Francis B. 1989. "Mousterian, Chatelperronian and Early Aurignacian in Western Europe: Continuity or Discontinuity?" in *The Human Revolution—Behavioral and Biological Perspectives on the Origins of Modern Humans*, P. A. Mellars and C. Stringer, eds., Princeton, N.J.: Princeton Univ. Press, pp. 677-713, esp. pp. 680-681.

Hartman, H., *et al.* 1987. *Search for the Universal Ancestors: The Origin of Life*, Palo Alto, CA: Blackwell, pp. 61-62.

Hasegawa, M., *et al.* 1984. "A new molecular clock of mitochondrial DNA and the evolution of the hominoids," *Proceed. Japan. Acad.*, 60B:95-98.

Hasegawa, M., *et al.* 1993. "Toward a more accurate time scale for the human mitochondrial DNA tree," *Journal of Molecular Evolution*, 37:347-354.

Hayasaka, K., *et al.* 1988. "Molecular phylogeny and evolution of primate mitochondrial DNA," *Mol. Biol. Evol.*, 5(6):626-644.

Haynes, C. V. 1984. "Stratigraphy and late Pleistocene extinctions in the United States," in *Quaternary Extinctions*, P. S. Martin and R. G. Klein, eds., Tucson, AZ: Univ. of Arizona Press.

Hecht, M. K., ed. 1989. *Evolutionary Biology at the Crossroads*, N.Y.: Queens College Press.

Hedges, S. B., and Stoneking, M. 1992. "Technical Comments: Human Origins and Analysis of Mitochondrial DNA Sequences," *Science*, 255:737.

Hedges, S. Blair, *et al.* 1996. "Continental breakup and the ordinal diversification of birds and mammals," *Nature*, May 16, 1996, 381:226-229.

Hellman, Prof. Kenneth (Smith College), personal communication, October 16, 1997.

Henderson, Lawrence J. 1913. *The Fitness of the Environment*, N.Y.: Macmillan, p. 248 (Boston: Beacon Press, 1958).

Hester, J. J. 1967. "The Agency of Man in Animal Extinctions," in *Pleistocene Extinctions*, P. S. Martin and H. E. Wright, Jr., eds., New Haven, CT: Yale Univ. Press

Hill, A., and Ward, S. 1988. "Origin of the Hominidae: the record of African large hominoid evolution between 14My and 4My," *Yearbook of Physical Anthropology*, 31:49-83.

Hillenius, Willem J. 1994. "Turbonates in therapsids: Evidence for late Permian origins of mammalian endothermy (with appendix)," *Evolution*, April, 1994, 48:207-229.

Holdaway, S. 1989. "Were There Hafted Projectile Points in the Mousterian?" *Journal of Field Archaeology*, 16:79-85.

Holland, P. 1992. "Homeobox genes in vertebrate evolution," *Bioessays*, 14:267-273.

Holloway, M. 1994. "Family Matters," *Scientific American*, May, pp. 31-32.

Holloway, R. L. 1972. "New Australopithecine Endocasts SK 1585 from Swartkrans South Africa," *Am. Jrnl. of Physical Anthropology*, 37:173-186.

Holloway, R. L. 1974. "The Casts of Fossil Hominid Brains," *Scientific American*, July, 106-115.

Holloway, R. L. 1978. "Problems of Brain Endocast Interpretation and African Hominid Evolution," in *Early Hominids of Africa*, C. J. Jolly, ed., London: Duckworth.

Holloway, R. L. 1980. "Within Species Brain Body Weight Variability," *American Journal of Physical Anthropology*, 52:109-121.

Holloway, R. L. 1983. "Cerebral Brain Endocast Pattern of `Australopithecus afarensis' Hominid," *Nature*, 303:420-422.

Holloway, R. L. 1983. "Human Paleontological Evidence Relevant to Language Behavior," *Human Neurobiology*, 2:105-114.

Hooton, E. 1946. *Up From the Ape*, N.Y.: Macmillan.

Horton, D. R. 1984. "Red Kangaroos: last of the Australian megafauna," in *Quaternary Extinctions*, P. S. Martin and R. G. Klein, eds., Tucson, AZ: Univ. of Arizona Press.

Howells, W. W. 1973. "Cranial Variation in Man: a study by multivariate analysis," *Peabody Museum Papers*, 67:1-259.

Howells, W. W. 1973. *The Evolution of the Genus `Homo'*, Reading, MA: Addison-Wesley.

Howells, W. W. 1988. "The Meaning of the Neanderthals in Human Evolution," in *L'Evolution dans sa Realite et ses Diverses Modalites*, Fondation Singer-Polignac ed., Paris: Masson, pp. 221-239, esp. 225.

Howells, W. W. 1989. "Skull Shapes and the Map: Craniometric Analyses in the Dispersion of Modern `Homo,'" *Papers of the Peabody Museum*, 79:1-189.

Hsu, C-h, Han, K.-x and Wang, L.-h. 1974. "Discovery of 'Gigantopithecus' teeth and associated fauna in western Hopei," *Vert. palasiat.*, 12:293-309.

Hublin, J.-J. 1993. "Recent Human Evolution in Northwestern Africa," in *The Origin of Modern Humans and the Impact of Chronometric Dating*, M. J. Aitken, C. P. Stringer, and P. A. Mellars, eds., Princeton, N. J.: Princeton Univ. Press, p. 128.

Hublin, J.-J., *et al.* 1996. "A Late Neanderthal Associated with Upper Paleolithic Artifacts," *Nature*, 5/16/96, 381:224-226 (*The New York Times* 5/16/96, (AP)).

Hublin, J.-J. 1997. Personal communication, 12/2/1997.

Hughes, A. 1990. "The Tuinplaas Human Skeleton from the Springbok Flats, Transvaal," in *From Apes to Angels, Essays in Honor of Philip Tobias*, Geoffrey Sperber, ed., N.Y.: Wiley-Liss.

Humphrey, N. K. 1978. "Nature's psychologists," *New Scientist*, 78, 900-903.

Huxley, T. 1863. *Zoological Evidences as to Man's Place in Nature*, London: Williams and Norgate.

Huxley, J. 1943. *Evolution: The Modern Synthesis*, N.Y.: Harper.

Huxley, J. C., *et al.*, eds. 1954. *Evolution as a Process*, London: Allen & Unwin.

Ingold, T., ed. 1994. *Companion Encyclopedia of Anthropology*, N.Y.: Routledge, pp. 33-78.

Irsigler, F. J. 1983. "The Role of the Temporal Lobe on Morphogenesis and Lateralization of the Human Brain," *Speculations in Science and Technology*, 6:445-453.

Irsigler, F. J. 1984. "Quantitative Morphogenesis and Lateralization of the Human Brain," in *Mankind Quarterly*, 25:3-46.

Ishida, H., *et al.* 1984. "Fossil anthropoids from Nichola and Samburu Hills, Samburu District, Kenya, *African Studies Monographs (Kyoto), Supplemental Issue* 2:73-85.

Itzkoff, S. W. 1971, 1997. *Ernst Cassirer: Scientific Knowledge and the Concept of Man*, Notre Dame, IN.: Univ. of Notre Dame Press.

Itzkoff, S. W. 1983, 1985, 1987, 1990. "The Evolution of Human Intelligence," *The Form of Man, the evolutionary origins of human intelligence; Triumph of the Intelligent, the coming of 'Homo sapiens sapiens'; Why Humans Vary in Intelligence; The Making of the Civilized Mind*, N.Y.: Peter Lang International Publishers.

Itzkoff, S. W. 1991. *Human Intelligence and National Power*, N.Y.: Peter Lang.

Itzkoff, S. W. 1991. "The Evolution of Human Intelligence: A Reply," in *Evolutionary Theory*, Jan., 10:63-64.

Itzkoff, S. W. 1992. "Mysterious Ethnicity," *The Road To Equality, Evolution and Social Reality*, Westport, CT: Praeger Publishers, Ch. 13, pp. 139-145.

Itzkoff, S. W. 1994. *The Decline of Intelligence in America, A Strategy for National Renewal*, Westport, CT: Praeger.

Jablonski, D. 1986. "Causes and Consequences of Mass Extinctions: A Comparative Approach," in *Dynamics of Extinction*, David K. Elliott, ed., N.Y.: John Wiley.

Jablonski, D. 1989. "The biology of mass extinction: a paleontological view," *Philosophical Transactions of the Royal Society*, Ser. B.: 325:357-368.

Jablonski, D., and Bottjer, D. J. 1990. "The origin and diversification of major groups: environmental patterns and evolutionary lags," in *Major Evolutionary Radiations*, P. D. Taylor and G. P. Larwood, eds., Oxford: Clarendon Press.

Jacobson, A. L. 1963. "Learning in Flatworms and Annelids," *Psychological Bulletin*, 60:74-94.

James, S., Martin, R., Pilbeam, D., eds. 1991. *The Cambridge Encyclopedia of Human Evolution*, Cambridge: Cambridge Univ. Press.

Jameson, J. Franklin, ed. 1959. "Letter of Isaack de Rasieres to Samuel Blommart, (1628?)," 'Narratives of New Netherlands' New York, in Patrick Malone. 1991. *The Skulking Way of War*, Lanham, Md.: Madison Books, p.62.

Janis, Christine. "Victors by Default," in *Life*, S. J. Gould, ed., N.Y.: W. W. Norton.

Janke, A., *et al.* 1994. "The Marsupial Mitochondrial Genome and the Evolution of Placental Mammals," *Genetics*, May, 1994, 137:243-256.

Janvier, P. 1984. "The relationship of the Osteostraci and the Galeaspida," *Journal of Vertebrate Paleontology*, 4:344-358.

Janvier, P. (Paris), in John A. Long, 1995, *The Rise of Fishes*, Baltimore: Johns Hopkins Univ. Press

Jenkins, R. J. F. 1988. "Functional and Ecological Aspects, Ediacaran Assemblages," in B. C. Klein-Helmuth and D. Savold, compilers, *AAAS Publications*, 87-30 Washington, D.C.: AAAS.

Jensen, A. R. 1998. *The g Factor*, Westport, CT: Praeger.

Jepson, G. L., Simpson, G. G., Mayr, E., eds. 1949. *Genetics, Paleontology, and Evolution* N.Y.: Atheneum.

Jepson, G. L., *et al.*, eds. 1963. *Genetics, Paleontology, and Evolution*, N.Y.: Atheneum

Jerison, H. J. 1973. *Evolution Of The Brain And Intelligence*, N.Y.: Academic Press.

Jerison, H. J. 1977. "The Theory of Encephalization," *Annals of the New York Academy of Sciences*, Vol. 299.

Jerison, H. J. 1982. "The Evolution of Biological Intelligence," in *Handbook of Human Intelligence*, Robert J. Sternberg, ed., Cambridge: Cambridge Univ. Press.

Jerison, H. J. 1983. "The Evolution of the Mammalian Brain as an Information Processing System," in *Advances in the Study of Mammalian Behavior*, J. F. Eisenberg and D. G. Kleinman, eds. Special Publication No. 7, March 11, 1983, Shippensburg, PA: The American Society of Mammalogists.

Johanson, D. C. 1976. "Plio-Pleistocene Hominid Discoveries in Hadar, Ethiopia," *Nature*, March, 25, pp. 293-297.

Johnson, G. 1999. "Building a Cosmic Tape Measure," *The New York Times*, 6 June, Sections 4, 6.

Johnson, M. L., *et al.*, eds. 1954. *New Biology*, 16:41-53.

Jolly, C., ed. 1974. *Early Hominids in Africa*, London: Duckworth.

Jones, R. 1995. "Tasmanian Archaeology: Establishing the Sequences," *Annual Review of Anthropology*, 24:423-446.

Jones, S., Martin, R., Pilbeam, D., eds. 1992. *The Cambridge Encyclopedia of Human Evolution*, Cambridge: Cambridge Univ. Press.

Joseph, R. 1993. *The Naked Neuron*, N.Y.: Plenum.

Joysey, K. A., and Kemp, T. S., eds. 1972. *Studies in Vertebrate Evolution*, Edinburgh: Oliver and Boyd.

Kaas, J. H. 1989. "The Evolution of Complex Sensory Systems in Mammals," *Jnl. Exp. Biol.*, 146:170.

Kaiser, M., and Shevoroshkin, V. 1988. "Nostratic," *Ann. Rev. Anthropology*, 17:309-329.

Kaminga, J., and Wright, R. V. S. 1988. "The Upper Cave at Zhoukoudien and the Origins of the Mongoloids," *Jnl. of Human Evolution*, 17:739-767.

Kandler, O. 1993. "The Early Diversification of Life," in S. Bengtsen, *Early Life on Earth*, N.Y.: Columbia Univ. Press.

Kandler, O. 1993. (*Progr. Botan*, 54 {1993}:1-24).

Kano, Takayoshi. 1991. *The Last Ape: Pygmy Chimpanzee Behavior and Ecology*, Stanford: Stanford Univ. Press.

Kant, I. 1755. *Universal Natural History and Theory of the Heavens*.

Kant, I. 1758. *New Theory of Motion and Rest*.

Kasha, M., and Pullman, N., eds. 1962. *Horizons in Biochemistry*, N.Y.: Academic Press.

Kauffman, S. A. 1993. *The Origins of Order: Self-organization and Selection in Evolution*, New York: Oxford Univ. Press, p. 643.

Keeley, L. 1996. *War Before Civilization*, N.Y.: Oxford Univ. Press.

Kekoni, K. 1997. "Where Do Words Come From?" *Mankind Quarterly*, Spring, 37:3:283-315.

Kellert, S. and Wilson, E. O., eds. 1993. *The Biophylia Hypothesis*, Washington, D.C.: Island Press, p. 435.

Kemp, T. S. 1982. *Mammal-like Reptiles and the Origin of Mammals*, N.Y.: Academic Press.

Kermack, K. A., Mussett, F., Rigney, H. W. 1981. "The skull of Morganucodonton," *Jnl. Zool. J.Linn.Soc.*, 71:1-58.

Kerr, R. 1998. "Pushing Back the Origin of Animals," *Science*, 2/6/98, 279:803-804.

Kielan-Joworowska, Z., Crompton, A. W., Jenkins, F. A., Jr. 1987. "The origin of egg laying mammals," *Nature*, 326:871-873.

Kingdom J. 1993. *Self-Made Man*, N.Y.: John Wiley, p. 258.

Kious, W. J., and Tilling, R. T. 1996. *This Dynamic Earth: The Story of Plate Techtonics*, Washington, D. C.: U.S. Geological Service.

Kitching, J. W. 1977. "The distribution of the Karroo vertebrate fauna," *Mem. #1*, B. Price Institute for Paleontological Research, University of Wittwatersrand, 131.

Klein, R. G. 1989. *The Human Career*, Chicago: Univ. of Chicago Press, p. 48.

Klein, R. G. 1992. "The archaeology of Modern Human Origins," *Evolut. Anthr.*, 1:5-14.

Klein, R. G. 1995. "Anatomy, Behavior, and Modern Human Origins," *Journal of World Prehistory*, 9:2:167-197, esp. p. 191.

Klein-Helmuth B. C., and Savold, D., compilers. 1988. *AAAS Publications*, 87-30 Washington, D.C.: AAAS.

Knoll, A. 1992. "The early evolution of eukaryotes: a geological perspective," in *Science*, 256:622-627.

Koenigswald, G. H. R., von. 1952. "'Gigantopithecus blacki von Koenigswald,' a giant fossil hominoid from the Pleistocene of southern China," *Anthrop. Papers. Amer. Mus. Nat. Hist.*, 43:291-326.

Koenigswald, G. H. R., von. 1962. *The Evolution of Man*, Ann Arbor: Univ. of Michigan Press.

Kondo, S. ed. 1985. *Primate Morphophysiology, Locomotor Analyses, and Hominid Bipedalism*, Tokyo: University of Tokyo Press.

Korzybski, A. 1941. *Science and Sanity*, Lancaster, PA: .

Kozlowski, S. 1994. In *Late Quaternary Chronology and Paleoclimates of the Eastern Mediterranean*, O. Bar-Yosef, and R. S. Kra, eds., Tucson, AZ: Radiocarbon, University of Arizona, personal communication to Bar-Yosef.

Kramer, A. 1986. "Hominid-pongid Distinctiveness in the Miocene-Pliocene Fossil Record: the Lothagam mandible," *Amer. Jrnl. of Phys. Anthrop.*, 31:49-83.

Kumar, S., and Hedges, S. B. 1998. "A molecular timescale for vertebrate evolution," *Nature*, 392:917-920.

Laitman, J. T. 1985. "Evolution of the Hominid Upper Respiratory Tract: The Fossil Evidence," in *Hominid Evolution: Past, Present, Future*, P. V. Tobias, ed., N.Y.: Alan Liss, pp. 281-286.

Lake, J. A. 1988. "Origin of the eukaryotic nucleus determined by the rate-invariant analysis of rRNA sequences," *Nature*, 331:184-86.

Lake, J. A. 1989. "Origin of the eukaryotic nucleus: Eukaryotes and eocytes are genotypically related," *Can. J. Microbiol.*, 35:109-18.

Langer, Susanne. 1953. *Feeling and Form*, N.Y.: Scribner's;

Langer, Susanne. 1967-1982. *Mind: An Essay on Human Feeling*, 3 vols., Baltimore: Johns Hopkins Univ. Press.

Langer, Susanne. 1962. *Philosophical Sketches*, Baltimore: Johns Hopkins Univ. Press.

Larwood, G. P., ed. 1988. *Extinction and Survival in the Fossil Record*, N.Y.: Oxford Univ. Press.

Latimer, B., and Ward, C. 1993. "The Thoracic and Lumbar Vertebrae," in *The Nariokotome `Homo erectus' Skeleton*, A. Walker and R. Leakey, eds., Cambridge, Mass.: Harvard Univ. Press, pp. 266-293, esp. 292-293.

Latimer B., *et al.* 1987. "Talocrural Joint in African Hominoids: Implications for Australopithecus afarensis," *Amer. Jrnl. Phys. Anthrop.*, 74:2:155-175.

Le Gros Clark, W. E. 1947. "Observations on the Anatomy of the Fossil Australopithecinae," *Anatomy*, 81:300-334.

Leakey, R. 1981. *The Making of Mankind*, N.Y.: Dutton, pp. 193-196.

Leakey, R., and Walker, A. C. 1993. "The Skull," in *The Nariokotome Homo erectus Skeleton*, A. C. Walker, and R. Leakey, eds., Cambridge, Mass.: Harvard Univ. Press, pp. 64-96, p.76.

Lentz, T. L. 1968. *Primitive Nervous Systems*, New Haven: Yale Univ. Press.

Lewontin, R. 1979. "Sociobiology as an adaptationist program," *Behavioral Science*, 24:5-14.

Li, Chia-Wei, Hua, Tzu-En, and Chen, Jun-Yuan. 1998. "Precambrian Sponges with Cellular Structures," *Science*, 2/6/98, 279:879-882.

Li, Wen Hsing, *et al.* 1993. *Nature*, 362:745-747.

Lieberman, P. 1984. *The Biology and Evolution of Language*, Cambridge, Mass: Harvard Univ. Press.

Lieberman, P. 1991. *Uniquely Human: The Evolution of speech, Thought and Selfless Behavior*, Cambridge, MA: Harvard Univ. Press.

Lieberman, P. 1993. "On the Kebara KMH 2 Hyoid and Neanderthal Speech," *Current Anthropology*, 34:2:172-177.

Lieberman, P. 1994. "The Origin and Evolution of Language," in *Companion Encyclopedia of Anthropology*, T. Ingold, ed., N.Y.: Routledge, pp. 108-132.

Lieberman, P. and Crelin, E. S. 1971. "On the speech of Neanderthal man," *Linguistic Inquiry*, 2:203-222.

Liem, K. 1988. "Form and function of lungs: the evolution of air breathing mechanisms," *Amer. Zool.*, 28:739-759.

Lindgren, C. 1957. "The Role of the Gene in Evolution," in R. Nigrelli, ed., *Modern Ideas on Spontaneous Generation*, N.Y.: Annals of the New York Academy of Sciences," pp. 338-351.

Linton, R. D. 1956. *The Tree of Culture*, N.Y.: Knopf, p. 527.

Littleton, C. S. 1985. "The Indo-European Strain in Japanese Mythology," *Mankind Quarterly*, 26:152-174.

Long, John A. 1995. *The Rise of Fishes*, Baltimore: Johns Hopkins Univ. Press.

Lovejoy, C. O. 1974. "The Gait of Australopithecus," *Yearbook of Physical Anthropology*.

Lovejoy, C. O. 1978. "A Biomechanical View of the Locomotor Diversity of Early Hominids," in *Early Hominids in Africa*, C. Jolly, ed., London: Duckworth, pp. 403-429.

Lovejoy, T. E., and Salati, Eneas. 1983. "Precipitating Change in Amazonia," in *The Dilemma of Amazonian Development,* p. 211.

Lovejoy, T. E., Bierregaard, R. O., Rankin, J. M., and Schubart, H. O. R. 1983. "Ecological dynamics of forest fragments," in *Tropical Rain Forest: Ecology and Management*, S. L. Sutton, T. C. Whitmore, and A. C. Chadwick, eds., Oxford: Blackwell, pp. 377-384

Lovejoy, T. E., *et al.* 1984. "Ecosystem Decay of Amazon Forest Remnants," in *Extinction*, Matthew Nitecki, ed., Chicago: Univ. of Chicago Press, pp. 295-325.

Lovejoy, T. E., *et al.* 1986. "Edge and Other Effects of Isolation on Amazon Forest Fragments," in *Conservation Biology: The Science of Scarcity and Diversity*, Michael Soule, ed., Sunderland, MA: Sinauer, pp. 257-285.

Lovelock, J. 1987. *Gaia: a new look at life on Earth*, Oxford: Oxford Univ. Press.

Lowenstein, J. 1980a. "Immunospecificity of Fossil Proteins," in *Biogeochemistry of Amino Acids*, P. E. Hare, ed., N.Y.: John Wiley.

Lowenstein, J. 1980b. "Species-specific proteins in fossils," *Naturwissenschaften*, 67:343.

Lowenstein, J., *et al.* 1982. "Piltdown jaw confirmed as orang," *Nature*, 299:294

Lowenstein, J. 1983. "Fossil proteins and evolutionary time," *Pontif. Acad. Sci. Scripta. Varia.*, 50:151.

Lowenstein, J. 1985. "Radioimmunoassay of Extinct and Extant Species," in *Hominid Evolution: Past, Present and Future*, P. V. Tobias, ed., N.Y.: Alan R. Liss, p. 401.

Luckett, W. P., and Szalay, F. S., eds. 1975. *Phylogeny of the Primates*, N.Y.: Plenum Press, pp.405-406.

Lumsden, C., and Wilson, E. O. 1981. *Genes, Mind, and Culture: The Coevolutionary Process*, Cambridge, MA: Harvard Univ. Press.

Luo, Z. 1996. "Relationship and Morphological Evolution of Early Mammals," in *Carnegie Museum of Natural History Home Page*, Pittsburgh, PA.

MacLatchy, Laura. 1997. "Fossil Shows Apes Emerged Far Earlier," *The New York Times*, (AP), 4/17/97.

MacLean, Paul. 1986. "Culminating developments in the evolution of the limbic system: The thalamocingulate division," in *The Limbic System: Functional Organization and clinical Disorders*, B. K. Doane and K. F. Livingston, eds., N.Y.: Raven Press, pp. 1-28.

MacLean, Paul. 1990. *The Triune Brain in Evolution*, N.Y.: Plenum.

Maddison, D. R. 1991. "African Origin of Human Mitochondrial DNA Reexamined," *Syst. Zool.*, 40:355-363.

Mai, L. 1983. "A model of chromosome evolution and its bearing on cladogenesis in the hominoideia," in *New Interpretations of Ape and Human Ancestry*, R. L. Ciochon and R. S. Corruccini, eds., N.Y.: Plenum.

Margulis, L. 1992, 2nd ed. *Symbiosis and Cell Evolution*. San Francisco: W. H. Freeman.

Margulis, L., ed. 1989. *Handbook of Protoctista*, Boston: Jones and Bartlett.

Marks, A. E. 1990. "The Middle Paleolithic of the Near East and the Nile Valley: The Problem of Cultural Transformations," in *The Emergence of Modern Humans*, P. A. Mellars and C. B. Stringer, eds., Edinburgh: Univ. of Edinburgh Press, pp. 56-80.

Marks, A. E., and Monigal, Kathryn. 1995. "Modeling the Production of Elongated Blanks from the Early Levantine Mousterian at Rosh Ein Mor," in *The Definition and Interpretation of Levallois Technology*, H. L. Dibble and O. Bar-Yosef, eds., Madison, WI: Prehistory Press, pp. 267-277, esp. p. 267.

Marshack, A. 1972. "Cognitive Aspects of Upper Paleolithic Engraving," *Current Anthropology*, June-October, 13:3-4:445-477, esp. p. 449.

Marshack, A. 1972. *The Roots of Civilization*, London: Weidenfield and Nicolson.

Marshack, A. 1974. "The Meander as a System, An Analysis in Recognition of Iconographic Units in Upper Paleolithic Composition," in Ucko, P., ed., *Biennial Conference of the Australian Institute of Aboriginal Studies*, May-June, 16, Canberra, Australia

Marshack, A. 1976. "Some Implications of the Paleolithic Evidence for the Origin of Language," *Current Anthropology*, June, 17:2:274-282.

Marshack, A. 1979. "Upper Paleolithic Symbol Systems of the Russian Plain: Cognitive and Comparative Analysis" *Current Anthropology*, June, 20:2:271-311.

Martin, L. 1985. "Significance of enamel thickness in hominoid evolution," *Nature*, 314:260-263.

Martin, P. S. 1984. "Prehistoric overkill: the global model," in *Quaternary Extinctions*, P. S. Martin and R. G. Klein, eds., Tucson, AZ: Univ. of Arizona Press.

Martin, P. S., and Klein, R. G., eds. 1984. *Quaternary Extinctions*, Tucson, AZ: Univ. of Arizona Press.

Martin, P. S., and Wright, H. E., Jr., eds. 1967. *Pleistocene Extinctions*, New Haven, CT: Yale Univ. Press.

Martin, R. D. 1968. "Toward a New Definition of Primates," *Man*, 3:377-401.

Martin, R. D. 1990. *Primate Origins and Evolution, a Phylogenetic Reconstruction*, Princeton N.J.: Princeton Univ. Press.

Matsuda, T., *et al.* 1986. "Geochronology of Miocene Hominids East of the Kenya Rift Valley," in *Primate Evolution*, J. G. Else and P. C. Lee, eds., Cambridge: Cambridge Univ. Press.

Matsuoka, L. Y., *et al.* 1991. "Racial Pigmentation and the Cutaneous Synthesis of Vitamin D," *Archives of Dermatology*, 127:536-538.

Mayer, A. 1988. *Why Did The Heavens Not Darken?*, N.Y.: Pantheon.

Mayr, E. 1954. "Change of genetic environment and evolution," in *Evolution as a Process*, J. Huxley, A. C. Hardy, E. B. Ford, eds., London: Allen and Unwin, pp. 206-207.

Mayr, E. 1963a. *Animal Species and Evolution*, Cambridge, MA: Harvard Univ. Press.

Mayr, E. 1963b "Speciation and Systematics," in *Genetics, Paleontology, and Evolution*, G. C. Jepson, *et al.*, eds., N.Y.: Atheneum, pp. 281-298.

Mayr, E. 1963c. "The Taxonomic Evolution of Fossil Hominids," *Classification and Human Evolution*, in S. L. Washburn, ed., Chicago: Aldine, pp. 332-346.

Mayr, E. 1982. *The Growth of Biological Thought, Diversity, Evolution, and Inheritance*, Cambridge, MA: Harvard Univ. Press.

Mayr, E. 1983. "How to carry out the adaptationist program," *The American Naturalist*, 121:324-334.

Mayr, E. 1988. *Toward a New Philosophy of Biology*, Cambridge, MA: Belknap Press of Harvard Univ. Press.

Mayr, E. 1991. *One Long Argument: Charles Darwin and the Genesis of Modern Evolutionary Thought*, Cambridge: Harvard Univ. Press, pp. 141-164.

Mayr, E. 1997. *This Is Biology*, Cambridge, Mass.: The Belknap Press/Harvard Univ. Press.

Mayr, E. 1998. Personal communication, 27 June.

Mayr, E., and Provine, W., eds. 1980. *The Evolutionary Synthesis: Perspectives on the Unification of Biology*, Cambridge, MA: Harvard Univ. Press.

Mayr, E., ed. 1957. *The Species Problem*, Washington, D.C.: AAAS.

McCowen, T. D., and Keith, A. 1939. *The Stone Age of Mount Carmel* Vol.2, *The Fossil Remains from the Levalloiso-Mousterian*, Oxford: Clarendon Press.

McCrossin, M. L., and Benefit, B. R. 1993. "Recently recovered Kenyapithecus mandible and its implications for great ape and human origins," *Proc. Natl. Acad. Sci. U.S.A.*, Mar. 1993, 90:1962-1966.

McDonald, J. N. 1984. "North American Selection Regime," in *Quaternary Extinctions*, P. S. Martin and R. G. Klein, eds., Tucson, AZ: Univ. of Arizona Press

McEvedy, C., and Jones, R. 1978. *Atlas of World Population*, N. Y.: Penguin, p.14.

McHenry, H., & Berger, L. 1998. *National Geographic*, August.

McKinney, M. L., ed. 1988. *Heterochrony in Evolution: A Multidisciplinary Approach*, N.Y.: Plenum.

McKinney, M. L. 1993. *Evolution of Life*, Englewood Cliffs, N.J.: Prentice Hall, pp. 106-112.

McKinney, M. L., and McNamara, K. J. 1991. *Heterochrony: The Evolution of Ontogeny*, N.Y.: Plenum, esp. pp. 291-326.

McLaren, D. J. 1986. "Abrupt Extinctions," in *Dynamics of Extinction*, David K. Elliott, ed., N.Y.: John Wiley.

McMenamin, Mark A. S., and McMenamin, Dianna L. S. 1990. *The Emergence of Animals, the Cambrian Breakthrough*, N.Y.: Columbia Univ. Press.

McNab, B. K., and Eisenberg, J. F. 1989. "Brain Size and its Relation to the Rate of Metabolism in Mammals," *The American Naturalist*, Feb., 1989, 132:2:166.

McNamara, K. 1990. *Evolutionary Trends*, Tucson, AZ: Univ. of Arizona Press.

McNamara, P. 1998. *Mind and Variability: Mental Darwinism, Memory and Self*, Westport, CT.: Praeger Publishers.

Mellars, P. A. 1989. "Technological Changes across the Middle-Upper Paleolithic Transition: Economic, Social and Cognitive Perspectives," in *The Human Revolution — Behavioral and Biological Perspectives on the Origins of Modern Humans*, P. A. Mellars and C. B. Stringer, eds., Princeton, N.J.: Princeton Univ. Press, pp. 338-365, esp. p. 339f.

Mellars, P. A. 1996. *The Neanderthal Legacy*, Princeton, N.J.: Princeton Univ. Press.

Mellars, P. A., and Stringer, C. B., eds. 1989. *The Human Revolution — Behavioral and Biological Perspectives on the Origins of Modern Humans*, Princeton, N.J.: Princeton Univ. Press.

Mellars, P. A., and Stringer, C. B., eds. 1990. *The Emergence of Modern Humans*, Edinburgh: Univ. of Edinburgh Press, pp. 56-80

Mellars, P. A., Aitkin, M. J., Stringer, C. P. 1993. "Outlining the Problem," in *The Origin of Modern Humans and the Impact of Chronometric Dating*, M. J. Aitken, C. P. Stringer, and P. A. Mellars, eds., Princeton, N. J.: Princeton Univ. Press, p. 8, fig. 1.

Miao, D. 1993. "Cranial Morphology and Multituberculate Relationships," in *Mammal Phylogeny*, F. S. Szalay, M. J. Novacek, M. C. McKenna, eds., N.Y.: Springer-Verlag, pp. 63-74.

Miyamoto, M. M., *et al.* 1988. "Molecular systematics of higher primates: genealogical relations and classification," *Proceedings of the National Academy of Sciences*, 85:7627-7631.

Monod, Jacques. 1971. *Chance and Necessity*, N.Y.: Knopf, p. 197.

Mooers, Arne O., and Redfield, Rosemary J. 1996. "Digging Up the Roots of Life," *Nature*, 379:587-588.

Moorehead, A. 1966. *The Fatal Impact*, N.Y.: Harper and Row.

Morell, Virginia. 1995. "African Origins: West Side Story," *Nature*, 11/16/95; and *Science*, 11/17/95, p. 1117.

Morell, Virginia. 1995. "Siberia: Surprising Home for Early Modern Humans," *Science* 6/2/95, 268:1279, reporting on research of Ted Goebel, Oregon State College, and M. Aksenov, Irkutsk Univ., *Antiquity*, June, 1995.

Morowitz, H. J. 1992. *Beginnings of Cellular Life*, New Haven: Yale Univ. Press, p. 174.

Morris, Conway. 1987. "The Search for the Precambrian-Cambrian Boundary," *American Scientist*, 75:157-167.

Morton, D. J. 1924. "Evolution of the Human Foot, 2," *Am. Jnl. Phys. Anthr.*, 7:1-52, p. 39.

Morton, D. J. 1924. "Evolution of the Longitudinal Arch of the Human Foot," *Jrnl. Bone and Joint Surg.*, 6:56-90, esp. p. 88.

Mountain, J. L., and Cavalli-Sforza, L. L. 1993. "Evolution of Modern Humans: Evidence from Nuclear DNA Polymorphosis," in *The Origin of Modern Humans and the Impact of Chronometric Dating*, M. J. Aitken, C. B. Stringer, and P. A. Mellars, eds., Princeton, N.J.: Princeton Univ. Press.

Mountain, J. L., Lin, A. A., Bowcock, A. M., Cavalli-Sforza, L. L. 1993. "Evolution of Modern Humans: Evidence From Nuclear DNA Polymorphisms," in *The Origin of Modern Humans and the Impact of Chronometric Dating*, M. J. Aitken, C. P. Stringer, and P. A. Mellars, eds., Princeton, N. J.: Princeton Univ. Press.

Moya-Sola, S. 1995, *Jnl. Hum. Evol.*, 29:101-139.

Moya-Sola, S., and Koehler, M. 1993. *Nature*, 365:543-545.

Moya-Sola, S., and Koehler, M. 1996. *Nature*, Jan. 11, 379:156-159.

Mungall, C., and McLaren, D. J., eds. n.d., ca. 1990. *Planet Under Stress*, Toronto: Oxford Univ. Press, pp. 192-197.

Murray, P. 1984. "Extinctions Downunder: a bestiary of extinct Australian late Pleistocene monotremes and marsupials," in *Quaternary Extinctions*, P. S. Martin and R. G. Klein, eds., Tucson, AZ: Univ. of Arizona Press.

Napier, J., and Napier, P., eds. 1970. *Old World Monkeys*, N.Y.: Academic Press, p. 194.

Nei, M. 1987. *Molecular Evolutionary Genetics*, N.Y.: Columbia Univ. Press.

Nei, M.. and Roychoudhury, A. K. 1993. "Evolutionary relationships of human populations on a global scale," *Molecular Biology and Evolution*, 10:927-943.

Nigrelli, Ross F. ed. 1957. *Modern Ideas on Spontaneous Generation*, N. Y. Annals of the New York Academy of Science, pp. 369-376.

Nisbet, E. G. 1991. *Living Earth*, N.Y.: Harper Collins, p. 4.

Nishida, T., *et al.* 1992. "Meat sharing as a coalition strategy by an alpha male chimpanzee?" in *Topics in Primatology, Vol. 1: Human Origins*, T. Nishida *et al.*, eds., Tokyo: Univ. of Tokyo Press.

Nitecki, M. H., and Nitecki, D. V., eds. 1994. *Origins of Anatomically Modern Humans*, N.Y.: Plenum Press.

Nitecki, M. H., ed. 1984. *Extinction*, Chicago: Univ. of Chicago Press.

Nordstrom, F. 1984. *Medieval Baptismal Fonts: An Iconographical Study*, Stockholm.

Nougier, L. R. 1966. *L'Art Prehistorique*, Paris.

Novacek, M. J. 1996. *Dinosaurs of the Flaming Cliffs*, N.Y.: Anchor-Doubleday.

Novacek, M. J. 1996. Commentary on Hedges, quoted by Associated Press in *The New York Times*, May 16, 1996, p. 228.

Novacek, M. J. 1997. "Ukhaatherium nessovi," *Nature*, 10/2/97, 390:6650, Oct.2, reported by Browne, M. 1997. "Old Bones From Gobi Desert Spur a New Look at Evolution," *The New York Times*, 10/5/97, p. 14.

Novacek, M. J., *et al.* 1997. "Epipubic Bones in Eutherian Mammals from the Late Cretaceous of Mongolia," *Nature*, 10/2/97, 389:483-486.

Nurse, G. T., *et al.* 1985. *The Peoples of Southern Africa and their Affinities*, Oxford: Clarendon Press.

Oakley, K. 1959. *Man the Tool-maker*, Chicago: Univ. of Chicago Press.

Obayashi, T. 1984. "Japanese Myths of Descent from Heaven and Their Korean Parallels," *Asian Folklore Studies*, 43:171-184.

Olson, E. C. 1944. "Origin of mammals based on the cranial morphology of therapsid suborders," *Geol. Soc. of America. Spec. Papers*, 55:1-136.

Olson, E. C. 1974. "On the source of the therapsids," *Ann. of the South African Museum*, 64:27-46.

Oparin, A. I. 1938. *The Origin Of Life*, N.Y.: Dover (1953).

Otte, Marcel. 1995. "The Nature of Levallois," in *The Definition and Interpretation of Levallois Technology*, H. L. Dibble and O. Bar-Yosef, eds., Madison, WI: Prehistory Press, pp. 117-124, esp. p. 122.

Oxnard, C. E. 1969. "Evolution of the human shoulder; some possible pathways," *Amer. Jrnl. Phys. Anthrop.*, 30:319-322.

Oxnard, C. E. 1985. "Hominids and Hominoids, Lineages and Radiations," in *Hominid Evolution: Past, Present, Future*, P. V. Tobias, ed., N.Y.: Alan Liss, pp. 271-278.

Paabo, Svante. 1995. "The Y Chromosome and the Origin of All of Us (Men)," *Science*, May 26, 1995, 268:1141-42.

Paabo, Svante. 1997. "Neanderthal DNA Sheds New Light On Human Origins," N. Wade, *New York Times*, 7/11/97, in *Cell*, issue of 7/11/97.

Padian, K., ed. 1986. *The Beginning of the Age of Dinosaurs*, Cambridge: Cambridge Univ. Press.

Padian, K., *The New York Times*, 11/3/96, #4, p. 14.

Padian, K., and Clemens, W. A. 1985, in *Phanerozoic Diversity Patterns*, J. W. Valentine, ed., Princeton: Princeton Univ. Press, pp. 41-96.

Pagel, M. D., and Harvey, P. H. 1988. "How Mammals Produce Large-Brained Offspring," *Evolution*, 42(5):948-957.

Pagel, M. D., and Harvey, P. H. 1989. "The Taxon-Level Problem in the Evolution of Mammalian Brain Size: Facts and Artifacts," *The American Naturalist*, Sep., 132:3:355.

Pagel, M. D., and Harvey, P. H. 1990. "Diversity in the Brain Sizes of Newborn Mammals, Allometry, Energetics, or Life History Tactics," *BioScience*, Feb., 1990, 40:2:121-122.

Panchen, A. L. 1972. "The interrelationships of the earliest tetrapods," in *Studies in Vertebrate Evolution*, K. A. Joysey and T. S. Kemp, eds., Edinburgh: Oliver and Boyd.

Papez, J. W. 1967. *Comparative Neurology*, N.Y.: Hafner.

Partridge, T. C. 1985. "Spring Flow and Tufa Accretion at Taung," in *Hominid Evolution: Past, Present and Future*, P. V. Tobias, ed., N.Y.: Alan R. Liss, pp. 171-187.

Patterson, B., and Olson, E. C. 1961. "A triconodontid mammal from the Triassic of Yunnan," in *Int. Colloq. of Lower and Non-specialized Mammals*, G. Vanderbroeh, ed., Brussels: KonVlaamse Acad. Wetensch Lett. Sch. Kunsten, pp. 129-191.

Peterson, S. E., *et al.* 1989. "Positron Emission Tomographic Studies of the Processing of Single Words," *Journal of Cognitive Neuroscience*, 1:163-170.

Phillips, James. 1994. "Upper Paleolithic Chronology in the Levant and Nile," in *Late Quaternary Chronology and Paleoclimates of the Eastern Mediterranean*, O. Bar-Yosef, and R. S. Kra, eds., Tucson, AZ: Radiocarbon, University of Arizona, pp. 169-176.

Pianka, E. 1983. *Evolutionary Ecology*, 3rd ed., N.Y.: Harper and Row.

Pickford, M. 1985. "Kenyapithecus: A Review of its Status Based on Newly Discovered Fossils from Kenya," in *Hominid Evolution: Past, Present, and Future*, P. V. Tobias, ed., N.Y.: Alan R. Liss.

Pilbeam, D. 1969. *Tertiary Pongidae of East Africa*, New Haven: Yale Univ. Press.

Pilbeam, D. 1972. *The Ascent of Man*, N.Y.: Macmillan.

Pilbeam, D. 1979. "Recent Finds and Interpretations of Miocene Hominoids," *Annual Review of Anthropology*, 8:333-352.

Pilbeam, D. 1982. "New hominoid skull material from the Miocene of Pakistan," *Nature*, 295:232-234.

Pilbeam, D. 1989. "Human Fossil History and Evolutionary Paradigms," in *Evolutionary Biology at the Crossroads*, M. K. Hecht, ed., N.Y.: Queens College Press, pp. 117-138.

Pilbeam, D. 1996. "Genetic and Morphological Records of the Hominoidea and Hominid Origins," A Synthesis, *Molecular Phylogenetics and Evolution*, 5:1:155-168.

Pilbeam, D. 1997. "Research on Miocene Hominoids and Hominid Origins: The Last Three Decades," in *Function, Phylogeny and Fossils*, ed. D. R. Begun, *et al.*, N.Y.: Plenum Press.

Pilbeam, D., *et al.* 1977. "New hominoid primates from the Siwaliks of Pakistan and their bearing on hominoid evolution," *Nature*, 270:689-695.

Pinker, S. 1997. *How The Mind Works*, N.Y.: W. W. Norton, pp. 163-164.

Pirie, N. W. 1954. "On Making and Recognizing Life," in M. L. Johnson *et al.*, eds., *New Biology*, 16:41-53.

Pirie, N. W. 1957. "Some Assumptions Underlying Discussion of the Origin of Life," in *Modern Ideas on Spontaneous Generation*, Ross F. Nigrelli, ed., N. Y. Annals of the New York Academy of Science, pp. 369-376.

Pirie, N. W. 1959. "Chemical Diversity and the Origin of Life," in *The Origin of Life on Earth*, F. N. Clark and L. M. Synge, N.Y.: Pergamon Press, pp. 76-83.

Ploog, D. W. 1992. "Neuroethological Perspectives on the Human Brain: From the Expression of Emotion to Intentional Signing and Speech," in *So Human A Brain*, Anne Harrington, ed., Boston: Birkhauser, pp. 3-13.

Portmann, A. 1941. "Die Tragzeiten der Primaten und die Dauer der Schwangerschaft beim Menschen: Ein Problem der Vergleichen Biologie," *Rev. Suisse. Zool.*, pp. 511-518, 516

Prance, G. T. 1982. "Forest refuges: Evidence from woody angiosperms," in *Biological Diversification in the Tropics*, Prance, G. T., ed., N.Y.: Columbia Univ. Press, pp. 137-159.

Prance, G. T. 1983. N.Y. Botanical Garden, cited in Thomas Lovejoy and Eneas Salati, 1983, *The Dilemma of Amazonian Development*, pp. 214-215.

Prigogine, I., and Stengers, I. 1984. *Order Out of Chaos, Man's New Dialogue with Nature*, N.Y.: Bantam Books.

Prost, H. 1980. "Origin of Bipedalism," *Am. Jrnl. Phys. Anthrop.*, 52:175-189.

Prost, H. 1985. "Chimpanzee Behavior and Models of Hominization," in *Primate Morphophysiology, Locomotor Analyses, and Hominid Bipedalism*, S. Kondo, ed., Tokyo: University of Tokyo Press.

Prothero, D. R. 1994. *The Eocene-Oligocene Transition*, N.Y.: Columbia Univ. Press.

Purves, D. 1988. *Body and Brain*, Cambridge, Mass.: Harvard Univ. Press.

Quiroga, J. C. 1979. "The brain of two mammal-like reptiles (Cynodontia-Therapsida)," *J. Hirnforsch*, 20:341-350.

Quiroga, J. C. 1980. "The brain of the mammal-like reptile Probainognathus jenseni (Therapsida-Cynodonta). A correlative paleo-neoneurological approach to the neocortex at the reptile-mammal transition," *J. Hirnforsch*, 21:299-336.

Qumsiyeh, M. B. 1994. "Evolution of Number and Morphology of Mammalian Chromosomes," in *Jnl. of Heredity*, 85:459.

Radinsky, Leonard. 1987. *The Evolution of Vertebrate Design*, Chicago: The Univ. of Chicago Press, Chap. 3, "The Basic Vertebrate Body Plan."

Raff, R. A. 1996. *The Shape of Life: Genes, Development, and the Evolution of Animal Forms*, Chicago: Univ. of Chicago Press.

Raff, R. A., and Raff, E. C., eds. *Development as an Evolutionary Process*, N.Y.: Alan R. Riss, pp. 71-107,

Rak, Y. 1983. *The Australopithecine Face*, N.Y.: Academic Press, p. 122.

Rak, Y. 1985. In *Hominid Evolution: Past, Present and Future*, P. V. Tobias, ed., N.Y.: Alan R. Liss, pp. 233-237.

Ranov, V. A. 1995. "The Levallois Paradox," in *The Definition and Interpretation of Levallois Technology*, H. L. Dibble and O. Bar-Yosef, eds., Madison, WI: Prehistory Press, pp. 69-78.

Raup, D. M., and Boyagian, G. E. 1988. "Patterns of generic extinction in the fossil record," *Paleobiology*, 14:109-125.

Raup, D. M. 1991. *Extinction: Bad Genes or Bad Luck?*, N.Y.: Norton.

Renfree, M. B. 1993. "Ontogeny, Genetic Control, and Phylogeny of Female Reproduction in Monotreme and Therian Mammals," in *Mammal Phylogeny*, F. S. Szalay, M. J. Novacek, McKenna, M. C., eds., N.Y.: Springer-Verlag.

Rensch, B. 1959. *Evolution Above the Species Level*, N.Y.: Columbia Univ. Press.

Richards, M., *et al.* 1996. "Paleolithic and Neolithic Lineages in the European Mitochondrial Gene Pool," *Am. Jrnl. Hum. Genetics*, July, 59:185-203.

Richards, R. R. 1997. "Neanderthals Need Not Reply," in *The New York Times Sunday Book Review*, 8/17/97, p. 10.

Rightmire, C. P. 1978. "Human Skeletal Remains from the Southern Cape Province and Their Bearing on the Stone Age Prehistory of South Africa," *Quaternary Research*, 9:219-230.

Rightmire, C. P. 1985. "The Tempo of Change in the Evolution of Mid-Pleistocene Homo," in *Ancestors: The Hard Evidence*, E. Delson ed., N.Y.: Alan R. Liss, pp. 255-264.

Rightmire, C. P. 1989. "Middle-Stone Age Humans from Eastern and Southern Africa," in *The Human Revolution — Behavioral and Biological Perspectives on the Origins of Modern Humans*, P. Mellars and C. Stringer, eds., Princeton: Princeton Univ. Press, pp. 109-122, esp. p. 109.

Rightmire, C. P. 1990. *The Evolution of Homo erectus*, Cambridge, Eng.: Cambridge Univ. Press, pp. 34-52.

Roberts, D. F. 1978. *Climate and Human Variability*, 2nd ed. Menlo Park. CA: Cummings Pub. Co., p. 90.

Roberts, M. B., Stringer, C. B., Parfitt, S. A. 1994. "A Hominid Tibia from Middle Pleistocene Sediments at Boxgrove UK., *Nature*, 369:311-313.

Roberts, R. G., and Jones, R. 1994. "Luminescent Dating of Sediments: New Light on the Human Colonization of Australia," *Australian Aboriginal Studies*, 1994/2:2-17.

Roberts, R. G., *et al.* 1990. "Thermoluminescence Dating of a 50,000 Year Old Human Occupation Site in Northern Australia," *Nature*, 345:153-156.

Robinson, P. L. 1971. "A problem of faunal replacement on the Permo-Triassic continents," *Paleontology*, 14:131-153.

Rogers, A. R., and Jorde, L. B. 1995. "Genetic Evidence on Modern Human Origins," *Human Biology*, Feb., 67:1:1-36.

Romer, A. S. 1963. "Time Series and Trends in Animal Evolution," in *Genetics, Paleontology, and Evolution*, G. L. Jepson, *et al.*, eds., N.Y.: Atheneum, p. 107.

Romer, A. S. 1966. *Vertebrate Paleontology*, 3rd. ed., Chicago: Univ. of Chicago Press.

Ross, John T., ed. 1982. *International Encyclopedia of Population*, Vol. 2, N.Y.: Free Press, Macmillan Pub., p. 679.

Rowe, T., "Phylogenetic Systematics and the Early History of the Mammals," in *Mammal Phylogeny*, F. S. Szalay, M. J. Novacek, M. C. McKenna, eds., N.Y.: Springer-Verlag.

Rudenko, S. 1970. *Frozen Tombs of Siberia*, London: J. M. Dent.

Rukang, W., and Olsen, J. W., eds. 1985. *Paleoanthropology and Palaeolithic Archaeology in the People's Republic of China*, N.Y.: Academic Press.

Rummel, R. J. 1994. *Death By Government*, New Brunswick, N.J.: Transaction Publishers.

Russell, D. A. 1981. "Speculations on the evolution of intelligence in multicellular organisms," in *Life in the Universe*, J. Billingham, ed., Cambridge, Mass.: MIT Press, pp. 259-275.

Ruvolo, M., *et al.* 1993. "Mitochondrial COII sequences and modern human origins," *Molecular Biology and Evolution*, 10:1115-1135.

Salvini-Plawen, L. V., and Mayr, E. 1977. "On the evolution of photoreceptors and eyes," *Evolutionary Biology*, 10:207-263.

Salzano, F. M., ed. 1975. *The Role of Natural Selection in Human Evolution*, Amsterdam: North Holland.

Santa Luca, A. P. 1978 "A Reexamination of Presumed Neandertal-Like Fossils," *Journal of Human Evolution*, 7:619-636.

Santa Luca, A. P. 1980. *The Ngandong Fossil Hominids: A Comparative Study of a Far Eastern Homo Erectus Group*, New Haven, CT: Yale Univ. Publications in Anthropology, no. 78.

Sarich, V. 1970. "Primate systematics with special reference to Old World monkeys, a protein perspective," in *Old World Monkeys*, J. Napier and P. Napier, eds., N.Y.: Academic Press, p. 194.

Sarich, V., and Cronin, J. E. 1977. "Generation lengths and rates of hominid molecular evolution," *Nature*, 269:354-355.

Sarich, V., and Wilson, A. C. 1966. Quantitative immunochemistry and the evolution of primate albumins: microcomplement fixation, *Science*, 154:1564-65.

Sarich, V., and Wilson, A. C. 1967. "Rates of Albumin Evolution in Primates," *Proc. Nat. Acad. Sci. U.S.*

Sato, Hiroyuki, *et al.* 1995. "Lithic Technology of the Japanese Middle Paleolithic: Levallois in Japan?" in *The Definition and Interpretation of Levallois Technology*, H. L. Dibble and O. Bar-Yosef, eds., Madison, WI: Prehistory Press, pp. 485-500.

Savage, R. J. G. 1988. "Extinction and the fossil mammal record," in *Extinction and Survival in the Fossil Record*, G. P. Larwood, ed., N.Y.: Oxford Univ. Press.

Schild, R. 1976. "The Final Paleolithic Settlements of the European Plain," *Scientific American* (February), 234:2:88-99.

Schmid, P. 1983. "Ein Rekonstruction des Skelletes von A. L. 286-1 (Hadar) und deren Konsequenzen," *Folia primat*, 40:283-306.

Schopf, J. W., ed. 1983. *The Earth's Earliest Biosphere*, Princeton, N.J.: Princeton Univ. Press.

Schopf, J. W., ed. 1992. *Major Events in the History of Life*, Boston: Jones and Bartlett.

Schopf, J. W. 1999. *Cradle of Life*, Princeton, N.J.: Princeton Univ. Press.

Schultz, A. H. 1926. "Fetal Growth of Man and other Primates," *Quarterly Review of Biology*, 1:4:465-521.

Schultz, A. H. 1927. "Observations on a Gorilla Fetus," *Eugenical News*, 12:37-40, p. 40.

Shultz, A. H. 1930. "The Skeleton of the Trunk and Limbs of Higher Primates," *Human Biology*, 2:203-438.

Schultz, A. H. 1936. "Characters Common to Higher Primates and Characters Specific for Man," *Quarterly Review of Biology*, 11:259-283, 425-455.

Schultz, A. H. 1938. "The Recent Hominoid Primates," in *Perspectives on Human Evolution*, Vol. 1, S. L. Washburn and P. C. Jay, eds., N.Y.: Holt, Rinehart and Winston.

Schultz, A. H. 1968. "The Recent Hominoid Primates," in *Classification and Human Evolution*, S. L. Washburn, ed., Chicago: Aldine.

Schultz, A. H. 1969. *The Life of Primates*, N.Y.: Universe Books, p. 251.

Schwarcz, H. P. 1994. "Chronology of Modern Humans in the Levant," in *Late Quaternary Chronology and Paleoclimates of the Eastern Mediterranean*, O. Bar-Yosef and R. S. Kra, eds., Tucson, AZ: Radiocarbon, University of Arizona, pp. 21-32, esp. 27, also "Introduction," above volume, p. 12.

Schwartz, Jeffrey. 1984a. "The evolutionary relationship of man and orang-utans," *Nature*, 308:501.

Schwartz, Jeffrey. 1984b. "Hominoid evolution: a review and a reassessment," *Current Anthropology*, 25:655.

Schwartz, Jeffrey. 1985. "Toward a Synthetic Analysis of Hominoid Phylogeny," in *Hominid Evolution, Past, Present, and Future*, P. V. Tobias, ed., N.Y.: Alan R. Liss, pp. 265-269 (esp. pp. 267-268).

Schwartz, Jeffrey. 1987. *The Red Ape*, London: Elm Tree Books.

Schwartz, Jeffrey. 1993. *What the Bones Tell Us*, N.Y.: Henry Holt.

Schwartz, Jeffrey, *et al.*, and Wanpo, H., *et al.* 1996. "Whose Teeth?" *Nature*, 5/16/96, 381:201-202.

Sepkoski, J. J., Jr. 1984. "A kinetic model of Phanerozoic taxonomic diversity: Post Paleozoic families and mass extinctions," *Paleobiology*.

Sepkoski, J. J., Jr., and D. M. Raup. 1986. "Periodicity in marine extinction events," in *Dynamics of Extinction*, David K. Elliott, ed., N.Y.: John Wiley, pp. 3-36.

Sepkoski, J. J., Jr. 1990. "The taxonomic structure of periodic extinctions," in *Global Catastrophes in Earth History*, V. L. Sharpton and P. D. Ward, eds., Boulder Colo.: Geological Society of America, Geological Society of America Special Paper 247, pp. 33-44.

Sepkoski, J. J., Jr. 1993. "Foundations: Life in the Oceans," in *Life*, S. J. Gould, ed., N.Y.: W. W. Norton, p. 38.

Sharpton, V. L., and Ward, P. D., eds., *Global Catastrophes in Earth History*, Boulder Colo.: Geological Society of America, Geological Society of America Special Paper 247, pp. 33-44.

Shea, B. T. 1988. "Heterochrony in Primates," in *Heterochrony in Evolution: A Multidisciplinary Approach*, McKinney, M., ed., N.Y.: Plenum.

Shea, John J. 1989. "A Functional Study of the Lithic Industries Associated with Hominid Fossils in the Kebara and Qafzeh Caves, Israel," in *The Human Revolution — Behavioral and Biological Perspectives on the Origins of Modern Humans*, P. A. Mellars and C. Stringer, eds., Princeton, N.J.: Princeton Univ. Press, pp. 611-625. See fig. 31.1, p. 615, p. 622.

Shea, John J. 1995. "Behavioral Factors Affecting the Production of Levallois Points in the Levantine Mousterian," in *The Definition and Interpretation of Levallois Technology*, H. L. Dibble and O. Bar-Yosef, eds., Madison, WI: Prehistory Press, pp. 279-292.

Shreeve, J. 1994. "Lucy, Crucial Human Ancestor, Finally Gets a Head," *Science*, 4/1/94, 264:34-35, D. Johanson, William Kimball, Yoel Rak, of IHO in Berkeley, and Sackler School of Medicine, Tel Aviv.

Shreeve, J. 1996. "Sunset on the Savanna," *Discover*, July 1996, pp. 116-125.

Sibley, C. G., and Ahlquist, J. E. 1984. "The phylogeny of the hominoid primates, as indicated by DNA-DNA hybridization," *Jnl. Mol. Evol.*, 20:2-15.

Sibley, C. G., Comstock, J. A., Ahlquist, J. E. 1990. "DNA hybridization evidence of hominoid phylogeny: a reanalysis of the data," *Jnl. Mol. Evol.*, 30:202-236.

Siddall, M. E., *et al.* 1992. "Phylogenetic analysis of Diplomonida...," *Jrnl. Protozool.*, 39:361-367.

Sigogneau-Russell, D. 1989. "Haramyidae (Mammalia Allotheria) en provenance du Tria superior de Lorraine (France)," *Paleontographica Abt.*, A 206:137-198.

Simeons, A. T. S. 1962. *Man's Presumptuous Brain*, N.Y.: Dutton, p. 276.

Simmons, N. 1993. "Phylogeny of Multituberculata," in *Mammal Phylogeny*, F. S. Szalay, M. J. Novacek, M. C. McKenna, eds., N.Y.: Springer-Verlag, p. 148 (pp. 146-164).

Simons, E. L. 1976. "The nature of the transition in the dental mechanism from pongids to hominids," *Jnl. Hum. Evol.*

Simons, E. L. 1985. "African Origin, Characteristics and Context of Earliest Higher Primates," in Tobias, P. V., ed., *Hominid Evolution: Past, Present, and Future.*

Simons, E. L. 1986. "'Parapithecus grangeri' of the African Oligocene: an archaic catarrhine without lower incisors," *Jnl. of Hum. Evol.*, 15:205-213.

Simons, E. L. 1987. "New faces of `Aegyptopithecus" from the Oligocene of Egypt," *Jnl. of Hum. Evol.*, 16:273-289.

Simons, Marlise. 1996. *The New York Times*, 5/23/96.

Simons, Marlise. 1996. "Why Ancient Images Haunt Modern Minds," *The New York Times*, 6/30/96.

Simpson, G. G. 1927. "Mesozoic Mammals IX. The Brain of Jurassic Mammals," *Am. Jrnl. of Science*, 214:259-268.

Simpson, G. G. 1944. *Tempo and Mode in Evolution*, N.Y.: Columbia Univ. Press.

Simpson, G. G. 1945. "The principles of classification and a classification of mammals," *Bull. Am. Mus. Nat. Hist.*, 85:1-350.

Simpson, G. G. 1952. *The Meaning of Evolution*, New Haven: Yale Univ. Press, pp. 62-63.

Simpson, G. G. 1953. *The Major Features of Evolution*, N.Y.: Columbia Univ. Press.

Singer-Polignac, ed., Fondation. 1988. *L'Evolution dans sa Realite et ses Diverses Modalites*, Paris: Masson.

Skelton, R., and McHenry, H. 1992. "Evolutionary relationships among early hominids," *Journal of Human Evolution*, 23:309-349.

Smith, D. G., ed. 1982. *The Cambridge Encyclopedia of Earth Sciences*, Cambridge: Cambridge Univ. Press, pp. 349-362.

Smith, F. H. 1993. "Models and Realities in Modern Human Origins: The African Evidence," in *The Origin of Modern Humans and the Impact of Chronometric Dating*, M. J. Aitken, C. B. Stringer, and P. A. Mellars, eds., Princeton, N.J.: Princeton Univ. Press, pp. 234-248.

Smith, F. H., and Spencer, F., eds. 1984. *The Origins of Modern Humans: A World Survey of the Fossil Evidence*, N.Y.: Alan Liss.

Smith, F. H., *et al.* 1989. "Geographical Variation in Supraorbital Torus Reduction during the Later Pleistocene (c. 80,000-15,000 B.P.)" in *The Human Revolution — Behavioral and Biological Perspectives on the Origins of Modern Humans*, P. Mellars and C. Stringer, eds., Princeton: Princeton Univ. Press.

Smith, Homer W. 1961. *From Fish To Philosopher*, N.Y.: Anchor-Doubleday.

Smith, J. M., *et al.* 1993. In *Science*, 10/1/93, p. 27.

Smith, P. E. L. 1986. *Paleolithic Archaeology in Iran*, Philadelphia: Univ. Museum, Univ. of Penn.

Soffer, Olga. 1989. "The Middle to Upper Paleolithic Transition on the Russian Plain," in *The Human Revolution — Behavioral and Biological Perspectives on the Origins of Modern Humans*, P. A. Mellars and C. Stringer, eds., Princeton, N.J.: Princeton Univ. Press, pp. 714-742, esp. p. 736.

Sogin, M. 1991. "Early Evolution and the Origin of Eucaryotes," *Curr. Opin. in Gen. and Dev.*, 1:457-63.

Solecki, R. 1975. "Shanidar 4, a Neanderthal Flower Burial in Northern Iraq," *Science*, 190:880-881.

Sonneville-Bordes, D., de, and Perrot, J. Perrot. 1954-1956. "Lexique Typologique du Paleolithique Superieur," *Bulletin de la Societe Prehistorique Francaise*, 51:327-335; 52:76-79; 53:408-412, 547-549.

Soule, Michael, ed. 1986. *Conservation Biology: The Science of Scarcity and Diversity*, Sunderland, MA: Sinauer.

Soule, Michael, 1987, cited in C. Tudge, *Evolution and Extinction*, W. G. Chaloner and A. Hallam, eds., 1994, N.Y.: Cambridge Univ. Press, p.485; *World Almanac*, 1995, p. 510, says 200 million.

Sperber, G. H. 1985. "Comparative primate dental enamel thickness: radiodontological study," in *Hominid Evolution: Past, Present, Future*, P. V. Tobias, ed., N.Y.: Alan Liss.

Sperber, G. H., ed. 1990. *From Apes to Angels, Essays in Honor of Philip Tobias*, N.Y.: Wiley-Liss.

Stanley, S. M. 1988. "Paleozoic mass extinctions: shared patterns suggest global cooling as common cause," *American Journal of Science*, 288:334-352.

Stanley, S. M. 1996. *Children of the Ice Age*, N.Y.: W. H. Freeman.

Stebbins, G. Ledyard. 1982. *Darwin to DNA, Molecules to Humanity*, San Francisco: W. H. Freeman.

Stephan, H. 1975. "Allocortex," in *Handbuch der Mikroskopischen Anatomie des Menschen*, 4/9, Bargmann, W., ed., Berlin: Springer.

Stern, J. T. 1975. "Before bipedality," *Yearbook of Phys. Anthropol.*, 19:59-68.

Stern, J. T., and Susman, R. L. 1983. "The Locomotor Anatomy of *Australopithecus afarensis*," *Am. Jrnl. Phys. Anthrop.*, 60:279-318.

Sternberg, Robert J., ed. 1982. *Handbook of Human Intelligence*, Cambridge: Cambridge Univ. Press.

Stevens, W. K. 1998. "One in Every 8 Plant Species Is Imperiled, a Survey Finds," *The New York Times*, April 9, A1.

Stoneking, M., Cann, R. L. 1989. "African Origin of Mitochondrial DNA," in *The Human Revolution — Behavioral and Biological Perspectives on the Origins of Modern Humans*, P. Mellars and C. Stringer, eds., Princeton: Princeton Univ. Press, pp. 17-30.

Stoneking, M., *et al.* 1993. "New Approaches to Dating Suggest a Recent Age for the Human mtDNA Ancestor," in *The Origin of Modern Humans and the Impact of Chronometric Dating*, M. J. Aitken, C. Stringer, P. A. Mellars, eds., Princeton, N.J.: Princeton Univ. Press, pp. 84-103.

Stoneking, M., Sherry, S. T., Vigilant, L. 1992. "Geographic Origin of Human Mitochondrial DNA Revisited," *Syst. Biol.*, n.d.

Strait, D. S. *et al.* 1997. *Jnl of Human Evolution*, 32:17.

Straus, W. L. 1949. "The riddle of man's ancestry," *Quart. Rev. Biol.*, 24:200-223.

Stringer, C. B., ed. 1981. *Aspects of Human Evolution*, London: Taylor and Francis.

Stringer, C. B. 1989. "The Origin of Early Modern Humans: A Comparison of the European and non-European Evidence," in *The Human Revolution — Behavioral and Biological Perspectives on the Origins of Modern Humans*, P. Mellars and C. B. Stringer, eds., Princeton: Princeton Univ. Press.

Stringer, C. B. 1990. "The Emergence of Modern Humans," *Scientific American*, 262:98-104.

Stringer, C. B. 1993. "Reconstructing Recent Human Evolution," in *The Origin of Modern Humans and the Impact of Chronometric Dating*, M. J. Aitken, C. P. Stringer, and P. A. Mellars, eds., Princeton, N. J.: Princeton Univ. Press.

Stringer, C. B. 1994. "Out of Africa--A Personal History," in *Origins of Anatomically Modern Humans*, M. H. Nitecki and D. V. Nitecki, eds., N.Y.: Plenum pp. 149-172.

Stringer, C. B., and Andrews, P. 1988. "Genetic and Fossil Evidence for the Origin of Modern Humans," *Science*, 239:1263-1268.

Stringer, C. B., and Gamble, C. 1993. *In Search of the Neanderthals: Solving the Puzzle of Human Origins*, London: Thames and Hudson.

Stringer, C. B., and Gamble, C. 1994. "Reply: Confronting the Neanderthals," *Cambridge Archaeological Journal*, 4:1:112-119.

Stringer, C. B., and Gamble, C. 1994. "The Neanderthal World: Flat Earth or New Horizons," *Cambridge Archaeological Journal*, 4:1:96.

Stringer, C. B., and McKie, R. 1996. *African Exodus: the Origins of Modern Humanity*, London: Jonathan Cape, p.185.

Susman, R. L. 1984. In *The Pygmy Chimpanzees*, R. L. Susman, ed., N.Y.: Plenum.

Sutton, S. L., Whitmore, T. C., and Chadwick, A. C., eds. 1983. *Tropical Rain Forest: Ecology and Management*, Oxford: Blackwell, pp. 377-384.

Suwa, G., *et al.* 1997. "Robust Australopithecine Skull of Konso, Ethiopia," *Nature*, 10/2/97, Vol. 389, No. 6650.

Suwa, G., *et al.* 1997. "The first skull of *Australopithecus boisei*," *Nature*, 10/2/97, 389:489-492

Swisher, C. C., and Anton, S. 1996. "Ngandong, Solo River H. Erectus Sites Redated," *Science*, 12/13/96, 274:1870.

Swisher, C. C., *et al.* 1994. "Age of the Earliest Known Hominids in Java, Indonesia," *Science*, 2/25/94, 263:1118-1121.

Szalay, F. S. 1993. *Evolutionary History of the Marsupials and an Analysis of Osteological Characters*, N.Y.: Cambridge Univ. Press.

Szalay, F. S. 1993. "Metatherian Taxon Phylogeny: Evidence and Interpretation from the Cranioskeletal System," in *Mammal Phylogeny*, F. S. Szalay, M. J. Novacek, M. C. McKenna, eds., N.Y.: Springer-Verlag, pp. 234-240.

Szalay, F. S., and Delson, E. 1979. *Evolutionary History of the Primates*, N.Y.: Academic Press.

Szalay, F. S., M. J. Novacek, McKenna, M. C., eds. 1993. *Mammal Phylogeny*, N.Y.: Springer-Verlag.

Takahata, N., Satta, Y., Klein, J. 1995. "Divergence Time and Population Size in the Lineage Leading to Modern Humans," *Theoretical and Population Biology*, quoted in "The Mystery of Humanity's Missing Mutations," Ann Gibbons, *Science*, 1/6/95, 267:35-36.

Tattersall, I. 1986. "Species Recognition in Human Paleontology," *Journal of Human Evolution*, 15:165-175.

Tattersall, I. 1995. *The Fossil Trail*, N.Y.: Oxford Univ. Press.

Tattersall, I. 1995. *The Last Neanderthal*, N.Y.: Macmillan/USA.

Tattersall, I. 1998. *Becoming Human*, N.Y.: Harcourt Brace.

Taylor, P. D., and Larwood, G. P., eds. 1990. *Major Evolutionary Radiations*, Oxford: Clarendon Press.

Tchernov, E. 1992. "Mammalian Migration and Dispersal Events in the European Quaternary," W. von Koenigswald, and L. Werdelin, eds., pp. 103-123, *Cour. Forschungsinst. Senckenberg*, 153.

Templeton, A. 1983. "Phylogenetic Inference from Restriction Endonuclease Cleavage Site Maps with Particular Reference to the Evolution of Humans and Apes," *Evolution*, 37:221-244.

Templeton, A. 1992. "Technical Comments: Human Origins and Analysis of Mitochondrial DNA Sequences," *Science*, 255:737.

Thackery, J. F., and Kieser, J. A. 1993. "Variability in shape of dental arcade of *Homo sapiens* in Late Pleistocene and modern samples from southern Africa," *Paleontologia africana*, in *The Runaway Brain*, C. Wills, N.Y.: Basic Books, p. 302.

Theunissen, B., *et al.* 1990. "The establishment of a chronological framework for the hominid-bearing deposits of Java; a historical survey, in *Establishment of a Geologic Framework for Paleoanthropology*, L. F. Laporte, ed., Boulder: Geologic Society of America, pp. 39-54.

Thoma, A. 1957-58. "Essai sur les Hommes Fossiles de Palestine," *L'Anthopologie*, 61:470-502, 62:30-52.

Thoma, A. 1962. "Le Deploiement Evolutif de l'Homo Sapiens" *Anthropologia Hungarica*, 5:1-179.

Thoma, A. 1963. "La Definition des Neandertaliens et la Position des Hommes Fossiles de Palestine," *L'Anthropologie*, 69:519-534.

Thorne, A. G. 1980. "The Longest Link: Human Evolution in Southeast Asia," in *Indonesia: Australian Perspectives*, J. J. Fox, *et al.*, Canberra: Australian National University Press.

Thorne, A. G., and Macumber, P. G. 1972. "Discoveries of Late Pleistocene Man at Kow Swamp Australia," *Nature*, 238:316-319.

Timei, C., *et al.* 1994. "Antiquity of Homo sapiens in China," *Nature*, 368:55-56.

Tishkoff, S. *et al.* 1996. *Science* 3/8/96, and as reported in *The New York Times*, 3/8/96.

Tobias, P. V. 1971. *The Brain in Hominid Evolution*, N.Y.: Columbia Univ. Press.

Tobias, P. V. 1975. "Brain Evolution in the Hominoidae," in *Primate functional Morphology and Evolution*, R. H. Tuttle, ed., The Hague: Mouton.

Tobias, P. V. 1975. "Long or short hominid phylogenies? Paleontological and Molecular Evidences," in *The Role of Natural Selection in Human Evolution*, Salzano, F. M., ed., Amsterdam: North Holland.

Tobias, P. V., ed. 1985. *Hominid Evolution: Past, Present and Future*, N.Y.: Alan R. Liss.

Tobias, P. V. 1994. "The Evolution of Early Hominids," in *Companion Encyclopedia of Anthropology*, T. Ingold, ed., N.Y.: Routledge, pp. 33-78.

Tobias, P. V. 1999. "3.0 mya australopithecine skeleton at Sterkfontein," Blaine, WA: *Foundation for the Future, Lecture, 13 Apr.*

Tobias, P. V. 1999. Personal communication, 11, 12 Apr.

Tobias, P. V., and Clarke, R. 1995. "New Foot Steps into Walking Debate," *Science*, 7/28/95, 269:476, 521.

Torroni, A., *et al.* 1994. "mtDNA and the Origin of the Caucasians: Identification of Ancient Caucasian-specific Haplogroups, One of Which Is Prone to a Recurrent Somatic Duplication in the D-Loop Region," *Am. Jnl. Hum. Gen.*, 55:760-766.

Toth, N. 1982. *The Stone Technologies of Early Hominids at Koobie Fora, Kenya: An Experimental Approach*, Ann Arbor: Univ. of Michigan Microfilms International.

Toth, N. 1985. "The Oldowan Reassessed: A Close Look at Early Stone Artifacts," *Jnl. of Archaeological Science*, 12:2:101-120.

Travis, J. 1994. "Hubble War Moves to High Ground," *Science*, 10/28/94, 266:539-41.

Trinkaus, E. 1981. "Neanderthal Limb Proportions and Cold Adaptation," in *Aspects of Human Evolution*, Stringer, C., ed., London: Taylor and Francis, pp. 187-224.

Trinkaus, E. 1983. *The Shanidar Neanderthals*, N.Y.: Academic Press.

Trinkaus, E., ed. 1989. *Patterns and Processes in Later Pleistocene Human Emergence*, Cambridge: Cambridge Univ. Press.

Trinkaus, E., ed. 1989. *The Emergence of Modern Humans*, Cambridge, Eng.: Cambridge Univ. Press.

Trinkaus, E., and Howells, W. W. 1979. "The Neanderthals," *Scientific American*, 241(6):118-133.

Trinkaus, E., and Shipman, P. 1993. *The Neanderthals*, N.Y.: Knopf.

Trinkaus, E., and Zilhao, J. *Proceedings of the National Academy of Sciences*, forthcoming, 1999-2000.

Trotter, M. M., and McCulloch, B. 1984. "Moas, Men and Middens," in *Quaternary Extinction*, P. S. Martin and R. G. Klein, eds., Tucson: Univ. of Arizona Press.

Tudge, C. 1994. *Evolution and Extinction*, Chaloner, W. G. and Hallam, A., eds., N.Y.: Cambridge Univ. Press.

Tuttle, R. H. 1974. "Darwin's Apes, Dental Apes, and the Descent of Man: Normal Science in Evolutionary Anthropology," *Current Anthropology*, 15:389-398.

Tuttle, R. H. 1975. "Parallelism, Brachiation and Hominoid Phylogeny," in *Phylogeny of the Primates*, W. P. Luckett and F. S. Szalay, eds., N.Y.: Plenum Press.

Tuttle R. H., ed. 1975. *Primate functional Morphology and Evolution*, The Hague: Mouton.

Tuttle, R. H. 1981. "Evolution of Hominid Bipedalism and Prehensile Capabilities," *Phil. Transact. R. Soc. London.*

Tuttle, R. H. 1985. "Ape Footprints and Laetoli Impressions," in *Hominid Evolution: Past, Present, Future*, P. V. Tobias, ed., N.Y.: Alan Liss.

Tuttle, R. H. 1985. "Darwin's Apes, Dental Apes, and the Descent of Man: Normal Science in Evolutionary Anthropology," in *Primate Evolution and Human Origins*, R. L. Ciochon and J. G. Fleagle, eds., Menlo Park, CA: Benjamin/Cummings Publishing, pp. 333-342.

Ucko, P., ed. 1974. *Biennial Conference of the Australian Institute of Aboriginal Studies*, May-June, 16, Canberra, Australia.

Ueda, S., *et al.* 1988. "Multiple recombinational events in primate immunoglobulin epsilon and alpha genes suggest closer relationship of humans to chimpanzees than to gorillas, *Jnl. Mol. Evol.*

Upchurch, G. R. 1989. "Terrestrial Environmental Changes and Extinction Patterns at the Cretaceous-Tertiary Boundary, North America," in *Mass Extinctions: Process and Evidence*, S. K. Donovan, ed., N.Y.: Columbia Univ. Press.

Vrba, E., cited in Eldredge, N. 1991. *The Miner's Canary*, N.Y.: Prentice Hall, pp. 183, 187.

Vrba, Elizabeth S. 1979. "A new study of the scapula of *Australopithecus africanus* from Sterkfontein," *American Journal of Physical Anthropology*, 51:117-130.

Vrba, Elizabeth S. 1985. "Early Hominids in South Africa...," in *Hominid Evolution: Past, Present and Future*, P. V. Tobias, ed., N.Y.: Alan R. Liss, pp. 195-200.

Valentine, J. W. 1969. "Patterns of taxonomic and ecologic structure of the shelf benthos during Phanerozoic time," *Paleontology*, 12:684-709.

Valentine, J. W., ed. 1985. *Phanerozoic Diversity Patterns*, Princeton: Princeton Univ. Press.

Valentine, J. W., and D. H. Erwin. 1987. "Interpreting Great Developmental Experiments: The Fossil Record," in *Development as an Evolutionary Process*, R. A. Raff and E. C. Raff, eds., N.Y.: Alan R. Riss, pp. 71-107.

Vanderbroeh, G., ed. 1961. *Int. Colloq. of Lower and Non-specialized Mammals*, Brussels: KonVlaamse Acad. Wetensch Lett. Sch. Kunsten, pp. 129-191.

Vandermeersch, B. 1978. "Le Crane Pre-Wurmien de Biache-Saint Vaast (Pas de Calais)." In D. J. Chivers and K. A. Jousey, eds., London: Academic Press, pp. 345-418.

Vandermeersch, B. 1989. "The Evolution of Modern Humans: Recent Evidence from Southwest Asia," in *The Human Revolution—Behavioral and Biological Perspectives on the Origins of Modern Humans*, P. Mellars and C. Stringer, eds., Princeton: Princeton Univ. Press, pp. 155-164, esp. p. 156.

Van Valen, L. 1960. "Therapsids as mammals," *Evolution*, 14:304-313.

Van Valen, L. 1973. "A New Evolutionary Law," *Evolutionary Theory*, 1:1-30.

Van Valen, L. 1974. "Two Modes of Evolution," *Nature*, 252:298-300.

Vereshchagin and Baryshnikov. 1984. "Quaternary Mammalian Extinctions in Northern Eurasia," in *Quaternary Extinction*, P. S. Martin and R. G. Klein, eds., Tucson, AZ: Univ. of Arizona Press.

Vermeig, G. J. 1996. "Animal Origins," *Science*, Vol. 274, 25 Oct., 525-526.

Vigilant, L., *et al.* 1989. Mitochondrial DNA Sequences in Single Hairs from a Southern African Population," *Proc. Nation. Acad. of Sciences*, 86:9350-9354.

Vigilant, L., Stoneking, M., Wilson, A., Harpenden, H., and Hawkes, K. 1991. "African Populations and the Evolution of Mitochondrial DNA," *Science*, 253:1503-1507.

Vogel, J. C. 1985. "Further Attempts at Dating the Taung Tufas," in *Hominid Evolution: Past, Present and Future*, P. V. Tobias, ed., N.Y.: Alan R. Liss, pp. 189-194.

Vogel, J. C., ed. 1984. *Late Cenozoic Paleoclimates of the Southern Hemisphere*, Rotterdam: A. A. Balkema.

Vogel, J. C., and Partridge, T. 1984. "Preliminary Radiometric Ages of the Taung Tufas," in *Late Cenozoic Paleoclimates of the Southern Hemisphere*, J. C. Vogel, ed., Rotterdam: A. A. Balkema, pp. 507-514.

Wade, N. 1997. "Man Has Older Friend Than Thought," *The New York Times*, 1/13/97, p. A-12.

Wade, N. 1997. "Neanderthal DNA Sheds New Light On Human Origins," *The New York Times*, 7/11/97.

Wade, N. 1998. "Tree of Life Turns Out to Have Surprisingly Complex Roots," *The New York Times*, April 14, C1.

Wade, N. 1999. "Study Gives New Time Line for Human Population Split," *The New York Times*, 16 Mar., A-14.

Waddington, C. H. 1957. *The Strategy of the Genes*, London: Allen & Unwin.

Wainright, P. O., *et al.* 1993. *Science*, (1993):340-342.

Wald, G. 1945. "Human Vision and the Spectrum," *Science*, 101:635-658.

Walker, A. C., and Andrews, P. 1973. "Reconstruction of the dental arcades of 'Ramapithecus wickeri,' *Nature*, 244:313-314

Walker, A. C., and Leakey, R., eds. 1993. *The Nariokotome Homo erectus Skeleton*, Cambridge, Mass.: Harvard Univ. Press.

Walker, A. C., and Pickford, M. 1983. "New postcranial fossils of 'Proconsul africanus' and 'Proconsul nyanzae,'" in R. L. Ciochun, and R. S. Corruccini, eds., *New Interpretations of Ape and Human Ancestry*, N.Y.: Plenum Press.

Walker, A. C., and Shipman, P. 1996. *The Wisdom of the Bones*, N.Y.: Knopf.

Wallace, D., *et al.* 1985. "Dramatic Founder Effects in Amerindian Mitochondrial DNAs," *American Journal of Physical Anthropology*, 68:149-155.

Walls, G. 1942. *The Vertebrate Eye and its Adaptive Radiation*, Bloomfield Hills, Michigan: Cranbrook Press.

Wanpo, H., and Ciochon, R., *et al.* 1996. "Whose Teeth?: Reply to Schwartz & Tattersall," *Nature*, 5/16/96, 381:202.

Ward, C. V. 1993. "Torso morphology and locomotion in Proconsul Nyanzae," *Am. Jrnl. Of Phys. Anthropology*, 92:291-328.

Ward, Peter. 1994. *The End of Evolution*, N.Y.: Bantam Books, pp. 242-243.

Ward, S., *et al.* 1999. "Equatorius: A New Hominid Genus from the Middle Miocene of Kenya, *Science*, 8/27/99, 285:1382-1386.

Washburn, S. L., ed. 1963. *Classification and Human Evolution*, Chicago: Aldine, pp. 204-234.

Watson, D. M. S. 1913. "Further notes on the skull, brain, and organs of special sense in Diademodon," *Ann. Magaz. Nat. Hist.*, 12:217-228.

Weidenreich, F. 1942. "The Skull of 'Sinanthropus pekinensis,'" *Paleontologia Sinica*, new series D., 10:1-291.

Weidenreich, F. 1946. *Apes, Giants, and Man*, Chicago: Univ. of Chicago Press.

White, Randall. 1982. "The manipulation of burins and incision and notation," *Canadian Jrnl. of Anthropology*, 2:129-135.

White, Randall. 1989. "Production Complexity and Standardization in Early Aurignacian Bead and Pendant Manufacture: Evolutionary Implications," in *The Human Revolution — Behavioral and Biological Perspectives on the Origins of Modern Humans*, P. A. Mellars and C. B. Stringer, eds., Princeton, N.J.: Princeton Univ. Press, pp. 366-390.

White, Randall. 1989. "Toward a Contextual Understanding of the Earliest Body Ornaments," in *Patterns and Processes in Later Pleistocene Human Emergence*, E. Trinkaus, ed., Cambridge: Cambridge Univ. Press

White, T. D. 1987. "Cannibals at Klasies?" *Sagittarius*, 2:1:6-9.

White, T. D. *et al. 1994. "Australopithecus ramidus,* A new species of early hominid from Aramis, Ethiopia," *Nature*, 22 Sept., 371:306-312

White, T. D.. 1995. *Science*, 8/18/95, 269:918.

Whitfield, L. S., and Goodfellow, P. N. 1993. *Nature*, 364:713.

Wible, J. R. 1991. "Origin of Mammalia: The craniodental evidence reexamined," *Jnl. Vert. Paleontol*, 11:1-28.

Wilford, J. N. 1996. "`American' Arrowhead Found in Siberia," *The New York Times*, 8/2/96, from article in *Science*, described by M. King and S. B. Slobodin.

Wilford, J. N. 1996. "In an Amazon Cave, Light Is Shed on Early Americans," *The New York Times*, April 19, p. A10.

Wilford, J. N. 1996. *The New York Times*, from *Science* August 2.

Wilford, J. N. 1996. "First branch in Life's Tree Was 2 Billion Years Old," *The New York Times*, 1/30/96.

Wilford, J. N. 1996. "Mummies, Textiles Offer Evidence of Europeans In Far East," *The New York Times*, 5/7/96. Discusses Victor Mair's work from Univ. Of Penn. Museum written up in *The Journal of Indo-European Studies*.

Wilford, J. N. 1996. "Playing of Flute May Have Graced Neanderthal Fire," *The New York Times*, 10/29/96.

Wilford, J. N. 1996. "3 Human Species Coexisted on Earth, New Data Suggest," *The New York Times*, 12/13/96.

Wilford, J. N. 1997. *The New York Times*, 2/28/97, in *Science*, 2/28/97.

Wilford, J. N. 1997. "African Skull Suggests Diversity of Early Human Relatives," *The New York Times* 10/7/97, p. C9.

Wilford, J. N. 1997. "Ancient German Spears Tell of Mighty Hunters of Stone Age," *The New York Times*, 3/4/97.

Wilford, J. N. 1997. "Fossils Called Limb in Human Family Tree," *The New York Times*, 5/30/97.

Wilford, J. N. 1997. "Human Presence in Americas Is Pushed Back a Millennium," *The New York Times*, Feb. 11, p. A1.

Wilford, J. N. 1998. "Fossils Take Scientists Past Biology's Big Bang," *The New York Times*, 2/5/98.

Wilford, J. N. 1998. "New Analysis of Fossils May Muddy Accepted Path of Human Evolution," *The New York Times*, July 28.

Wilford, J. N. 1999. "Discovery Suggests Man Is a Bit Neanderthal," *The New York Times*, 4/25/99, 1, 19.

Williams, G. C. 1975. *Sex and Evolution*, Princeton, N.J.: Princeton Univ. Press.

Wills, C. 1993. *The Runaway Brain*, N.Y.: Basic Books, p. 253.

Wills, C. 1998. *Children of Prometheus*, Boston: Perseus Books.

Wilson, A. C., *et al.* 1977. "Biochemical Evolution," *Ann. Rev. Biochem.*, 46:573-639.

Wilson, A. C., and Cann, R. L. 1992. "The Recent African Genesis of Humans," *Scientific American*, April, 266:4, 22-27.

Wilson, A. C., and Sarich, V. M. 1969. "A molecular time-scale for human evolution," *Proc. Nat. Acad. Sci. U.S.*, 63:1088-1093.

Wilson, E. O. 1979. *On Human Nature*, Cambridge, MA: Harvard Univ. Press.

Wilson, E. O. 1992. *The Diversity of Life*, Cambridge, MA: Harvard Univ. Press.

Wilson, E. O. 1996. *In Search of Nature*, Washington, D.C.: Island Press.

Woese, C. R. 1981. "Archaebacteria," *Scientific American*, Vol. 244, No. 6.

Woese, C. R. 1987. "Bacterial Evolution," in *Microbiol. Rev.*3, 51:221-271.

Woese, C. R., and Fox, G. E. 1977. "Phylogenetic structure of the prokaryotic domain: The primary kingdoms, *Proceed. Nat. Acad. Sci.*, 74:5088-5090.

Woese, C. R., Kandler, O., and Wheelis, M. L. 1990. "Towards a Natural System of Organisms: Proposal for the Domains Archea, Bacteria and Eucarya," in *Proc. Natl. Acad. Sci. USA*, 87:4576-79.

Wolpoff, M. H. 1989. "Multiregional Evolution: The Fossil Alternative to Eden," in *The Human Revolution—Behavioral and Biological Perspectives on the Origins of Modern Humans*, P. Mellars and C. Stringer, eds., Princeton: Princeton Univ. Press, pp. 62-108.

Wolpoff, M. H. 1992. "Theories of Modern Human Origins," In *Continuity or Replacement: Controversies in Homo Sapiens Evolution*, G. Brauer and F. H. Smith, eds., Rotterdam: Balkema.

Wolpoff, M. H. 1994. "The Calm Before the Storm," *Cambridge Archaeological Journal*, 4:1:97-103.

Wolpoff, M. H. 1997. "No `Homo erectus' at Ngandong," in *Human Origins News*, 1/4/97, 6pp, esp. p. 4.

Wolpoff, M. H., and Caspari, R. 1997. *Race and Human Evolution*, N.Y.: Simon and Schuster.

Wolpoff, M. H., Xinzhi, Wu, Thorne, A. G. 1984. "Modern Homo Sapiens Origins: A General Theory of Hominid Evolution Involving the Fossil Evidence from East Asia," in *The Origins of Modern Humans: A World Survey of the Fossil Evidence*, F. H. Smith and F. Spencer, eds., N.Y.: Alan Liss, pp. 411-483.

Wood, B. A. 1985. In *Hominid Evolution: Past, Present, and Future*, P. V. Tobias, ed., N.Y.: Alan R. Liss, pp. 227-232, esp. p. 231.

Wood, B. A. 1992. "Evolution of Australopithecines," in *The Cambridge Encyclopedia of Human Evolution*, S. Jones, R. Martin, D. Pilbeam, eds., Cambridge: Cambridge Univ. Press, pp. 231-240.

Wood, B. A. 1992. *Nature*, 355:783-790.

Wood, B. A. 1997. "Ecce Homo — behold mankind," *Nature*, 11/13/97, 390:120-121.

Wood, B. A., and Turner, A. 1995. "Out of Africa and into Asia," *Nature*, 11/16/95, 378:239-240.

Wood, B. A., Martin, L. B., and Andrews, P. J., eds. 1986. *Major Topics in Primate and Human Evolution*, Cambridge Univ. Press.

Wood, B. A., and Collard, M. 1999. "The Human Genus," *Science*, 2 Apr., 284:65-71.

World Almanac, 1995, p. 510.

Wray, G. A. *et al.* 1996. "Molecular Evidence for Deep Precambrian Divergences among Metazoan Phyla," *Science*, Oct. 25, 568-573.

Wright, S. 1963. "Adaptation and Selection," in *Genetics, Paleontology, and Evolution*, G. L. Jepson, G. G. Simpson, E. Mayr, E., eds., N.Y.: Atheneum, pp. 365-391.

Wu, X. 1988. "The relationship between Upper Paleolithic fossils from China and Japan," *Acta. Anthr. Sinic.*, 7:235-238.

Wu, X. 1990. "The evolution of humankind in China," *Acta. Anthrop. Sin.*, 9:312-322.

Wu, X., and Zhang, Z. 1985. "Homo Sapiens Remains from the Late Paleolithic and Neolithic China," in *Paleoanthropology and Paleolithic Archaeology in the People's Republic of China*, R. Wu and J. W. Olsen, eds., London: Academic Press, pp. 107-133.

Wu, Xinzhi, and Wu, Maolin. 1985. "Early Homo Sapiens in China," in *Paleoanthropology and Palaeolithic Archaeology in the People's Republic of China*, W. Rukang and J. W. Olsen, eds. N.Y.: Academic Press, pp. 91-106.

Xiao, S., Zhang, Y., Knoll, A. H. 1998. "Three-dimensional preservation of algae and animal embryos in a Neoproterozoic phosphorite," *Nature*, 2/5/98, 391:553-558.

Yearbook Of Physical Anthropology, 1988, 31:49-83.

Yellin, J., *et al.* 1995. "A Middle Stone Age Worked Bone Industry from Katanda, Upper Semlike Valley, Zaire," *Science*, 268:553-556.

Yoder, A. D., *et al.* 1996. "Ancient single origin for Malagasy primates," *Proc. Natl. Acad. Sci. U.S.A.*, (May) 193:5122-5126.

Yoshida, A. 1977. "Japanese Mythology and the Indo-European Trifunctional System," *Diogenes*, 98:93-116.

Yunis, J., and Prakash, O. 1982. "The origin of man: a chromosomal pictorial legacy," *Science*, 215:1525.

Zihlman, Adrienne L., *et al.* 1978. "Pygmy Chimpanzee as a Possible Prototype for the Common Ancestor of Humans, Chimpanzees and Gorillas," *Nature*, 275:744-746.

Zihlman, Adrienne L. 1985. "A. afarensis: Two Sexes or Two Species," in *Hominid Evolution: Past, Present, Future*, P. V. Tobias, ed., N.Y.: Alan Liss, pp. 213-220.

Zihlman, Adrienne L. 1990. "Knuckling Under, Controversy Over Hominid Origins," in *From Apes to Angels, Essays in Honor of Philip Tobias*, Geoffrey Sperber, ed., N.Y.: Wiley-Liss, pp. 187-188.

Zihlman, Adrienne L., and Brunker, L. 1979. "Hominid Bipedalism: Then and Now," *Yearbook Phys. Anthrop.*, 22:132-162.

Zimmer, Carl. 1995. "Coming Onto the Land," in *Discover*, June 1995, 9 pp.

Zubrow, E. 1989. "The Demographic Modeling of Neanderthal Extinction," in *The Human Revolution*, P. A. Mellars, and C. B. Stringer, eds., Princeton, N.J.: Princeton Univ. Press, pp. 212-231.

Zuckerkandl, E., and Pauling, L. 1962. "Molecular disease, evolution, and genetic heterogeneity," in *Horizons in Biochemistry*, M. Kasha and N. Pullman, eds., N.Y.: Academic Press.

Zuckerkandl, E., and Pauling, L. 1965. "Evolutionary divergence and convergence in proteins," in *Evolving Genes and Proteins*, V. Bryson and H. J. Vogel, eds., N.Y.: Academic Press, p. 97.

Illustration Acknowledgments

Estate of Carleton Coon..17.2
John Wiley..2.1
....6.1
....10.4
....12.2
Johns Hopkins University..5.1
....5.3
Jones and Bartlett...10.2
....13.5
Journal of Indo-European Studies...17.7
Macmillan...2.2
....16.6
McGraw Hill Publishers ....A and B: 16.7
Merrill Publishers 2.3
Musée des Antiquités Nationales, Paris.................................... Frontispiece
.... A and B: 16.2
Nelson Hall Publishers..13.2
Patterson Publishers...3.2
....3.3
Peter Yates..13.4
Prentice Hall 6.2
....9.1
Princeton University Press...14.1
....14.2
....14.3
....14.4
....15.5
....16.3
Scientific American Press..4.2
....16.5
Transaction Publishers..2.4
University of Chicago Press 5.2
....9.2
....12.1
....15.4
....17.1
....17.4
....A: 18.2

Subject Index

Orthoselection *(Continued)*
  and brain development, 74, 199
  in human evolution, 314
Osteichthyes (bony fish), 56–59
Osteolepiformes, 81–82
Out of Africa model. *See also Homo sapiens
  sapiens,* Eur-Asian origins of; Humans,
  African Eve hypothesis for
  and Cro-Magnon man, 264–265
Outlanders, 127–137
Outliers, 130–131, 313
Ox *(Bos primigenius),* extinction of, 17
Oxyclaenus (arctocyonids), 110, 115
Oxygen
  atmospheric extraction of, 60–61
  in brain development, 68–69
  in Cambrian era, on animal proliferation,
    43, 48
  on eukaryote cells, 31
Oxygen/isotope 6, 324–325

P
Paedomorphosis, 311–313
Paintings, in Aurignacian civilization,
  278–280
Palate, of therapsids, 84
Paleocene period
  Cretaceous holdovers in, 115
  fossils of, 112
Paleolithic period
  cultural development in
    chronology for, 270–272
    material, 272–275, 273f, 274f
  Levant sites of, 286, 287f
Pan paniscus, 186
Pan troglodytes, 186
Panderichthyids, 64
Pangea, mass extinctions of, 77–78
Paranthropus, 180
Pelycosaur, 82
Peramorphosis, 312
Permian period, 41
  cynodonts in, 82–83, 132
  extinction in, 74–75, 75f, 78
  therapids in, 82
Photosynthesis, on Cambrian vertebrate
  differentiation, 48
Phylogeny(ies)
  of bovids, 159f
  of *Homo,* complications in, 219

of human ancestors, 140–142
of mammals, 92f
nuclear DNA diversity in, 228–231, 229f,
  231f
of primates, molecular clock in, 147–149
Pikaia, 47, 54f, 55
Pithecanthropus erectus, 206–207
Placentals, 94–96
  adaptive reproductive patterns of, 111–112
  divergence from, 110
  genetic memory of, 133
  mid-Cretaceous restructuring of, 113–114
Placoderms, 56, 59
Planaria flatworms, neurological pathways of,
  69–70
Plants, land development of, 66
Pleistocene period
  fossils of, in multiregional question, 323
  Homo in, 213
  Ice Age of, 169
    on Caucasoid migrations, 304
    Cro-Magnon arrival in, 8–13
  mammal extinction in, 9f
  Neanderthal/Cro-Magnid relationship in,
    292–293
  Old World sites in, 257f
  racial types of, 219
Plesiadapiforms, 116, 116f
Plesiadapids, 109–110
Plesiadapis, 109
Pliocene era, animal extinction in, 9
Political considerations, in evolution debate,
  204
Pongid relationships, in primate origin and
  radiation, 122
Pongid to hominid transitions, 168–182. *See
  also* Transitions, from pongid to hominid
Population
  East Asian shifts of, Caucasoids in, 302–303
  growth of, 14–15, 14f
  stagnancy of, in African Eve hypothesis,
    231–232
Porifera (sponges)
  establishment of, 44
  neurological pathways of, 69
Post-erectine gap, 211
Predators
  -prey cycle, in Cambrian era, 43, 47
  humans as, 8–24 (*See also* Humans, as
    predator)